Worlds Apart?

A Review of Research into the Education of Pupils of
Cypriot, Italian, Ukrainian and Vietnamese Origin,
Liverpool Blacks and Gypsies

Monica J. Taylor

NFER-NELSON

Published by The NFER-NELSON Publishing Company Ltd.,
Darville House, 2 Oxford Road East,
Windsor, Berkshire SL4 1DF, England.

First Published 1988
© 1988, National Foundation for Educational Research

Typeset by First Page Ltd., Watford.
Printed in Great Britain by
Antony Rowe Ltd, Chippenham, Wiltshire

ISBN 0 7005 1043 5
Code 8241 02 1

CONTENTS

TABLES IN THE TEXT

PREFACE AND ACKNOWLEDGEMENTS

This is the fourth and, thankfully, final report in a series of reviews of research commissioned by the Committee of Inquiry into the Education of Children from Ethnic Minority Groups (Swann Committee). The review was originally undertaken in three months during 1983 and has been revised and updated in 1986 whilst I have been engaged in full-time employment on a research project. This accounts for the publication delay.

The research reviewed here relates to the education of children from several numerically smaller ethnic minority communities who, given the predominant focus on pupils of West Indian and South Asian origin (see Taylor, 1981; Taylor with Hegarty, 1985), have often been overlooked. The minority groups represented are those selected by the Swann Committee, 'either as exemplars of particular types of communities or whose needs we considered to be particularly deserving of attention in their own right' (GB. P. H of C, 1985, p.649). Among these was the dispersed Chinese community, which formed the subject of the third in this series of reviews of research (Taylor, 1986). Here consideration is given to research evidence on the education of pupils of Cypriot, Italian, Ukrainian and Vietnamese origin, Liverpool blacks and gypsies. Dr Seamus Hegarty was responsible for the research reviews on pupils of Vietnamese origin and gypsies.

As before, the review, which draws upon a range of published sources, many now dated though supplemented by some new unpublished material, usually employs the terminology of the research studies themselves. These are of variable quality and often of a qualitative rather than quantitative kind. Nevertheless, taken cumulatively, the evidence clearly shows that the issues which emerge in the education of these 'other' ethnic minority pupils, particularly in respect of language and culture, racism and ethnic identity, and their interrelation with academic performance, experience of schooling and educational policies and practices, though differing in emphasis for individuals and groups, are both common to the education of pupils from more numerous ethnic minority groups and in some cases, especially Liverpool blacks and gypsies, heightened to an extreme degree and hence deserving of even greater attention. Whilst the debate fostered by the Swann Committee and its Report has served to raise consciousness of these issues and to make them more widely known with, for example, consideration being given to both an anti-racist and multicultural curriculum, the challenge of continuing provision which meets both the differentiated needs of individual pupils – which for some may include special interests on account of their ethnic minority origin – and a broad, balanced and relevant education for all, remains a daily educational reality. These reviews have drawn together research evidence of needs, interests and concerns on the part of pupils, parents, communities, teachers and LEAs and indicated areas for urgent consideration and further inquiry. Among these it is especially to be hoped that good practice may be identified and disseminated to the benefit of all, ethnic minority and majority alike.

Undertaking reviews of research draws considerably on library facilities and, once again, I should like to thank staff in the library and information services, particularly latterly, Pauline Benefield and Tony Gwilliam, for their ready and unstinting help. Acknowledgements are also due to Terence Organ, who compiled the index, and Michael Halson, Carolyn Richardson and Roda Morrison, who coped with postponed deadlines and competently facilitated the publishing arrangements. My thanks also go to Mary Dyer and Annie Cridge, who typed the first draft of the manuscript. My special debt of gratitude is owed to Lynn Fardell, who with great patience, loyalty and fortitude not only took pride in speedily transforming an extremely tatty revised draft into the final manuscript, but also offered careful encouragement. This, together with the interest of other friends and colleagues within and outside the NFER, and above all the enduring material and moral support of my mother, has enabled me to complete this review. With it draws to a close an undertaking, which for a not inconsiderable time became a preoccupation, in itself educative but often disturbing in terms of the conclusions which can be drawn from research into past policies and practices, and demanding in its educational implications for the future of Britain as a multiracial, multiethnic and multicultural society.

MJT

February 1987

Part One
Pupils of Cypriot Origin

Introduction and Background

Other than in certain areas of north London and gradually extending into the suburbs, the presence of a considerable number of pupils of Cypriot origin over the last 35 years has largely been overlooked. Although a few Cypriots had settled in Britain before the 20th century (Constantinides, 1977; George, 1960), it was not until well after Cyprus had come under British colonial rule that Cypriots migrated to Britain in significant numbers. To set in context the contemporary position of pupils of Cypriot origin, their families and their communities in Britain, it is necessary to outline the historical background to the circumstances of emigration from Cyprus to the UK.

HISTORY   The location of Cyprus (3,572 square miles) in the eastern Mediterranean, at the boundaries of Europe, Asia and Africa, has been an important factor in its embattled history since 6,000 BC. The Greeks were early colonizers – around the second century BC – but became subject to successive invasions and occupations by, amongst others, the Egyptians, Persians, Romans, Byzantines and, after the Crusades, the conquering Richard I sold Cyprus to the Franks who were followed by the Venetians. In 1571 Cyprus fell to the Turks who recognized the Greek Orthodox faith and the Archbishop as leader of the people, but under the Ottoman Empire the island did not keep pace with social and political developments in Europe (London Council of Social Service, 1967; Alkan and Constantinides, 1981). When in the 19th century Greece gained independence from the Ottoman Empire the Cypriot uprising was unsuccessful and Cyprus was leased by Turkey to Britain in 1878, under the Treaty of Berlin, whereby Britain undertook to protect Cyprus against other powers. In 1914 (when Armenians arrived in Cyprus) Britain annexed the island as Turkey joined in the First World War on the side of Germany. In 1925 Cyprus became a British colony.

Various unsuccessful attempts were made for independence during the 1920s and 1930s. Some Cypriot leaders were exiled until the start of the Second World War, when many thousands of Cypriots joined the British army. During British rule Cyprus received considerable agricultural, educational and economic aid (Oakley, 1968). Sources are generally agreed that despite the long years of Turkish and British rule the Greek majority had preserved their Greek identity and culture and, once again, at the end of the war Greek Cypriots began campaigning for independence on the basis of union with Greece *(enosis)*. This, however, was unpopular with Britain which wished to retain its military base on the island, and was opposed by Turkish Cypriots who were in a minority of approximately one to four. In 1954 the matter was taken to the United Nations, but in April 1955, while still unresolved, Cypriots led by Greek EOKA terrorists began a campaign of civil uprisings which lasted for four years, causing great hardship and loss of life. A compromise agreement was finally reached in 1959 when Britain, Greece and

Turkey guaranteed the constitution of an independent Cyprus which became a republic in 1960 under its President Archbishop Makarios, the leader of the Greek Cypriots. At that time, about two-thirds of the population of 577,615 (Greek Cypriots 442,521, Turkish Cypriots 104,350, Maronites 2,708, Armenians 3,628 and British 24,408) lived an agrarian life in 600 scattered villages, 100,000 lived in the capital Nicosia and district and the remainder in five other district towns which acted as administrative and market centres (Alkan and Constantinides, 1981; Krausz, 1971; Oakley, 1979).

The constitution, which included laws for the protection of the minority Turks and separate responsibility for schools of the Greek and Turkish communities was unacceptable to the majority of Cypriots as independence was limited by the involvement of outside interests. In 1963 Archbishop Makarios proposed modifications to the constitution which included unification of the army and municipalities divided according to their majority population. However, the situation deteriorated into violent clashes and the setting up of enclaves by the Turkish Cypriots for the protection of isolated groups and villages throughout the island which disrupted communications and public services, including education (Crellin, 1979). In 1964 UN troops intervened in an attempt to keep peace between the two communities. However, the separation of the Turks and economic restrictions placed on them between 1963–7 increased feelings of insecurity and resentment (Ladbury, 1977) and hostilities continued amidst continuing discussions involving Greek and Turkish Cypriots, Greece, Turkey, the UK and the United Nations.

In July 1974 a short-lived coup, supported by the then ruling military junta of Greece, aimed at overthrowing the Makarios government and its policy for an independent Cyprus. Fighting broke out between rival Greek factions and between Greeks and Turks. Shortly thereafter, there was an invasion and occupation by mainland Turkish forces, which was regarded by the Turks as in accordance with the tripartite agreement setting up the Republic of Cyprus but was seen by the Greek and Cypriot governments as an unjustified act of aggression. The intercommunal fighting, atrocities and enforced evictions resulted in the division of the population and the island into the Turkish north and Greek south. In 1975 a separate administration was set up by the Turkish Federated State of Cyprus. The population of Cyprus in 1974 was 645,000 comprised of Greek Orthodox 501,000, Turkish Muslims 118,000 and others 26,000. Following an agreement for an official population exchange, about 65,000 Turks previously resident in the south moved to the north and about 200,000 Greeks moved south of the new boundary. As a result, the Greeks who constituted 78 per cent of the population were confined to 60–65 per cent of the island and, according to Ladbury, personal relationships between Greeks and Turks almost completely terminated. Incentives were offered to emigrant Turkish Cypriots to return to build up the economy in the 40 per cent of land owned by the Turks, representing 20 per cent of the Cyprus population, but the number of returnees from the UK though uncertain was unlikely to have been large. Instead the Turkish population has been augmented by immigrants from the mainland upon which the Turkish community remains economically and educationally dependent. Clearly these events had 'far reaching and traumatic effects on the folk memories of the people involved' (Crellin, 1979, p.7). Constantinides (1977) has described the immediate impact on Greek Cypriots in London, and Ladbury (1977) has offered a fascinating analysis of interethnic relations between Turkish and Greek Cypriots and Cypriot and mainland Turks in Cyprus and London in the years immediately after partition.

EMIGRATION   Emigration from Cyprus to Britain can be divided into three phases: pre-1939, post-war (1945–74) and post-1974. The first Cypriot immigrants to Britain were young men mainly of Greek origin and came as British subjects when Cyprus was a Crown Colony with a mostly subsistent agricultural economy. Although some were merchants, sailors or students, most came to seek employment often in catering, though many suffered acute hardships in the early years. After the depression, the British administration in Cyprus promoted an alluring image of prosperity in England. But a Cypriot government emigration liaison officer based in London checked on conditions of passage – the ability to speak some English, a deposit of £30 and the certainty of work or friends or relatives who could guarantee accommodation or financial support – before issuing an affidavit of support. Women were also encouraged to join their husbands (George, 1960). The Censuses showed the number of Cypriots as 208 in 1911, 334 in 1921 and 1,059 in 1931. With the arrival of an increasing number of immigrants in the 1930s, an estimated 8,000 Cypriots were in full employment in the UK at the outbreak of the Second World War.

The main phase of post-war Cypriot immigration occurred on account of several social, economic, political and administrative reasons. The war brought comparative, but temporary, prosperity to Cyprus and increased employment. It was followed by post-war urbanization but expansion was not maintained at a high enough level to satisfy the newly acquired social and economic aspirations of the people (George and Millerson, 1967; Oakley, 1968). During the 1940s and early 1950s there was a rising population level and movement to the towns, with the most depopulated rural districts, especially in the plains, providing the majority of 'disgruntled, frustrated and enterprising' emigrants to the UK. Post-war economic conditions in the UK favoured immigration and Cypriot businesses which had increased and prospered (see p. 14) were able to offer employment to immigrants. The affidavit system reinforced family links and formalized a patronage system (Oakley, 1979), but also restricted the flow of immigrants, on average 1,000 per year, until the more stringent requirements, such as knowledge of English, were lifted in 1954 (George, 1968). Political unrest, violence, curfews and economic stagnation in the late 1950s also contributed to emigration (Krausz, 1971). At this time, Turkish Cypriot emigration, which started later, was almost in proportion to their numbers in the Cyprus population (George and Millerson, 1967).

Independence brought a brief slackening off of emigration but with the abolition of affidavits, which allowed Cypriots free access to the UK like other Commonwealth members, 1960–1 saw the peak of immigration with 25,000 Cypriots entering Britain (Oakley, 1970; see also OPCS, 1984, Table 14). Most came for economic reasons – to obtain stable and better jobs, which had not resulted from the British withdrawal – though some had educational aspirations for their children (Butterworth and Kinnibrugh, 1970; Triseliotis, 1976) and a few had political motives. For some, migration was a way of improving status or associated with marriage prospects (Oakley, 1970). Although the presence of relatives in Britain facilitated 'chain' migration, 'a means of locating or creating opportunities and also a social context within which migration and settlement' could take place, the decision to migrate was that of the immediate family. Whereas the original migrants tended to be service or white-collar workers (Oakley, 1971), Constantinides (1977) found that most of the emigrants from two Greek Cypriot villages were from landless families or families with small non-viable holdings (see LCSS, 1967), typically young men with only elementary school education and no formal training and often already married with a young family. Ladbury (1977) has described how for Turkish Cypriots migration was a matter of personal choice for the individual who regarded it as an economic opportunity, not a necessity to support relatives by remittance. She claimed that Turkish Cypriot emigrants to the UK represented a cross section of the population. Generally the migrants were young – about half under 35 – some single men and women, but many already married, some of whom initially came alone and within a year or two sent for their wives and others who migrated with their small children – practices which were reinforced by the Department of Social Welfare Services in Cyprus and the Cyprus Office which had responsibility for supervising the welfare of migrants' children and promoting family reconciliation (George, 1960; Oakley, 1979). Some elderly widows followed later when families were securely established.

It has been suggested that every adult Cypriot probably weighed the pros and cons of emigration. However, the introduction of the Commonwealth Immigration Act in 1962 reduced the number of immigrants to an average of less than 2,500 per annum (Oakley, 1970). Oakley (1971) and Constantinides (1977) agree that this fall off was due more to the perceived decline in economic opportunities. Some families (especially children of primary school age) were reunited, but the introduction of the voucher system, which meant that 90 per cent of new immigrants came to specific jobs and sometimes had their passage paid, reinforced the family networks and virtually completed Cypriot immigration by 1966 (Oakley, 1979; see also Rose *et al.*, 1969). By 1970 one in six Cypriots was in Britain (Oakley, 1970).

The pre-war immigrants had been prevented from returning even to visit their families, but many of the migrants in the post-war migration intended to return (LCSS, 1967; Butterworth and Kinnibrugh, 1970). Few in fact did so by the mid-1960s (George and Millerson, 1967) and Oakley (1968) claimed that those with school-age children who did so counted their return as a serious mistake. Most returned only for holiday visits (George, 1960; Constantinides, 1977), although some Greek Cypriots made capital investments in developing tourist areas and remittances and others had business or retirement dreams. Ladbury (1977) also indicated that despite considerable contact between Turkish Cypriots in London and Cyprus the majority would be unlikely to return there to live. Whatever the short- or long-term intentions of the migrants, many found increasing ties of settlement with the growth of UK-born families. Moreover, the Civil War in Cyprus, in 1974, meant that for those whose home villages were in the occupied areas return became a physical impossibility and others came to see their futures in the UK. Indeed an estimated 10,000–12,000 refugees (GB.P. H of C, 1985; CRC, quoted by Clough and Quarmby, 1978; World University Service, 1977) arrived in the UK. The majority were Greek Cypriots but included those who had returned to Cyprus to retire and had lost everything and had to start afresh – whole families, mothers and children and children and teenagers on their own – who numbered 2,000 (McCarty and Christoudoulou, 1977; Constantinides, 1977; Alkan and Const-antinides, 1981). Some of those 'refugees' who were never officially recognized as such stayed only a short while and returned home, sometimes under threats of deportation due to *ad hoc* government policies (Gordon, 1983). But some 2,000–3,000 visitors and British passport holders remained to start a new life. Even so, a 'home orientation' and 'ideology of return' continues to exist (Anthias, 1983).

DEMOGRAPHY AND COMMUNITY COMPOSITION   Immigration patterns are reflected in a demographic analysis of the Cypriot community in the UK over the last 35 years. In preface, it is however necessary to draw some important distinctions in terms of community composition and characteristics and to point to certain data limitations which have a significant bearing on an interpretation of demographic trends.

Many Cypriots are British citizens, although a high proportion of the refugees in

1975 held Cypriot passports (Alkan and Constantinides, 1981). The Cypriot community in the UK was roughly representative of the population in Cyprus itself: about four-fifths Greek Cypriots and one-fifth Turkish Cypriots (Oakley, 1970) – though this may have changed in recent years (see GB P. H of C, 1985). Despite common birthplace, background, appearance and many customs, there are significant differences of language, religion and kinship between the Greek and Turkish Cypriots. Social anthropologists have debated the relative emphasis given to ethnic and national consciousness and identity in the beliefs of and interaction between members of the two groups (see pp. 33–5). Until the mid-1970s at least it appears that generally an ethnic identification predominated. Within this, the communities are divided on social class lines. The Greek Cypriot community in the UK was mainly composed of 'ordinary immigrants', but also included officials in government, banking, tourism and academics – groups distinguished by their education, status and reason for being in the UK (Constantinides, 1977). Within the Turkish Cypriot community there was also an urban educated élite, including students involved in government or ethnic associations and organizations, but distinguished from and having little influence on the majority of working-class Turkish Cypriots (Ladbury, 1977). Events in Cyprus and community developments in the UK over the last decade may, however, have modified these distinctions and relationships.

Ethnic and national boundaries are, moreover, complicated by the presence in the UK of mainland Greeks and Turks with whom Greek and Turkish Cypriots have complex interrelationships but generally limited interactions. Although Greek and Turkish Cypriots may emphasize their ethnic identity with their respective mainlanders – they share a common language, religion and kinship system – they in fact differ in dialect, details of custom, political ideology and religious practices (Constantinides, 1977; Ladbury, 1977) (see also pp.26–8). The mainland Greeks are mostly shipowners, big business people, white-collar office workers and middle-class professionals, some associated with the Embassy, or students. Generally they have a different socioeconomic background from most Greek Cypriots and live in more affluent areas of London. There are also some Greek immigrants who have arrived under EC legalization of labour mobility. Similarly, ordinary Turkish Cypriots had no contact with the 1,000-plus students or 300 or so government and administrative personnel from the mainland in London in the mid-1970s. At that time, an estimated 4,000 mainland Turks – only a fraction of Turkish workers in Europe (Paine, 1974; Berger, 1975) – were also working, usually in catering, and living in the same areas of London, though they were apparently not generally seen as economically or culturally threatening (Ladbury, 1977) (see p. 31). The extent to which perceptions of and interactions with their respective mainlanders by Greek and Turkish Cypriots may have been modified in the light of community developments in Cyprus and the UK during the last decade is unclear from research sources. However, it is important to be aware of ethnic and cultural links between Greek and Turkish Cypriots and Greeks and Turks from the mainland in considering recent population trends and, in educational terms, in respect of language surveys.

There are additional complications in attempting to describe the demographic evolution of the Cypriot community in the UK arising from data inadequacies. Every decade the Census provides data on country of birth; information is also available on the Cypriot population in the UK from their inclusion in the category 'Mediterranean Commonwealth origin' or 'New Commonwealth Mediterranean'. However, like the birthplace figures, this heterogeneous category also comprises people born in Gibraltar, Malta and Gozo including significant numbers of British service personnel. Consideration of such figures requires that these other groups be weighted in order to estimate the Cypriot population. In any case, Census data are increasingly inaccurate as they fail to distinguish the growing number of UK-born Cypriots. Nor, moreover, are the usually helpful Labour Force Survey figures on ethnic origin of assistance since their inclusion in the categories 'white' or 'European' renders Cypriots indistinguishable as a group. Whilst national data do not distinguish the numbers of Greek and Turkish Cypriots in the population, Census figures do permit certain comparisons between the populations born in Cyprus, Greece and Turkey now resident in the UK. For all these reasons the account which it is possible to offer of the demographic characteristics of the Cypriot community in the UK is seriously flawed and must be regarded with extreme caution, bearing in mind the above caveats.

Census figures show that the Cyprus-born population resident in the UK increased by about 30,000 in each of the two decades between the Censuses 1951–71 (Table 1). According to an analysis by George and Millerson (1967), by 1961 the sex ratio of the Cypriot immigration had narrowed to five to four and could be considered normal for an immigrant community. Apart from the lower percentage of persons over 65 (1.2 per cent), the age structure was almost identical to that in Cyprus but predominantly youthful – 37.2 per cent were under 14 and 61.6 per cent up to 64. The 1971 Census data show that there was an almost even sex ratio in the population born in the Mediterranean New Commonwealth, with 85 per cent being under 45 (CRE, 1978).

Table 1:   Cypriot-born population resident in Britain, by sex, 1951, 1961, 1971 and 1981

	1951	*1961*	*1971*	*1981*
Total	10,208	41,898	73,295	84,327
Males	6,494	23,468	39,425	44,585
Females	3,714	18,430	33,870	39,742

Sources: Census 1951, 1961, 1971, 1981; GRO, 1956, 1964; OPCS, 1974, 1983a.

The 1981 Census data based on the head of household's birthplace in the Mediterranean (50,863 persons) and household members born inside or outside the UK gives some indication of changing age structure as well as the increasing number of UK-born (Table 2). It must be remembered that although these figures include an unknown number of persons other than Cypriots born in the Mediterranean Commonwealth, the figures also exclude an increasing number of third- (or even fourth-) generation with Cypriot origins born to UK-born heads of household.

Table 2:   Persons born inside or outside the UK, by age, by birthplace of head of household in Mediterranean, 1981

	UK-born	*Born outside UK*
0–4	13,625	400
5–15	30,796	2,891
16–19	11,113	2,946
20–29	12,970	19,916
30–44	6,376	31,390
45–60/65	2,752	24,074
60/5+	1,683	9,146
All	79,315	90,763

Sources: Census 1981; OPCS, 1983a, adapted from Table 3.

Table 2 suggests that by 1981 almost half the members of households whose heads were Mediterranean-born were born in the UK. Moreover, some 47,000 were under

16, the overwhelming majority UK-born. This appears to be corroborated by other data from the 1981 Labour Force Survey (OPCS, 1982a, Table 5.19; OPCS, 1983b, Table 12). However, the imprecision of these data with the inclusion of a few thousand non-Cypriots must be emphasized.

The 1981 Census data do, however, allow comparisons to be made between the sex and marital status of the Cyprus-, Greek- and Turkish-born populations resident in the UK (Table 3). In 1986 their respective Embassies estimated that there were 20,000 Turkish and 35,000–40,000 Greek nationals in the UK.

Table 3: Cyprus-, Greek- and Turkish-born population in the UK, by sex and marital status, 1981

| | | Country of birth | | |
		Cyprus	Greece	Turkey
	Total	44,585	5,840	6,772
	Single	13,711	2,192	2,718
Males	Married	29,488	3,421	3,820
	Widowed	512	74	74
	Divorced	874	153	160
	Total	39,742	6,272	5,076
	Single	10,439	1,179	1,492
Females	Married	25,549	4,119	2,861
	Widowed	2,202	594	570
	Divorced	1,552	380	153
Total persons		84,327	12,112	11,848

Source: Census 1981; OPCS, 1983a, Table 1.

Owing to the impossibility of obtaining precise figures on the Cypriot population in the UK, researchers and Cypriot sources have from time to time suggested estimates based on country of origin or language spoken. Oakley (1970) has calculated a Cypriot population of 110,000, and Markopoulou (1974) suggested 120,000. Several sources have quoted the Cyprus High Commission's estimate in 1976 of 130,000–140,000, including 40,000 Turkish Cypriots and 1,000 Armenians from Cyprus, although some (eg. Triseliotis, 1976) put the estimate as high as 160,000. In 1980 there were estimated to be 80,000 Greek speakers in London and 7,000 Turkish speakers in Haringey alone (Reid *et al.*, 1985). An estimate in 1984 of the Cyprus High Commission of the Greek-speaking population (Greek Cypriots and mainland Greeks) has been variously reported as 160,000 (*Mother-Tongue News*, 4 May 1984 and 5 September 1984) and 200,000 (Tansley, 1986). Anthias (1982) estimated 180,000–200,000 Greek Cypriots, and Krokou (1985) calculated that the UK Cypriot population is now over 200,000. In 1986 the office of the London representative of the Turkish Federated State of Cyprus estimated that there are 50,000–80,000 Turkish Cypriots in Britain and the Turkish Cypriot Cultural Association and Cyprus Turkish Association estimated 85,000 with 145,000 Greek Cypriots. Although the UK Cypriot population is only a small percentage of the total UK population (0.14 per cent based on 1971 figures – see Littlewood and Lipsedge, 1982), and is small compared with the UK, West Indian and Asian populations, nevertheless the current estimates equal one-third of the total population of Cyprus (Krokou, 1985). As Constantinides (1977) has observed, considering the majority of Cypriots had village origins the way in which they have established themselves in an alien metropolis is of great interest.

SETTLEMENT   The settlement patterns of the Cypriots in the UK initially reflected the kinship-sponsored immigration linked to employment availability and accommodation (see pp. 11, 13–14). Subsequently it appears settlement was associated with the desire for the security of living within a distinct community with its own services, associations and lifestyle (see p. 29). Since from the earliest years of settlement Cypriots have lived predominantly in the Greater London area, it has been claimed that their 'degree of concentration in a single urban area is one of the highest for any ethnic minority in a modern industrial society' (Oakley, 1970). Even though in the last 20 years the Cypriot population has been characterized by socio-economic mobility, reflected in its geographical redistribution northwards of Greater London, it has been suggested that 'The Cypriot community remains probably the most concentrated of all Commonwealth-derived immigrant groups' (with the possible exception of recent Bangladeshi communities) (GB. P. H of C, 1985). By drawing on various research sources and demographic data, it is possible to give an account of Cypriot settlement over the last 60 years from the early settlements in London, augmented by post-war immigrants to show the national distribution of the Cyprus-born population, its changing distribution within Greater London and the location of the Greek and Turkish Cypriot communities (Table 4).

The pre-war male immigrants settled in lodging-houses in the West End near the hotels and restaurants where they worked. With the growth of new immigrants and the arrival of women and children many moved out of the increasingly expensive and unsuitable premises to Camden. Many mothers and children were evacuated during the war to places such as Rickmansworth and Bedford and to Northamptonshire. At the end of the war many returned to Camden and a few families went to the outskirts of London. Later, in the hope of improved business prospects, some Cypriots moved out of London to seaside towns such as Margate, Bournemouth and Southend (Alkan and Constantinides, 1981; George and Millerson, 1967).

The organization of post-war emigration in the 1950s (p.3) meant that the large number of Cypriot immigrants and their families swelled the density of Cypriot populations in central London which were already moving north and north-west. Over the past 50 years various sources, using the Census data for each decade (except 1941), have demonstrated that at least two-thirds to three-quarters of the Cyprus-born population in the UK have resided in London, Greater London or the south-east. The concentration in Greater London was particularly dense in 1961 – over 80 per cent – and remained at about 70 per cent in 1981. The last two Censuses demonstrate further movement outwards into the south-east.

It appears that the 20–25 per cent of the Cypriot population residing out of Greater London have always been widely dispersed, like the Chinese, for occupational reasons. In the 1930s on account of seafaring and business connections they were to be found in cities such as Southampton, Liverpool, Manchester, Cardiff and Glasgow (George, 1960). By the 1960s their involvement in catering had extended their dispersal to seaside towns (see above and p. 10) and other cities such as Leeds and Bristol (Oakley, 1968). The majority living outside London are Greek Cypriots, though there are Turkish Cypriots in the Home Counties and settlements in Birmingham and Manchester (Ladbury, 1977). By the 1971 Census only nine cities and towns outside Greater London had Cyprus-born populations of over 200: Birmingham 1,030, Manchester 490, Bristol 375 and Liverpool 345 and Coventry, Glasgow, Leeds, Plymouth and Brighton (Campbell-Platt, 1978). CRC (1974) and CRE (1978, Tables 6 and 7) provide further county and district breakdowns. Only a few refugees arriving in the mid-1970s joined relatives outside London (Triseliotis, 1976). Data from the 1981 Census show the regional settlement of the Cyprus-born population, compared with that of the Greek and

Table 4:   Regional settlement of the Cyprus-, Greek- and Turkish-born populations in the UK, 1981

Country of birth and total Great Britain	England total	North	Yorkshire and Humberside	East Midlands	East Anglia	Greater London	South East — Outer Metropolitan	South East — Outer SE	South-west	West Midlands	North-west	Wales	Scotland
Cyprus (84,327)	82,120	779	2,099	2,488	1,667	58,453	4,126	3,794	3,168	3,033	2,513	943	1,264
						{ 66,373 }							
Greece (12,112)	11,048	337	444	325	292	6,083	1,080	872	450	408	757	690	374
						{ 8,035 }							
Turkey (11,848)	11,490	142	352	226	155	7,955	958	593	343	271	489	87	271
						{ 9,512 }							

Sources: Census 1981; OPCS, 1983a, adapted from Table 1.

Turkish populations, confirming the residential concentration of all these groups in the south-east (Table 5). Outside this area the largest Cyprus-born populations occur in the south-west, the West and East Midlands and the north-west.

Not surprisingly, analyses of the Cypriot population have focussed on London and Greater London in terms of movement between districts and boroughs and concentrations within these localities. An analysis by George and Millerson (1967) showed that between 1931 and 1961 the main location of Cypriot population changed from St Pancras to Islington. But although Cypriot immigrants in the 1950s congregated in Islington, Camden and Hackney, with smaller populations to the south of the Thames, Camden remained the 'heart' of Greek Cypriot settlement (Constantinides, 1977). During the early 1960s there was a considerable northward movement of Cypriot families. A detailed analysis of trends in the distribution of the Cypriot/Maltese population in London between 1961 and 1971 showed that the concentration in Islington and Camden declined sharply, whilst Haringey and Enfield experienced large increases (Lee, 1973). This was clearly reflected in the 1971 Census when the Cyprus-born population of Greater London totalled 53,095 with 13 boroughs having over 1,000 Cypriots. The largest were: Haringey 11,865, Islington 7,300, Enfield 4,020, Hackney 3,985, Southwark 3,310, Camden 2,850, Barnet 2,640 and Lambeth 2,265 (Campbell-Platt, 1978). In a ward analysis of Haringey using 1971 Census data Leeuwenberg (1979) demonstrated the concentration of the Cypriot population in and around the Green Lanes area.

In the mid-1970s Cypriot refugees joined families in Haringey, Camden, Islington, Enfield and Hackney (Alkan and Constantinides, 1981). The movement northwards continued out to Enfield, Barnet, Brent and Waltham Forest (Constantinides, 1977). This was in fact reflected in the ILEA Literacy Survey (ILEA, 1977), in which fewer than two-thirds of the Greek and Turkish Cypriot pupils tested in 1971 remained in the authority in 1976. In the 1981 Census Haringey still had the largest Cyprus-born population – 11,671 – with 9,240 in Enfield, but only 1,837 in Camden the original area of settlement (Krokou, 1985). However, Alkan and Constantinides (1981) have estimated that the true Cypriot population of Haringey in 1980 was more like 30,000–35,000 out of an estimated total of 228,000. Data from these research papers suggest that, although there is a movement into Haringey from Camden, Enfield is likely to have the greatest number of children of Cypriot origin in its schools in the future as newly weds and business people have been tending to move out of Haringey to Enfield. Alkan and Constantinides (1981) estimated that the population of Enfield with origins in Cyprus is about 10,000. Indeed the more affluent are moving out further into Hertfordshire.

Within the London area there are certain differences with respect to the settlement of the Greek and Turkish Cypriots and Greeks and Turks from the mainland. There are few Turkish Cypriots outside London: about 5,000 scattered between Birmingham, Manchester, Liverpool, Newcastle, Nottingham, Derby, Southend-on-Sea, Brighton, etc. (Memdouh, 1981). In the 1950s to mid-1960s they tended to be in London boroughs to the east and south-east of the centres of Cypriot settlement (George, 1960) and fairly evenly distributed north and south of the river (Oakley, 1971). In the 1970s the Turkish population expanded northwards but remained relatively scattered even in Haringey, with its considerable Turkish population. Turkish Cypriots south of the river were likely to be more isolated from one another and other Cypriots. In the mid-1970s the majority of Turkish Cypriots lived in Haringey, Islington, Lewisham and Southwark (Ladbury, 1977), together with working-class Turks from the mainland. In the 1980s Turkish Cypriots are concentrated in Hackney (GB. P. H of C, 1985) and in the poorer housing in the east of Haringey (Reid *et al.*, 1985) (see p. 13). Although Leeuwenberg (1979) and

Beetlestone (1982) found that Turkish Cypriots in Haringey were less socially mobile than Greek Cypriots, they too now appear to be moving out to Barnet and Enfield. According to Anthias (1983), certain suburbs of London such as Hendon, Finchley and Barnet are designated as status areas, and the woman's income may contribute to relocation. Mainland Greeks tend to live in Central London – especially Queensway in Bayswater and the more affluent in Hampstead – and have little contact with Greek Cypriots in north London (Tsatsaroni, 1983).

HOUSING   The housing situation of the Cypriot population has been closely linked to their economic development and changes in settlement patterns. It is characterized in London by an initial need for cheap, rented accommodation near the workplace, then a high motivation towards owner occupation, at first in the larger, often poorer-quality housing of the community heartlands and more recently, with changes in household size, in smaller, better-quality housing in the outer London boroughs. Not surprisingly in view of the concentration of Cypriots in Greater London, research has focussed on this area in relation to housing tenure, household size and housing standards, but it is also possible to draw some national comparisons.

Pre-war migrants faced housing problems, accommodation was scarce and run down and many rented single rooms. After the war, many families lived in multi-occupied accommodation often rented from a few Cypriot owner-occupiers, sometimes on account of the guarantor system but this also enabled them to pay mortgages (George, 1960; Constantinides, 1977, Alkan and Constantinides, 1981; Kroukou, 1985). There was a strong motivation towards house ownership which, as George (1960) discovered, was due to several factors including the reported reluctance of British landlords to accept large Cypriot families and the fact that owner–occupation was seen as an economic asset and an enhancement of social status – in fact a goal of emigration. At that time there were only a few Cypriots in council housing owing to long waiting-lists, changes of address, failure to register and ineligibility, but council tenancies were more likely to be overcrowded on account of family size. Furnishing was often sparse and utilitarian, but usually included a TV or gramophone. Few Cypriots adopted British cultural habits, such as gardening or keeping pets, and interactions with British neighbours were minimal. Constantinides (1977) confirmed that in the late 1950s when, for economic reasons, Cypriots sought accommodation near their workplaces in the 'twilight zones', they often felt their friendly overtures rebuffed by English neighbours, which may have been due to cultural misunderstanding or hostile feelings during the EOKA period in Cyprus; and they often felt culturally or morally superior to other immigrants in these localities (see also pp. 36–7).

The strong aspirations of Cypriots to home ownership coincided in the late 1950s and early 1960s with lack of housing in inner London boroughs, rebuilding and, in some areas, the removal of some of the indigenous population to outer London boroughs or smaller houses (Alkan and Constantinides, 1981). Lower-cost housing – often larger terraced properties in Haringey and Hackney – became available when Cypriots were seeking housing, and these areas still permitted easy access to work in the West End (Clough and Quarmby, 1978). High mortgages and overheads meant that families sometimes took on joint mortgages or that they, in turn, sub-let to relatives or other Cypriots.

These attitudes, aspirations and practices are reflected in housing data on patterns of tenure, standards and household size in the 1960s, which set the trend towards improved housing status in the 1970s and 1980s. According to Dench (1975), the 1961 Census showed that in Greater London 38 per cent of Cypriot households were in owner-occupied housing, 28 per cent in private unfurnished, 25 per cent in private furnished accommodation and only five per cent in council housing. By the ten per cent Sample Census in 1966 44 per cent of Cypriot householders in London were owner-occupiers (Oakley, 1970). This was similar to the figure for Cypriot households nationally (46.2 per cent) and almost identical to the national percentage for all households. At that time, 23 per cent of Cypriot households (nationally) lived both in private rented unfurnished and furnished property and only 7 per cent lived in local authority housing (Collison, 1969). However, Cypriot households, like other ethnic minority families, but to a lesser extent than Caribbean immigrants, suffered a degree of overcrowding – 31 per cent nationally having more than one person per room, compared with 6.5 per cent of all households. Rose *et al.* (1969) undertook an analysis of the 1966 Sample Census data for the West Midlands and London as a whole and for selected wards and boroughs, making comparisons with Davison's (1966) analysis of 1961 Census figures for seven London boroughs. In 1966 Cypriot household size in London was 3.89 persons with 4.11 rooms per household and 55 per cent of Cypriot households shared accommodation. In the seven selected London boroughs the percentage of Cypriot households sharing accommodation had increased between 1961 and 1966, but the housing density had declined. Yet Cypriots in fact had a reduced level of housing amenity – one-fifth of Cypriot households had no bath and almost half did not have exclusive use of a WC.

It appears that, unlike West Indian and Asian immigrants at this time, Cypriots did not particularly suffer discrimination in housing. A study in 1966–7 by Daniel (1968) found that only eight per cent of Cypriots compared with 39 per cent of West Indians, and 19 per cent of Indians, claimed and produced evidence of personal experience of discrimination in applying for privately rented accommodation (see McIntosh and Smith, 1974). Relatively few claimed discrimination in applying for a mortgage and only nine per cent, like Asians rather than West Indians (23 per cent), had ever considered applying for council housing. By the late 1960s the existence of Cypriot estate agents and a supporting internal economy (Oakley, 1970) may have assisted in housing acquisition. However, there were some claims of exploitation by Cypriot landlords (Markopoulou, 1974). Alkan and Const-antinides (1981) pointed to difficulties where households with growing families included relatives and/or other Cypriots as tenants who could not leave due to the diminishing private rented sector. Multi-occupancy, larger household size and greater than normal density of persons per room, reported in some educational investigations (see e.g. Bhatnagar, 1970; MacDonald, 1975), have implications for opportunities for study.

The 1971 Census showed that although the number of persons per household whose chief economic supporter was born in Cyprus, Gibraltar and Malta had declined further to 3.74, over 20 per cent of these households still lived in shared dwellings, a few without exclusive use of cooking facilities (CRE, 1978, Table 17). As interviews with 181 families in Haringey, Islington and Camden in 1975 showed, the arrival of refugees put a further strain on relatives' households, especially when they were in privately rented accommodation or renting on their own, when they were often subject to very high rents or frequent changes of address (Alkan and Constantinides, 1981). During the 1970s, with increasing financial security, some Cypriot families have moved to smaller but better-quality homes, particularly as the second generation have grown up and married. According to Constantinides (1977), there continues to be a small percentage of Cypriots in public housing, usually due to compulsory purchase by the local authority of the property in which they were living. She maintained that living in a council house or flat carries a stigma. However, Ladbury (1977) indicates that some newly married Turkish Cypriots take up such accommodation and families have also moved out of Haringey into council housing in Wood Green and Tottenham.

Data for 1981 (see p. 6) show that the average size of households where the head was born in the Mediterranean Commonwealth has declined further to 3.2 persons (OPCS, 1982a, Table 5.19). The largest number of households with a head born in the Mediterranean comprised three adults with or without one or two children or two adults with two children (OPCS, 1983a, Table 6). Demographic data from the Linguistic Minorities Project suggest that Turkish-speaking households may be larger (see also Beetlestone, 1982) but confirm the very high proportion of Greek and Turkish-speaking households in London – over four-fifths in their sample – in owner occupation and less than one-tenth in council housing (see Table 8, p. 54). To this extent, the Cypriots must largely be regarded as satisfying one of their own objectives of emigration.

EMPLOYMENT   The employment position of the Cypriots in the UK is characterized by a high degree of occupational mobility, flexibility and diversification, with highly developed internal and external economies. Thus in terms of type of work and socio-economic status since their early involvement, predominantly in catering, the Cypriots have developed a whole range of service industries, especially clothing, in businesses which are often owned, run by and employ Cypriots. This is one reason why Cypriots appear to have suffered less discrimination in employment than some other post-war immigrants. A major economic shift within the Cypriot community since being in the UK is the involvement of women in paid employment. There are strong similarities in the employment patterns of the Greek and Turkish Cypriots and an important interdependence. These features can be examined in relation to the employment background in Cyprus, early employment in the UK and the way in which post-war trends have become established and modified in the 1970s and 1980s.

The employment background from which many of the Cypriot emigrants came was that of an agrarian economy, based on increasingly fragmented peasant land holdings, where families, including women and children working in the fields, were accustomed to working on their own. After the economic depression of the 1950s, there was expansion and diversification in the 1960s, with increasing mechanization of agriculture which engaged 40 per cent of the economically active population, and the development of industry, mining and tourism (LCSS, 1967). The British military base was also a major source of employment (Oakley, 1979). However, underemployment was widespread and families generally had a low annual income. Urban developments encouraged some migration from rural areas for employment. Generally women occupied themselves with household tasks, especially sewing, though in the 1960s some in towns took up clerical work. Some men had worked in the towns before emigrating to Britain, but Oakley (1970) found that those with jobs stayed even if they had relatives abroad. In one sample in the UK Daniel (1968) found that 78 per cent had been working before emigrating. The 'Demographic Report' for Cyprus in 1963 (quoted by George and Millerson, 1967) showed that about a third of emigrants to the UK from 1959 to 1963 were craftsmen or tradesmen and about 15 per cent were in catering, but about half were classified as unskilled or had skills which would not necessarily be directly useful to them in the UK.

The post-war immigrants came to join relatives and friends, most of whom were already established in catering. In the 1930s they had lacked opportunities other than as unskilled workers or kitchen hands in West End restaurants where they were not handicapped so much by lack of English. A few managed to start their own businesses – cafés, restaurants, hairdressers and tailors. The war marked an economic turning-point for the Cypriots, for the internment of many Italians provided those Cypriots who were not conscripted with the 'long sought' opportunity to oust their Italian superiors from the catering trade; until then Italians had owned and held most of the managerial posts in the restaurants since they had been established longer in London (George, 1960). Whereas in 1939 there had been 29 Cypriot restaurants in London, there were 200 by 1945. In the immediate post-war years the Cypriot community experienced remarkable business prosperity and expansion, so that by 1950 there were some 280 restaurants and cafés in London, and 230 in the provinces; the Cypriot restaurants were said to be amongst the best in London and to have a wide clientele. There were also said to be about 60 Cypriot hairdressing businesses, 22 shoemakers and 15 grocers (ibid; George and Millerson, 1967).

The affidavit system of emigration reinforced recruitment amongst the post-war immigrants into these occupations, especially catering, although unlike the other personal service trades, the majority had no previous experience in this area and came from varied educational and occupational backgrounds (see e.g. Martianou, 1981). By 1958 there were 350 Cypriot restaurants and cafés, 182 hairdressers, 150 tailors, 78 grocers, 72 shoemakers and 38 other Cypriot businesses. Analysis of the occupations of an opportunity sample of callers at the London offices of the Cyprus government in 1952 and 1958 showed that, whereas in 1952 nearly half the 400 Cypriot men had been involved in catering, 30 per cent (of 1,000) were so employed six years later. There was also a decline in those men citing occupations in tailoring, hairdressing and shoemaking. However, a huge increase was reported in men engaged in factory work (eight to 30 per cent) and in food industries (5–10 per cent). The rise in factory employees was apparently due to the inability of the small-scale Cypriot businesses to expand fast enough to accommodate the growing number of immigrants. Turkish Cypriots were more likely to be employed in the factories and Greek Cypriots in catering.

Using a ten per cent sample of the 1961 Census figures, Davison (1966) calculated that in London 76 per cent of Cypriot men and 38 per cent of Cypriot women were economically active. However, 5.8 per cent of Cypriot men, the third highest percentage in London, were unemployed. An analysis of the ten per cent Sample Census in 1966 (Collison, 1969), based on socioeconomic group, confirmed that the Cypriot population in Britain had a high proportion of employers and managers, although most were in small firms, but a proportion in the professions smaller than that for any other group except the West Indians. By and large the socioeconomic distribution of Cypriot males in Greater London confirmed the national picture and also indicated a much higher proportion of Cypriot men in service industries (Table 5).

In 1966, according to Rose *et al.* (1969), 89 per cent of Cypriot men and 47 per cent of Cypriot women in Greater London were economically active. In terms of occupation a third of Cypriot men were in service work, mainly catering, 9.3 per cent in clothing, 9.1 per cent in engineering, 5.7 per cent in retailing, 3.6 per cent in the professions, 3.3 per cent in clerical work and 1.4 per cent were administrators and managers. As Oakley (1970) observed, although Cypriots continued in the traditional skills and crafts, chiefly tailoring, hairdressing and shoemaking, the increasing popularity of retail trades especially grocery and greengrocery, like catering, were newly acquired skills, often a response to the opportunities available but also motivated by a desire for independence rooted in traditional working patterns. Yet as Anthias (1983) has also observed, many Cypriots were excluded from other openings because of lack of language skills and qualifications.

Table 5: Socioeconomic grouping of Cypriot men, compared with the whole population in Greater London, 1966 (percentages)

	Whole population %	*Cypriot men* %
Professional workers	5.4	2.7
Employers and managers	11.8	11.0
Foremen, skilled manual and own-account workers (other than professionals)	34.1	41.8
Non-manual workers	23.1	6.4
Personal service, semi-skilled manual and agricultural workers	14.3	31.2
Unskilled manual workers	8.1	7.0

Sources: Census 1966; Collison, 1969, Table 2.

Indeed in 1966 one-fifth of all Cypriot men were self-employed – more than twice the national average (Oakley, 1970). Virtually all the Cypriot businesses were one-man or small family enterprises which absorbed migrant relatives who were trained in appropriate skills, before they in turn set up their own independent businesses. Alkan and Constantinides (1981) have described how in the 1960s as English retailers were selling out, due to increased competition from supermarkets, Cypriots took over shops in the Green Lanes area of Haringey and Seven Sisters in Islington where, being assured of a market from Cypriot customers and by drawing on family labour, they could reduce the overhead of wages and afford the rents. Thus, in addition to the traditional crafts, Cypriots 'established themselves in almost every conceivable kind of business which could possibly be of use to their community, estate agents, printers, garages, bookshops, travel agents, solicitors, driving schools, electrical shops, and many other kinds of business' (Oakley, 1968, p.26).

To this list for the 1960s, Alkan and Constantinides (1981) add greengrocers (retailing produce from Cyprus), grocers, butchers, pâtisseries, bakeries, dress shops, furniture shops, opticians, dentists, GPs and banks. According to Oakley (1968, 1970), these wide-ranging Cypriot businesses constituted both an external and an internal economy, predominantly the provision of personal services, for the general public and not just fellow members of the ethnic community. By means of this 'dual economy', Cypriots had been able to achieve a 'high degree of self sufficiency and autonomy for their community not to mention a moderate degree of affluence' (Oakley, 1970, p.101). The 1971 Census figures (quoted by Anthias, 1983) confirmed a marked self-employment of Cypriot men and the high proportion of service workers (just over one-fifth in each case).

As an outcome of the success of these independent family businesses, and the great concentration of Cypriots in the area of settlement (see p. 8), ethnic segregation both limited their exposure to the forces of assimilation (see p. 36) and reduced their contact with indigenous workers in British firms, unlike the experience of many other post-war immigrants (George and Millerson, 1967; Oakley, 1968). These factors probably account for less discrimination suffered by Cypriots in employment. George (1960) found little evidence of friction between Cypriot and British workers or difficulties with trade unions. In a study, in 1966–7, Daniel found that only six per cent of Cypriots, compared with nearly half the West Indians and over a third of Asians, claimed and provided evidence of discrimination in employment. Indeed almost two-thirds of Cypriots were uncertain of, or failed to believe in, such discrimination, and the remainder claimed to have avoided it personally, many suggesting that they belonged to an immigrant group which did not experience discrimination. However, less than one-fifth had used a labour exchange when last looking for work. A controlled study of job application (Jowell and Prescott-Clarke, 1970) discovered that Cypriots or Australians had a success rate of 74 per cent in applications for interview, compared with 52 per cent of West Indians and Asians. Moreover, in situation testing by actors applying for skilled and unskilled jobs (and housing), the net discrimination experienced by the Greek tester was just under half of that against the Asian and West Indian tester (McIntosh and Smith, 1974). Within the Cypriot community itself mutual assistance in finding a job lessened any language difficulties and reinforced social networks. Although Cypriots are industrious, over the last 20 years there have been reports of exploitation within the Cypriot community, that working conditions in restaurants, tailoring and factories are poor, with long hours and wages sometimes very low, especially for women in dressmaking (George and Millerson, 1967; Markopoulou, 1974; Constantinides, 1977). Anthias (1983) shows how family 'honour' and that of the community often prevents complaints being made or mainstream unionization.

It has been suggested that it is the economic role of women which has changed the most in the immigration process (Constantinides, 1977). Even before the war, the availability of work in tailoring and dressmaking in Cypriot and Jewish firms permitted the emigration of Cypriot women and girls, despite cultural sanctions (Oakley, 1979), as most girls in the villages in Cyprus had learned to sew as part of their preparation for marriage. George and Millerson (1967) found that in the 1950s the great majority of Cypriot women in work – as many as three-quarters of the wives of callers at the Cyprus High Commission office and half with children under five – were employed in dressmaking. In the late 1950s and early 1960s, with the boom in fashion and ready-to-wear clothes, the Cypriots were able to consolidate the niche being vacated by Jewish workers aspiring to white-collar jobs (Alkan and Constantinides, 1981). They were thus able to draw upon traditional skills in work where lack of fluency in English was no handicap, women were able to observe cultural norms by sewing in workshop groups or in family businesses – where they were able to develop some social life – or by doing piece-work at home, and so contributed to the family income.

By 1966 two-thirds of Cypriot women in work in Greater London were employed in the clothing industry – the greatest concentration of all groups of workers. (A further 13.6 per cent were engaged in service work, 8.1 per cent in clerical work and 3.3 per cent in sales, (see Rose *et al.*, 1969). A number of Cypriot clothing firms had become large and very profitable and the wages had risen due to a shortage of labour (Oakley, 1970). Census data for 1971 show that the economic activity rate of Cypriot women aged 15–45 ranged from 29 to 48 per cent, according to the area of the county; they were more likely to be working than Pakistani women but less likely than African and West Indian women (CRC, 1976). Cypriot women were more clustered in the skilled (16.9 per cent) and semi-skilled (32.5 per cent) social class categories than other New Commonwealth women and, in this sense, may be in a more subordinate position (Anthias, 1983).

The majority of Cypriot women over 25 work for Cypriots in the clothing industry and many, especially with pre-school children, do dressmaking outwork at home (Bhatnagar, 1970; Figueroa, 1974; Reid *et al.*, 1985; and see p. 22). Working at home allows flexibility to attend to domestic and family needs and avoids the need to cope with travel to work and workplace relationships. On the other hand, it may lead to social isolation and overwork with long hours in order to increase income from low piece-work rates; and some councils have imposed fines on outworkers after investigating complaints of noise by neighbours. Moreover, home machinists are self-employed, do not always receive holiday or sick pay and are the first to be laid off in slack periods (Constantinides, 1977; Alkan and Constantinides, 1981; Anthias, 1983). In 1981, 80 per cent of the clothing trade was said to be run by Cypriots in small family businesses and factories employing 40 or more people in Haringey, Islington, Hackney and Camden, with associated wholesale outlets. There have been changes in the clothing trade with the recession, such as pay cuts to women workers, and it is difficult to estimate the current size of the workforce especially as many women working as machinists or finishers are unregistered (Anthias, 1983). Generally they are susceptible to high unemployment and low job security and have little protection or power, but ethnic identification and, within that, acceptance of social role definition prevent them from reconceptualizing their employment rights or an employment progression. As a result of research including participant observations in factories and home interviews over two years, Anthias (ibid) has argued strongly that women have borne the brunt of the migrant adaptation of a fairly significant proportion of men who have used their ethnicity successfully in the clothing trade in Britain. The entry of Cypriots into this section depended on the skills of women, their need to work and the overriding economic motivation for migration. Cypriot women are a source of cheap labour, totally controlled by the employer and the demand for labour and, as Anthias shows through case-study data, their employment often involves the extension of the patriarchal relations of the family to those at work. In the clothing industry men tend to have different jobs, as pressers and cutters, and to earn much more. Yet even the men, she argues, have experienced cultural and personal impoverishment by their involvement in a spiral of money-making in the all-demanding but highly unstable and competitive clothing and service sectors.

The employment sphere has highlighted the ethnic interdependence of Greek and Turkish Cypriots. It has been suggested that the generally later arrival of the Turkish Cypriots affected their economic, financial and social stability *vis-à-vis* the Greek Cypriots. According to Ladbury (1977), since the majority of Turkish Cypriots had migrated from ethnically mixed villages, some of the first migrants turned to Greek Cypriots for employment when there were no Turks available to help. Despite political tensions during intercommunal fighting in the 1960s and 1970s, Greek and Turkish Cypriots continued working together in factories and small businesses with good, firm individual and working relationships (see Constantinides, 1977). In the mid-1970s Turkish Cypriots maintained work ties with Greek Cypriots both because there were insufficient Turks in varied occupations to be ethnically self-reliant and their relationship was mutually beneficial and economically viable. This interdependence even if unequal – since the more numerous Greek Cypriots were more likely to be employers of Turkish Cypriots – made discrimination untenable. Ladbury (1977) cited several examples of the economic and cultural importance of the patron–client relationships built up between Greek and Turkish Cypriots in terms of employer–employee or vendor–customer at the individual level (see also Leeuwenberg, 1979). She considered that the fact that it was economically advantageous for Turkish Cypriots to choose to play down their differences and continue contact with Greek Cypriots also partly accounted for the concentration of both groups in the same type of employment. In 1975 the Kimon trade and service directory listed a range of over 3,000 Greek Cypriot businesses in London and a Turkish trade directory listed 500 Turkish businesses, mainly dress factories and catering establishments, suppliers and services. From a study in Haringey, Leeuwenberg suggested that Turkish Cypriots were less likely than Greek Cypriots to be self-employed in the professions, or to work with other Turkish Cypriots, but that many had been economically successful.

The Linguistic Minorities Project survey in Haringey, in 1981, discovered that the work environment for Turkish-speaking respondents was less likely to be supportive of the use of the minority language than it was for Greek speakers; in particular, Turkish speakers were less likely to have a Turkish-speaking boss, at least one Turkish-speaking fellow worker or a job where it was essential to speak Turkish (Reid *et al.*, 1985) (see p. 71). Even so, it has been claimed that there are at least 1,500 Turkish Cypriot/Turkish owned businesses in London (Memdouh, 1981).

During the 1970s and 1980s the employment trends established in the early years of immigration appear to have been consolidated. Several sources have remarked upon the Cypriots' capacity for long hours of hard work and their versatility. Constantinides (1977) noted the occupational mobility of many Greek Cypriots who were usually prepared to try a wide range of jobs and experiment with several types of small enterprises before finding what suited them best. This accounted for much of the further diversification of Cypriot service and manufacturing businesses in the 1970s which strengthened the 'internal economy'. Thus, although the 'ethnic economic niche' was being eroded as Cypriot foods were becoming attractive to a wider British public and Cypriots were not exclusively patronizing their own stores, the internal economy was still strong enough to employ the second generation. Many of the Cypriot refugees in 1975 were absorbed into the clothing trade (Alkan and Constantinides, 1981).

It is generally agreed that there are still comparatively few Cypriots in professional occupations such as teachers, lawyers, doctors, architects, social workers or accountants. This was confirmed in an analysis by Leeuwenberg (1979) which also indicated that in Haringey, compared with the general population, there were three times as many self-employed Cypriots including more employers and managers and more skilled and semi-skilled service workers. Although he suggested that the number of self-employed Cypriots may have been levelling off, as many as half the Cypriots in a Commission for Racial Equality (CRE) survey based on a quota sample in 1981 (CRE, 1981a) claimed to be self-employed. Anthias (1983) suggests that 20 per cent of Cypriot men are self-employed (including small-scale employers), 20 per cent are service workers and in distribution trades, and nine per cent are construction workers. The LMP survey in Haringey, in 1981, of about 100 of both Greek and Turkish Cypriot respondents found that they were predominantly in manual work (three-fifths Greek, four-fifths Turkish Cypriots) and a high proportion were in manufacturing (just less than two-fifths Greek, a half Turkish Cypriots) especially in clothing and were self-employed or worked in the family business (over one-third of Greek and a quarter of Turkish Cypriots) (Reid *et al.*, 1985). Evidence generally suggests that there may have been further intensification of the involvement in the clothing trade, using women's traditional skills, perhaps in response to increased competition in catering from other more recent immigrant groups. However, this sector is particularly vulnerable at times of economic recession.

FAMILY LIFE AND STRUCTURE   The family is of great, if not paramount, importance to Cypriots. In order to appreciate the home background of pupils of Cypriot origin, it is therefore necessary to consider the family structure, lifestyles and values of the traditional village communities from which the emigrants came, and the recreation and modification of these practices and relationships in the domestic arrangements of urban living in London, and later to examine implications for child care (pp. 23–4), health (pp. 24–5) and social services (pp. 25–6).

Several sources, notably Oakley's research (1968, 1979; see also LCSS, 1967) have described the traditional village society and family lifestyles and values in which Cypriot migrants had their roots, even though post-war life in Cyprus with new economic and educational opportunities, especially in the towns, was already changing as the migrants left in the 1950s and 1960s, and family ties were extended and loosened with emigration itself. In Cyprus urban and rural life were in sharp contrast, especially in terms of employment, education, social interaction and the pace of life (George, 1960; LCSS, 1967; Butterworth and Kinnibrugh, 1970). The majority of emigrants came from the villages – communities of 200–3,000 people – where life centred upon the church, school and coffee houses, and had varying degrees of contact with the towns. Until the 1960s Greek and Turkish Cypriots in mixed or separate villages had a similar way of life in respect of work, recreation and food habits, though they differed in language and religious practices (George, 1960). Oakley (1968) claimed that the different historical and cultural traditions radically affected individual character and family life and education. The village communities 'demanded of their members fairly rigid adherence to a set of social practices and associated values' (Constantinides, 1977, p.23) which were closely associated with family honour, loyalty and kinship ties and 'gender-differentiated cultural ideals' (Oakley, 1979, p.17), especially the social importance of female sexual purity (see Anthias, 1983). The moral influence of the community can be appreciated through an outline of traditional family structure, marriage and child care practices.

A number of small autonomous family groups, closely connected by ties of marriage and descent make up the Cypriot village. The family is a nuclear unit of married parents and children, possibly with elderly or widowed grandparents. A married brother and his family may live in the same household, but each family aims to be a sovereign and self-reliant unit. Family loyalty, a 'paramount virtue' (Oakley, 1979), involves the obligation to put the immediate family first and kin generally before others. Every individual member is expected to maintain and promote the honour, reputation and welfare of the family group by discharging roles and responsibilities in line with gender expectations. The male head of the family has a particular responsibility to represent the family in public and, in the village, family life and conduct is very much open to public scrutiny and criticism so many individual problems are only revealed and treated within the immediate family (Oakley, 1968). Ties with near kin, especially married siblings, are close and important, especially where economic and educational opportunities require reliable relationships outside the village. This may result in cementing ties with more distant kin or creating 'pseudo-kinship' in terms of godparenthood or wedding sponsorship which may lead to more contractual relationships of patronage.

The nuclear family and household is usually established on marriage. Traditionally, in Greek Cypriot families, marriages were arranged between families in the same village by parents, sometimes with the help of a go-between, but Constantinides (1977) suggests that young people now have a greater degree of initiative before parents institute formal proceedings. It is important that the economic and social standing of the couple's families are evenly matched (Oakley, 1968). The bride's dowry and other property agreements whereby the groom receives his share of the parental estate are pledged at the religious betrothal ceremony followed a year or so later by the marriage itself. The breaking of an engagement brings great dishonour to the participants, and the Greek Orthodox Church recognizes few grounds for divorce. The ideal bride is said to be diligent and chaste as all her early training has led towards marriage and motherhood. Traditionally the sexes are thought to be essentially different in nature and temperament and only in private family life is their complementary interdependence recognized. Even so, there is strict division of labour between husband and wife, and the wife is under the authority of the husband, the source of family discipline. The wife's role is domestic, not public, and to uphold the family honour through her industrious, modest and virtuous behaviour (ibid).

Within the patriarchal family traditional differences in attitudes to and expectation for boys and girls have been observed. On the whole boys are preferred to girls: there is an emphasis on masculinity in Greek society; sons symbolize family vigour and the continuity of patronymy and they are an economic asset whereas daughters require a dowry to take to their husband's families and villages. The mother is totally responsible for the children: though she expects obedience, she is also the provider of emotional warmth and security, and Oakley (ibid.) maintains that she feels especially close to her sons. Triseliotis (1976) indicates that the fathers' fondness is shown more in symbolic interaction with the children, which takes precedence over the husband–wife relationship. Babies and toddlers receive much indulgent attention but more firm discipline by the age of four, so that they develop a sense of personal responsibility, morality and authority sanctioned by limited physical punishments. Older children are often responsible for younger brothers or sisters. Child care may also be shared with grandmothers, other relatives and neighbours. By school age, when children are made to feel a wider responsibility to the family, they have also adopted gender-differentiated duties on the land or in the home as mini-adults. These rules and responsibilities develop further into adolescence when young men are traditionally allowed greater freedom whereas the girls live a more home-based life preparing for marriage – the final step to adult status. Traditionally until then children remained economically and psychologically dependent on their parents. Only with the extension of secondary education to the majority, and in the struggle for independence, has there developed a concept of youth and adolescence (Oakley, 1968).

Since the post-war emigrants left Cyprus there have been further changes in the traditional patterns of family and social life, but the extent to which Cypriots in the UK are aware of these will depend on contacts through family letters and visits. Whether family life has been recreated or modified in the UK depends on individual families and factors such as rural or urban origins, family involvement in the migration process itself, length of time and family contact in the UK. However, sources are generally agreed that there is a strong sense of family solidarity and family-centredness amongst Greek Cypriots in the UK (ibid.). Through business, accommodation and social links families have been able to reinforce traditional values in the minds of members and for first-generation migrants the traditional way of thought and behaviour is a reference point and guideline. Constantinides (1977) has suggested that Greek social customs and institutions have thrived due to the strength of certain basic values, the emigrants' arrival together over such a short time and a balanced sex ratio. Allegiances among the first-generation are primarily to the family, village and Cyprus itself. The recreation and modifications of traditional family and social practices may be examined in respect of evidence on marriage, relationships between families, male–female roles within the family and the position of the elderly.

With the exception of the early pre-war immigrants, the majority of Cypriots appear to have married compatriots within their own ethnic group. The imbalance in the sex ratios of the pre-war migrants – 2:1 in 1921, 5:1 in 1931 – meant that if they did not return to their home villages or send for future brides, some young Cypriot men, especially in London where the sex ratio was even greater, married British girls. But even in the 1950s it was suggested that such mixed marriages amounted to only four per cent (George, 1960). Both Greeks and Turks married out, but Cypriot marriage with the British was relatively low compared with that of another Mediterranean group, the Maltese (Dench, 1975). By 1961 the sex ratio was almost balanced (see p. 6) as also among the immigrants between 1955 and 1966, who were divided between single persons and those with wives and young families (Oakley, 1979). Intermarriage between Greek and Turkish Cypriots in the UK has not been favoured by either ethnic group for religious, social and, latterly, political reasons. Although Constantinides (1977) claimed such intermarriage or cohabit- ation exists and more commonly than in Cyprus, Ladbury (1977) found very few examples during an 18-month study of Turkish Cypriots in London. There is some intermarriage between Greek Cypriots and mainland Greeks in the UK, but this is generally regarded unfavourably by mainlanders (Archimandritou- Xefteris, 1977). Intermarriage with the British, Irish, Spanish and Italians is greater, but even so, a relatively small proportion of all marriages. More men marry out. Parents may disapprove, but become reconciled to marriage to an Englishman or woman (Anthias, 1983).

Amongst Turkish Cypriots in the 1970s in London marriages were no longer arranged between members of families who originally migrated from the same village in Cyprus, but certain kin relationships were strengthened and new relationships formed on the basis of status in the UK (Ladbury, 1977). There is a preference for a Turkish Cypriot brought up in Britain and hence a better chance of mutual understanding, although sometimes a marriage is arranged with a partner in Cyprus. Ulug (1981), a young Turkish Cypriot, has pointed to the linguistic and cultural difficulties of such a match. However, this is currently much more acceptable than marriage to a Britisher, 'an additional threat to Turkish self-ident- ity' (p.36). Since, apart from school, interaction between the sexes is limited to community functions such as cinema going and weddings, a go-between usually contacts the girl's family and arranges a meeting between both families. The courting period is closely controlled and chaperoned, but may be a stressful and confusing time for the girls due to previous limited contacts with the opposite sex and the difference in expected and accepted behavioural norms in Turkish and British society. Ulug provides some interesting data on young Turkish Cypriots' views on arranged marriages and relationships between the sexes (see p. 180). Certain practical compromises have however been effected, such as the optional registration of the marriage and the wedding feast itself within a month rather than a year, thereby facilitating house purchase and restricting the former ceremony to a family event, followed by a celebration by up to 400 guests.

Similarly, Greek Cypriots tend to marry other Greek Cypriots, and this is the preference of the second generation. Constantinides (1977) reported that although the UK-born often inveighed against arranged marriages, many were prepared to accept this in practice providing they were allowed to express an opinion (see Alkan and Constantinides, 1981; Anthias, 1983). Marriage patterns are increas- ingly pan-Cypriot and there have been changes relating to engagement, marriage and the dowry. According to Constantinides, in the 1970s, engagements, which were often at an early age in an attempt to safeguard reputation and the marriage pattern were more likely to be celebrated by a secular party than a church blessing. Hence less dishonour accrues to the parties of a broken engagement. Sometimes the arrangement was abused as a way of permitting greater freedom for Cypriot girls outside the home (see p. 160). Although register office marriage has become more common, it is regarded with disfavour, and family pressure is brought to bear to solemnize the marriage in church. The dowry system in the UK has to some extent been supplanted by wedding parties, though both sets of parents usually help substantially in setting up the couple's independent household. Generally practices vary from family to family and there is increasing flexibility in marriage 'arrangements', greater freedom and more opportunities to exercise independent judgement (Anthias, 1983).

It has been said that the Cypriots are more family-centred than any other large ethnic minority group in Britain, or the indigenous population (Oakley, 1970). That this has been possible in Britain is partly due to the process (see pp. 3–4) and pattern of emigration itself which favoured the emigration of nuclear family units or their reunion within a relatively short time. Moreover, according to Oakley (1979), a survey of Commonwealth immigrants in 1961 revealed that two-thirds of Cypriot immigrants had one or more siblings living in the UK and almost half had at least two other siblings in Britain. Oakley's own research confirmed that often other extended kin were also in the UK. Several studies have reported that any spare leisure-time is spent relaxing with the immediate family or visiting relatives and have remarked upon the intensity of family relationships (George, 1960; Hylson-Smith, 1968; Constantinides, 1977). Greek Cypriots claimed that their most important leisure activity was visiting relatives and friends – close kin, wedding sponsors and godparents. For many, wedding parties with as many as a thousand guests were the principal or only type of family outing and the most important and ostentatious social function reinforcing old ties and establishing new ones (Constantinides, 1977). Alkan and Constantinides (1981), however, suggest that these parties are not now so elaborate. According to Ladbury (1977), many Turkish Cypriots have established new kin relationships, the most relevant being those with other Turkish families in the neighbourhood who visit most frequently. In addition, communication between Cypriots in the UK and their families and kin in Cyprus is maintained by letters and visits in both directions (Oakley, 1979, and Constantinides, 1977, give details of increasing visits between the early 1960s and 1970s) and, in some cases, remittances and business transactions. Often news and information are spread widely and publicly in the two communities.

However, adapting to life in an urban environment in the UK has also been accompanied by some stresses and tensions within families and households. For example, there have been significant changes in male and female roles. Even in the 1950s, George (1960) found that although the man was still in a position of moral and financial authority, there were beginning to be changes in the authority structure due to modifications of habits and especially the economic influence of working wives (see Markopoulou, 1974). Women working, especially outside the home, has implications for child care, but according to Alkan and Constantinides (1981) this has also contributed to an accelerated rate of marital breakdown. Although a second wage contributes to the family income, it brings a certain independence to the women which many Cypriot men cannot cope with or understand as, traditionally, male 'honour' is related to the role of chief provider. Men socializing out of the home with friends and sometimes gambling rather than having a social life within the family is also said to cause marital stress, and some women are no longer prepared to tolerate this situation. Divorce, though greater than in Cyprus, is relatively uncommon (see Table 3); Anthias (1983) shows how divorced and separated women are subjected to social abuse and lack supportive frameworks within the Cypriot communities.

Whilst some (especially older women) suffer isolation from family and the Cyprus lifestyle, a source of tension for others is the very presence of members of the extended family, often an elderly grandparent, uncle or aunt, in the household (see household size figures, pp. 11–13). Although they are often able to assist with child care, their traditional role as advisers to the community and their families may not be easily accepted by young people who may also experience intergenerational and cultural differences with their parents (see pp. 158–65). In addition, housing in the UK is more spatially confined and the lifestyle more an indoor one than in Cyprus (Oakley, 1979; Alkan and Constantinides, 1981). The arrival of refugees, many of whom continued to live with relatives, and some of whom became responsible for child care and upkeep, caused additional pressures.

CHILD CARE   Traditionally in Cyprus young children were used to a wide network of relationships and group care in the village. Although close observational structures of families do not appear to have been undertaken in the UK, some research sources permit an examination of child care and rearing practices in the newly constituted nuclear families within an urban environment; Ulug (1981) indicates that child care patterns are similar for Greek and Turkish Cypriots.

Triseliotis (1976) warned that urban life in Britain might bring about a loss of kinship and neighbourhood support especially detrimental to children, yet even in the late 1950s George (1960) discovered that most of the pre-school children whose mothers worked (see p.16) were looked after by their grandmothers who had come over specifically for this purpose. Other children were placed in day nurseries. Some of school age were 'latch-key' children. In an inquiry in 1967–8 Stoker (1969) discovered that few infant headteachers had explained the availability of nursery schools and some claimed that Greek Cypriot parents preferred full-time care in order to work. However, Triseliotis (1976) reported that because of inadequate day-care facilities, many young children were looked after by a succession of unregistered child-minders in unsuitable premises and lacked continuity of care. Hunter-Grundin (1982) described the South Haringay Pre-School Centre, set up in 1978, to foster child development, adult education and community support. Mothers from many ethnic groups, including Cypriots, were able to discuss different child-rearing practices and child-minders also appreciated the support and facilities. Indeed a report from the Cyprus High Commission (Aristodemou, 1979) indicated that consideration was being given to setting up community nurseries – if the Cyprus government would supply personnel the Cypriot community would provide buildings and furnishings – in order to offer 'care for those children whose mums are working and often leave them unattended or to unreliable hands' and to ease the transfer from home to school. However, in 1981 Alkan and Constantinides reported increasing difficulties for mothers sewing at home or working away from home, owing to a lack of nursery provision in Haringey (with priority being given to one-parent families) and the short hours of pre-school playgroups. Mothers either worked at home or tended to leave children until the early evening with unregistered child-minders – often other Cypriot mothers working at home, relatives or friends – who might be looking after several children (see Anthias, 1983). However, these community liaison officers recommended that there should be more day nurseries and playgroups to facilitate the pre-school child's socialization and language development – both English and their mother-tongue – and again suggested that the community itself or even Cypriot factories should make provision. Anthias has supported this, also in order to allow mothers greater choice in their type of work. Turkish Cypriot sources too have expressed concern at the lack of pre-school facilities (Memdouh, 1981).

Relatively little specific information exists in child rearing practices in the UK. George (1960) indicated that, as in Cyprus, young children were indulged and gradually encouraged to take on some responsibilities, and discouraged from being inquisitive. Physical punishment was sometimes meted out. Triseliotis (1976), using case-study examples, pointed to the difficulties some children and adolescents experienced on migration to the UK and their responses to family reunions. Moreover, he claimed for example that often parents were so preoccupied with making a living that they were too tired to play or stimulate young children after work and found it difficult to cope with the greater tendency to question and challenge of the children who were growing up in the UK. Alkan and Constantinides (1981) have remarked on the immense concern, pride and affection for children within the family and the keenness for them to do well at school. Growing children begin to take some responsibility for younger members of the family. However, the undivided attention which children receive from all family members sometimes makes the transition to school a little daunting and they recommended that mothers should be encouraged to visit schools to develop the child's confidence to settle.

HEALTH   Some researchers have reported on aspects of the mental and physical health of Cypriots and their families, focussing particularly on their adjustment to life in the UK. In two articles Triseliotis (1968, 1976), an experienced social welfare worker with the Cypriot community, and a psychiatric social worker at a child guidance clinic, analysed the cultural and pathological aspects of the mental health of immigrants, with particular reference to Cypriots and including case-study material. Importantly, he pointed to the cultural taboo on talking about personal and family problems unless the situation is severe. Women were unlikely to discuss difficulties unless the husband was present or had been consulted. It was, moreover, useful to contact and liaise with the Cypriot father first, in recognition of his responsibility for matters outside the family, and it was he who usually accompanied a child to the clinic. Sources have observed the tendency of Cypriots to give greater expression to their feelings than the indigenous population, and their tendency to be more emotional and voluble has also been compared to West Indian rather than South Asian behaviour (Triseliotis, 1968; Cheetham, 1972). In line with this, for example, Triseliotis (1976) claimed that Cypriot children were more often referred to social agencies for behaviour rather than emotional problems. Psychological problems may only be recognized by parents if the child is extremely disobedient or delinquent and not amenable to external control and discipline. In particular, Triseliotis reported the emotional disturbances of Cypriot refugee children resulting from the experience of civil war and its profound psychological effect on the Cypriot community in the UK. In this and other cases confusion, depression, isolation and frustration were sometimes projected onto children who could not fully identify with their parents' sense of loss. However, Littlewood and Lipsedge (1982) reported that Cypriot immigrants – even refugees – were unlikely to have feelings of persecution, unlike some other psychotic patients from the New Commonwealth, possibly because they did not experience discrimination. Bagley (1971) reported a low rate of mental illness amongst Cypriot immigrants. But Markopoulou (1974) noted cases of mental illness and disorder amongst individuals and families who were trying or had failed to adjust to life in the UK and reported attempts to help them (see p.25). There is a reported need for Greek- or Turkish-speaking psychiatric help for Cypriot 'wives in particular who are under the most pressure' (Alkan and Constantinides, 1981), and who due to their lifestyles, are often dissatisfied and frequently suffer from ailments and depression (Anthias, 1983). There are support groups for women, and especially in relation to health, at the Cypriot Community Centre in Haringey (see p.32).

There is little information about the physical health of the Cypriot population. They may prefer a Greek- or Turkish-speaking GP, where one exists (Leeuwenberg, 1979). In the LMP survey a third of Greek-speaking and nearly half of the Turkish-speaking respondents had a doctor who spoke their language. However, other medical services, for example, family planning, may not be available in the community languages (Alkan and Constantinides, 1981). A particular health problem for Cypriots is thalassemia, an inherited blood disease passed on by healthy people who do not themselves suffer from it. Some 15–20 per cent of Cypriots are carriers and in Britain, in 1977, 60 per cent of 300 children with thalassemia were Greek Cypriots (Lobo, 1978). Several sources include information about this disease which starts in infancy, restricting growth and sleep, and requires regular blood transfusions and subsequently iron removal therapy (Alkan and Constantinides, 1981; Lobo, 1978). Miles (1983) discusses the educational implications, including the need to include such information on the medical record card and to take account of time off school for transfusions and lack of energy for PE or concentration. Research directed towards better diagnosis and treatment is ongoing. Lobo has advocated the screening of Cypriots on school transfer or leaving or in a medical examination often demanded before marriage in order to detect carriers. But Alkan and Constantinides (1981), reporting a pilot blood testing in a Haringey school in 1977, pointed to the sensitivity of such information in the community and especially in terms of its implications for arranged marriages. The UK Thalassemia Society aims to promote awareness and understanding of the disease.

SOCIAL SERVICES Consideration of social services provision and take-up revolves around awareness of and access to facilities and the extent to which these meet needs. There is a reluctance by Cypriots to seek professional help outside the family (Oakley, 1968). Markopoulou (1974) reported that a social work project initiated by the Camden Council of Social Service in 1965 for Cypriot immigrants was often ignored because of lack of English, shyness, fear of seeking help or ignorance of rights. Publicity in Greek drew more Cypriots to the Citizens' Advice Bureau (CAB) when advice was available in Greek on financial, family, health, social and legal problems. This acted as a bridge between the Cypriot community and statutory services. Markopoulou, a Greek-speaking social worker, was employed to deal with special long-term case work concerning mental health, delinquency and child care problems, which involved home visiting and liaison with the community, other welfare bodies and professionals (see p.149). Although she was initially regarded with suspicion, she was gradually accepted and respected, not least for assistance independent of any national group, the church or the High Commission. Finally, with the exception of the elderly, many cases were transferred to statutory social services but also within a more supportive community network.

Other researchers a decade or so later have commented on provision in Haringey. Leeuwenberg (1979) recorded that the borough published information in Greek and Turkish on education, housing, dental treatment and medical facilities and made available Department of the Environment information on housing as well as some translation and interpretation services. Even so, difficulties of access to information on taxation and legal matters were experienced. Pre-school centre provision also offered a consultancy service to parents on social and welfare services and aimed to foster interethnic, and inter-parental, support (Hunter-Grundin, 1982). In 1981 three Cypriots worked as liaison officers in the Social Services Centre, covering all aspects of social services, education, community work, health, etc., and monitoring contact with a wide range of statutory and voluntary agencies. Alkan and Constantinides (1981) reported continuing and acute language or culture problems, sometimes involving whole families, and in particular growing problems with social service, day care and housing provision for the elderly. They point to the increasing numbers of Cypriot elderly and the expansion of facilities required. For the elderly, above all, information about provision needs to be translated, and also interpreted on tape and radio. But documents on all aspects of education and social services should be translated automatically if the Cypriot community is to have greater awareness of available support and entitlements.

RELIGION   The significance of religion to Cypriots can be considered by outlining its role in social life in Cyprus and the existence of facilities, associated social functions and the extent of religious practice in the UK. Religion is one of the most obvious points of difference between the two ethnic groups. Greek Cypriots are Christians belonging to the Greek Orthodox Church, their religion being mystical and highly ritualistic, whereas Turkish Cypriots are Muslims, believers in the Koran, which contains detailed instructions for the conduct of life. The separate religious traditions have co-existed in Cyprus since 1571, although George (1960) claimed that the Christians were very sensitive to any moves to undermine the authority of the church, a very conservative institution. Indeed for Greek Cypriots the church has always given spiritual and temporal leadership (see p.2), associated with the Hellenist culture and traditions (LCSS, 1967). Since the establishment of monasteries in the 11th century the church has served a social welfare function and is the focal point of village life and festivals.

The Greek Orthodox faith has been practised at least since the 1600s in Britain and the centre for worship, St Sophia's in Bayswater, London, built in 1877 was designated as a cathedral in 1922. This church has always been patronized by upper-class Greek merchants and has come under the jurisdiction of mainland Greece. The arrival of Greek Cypriots with a different cultural background led to continuing friction over representation and control of the lay aspects of the church (George, 1960; Constantinides, 1977). As a result, Cypriots began to establish their own churches; however, according to Constantinides, the fact that their churches are not under the authority of an independent Church of Cyprus, but rather of mainland Greece whence most of the clergy came, has been a continuing problem. The first church for Cypriots was formed in Camden Town in 1948 and this was followed, in 1959, by a second in Kentish Town, a third in 1963 in Camberwell and a fourth in 1965 in Hammersmith. Moreover, at the beginning of 1965, 13 Greek Orthodox churches existed in other parts of the country and five were being established (George and Millerson, 1967). Despite ongoing disputes within the church, Greek Cypriot communities continued to petition for the services of a priest and use of a church, often on lease from the Church of England, wherever they inhabited new areas, so that by 1974 there were 22 Greek Orthodox churches in Greater London and 29 throughout Britain (Constantinides, 1977). There are three Greek Orthodox churches in Haringey, two in Wood Green and one in the Green Lanes area (Alkan and Constantinides, 1981). An Orthodox monastery exists in Essex and a convent in Buckinghamshire.

By contrast in the 1950s and 1960s Turkish Cypriots lacked a mosque for formal religious observance. Islamic associations hired halls to celebrate religious festivals. By the late 1970s some Turkish Cypriots attended the mosque in Regent's Park (Leeuwenberg, 1979) and a small mosque existed in Newington Green (Ladbury, 1977). Eventually the Turkish Cypriot community agreed on a suitable site for a mosque in Stoke Newington which opened in 1977, but there was no mosque for Turkish Cypriots in Haringey (Alkan and Constantinides, 1981).

Especially in the early years of settlement, but also continuing into the 1980s, the Orthodox churches have served not only as places of worship, but as focal points for local communities of Greek Cypriots and their way of life and as a means of preserving their ethnic and cultural identity. In addition to their religious functions, the churches have also been actively engaged in social welfare in the community, politics, language maintenance and the arts. Indeed several researchers in the 1950s and 1960s saw the role of the church in helping Greek Cypriots to maintain their national, cultural and ethnic identity as equally if not more significant than its specifically religious role (George, 1960; George and Millerson, 1967; Oakley, 1970); however, its religious and secular interests have often been in conflict for Greek Cypriots. There have been some social welfare activities, but these have not been well developed (Markopoulou, 1974; Constantinides, 1977). The Greek Orthodox Church has always been politically involved, reflecting events in the complex politics of Cyprus and mainland Greece (and Turkey). During the 1950s clergy actively supported EOKA (George and Millerson, 1967). By the late 1960s the church's interests were closely linked with those of the wealthy and more conservative Cypriots who financed and administered individual churches (Oakley, 1970). Before 1974, the Greek–Cypriot left-wing press had strongly criticized the church hierarchy for its allegedly anti-Makarios stance (Constantinides, 1977). Some anti-church feeling remains on political grounds (Leeuwenberg, 1979). From the early years of settlement there was competition between the church and left-wing and Communist groups in running part-time schools and classes for the teaching of the Greek language and culture (see pp.80–81). In 1981 the 21 Orthodox churches each had mother-tongue classes (Martianou, 1981). The churches have also patronized arts and youth activities in an attempt to retain the religious allegiance of the second generation (Khan, 1976).

Over the years sources have given various indications of the extent of religious practices amongst Greek and Turkish Cypriots and the significance of religion *per se* in their lives. In the 1960s the prestige of the church was said to be high and attendances good, especially on religious and national holidays (George and Millerson, 1967). However, Oakley (1970) maintained that the church was less influential than commonly supposed and that only the older Greek Cypriot women had any deep religious involvement. Although the church has continued to play a role in the life-cycle rituals of baptisms, weddings and funerals, at festival time and in Sunday Schools, church attendance and weekly services may be an ethnic or cultural rather than a religious experience. The main religious events and practices in the Greek Orthodox and Islamic calendars are briefly outlined by Alkan and Constantinides (1981).

Clearly, by comparison, Turkish Cypriots have lacked opportunities for formal religious practice and in the 1950s George (1960) reported some adjustments in observance of customs, festivals, fastings and dietary requirements. In the 1970s the small mosque was only full on Fridays, though prayers were held each evening, and according to Ladbury (1977), this was indicative of the fact that only a tiny minority of Turkish Cypriots in London attended a mosque or said prayers at home. Rather they drew upon the greater religiosity of mainland Turks to conduct occasional religious ceremonies at home, for example, a memorial ceremony or thanksgiving for a new-born child or new house (Alkan and Constantinides, 1981). According to Ulug (1981), Turkish Cypriots are less devout than Asian Muslims or Turkish mainlanders.

Religious observance amongst the second generation of Greek and Turkish Cypriots is generally said to be in decline although Beetlestone (1982) has reported that church services are always well attended by a wide cross-section of the Greek–Cypriot community. However, somewhat curiously, two studies (Marvell, 1974; Leeuwenberg, 1979) found a much higher identification on the part of Turkish than Greek Cypriots of their religious leaders as 'important people' and with religion. Recently the Swann Committee (GB. P. H of C, 1985) claimed in its Report that, from the evidence received, it seemed that the influence of religion was not central in either community (see LMP, 1985). Yet Krokou (1985) has asserted that 'maintenance of identity is inextricably linked to religious identity for both Greek and Turkish Cypriots'. It may be that religious beliefs and practices are more important in maintaining ethnic and cultural identity rather than on their own account and that those who assert their religious affiliation may be attempting to uphold their ethnic identity in as pure a form as possible. This may be particularly salient for certain Turkish Cypriots who, in a minority, have over many years generally lacked as supportive or wide ranging an ethnic community network as their Greek Cypriot compatriots.

Two other factors which considerably affect adaptation to a new life in the UK are language and education. The language knowledge, use and attitudes of Cypriot adults and children are reviewed in detail elsewhere (see pp.51–78). Parents' own educational experiences are considered in relation to their attitudes to their children's education (see pp.139–68).

COMMUNITY ASSOCIATIONS   One way in which Cypriots have sought to establish their community in the UK is through various voluntary associations with the objective of keeping alive and re-creating traditional cultural practices, values and activities, or, latterly, developing new leisure interests. These associations can be divided along ethnic, religious, political or class lines. Above all, immigrants needed to be able to spend their leisure time as in Cyprus and hence early associations were ethnocentric and reflected the increasingly political dimension in social life (George and Millerson, 1967). Since these factors have influenced the subsequent development of associations, the nature and meaning of ethnic associations and cultural practices will be considered separately here for Greek and Turkish Cypriots, prior to examining the extent to which such activities may take place on national lines and in conjunction with the wider society.

Even in the 1930s the few hundred Cypriots in London began setting up their own clubs and societies, and during the 1940s and 1950s the post-war immigrants established churches (see p.26), language classes (see p.27) and other associations to meet their needs. This support network was highly influential in terms of retaining their cultural outlook and habits although domestic and work routines predominated and leisure was primarily family-centred (see pp.22). Initially, reflecting the traditional public–private lifestyles of men and women, the associations were for men only, suffered from feuds and only engaged a minority of the community, according to George and Millerson. However, over the years as associations have developed to cover all ethnic and leisure interests the majority, including women and children, are usually occasional participants, if not members of at least one group (Leeuwenberg, 1979; Martianou, 1981).

Amongst the earliest associations were two pre-war political clubs, determined by the structure of politics in Cyprus, the Cypriot Communist Party existing since 1931 and the right-wing, pro-Greece Cyprus Brotherhood established in 1934. The latter concerned itself primarily with events in Cyprus and grew in strength, having 3,000 members in 1960, with businessmen and professionals amongst the more active. The Communist Party had a more dynamic organization based on the Cyprus Community Centre in Camden, spread through local groups with 1,250 active members in 1965 and took a wider interest in issues other than the union of Cyprus with Greece. Both groups tended to support the Labour Party in British elections. Both provided facilities for social, cultural and welfare activities aiming to preserve ethnic characteristics. Several other societies, particularly concerned with youth work and students, were also connected with these political associations, which generally reflected the dichotomy of left and right characteristic of social life in Cyprus (George and Millerson, 1967; Oakley, 1970). Even in the 1970s, although some of the variety of clubs claimed to be free of overt political alliance, many were at least loosely associated with the politics of left or right. Constantinides (1977) has also described how just as ethnic consciousness was at its height for Greek Cypriots in 1974 many, especially of the second generation, prompted by concerns for Cyprus, became more politically active in Britain. Leeuwenberg (1979) asserted that by the late 1970s right-wing, Cypriot-orientated political divisions were less prominent, and in 1981 Martianou reported that there was some allegiance to four political organizations representing the main groups in Cyprus, but also a growing interest in British politics. Student organizations are, however, generally energetically orientated towards politics in Cyprus, Greece or Turkey.

Other recreations of Cypriot social life which occurred with the main post-war arrival of Cypriot immigrants were the village associations open only to immigrants from specific villages. Many of these clubs were based on a café or restaurant owned by a member of the former village and their aim was to act as social and welfare bodies for members in London and to assist financially their villages in Cyprus – some making substantial contributions such as churches, youth centres and sportsfields (George and Millerson, 1967; Constantinides, 1977).

During the 1950s and 1960s a whole range of ethnic services, catering for all kinds of personal, social, domestic and leisure needs of daily life, were developed, further reinforcing community networks and interdependence (see p.17). Even in the mid-1970s Constantinides (1977) found that despite increased proficiency in English, and although Greek Cypriots did the bulk of their weekly shopping in supermarkets, most used a Cypriot butcher or grocer from time to time not just for economic reasons, but because of the personalized services which afforded opportunities for a renewal of contacts, the upholding of values and the exchange of news (see pp.15–18).

Amongst the provisions regularly available in Cypriot grocers and coffee shops are a range of Cypriot newspapers and magazines produced in Cyprus and the UK. The newspapers have a definite political orientation. The number of Greek Cypriot newspapers available seems to have fluctuated over the years (George, 1960; George and Millerson, 1967; Constantinides, 1977; Leeuwenberg, 1979), but the most persistent and widely circulated seems to be *Vema* which first appeared in 1939, has a left-wing orientation and has increased its sales from 3,500 in 1954 to 9,500 in 1979 including 2,500 to Manchester and Birmingham. Although it includes local Greek Cypriot news, especially advertisements for accommodation and jobs (and more recently for local authority posts – see Alkan and Constantinides, 1981), it deals mainly with events in Cyprus and communist countries. Events in Britain and overseas generally tend to be dealt with incidentally and ideologically in connection with Cypriot politics or the local community, for whom the paper is reported to have great concern. Interestingly, in the 1950s the Cypriot press supported the 'accommodation' of the Cypriot community but strongly opposed its 'assimilation'. Cypriots were exhorted to be law abiding, learn English, improve their employment prospects and avoid racialist provocation, whilst being reminded of their obligations to Cyprus and Greece and the need to maintain religious and linguistic traditions especially amongst the second generation. Apparently there are now at least two main weekly Greek Cypriot newspapers and one fortnightly, which tend to include sections in English for the British-born (see CILT 1982 for information on Greek newspapers and periodicals).

Even in the 1950s, there were apparently three Greek bookshops. Leeuwenberg (1979) lists: Kimon, in Camden, which has a range of books including children's books; Zeno, for antiquarian books; and the Hellenic Book Services, which also sells to libraries (see CILT, 1982). Apparently there are two small Greek Cypriot publishers which mainly produce books on religion and history. In another library study Clough and Quarmby (1978) reported some difficulties in meeting the needs of Cypriot users and that, with the exception of academic books and books on art and architecture, standards of book production were poor. Cooke (1979) noted that only two local authorities in the UK, replying to a survey, provided children's books in Greek, but Elliott (1981) found that variously sized collections of Greek books existed in public libraries in Haringey, Hackney, Islington and Brent. With increasing awareness of library needs in recent years, provision now seems to be more extensive. The CILT Language and Culture Guide for Modern Greek (CILT, 1982)also lists many academic and public libraries with Greek collections, for example, in Enfield, Redbridge, Camden, Lambeth, Waltham Forest, Westminster and Hertfordshire. But it may also be important to publicize the availability of books to local organizations in order to stimulate demand (Clough and Quarmby, 1978; Leeuwenberg, 1979; see p.72–4).

The performing arts, especially dance but also theatre and music, have always been popular. Apparently in the 1950s there were as many as 60 Cypriot dancing groups but, by the mid-1970s when Khan (1976) investigated the state of ethnic minority arts in Britain, she reported only five dance classes in London due to lack of community organization and outside support. Accommodation was a particular problem, and there was no centre for the 37 organizations then affiliated to the Greek Cypriot Co-ordinating Committee. For many years Theatro Technis, based in Camden, a pan-Cypriot experimental theatre and arts group, particularly involving the second generation, has had mixed success. It played a leading role in establishing a 'Cyprus week' for the arts in Camden which was open to the general public, and in 1981 was expanding its activities for young and old and addressing traditional as well as contemporary issues (Constantinides, 1977; Alkan and Constantinides, 1981). Music is also important in the lives of Cypriots, and the most authentic music, dance and songs are often to be found at weddings or festivals. In a survey, in Haringey, Leeuwenberg (1979) found that the majority listened to mainly ethnic music and overwhelmingly wanted easier access to music, the Greek Cypriots especially wanting modern music. Clough and Quarmby (1978) also noted a need for greater library provision for music. In the 1970s cinema-going was popular, local cinemas in centres of Greek Cypriot population being hired for weekend showings of Greek films, but there is no evidence to indicate how the availability of home videos may have affected these communal gatherings.

Over the years the number of interest groups has grown and diversified to cover sports clubs, youth clubs (see pp.157–8) and parents' associations as well as social and cultural clubs. Sports are popular amongst the second generation and there exist, for example, London-wide Greek and Turkish football leagues composed of 22 borough clubs (Leeuwenberg, 1979; Alkan and Constantinides, 1981). There are a number of Greek parents' associations in several boroughs which aim to promote educational, cultural and social activities and are particularly involved with the organization of 'mother-tongue' teaching for the second generation (see pp.80–3). Clearly the number and range of associations varies over time and locality. For example, Leeuwenberg (1979) discovered more Greek-Cypriot organizations in Haringey: two youth groups, two religious groups, one parents' association, one social club, one cultural association, one political group and one neighbourhood association (see Alkan and Constantinides, 1981) (see also pp.43–5).

There is generally less research evidence on Turkish Cypriot organizations and associations. It is unclear to what extent the formation of such groups has been affected by their smaller numbers, more scattered settlement and the greater difference in their religious background compared with that of the indigenous population, but it has been claimed that their later emigration hindered their financial and social situation *vis-à-vis* Greek Cypriots. In 1951, in the early days of migration when other kin were not already in the UK, there was, for example, a club which aimed to address the political, cultural, educational, recreational and welfare needs and interests of Turkish Cypriots (George, 1960). However, Ladbury (1977) has claimed that in the 1970s organizational activity did not provide a centralizing focus for Turkish Cypriots in London, who derived this on an individual rather than a group basis from kinship ties and neighbour interdependence. Even in Haringey, with a considerable Turkish population, there was no specifically Turkish business district, cultural or social centre. However, one street in Newington Green offered a coffee shop, records and paperbacks, and Turkish films were shown at two north London cinemas at weekends. Ladbury maintained that most of the Turkish associations such as the Turkish Islamic Association, the Ladies' Association, the Turkish Arts Society and several students' political associations were run by the urban educated élite and tended to cater for the middle class. Most working-class Turkish Cypriots were little influenced by these organizations, and, she claimed, had little contact with them other than in connection with provision of Turkish lessons for children and social functions on national holidays by the Cyprus Turkish Association which had publications in Turkish and English (CILT, 1983) and took the official political line on Cyprus. It is possible that the position may have changed in the last decade. The Turkish Cypriot respondents in Leeuwenberg's (1979) survey were much more likely than the Greek Cypriots actively to support other Turkish Cypriots when shopping or needing medical help and legal advice or travel facilities. They were also more active in community organizations, especially connected with politics and religion. At that time, there were five Turkish associations in Haringey concerned with the theatre, religion and culture, arts, women's issues and politics, and the list supplied by Alkan and Constantinides (1981) suggests that the number may have grown (see CILT, 1983). Indeed Ulug (1981) has claimed that Turkish Cypriot families no longer suffer a lack of Turkish amenities or contact with other Turkish Cypriots. Although organizers of Turkish community groups devote much time and energy to maintaining a feeling of unity, a unified and stable organization satisfying all interests does not always result.

Since 1959 there has been at least one weekly newspaper – now printed in Turkish and English and supplied from Germany – and whilst it gives news of Cyprus, there is inadequate coverage for Turkish Cypriots in the UK (Leeuwenberg, 1979; Alkan and Constantinides, 1981). (The CILT Language and Culture Guide on Turkish – CILT, 1983 – in fact lists five Turkish newspapers.) Leeuwenberg (1979) recorded that there were no Turkish publishers or booksellers in the UK, that books were difficult to obtain and stocks in Turkish newsagents were small, dated, of a limited range and expensively priced. However, there is now a Turkish bookseller, Basan Turk Kitabevi in Green Lanes, Haringey. Other library surveys revealed that only one local authority kept children's books in Turkish (Cooke, 1979), although Elliott (1981) recorded collections in Haringey and Hackney (see pp.74). More recently, the CILT guide (1983) lists some booksellers specializing in Turkish books, and university and some other public libraries, including Barnet and Kensington and Chelsea with Turkish collections. Access to greater music provision, especially traditional Turkish music, was identified as a library need in Leeuwenberg's study.

It is interesting to note how after 'unhappy' and 'misguided' attempts at promoting Anglo-Cypriot societies in the early 1930s, Cypriot associations and organizations in recent years have become less ethnocentric and also relate to the wider society.

George and Millerson (1967) recorded how concern for the welfare of Cypriot immigrants by the Colonial Office, British Council and Cyprus government – aimed at quickly integrating Cypriots – led to the establishment of a reception hostel and a non-political, non-religious Cyprus Association. Both failed owing to the lack of appreciation of the immigrants' need to spend leisure-time as in Cyprus and their strong political concerns. Relations with the Cyprus High Commission, for example, with respect to social welfare, were not always co-operative, sometimes for political reasons (Markopoulou, 1974), though it is now closely associated with parents' associations in the organization of language teaching (see pp.80–3). Contact with British officialdom is often avoided (Leeuwenberg, 1979). According to Constantinides (1977), some Cypriots who through education, status and linguistic fluency moved easily within the ethnic and wider society have tended to act as 'brokers' for other members, for example, in dealing with the complexities of the welfare state or local authority bureaucracy. They often used office in Cypriot associations as a training-ground for active participation in the institutions of the wider society.

It appears that sports and the arts began to bridge the social and cultural gap between Cypriots and the general public. George (1960) reported that there was some participation in British sports activities, but no membership of sports or social clubs, though it seems that this has changed with the education of the second generation (Aristodemou, 1979). Cypriot dancing, music and theatre has been made available to a wider British audience through various local community festivals and, in particular, the work of the Theatro Technis which 'aims to create the understanding and cultural exchange between the Cypriot community and its host community', with plays in Greek, Turkish and English. Several of the wide-ranging Cypriot associations and organizations listed by Alkan and Constantinides (1981) in Haringey and neighbouring boroughs aim to promote harmonious relationships and engage in joint social and cultural activities with other ethnic minority groups and society at large. Some raise funds for charities (see Miles, 1983). An interesting development in Haringey was the joining together of the main Greek and Turkish Cypriot organizations, in 1981, to form the Cypriot Community Centre in Wood Green, a community project backed by the Borough and Department of the Environment. The Centre aims to 'provide a base where the Cypriot community can maintain and develop its own identity, a bridge of communication between all sections and religious denominations within the Cypriot community and all other communities in Haringey; and to strengthen links amongst all generations of the Cypriot family'. In 1986 it began a project to help the unemployed to gain jobs or entry to courses and held a festival of Cypriot culture. Ongoing activities include a young women's and girls' committee, luncheon club for the elderly, youth activities, language classes and an advice bureau. Clearly the existence and expansion of Cypriot voluntary associations over many years demonstrate community strengths, and, as Alkan and Constantinides observed, they have 'become stable enough to allow these organizations to increasingly take part in the work of the wider community, from borough matters to cultural events and also to reach out to other communities' (1981, p.2). Although Anthias (1984) considers Cypriots have become less community- and more family-centred, she considers that the importance of groups which have increasingly become concerned with managing and reaffirming the interests of the community *vis-à-vis* the British state cannot be overestimated, even though actual participation by most Greek Cypriots is fairly low. Such organizations have a dual function: to reaffirm ethnicity and culture, and to act as political agencies.

COMMUNITY PERCEPTIONS   Finally, in considering the social background of Cypriots in the UK, it is important to examine the interrelation of community and inter-ethnic perceptions: Greek and Turkish Cypriots' self-perceptions, inter-ethnic perceptions and perceptions of their respective mainlanders in the UK; inter-ethnic perceptions of the British and Cypriots; and Cypriots' perceptions of other minority groups. Once again, many research sources, as in other aspects of Cypriot social life, are now somewhat dated. However, they usefully complement educational sources from the same period and provide a context in which to locate self- and inter-ethnic perceptions of the second generation (see pp.174–85, 169–74).

The relatively small number of pre-war Cypriots desired not to appear 'foreign', often adapted their names, lacked ready access to ethnic goods, such as food, and suffered from poor communications with their home country (Alkan and Constantinides, 1981). Both Greek and Turkish Cypriots maintained strong pride in their respective heritages and did not regard themselves as culturally inferior, and hence preferred accommodation to assimilation (see p.29). The greater number of post-war migrants thus made a deliberate attempt to develop their own community, to maintain loyalties to Cyprus and to resist Anglicization: 'They want to live their lives according to their own traditions within the prescribed limits of English society' (George, 1960, p.236). Moreover, the characteristic desire for independence and the economic success of the first-generation immigrants, often in their own businesses, produced a 'remarkably self-sufficient ethnic community' which was 'consequently less exposed to the forces of assimilation' (Oakley, 1968, p.26). Social interaction was within their own group, not with the British or other local minority groups (Hylson-Smith, 1968). Within the Cypriot community strong religious, linguistic and kinship differences between Greek and Turkish Cypriots and the importance of family life (see pp.21–2) served to perpetuate ethnic distinctiveness despite a certain economic interdependence (see p.17).

For the Greek Cypriots, it is ironical that when consciousness of specifically Greek Cypriot identity was at its height, at the time of the Turkish invasion of Cyprus, so too was their awareness that in reality their future lay in the UK. Yet this did not apparently diminish the desire to maintain a strong ethnic identity, especially through family and community associations (see pp.20,29). As Constantinides (1977) has pointed out, the extent to which Greek Cypriots are and wish to be differentiated depends on which of their physical and cultural features – skin colour, religion, names and language – Cypriots and those in contact with them wish to stress as, unlike some other immigrants, they are 'invisible' within the British majority population. She suggested that Greek Cypriots maintained such a strong sense of ethnic identity not just because of their residential proximity, daily social interaction or economic niche, but because their social norms and values, so important to a sense of identity, were felt to be superior to the values of the wider society and hence reinforced the distinctiveness of their identity. This sense of a 'moral community', in which Greek Cypriots judge one another according to strict moral and economic criteria, is closely linked to family-centred values and roles, which have been supported initially by the character of the migration and subsequently by the balanced sex ratio which facilitated and reinforced ethnic intermarriage. More recent evidence suggests that, even though Cypriot adults may be divided about the present state of the Cypriot community and the leadership of its organizations, they wish to perpetuate the community institutions. Their strong community spirit is reflected in their determination to retain their Greek Cypriot identity and above all to convey this to their children, especially through language classes (Martianou, 1981; Miles, 1983). However, some consider that it is possible to retain a Cypriot identity and play a part in the community at large (see Anthias, 1984).

Generally Greek Cypriots distinguish themselves from mainland Greeks, though their origins are rooted in a common language, religion and kinship system. Political ideology influences the extent to which distinctions are felt or stressed: some Greek Cypriots wish to emphasize the Cypriot connection, others consider themselves as Greeks from Cyprus (Constantinides, 1977). Social class distinctions are also strong (see pp.5, 10–11). These, together with dialect differences, may be emphasized by the second generation. For example, Greek Cypriot children asked if they felt they were the same as Greeks from the mainland said: 'They are more posh.' 'They are ruder and noisier.' 'They speak faster and use a different language, language with different words and meanings.' 'The Greeks look down on the Cypriots and say they are peasants' (Georgiou, 1983, p.21).

The ethnic identity of Turkish Cypriots and their relationships with mainland Turks both in London and Cyprus in the mid-1970s have been explored by Ladbury (1977). Like the Greek Cypriots, Turkish Cypriots in London were retaining their identity as a distinct ethnic group. According to Ladbury, Turkish Cypriots were distinguished from Greek Cypriots and mainland Turks by their informal organization, a shared common cultural heritage and value system, or one perceived as such by its members, and individuals who stress or play down their ethnic identity for a reason, possibly without any understanding that they are actually maintaining or diminishing the group's distinctiveness in the process. Yet apart from one north London location where ethnic distinctiveness was maintained by local facilities (see Hylson-Smith, 1968), Ladbury considered that, compared with Greek Cypriots, working-class Turkish Cypriots lacked group organization socially and culturally as associations were largely run and patronized by the middle class (see p3). For the majority interaction, though frequent, was limited in scope other than at weddings or visits to the cinema. Nevertheless, as for their Greek compatriots, ethnic identity was sustained by day-to-day individual relationships with kin, Turkish neighbours and workmates: 'From these people every service can usually be obtained, be it a case of finding a job, a husband, or someone to mend the roof. They constitute the individual's social universe in the context of which his behaviour as a Turk is judged, and his attitudes to non-Turks are formed' (Ladbury, 1977, p.312).

In London the majority of Turkish Cypriots have relatively little contact with mainland Turks, even those living in the same areas or also employed in catering (see p.31), although some visiting occurs and occasionally marriages are arranged. Ladbury explained how even though derogatory stereotypes may not exist at a group level – mainland Turks are not seen by Turkish Cypriots as a threat to their interests as individuals in economic, cultural or religious terms – nevertheless individual situations of conflict or disagreement from time to time may be explained by differences in attitudes and standards. By contrast, the cultural differences between Turkish Cypriots and mainland Turks in Cyprus was often exaggerated and emphasized and discriminatory attitudes or derogatory stereotypes displayed often on account of perceived economic advantages to the mainlanders. Indeed Ladbury suggests that since 1974 in Cyprus Turkish mainlanders fulfil the important social role of scapegoat – normally reserved for Greek Cypriots – to maintain ethnic distinctiveness.

Despite differences of kinship, language and religion, relations at the individual level between Greek and Turkish Cypriots in London before 1974 were very good. Both Constantinides and Ladbury agree that, despite the intercommunal hostilities of 1963 and the subsequent fluctuating nature of Greek–Turkish relations on Cyprus, this did not have profound consequences for inter-ethnic relations in Britain. Many of the migrants, who may have come from ethnically mixed villages, had already established working relationships together in London (see pp.17–18). Also many Greek Cypriots held left-wing political views, like the Turkish Cypriots, wanting independence from Britain, but not necessarily union with Greece. Although events in 1974 imposed a strain on relationships between Greek and Turkish Cypriots in Britain, it would have been detrimental to the nature of and shared roles in economically viable working relationships if the war and partition in Cyprus had caused them to terminate relations in London. In the mid-1970s the nature of individual Greek–Turkish relations in London also varied according to factors such as the ratio of Greeks to Turks in a neighbourhood, the length of time they had lived as neighbours and the current situation in Cyprus. Although ethnic differences were played down in working arrangements and the neighbourhood, relationships mostly remained public, confined to classroom, factory or street. It was rare, for example, for family visiting to take place between Greek and Turkish Cypriots, even if they had known each other for years, and any relationships overstepping conventional behaviour caused ethnic boundaries to be redrawn with renewed vigour. Interethnic marriage, for example, was seen as neither socially possible nor ethnically desirable. Community sanctions were exercised in accordance with the extent to which the liaison was perceived as threatening ethnic distinctiveness. Ethnicity is of course a relative and dynamic phenomenon which can be used and can change differentially over time, in various environments and between different individuals and groups of individuals. It is only possible to speculate to what extent a *rapprochement* between or hardening of ethnic boundaries has taken place in the light of the current economic climate in Britain, the political situation in Cyprus and the attitudes of Greek and Turkish Cypriot political factions. It may, however, be noted that the Swann Committee reported 'little real antipathy between Greek and Turkish Cypriots in this country' (GB.P. H of C, 1985 p.691). Beetlestone (1982) reported that in comparison with Greek Cypriots, Turkish Cypriots were less well organized and saw themselves as less powerful economically and politically and as little able to make their views known.

The nature of interethnic relationships between Greek and Turkish Cypriots in the UK and their ethnic identities have also been influenced by mutual perceptions of and relationships with other ethnic – majority and minority – groups. Research evidence indicates that interethnic perceptions between the British and Greek and Turkish Cypriots amongst the first generation have in general been characterized by little genuine reciprocal knowledge or understanding, but this may increasingly overlook individual relationships at a personal level. During the pre-war years there was general ignorance of Cyprus, Cypriot food and customs, and whilst darker-haired Cypriots were mistaken for Italians or Jews, the fairer were taken for Germans (Alkan and Constantinides, 1981). In the 1950s new migrants found work in the expanding labour market and settled 'unnoticed'. Cypriots were seen as law-abiding and any, generally mild crime was kept within the Cypriot community and guided by the social values of Cyprus (George, 1960). In the 1960s the British did not see the Cypriots as an economic or employment threat, but often held largely hostile stereotypes based on the Cypriots' perceived exclusivity, partly due to the barrier of language, but also to different social and cultural practices (Hylson-Smith, 1968). There was a lack of intensive social interaction between the British and Cypriots and any relationships between individual families rarely extended to home visiting (Bhatnagar, 1970). It appears that Cypriots were generally perceived as 'white' and hence did not suffer prejudice as some other minority groups. However, there was also little awareness of ethnic differences within the Cypriot community and what these might imply and signify in daily life.

From the Cypriot perspective, contact with the British was extended through the post-war expansion of catering and other services in areas of Cypriot settlement. Oakley (1968) emphasized that Greek Cypriots were friendly and well-disposed towards the English whom they met, having a high regard for the British people and for their way of life in general. Yet other sources have claimed that the social isolation of first-generation Cypriots and their lack of institutional contact with the wider society in clubs, associations and organizations led to stereotypical views of British culture (Hylson-Smith, 1968). Cypriot and British cultures were seen as differing fundamentally in respect of social and moral values and, in particular, the concept of romantic love and equality of the sexes was seen as tantamount to sexual immorality (George and Millerson, 1967). Even in the 1970s, Constantinides (1977) was surprised to find that, although Cypriots had clear, if occasionally conflicting, stereotypes of the British, based on their colonial experiences and contact through work and business, they had little intimate knowledge of individual Britons and were often unaware of British social conventions. Ladbury (1977) reported that Turkish Cypriots' attitudes to the British seemed vague and ambivalent: occasionally the British were seen to epitomize modernity, which was sometimes seen as commendable, but at other times reinterpreted as immorality. According to Ulug (1981), Turkish Cypriots fear the loss of their moral standards and 'way of life', so the 'outgroup' is devalued and strong measures are sometimes taken to retain social distance. However, Ladbury reported such reactions were not sustained on personal acquaintance with British people. Yet even friendships developed at school did not usually survive adulthood or marriage with reabsorption into the ethnic community. Anthias (1983) has also emphasized the reversion of Greek Cypriot girls to the environment of their community and its activities after school for economic, disciplinary and cultural reasons enforced by community sanctions.

The strong preferences of first-generation Greek and Turkish Cypriots for the company of their own kin and cultural institutions have also comforted them and confirmed their ethnic identity in the face of any perceived lack of sympathy, reserve, hostility or rejection by the British (Triseliotis, 1968; Constantinides, 1977; Leeuwenberg, 1979). However, claimed discrimination has generally been low (see pp.12, 15–16). In the mid-1960s Daniel (1968) discovered that, with the exception of the climate and food, Cypriots had a favourable reaction to living in England, although to a certain extent they found social life disappointing and experienced problems of adjustment. None claimed personal abuse or prejudice, believing that discrimination existed but not in relation to themselves. Certain periods of high unemployment or unclear immigration status have sometimes given rise to concern (Markopoulou, 1974; Alkan and Constantinides, 1981). In a Commission for Racial Equality (CRE) survey, in 1980, more than half the Cypriots – the highest proportion of any ethnic minority group surveyed – claimed that the police try to be fair and, conversely, the Cypriots were less likely to blame the police for any trouble between ethnic minorities and the police force. In these judgements they tended to identify more with the white majority. However, amongst the ethnic minorities, the Cypriots, like the West Indians, were marginally more likely to think race relations had become worse (CRE, 1981a). Anthias (1984), whilst acknowledging that Cypriots do not experience the 'immediate' racism suffered by black people, states that many Cypriots claim to have experienced racism: they speak in a foreign accent, may look darker, have names which are difficult to pronounce – all factors which 'exclude them from the English national collectivity'. Beetlestone's (1982) research also shows that stereotypes of Greek and Turkish Cypriots are prevalent amongst educationists and that these are often negative with respect to Turkish culture.

Cypriots' perceptions of other ethnic minority groups, often living in the same areas of settlement and especially in Greater London, are also interesting. Daniel (1968) noted that 'it is apparent that many of the Cypriots share what they believe is the general British antipathy to coloured people' (p.40). A study of immigrant group relations in north London in the mid-1960s (Hylson-Smith, 1968) found little inter-racial mixing between Cypriots and West Indians. Indeed, according to Constantinides (1977), the Cypriots, who for economic reasons initially lived in 'twilight zones' near their workplaces, often found themselves 'co-resident with other groups to whom they felt both morally and culturally superior'. By moving out northwards, she claimed Greek Cypriots were moving into neighbourhoods where their 'middle-class aspirations' were shared. Ladbury (1977) has claimed that Turkish Cypriots have adopted racist attitudes towards members of other ethnic groups, particularly West Indians and Africans. Interestingly, Turkish Cypriots expressed less prejudice towards Pakistanis, partly because settlement patterns did not coincide, partly because they are Muslim and partly because they were perceived as 'less black'. According to Ladbury, these ethnic stereotypes have been acquired in the UK. Yet Cypriots do not see these minority groups as a threat to their own individual economic interests as Turks or Greek Cypriots, or challenges to their moral interests as the British are sometimes perceived. Ladbury suggests that Turkish Cypriots, when working with or getting to know British people, find it expedient to identify with the British majority by adopting stereotypes already in use to create a common outgroup based on colour. By so doing, they also seek to divorce themselves from the term 'immigrant' together with its associations.

The extent to which these interethnic perceptions have persisted between Greek and Turkish Cypriots, their respective mainlanders, the indigenous British and other ethnic minority groups amongst the second-generation and their peers is examined elsewhere according to available research evidence (see pp.169-74, 191–5). Early studies suggested that the degree of social and cultural differentiation would not last and that greater assimilation would occur with the second generation and when ethnic cultural traits were in decline (Oakley, 1970; George, 1960). Whilst evidence indicates that ethnic identity, at least among the first generation, is still strong, and persistent attempts are made to transfer cultural values to the second generation through return visits and not least language classes, some community associations in the 1980s aim to reach out to a wider multicultural, multiethnic British community. Another key factor in the modification of ethnic identity and community perceptions, especially of the second and subsequent generation, is mainstream education, to which we now turn.

Education

Quality of Research Data

Pupils of Cypriot origin are distinguished amongst ethnic minority pupils by their concentration in Greater London. Over three-quarters live in this area, most in the northern boroughs. In the 1950s and 1960s the main areas of Cypriot settlement gradually changed from Camden, Islington and Hackney to Haringey and continued, in the 1970s, to spread out west, north and east to Brent, Barnet, Enfield and Waltham Forest (see pp.10–11). This relative concentration has meant that pupils of Cypriot origin have become the subjects of educational research to a greater extent than other pupils from the smaller ethnic minority groups. In these areas, where they are sometimes the largest group of all ethnic minority pupils, their stronger presence has facilitated the conduct of research. By contrast, very little research has included pupils of Cypriot origin living in south London boroughs, for example, Southwark, Lambeth or, more recently, Lewisham. As with socioeconomic research, a particular gap in educational research data exists with respect to pupils of Cypriot origin elsewhere in Britain, especially in seaside towns. Given their smaller numbers, their experience of education may be different from that of pupils of Cypriot origin in London.

Although research including pupils of Cypriot origin relates to the localities where they are most numerous, they are not necessarily represented in large numbers in the research itself. Inadequate numbers may not, for example, always make statistical comparisons possible. Usually pupils of Cypriot origin are considered alongside white British and ethnic minority pupils, or as a third group, in studies concerning ethnic minority pupils, where they are more often compared with pupils of West Indian origin than pupils of Asian origin. But data on pupils of Cypriot origin are frequently obscured in the oft-used category 'other', where they form a composite but disparate group with other ethnic minority pupils with diverse origins. Sometimes they are included in a group of pupils with European origins, often comprising pupils of Italian origin (see p.213). However, such general categories are unhelpful when evaluating the educational experience and achievement of pupils of Cypriot origin *per se*. Indeed, although there exists a certain body of educational research which includes data on pupils of Cypriot origin, the reasons for a lack of specific focus on this group are unclear. It may be the case, as Krokou (1985) has suggested, that their numbers overall are 'too small to warrant serious attention', or that pupils of Cypriot origin are not perceived as 'problems' in school and can be ignored by local education authorities (LEAs) or the Department of Education and Science (DES). However, this suggests that their distinctive educational needs as a group and in comparison with other minority and majority peers may have been overlooked.

Much mainstream research on pupils of Cypriot origin is now ageing since it was largely conducted in the late 1960s and early 1970s. Moreover, it has tended to focus on the affective and attitudinal aspects of their educational experience. Evidence on educational performance, in school subjects or examinations and the actual transition from school to work is generally slight. Fortunately, however, with the growing interest in language learning in mainstream and community schools more up-to-date research data have recently become available on the language backgrounds of Greek- and Turkish-speaking pupils, in terms of their language knowledge, use and attitudes, which usefully complement earlier information on English as a second language (E2L) and reading performance. Research on language teaching, especially of Greek and Turkish, is now beginning to be available from both mainstream and community sources.

Yet even though research on pupils of Cypriot origin is fairly localized, the lack of longitudinal research, especially in recent years, means that findings from discrete studies have to be considered as a whole in order to achieve some continuity. The significance of the implications of earlier research findings may need to be reassessed in the light of educational developments in the research localities, the changing intraethnic relationships in the Cypriot community and interethnic relationships in the wider community during the last decade or so. Despite the extant research, it is, for example, not possible to provide evaluative evidence of the impact of an LEA's or school's multicultural or anti-racist education policy (or the absence of such) on the educational experience of pupils of Cypriot origin and their peers. Even though good practice may exist, the absence of publicly available information makes for a lack of awareness of specific pedagogic skills. However, a growing number of second-generation Greek and Turkish Cypriots are becoming involved in research in their communities and their observations provide helpful insights which augment and complement mainstream educational research data.

In considering educational research on pupils of Cypriot origin, a number of qualifications should be made. Pupils of Cypriot origin currently in schools are almost all UK-born since, in recent years, very few school-age pupils have arrived directly from Cyprus. Yet many research subjects, especially in the 1960s, will have been born in Cyprus, although they may have arrived in the UK at a very early age. Moreover, in the last few years a third generation of Cypriot pupils, children whose parents themselves arrived as children in the 1950s, will have been starting school. Indeed first-, second- and third-generation pupils may all have been receiving education concurrently and even occasionally alongside each other in a few schools. Whilst by far the majority of these children will either be of Greek or Turkish Cypriot origin, a few second- and third-generation pupils may come from mixed Greek or Turkish Cypriot and British or Cypriot and other Mediterranean or southern European backgrounds. Thus research evidence spans three generations, it focusses upon first- and second-generation pupils of Cypriot origin though they are rarely, if ever, distinguished.

In addition to distinguishing between the generations of pupils of Cypriot origin, it is also important to be aware of a further distinction – though, once again, often ignored by educational research – within the group as a whole, according to whether their origins and home backgrounds are Greek or Turkish Cypriot. Since the proportion of Greek Cypriots to Turkish Cypriots has generally been thought to be four to one, as in Cyprus, it would seem probable for a similar proportion to have obtained amongst pupils of Cypriot origin, at least during the late 1960s and early 1970s. However, some have suggested that this has underestimated the size of the Turkish Cypriot community (GB.P. H of C, 1985). Greek and Turkish Cypriots share a common birthplace, background, appearance and many customs and attitudes. Yet they differ in respect of language, religion and kinship. The significance of these similarities and differences may have been modified by the experiences of living in the UK. Socioanthropological research in the UK and Cyprus (see Oakley, 1971; Constantinides, 1977; Ladbury, 1977) has indicated that despite a complex set of interrelationships between Greek and Turkish Cypriots a separate ethnic consciousness has persisted in the UK for the first generation, at least, though this may be emphasized or played down in different circumstances, at different times and by individual members of the two groups (see pp.34–5). Yet although first-generation Cypriots may stress the Greek-ness or Turkish-ness in their identity, they in turn both share certain similarities with their respective mainlanders and differ from them in other respects (see pp.33–4). In the mid-1970s interactions between Cypriots and mainland Greeks or Turks were generally limited.

It is important to draw these distinctions, for just as ethnic boundaries may be maintained or eroded by adult Greek and Turkish Cypriots and these may be communicated to and experienced in the UK by their children, so they also may vary in the extent to which in different locations and at different times they may choose to assert their Greek, Turkish or Cypriot origins. Thus Oakley's (1968) statement that it was 'significant that many of the migrants, and especially their children, refer to themselves as simply "Greek" or "Turkish": a fact which misleads many English people into thinking that they are immigrants from Greece or Turkey' now needs to be re-examined in the light of subsequent political developments in Cyprus and the ongoing evolution of the Cypriot community in the UK. Indeed the position is even more complex. It is not merely a question of the extent to which pupils of Cypriot origin identify themselves as Greek or Turkish, as Greek Cypriots or Turkish Cypriots, or as Cypriots, for the experience of living, and for many having been born in Britain affects their self-perceptions and the way in which they are perceived by others, so that their 'British-ness' is also an influential factor in their identity. In fact their European origin, on account of which they are less easily distinguished than some other ethnic minority pupils by their physical appearance, means that they may indeed pass as indigenous British. This, in itself, may go some way to explaining why educational research has given less attention to pupils of Cypriot origin and within-group differences compared with pupils from West Indian or Asian backgrounds. The significant point remains: even when pupils of Cypriot origin have been considered as a distinct ethnic group in educational research literature, the common identity of Cypriots has largely been assumed and important differences – linguistic, religious and familial – between Greek and Turkish Cypriots as they affect pupils of Cypriot origin have, for the most part, been overlooked. It is to be hoped that schools in the areas of settlement have had a greater awareness of these differences (and the similarities) and an appreciation of their potential implications in practice for interaction both within and beyond the life of the school.

Numbers and Distribution of Pupils of Cypriot Origin

It is always notoriously difficult to attempt to marshal figures on the numbers of pupils from an ethnic minority group which have any degree of accuracy because no records are available on a national scale. But in the case of pupils of Cypriot origin, this process is even more hazardous and unsatisfactory. Census figures based on country of birth are increasingly inaccurate as the overwhelming majority of pupils of Cypriot origin are now British-born and the category 'New Commonwealth Mediterranean' is non-specific (see pp. 5–6). Although Labour Force Surveys have usefully included a question on ethnic group membership, Cypriots cannot be distinguished because they are counted as 'white' or European. Clearly it would be impossible to give precise numbers for pupils of Greek or Turkish Cypriot origin within the Cypriot population. DES figures for the number of 'immigrant' pupils who had arrived in the UK in the previous ten years were collected from 1966 to 1972, but their accuracy was widely disputed and this eventually led to their abandonment. Fortunately, in the last decade language censuses in ILEA and five other LEAs, including Haringey and Waltham Forest, provide useful data on the numbers of Greek- and Turkish-speaking pupils. However, whilst these surveys have taken place in some of the main areas of Cypriot settlement, figures on language speakers or pupils of Cypriot origin *per se* from other adjacent LEAs with large Cypriot populations are not publicly available. Hence the lack of continuity and LEA-wide data only makes it possible at present to provide a piecemeal account and estimate of the number of pupils of Cypriot origin in UK schools over the last 25 years or so.

In recent years, there has been renewed debate about the possibility of collecting statistics on pupils' ethnic origins. A government working party has recently recommended that LEAs should monitor pupils' ethnic origins, mother tongue and religious affiliations on a voluntary basis as 'a base for making appropriate provision and for monitoring achievement' (Thompson, 1986). Whether such monitoring will commence is unknown at the time of writing, and doubts have been expressed by some teachers about the validity of the voluntary nature of the exercise. However, the Swann Report noted that representatives from Greek and Turkish Cypriot communities, 'while appreciating the concerns expressed by other ethnic minority groups, were firmly in favour of the collection of ethnically-based statistics in the education system, on the grounds that "needs could not be met until they were quantified"' (GB. P. H of C, 1985, pp. 685–6).

In 1961, using available Census data on 36,873 out of a total of 41,898 Cypriots, George and Millerson (1967) calculated that 20.9 per cent of the Cypriot community were aged 0–14. When the number of Cypriot children born in the UK (calculated from the numbers of children baptised at the Greek Orthodox churches in London, covering 83 per cent of Cypriots in the UK and 95 per cent of baptisms) were taken into account, the proportion of 0–14-year-olds in the Cypriot community rose to 37.2 per cent. The number of Turkish Cypriot children was estimated, taking into account the fact that up to 1950 there were about one-tenth as many Turkish Cypriots as Greek Cypriots, whilst between 1951 and 1961 the proportion rose to about one-fifth. According to George and Millerson, some 14,733 Greek Cypriot children and 2,808 Turkish Cypriot children were born in the UK between 1938 and 1964. Table 6 shows DES figures for the number of pupils of Cypriot origin, Greek and Turkish, boys and girls for 1967, 1970 and 1972.

Table 6:   Number of pupils of Cypriot origin in schools in England and Wales, by sex, 1967, 1970 and 1972

Year	Total Cypriots	Total Greek	Boys/ girls	Total Turkish	Boys/ girls
1967	13,835	9,826	4,955	4,009	2,060
			4,871		1,949
1970	14,798	9,891	5,031	4,907	2,568
			4,860		2,339
1972	13,965	9,504	4,806	4,461	2,298
			4,698		2,163

Source: GB. DES, 1968, Table 27, 1971, 1973, Table 38.

From the figures in Table 6, it appears that the number of pupils of Cypriot origin classified as immigrant pupils did not increase greatly during the period 1967–72. Their numbers peaked in 1970, according to this classification, due to a slight increase in Turkish Cypriot pupils, though generally the proportions of Greek to Turkish pupils remained similar, roughly 2:1. However, these figures may have been distorted owing to the confusion in interpretation of the DES definition of 'immigrant' pupils, and may well have under-enumerated pupils of Cypriot origin as they increasingly failed to pick up children born in the UK to parents who arrived over ten years earlier. In view of the migration pattern and immigration peak in 1960–1 the DES figures could have been a considerable underestimate of pupils of Cypriot origin then in schools. In 1972 official figures for Cypriot pupils were 6,170 in primary education and 3,334 in secondary education, a total of 3.4 per cent of all immigrant pupils.

However, it has subsequently proved even more difficult to gauge the number of pupils of Cypriot origin as they become increasingly UK-born. Using the ten per cent GLC sample 1971 Census data, Leeuwenberg (1979) calculated that there would be some 17,394 Cypriot children in the UK if these figures were re-weighted for the whole population. He found it difficult to extrapolate this figure further into the 1970s because of the number of births, new immigrants and mobility, but estimated that there were around 20,000 Cypriot children, some 13,000 Cyprus-born and 7,000 UK-born, possibly about 15,000 of Greek Cypriot origin and 5,000 of Turkish Cypriot origin. During the 1970s Cypriot children continued to arrive from Cyprus albeit in decreasing numbers, and the political upheaval in 1974 led to the admission of some 2,000 Cypriot children to Britain in 1975, though they tended to be afforded only six-month visitors' visas rather than refugee status (McCarty and Christoudoulou, 1977).

The 1981 Census data (OPCS, 1983a, Table 5) show that in 1980 there were some 1,002 0–19-year-old immigrants of New Commonwealth Mediterranean origin. This figure includes young people of other than Cypriot origin, but it does demonstrate that there are currently very few young Cypriots of school age arriving in the UK. The 1981 Census figures (ibid., Table 2), available since the entry of Greece into the European Community, show that there were 1,061 0–19-year-olds of Greek origin resident in the UK, some 488 of them aged five to 15. Unfortunately, the Census does not provide similar figures for Turkish youngsters. Regrettably, the nature of Census data only make it possible to suggest a figure for pupils of Cypriot origin in schools in Britain, in the early 1980s, which has a limited accuracy. Though there are problems with the Census classification, figures based on head of households' birthplace which are apparently corroborated by Labour Force Survey (LFS) data (see pp. 6–7) suggest a school-age population of over 30,000, overwhelmingly British-born. Indeed in 1984 the Cyprus High Commission estimated the school population of Greek origin to be about 25,000 pupils (Tansley, 1986), so perhaps the larger figure is not over-inflated for pupils of Cypriot origin as a whole.

Recent language censuses provide location–specific numbers of Greek- and Turkish- speaking pupils. In the first ILEA survey, in 1978, teachers estimated the number of pupils whose first language was Greek or Turkish and in subsequent surveys pupils who spoke either of these languages other than or in addition to English at home (Table 7).

Table 7:   Numbers of Greek- and Turkish-speaking pupils in ILEA, 1978, 1981, 1983 and 1985

Language spoken	1978	1981	1983	1985
Greek	3,802	3,859	3,410	3,033
Turkish	3,587	4,418	4,316	4,383
Total	7,389	8,277	7,726	7,416

Source: ILEA language censuses 1979, 1982, 1983 and 1986.

In combination Greek- and Turkish-speaking pupils, the overwhelming majority of whom are of Cypriot origin, have formed from nearly 20 per cent of overseas language speakers in ILEA in 1978 to 13 per cent in 1985. Although Greek-speaking pupils were the largest group of overseas language speakers in 1978, they have since declined to seventh position, whereas Turkish speakers have always ranked as the second largest group, latterly after Bengali speakers (see pp. 55–7). Evidence from the Schools Language Survey (SLS) of the Linguistic Minorities Project (LMP), undertaken in five LEAs in 1980–1, is also of interest since Haringey, the largest area of Cypriot settlement, and Waltham Forest, where many Cypriots also live, were two of the survey areas (see also pp. 43–6). According to six to 16-year-old pupils' self-reports, 2,521 spoke Greek and 1,091 Turkish at home in Haringey, where together they formed 48 per cent of the borough's 30 per cent of speakers of a language other than English. In Waltham Forest there were 431 Greek speakers and 239 Turkish speakers, who together formed 12 per cent of the borough's 18.8 per cent of speakers of a language other than English at home. There were very few Greek- or Turkish-speakers in the other three LEAs surveyed, in Bradford, Coventry and Peterborough (93 in total) (Couillaud and Tasker, 1983). Cumulatively these surveys alone revealed that in 1981 some 12,672 pupils spoke Greek or Turkish to some degree. Since by far the majority of these pupils have Cypriot backgrounds, and given that according to the 1981 Census figures, some 70 per cent of Cypriots live in the Greater London area, these surveys have gone some considerable way to uncovering the number of pupils of Cypriot origin in this area. Unfortunately, it is only possible to speculate upon their numbers in the adjacent boroughs of Enfield, Barnet and Brent where there are known concentrations of Cypriot settlement.

In view of the overwhelming concentration of pupils of Cypriot origin in schools in the Greater London area from the earliest times of settlement, and since much of the educational research evidence relates to north London and particularly the borough of Haringey, it may be of interest to examine what is known about the numbers of such pupils and their concentration in this locality. In the early 1960s Islington was the main area of Cypriot settlement, and in 1965 Truman (cited by Krausz, 1971) found ten schools in Islington which each had over 40 per cent immigrant children totalling 6,000, half of whom were Greek- or Turkish-speaking Cypriots. About this time also, the gradual movement of Cypriot settlement northwards into Haringey was beginning to be reflected in the proportion of Cypriot pupils in schools in that borough. According to Figueroa (1974), in 1967 Cypriot pupils, numbering 2,689 (Greek 2,079, Turkish 610), comprised 35 per cent of the immigrant pupils in Haringey. In the following year Haringey had the highest percentage of immigrant children in its schools of any LEA in the UK – some 26.9 per cent (9,241 of 33,842) (Hill, 1970). Of the immigrant pupils, Cypriots numbered 3,013 (2,214 Greeks, 799 Turkish) and were only exceeded by pupils of West Indian origin. Haringey continues to have a large proportion of pupils of Cypriot origin relative to their numbers as a whole. Their concentration varies according to the wards within this borough and hence in different schools. For example, in 1974 Clough and Quarmby (1978) noted that in one junior school with pupils from 28 countries Cypriots, numbering 145, were the predominant group on the roll of 359. More recently, Hunter-Grundin (1982) noted that pupils from Cypriot backgrounds comprised 65 per cent of the rolls of a pre-school centre, infant and junior school in the South Harringay area of Haringey. However, data from the SLS of the LMP, cited above (Couillaud and Tasker, 1983), showed that Greek- and Turkish-speaking pupils constituted in 1981 some 15 per cent of the school population of the borough of Haringey as whole.

For many years Haringey, as an outer London borough responsible for its own educational system, has been one of the most ethnically and linguistically diverse areas of England. It is of relevance here to outline what is known of Haringey's educational policies and practices as charted by the literature over the years as a context in which to consider research findings on pupils of Cypriot origin within its boundaries. Milstead (1981) undertook a review of multicultural education in Haringey, 1965–81. During the mid-1960s Haringey had ignored the DES recommendation, made in 1965, that schools should not contain more than one-third immigrant pupils and had operated a *laissez-faire* policy. However, in 1969 the borough changed its policy towards immigrant children, and this was the cause of much controversy both locally and nationally (Hill, 1970; Bhatnagar, 1970). Following comprehensivization in 1967 and growing concern about the development of 'ghetto' schools, a system of selection by verbal reasoning tests on transfer to secondary schools was implemented, so that pupils would be banded by ability and placed proportionally in each comprehensive school in order that all schools might have similar ability ranges. However, it was claimed that the criteria used in the assessment of intelligence were operating unfairly for immigrant children who would be separated in school from other children. These factors might have a bearing on the assessment of educational research in this area during this time.

Since 1970, Haringey has had an English Language Resource Centre to support the teaching of English as a second language. Between July 1974 and February 1975 Haringey was preoccupied with responding to the needs, especially for E2L teaching, of a large influx of Cypriot children and their families fleeing the civil war in Cyprus. A decade later a team of over 30 peripatetic teachers based there followed a policy of working alongside teachers in their classes in all primary schools and most secondary schools, although there was still some withdrawal of pupils in this sector (LMP, 1985).

It is most interesting to note that as early as 1978 Haringey published a pamphlet on its policy on racialist activities in schools (London Borough of Haringey, 1978). This states the borough council's aim 'to foster good relations between all sections of the community' and 'take every opportunity to oppose racialism in all its forms'. It notes certain rights and freedoms for all individuals and groups and recognizes the enrichment of cultural diversity. It stresses the responsibilities of heads and teachers to ensure 'that all children have the right to be educated towards an understanding of and commitment to a multi-cultural/multi-racial society', and this should lead to 'a genuine sensitivity for the needs of others, and tolerance of all races and religions'. In particular, the policy claims that 'schools should aim to teach every individual pupil self-respect, respect for others and respect for the truth', and it encourages positive resistance to racialist statements and activities, especially attempts to recruit children to the membership of quasi–political organizations.

Haringey also has an equal opportunities policy (London Borough of Haringey, n.d.) and in line with this financial priorities have been reordered and evaluations made of ways in which education and community services can be improved (Hunter-Grundin, 1982). The policy document is concerned with equal opportunities in employment, in the educational service and in the provision of educational services. It requires 'all educational establishments and services to review their aims and objectives, their employment, organizational and curricular practices to secure on a whole institution basis an effective framework to combat disadvantage and provide equal opportunities'. In relation to the employment of teachers the council's policy makes a strong stand against racism, sexism, ageism and disability and asserts affirmative action 'to remove those unjust discriminatory influences which have hindered the recruitment and development of a Council workforce reflecting the diversity of the Community it serves' and 'to ensure that only job-related criteria are used in recruitment and other employment procedures and practices'. The document also points out the general responsibilities of governors, heads, teachers, advisers and others in the education service to fulfil the council's policy and, in addition to provision of training programmes, the education committee undertakes to make available clear policy statements and guidelines to exemplify good practice. Each educational establishment and service was expected to draw up its own statement of policy to combat the discriminatory attitudes and practices of individuals or institutions and to engage in continuous review of the content and expression of the curriculum to promote equal opportunities. Indeed since 1977 there has been an Adviser for Multicultural Education and a Multicultural Support Group to work with schools on curriculum development and in-service training (Beetlestone, 1982; LMP, 1985). However, there have been repeated recommendations in the literature that day care and nursery facilities should be available to children of Cypriot origin and that in-service training should be more widespread (Alkan and Constantinides, 1981; Beetlestone, 1982).

Haringey is also committed to a positive attitude towards bilingualism. Indeed in 1981 nearly one-third of its 32,000-plus pupils were bilingual and spoke between them 87 languages. Speakers of Greek and Turkish constituted nearly half of these bilingual pupils in the borough's 81 primary, 14 secondary and five special schools. For some time, the borough has had a standing committee which acts as a consultative committee on mother-tongue teaching and consists of representatives from all minority language groups (Tansley, 1986; Christodoulides, 1984). In recent years the LEA has also co-operated with several projects concerned with bilingualism, language awareness and language development. In 1980–1 three surveys of the Linguistic Minorities Project – the Adult Language Use Survey, the Schools Language Survey and the Mother–Tongue Teaching Directory took place there (see. p.53). In 1981–3 the Schools Council Language in the Multicultural Primary Classroom project (see p.122) included class teachers in Haringey, and since 1982 the Learning Materials for Ethnic Minority Groups Project has also collected oral material and worked in a range of schools in Haringey (see pp.123). In 1982–3 the Mother Tongue Project (1981–5) (see pp.96–7) worked closely with Haringey in trialling mother–tongue teaching materials for Greek and the Children's Language Project (see pp.122–3) activity cards in community and primary schools. Since the LEA did not have primary school classes in which this work could easily be included, involvement with the project raised many educational and organizational issues related to mother–tongue teaching, in addition to the development of positive attitudes to mother–tongue teaching in the project schools (Tansley, 1986). The project enabled the LEA to assess the policy and practical implications of this type of work, and together with the influence of the LMP project and general pressure from organizations like the National Council of Mother–Tongue Teaching and community groups, stimulated the LEA to formulate a policy on bilingualism and to acknowledge that it must make a commitment to the development of mother–tongue teaching itself rather than relying on community initiatives.

The LEA's policy statement on bilingualism 'recognizes the importance and value of the languages spoken within the borough boundaries' and acknowledges that the employment of bilingual staff, provision of language awareness courses and specialist teaching are necessary for the education service to assist 'all members of the community to maintain and develop their knowledge of oral/written fluency in the language of their home and community' (quoted by Tansley, ibid., p. 36). The LEA agreed to purchase books and materials; provide free use of school premises for affiliated classes; set up a Community Language Panel, comprising members of the Standing Committee and education officers and advisers, to monitor and develop policy; establish criteria for the affiliation of community classes; and with Education Support Grant and Section 11 money fund a centre for bilingualism with some 15 teachers. An adviser has responsibility for community languages and liaison with E2L staff, and there were plans for a coordinated approach to language teaching and a language across the curriculum policy. There is strong liaison with the language communities, and the centre for bilingualism is to serve both voluntary and mainstream sectors for in–service training and resources (Keen, 1985). Clearly, and especially in recent years, the direction of Haringey's policy shows considerable awareness of the needs and interests of its multiethnic, bilingual pupils (including pupils of Cypriot origin). It remains for further research to assess the extent to which changes in policy affect practices and these, in turn, influence the pupils' educational experience and performance.

Whilst virtually all pupils of Cypriot origin now starting school will have been born in this country, during the years covered by this review many Cypriot children would have arrived in Britain in the course of their schooling. However, it was less usual than with many other ethnic minority pupils for them to arrive during secondary schooling; they tended to migrate as small children with their families, or with their mothers, usually a relatively short time after their father had established himself in the UK (see p.4, and Butterworth and Kinnibrugh, 1970). Triseliotis (1976) analysed through case studies the difficulties which some children experienced in the reunion with their families. The need to renew relationships within the family was an additional difficulty in adapting to different cultural and educational environments and adjustment problems within the home sometimes extended to school. Some Cypriot teenagers who arrived in the UK after having left school at the age of 12 when it was no longer compulsory and had been working for one or two years in Cyprus found it necessary to attend school again, and this sometimes led to resentment, truancy and other behaviour problems (Butterworth and Kinnibrugh, 1970). But perhaps the greatest contrast for any newly arrived Cypriot child was between his rural village background – a known community with wide open spaces for play – and the cramped housing conditions in an impersonal urban environment which was the initial experience of living in London (LCSS, 1967; Butterworth and Kinnibrugh, 1970). Also in the school environment newly arrived Cypriot pupils were often bemused by the apparently more liberal atmosphere and more individual teaching methods, contrasting with the more formal and strictly disciplined approach which they were used to in their schooling in Cyprus (see pp.140–1).

English would only have been learned at secondary school. For newly arrived pupils of Cypriot origin, even those of the third generation and particularly Turkish-speaking pupils who continue to start school speaking little English (Beetlestone, 1982), learning a new language is of prime significance in their adaptation to school. In the early 1970s, although provision was made for special English teaching for pupils of Cypriot origin in some London LEAs, newly arrived Cypriot children scattered across the country often did not receive the same kind of attention (Triseliotis, 1976). Such pupils, claimed Triseliotis, could be lost sight of, and since their teachers often had no E2L teaching experience, the children were sometimes left to manage as best they could. But unable to communicate, their lives in school were at least initially sometimes isolated and apathetic. Some LEAs, especially in north London and the Midlands, received hundreds of Cypriot refugee children in 1975 (Derrick, 1977) and some were particularly stretched in attempting to meet their linguistic needs. Whilst an LEA such as Haringey made special provision for language teaching for refugee children, others used their status as 'visitors' to deny them education (McCarty and Christoudoulou, 1977). A World University Service document (1977) argued that at that time some LEAs with a concentration of newly arrived refugee pupils needed additional funds in order to provide adequate teaching and community care.

In recent years, as pupils of Cypriot origin starting school have been mainly British–born, the kinds of difficulty outlined here may have receded or at least changed in emphasis. But it is important that they be taken account of when evaluating the research evidence on pupils of Cypriot origin since this largely pertains to the late 1960s and early 1970s. Indeed it is of interest to compare the extent to which Cypriot pupils now starting infant school experience similar difficulties in terms of language and differences in the cultural values and attitudes transmitted by parents and schools. The following section examines the educational experience of pupils of Cypriot origin and the extent to which teachers and LEA administrators have appreciated their distinctive educational needs and potential contribution to multicultural education. Perhaps at least those pupils of Cypriot origin in north London (though can the same be said for those in smaller numbers across the country?) have not suffered in the last 25 years from the lack of recognition experienced by Cypriot children in the 1940s who, according to Alkan and Constantinides (1981), 'at school never mentioned that their parents were from Cyprus because no-one of the ordinary public appeared to know where Cyprus was' (p.9).

IQ and Cognitive Ability
Few statements about the general educational ability or achievement of pupils of Cypriot origin appear in the literature on ethnic minority pupils. Oakley (1968) considered that several features of traditional Greek Cypriot family upbringing such as discouragement given to play and encouragement to help with practical tasks limited the educability of the Cypriot child. Although children were included in adult discourse, the linguistic code, in Oakley's view, was relatively restricted in vocabulary, abstract concepts, sentence structure and range of tenses. Oakley suggested that in British educational terms the child from such a background tended to be disadvantaged from the outset in linguistic and intellectual development, but that it would be wrong to conclude that Cypriot children were unintelligent and destined to perform poorly in school. Indeed he claimed that in the mid-1960s evidence from schools in north London with many Cypriot children suggested that their performance compared very favourably with other children in these schools. By contrast, more recent responses from the LEA survey by Little and Willey (1983) suggested that there should be less complacency even about the achievement of third-generation European pupils whose home background maintained the mother tongue and the cultural traditions of their village origins. It is important, therefore, to attempt to evaluate these respective claims in consideration of the available research data on the performance of Cypriot pupils.

One way in which ability and potential to benefit from schooling traditionally have been assessed is through measurements of IQ in verbal and non-verbal reasoning tests. It is now widely recognized that IQ tests in common use in Britain contain a significant cultural bias (Hegarty and Lucas, 1978) and they are not generally considered to lead to a proper assessment of ethnic minority pupils, especially those whose first language is not English. Nevertheless, these tests were employed, in the 1960s, in a few research studies involving Cypriot pupils. It is doubtful whether it is possible to construct a genuinely culture-free test, though tests have been devised to assess learning ability rather than intelligence. As yet little experimental investigation with such tests has been undertaken, though one small-scale study used these procedures with Cypriot pupils.

As part of a survey of the transfer of ten-year-old pupils to secondary education in 1966, the ILEA administered verbal reasoning tests to 1,038 immigrant pupils in 52 schools with more than one-third immigrant pupils. Cypriot pupils formed 21 per cent of all the immigrant pupils of this age in ILEA schools, and 23 per cent of the sample tested. The performance of the 232 Cypriot pupils, like that of other immigrant pupils, was significantly lower on verbal reasoning tests than that of all ILEA pupils. A mere six per cent of Cypriot pupils were ranked in groups 1 and 2 (the top 25 per cent) of the seven profile groups and 57 per cent fell into groups 6 and 7. Their ranking of performance on verbal reasoning tests was inferior to that of Indian and Pakistani pupils, but better than that of West Indian pupils. When a further analysis was undertaken on those pupils considered by their teachers to be English speaking, the 124 Cypriot pupils' performance on verbal reasoning again fell between that of Asian and West Indian pupils, but with twice as many (12 per cent) than in groups 1 and 2, though 41 per cent still in groups 6 and 7. Unfortunately, performance of pupils of Cypriot origin, according to length of schooling, was not analysed. However, the findings demonstrated that language was a factor in performance on verbal reasoning tests (Little *et al.*, 1968).

In 1968 a further transfer survey was undertaken in which 4,269 immigrant pupils and 22,023 non-immigrant pupils entering secondary schools in ILEA were given verbal reasoning tests. Unfortunately, the number of Cypriot pupils involved were not recorded (Little, 1975a), though Greek and Turkish Cypriot pupils were distinguished in an analysis of results. Once again, none of the groups of immigrant pupils had a distribution of performance similar to that of non-immigrant pupils. The difference was particularly marked on the verbal reasoning test. Only 5.9 per cent of Greek Cypriot pupils fell into groups 1 and 2, compared with 19.8 per cent non-immigrant pupils and 6.7 per cent of immigrant pupils as a whole. Only 3.5 per cent of Turkish Cypriot pupils were ranked in groups 1 and 2 – the lowest percentage of immigrant pupils. Similarly, the Greek Cypriot pupils occupied a mid-position for immigrant pupils assigned to groups 6 and 7 on the verbal reasoning test (55.6 per cent), whereas 70 per cent of Turkish Cypriot pupils, the highest percentage of any immigrant group, were so assigned. Compared with the 1966 transfer study, the performance of Greek and Turkish Cypriot pupils was on average lower on verbal reasoning tests in 1968. Moreover, the performance of Turkish Cypriot pupils was clearly inferior to that of Greek Cypriot pupils and slightly inferior to that of West Indian pupils.

Turning to a consideration of findings on non-verbal reasoning tests, some information on the performance of Cypriot pupils is available from a survey of the ten-year-olds in 1970, in one London borough (Yule *et al.* 1975). Some 1,341 UK-born 'British' children, 354 children of West Indian parents, 34 of Greek Cypriot parents and 43 of Turkish Cypriot parents were group-tested on the NFER NV5 non-verbal reasoning test. Once again, the mean score of the immigrant children was significantly lower than that of the indigenous children. Greek Cypriot children had a mean score of 85 and Turkish Cypriot children a mean of 82, compared with 92 for the indigenous children (<0.001), and a mean score for West Indian pupils of 82. There was no significant difference between the mean scores of the Greek Cypriot and the Turkish Cypriot pupils. However, when the scores of the Greek and Turkish Cypriot pupils were analysed separately according to whether they were born in the UK or had immigrated, an interesting result emerged – though this must be regarded with caution because of the small numbers of pupils involved. There was a significant difference (<0.05) between the two groups of Greek Cypriot pupils: those who were born in the UK had a mean score of 90.65, almost that of the mean of the indigenous pupils, and some ten points greater than that of the Greek Cypriot immigrant pupils (80.18). By comparison, there was only a non-significant four-point difference in the mean score of the UK-born and immigrant Turkish Cypriot pupils. These findings tentatively suggested the significance of length of residence, if not of schooling, on performance on non-verbal reasoning tests.

Similar evidence of performance by Cypriot pupils on non-verbal reasoning tests is indicated by a small-scale study in 1966 in one secondary modern mixed school with 40 per cent immigrant pupils in Haringey (Bhatnagar, 1970). Ravens Progressive Matrices (RPM) test was administered to 174 West Indian pupils, 76 Cypriot pupils (66 Greek and ten Turkish Cypriot; 38 boys and 38 girls) and a control group of 100 English pupils. The school's entire immigrant population covering the complete age range was tested. Cypriot pupils obtained the lowest mean score (33.85) of the three groups, though the West Indian pupils' mean score (36.15) was only slightly greater. When these scores were converted to IQ scores, there was a significant difference at the one per cent level between the English and the Cypriot pupils as a whole and for boys and girls separately, but not between the Cypriots and West Indians. There was little difference in the mean IQ score of the Cypriot boys (84.15) and that of the Cypriot girls (85.15). However, Bhatnagar did not consider this test to be a proper measure of the intelligence of the immigrant pupils.

In an investigation into the language acquisition of a multicultural group of further education students, in 1972-3 and 1973-4, MacDonald (1975) administered Ravens

Standard Progressive Matrices (RSPM) to 114 Jamaican, 55 British and 65 Greek and Turkish students (49 Greek and 16 Turkish, some of whom had parents from mainland Greece and Turkey). The performance of the Greek and Turkish students was significantly greater than that of the Jamaican students (0.05) and not significantly less than the performance of the UK students. For each of the two year groups, the Greek students performed significantly better than the Turkish students (at the 0.01 and 0.05 levels). But in view of the small number of Turkish Cypriot pupils, this finding must be treated with great caution.

Due to the known dissatisfaction with using verbal and non-verbal reasoning tests to assess ethnic minority pupils, a test of learning ability was devised to avoid measurement of what a child had already learnt and instead to measure response to a series of contrived teaching–learning situations (see Hegarty and Lucas, 1978). The test covers conceptual, verbal, numerical and visual–perceptual learning and is administered on a teach–practice–test basis with a minimum of verbal instructions. Ward (1982) reported on the use of this test with some children aged seven to eight whose mother tongue was not English, including a Greek-speaking child, in a special school for pupils with moderate learning difficulties in south-west Hertfordshire. There was no significant correlation between performance on Ravens Coloured Progressive Matrices (RCPM) or the Learning Ability Test with length of experience of English schooling. The numerical and visual perceptual learning sub-scales of the Learning Ability Test appeared to be the most culturally independent tests, but the author pointed to the need to confirm this with a wider sample and to take into account such factors as proportional use of English and mother tongue in the home. Using the scoring profile on the Learning Ability Test to compare the scores of ethnic minority children with a standard profile and to identify relative strengths and skills requiring extra attention, Ward described an interesting diagnosis of and remedial activities for the Cypriot child.

This study indicates ways in which the Learning Ability Test can usefully assess learning difficulties and potential in a way that verbal and non-verbal reasoning tests cannot. However, it is clear that when 15-20 years ago Cypriot pupils were involved in research which tested verbal and non-verbal reasoning, their performance within the group of immigrant pupils as a whole was relatively low and inferior to that of British subjects. Moreover, and perhaps more significantly, Greek Cypriot pupils tended to score at a higher level than Turkish Cypriot pupils on such tests. Indeed the performance of Turkish Cypriots at a level similar to, if not lower than, that of West Indian pupils might have given rise to some concern, especially when taken in conjunction with other test performance on reading and mathematics (see pp.126–30, 130–1).

Language

Language is obviously a key issue in the consideration of the education of pupils of Cypriot origin. Knowledge, use of and attitudes to language on the part of Greek and Turkish Cypriot adults and children are matters of considerable complexity and subtlety. A review of research studies over a 25-year period reveals significant differences according to the time when the research was undertaken, its particular focus and the context of language use according to the linguistic group and generation under consideration. This reflects the language development of these linguistic minority communities in a monolingual country such as Britain. Moreover, since research into the language knowledge and use of Greek and Turkish Cypriots has only been undertaken during the past decade, there is generally inadequate documentation based on subjective statements and social anthropological descriptions for earlier linguistic generations. There is a certain ambiguity in the evidence, lack of longitudinal data and inadequate assessment of linguistic competence. Above all, however, the research evidence reveals the evolution of language and the interdependence of language knowledge use and attitudes, and also the importance of setting consideration of language shift and of the linguistic competence of pupils of Cypriot origin in a wider sociological and interethnic context.

The complexity of the linguistic considerations can be seen from the range of languages or dialects involved. In London there are speakers of Standard Greek and Turkish, Cypriot dialects and other dialects. Hence an analysis of knowledge and use of, and attitudes to, language by Cypriot adults and children must take account of: the Greek Cypriot dialect in relation to Modern Greek and the Cypriot dialect of Western Turkish in relation to Standard Turkish, each in relation to English, particularly London dialects of English, and the other languages spoken in the localities in which Cypriots live, at the workplace and, for some, in the homes.

Although in Cyprus there has been considerable emphasis on respective national links with, and cultures of, mainland Greece and Turkey, geographical separation and a different history of language contacts means that the forms of Greek and Turkish spoken in Cyprus and by Cypriots in Britain are significantly different from the mainland standard languages (Wright, 1983; LMP, 1985). Modern Greek originated in Classical Greek, and is spoken by some 12 million people, ten million in Greece and half a million in Cyprus. Katharevousa 'purified' Greek, which draws heavily on Classical Greek in lexis, grammar and the written system, was created in the early 19th century as part of Greece's struggle to develop a pan-Hellenic identity after freeing itself from Ottoman rule. It was adopted as the medium for official writing, legal documentation and public speaking in contrast to the various demotic or 'popular' forms of Greek. Language became a political issue in Greece, the demotic being associated with liberalism and modernism, Katharevousa with conservatism and nationalism. In the past decade Athenian demotic has been adopted as the basis for the national written and spoken Standard Greek both for official and everyday purposes. In 1982 further simplification of accents and breathings were made, rendering spelling easier to teach (Wright, 1983). The demotic is now recognized as the standard language by Greek Cypriots, although there are lexical, phonological and syntactical differences in the Cypriot dialect, which has also incorporated some features of French, Italian and English during its history (see pp. 1–2).

The Cypriot form of Turkish is a dialect of Western Turkish and differs mainly in pronunciation from the standard form which is based on the speech of an educated élite and spoken by about 50 million people. The written form of Turkish used the Arabic script and included a high lexical content from Persian and Arabic until the end of the Ottoman Empire. Ataturk's reform in the 1920s led to the adoption of a modified Roman alphabet for written Turkish, and non-Turkish words were replaced by Turkish equivalents, a process which continues (CILT, 1983). This linguistic evolution reflects a move towards nationalism and democratization, attempting to make the standard language more accessible to the less educated.

These linguistic differences have an important bearing on the language backgrounds of Cypriot adults and children. Although the Cypriot dialects have roots in their respective mainland language forms, significant differences mean that dialects have acquired a lower status in oral and uncommon written form (Roussou, 1984a; Wright, 1983). The attitudes of speakers of non-standard forms to their language are influenced by others' perceptions of inferiority. Ladbury (1977), for example, reported that Turkish Cypriots sometimes admired the clean pronunciation of Turkish mainlanders. Moreover, in Britain the Greek Cypriot dialect has further developed into a London Cypriot dialect – 1950s and 1960s with English loan words. Unfortunately, this has not been described linguistically, nor well documented. Such factors have a bearing on the education of pupils of Cypriot origin, particularly with respect to language development, in mainstream and community schooling and second language learning, whether this be English or Standard Greek or Turkish.

This review draws chronologically upon various investigations into several linguistic communities, including Greek- and Turkish-speaking Cypriots, mainly in the most concentrated areas of settlement in Greater London. It attempts to disentangle data on the language knowledge, use and attitudes of Cypriot adults and children with respect to dialect forms of Greek, Turkish, their standard forms and English in order to assess the effect of the linguistic background of pupils of Cypriot origin on their ability to benefit from education in English-medium mainstream schooling. A major influence is that of community language classes, which are examined on (pp.78–102), as are mainstream provision for Greek and Turkish (pp. 102–17) and the teaching of English as a second language (pp. 117–23).

LANGUAGE KNOWLEDGE

This section considers Cypriot adults' and children's range of language knowledge in Greek, Turkish and English. Oral–aural competence and literacy skills as assessed by self-reports, interviewers' judgements and teachers' assessments are reviewed. Knowledge of Greek and Turkish are here considered separately from English and the evidence is reported chronologically. Research does not usually distinguish knowledge of dialect or standard forms of Greek or Turkish, though the spoken form will usually be the Cypriot dialect increasingly as modified by living in London. Literacy, especially for the second generation, is more likely to be in the standard language forms. Their performance on large-scale, in-school tests and assessment of English and reading is considered subsequently (see pp. 123–35).

Knowledge of Greek and Turkish

There is no national information about the extent to which Greek or Turkish in standard or dialect forms are spoken, read, written or by whom in the UK. Census figures based on country of birth and other official surveys categorizing ethnic origin (see pp. 5–7) are unhelpful with respect to linguistic affiliation as they offer no way of distinguishing between Greek-speaking and Turkish-speaking Cypriots. Language statistics for Greek and Turkish speakers are, moreover, complicated by the presence in the UK of speakers of these languages from Greece and Turkey (see p.5). It has generally been thought that until the mid-1970s Greek- and Turkish-speaking Cypriots in the UK were roughly in the same proportion as in Cyprus at 1960, namely, four-fifths to one-fifth (Oakley, 1979). But more recent estimates have suggested that there may be a greater proportion of Turkish-speaking Cypriots: Anthias (1983), for example, suggests that the Cypriot population in the UK may be three-quarters Greek Cypriot and one-quarter Turkish Cypriot. In the absence of accurate Census data estimates, covering two or three generations of Cypriot or mainland origin, abound (see pp. 4–7). For example, two language and culture guides from the Centre for Information on Language Teaching recently estimated that there are about 100,000 Greek speakers of Cypriot origin in the UK (CILT, 1982) and 150,000 Turkish speakers in Britain both from Turkey and Cyprus (CILT, 1983). However, given the 1981 Census figures (see Table 3), this latter figure may be inflated. Conversely, the Greek-speaking population may be an underestimate, as in 1984 the Cyprus High Commission estimated 200,000 Greek speakers from Cypriot and mainland backgrounds (Tansley, 1986). Given the concentration of Greek and Turkish speakers in London – and, in particular, in Haringey – in the early 1980s, it is interesting to note that the Linguistic Minorities Project (LMP) estimated that in 1980 there were at least 80,000 Greek speakers in London where they formed one of the largest linguistic minorities, and that there were about 7,000 Turkish speakers in Haringey where they were probably the second largest linguistic minority. In terms of the school population of Haringey, in 1981, the ratio of Greek to Turkish speakers was 70:30, whereas in the adjacent borough of Hackney in the same year the proportions were roughly reversed (Reid *et al*, 1985).

Irrespective of the *exact* proportion of Greek and Turkish Cypriots in the UK, the predominance of Greek Cypriots in Cyprus and the power imbalance which existed between the two communities up to and during the main years of emigration in the early 1960s influenced patterns of language knowledge and use which are reflected in the UK. Although there was a certain interdependence between Greek and Turkish speakers in Cyprus, the members of the minority Turkish community were much more likely to know Greek than Greeks were to know Turkish. As Ladbury (1977) has observed, the Turkish Cypriot emigrant of the 1950s and early 1960s would probably have migrated from a mixed village in which, as a member of a minority population, he would normally have spoken Greek as a second language. Thus in the UK Alkan and Constantinides (1981) have claimed that, in Haringey, elderly Cypriots are more likely to know both Greek and Turkish and that most Turkish Cypriots over 30 years old, in addition to Turkish, also know Greek, though fluency depends on their education and where they lived in Cyprus. However, other young Cypriots who may have grown up in Britain, or have come from those parts of Cyprus where the Greek and Turkish Cypriot communities were separated in the 1960s after the intercommunal hostility following Independence, are more likely to know either Greek or Turkish, rather than both languages. To a certain extent, the greater number of Greek Cypriots and the wider knowledge of Greek in the UK are mirrored in the emphasis of available research evidence.

The literacy of first-generation Cypriot adults in Greek or Turkish is closely connected with their length of schooling in Cyprus prior to emigration. Each community has maintained a separate system of schooling emphasizing its respective mainland links in terms of language, culture, religion and history. Neither system has included the teaching of the island's other main language in its curriculum. Moreover, although post-war education expanded rapidly in Cyprus, even until the late 1960s secondary education was neither free nor universal. Educational opportunities will have been affected by age, gender, access and attendance rates. Most of the post-war emigrants, however, especially men, will have experienced at least elementary if not some secondary education (see pp. 140–2). Several sources provide information on the illiteracy rates in Cyprus considered in relation to the emigrants. According to Oakley (1968), illiteracy in Cyprus was 73 per cent in 1911, compared with 33 per cent in 1946. George (1960) claimed that women and the elderly were more likely to be illiterate on account of previously poor educational facilities and the fact that less importance was placed on the attendance of girls at school. Although these factors may have affected the literacy of some of the earliest Cypriot migrants in the pre-war period, George suggested that the literacy of immediately post-war emigrants was likely to be higher, as most were not from the lowest social group and because the very process of emigration itself required a certain literacy in terms of form-filling and other bureaucratic matters. According to Oakley (1968), illiteracy fell to 18 per cent in Cyprus by 1960 and was then more or less confined to the elderly female section of the population, so that the Cypriot migrants of the late 1950s and early 1960s – at least the young adult males – are likely to have been literate to some degree in Greek or Turkish. By 1970 illiteracy in Cyprus had declined still further (Leeuwenberg, 1979), so that only two per cent of 17–24-year-olds, 3.4 per cent of those aged 25–39, 17.2 per cent aged 40–59 and 34.8 per cent of 60–69-year-olds were illiterate. In the UK, Alkan and Constantinides (1981) have claimed that a small percentage of Cypriot mothers and some elderly women are illiterate in Greek or Turkish and they suggest that Cypriot adults, both men and women, find it easier to read in their mother tongue.

Although such statements have been made from first-hand experience with the Cypriot community in north London, it is fortunate that some more detailed quantitative data on knowledge of Greek and Turkish are available from the recent Linguistic Minorities Project (LMP) survey which involved Cypriots in Haringey in 1980–1. The LMP survey (1979–83) (LMP, 1983a, 1985) represents a major contribution to establishing a sociolinguistic baseline of linguistic diversity and patterns of language use for several linguistic minorities. The LMP survey had four components: the Schools' Language Survey (SLS) documenting the linguistic diversity and extent of literacy in five LEAs; the Secondary Pupils Survey (SPS), a sample survey in two LEAs of language use and perceptions; the Adult Language Use Survey (ALUS) of patterns of adult language skills and use in three cities; and the Mother-Tongue Teaching Directory Survey (MTTDS), which gathered information about mother-tongue teaching provision in the same three areas. Two of these surveys, ALUS and SLS, provide information on Cypriot adults' and children's knowledge of Greek and Turkish. In the context of establishing adult language knowledge it is relevant to describe the ALUS and its findings in further detail here; reference is made in this and subsequent sections to other survey findings.

The ALUS involved several linguistic minorities, including Greek and Turkish speakers in London. Interviews took place in Greek or Turkish, English was only used when the respondent asked to do so, or initiated a language switch. A section of the questionnaire investigated respondents' self-assessments of language skills, including literacy. Although it was not possible to estimate the total population of Greek speakers in Haringey, a random sample of 193 were eventually interviewed in late 1980, despite a low response rate due to out-of-date addresses and a high number of refusals, probably linked to adverse publicity in a local Greek-language newspaper. There were estimated to be about 7,000 Turkish speakers in Haringey and a random sample of 197 were eventually interviewed in late 1981, despite out-of-date addresses, contact difficulties and refusals. Table 8 shows the main demographic features of the Greek- and Turkish-speaking respondents in Haringey. An age and sex balance was largely achieved. The household members of respondents in the two groups were largely middle-aged migrants and their children in their late teens and twenties, and in the Turkish-speaking households especially there were sizeable numbers of people in their thirties and younger children (Reid *et al.*, 1985). Findings should, however, not be interpreted as necessarily representative for Greek and Turkish speakers in London or England as a whole.

Naturally the main languages spoken by the respondents were the language of the interview, Greek or Turkish, and English. Almost all of the respondents had at least a little Greek or Turkish and English. Most of the Greek speakers knew only Greek and English, but 17 per cent knew three or more languages, usually school-learned languages such as French or German. By contrast, some 51 per cent of the Turkish speakers claimed to know three or more languages, with 44 per cent of respondents knowing some Greek. This knowledge of Greek by the Turkish-speaking

Table 8: Demographic features of the Greek- and Turkish-speaking respondents in the Adult Language Use Survey, Haringey

	Speakers of:	
	Greek	Turkish
Estimate of total population	–	7,000
Number of households with member interviewed	193	197
Number of people in respondents' household	758	822
% of people in respondents' household aged below 17	25	30
% of people in respondents' household aged over 50	16	11
% of households in owner occupation	86	84
% of households in council housing	8	9
% of males aged 17–65 at work outside home or in family business	76	76
% of females aged 17–60 at work outside home or in family business	43	32
% of people in respondents' household brought up overseas	52	48

Sources: Adapted from LMP, 1983a, Table 5.3, and Reid *et al*, 1985.

respondents, and the absence of significant mention of Turkish by the Greek-speaking respondents, is probably more a reflection of the Cyprus-based pattern of relationships than of the situation in London in the 1970s and 1980s (see p. 52). Another survey in Haringey in 1978–9 (Leeuwenberg, 1979; see p. 63) also revealed multilingualism: more than one-fifth of the 168 Greek and Turkish speakers spoke, and more than one-eighth read, three or more languages – seven in all. Moreover, almost a quarter of a small sample of mainland Greeks involved in another study of library users (Clough and Quarmby, 1978) claimed to speak, and one-sixth to read, a third language, French, in addition to Greek and English.

Greek- and Turkish-speaking respondents in the ALUS also reported on the oral skills of household members, including children and non-family members, said to know Greek or Turkish very or fairly well:

Greek speakers   (N = 673)   82 per cent
Turkish speakers   (N = 761)   87 per cent

The ALUS also provides information on respondents' self-reported competence in Greek or Turkish (Table 9). Almost all respondents reported understanding and speaking Greek or Turkish fairly or very well; the remaining six per cent of Greek speakers who considered their Greek language skills were weaker were either dialect speakers who answered with reference to Standard Greek or younger respondents who felt their Greek was weak in comparison with their English. For both Greek and Turkish speakers, oral skills varied mainly according to place of upbringing. Some two-thirds of Greek speakers, compared with a notable four-fifths of Turkish speakers, reported fair or good literacy skills; for both groups, these varied mainly according to place of upbringing with those brought up in the UK reporting lower skills, but length of schooling was also influential. Further information on literacy is given in Table 11 (see also pp. 63–4, 72–3).

Given this account of Cypriot adults' knowledge of and competence in Greek and/or Turkish, how is this likely to influence their children's knowledge of these languages, particularly in their pre-school years and in out-of-school hours? Various factors such as generation, cultural orientation of the home, the language in question (Greek or Turkish) and the extent to which there is family and

Table 9: **Adults' competence in Greek or Turkish**

Speakers of:	N	% respondents answering fairly or very well	
		Understand and speak	Read and write
Greek	193	94	66
Turkish	197	98	80

Source: Adapted from LMP , 1983a, Table 5.5.

community support for mother-tongue maintenance – factors which may not have been adequately taken into account in research – are likely to have a bearing on any evaluation of available evidence. For example, in 1960 George found that Cypriot children born in the UK tended to be bilingual but often had little Greek. By 1968 Hylson-Smith claimed that many of the Greek Cypriots attending youth clubs in the Islington–Stoke Newington area spoke almost no Greek. From a socio-anthropological study in the mid-1970s Constantinides (1977) also claimed that the second generation, in spite of parents' efforts, often spoke very little Greek. More recently, Constantinides (1984) and others have drawn attention to the complex language background of some children, from the rising number of second-gener-ation mixed marriages. These children normally have fathers of Greek Cypriot origin and mothers from the English-language majority or other ethnic minority groups, thus introducing a third language to the child. In such cases Greek, for example, would be the 'father tongue', thus having different implications for early language exposure and learning. Although at pre-school age the language exposure of children of Cypriot origin will depend largely on the home language background, this is likely to vary to some extent from family to family and by generation. Oral and literacy skills are likely to be age-related and affected by community and mainstream educational experience. A range of research evidence permits con-sideration of the extent to which Greek and Turkish are claimed as spoken languages for pupils of Cypriot origin. Most of this information comes from research surveys and studies in Greater and inner London, where the majority of pupils of Cypriot origin are to be found.

Four language censuses, covering the whole of ILEA in 1978, 1981, 1983 and 1985 (ILEA, 1979, 1982, 1983, 1986), provide evidence of considerable and increasing linguistic diversity amongst London schoolchildren and of the numbers of Greek and Turkish speakers (see also Table 7, p. 42) analysed according to their distribution within the ILEA and by age. Unfortunately, however, no distinction is made between Cypriot dialect forms and Standard Greek and Turkish, let alone London dialect forms, nor is any assessment available of competence in these languages, as it is for English (pp. 66–7). In the first language census, in 1978, teachers in all primary and secondary schools collected information on a class basis for every pupil for whom English was not a first language. Greek speakers (3,802) and Turkish speakers (3,587) formed the first and second largest groups of speakers of the 128 languages recorded. The survey revealed the different distribution of Greek- and Turkish-speaking pupils. Some 65 per cent of the Greek-speaking pupils were found in the Islington (1,277 pupils), Hackney (613) and Camden (592) divisions of the ILEA, with fewest Greek speakers in Greenwich (53). By contrast, Turkish speakers predominated in Hackney (1,118) and in Southwark (782), though there were also 538 Turkish speakers in Islington schools, with fewest Turkish speakers in the Borough of Wandsworth (73). A lower proportion of Greek-speaking pupils (54 per cent), compared with speakers from some more recently established linguistic minority communities, were of primary school age, but it was unclear whether this was because the Cypriot community had given birth to fewer children in this age range or whether a higher proportion of such children had acquired English as a first language (ILEA, 1979).

In the second ILEA survey, in 1981, teachers in all primary and secondary schools recorded the number of pupils who used a language other than, or in addition to, English at home. The number of both Greek and Turkish speakers had increased and Turkish speakers (4,418) outnumbered Greek speakers (3,859). They formed respectively the second and third largest group of speakers of 131 overseas languages, constituting respectively 9.8 and 8.6 per cent of the total number of 44,925 foreign language speakers. Once again, there was a notable concentration of Greek-speaking pupils in Islington (1,186), and large numbers in Camden (661) and Hackney (572), with fewest in Greenwich (64). Turkish speakers were again concentrated in Hackney (1,295), with large numbers in Southwark (862) and Islington (665). There had also been a considerable increase over the 1978 figure (422) in Lewisham (611). Wandsworth again had the smallest number of Turkish-speaking pupils (184). Although year-by-year fluctuations in the number of Turkish-speaking pupils obscured any age-related trends, there were by contrast a decreasing number of Greek speakers in the younger age-groups – pupils aged five constituting only about 75 per cent of those aged 15. Another difference was that whereas Greek-speaking 16–19-year-olds formed 66.8 per cent of the number of Greek-speaking pupils aged 15, Turkish speakers aged 16–19 constituted only 46.3 per cent of the number of Turkish speakers at 15. In fact, out of the 12 main foreign language-speaking groups, only the Turkish speakers had a lower percentage of 16–19-year-olds in relation to 15-year-olds in school than that of the ILEA as a whole (52.2 per cent). This suggested that they had a lower rate of staying on at school after the legal school-leaving age, a pattern which continues (see p.138). A third difference between the Greek and Turkish speakers was that whereas in 1981 the Turkish speakers increased by 23.2 per cent over the 1978 figure, the Greek speakers only increased by 1.5 per cent overall – by far the smallest increase for any of the main foreign language-speaking groups. Whilst it was not possible to be certain whether the increases were due to a change in population or definition employed in the Census, it is interesting to note that only in the Greek-speaking group was there a small decrease in the actual number of children recorded in primary schools (−2.5 per cent) (ILEA, 1982). This might also suggest either a declining birth rate or moving out of the ILEA area.

Further evidence of changing age patterns of and between Greek- and Turkish-speaking pupils in the ILEA are apparent from subsequent surveys. The 1983 survey employed the same definition as the 1981 survey, but extended its scope to include pupils in nursery and special schools. A total of 147 languages was recorded, and although the number of Turkish speakers (4,316) declined slightly, they maintained their position as the second largest group (8.6 per cent) of all foreign language speaking pupils (50,353). The number of Greek speakers had declined further to 3,410, the fifth largest group (6.8 per cent) of foreign language speakers. As before, the largest number of Greek speakers were to be found in Islington (1,000), Camden (602) and Hackney (480) with fewest in Greenwich (47). The greatest number of Turkish speakers was again to be found in Hackney (1,234) and Southwark (795), and by 1983 almost as many in Lewisham (632) as Islington (647), with fewest in Wandsworth (101) as before. In relation to 1981 the number of both Greek and Turkish speakers declined by 14.3 and 4.7 per cent respectively, compared with a declining roll of eight per cent in the ILEA as a whole. The ILEA report (1983) indicates that although there were again no discernible age-related trends for Turkish speakers, there were again more Greek speakers aged 15 than five and it was anticipated that, as with Italian speakers, their numbers in ILEA schools would continue to decline.

This was confirmed in the 1985 census (ILEA, 1986), when there were found to be fewer Greek speakers (3,033), now the seventh largest group (5.4 per cent) of pupils speaking a language other than English at home (56,607). By comparison, there was a slight increase in the number of Turkish speakers (4,383), who again maintained their position as the second largest group of 161 overseas language speakers, though they constituted only just over a third of the number of Bengali speakers. Greek speakers were again concentrated in Islington (867), with a sizeable number in Camden (573) as before, though proportionately fewer in Hackney (390), whose numbers were being approached by Southwark (309). However, as before, there were more than twice as many Turkish speakers in this location (763) and, in turn, consistently outnumbered by Turkish speakers in Hackney (1,218), though fast approached by Lewisham (700) which had overtaken Islington (645). The overall decline of Greek speakers (-11.1 per cent) was second only to that of Italian speakers and like that group Greek speakers were more numerous in older than younger age-groups, except at the beginning of primary school where there were quite small differences. Thus, in contrast to Turkish speakers, a continuing decline in the number of Greek speakers, especially in secondary schools, is predicted. This suggests that the majority of second-generation Greek speakers have almost completed their schooling and that the third generation are only just commencing school, whereas there are consistently considerably more Turkish speakers in the primary-age range (see also p. 53). However, it will be of interest to monitor to what extent Greek and Turkish continue to be represented as languages spoken at home by ILEA pupils.

The Schools Language Survey (SLS) of the LMP, undertaken in 1980–1 in five LEAs, also records the number of pupils speaking Greek or Turkish at home and confirms the ILEA trend to declining numbers of Greek-speaking pupils in the lower age ranges in two north London outer boroughs (Couillaud and Tasker, 1983). The SLS, developed to assist LEAs to document linguistic diversity, was administered by teachers and records pupils' self-reports of the language(s) they spoke at home and their language(s) of literacy. Table 10 provides information on the number of pupils speaking Greek or Turkish, and whether or not Cypriot dialect forms of these languages were specified, the pupils' age and sex and literacy (see p. 60) and their percentage of that of all minority language groups in two LEAs, Haringey and Waltham Forest. In Haringey, Greek and Turkish speakers together represented 48.8 per cent of the borough's 30.7 per cent of pupils who used a total of 87 languages other than English at home. Greek and Turkish speakers were less dominant in Waltham Forest, together representing 12.1 per cent of that borough's 18.8 per cent of pupils who used a total of 65 languages other than English at home. In both boroughs there were fewer Greek speakers in the younger age ranges, as also of Turkish speakers in Waltham Forest, with age-group fluctuations in the number of Turkish speakers in Haringey. Interestingly, roughly half of each group of language speakers in each of the LEAs reported speaking Cypriot dialects of the standard languages. It is also worthy of note that in Haringey 196 pupils (2.7 per cent) of the speakers of languages other than English at home also reported a second spoken language, of which Greek was the most frequently mentioned. In contrast to the large numbers of Greek and Turkish speakers in Haringey and Waltham Forest, there were very few such speakers in the three other LEAs which took part in the SLS:

	Bradford	*Coventry*	*Peterborough*
Greek speakers	27	41	18
unspecified	18	27	11
Cypriot	9	14	7
? Hellenska	1	–	–
Turkish speakers	2	2	3

Table 10:   Pupils' knowledge of Greek and Turkish in Haringey and Waltham Forest, 1981

		Haringey		Waltham Forest	
		Greek	Turkish	Greek	Turkish
1	Pupil numbers	2,521	1,091	431	239
2	% of all language groups in schools	34.1	14.7	7.8	4.3
3	Literacy*, % of total Greek/Turkish speakers	60	49	55	46
4	Sex ratio: boy/girl	51/49	50/50	49/51	47/53
5	Age-groups 6–8	614	199	104	57
	9–11	643	163	120	60
	12–14	784	225	121	66
6	Language form:				
	standard or unspecified	1,432	730	278	156
	Cypriot dialect	1,089	361	152	83
	From Turkey		1		

*'Literacy' here means reading or writing in one of the spoken languages given as a separate language of literacy.

Sources: Adapted from Couillaud and Tasker, 1983; LMP, 1983a, Table 2.5.

The relative concentration of Greek- and Turkish-speaking pupils is illustrated by the fact that in a nation-wide survey, in 1983, only seven out of 56 LEAs with primary schools with at least ten per cent bilingual pupils named Greek and only three LEAs named Turkish as two most frequently spoken languages (Tansley and Craft, 1984). Moreover, in a national survey, in 1979, only 11 per cent of 118 schools reported having speakers of Greek as a first language (Little and Willey, 1983).

Unfortunately, no research appears to have assessed the oral skills of pupils speaking Greek or Turkish or Cypriot dialect. However, a few studies have considered the relative dominance of Greek and English or Turkish and English for pupils speaking these languages (see also pp. 65–7). As part of a large-scale research project into the library use of ethnic minorities in six London boroughs – Brent, Camden, Haringey, Islington, Wandsworth and Westminster in 1975 – Clough and Quarmby (1978) interviewed 397 ethnic minority children (average age 11), ten per cent of whom were of Greek Cypriot origin. Of these 39 children, 24 male and 15 female, 36 had been born in the UK, 38 had Greek Cypriot fathers and 34 Greek Cypriot mothers. All claimed to speak English and 94.9 per cent spoke Greek, apparently one of the highest percentages of children from minority groups who claimed to speak two languages. In addition, two children with mothers of other European origins also claimed to speak another language. In another study, in a school in Waltham Forest, Prager (1977) found that slightly more than half of the small number of Greek speakers claimed to speak Greek better than or as well as English, and a similar proportion of Turkish speakers claimed to have a better command of Turkish than English. The most informative data come from an investigation in 1977–8 of the linguistic competence of 4,600 11–12-year-olds in 28 secondary schools in 11 London boroughs (Rosen and Burgess, 1980). Five of the schools are reported to have been in Haringey (Leeuwenberg, 1979). Greek was spoken by 165 (22 per cent of the sample) and Turkish by 97 (13 per cent) of the 749 bilingual pupils. According to their teachers, some 65 per cent of the Greek-speaking pupils were bilingual and regularly spoke Greek. Of the remainder, only five per cent had Greek as their dominant language and 30 per cent spoke only a little. By comparison, 61 per cent of the Turkish speakers were rated as bilingual and 39 per cent as speaking only a few phrases. Rosen and Burgess suggested that, in the case of Greek- and Turkish-speaking pupils, substantial language communities or strong cultural interest served to maintain their mother tongues. Yet these were by no means dominant at age 11. Taken together with other assessments of their perceived competence in English (see p. 65), it appeared that bilingualism as such might be significant for a fair proportion of Greek and Turkish speakers.

Given these data on children's oral–aural skills, and bearing in mind the likely influence of spoken dialect forms rather than the standard language in domestic use, to what extent are they literate in Greek or Turkish? Also, how do the literacy skills of Greek- and Turkish-speaking pupils compare with those of adult speakers of these languages (see pp. 54, 64)? In the pre-war and immediately post-war years of settlement, although a few Cypriot children retained a little of their mother tongue, they did not necessarily learn to read and write it (Alkan and Constantinides, 1981). There was then a lack of opportunity for formal mother-tongue maintenance, compared with the community network which now makes it possible for Greek- and Turkish-speaking Cypriot children to attend mother-tongue classes to maintain and improve oral skills and to learn to read and write Standard Greek and Turkish (see pp.78–102). Such classes must be the major influence on the development of literacy skills for pupils of Cypriot origin, especially given the general relatively low educational standard of their parents and their employment preoccupations. However, Cronin (1984, reporting an investigation by Jones, J., 1982) noted that two-thirds of the few Turkish children interviewed in a Turkish supplementary school had been taught to write by, and had learnt songs, rhymes and stories from, their parents from mainland Turkey, who were mainly working class or who ran small businesses.

Evidence of pupils' literacy in Greek or Turkish, compared with English, is available from the same few studies. Clough and Quarmby (1978) found that all the 39 Greek Cypriot children aged 11 claimed to read English and 20 claimed to read Greek. In fact exactly the same number attended mother-tongue classes. Of those who could read Greek, all except two preferred to do so. One child also claimed to read in his mother tongue (German). However, in another part of the survey a few Greek Cypriot mothers who were themselves learning English were more likely to read in English than in Greek. Similarly, in Prager's (1977) study two-thirds of the relatively small number of Greek- and Turkish-speaking pupils in one secondary school in Waltham Forest claimed to read and write less well in their mother tongue than in English. Rosen and Burgess's (1980) study is again the most illuminating in this context, providing assessments of reading and writing skills, enabling comparisons to be made with oral competence and with other language speakers, and revealing further differences between Greek- and Turkish-speaking pupils in their proficiency in their respective mother tongues. Some 42 per cent of the 97 Turkish-speaking pupils aged 11 were estimated by their teachers as reading and writing Turkish, compared with some 37 per cent of 165 Greek-speaking pupils who were said to read and write Greek. A further 16 per cent of the Greek-speaking pupils were assessed as reading but not writing Greek, compared with 12 per cent of Turkish-speaking pupils who were thought to read but not write in Turkish. Since 61 per cent of Turkish speakers and 65 per cent of Greek speakers were considered bilingual, it seems that these language speakers were more likely to have greater oral than literacy skills in Greek and Turkish. Nevertheless, about half of each group of language speakers had at least some literacy skills, which were greater in reading than writing. Their literacy skills were like those of Portuguese speakers (43 per cent able to read and write their mother tongue) rather than French speakers (53 per cent) or Italian speakers (21 per cent) (see p. 65). Unfortunately, these figures give no impression of the degree of literacy for Greek- and Turkish-speaking pupils.

Importantly, teachers' estimates of pupils' literacy are supplemented by other pupils' self-reports in both community and mainstream schools. As part of an investigation into the library needs of mother-tongue schools in London, Elliott (1981) interviewed some 20 Greek-speaking Cypriots and 20 Turkish-speaking Cypriots out of a total of 200 seven to 18-year-old pupils in ten mother-tongue schools. All but one of the Greek speakers were second generation, seven of primary school and 13 of secondary school age. Although the Turkish speakers were divided evenly by age-group, three of primary and four of secondary age were first generation. All the Greek and Turkish speakers claimed to read English, but the Greek-speaking pupils were more likely to say that they read Greek (17 and three a little) than the Turkish-speaking pupils were to claim to read Turkish (13, six a little, one not at all).

Further interesting data on the literacy of Greek- and Turkish-speaking pupils are available from the Schools' Language Survey. Over the five LEAs the average reported literacy rates were 60 per cent for Greek-speaking pupils and 50 per cent for Turkish-speaking pupils (LMP, 1983a, Table 2.5). These rates were in the middle range for the average reported literacy of 12 language of literacy groups. Data from Haringey and Waltham Forest, the two LEAs with most of the Greek- and Turkish-speaking pupils in the SLS, reveal further contrasts in the reported literacy of pupils from these two language groups and also by age and sex. The reported literacy rates of Greek speakers were higher than those of Turkish speakers both in Haringey and Waltham Forest (see Table 10, p. 58). There was a clear, straightforward increase in reported literacy with age for both Greek- and Turkish-speaking pupils aged six to 15+ in Haringey and Greek speakers in Waltham Forest (Couillaud and Tasker, 1983). But amongst the Turkish-speaking pupils in Waltham Forest there was a tendency for those in the 14 plus age-group to report a lower literacy rate than those in the younger age-groups. It was not possible to tell whether this was due to under-reporting of literacy skills or whether it was a particular feature of this age cohort or a combination of these and other factors, such as lack of access to mother-tongue support in community or mainstream schools. Moreover, Greek-speaking girls in both LEAs and Turkish-speaking girls in Haringey had a statistically significant higher reported literacy rate compared with that of their male peers. This corresponds to widespread evidence of such differences in the educational literature on language achievement in general, and literacy in particular. Furthermore, it is possible that some Turkish Cypriot pupils from devout Muslim backgrounds may have an additional language of literacy, Quranic Arabic, acquired for study of religious texts. Although the SLS notes that some pupils reported this as an additional language of literacy, it is unfortunately unclear whether, or to what extent, this was the case for Turkish-speaking pupils.

Overall research on the literacy of Greek- and Turkish-speaking pupils does not lend itself to easy generalization, especially since competence in reading and writing is unclear. Moreover, even the relatively limited evidence available indicates that there are complex differences and similarities in the language knowledge, and especially literacy of Greek- and Turkish-speaking pupils. Thus, for example it may appear as if the proportion of Greek-speaking adults and children reporting literacy is much closer than that of Turkish-speaking adults and children. However, this fails to take account of level of skills. Although there are implications that children's reading skills are greater than writing skills, research evidence is only based on adults' and children's self-reports and teachers' subjective assessments. Pupils from Greek- or Turkish-speaking backgrounds are less likely to be literate in their respective languages than to speak these languages. Research is not unambiguous about whether Greek-speaking pupils are more likely to be literate in Greek than Turkish-speaking pupils are to be literate in Turkish. However, it would appear that when Greek-speaking pupils are literate, girls are more likely to be literate than boys, and literacy, at least for Greek-speaking pupils, is likely to increase with age. This suggests that literacy in Standard Greek and Turkish must depend to a great extent on persistence with learning, and hence the likely influence of language classes in community and mainstream schools, their accessibility, and attitudes towards language maintenance and development (see pp.75–7).

In conclusion, the situation with respect to Cypriot adult's and children's knowledge of Greek and Turkish is very complex and as yet inadequately researched. Cypriot adults appear more likely to have oral skills in the Cypriot dialects of Greek and Turkish, and as further modified in London, than in the standard forms of these languages. Unfortunately, however, there is no research evidence, as there is for Italian adults with respect to dialect and standard language forms (see pp.221–4), on the factors influencing and the extent of knowledge of Standard Greek and Turkish by Cypriot adults. The numerical concentration of dialect speakers may be sufficient to sustain the dialects. The fairly high proportion of Turkish-speaking adults reporting a knowledge of Greek, but not vice versa, is a reflection of the demographic and political situation in Cyprus prior to emigration. Yet the fact that in Haringey some pupils speaking a language other than English have reported in addition a knowledge of Greek as a second spoken language suggests that Greek may still have a certain currency in communications between Greek and Turkish Cypriots in London. Moreover, a notably higher proportion of Turkish-speaking adults claimed fair or good literacy skills in the mother tongue than did Greek-speaking adults. Place of upbringing and length of schooling are clearly influential. These factors also appear to apply to the second generation, in so far as location of residence may affect the extent to which there is access to community and mainstream educational support for mother-tongue maintenance and development. This may be the case to a greater extent for Turkish- than Greek-speaking pupils and for both language speakers living outside Greater London – though there is no explicit research evidence on this. Clearly the development of literacy in Standard Greek or Turkish by the second generation is likely to depend particularly on educational opportunities and attitudes to language in the home, community and school. There is widespread evidence from the London-based researches reviewed here of the extent to which pupils claim a knowledge of Greek and Turkish as languages spoken at home, though unfortunately no indication of their aural–oral competence. However, it appears that overall between a half and three-fifths of Turkish- and Greek-speaking pupils report some literacy skills in their respective languages. However, it is also important to consider pupils' skills in Greek and Turkish in relation to their knowledge of and competence in English.

Knowledge of English
The remainder of this sub-section focusses on Cypriot adults' and children's knowledge of English and considers to what extent skills in Greek and Turkish interact with oracy and literacy in English. Bilingualism is likely to be a matter of the degree to which languages are spoken, ranging from minimum competence to complete mastery. Most bilinguals are likely to have a dominant language and those who speak English as a second language are likely to have degrees of mastery. Fluency is sometimes deceptive and literacy more difficult to assess.

Again, Cypriot adults' and children's knowledge of English is reviewed through local studies and surveys, mostly in inner and Greater London. A subsequent section examines complementary evidence of the performance of pupils of Cypriot origin on tests of English proficiency and reading in large-scale and longitudinal surveys in a school context (pp.123–30). The teaching of English as a second language to pupils of Cypriot origin will also be considered (see pp.117–23).

An examination of Cypriot adults' knowledge of and competence in English indicates that this is likely to vary at least according to the time when research is conducted, the generation of the subject, length of residence, area of settlement and degree of interaction with the wider community. For Cypriot emigrants, contact with English in Cyprus was as the language of rule connected with the country's history of colonization. George (1960) claimed that Cypriot immigrants in the 1930s had a poor knowledge of English. However, Alkan and Constantinides (1981) have suggested that by the end of the Second World War most of the men in this group spoke adequate to fluent English, although Cypriot women were less proficient in English. Cypriot adults who emigrated to the UK in the 1950s may have had more opportunity to benefit from secondary education which included English in the curriculum, though secondary schooling was neither free nor compulsory. Yet according to George, few spoke English on arrival. By 1960 Oakley (1968) reported that more than one in every seven Cypriots in Cyprus over the age of ten had a knowledge of spoken English, and almost twice as many in the urban areas. He suggested that it was likely that the majority of young male Cypriot immigrants to Britain at that time would have at least an elementary knowledge of English, whilst Greek Cypriot women rarely spoke much English.

Clearly the length of residence and area of settlement have some part to play in the development of English skills of the adult Cypriot population. Cypriot immigrants in the 1930s and 1940s, even the women, gradually came to acquire some knowledge of English simply because of a need to function when there was less support from a smaller Cypriot community (Alkan and Constantinides, 1981). The more numerous Cypriots who migrated to the UK in the 1950s and 1960s formed large concentrated settlements, with supporting networks and services, which made it unnecessary to go beyond the Cypriot community to speak English to meet daily needs. Hence, for example, Hylson-Smith (1968) claimed that a large percentage of first-generation Cypriots who lived on the borders of Islington and Stoke Newington spoke very little English. In particular, Cypriot women because of their confinement to home or the Cypriot-owned factory often had fewer opportunities for learning English. However, by the mid-1970s Constantinides (1977) reported that most Greek Cypriot women had some proficiency in English. The mere fact that the majority of Cypriots have lived in the UK for 20 years or so might in itself be thought likely to have developed their skills in English. Yet Hunter-Grundin (1982) has claimed that, although most of the Cypriot fathers of children in the concentrated Cypriot area of the South Harringay district of Haringey understand and have some command of spoken English, this is not the case for the Cypriot mothers. Ulug (1981) has also observed that many Turkish Cypriot women despite having lived in London for over a decade cannot speak English. A limited command of English gives rise to communication problems with children whose first language has become English rather than Turkish. Other Turkish parents from the mainland have also been reported by their children to have little or no command of English (Cronin, 1984). It is likely that the extent to which Cypriot adults live within their own ethnic community, with its supporting shops, employment and social network, will have a considerable effect on the degree to which they acquire a knowledge of and proficiency in English. Moreover, even if aural–oral English skills are acquired, literacy in English may not be. Cypriots who are literate in Greek or Turkish may not be fluent or literate in English (Alkan and Constantinides, 1981).

Data from two surveys in Haringey enable these observations on Cypriot adults' knowledge of and competence in English to be explored further. A relatively small-scale survey undertaken by Leeuwenberg (1979), in 1978–9, one of an informative series of library surveys planned as a sequel to the research of Clough and Quarmby (1978), aimed to study the literacy and reading habits of Greek and Turkish Cypriots so as to enable more appropriate library provision to be made. Despite an overrepresentation of young Cypriots in the age-group 15–24, and of those with urban origins in Cyprus and hence an inadequate statistical basis to relate to Haringey's Cypriot population as a whole, this survey provided some interesting data on language. Of the 84 Greek and 84 Turkish Cypriots interviewed, 43 per cent had been educated wholly in Cyprus, 30 per cent in Cyprus and the UK, and 25 per cent in the UK only. Over two-fifths of the Greek Cypriots compared with less than one-fifth of the Turkish Cypriots had remained in education to the age of 19. Some 61 per cent of Greek Cypriots claimed to be bilingual in Greek and English and 69 per cent of Turkish Cypriots claimed to be bilingual in Turkish and English. Of the remainder, a quarter of each language group had Greek or Turkish as their dominant spoken language, whereas 14 per cent of Greek Cypriots compared with six per cent of Turkish Cypriots claimed to speak mainly or only English (see pp.69–70). Some 88 per cent of Turkish speakers and 85 per cent of Greek speakers could read easily in at least one language. Half to two-thirds were to a fair degree biliterate: 64 per cent of Turkish speakers claimed to read both Turkish and English, compared with 51 per cent of Greek speakers who read in Greek and English. Of the remainder, about a quarter of each language group read mainly or only in Greek or Turkish, whereas over one-fifth of Greek speakers compared with fewer than one-tenth of Turkish speakers read mainly or only in English (see pp.72). It is interesting that this study found that this sample of Greek- and Turkish-speaking adults had a very similar pattern of knowledge of English in terms of spoken and written skills, with a slightly greater shift towards English amongst Greek Cypriots, which may have been influenced by their tendency to remain in education longer. However, of those who claimed to speak English, some 40 per cent of Turkish speakers and 31 per cent of Greek speakers said that they experienced difficulties in obtaining information, particularly of a specific kind, and especially in relation to taxation, legal matters, social services, education and medical concerns.

The ALUS of the LMP (1983a) provides up-to-date information on the oracy and literacy of Greek- and Turkish-speaking adults in English (see pp. 53–4 for survey and sample details). Almost all of the Greek- and Turkish-speaking respondents in Haringey claimed some knowledge of English. It is interesting to note that, in contrast to most respondents from the other linguistic minorities, as many as 18 and 19 per cent of the Greek- and Turkish-speaking respondents respectively said that they had started to learn English at home. Like some other language speakers, over 50 per cent of both Greek- and Turkish-speaking respondents had started to learn English at school (LMP, 1985). Although self-rated ability to understand and speak English amongst these adult respondents was lower than for the same skills in the minority languages (see Table 9), Turkish and Greek speakers reported high rates of oral–aural skills in English (Table 11), exceeded only by Polish, Gujerati and Italian speakers in Coventry.

Literacy skills in English, defined as an ability to read and write at least fairly well, were lower than aural–oral skills in English and literacy skills in Greek or

Table 11:   Greek- and Turkish-speaking adults' competence in English

| Speakers of: | N | *% respondents answering fairly or very well* | |
		Understand and speak	Read and write
Greek	193	72	57
Turkish	197	75	46

Source: Adapted from LMP, 1983a, Table 5.5.

Turkish (see Table 9). However, it is interesting to note that the literacy skills of Greek speakers in English and Greek were not too dissimilar in contrast to the literacy of Turkish speakers, whose skills in English were considerably inferior to those in Turkish. For both language groups, English skills related very closely to country of upbringing and also to length of formal schooling. Only three per cent of speakers had no literacy in either Greek or Turkish, or English. In fact 63 per cent of Greek and 61 per cent of Turkish speakers had at least minimal reading and writing skills in one of these languages and English.

Finally, the spoken language skills of respondents' household members, including children and non-family members, who were said to know English or English and Greek or Turkish very or fairly well, are shown in Table 12. At least four–fifths of both Greek- and Turkish-speaking respondents' household members in Haringey were said to know English at least fairly well. For both groups of language speakers, English skills depended on whether upbringing was totally or partly in the UK, and males had significantly higher reported levels of skills than females, probably due to the combination of shorter formal schooling for women and fewer opportunities to acquire English at work outside the home (LMP, 1985). Just under two-thirds of members of Greek-speaking respondents' households and over two-thirds of members of Turkish-speaking respondents' households were said to be bilingual in the sense of knowing either Greek or Turkish and English fairly well and hence had, in principle, the possibility of speaking these languages in the home. The pattern of bilingualism also suggests that, for many people of Greek and Turkish origin in London, English has become a major element in their linguistic repertoire but that they have retained at least a very strong base in Greek or Turkish (Reid *et al.*, 1985) (see p.54). Overall the evidence from these samples also suggests a slightly greater linguistic shift towards English as such for Greek speakers.

Table 12:   English and bilingual skills of household members of Greek- and Turkish-speaking respondents

Speakers of:	N	*English%*	*Bilingual%*
Greek	673	79*	63
Turkish	761	80	70

*Reid *et al.*(1985), Table G5, give this figure as 89 per cent.
Source: Adapted from LMP, 1983a, Table 5.7.

The aural–oral English skills of pupils of Greek or Turkish Cypriot origin, at least in their early years, are likely to depend on a number of factors such as generation, extent of contact with the wider English-speaking community, the extent to which English is spoken in the home and position of child in the family. Some general evidence exists on the dominance of Greek or Turkish for pupils of Cypriot origin in the pre–school years and of the extent to which such a child is prepared to receive schooling in the medium of English. Alkan and Constantinides (1981) have commented that the first generation of Cypriot children in the 1940s and 1950s soon learnt English as there was less of a Greek–speaking community and they usually played with English children. They generally only experienced a little difficulty with English once they entered primary school. In fact it was less likely that these children were able to retain their mother tongue because of the lack of availability of formal mother–tongue teaching. Yet by 1968, Oakley, writing of the majority of children of Cypriot origin who had arrived in the UK as young children or had been born here to recently immigrated parents, claimed that few would know any English before starting school. Those who did were usually the children of mixed marriages, particularly those with an English mother, or perhaps with older brothers or sisters who had themselves already acquired some knowledge of English. In confirmation Alkan and Constantinides have suggested that it is because of the close-knit community that second-generation children of Cypriot origin, especially the eldest, speak Greek or Turkish at home until the age of five when they go to school. This was borne out by Hunter-Grundin's (1982) study of pre-school and primary education in the South Harringay district of Haringey where it was quite common for Cypriot children to speak no English at all on commencing schooling. However, Beetlestone (1982) has claimed that whilst children of Greek Cypriot origin tend to be bilingual to some degree at the age of four, third-generation pupils of Turkish Cypriot origin tend to speak only Turkish on starting school. Clearly the home language background of children of Cypriot origin will greatly influence whether they enter school with some knowledge of English. The relative dominance of Greek or Turkish and English will vary from family to family, and for individuals within a family, especially by generation, at different times. However, there is some evidence to suggest that children from Turkish Cypriot backgrounds may be less likely than those from Greek Cypriot backgrounds to experience the use of English alone or in some mixed form with the mother tongue in the home (see p. 70). Hence needs with respect to language development on entry to school may be diverse. Some approaches to the teaching of English as a second language to pupils of Cypriot origin are discussed elsewhere (see pp. 117–23), as is their performance on standard tests of English and reading (see pp. 123–30).

One smaller investigation and the language censuses in London provide evidence of Greek- and Turkish-speaking pupils' developing proficiency in English during the course of primary and secondary education. These teachers' assessments of the English language knowledge of Greek- and Turkish-speaking pupils may be compared with assessments of their knowledge of Greek and Turkish (see pp.58–9). In 1978 Rosen and Burgess found that teachers considered some 72 per cent of 165 Greek-speaking and 60 per cent of 97 Turkish-speaking pupils as unambiguous speakers of English. The remainder of each group were considered to incorporate some features from Greek or Turkish in their spoken English. Eighty-eight per cent of both the Greek- and Turkish-speaking 11-year-olds were rated by their teachers as fluent speakers of English and the remainder, with the exception of one per cent of the Turkish speakers, were rated at an intermediate level of competence. Thus, in comparison with other minority language speakers, a lower proportion of Greek and Turkish speakers than German, Italian or French speakers were considered unambiguous speakers of English. However, a similar proportion of Greek and Turkish speakers and these other minority language speakers were estimated to be fluent in English. Indeed a much higher proportion of Greek and Turkish speakers were considered to be bilingual (see pp.58–9). More Greek speakers were considered unambiguous speakers of English than bilingual (almost three-quarters compared with two-thirds). By contrast, a similar proportion of Turkish speakers (three-fifths) were regarded as both unambiguous speakers of English and bilingual. These assessments indicate that by secondary school age a large majority of Greek- and

Turkish-speaking pupils have acquired fluency in spoken English, but fewer, especially Turkish speakers, are considered unambiguous speakers of English. This lends support to the LMP (1985) observation that 'the English spoken by many bilinguals in England is often different from that spoken by their monolingual peers. It may be a form of "Greek London English" reflecting the new social reality of its speakers, and their use of particular discourse strategies such as code-switching skills' (p.7). However, the detailed sociolinguistic position of Greek- and Turkish-speaking Cypriot pupils largely awaits description.

English competence has also been assessed by teachers in four ILEA language censuses in 1978, 1981, 1983 and 1985 (ILEA, 1979, 1982, 1983, 1986). In the 1978 census teachers assessed the number of pupils whose first language was not English and who were in need of additional English teaching. At that time, Greek-speaking pupils formed the largest group of overseas language speakers, but they fell numerically to third position in terms of need of additional language teaching. However, both numerically (1,595) and proportionately (44.5 per cent) more Turkish speakers than Greek speakers (1,203 or 31.6 per cent) were considered to need additional help with English. The proportion of Turkish speakers in need of additional English was between that of Spanish and Portuguese pupils, whereas the proportion of Greek speakers was only slightly greater than that of French or Italian speakers in need of help with English. Nevertheless, it is clear that almost a third of Greek speakers and almost a half of Turkish speakers were considered by their teachers to be in need of additional English tuition. Generally Greek- and Turkish-speaking pupils considered to be in need of additional English teaching were found roughly in proportion to their distribution throughout the ILEA divisions.

In the subsequent surveys the fluency in English of pupils who used a language other than or in addition to English at home was assessed by teachers according to four categories: beginners with very restricted spoken English and only slight understanding, so that the diversity of linguistic demands in the classroom are significantly problematic; second-stage learners quite fluent in spoken English, with a high proportion of non-native errors and an uneven vocabulary and syntax; third-stage learners, with spoken and written English with few signs of non-native use, though lacking the full language range of English speakers of the same age and ability and thus tending to underachieve in language-based subjects; and those with full competence, having a command of written and spoken English comparable to that of native speakers of the same age and ability; thus findings in 1981, 1983 and 1985 may be directly compared (Table 13).

Table 13: **Stages of competence in English of Greek- and Turkish-speaking pupils in ILEA, 1981, 1983 and 1985**

Year	Speakers of:	Beginners %	Second stage %	Third stage %	Fluent %	Total No.
1981	Greek	5.3	15.3	21.3	58.1	3,859
	Turkish	13.4	20.5	24.9	41.1	4,418
1983	Greek	5.1	13.3	21.6	59.5	3,410
	Turkish	9.9	21.0	26.2	42.5	4,316
1985	Greek	5.0	15.9	25.8	52.8	3,033
	Turkish	12.5	23.7	29.0	34.3	4,383

Sources: ILEA language census 1981, 1983 and 1985, adapted from ILEA, 1982, 1983, Appendix 4; 1986, Appendix 5.

Across the three language census years the percentage of Greek-speaking pupils rated as fluent in English has consistently been slightly, but increasingly, less than that of European language speakers as a whole – amongst whom Greek speakers have most resembled Spanish speakers in their competence in English; secondly, much greater than that of all overseas language speakers in ILEA as a whole; thirdly, much (and increasingly) greater than the percentage of Turkish-speaking pupils rated as fluent in English. By contrast, the percentage of Turkish-speaking pupils rated as fluent in English has been slightly higher than that of Middle East language speakers as a whole in 1981 and 1983, but not in 1985; secondly, consistently slightly lower than that of all overseas language speakers in ILEA as a whole; thirdly, considerably lower than the percentage of Greek speakers rated as fluent in English. It is possible that the difference in the proportion of Greek- and Turkish-speaking pupils rated fluent in English (approximately three-fifths to two-fifths in 1981 and 1983, and a half to a third in 1985) can be partly explained by the age distributions of the two groups (see pp.56–7), given that fluency is likely to increase with age, since in 1981 and 1983 there were far more Greek-speaking pupils aged 15 than five, whereas Turkish-speaking pupils were more evenly distributed across the age range. In 1985 the relatively small differences in the numbers of Greek-speaking pupils at the beginning of primary school and the end of secondary school might also account for the smaller percentage of Greek-speaking pupils rated as fluent in English compared with the two previous censuses. However, the consistency of the difference in the percentage of Greek- and Turkish-speaking pupils placed in the three stages of learning English and rated as fully competent across these three censuses suggested, especially when taken together with other evidence, that there is a real difference in the fluency in English of pupils from these two language groups as perceived by their teachers (see pp.118–19). Moreover, in ILEA, in 1985, almost half of Greek-speaking and two-thirds of Turkish-speaking pupils were lacking full competence in English and thus in some degree of need of language support.

Overall the limited research evidence indicates considerable skills in English for Greek- and Turkish-speaking adults and children. On the whole Greek- and Turkish-speaking adults are likely to have lower levels of skill in English than their mother tongue. Their aural–oral skills in English are greater than their literacy skills in English. It appears that a large majority of Greek and Turkish speakers may have at least a fair knowledge of spoken English and many have high levels of skill. Skills are likely to depend on place of upbringing and length of formal schooling, with adult females having lower reported levels of English skills. There is some evidence of a slightly greater shift to English amongst both Greek-speaking adults and children compared with Turkish speakers. This is particularly reflected in Greek-speaking adults' literacy skills in English (see p.64) and the greater proportion of Greek-speaking pupils assessed as fluent in and unambiguous speakers of English. However, despite the significance of English in the linguistic repertoires of many Greek and Turkish speakers, bilingualism and even biliteracy in Greek or Turkish and English appear to be important as such – minimally, at least, for perhaps as many as three-fifths of Greek and Turkish speakers. This pattern of language knowledge and the relative significance of developing and maintaining competence in Greek or Turkish and English are likely to be considerably influenced by attitudes to these languages, opportunities to learn them and the need, occasion and motivation for using them. Hence it is of interest to examine research evidence on these matters.

LANGUAGE USE

An examination of reported uses of Greek, Turkish and English in different contexts can be a means of cross-checking claims made by researchers, teachers, Greek- and Turkish-speaking adults and children about language knowledge and competence. Several researches, usually the same studies and surveys from which information has been drawn regarding language knowledge and skill, have attempted various sociolinguistic assessments of patterns of language use amongst Greek and Turkish Cypriot communities and households in London, occasionally on the basis of involvement or observation over time, or more frequently by questionnaire. Research evidence on language use in the community, between parents and children, siblings and other household members, reveals changing patterns over time and some of the factors influencing an increasing degree of choice in language employed in oral communications. A few studies which have investigated use of literacy in terms of the reading habits of Greek- and Turkish-speaking adults and children in the context of reviewing library provision are also considered. Data are not divided here according to use of English, Greek or Turkish because the studies, largely reflecting practice, make no clear division. Language use is obviously closely related to proficiency in and attitudes to language (pp.51–67, 75–8).

Amongst Cypriot adults in the 1950s and 1960s Greek and Turkish were reported to be the languages of daily conversation even by those who had been in London for 20 years or more (George, 1960; Hylson-Smith, 1968). However, Alkan and Constantinides (1981) have suggested that there was a difference in the extent to which the early settlers in the pre and post Second World War period and the majority of immigrants in the late 1950s and early 1960s used their mother tongues and English in daily life. Although the women amongst the first group were not so conversant with English as their menfolk, the need in the absence of a supporting Cypriot community to operate in the wider community on a daily basis meant that English had to be used. However, this was not the case for the large majority of Cypriots who migrated in the late 1950s and early 1960s and lived, worked and formed communities in certain areas of London. Hence Alkan and Constantinides claim that in most Cypriot households Greek and Turkish is spoken continuously. To an extent, these languages are perpetuated because of the close knit Cypriot community which makes it unnecessary to use English in daily life since it is now possible to shop in Cypriot stores or in self-service supermarkets, Greek and Turkish films are shown regularly, Cypriots often work together in factories where Greek and Turkish are spoken, and Cypriot women work sewing, often at home, all minimizing the need to use English. But despite this ethnic framework supporting mother-tongue use, observational evidence suggests that English is increasingly used by adult Cypriots. For whereas George (1960) claimed that English was only used by Cypriots in formal association with the British, even in the mid-1970s Constantinides (1977) noted that second-generation Greek Cypriot adults often spoke to each other in a mixture of colloquial English and Cypriot Greek liberally sprinkled with Hellenized terms invented by first-generation Cypriots to describe aspects of the dressmaking and restaurant trades. It is of course this generation who are now raising their own children, the third generation, who are, in turn, embarking upon their English schooling.

As Cypriot adults' language use has changed over the years of residence in Britain, so the language use of second-generation children of Cypriot origin has changed from that of the mother tongue in the early years before school to an increasing knowledge of and use of English with schooling. Even in the 1950s George (1960) noted that Cypriot children born in the UK tended to be bilingual but with rather less Greek. They spoke Greek at home and English at school. Commenting on this situation-specific use of Greek and English, George wryly observed 'it would be interesting to know whether educational achievement suffers from this shift between two languages'(p.164). Though educationists have long been aware of the bilingual background and use of at least two languages in different contexts by Greek- and Turkish-speaking linguistic and other minority pupils – and this review constitutes a general attempt to answer that very question –

the lack of research examining the links between pupils' language competence and use and their educational achievement in terms of subjects or examinations still does not enable a proper evaluation of this issue to be undertaken. A decade after George's research there had been some shift towards speaking English at home by pupils of Cypriot origin; for example, although the overwhelming majority of Greek and Turkish Cypriot pupils whom Bhatnagar (1970) studied, in a secondary modern school in Haringey, claimed to speak their mother tongue at home, seven per cent claimed to speak English at home. Other studies reported that Greek-speaking children spoke English at home or replied to their parents' Greek with English (Clough and Quarmby, 1978; Oakley, 1970). Yet in view of the evidence collected by school-based language censuses, English is obviously not the only language used at home by pupils of Cypriot origin. Indeed Rosen and Burgess's claim seems to ring true:

> It is clear that there is no single, mother tongue or language of the home for the many Greek pupils who speak Greek all the time to one parent (who is perhaps still not a very fluent English speaker), English some of the time to the other parent (except at family, communal occasions, perhaps) and English *all* of the time with brothers and sisters at school. (Rosen and Burgess, 1980, p.60)

At some point, probably during primary schooling, many pupils from Cypriot backgrounds acquire a fluency in English which they assert in their predominantly Greek- or Turkish-speaking homes and converse increasingly in English, especially with their siblings (as do mainland Turkish children – see Cronin, 1984). The younger children in the family learn some English from older siblings who have already started school. According to Alkan and Constantinides (1981), Cypriot children who arrived as refugees in the mid-1970s are more likely to use both Greek or Turkish and English. But within the peer group use of English for pupils of Cypriot origin may become so commonplace that it is even employed in mother-tongue schools (Elliott, 1981). Interestingly, Hewitt (1982) cited cases of Turkish- and Greek-speaking children who have been attracted by the 'street credibility' of Creole forms of English and have not uncommonly been found to employ 'London Jamaican' speech. This is clearly an area for further sociolinguistic exploration. In sum, limited observational studies suggest that children of Cypriot origin often have a certain fluency in Greek or Turkish but may choose, except in cases where it is not possible to make themselves understood, to communicate in English, especially within the peer group, both at home and at mainstream and community schools.

These general observations are usefully complemented by other quantitative and more precisely categorized data. In an interview survey in Haringey, in 1977–8, Leeuwenberg (1979) found Greek and Turkish speakers used their mother tongues to a similar extent in various social contexts (see p.63 for sample details). Half the Greek and the Turkish speakers claimed to use these languages, half used English. As might be expected, there was a greater use of mother tongue with the first generation, as 85 per cent of the Greek speakers and 70 per cent of the Turkish speakers who had parents alive spoke to them only in Greek or Turkish. Similarly, the 63 per cent of Greek speakers and 55 per cent of Turkish speakers who were married claimed to speak mainly Greek or Turkish to their spouses unless they were non-Greek or Turkish speaking. But a different pattern of language use was demonstrated by the 40 Turkish and 39 Greek speakers with children: 45 per cent spoke to them only in Greek or Turkish, 45 per cent operated a mixed use of English, Greek or Turkish and ten per cent claimed to speak to them mainly in English. The interviewees thus seemed to be playing a significant strategic linguistic role as intermediaries between the first and third generation. A Commission for Racial Equality survey in 1981 (CRE, 1981a) which included a quota sample of 100 Cypriots, predominantly aged 40 plus, from the C1 social class, out of a sample of 1,057 ethnic minority respondents and 1,073 white British respondents, found that although 64 per cent of the Cypriots claimed to speak Greek at home and 11 per cent Turkish, 22 per cent reported that they spoke English mainly at home, again demonstrating increasing use of English in the home.

Table 14:   Languages used between Greek- and Turkish-speaking adults and their respective household members

Speakers of	N = household members excluding respondents	% of interlocutors using only or mostly minority* language reciprocally with respondents	% of interlocutors using only or mostly English recip- rocally with respondents	% of interlocutors using both English and minority language reciprocally with respondents
Greek	548	51	16	18
Turkish	607	60	7	16

*'Minority language' here means Greek for Greek speakers, Turkish for Turkish speakers.
Source: Adapted from LMP, 1983a, Table 5.8.

Fortunately more precise data from the ALUS of the Linguistic Minorities Project permit consideration of language use by Greek and Turkish speakers with other household members, according to language skills, in the community and in free-time activities, and between children in the household. Table 14 shows the patterns of language use between Greek- and Turkish-speaking adult respondents in Haringey (see pp.53–4 for sample and survey details) and their respective household members, regardless of language skills. All of these interactions involved at least one adult. These data show that in both Greek- and Turkish-speaking households these languages are used mostly by most household members. However, whereas in Turkish-speaking households in three-fifths of cases Turkish was used most of the time by both speakers, in Greek-speaking households only just over half the respondents spoke mostly Greek with other household members – the lowest proportion of minority language use for any of the linguistic minorities in London, except Italian speakers. In a third of cases in both Greek- and Turkish-speaking households there was some mixed pattern of language use in which both the minority language and English were spoken by both parties or where one person spoke in the minority language and the other in English (Reid *et al.*, 1985). The Greek-speaking households demonstrated a greater shift towards using English alone than the Turkish-speaking households. This may, in part, be related to the level of language skills available to speakers (see Table 12).

Further analysis of unconstrained choice of language use between respondents and family members with a fair knowledge of English and Greek or Turkish revealed that three-fifths of both Greek- and Turkish-speaking bilinguals used only or mostly the minority language (Table 15). However, of the linguistic minorities in London only among the Greek-speaking bilinguals with a real choice of language use did those choosing to speak English exceed five per cent. Thus overall these data indicate the predominant use of Greek or Turkish amongst bilingual members in Greek- or Turkish-speaking households, with about a third in each case employing a mixed pattern of language use of the minority language and English.

Table 15: **Languages used between bilingual Greek and Turkish speakers and other bilingual family members**

Speakers of:	No. of persons in households including respondents	A No. of pairs of interlocutors both knowing English and minority language* fairly or very well	B % of A where minority language used reciprocally all or most of the time	C % of A where English used reciprocally all or most of the time
Greek	758	167	59	6
Turkish	822	285	60	3

*'Minority language' here means Greek for Greek speakers, Turkish for Turkish speakers.
Source: Adapted from LMP, 1983a, Table 5.9.

Most interestingly, the ALUS also revealed some supplementary data on the language use of children in the Greek- and Turkish-speaking households. There was a considerable difference in the proportion of children from the two language groups who were reported as using only or mostly English when speaking to one another: 82 per cent of the 99 children from Greek-speaking households compared with 61 per cent of 120 children from Turkish-speaking backgrounds. In fact the percentage for children from Greek-speaking households equalled that for children from Italian-speaking households and was only exceeded by children from Polish-speaking households in Coventry. These findings tend to fit with other data on language skills (see pp.65–7).

Further analysis of language use (ibid.) revealed that whilst the working environment of Greek-speaking adult respondents was more likely to give some support to use of the minority language than the working environment of Turkish-speaking respondents, the community and free-time activities of the Turkish speakers indicated a slightly greater use of the minority language than did those of the Greek speakers. For example, three-quarters of Turkish speakers mentioned Turkish-speaking social clubs and associations and half were involved in at least one organized group, compared with two-thirds and two-fifths of Greek speakers. Most of the Turkish respondents said they spent time mainly with other Turkish-speaking friends and three-quarters used Turkish with the person they spent most free time with, compared with over half of the Greek speakers in each case. Turkish speakers were more likely to have seen a video or film in their language in the previous few weeks than Greek speakers and nearly half had neighbours speaking their language compared with only one in six Greek speakers. Nearly all respondents in both groups sometimes went to a shop where their language was spoken. Just less than a third in each group sometimes used an interpreter, usually a family member or friend. Sometimes children perform such a function at school, the hospital or whilst shopping, though they may not be able to cope with official documentation (Oakley, 1968; Alkan and Constantinides 1981; Cronin, 1984).

Fortunately, information on the use of literacy, reading habits and type of reading-matter enjoyed by Cypriot adults and children is available from several investigations, mostly conducted by researchers interested in library provision. Reading habits are obviously influenced by level of skill in a language, access to reading material and leisure-time. Clough and Quarmby's research (1978) includes information on mainland Greek adult library users, Greek Cypriot non-library users and Cypriot children who used libraries. Findings for the two small samples of adult Greek speakers highlight contrasting and possibly atypical uses of literacy. Just under half of the highly educated mainland Greeks in their early twenties preferred to read in English and three-quarters claimed to read a serious English newspaper, compared with almost two-fifths who read a newspaper in Greek. The same proportion had learned of the library from their families and had used it for about three years on average, just under one-third for lending and one-third for study purposes. Although just over three-fifths were satisfied with library provision and consulted library staff for help, they wanted a larger book stock, improved study facilities, materials for learning Greek and English and more information. Most importantly, some 85 per cent wanted more Greek books, particularly fiction, mythological and historical books. By contrast, half of the few Greek Cypriot mothers surveyed in language learning classes were unaware that the library provided any materials in Greek, although others did not use the library because of lack of time. Two-thirds, however, claimed to read the newspaper in Greek.

Leeuwenberg's survey (1979) also provides data on the reading habits of mainly young Cypriot adults. Some 23 per cent of Greek speakers and 11 per cent of Turkish speakers claimed to read these languages in their everyday work. Generally men and women read to a similar extent, though those over 25 and from the higher socioeconomic groups read more. Overall it appeared that Turkish readers read newspapers, magazines, books, circulars and newsletters to a much greater extent than Greek readers, though this may have been because it was necessary for them to look in more than one place for information. For example, 93 per cent of Turks, compared with 81 per cent of Greeks, read newspapers, about two-fifths of each group weekly and/or daily. Both Greek and Turkish readers were mainly interested in politics, news of Cypriots in London and sport. Neither Greek nor Turkish readers were heavy book readers as 58 per cent of Greek and 40 per cent of Turkish readers had not read any books in the month prior to the research, and only seven per cent of Greek and 11 per cent of Turkish readers had read five or more books in their language in that period. About four-fifths of Greek and Turkish readers read in English about Cyprus or Cypriot affairs, and the greatest demand, especially by young people, was for this type of reading-matter. Although a similar proportion claimed to buy books, Leeuwenberg found a small book-owning élite of teachers, doctors, journalists, lawyers and those connected with various Cypriot organizations, with only 27 per cent of Greek readers and 18 per cent of the Turkish readers having more than 30 books. This tends to bear out an early observation by George (1960) that 'very few Cypriots can afford or are interested in buying any books', though this must also be influenced by the availability in the UK of good-quality books in Greek and Turkish (see pp.30,31). Indeed Leeuwenberg claimed that by far the majority of the sample, especially Turkish readers, were anxious that more reading-matter, especially books and newspapers in their mother tongue, should be available in public libraries in Haringey.

The ALUS of the LMP also supplies information on contrasting patterns of library usage and reading habits amongst Greek and Turkish readers (Reid *et al.*, 1985). Less than half of the Greek speakers, compared with slightly more than a third of Turkish speakers, knew that libraries in Haringey stocked books in their language. About a third of both Greek and Turkish speakers sometimes used a library, a similar proportion of Turkish speakers sometimes borrowing books in Turkish, compared with a quarter of Greek speakers who borrowed books in Greek. Again, a greater proportion of Turkish-speaking than Greek-speaking respondents (86 compared with 78 per cent) read newspapers in the minority language, with just less than three-quarters in each case reading newspapers in English. About a third of Greek respondents read textbooks and novels in Greek and English, compared with less than a fifth of Turkish speakers reading textbooks in Turkish and just over a quarter in English, less than half reading novels in Turkish and less than a third in English.

Turning to children of Cypriot origin, two studies have considered their reading habits, library use and the extent of interaction between parents and children in the uses of literacy (see pp.126–30 for school-based assessments of reading skills in English). In Clough and Quarmby's (1978) investigation of library use by 39 Greek Cypriot children of average age 11 years, about two-fifths claimed to have learned of the library from their school and a similar proportion from their families. They seemed to have a high rate of library use compared with other linguistic minority children, with nearly one-quarter using it more than once a week and over one-third weekly, overall mainly for fiction. Almost all claimed to have books at home, three-fifths in English and just over a third in Greek and English. Just over four-fifths were satisfied with the library provision and three-fifths consulted staff when in difficulties. Yet only one-fifth had parents who were members of the library. On the other hand, three-fifths of the children claimed that their parents inspected the books which they selected from the library, over two-fifths claiming that both parents looked at their books. Yet only ten per cent of their parents were reported to read to them from these books.

Elliott's survey (1981) in 1980 which involved 20 Greek-speaking pupils and 20 Turkish-speaking pupils in ten mother-tongue schools found that Greek- and Turkish-speaking pupils had very similar reading habits. Three-fifths or more of Greek and Turkish speakers had read a book in their mother tongue up to six months before the interview and nine out of every ten had read a book in English. Almost all the Greek and Turkish speakers spoke in English of the books they had read, which, as Elliott points out, might indicate that English was preferred as a reading language by these pupils, that they wanted to show that they were more fluent in English or that there were not enough books in their mother tongues for the pupils to read at leisure. Both groups of children liked to read stories and magazines or comics in English and to read about their parents' country of origin in their mother tongue. There were differences, however, in the extent to which their parents encouraged them in language development and maintenance. Whereas six out of 20 Greek pupils claimed that their parents read to them and that one told stories in English, only two out of 20 Turkish pupils made similar claims. There was much greater encouragement in the mother tongue, with half of the Greek pupils reporting that their parents read to them and two-fifths that they told them stories in Greek, and almost two-fifths of the Turkish pupils said that their parents read to them and told them stories in Turkish. These were much higher levels of parental interaction than in Clough and Quarmby's survey.

During the last decade or so since these researches began it is likely that access to reading materials by means of library provision in Greek and Turkish for adults and children, at least in the main centres of population, has increased (see pp.30,31). In 1974 Clough and Quarmby found that only two of the six London boroughs where they interviewed the children's librarian had children's books in Greek, and these were mainly used by eight to 11-year-olds because there were few books for young children. In general, Greek materials were said to be difficult to obtain and of poor quality. Interestingly, however, the Greek books had been provided partly in response to requests from the children themselves, though similar requests had not been received from Turkish readers. By contrast, Leeuwenberg in Haringey, in 1979, found that Turkish Cypriots were particularly anxious to have more reading material in Turkish, especially for their children, and recommended that there should be much more reading material in Turkish and Greek available in the public library to satisfy the continuing demand. He suggested that special attention should be paid to reading and story-telling in Turkish as part of the library provision for Turkish Cypriot children, and that there should be greater liaison with schools to provide material on Cyprus in English which would interest both second-generation Cypriot pupils and their peers. Indeed only a short while later Elliott (1981) found that there were sizeable collections of Greek and Turkish books for children in Haringey, a small collection of Greek books in Brent, some children's books in Greek in Islington and a larger collection of books for adults, and for parents to read to children, in Greek and Turkish in Hackney. These findings suggest, therefore, that research undertaken by librarians has had some effect in increasing provision within the library service.

Overall the research evidence suggests that although there has been some movement towards use of English among the Greek- and Turkish-speaking population, there has been considerable maintenance of use of Greek or Turkish as such. It is much more likely that there will be some mixed use of English and either Greek or Turkish, especially among adults, rather than use of English alone. The continuing predominance of Greek and Turkish in communication between adults has gained support from the concentration of Greek and Turkish speakers in certain localities where the establishment of their own businesses, services and recreational facilities has enabled them to maintain their mother tongue in daily life outside the home. There is some evidence to suggest that Greek speakers have more support for the use of their language, in spoken and written forms, in the workplace, but that Turkish speakers may make greater use of their language in leisure-time. Research suggests that at home these languages are spoken only or mostly by about three-fifths of their speakers, with about a third of households having some form of mixed language use, with both interlocutors using Greek or Turkish and English or one speaker Greek or Turkish and the other English. Exchanges are of course influenced by language skills available to the speakers, and evidence indicates that a greater proportion of Greek than Turkish speakers use English alone, even when the interlocutors have a real choice of language. This appears to hold also for children speaking to one another in the home. Yet, although schooling and the peer group are important influences of children's use of English, language surveys demonstrate continuing use of Greek and Turkish at home, most likely with parents as the majority of Greek- and Turkish-speaking children appear to use English in communication with one another in the home, mainstream and community language schools. In terms of uses of literacy research evidence suggests that in general Greek- and Turkish-speaking adults tend towards more lightweight reading-matter, the great majority reading newspapers in their mother tongue and only slightly fewer in English. There is some evidence of greater use of literacy by Turkish speakers. This is dependent on skills, use of leisure-time and access to reading materials. Although the second generation of Cypriot origin may have learnt to read and write Greek or Turkish at language classes, they are likely to have greater literacy in English and hence their reading habits will tend to draw on skills in this language.

LANGUAGE ATTITUDES

Attitudes to language may be significant in affecting the acquisition of language skills and use of a language and also related to a sense of identity. It is, therefore, important to attempt to build up a picture of the language attitudes of Cypriot adults and children towards Greek, Turkish and English. However, in contrast to the fairly large-scale survey research evidence on language knowledge and use of Cypriot adults and children, the evidence on their attitudes to languages is somewhat fragmentary. Nevertheless, some account can be given from the observations, comments and claims made by researchers on the basis of socio-anthropological study or close personal acquaintance with Cypriot communities. Thus the attitudes of Cypriot parents and children to Greek, Turkish and English tend to be inferred from behaviour and practice rather than measured by specific investigations. Attitudes to language will, therefore, be considered through evidence on Cypriot parents' attitudes towards their children maintaining and developing a knowledge of Greek and Turkish; children's attitudes to these languages; and Cypriot parents' attitudes to their children and they themselves learning English.

One of the clearest impressions to emerge from the research literature on first-generation Cypriot adults is the significance for their identity and that of their communities of maintaining their knowledge and use of Greek and Turkish. For example, in the ALUS Turkish- and Greek-speaking respondents were almost unanimous in agreeing, or strongly agreeing, that they should make every possible effort to maintain the fullest use of their languages in Britain (Reid *et al.*, 1985). However, only two-fifths of Turkish speakers and fewer than a third of Greek speakers thought there was no problem in maintaining these languages. Around nine out of every ten Turkish and Greek speakers considered that the authorities should provide more support for their languages by producing official communications in Greek and Turkish, employing more Greek- and Turkish-speaking doctors, teachers and social workers and making mainstream provision for teaching these languages (see also p.103).

Related to these attitudes is the desire of Cypriot parents that their children should maintain their mother tongue and indeed extend their knowledge of the spoken language by acquiring a competence in reading and writing Greek or Turkish. Indeed parents seem to place a particular value on literacy in the standard form of the language and may even see it as a virtue (Beetlestone, 1982; Tansley, 1986; Oakley, 1968). In addition to helping and encouraging their children to read and write Greek or Turkish at home (Cronin, 1984; see p.59), many Cypriot parents send their children to community mother-tongue classes to further develop their language skills. These classes may extend children's language knowledge in a way which may not be possible within the home, and also convey a particular set of cultural values associated with Greek or Turkish which may differ from those espoused in mainstream schools. According to Alkan and Constantinides (1981), Cypriot parents' anxiety and desire for their children to maintain Greek or Turkish is both academic and practical. On the one hand, they may appreciate that learning two languages can prove both useful and satisfying if learnt well. On the other, they know that those who can converse in Greek or Turkish as well as English are able to enjoy communicating with their immediate and extended family and especially relatives in Cyprus when they go for holidays. Indeed it appears that the latter – more practical – reason is the main motivating force for the establishment of mother-tongue schools by community organizations. This may have been heightened by an increased awareness that by adolescence many children of Cypriot origin have communication problems with their parents, especially with their mothers, for it has been claimed that whilst the second generation may be able to use everyday words in Greek or Turkish they may be unable to express themselves with any subtlety of meaning in these languages. Hence, according to Alkan and Constantinides, many Cypriot parents believe that Greek or Turkish and English should be learnt simultaneously and used contemporaneously, otherwise Cypriot youngsters may be too shy to use their mother tongue later in life. However, Alkan and Constantinides claim that some Cypriot children can be confused by the multilingual environment which they experience in their early years and many Cypriot parents have begun to realize the difficulty of coping with learning two languages. Some, it is suggested, have commented that Greek or Turkish must be learnt first, then English and only in later years if there is a chance to study Greek and Turkish again, and if a child has the ability, should first-language knowledge be extended. However, Alkan and Constantinides have argued that it is not difficult for a child to learn two or even three languages, provided that they are taught correctly, simultaneously and continuously. Cypriot parents being used to bi- or trilingualism have a different attitude to language learning than British parents and do not see their own languages as a barrier to learning in the mainstream school (Beetlestone, 1982).

But what of the attitudes of children of Cypriot origin to their Greek or Turkish mother tongue? Many are exposed from their earliest years to one or other of these languages, often in some mixed form with English, especially if they have older brothers and sisters who bring English into the home. As they progress through the school system, they acquire greater proficiency in English, but this may not necessarily mean that they have a positive attitude towards it or a negative attitude towards their mother tongue. Clearly one individual may do well in coping with both languages, whereas another may be confused or bewildered by both, and a third opt for one rather than another. Hence, in a certain context, it may be easier to express a thought in English, whilst in another Greek or Turkish may seem more appropriate. Ulug's (1981) case study of five secondary-age pupils of Turkish Cypriot origin provides some interesting illustrations. Only one girl preferred talking English. Although one took pride in her literacy in Turkish and another preferred to speak Turkish in school, at home and to her friends, all four experienced some confusion with English, in 'both thought and speech': 'I have to think in English, then say it in Turkish'. 'I get it the wrong way round' and 'I speak half English, half Turkish'; and two girls experienced both languages in their dreams, 'it was usual to dream in "Turkish" if the subject was a Turkish event such as weddings involving relatives; but if the subject of the dream was school, then it would be dreamt in "English" (ibid., pp. 44–5). Moreover, as Alkan and Constantinides (1981) have observed, some children may be unwilling to spend more time learning by attending mother-tongue classes (see p.100) and may reach adolescence understanding their mother tongue but be too embarrassed to speak it in case of making mistakes. Cypriot Greek and Turkish speakers may be acutely conscious of speaking dialect forms of the standard language which they may come to see as inferior (Ulug, 1981). Turkish Cypriots were reported to admire mainlanders' clean pronunciation (Ladbury, 1977). Yet some children may resent having to speak to their parents in Turkish or Greek (Cronin, 1984). On the other hand, some children may delight in using Greek or Turkish, especially in the mainstream school environment where there may be few others who may understand. Some teachers have realized that Cypriot pupils have a pride in their mother-tongue knowledge and are keen to display their proficiency (Little and Willey, 1983). The teaching of Greek or Turkish in the secondary curriculum of mainstream schools (see pp.105–8) and the introduction of special language projects such as the Mother Tongue Project, which included the use of Greek materials in some Haringey primary schools, may lead pupils to have greater pride in their home language and their abilities in it, and the development of positive attitudes to bilingualism and awareness of languages other than English in the school (Tansley, 1986).

How, then, do Cypriot parents regard English and its acquisition, particularly by their children? According to Oakley (1968), although many Cypriot fathers at that time spoke some English, it was a matter of principle that they should not use it when talking with their children. However, Cypriot parents were well aware that proficiency in English was crucial to their children's future success and hence they were very keen to see their children perform well in mainstream school at the same time as encouraging their mother-tongue maintenance. They saw being literate in English primarily as a practical necessity and as instrumental to achieving success. Having surveyed infant schools in 11 LEAs in 1967–8 and evaluated the particular needs of non-English-speaking immigrant children, Stoker (1969) suggested that Cypriot parents, in contrast to some ethnic minority parents, would have prepared their child for a change of language and told the child that he or she would be going to school to learn English, though the child and perhaps even the parent would not have had a proper knowledge of what this meant. Indeed Oakley even suggested that the majority of Cypriot parents reluctantly allowed their desire for their children both to maintain their mother tongue and to acquire proficiency in English, which might sometimes conflict, to be resolved by the Anglicizing influences of education. Whilst none set out systematically to 'de-Hellenize' their children, Oakley observed that a small minority, usually those with a stronger allegiance to returning to Cyprus, had tended to discourage effort in English and focussed their child's interest on Greek. However, in recent years Alkan and Constantinides (1981) have claimed that as a community the Cypriots are realizing how important it is for children to acquire some knowledge of English before they enter school and some parents attempt to help their children with English, but as it is often incorrect this can lead to confusion. They also noted a problem of 'feigned' understanding of English which, they claimed, may happen if there is no support for learning English at home. Alkan and Constantinides argued for the provision of more pre-school playgroups and day nursery facilities with extended day care in order that young Cypriot children might socialize with other children, learn English and retain their home language.

Until relatively recently the suggestion that children from linguistic minority groups might attend such pre-school facilities both to retain their community language as a basis for learning English and to learn English would scarcely have been countenanced. Since the early 1970s the prevailing view has been that children from non-English-speaking homes should be encouraged to mix with native British speakers as early as possible in order to pick up Standard English. British society has been largely hostile to bilingualism and especially to language and culture maintenance. Indeed until recently the importance of encouraging non-English-speaking mothers to attend English language classes such that they might assist their children's learning of English was unquestioningly assumed. Whilst Cypriot men – despite their concentration in ethnic businesses – might have more opportunity to acquire some proficiency in English through their contact with the wider community in work, Cypriot women – heavily employed in the Cypriot clothing industry and often working at home – would have less occasion to develop a proficiency in English. To what extent, then, have Cypriot adults, especially women, perceived a need to learn English and what have been their attitudes towards doing so?

As early as 1960, George recorded that a number of special classes were organized to assist Cypriots to learn English. In 1967 a London Council of Social Service (LCCS) report argued that there was a case for English classes for parents to be arranged in schools attended by their children. In a survey in 1971 Townsend and Brittan (1972) reported that 12 out of 128 primary schools and 11 out of 93 secondary schools nationally had received requests for English-language tuition for adults from ethnic minority communities, including Greek and Turkish Cypriots, and that many of these requests had been implemented either in the school itself or by referring the Cypriot adults to further education colleges holding evening classes. At the end of the 1970s, Little and Willey (1983) found that some schools continued to arrange courses in English for Greek Cypriot mothers. In some cases, Cypriot associations, such as the Greek Parents' Association, organize English classes for their own community in conjunction with the LEA, sometimes in the same building and alongside the Greek mother-tongue classes for children (Leeuwenberg, 1979; Alkan and Constantinides, 1981; Christodoulides, 1984). But a national survey of English-language classes for women from ethnic minority groups (Mobbs, 1977) claimed that few classes were attended by substantial numbers of Cypriot women. According to Hunter-Grundin (1982), living in an ethnic community with its own social life and facilities has often meant a lack of motivation for Cypriot mothers to learn to communicate in English; or it may be that despite considerable efforts to learn English, many Cypriot mothers are too embarrassed or shy to attend classes, even though they may be informal and held in community centres, schools or clinics (Alkan and Constantinides, 1981). In such cases, home visiting by voluntary tutors working on a one-to-one basis may be particularly appropriate, especially since tutors are often Cypriots themselves who speak both languages fluently, and this personal contact can help to extend social contacts in both the Cypriot and British communities.

Generally, first-generation Cypriot adults have a natural and proper pride in their Greek or Turkish language and culture which, because of the support they receive from the surrounding community, may outweigh their perceived need to learn English. However, this may not mean that they have negative attitudes towards English, only that it is regarded as primarily a practical necessity, not integral to their identity. Thus they may attempt to encourage the retention and development of the mother tongue by their children in an attempt to ensure communication and community identity whilst, at the same time, appreciating the need for them to have opportunities to develop a knowledge of English from their early years in order to enhance their chances of educational and economic success. These attitudes and aims are not necessarily incompatible, though much will depend on the attitudes which Cypriot pupils themselves develop towards the majority and minority language and learning these languages. In this they are likely to be influenced not only by their parents, but also by the school system and the media which may reinforce the low or marginal status accorded to minority language use and teaching in British society at large. The following sub-sections consider the arrangements made by mainstream and community schools to teach English, Greek and Turkish to pupils of Cypriot origin and assessments of their levels of proficiency in these languages.

'MOTHER-TONGUE' TEACHING

Community provision
The foregoing review of language knowledge, use and attitudes demonstrates that Cypriot adults have a strong and positive sense of their mother tongue, either Greek

or Turkish, and this is felt to be closely bound up with the maintenance of ethnic identity. Favourable attitudes towards the mother tongue are further enhanced and reinforced by the surrounding community in which Greek and/or Turkish are in continual use. It is, therefore, important when considering the education of pupils of Cypriot origin to examine the extent to which this predisposition towards, and pride in their native tongue on the part of many Cypriot parents leads them to attempt to ensure that it is maintained by their children, not only through everyday communication in the home and community, but by specifically encouraging children to attend mother-tongue classes. Moreover, in view of the current educational debate as to whether provision should be made for teaching the languages of minority pupils in the mainstream curriculum, it will be of assistance to clarify the extent of existing community mother-tongue teaching provision for Greek- and Turkish-speaking pupils. The following analysis of the organization and nature of provision and the attitudes of participants and significant resource issues has been compiled from various research sources covering a 25-year period, and some unpublished information from community sources. Not surprisingly, perhaps, in view of the preponderance of Greek speakers amongst the Cypriot population, there is clearly both more community language teaching provision in Greek and better documentation of it. Nevertheless, available information on community provision for Turkish will also be cited. Indeed more information exists in both Greek and Turkish but was not accessible to be drawn upon for this review.

AIMS   What, then, are the aims of the mother-tongue classes? Since the earliest years of settlement Greek Cypriot parents have apparently been under pressure from the church, other community members and their families to ensure that their children not only retained, but also developed, their mother tongue. Indeed, according to George (1960), it was considered a national duty for parents to instruct their children in their language. George quotes the following exhortation to parents from the left-of-centre Cypriot newspaper, *Vema* (17 January 1959) 'The struggle for the Greek education of our community is one of a national nature, a struggle for the protection of our children against the danger of their anglicization that the conqueror of our suffering island so much desires'. Evidently nationalistic feelings were running particularly high at that time and the views of the Greek Orthodox Church were no less fervently held. According to George and Millerson (1967), in discussing the establishment of one mother-tongue school the calendar of All Saints' Church, Kentish Town, London, in 1959 declared 'the young Cypriot children of our community will be educated and strengthened with nourishment from the national and religious ideals of the Orthodox Church and the Greek Motherland and not with the lure of dehellinization and assimilation'. Indeed similar views may still be held: Tansley (1986) records that the contact person of the Mother Tongue Project at the Greek Embassy saw the current aim of mother–tongue teaching as 'to combine all Greeks abroad under the umbrella of Hellenism' (p. 187). This, however, may not be a shared perception.

It seems more likely that the aim of Cypriot parents in sending their children to such classes has been primarily to bridge an increasing linguistic and cultural gap between the first and second generation (George and Millerson, 1967). Even in the 1960s, it was not uncommon for the second generation to speak a hybrid dialect of Greek and English and some did not speak any Greek at all. Moreover, according to Oakley (1968, 1970), Greek Cypriot parents, by sending their children to mother-tongue classes, not only sought to counteract the Anglicizing influence of mainstream schooling but also attempted to ensure that they became literate in Greek since this was seen as a virtue. Their purpose was thus both to instil a sense of identity and to maintain a core element of Greek civilization. In addition, as Saifullah Khan (1977), for example, has pointed out, the status and orientation of the Cypriot population – especially for work-permit holders and refugees from Cyprus who arrived in the mid-1970s were accorded only visitor status and thus had feelings of insecurity and uncertainty about their place of settlement – might have influenced the desire and need for the development of mother-tongue schools. Indeed the entry of Greece into the EC in 1981 (and possible full admission of Turkey), and the increased opportunities for labour mobility thereby opened up, might lead to greater demand for mother-tongue provision from both Cypriots and mainland Greek and Turkish speakers. Most Greek parents, especially temporary residents, are anxious to have access to a mother-tongue school (Tsatsaroni, 1983). Evidence indicates that Cypriot, mainland Greek and Turkish speakers and exiles, temporary workers or settlers, may be very concerned to preserve their mother tongue and traditions. According to Constantinides (1977), Greek mother-tongue classes are specifically intended to keep alive a consciousness of belonging to a Greek-speaking ethnic group and to counteract some of the perceived effects of mainstream schooling which is thought by many Greek parents to bring about a loss of 'Greek identity' as individual children become more influenced by the values and behaviour of their school peers. Yet Miles (1983), concurring, states that parents in Weston-super-Mare were concerned that mother-tongue lessons should not interfere with their children's mainstream education, but rather be an 'addition' – a way of remaining Cypriot in British society. Beetlestone (1982) claims too, that Greek Cypriot parents in the past at least have seen mother-tongue classes as additional to the system, partly because they imply a concern for a different set of values, particularly in connection with respect for the family. Thus they attempted to remedy the perceived lack of Greek and Turkish teaching in the mainstream by making their own provision within the community.

ORGANIZATION AND FINANCE   The organizational arrangements for mother-tongue teaching for Greek and Turkish have always been quite distinct and will be treated separately here. The Greek Orthodox Church in the UK has always had an important role *vis-à-vis* the Greek Cypriot population both in maintaining culture and identity and in its political involvement in competition with left-wing and Communist groups. This role is particularly apparent with respect to the organization of Greek mother-tongue teaching which was first undertaken by the church and now also involves political parties and cultural groups. Greek mother-tongue classes are now arranged by several different organizational networks: the Greek Orthodox Church with the support of the Greek Ministry of Education through the Greek Embassy; the Greek Parents' Association which is affiliated to the left-wing Union of Greek Cypriot Educational Associations in Britain (OESEKA) and is supported by the Cypriot Ministry of Education through the Cyprus High Commission; and the Independent Parents' Association and other independent groups of parents which sometimes request support from the Greek Embassy or Cyprus High Commission (Roussou, 1984a; Tsatsaroni and Papassava, 1986). In addition, some LEAs organize mother-tongue teaching in mainstream schools during normal school hours, sometimes in conjunction with some of these groups (see p.107).

The first Greek mother-tongue classes were set up before the Second World War under the auspices of the Greek Orthodox Church (Anthias, 1984). According to George (1960), in 1950 the Greek Orthodox All Saints' Church in London arranged classes in Greek and religious education for children. Nowadays almost every church has its own school and, in some cases, these also offer part-time tuition in Greek for adults (Alkan and Constantinides, 1981). The church schools are administered under the auspices of the Archbishop of Thyateira and Great Britain and a Central Educational Council which has links with the Educational Councillor of the Greek Embassy (Tsatsaroni and Papassava, 1986). The alternative Cyprus-oriented Greek Parents' Association (GPA), formed in 1952, and the independent groups were apparently specifically set up to counter what was seen by some parents as the excessive stress on Greek nationalism present in the teaching in church schools, and have resisted attempts by the church organization to co-ordinate educational work in this field (Constantinides, 1977). In 1952 the Greek Parents' Association founded a mother-tongue school in Camden (George, 1960; Anthias, 1984) and for at least the following 15 years operated entirely on a voluntary basis funded by parents. Since Independence in 1960 the Ministry of Education of Cyprus apparently took an interest in the mother-tongue schools through the Cyprus High Commission. In 1968 the Greek Cypriot community requested assistance from the Cypriot government in organizing the teaching of Greek (Anthias, 1984). But it was not until the mid-1970s that a special educational department was set up to oversee and standardize the level of teaching (Constantinides, 1977; Aristodemou, 1979). In 1976 Haringey provided assistance with an urban aid grant which enabled the Greek Parents' Association to establish its area offices from which it administers 109 Greek-language classes, several youth clubs and a children's choir and orchestra (Christodoulides, 1984). Thus the Greek Parents' Association now appears to be a thriving and widespread national organization, which not only arranges Greek mother-tongue classes for children, but also classes for teaching both Greek and English to adults (Alkan and Constantinides, 1981; Leeuwenberg, 1979; Hunter-Grundin, 1982). The Greek Parents' Association also has a role liaising between the Greek Cypriot community and mainstream educational establishments, schools, LEAs and the DES.

The Cypriot High Commission, the Greek Embassy and the church provide important institutional backing and sources of funding. From the early days of the establishment of Greek mother-tongue classes parents have paid some fees (George and Millerson, 1967; Anthias, 1984). Generally, however, the Greek Embassy and Cyprus High Commission supply teachers and textbooks to the church or GPA schools and, in addition, offer advice to the independent schools (Roussou, 1984a). The funding of premises and the running of classes is generally undertaken by the church committees and GPAs (Tansley, 1986). Although parents who cannot afford to pay are subsidized (Singleton, 1979), parents' fees apparently continue to make a major contribution to the finances of the schools. Financial arrangements clearly vary from school to school, organization to organization and locality to locality. For example, parents may pay for textbooks and teachers, travelling expenses, as in the case of the Greek school in Coventry (LMP, 1982a), or they may generally complement the contribution of the Embassy, High Commission, church or the organization's own resources towards teachers' salary, rent for accommodation, stationery, textbooks and travelling expenses, as in the case of the Greek language school in Bradford (LMP, 1982b). The increase in support by some LEAs for mother-tongue teaching further complicates this picture. Some LEAs provide free accommodation for Greek classes, as in Coventry (LMP, 1982a), and occasionally give a grant towards a teacher's salary, as in the ILEA (Elliott, 1981). Encouragement from LEAs has principally taken the form of sponsorship of classes in 'twilight hours' and of grants-in-aid to community groups (Krokou, 1985). In a LEA with a large number of Greek classes the funding support may be particularly complex as the LMP MTTD Survey in Haringey revealed (LMP, 1983b). Of those responding, the mother-tongue teaching organizations (sometimes in conjunction with the Embassy) usually paid the teacher's travelling expenses, and accommodation was either supplied by the LEA or the organization itself, but parents were most likely to fund exercise books and paper. Funding for textbooks and teaching aids was most likely to be by the Embassy/High Commission or parents' fees or the organization's own resources. Teachers' salaries, the major financial input, were paid by some combination of the Embassy/High Commission, LEA, parents' fees, the organization's own resources and donations or fund raising, most usually a combination of the organizations', parents' and embassies' support (see p.108).

As Tansley (1986) has observed, although the involvement of two 'home' governments in mother-tongue teaching arrangements is largely beneficial, notably in respect of provision of teachers and teaching materials, it is also in some respects a disadvantage. It may represent a constraint on both the community itself and mainstream British education in encouraging support for children's home languages. The relationships between overseas governments and their expatriate communities in the UK and between the two home governments have to be taken into account. For example, Roussou (1984c) suggests that during the 1970s communication between the Greek and Greek Cypriot oriented mother-tongue teaching organizations and teachers were rare and not sufficiently close for an exchange of ideas, materials or in-service discussions, let alone to liaise with other similar minority organizations or mainstream authorities. However, awareness of administrative difficulties has apparently led to high-level meetings between the Greek Embassy and the Cyprus High Commission to discuss the setting up of a joint common agency to administer all Greek mother-tongue schools (Tsatsaroni and Papassava, 1986).

The organizational arrangements for Turkish mother-tongue teaching are less well documented and give the appearance of being less extensive and less supported than the Greek classes. Once again, there is varied involvement on the part of community associations and religious and government institutions in the organization of Turkish mother-tongue teaching. At least three community associations seem to be concerned with teaching Turkish. The largest organization, the Cyprus Turkish Association, was established in 1951, partly to promote mother-tongue teaching and the preservation of Turkish culture (Memdouh, 1981). From 1959 Turkish classes were set up in rented school premises in north London and there was further demand by the Turkish Cypriot communities in south London (George, 1960). The Cyprus Turkish Association has responsibility for organizing the classes, accommodation and overseeing the curriculum. It has received limited support since 1959 from the Turkish government, and since 1976 from the Turkish Federated State of Cyprus in terms of teachers, textbooks and teaching materials to augment its own resources. However, Ladbury (1977) doubted whether most Turkish Cypriots would have benefited from its activities, even though they would know of the Association because of the barriers of social distance between its organizers, the urban educated élite, and working–class Turkish Cypriot families. Indeed the Association itself has acknowledged the restrictions on its resources in providing Turkish classes and the need for more teaching and financial support to operate the classes efficiently (Memdouh, 1981). Another community association, the Turkish Cypriot Cultural Association, is involved with mother-tongue teaching and, like the Turkish Federated State of Cyprus, in the development of materials and language courses for teaching Turkish to children especially of primary age (CILT, 1983). In Haringey, Leeuwenberg (1979) noted that the Turkish Women's Philanthropic Association of Great Britain ran mother-tongue teaching classes, and Alkan and Constantinides (1981) reported that the mosque in Hackney also arranged Turkish language and religious classes.

However, despite inquiries, the extent and nature of involvement of these organizations and that of the Turkish Embassy and Turkish Federated State of Cyprus remain largely unclear.

Hence relatively little is known of the exact financial arrangements and support for Turkish teaching. In a survey in London Elliott (1981) found that some of the secular Turkish mother-tongue schools which responded claimed to be partly financed from 'home' government sources. Beetlestone (1982) reported that in Haringey the Turkish classes were not financed to the same extent as the Greek classes. Although parents did not pay fees, money had to be found for the rent of premises. The LMP survey in Haringey in 1982 (LMP, 1983b) confirmed this, and that the few Turkish classes were largely supported by the Embassy/High Commission in terms of teachers' salaries, textbooks and teaching aids and stationery. However Singleton (1979) reported that the Cyprus Turkish Association purchased some textbooks, and it also pays at an hourly rate the part-time teachers it employs in addition to those supplied. The Turkish Cypriot Cultural Association pays its volunteer teachers a nominal rate. These organizations are clearly aware of the need to enlarge the teaching force, make financial provision for accommodation, exercise more choice over class timing, operate transportation and provide more relevant materials if they are to attempt to cater for the expanding numbers of Turkish-speaking children even within London (Memdouh, 1981).

NUMBER AND LOCATION OF SCHOOLS, CLASSES AND COURSES   Given the variety of organizations involved in teaching Greek and Turkish, it is not surprising that there is no national or comprehensive information available on the number or location of Greek and Turkish mother-tongue schools, classes or courses. Indeed figures cited in the literature are often confused with regard to courses, classes and schools, for schools may have a number of classes or courses. Nevertheless, using several published sources, it is possible to construct a chronological account of the development of community provision for Greek and Turkish teaching over the past 25 years across the country and in specific locations.

Owing to the well-known concentration of Cypriot settlement in Greater London, and particularly North London, it is to be expected that the oldest and the majority of mother-tongue teaching classes are to be found in these locations. Recent research by the LMP revealed that in Haringey the earliest surviving Greek class had begun in 1955 and a Turkish class in 1959 (LMP, 1983b). With the exception of classes for Hebrew, these were by far the longest running classes. Towards the end of the 1960s, George and Millerson (1967) estimated that there were about 20 Greek mother-tongue classes in all, many throughout London. Indeed in 1967 there were 12 classes for Greek in Haringey alone, arranged under the auspices of the North London Cypriot Association, the Greek Parents' Association and St. Sophia's Cathedral, Bayswater, and held in four different school locations throughout the borough (Milstead, 1981).

Although for various reasons there is always a tendency for the number of schools and classes to fluctuate over time, there was considerable expansion throughout the 1970s, particularly towards the end of the decade. In 1977 Constantinides estimated that there were over 50 Greek mother-tongue schools run by various organizations in Britain. Leeuwenberg (1979) claimed that the Greek Parents' Association organized some 40 classes nationally and as many as 17 in the Borough of Haringey alone. According to the annual report of its education department, of the 42 community schools known to the Cyprus High Commission in 1978–9, the majority were in the London area, in Enfield (10), Barnet and north-west London (7), Haringey (6), south London (5), Islington and Hackney (5) and the East End of London (4) (Aristodemou, 1979). In 1980 Elliott (1981) located 41 Greek and 18 Turkish schools in London. From the response of 23 Greek and 11 Turkish schools to a questionnaire, Elliott was able to establish that over the previous decade there had been a steady increase in the number of Greek schools, from eight prior to 1970, and for Turkish schools, from three prior to 1970, with a more dramatic expansion towards the end of the decade. Of the 23 Greek mother-tongue schools, nine were located in Haringey, seven in Enfield, six in Barnet and five in Islington. The 11 Turkish schools were almost equally distributed between Haringey (six) and Hackney (five). Evidence from the Cyprus Turkish Association to the Swann Committee (Memdouh, 1981) shows that, at this time, this organization arranged ten schools, over half with more than one class, at various locations across London, mostly in north London. According to a Greek Embassy source (Tsatsaroni, 1983), in 1983 there were 14 schools run by the Greek Orthodox Church in London, in addition to the Greek Parents' Association schools and those known to the Cyprus High Commission. By 1986 the number of church schools in London had risen to 20. Two studies demonstrate the extent of provision for Greek and Turkish teaching in Haringey, the area of the greatest concentration of Cypriots. From their survey Alkan and Constantinides (1981) found 12 Greek schools in the borough, seven run by the Greek Parents' Association, three by the church and two by other community associations. There were also four mother-tongue schools for Turkish, all organized by the Cyprus Turkish Association. Another survey in 1982 (LMP, 1983b), based on the number of classes rather than schools, revealed five Turkish classes and a massive 90 classes for Greek throughout the borough, a few of which took place in mainstream school-time (see p.108).

Although outside London community provision for Greek mother-tongue teaching (and indeed Turkish on which there are no data) has been less widespread compared with that for some other linguistic minority groups and has largely been limited to towns or cities where there are relative concentrations of Greek speakers, as in Leeds (Saifullah Khan, 1977), there is evidence that there has also been expansion in the number of schools and classes nation-wide during the last decade. Indeed LMP research showed that one of the three Greek classes in Coventry has been running since 1963 (LMP, 1982a). Chapman (1976) reported that there was a flourishing Greek mother-tongue school in Birmingham. At this time, Saifullah Khan (1976) noted that there was no Greek-language school in Bradford, despite the existence of a small Cypriot community there; but a subsequent LMP survey revealed that a class started there in 1979, and by 1981 three classes were in operation. Five of the 42 Greek schools known to the Cyprus High Commission in 1978–9 were held outside London in Clacton-on-Sea, Manchester, Reading, Sheffield and Weston-super-Mare (Aristodemou, 1979). In 1983 as many as 29 Greek schools, either associated with the church or run by independent parents' associations, were known to the Greek Embassy (Tsatsaroni, 1983). These were located in Birmingham, Brighton, Bristol, Cambridge, Cardiff, Colchester, Coventry, Derby, Eastbourne, Folkestone, Glasgow, Great Yarmouth, Hastings, Leeds, Leicester, Liverpool, Luton, Manchester, Margate, Middlesbrough, Norwich, Nottingham, Oxford, Plymouth, Reading and Maidenhead, Southampton, Torquay and Weston-super-Mare. By 1986, although the schools in Derby and Folkestone had ceased, there had been a general increase to 35 schools, additionally located in Aylesbury, Bury St. Edmunds, Gillingham, Newcastle upon Tyne, Northampton and Southend, with two schools in each of Birmingham, Cardiff and Manchester (Tsatsaroni and Papassava, 1986). Wright (1983) also mentions classes in Bradford, Wakefield and various locations in Scotland. This information indicates that there are Greek-speaking communities in and around these towns which are sufficiently keen to support mother-tongue schools, though they may well vary considerably in size and status. Indeed, though the data are confounded by categorization according to school or class, clearly the more numerous Greek-speaking Cypriot communities have initiated, maintained and developed substantial provision for mother-tongue teaching over 20 years or more.

However, it appears from mainstream research evidence that, despite increased debate about mother-tongue teaching in recent years, and in connection with mainstream provision, LEAs may lack awareness of community provision for Greek and Turkish teaching. Given the concentration of the Cypriot community in and around London, it is to be expected that certain LEAs would be more likely to know of community provision. Evidence from national research surveys could be particularly skewed by the LEAs responding. However, the relative diversity of organizational support for Greek and Turkish teaching, compared with, for example, the strong central direction given by the Italian government to Italian classes, may also have had the effect of restricting local awareness of the diffusion of provision. Following a national survey of LEAs in 1970, Townsend (1971) reported that although there was very little evidence that any attempt was being made by LEAs to provide mother-tongue teaching in mainstream schools, the Greek community were particularly active in making community provision. It was known that one Cypriot community ran about 20 Greek classes after school hours by agreement with the LEA. In a follow-up survey of 230 primary and secondary schools with immigrant pupils, in 1971 (Townsend and Brittan, 1972), 24 schools reported that Greek-speaking communities made arrangements to teach Greek outside school hours. This was the largest number of schools to report community language teaching provision. Indeed, the researchers' comments suggest that the number of Greek mother-tongue schools may well have been higher. Only two schools reported similar arrangements by Turkish-speaking communities. Information about community mother-tongue provision may well be known more accurately by schools with which arrangements may be made directly for hire of premises, rather than LEAs as such. In another national survey, in 1979, only six out of 18 LEAs with ethnic minority concentrations of ten per cent or more reported that Greek was taught in out-of-school hours by the community and only two reported community provision for Turkish. In areas with between two-and-a-half and ten per cent of ethnic minority pupils only three out of 21 LEAs reported the teaching of Greek in mother-tongue schools (Little and Willey, 1983). In a further national survey, in 1983 (Tansley and Craft, 1984), only seven out of 63 LEAs responding mentioned Greek, and three Turkish, as languages occurring most frequently in their areas. Twelve of the 49 LEAs able to give details about community schools knew of a total of 28 Greek schools in their areas, and two LEAs knew of nine local Turkish schools. However, the addition of figures collected from the three LEAs (Coventry, Bradford and Haringey) surveyed by the Linguistic Minorities Project in 1981–2 boosted the total Greek schools/classes which could be listed to 124 and with the data from the Haringey survey the number of Turkish schools rose to 14. Apart from difficulties of classification, this serves to demonstrate the potentially inaccurate picture of community provision which may be gained from LEA sources alone. Moreover, in some LEAs with large numbers of Greek-speaking and/or Turkish-speaking pupils, both the extent and form of LEA support for community provision and mainstream teaching also need to be taken into account. Indeed there are some signs of increasing collaboration between mainstream and community providers, as in the case of the Mother

Tongue Project (1981–5) which was concerned with developing primary teaching resources (see pp.111–14).

PUPIL NUMBERS, AGES AND ATTENDANCE   Just as the number of Greek and Turkish classes in out-of-school hours grew, so the number of pupils studying their mother tongue increased over the years. Since no single authority has responsibility for organizing either Greek or Turkish mother-tongue classes, it is difficult to cite precise overall figures for the number of pupils enrolled in classes over the last 20 years or so. However, by drawing on various mainstream and community sources, it is possible to build up a chronological account demonstrating the increase in numbers of pupils on roll, indicating school or class size, according to location and community organization and the age range of pupils attending. Once again the overwhelming majority of research data relate to Greek-speaking rather than Turkish-speaking pupils.

In 1960, George recorded that the Greek Orthodox Church classes in nine areas of London were attended by about 600 pupils, and that a further 300 pupils throughout London studied in classes run by the Greek Parents' Association. By 1967 George and Millerson estimated that on average there were about 40 children attending each of the 20 Greek classes then held throughout London. By the mid-1970s the enrolment for schools and classes may well have risen. Saifullah Khan (1976) recorded that a Greek school in Haringey which had been running for ten years taught 100 children, and another school in Bayswater catered for 200 children in eight classes. Archimandritou-Xefteris (1977) reported that about 2,500 pupils of primary school age attended Greek classes, but that the number of pupils of secondary school age dropped off considerably and probably did not exceed 500 between the ages of 13 and 18. At about the same time, Constantinides (1977) estimated that about 4,000 children attended Greek schools throughout Britain. Data from the Cyprus High Commission (Aristodemou, 1979) revealed a dramatic increase of almost 300 per cent in the number of pupils attending Greek classes which it administered, from 854 pupils in 1977 to 2,534 pupils registered in July 1979. The largest number of pupils generally corresponded to the number of schools in the different localities across London (see pp.83–84). The largest school was in Enfield with 173 pupils out of the 680 registered in that area. Outside London three of the five schools had only 18 pupils, although the smallest school was in East Barnet with 13 pupils. The High Commission figures also confirmed earlier claims that the school rolls diminished markedly as the level or stage of teaching increased. Not only had there been huge increases in pupils registered as beginners, but at the same time there had also been a steady withdrawal of pupils from the higher stages. Aristodemou attributed the unwillingness of the older pupils to continue to attend primarily to the fact that the community school itself 'is not in a position to provide the kind and quality of work which would satisfy and attract its pupils'. According to Leeuwenberg (1979), over 1,000 pupils were registered in classes throughout Britain held by the Greek Parents' Association and there were said to be 500 such pupils in Haringey alone. Singleton (1979) reported that as many as 1,100–1,200 pupils attended all the Greek schools in that borough.

In 1980 Elliott (1981) discovered that 2,866 pupils attended 23 Greek mother-tongue schools and 1,306 pupils attended 11 Turkish mother-tongue schools contacted throughout the London area. These represented in 1981 just over two-thirds of all the Greek-speaking pupils and just under a third of all Turkish-speaking pupils in ILEA schools (ILEA, 1982). Evidence from the Cyprus Turkish Association at that time claims that due to the shortage of teachers, pupil numbers had to be restricted to 700. There were then in fact some 645 pupils in the Turkish schools, including children from mainland Turkish backgrounds (Memdouh, 1981). In 1983 there were 2,900 pupils enrolled in Greek classes organized by the Greek Orthodox Church. Tsataroni (1983) estimated that a further 4,500 attended classes organized by the Cyprus High Commission, and some 500 pupils registered at independent schools. Ninety per cent of the pupils attending classes organized by the Greek Orthodox Church are of Cypriot origin, the remainder hail from mainland Greece. Of the church schools, the largest is in Kentish Town and is the particular responsibility of the bishops. Singleton (1979) described the Greek Orthodox Church school, St. Barnabas in Wood Green, with over 900 pupils. Outside London the largest church school was in Reading, with 60 or more pupils, and the Cyprus High Commission report for 1978 showed that there were larger schools of 61 pupils studying Greek in Weston-super-Mare and 84 in Manchester. Clearly a large and apparently over the years increasing number of Greek-speaking pupils have been registered at mother-tongue schools. Indeed Wright (1983) claimed that as many as 9,000 Greek-speaking pupils attended classes in the London area alone. If correct, this is no mean indication of demand and the extent to which the Greek community and supporting institutions have been able to establish provision to meet this perceived need.

Greek and Turkish schools generally appear to cater for a maximum age range of pupils between five and 16 (e.g. LMP, 1982a, 1982b, 1983b). Some studies have found later starting ages and far earlier finishing ages – Greek, six to 14 (Saifullah Khan, 1976, and Turkish Cypriot sources); seven to 16 (Elliott, 1981, for Greek schools); and six to 15 for Turkish (Singleton, 1979). Milstead (1981) reported that in Haringey, in 1967, Greek mother-tongue teaching organizations had agreed with the LEA that pupils of infant age should not be admitted and that the attendance of seven to nine year-olds should be limited to once per week. Singleton (1979) found that in the GPA schools the common starting age was seven through to 15, but the church schools catered for a few five-year-olds through to 18 (see also LMP, 1983b).

Fortunately, data collected by the Linguistic Minorities Project in its Mother–Tongue Teaching Directory Survey (MTTD) in 1981 in Bradford and Coventry, in 1982 in Haringey and the Schools Language Survey in these areas in 1981 enable more illuminating consideration to be given to the extent to which local provision is taken up according to the potential number of students, their attendance rate and their age distribution (LMP, 1983a, 1982a, 1982b, 1983b). The MTTD covered classes provided by community organizations as well as those initiated by the LEA or its schools, inside or outside LEA premises and during and after school hours. Table 16 gives details of the number of Greek and Turkish classes, pupils and their ages in the three LEAs. The levels of attendance are of interest and especially the contrast between those of the Greek- and Turkish-speaking pupils. In both Coventry and Haringey over four-fifths of all the pupils who spoke Greek at home were enrolled in Greek classes and over nine out of every ten were said to be regular attenders. These attendance rates were amongst the highest for any of the linguistic minority pupils surveyed. In fact the Greek speakers in Haringey constituted the largest group across the three locations of minority language speakers attending mother-tongue classes. By contrast, fewer than two-fifths of the Turkish-speaking pupils attended Turkish classes in Haringey (although some travelled to a neighbouring borough) and their attendance was less regular than that of Greek speakers. These data suggest varying degrees of commitment on the part of parents, pupils and communities (see pp. 99,100) or that alternative opportunities exist. It is also interesting to find that across the locations, although

Table 16: Number of Greek and Turkish language classes, pupils and ages in three LEAs, 1981–2

		Bradford 1981	Greek Coventry 1981	Haringey 1982	Turkish Haringey 1982
1	Year in which first surviving class began:	1979	1963	1955	1959
2	Number of classes in 1981/2	3	3	90	5
3	Number of pupils on roll	33	35	2,073	139
4	Percentage of pupils attending regularly	100	91	97	78
5	Pupils on roll as % of pupils in the LEA using Greek/Turkish at home	*	85	82	13†
6	Age-group of pupils 5	–	1	15	–
	5–7	14	6	364	26
	8–10	9	13	533	46
	11–13	4	13	514	27
	14–16	1	2	331	32
	16+	–	–	131	1

* Greek classes in Bradford probably include pupils from a wider area beyond the city.
† Other Turkish classes are available in Hackney and some children travel there from Haringey.
Source: Adapted from LMP, 1983a, Tables 4.1, 4.2 and 4.3; 1982a, 1982b, 1983b, Table 6.

there was some decline in the number of both Greek- and Turkish-speaking pupils attending mother-tongue classes with increasing age, their numbers were fairly evenly divided between the five to ten and 11–16+ age-groups. Indeed the data reveal that not only do a few Greek-speaking children commence classes before the age of five, but a substantial number also continue to attend classes beyond mainstream school-leaving age. Again, this indicates a high level of commitment by some Greek speakers and the numbers of Greek speakers in the lower age ranges enrolled in mother-tongue classes suggests that the level of demand for provision is likely to continue (see also p.103–5).

ACCOMMODATION   It appears that from their earliest years the majority of Greek and Turkish mother-tongue schools have been held on LEA mainstream school premises after school hours. Rooms have usually been rented by the organizing associations or communities (George, 1960; George and Millerson, 1967; Townsend, 1971; Memdouh, 1981). However, as Milstead (1981) records, during the 1960s applications to LEAs to rent additional accommodation did not always meet with success and even provoked LEA inquiries into the running of the mother-tongue schools. Generally although most church schools have their own premises, the community schools run by the Independent and Greek Parents' Association in concert with the Cyprus High Commission, hire mainstream schools (Tsatsaroni and Papassava, 1986; Aristodemou, 1979). In common with other linguistic minority groups which depend on mainstream school accommodation (CRE, 1982) Greek and Turkish schools often experience problems with such facilities. According to Aristodemou:

Decoration is alien to the purposes of the community school. School keepers and heads often complain about damages and losses caused by the children and sometimes they make insulting remarks to the parents and teachers of the community school.
The teacher has no access to any of the teaching means of the school and he lacks the space to store his own. (Aristodemou, 1979, p.7.)

Other sources have confirmed difficulties in storing materials (Leeuwenberg, 1979), with unfriendly and unhelpful caretakers (Khan, 1976; GB.P.H of C, 1985; Christoudoulides, 1984) and even hostile mainstream teachers, lack of access to audio-visual aids or use of the blackboard or wall spaces in return for high rents (Christoudoulides, 1984). Against such adverse conditions Aristodemou (1979) questioned whether it was time for the Greek communities to acquire their own premises as, for example, in Weston-super-Mare, where classes are held in the community's own centre (Miles, 1983). However, it would appear that, on the whole, Greek mother-tongue classes continue to be accommodated in LEA premises, though whether these are provided free as in a growing number of cases, for example, in ILEA (Aristodemou, 1979) Hackney (Elliott, 1981) or Coventry (LMP, 1982a) or for rent as in Bradford (LMP, 1982b) will vary from locality to locality according to LEA policy, and may depend on whether classes take place partly in or after school hours as in Haringey (LMP, 1983b).

TRANSPORT   In the 1960s George and Millerson (1967) reported that transport facilities were provided for those Greek-speaking children attending mother-tongue schools who did not live nearby. It might be thought likely in view of the concentrated settlements of Greek Cypriots and the extensive provision of Greek schools in such localities that travelling distance, time and transport might not be a particular problem for Greek-speaking pupils compared with, for example, Chinese pupils attending mother-tongue classes. Apparently most pupils are transported by coaches or by their parents using their own transport (Singleton, 1979; Tsatsaroni and Papassava, 1986). However, out of London, where settlements of Greek Cypriots are less concentrated, pupils attending classes may be obliged to travel some distance, as in the case of pupils in and around Bradford where classes are organized on a regional basis (LMP, 1982b). Indeed the majority of Turkish Cypriot pupils are in a similar position since, compared with Greek Cypriots, the Turkish Cypriot population is smaller, more scattered and has access to fewer mother-tongue schools. Turkish-speaking pupils apparently have to travel long distances to attend classes, and no coach transport is available, although the Cyprus Turkish Association has been keen to provide such a facility (Singleton, 1979; Memdouh, 1981).

CLASS TIMING, DURATION AND FREQUENCY OF ATTENDANCE   From their inception both Greek and Turkish classes in London have tended to be held on weekday evenings (George, 1960), a practice which has continued (Tsatsaroni, 1983; Memdouh, 1981). However, some provision is also made at the weekends and this may be more likely to be associated with schools run by the church (Alkan and Constantinides, 1981; Tsatsaroni, 1983) and/or for classes in towns and cities across the country as, for example, in Weston-super-Mare (Miles, 1983) and Coventry and Bradford (LMP, 1982a, 1982b). Some classes meet at weekends and partly after school or in the evenings, as in the case of almost two-thirds of the Greek community classes in Haringey in 1982 (LMP, 1983b).

The majority of evening or post-school classes both for Greek and Turkish seem to be two hours long, although they may range from one-and-a-half to two-and-a-half hours in length. Classes tend to be held from 5 to 7 pm or 6 to 8 pm. Whilst it is reported that Church schools operate from 5 to 7 pm (Tsatsaroni and Papassava, 1986), Elliott (1981) found that a local community association Greek school ran from 6 to 8 pm. Turkish classes organized by the Cyprus Turkish Association are held from 6 to 8 pm. Memdouh (1981) indicated that the

Association had received requests from parents that classes should commence one hour later but that school caretakers were reluctant to extend school opening times. However, classes may be longer if held on Saturday – three to four hours for Greek and apparently two to three hours for Turkish, according to data on classes in Haringey (Alkan and Constantinides, 1981) and elsewhere (Saifullah Khan, 1976; Tsatsaroni and Papassava, 1986).

Whilst some Greek schools, especially large church schools, and some Turkish schools are open every weekday and on Saturday (Elliott, 1981; Tsatsaroni and Papassava, 1986) and there is a wide-ranging pattern (Elliott, 1981), most appear to run two or three times a week for one or more classes (George, 1960; George and Millerson, 1967; Saifullah Khan, 1976; Elliott, 1981; Memdouh, 1981). But some Greek schools only meet once a week (Elliott, 1981; Alkan and Constantinides, 1981; LMP, 1982a, 1982b). Although the schools may be open on several occasions, the classes are not necessarily always for the same group of pupils. Pupils usually attend Greek and Turkish classes twice a week, either on two weekday evenings or one evening and one Saturday morning, for two hours at a time. Others who attend once a week may attend for up to four hours on Saturday from 9 am to 1 pm (Tsatsaroni and Papassava, 1986). Indeed, the LMP Mother-Tongue Teaching Directory (MTTD) Survey found that pupils attended Greek classes for four hours per week in Coventry and three hours in Bradford. In Haringey whilst pupils attended Greek or Turkish classes for on average three hours per week, attendance ranged from one hour to four hours weekly (LMP, 1983a).

Over the years concern has generally been expressed by mainstream teachers about the attendance of pupils at community mother-tongue classes in terms of the demands made on the pupil, the tiredness which might ensue, implications for homework and especially interference with learning English (see p.198). An early document (LCSS, 1967) was quite explicit on this point: sometimes, it said, attendance at mother-tongue classes would 'hinder the children from learning English as they take place at the time when their understanding of English is beginning to dawn and this extra pressure to become literate in Greek results in their failing to comprehend fully in either language' (p.53). Indeed one LEA which rented school premises for about 20 Greek classes organized by the community restricted the attendance of junior school pupils to one lesson per week and that of secondary pupils to two lessons and did not allow infants to be accepted (Townsend, 1971; Milstead, 1981). Yet it is interesting to see how a different view has prevailed within the Cypriot community. In the annual report of the education department of the Cyprus High Commission for 1978–9, Aristodemou expressed concern that almost half the community schools known to the Commission operated for only two to two-and-a-half hours per week and recommended that, although the overall working hours of the schools had increased by up to 40 per cent in the two previous years, a four-hour week, divided between two or possibly three days, would be necessary to achieve satisfactory results. Evidence indicates that just as some parents are ambivalent about sending their children to mother-tongue classes (see p.99), so some pupils have mixed feelings about attendance (p.100); nevertheless, there is a strong commitment on the part of many parents and apparently a high attendance rate by the pupils enrolled (see Table 18). There has in fact been no study of the effect of attendance at mother-tongue classes on pupils' mainstream schooling. However, Georgiou (1983) carried out a small-scale investigation of the social and cultural effects of attendance at evening and weekend schools by Greek Cypriots in a north London comprehensive school.

THE TEACHING FORCE   The teaching staff of the Greek and Turkish schools are drawn from a range of backgrounds and have different teaching qualifications and degrees of experience. In the case of the Greek schools there are three main groups of teachers.

Qualified teachers of Greek, mostly primary school teachers, are seconded from Greece by the Greek Embassy and from Cyprus by the Cyprus High Commission to teach Greek in the church and community schools, usually for a period of five years. They are not recognized by the DES as qualified teachers. A second group of teachers is composed of bilingual mainstream teachers who have qualified in the UK. Although they have DES recognition, they have no specialist knowledge of teaching Greek. A third group of teachers are unqualified, but very enthusiastic parents and undergraduate bilingual students (Roussou, 1984a). According to George and Millerson (1967), in the 1960s, teachers from amongst the Cypriot community itself assisted priests in the teaching organized by the Greek Orthodox Church. In 1968 the Greek Cypriot community requested assistance from the Cypriot government, and in 1969 the first Cypriot Educational Group (KEA) of five teachers and an inspector arrived. A second group of six teachers and an education officer arrived in February 1977 (Anthias, 1984). The report of the Cyprus High Commission Education Department for 1978–9 shows that although the school year began with only seven members of staff, another 14 teachers were sent over from Cyprus enabling the community schools to be better staffed and, as a consequence, it was claimed this improved the quantity and quality of work which was carried out (Aristodemou, 1979). Even so, a further 26 teachers had to be hired: 12 were students or professionals without any teaching qualifications, four were teachers, often working in English secondary schools, and ten were Cypriot teachers with full qualifications living in Britain. According to research undertaken by the Organization of Greek Teachers in Britain, in 1982, there were 380 mother-tongue teachers based in classes organized by OESEKA and the church. The Ministry of Education of Cyprus supplied 23 teachers mainly to classes organized by OESEKA, and the Ministry of Education of Greece provided 60 teachers, who mainly teach in the church classes (Wright, 1983). Sometimes the Greek and Cypriot teachers teach in the same schools, and most schools also have unqualified teachers especially on Saturday to cope with the number of pupils attending. In 1986 the Greek Embassy supplied a team of 40 teachers. Apart from one teacher sent from the Cyprus High Commission to a Greek school in Bristol, the Greek Embassy supplied 15 teachers to the schools out of London. The Greek teachers also attend 15 out of 20 church schools in London, and there may sometimes be up to ten teachers in one place, as in the case of the largest school in Kentish Town (Tsatsaroni and Papassava, 1986).

As with the teachers for the Greek schools, qualified teachers to the Turkish schools are supplied by the Turkish government and the Turkish Federated State of Cyprus, but only to a very limited extent. Since 1959 the Turkish government has provided two teachers on four-year contracts to teach in the Cyprus Turkish Association classes in London, and since 1976 two teachers have been supplied on two-year contracts from the Turkish Federated State of Cyprus (Memdouh, 1981). The Cyprus Turkish Association also employs four part-time teachers. There is a need for more qualified teachers to be supplied or recruited but financial difficulties restrict this. The Association is aware of the importance of Turkish and Turkish Cypriot teachers from abroad and the UK being familiar with each of the educational systems.

The Annual Report of the Cyprus High Commission for 1978–9 offered some insight, at that time, into the amount of teaching time of the teaching force. Of the total teaching time of 431 hours per week, teachers sent by the Cyprus government taught for 46 per cent of the time, qualified teachers living in Britain 19.5 per cent and unqualified teachers 34.5 per cent. An analysis of the teaching hours according to district of school location and qualification of teaching staff showed that some mother-tongue schools clearly had an advantage in terms of the number of teaching hours taught by qualified staff. Aristodemou (1979) argued that more qualified teachers were required. Although the teaching time offered by teachers from Cyprus could be increased if the work of the community schools was more evenly dispersed across the days of the week, nevertheless, heads of community schools often had to undertake responsibilities in addition to their full-time teaching which prevented them from establishing proper contacts with other teaching staff, parents and children. It was suggested that by employing an additional floating teacher in the school, especially a much-needed specialist for teaching music or dance, better provision could be made through a further increase of teaching-time by qualified teachers. Singleton (1979) found that the teachers teaching at the Cyprus Turkish Association classes in Haringey taught four evenings a week at two schools, all day Saturday at a third, ran dancing classes for adults on Sundays and took part in other community activities.

In terms of teacher–pupil ratios Elliott's (1981) research in London showed that about half of 23 Greek schools had a teacher–pupil ratio of one to 20, which tended to be higher than ratios for mother-tongue classes for some of the other linguistic minority groups. In fact two classes had only one teacher for 50 pupils. Singleton (1979) described a church class with one teacher to 25–30 pupils. However, Elliott found that the teacher–pupil ratio was even worse for Turkish mother-tongue schools: on average one teacher to 35 or 40 pupils, and two schools had over 50 pupils per teacher. Cronin (1984) described a Turkish class of about 22 pupils. In both the Greek and Turkish classes pupils may be divided by age or level or in mixed groups where the teachers attempt to give individualized instruction (Tsatsaroni and Papassava, 1986; Beetlestone, 1982).

TEACHING METHODS AND LANGUAGE TAUGHT Although there is no first-hand research evidence on the teaching methods employed by the teachers in the Greek or Turkish schools, several commentators have suggested that they are generally considered to have a formal approach to language teaching. A question may be raised as to the extent to which this may be compatible with methodologies employed by mainstream teachers. Indeed Wright (1983) has commented that the teaching methods of community teachers seem quite strange to children used to the child-centred methodology of English primary schools. According to Roussou (1984a), the main reason for the Greek teachers' formal approaches are their lack of training and their very difficult working conditions. These include: a limited time for language activities, sometimes all at one session; limited resources in terms of textbooks and teaching aids; lack of storage for the teacher's own materials; constraints of space and number of pupils per class; and the demands of parents for quick, observable results in reading and writing (also confirmed by Tsatsaroni and Papassava, 1986). Some schools hold open evenings to explain their teaching methods and to encourage the active involvement and co-operation of parents.

One of the main aims of the classes is to teach language, but a major issue is the extent to which pupils attending Greek mother-tongue classes receive appropriate linguistic instruction. This question arises in connection with the language taught, the language used as the medium of instruction and the orientation of the classes in terms of curriculum content (see pp.94–5) and teaching materials (see pp.95–7). Although Greek-speaking Cypriot families in the UK trace their culture and language from roots in mainland Greece, in their Cypriot form these have developed and taken on different features by virtue of belonging to an independent island (Cyprus), with British and Turkish influences. In particular, the form of the Greek language spoken by Cypriots has many lexical, syntactical and phonological features distinct from Athenean Greek and rarely appears in written form. Moreover, since taking up residence in the UK many Cypriots have developed a London form of the Cypriot dialect of Greek. In a church school visited by Singleton (1979) the teachers had to deal with four Greek dialects: demotic mainland Greek, town Cypriot Greek, various types of village Cypriot Greek and London Greek. Thus there may be a difference between what are perceived by parents and pupils as their needs in language learning (Wright, 1983) and what the teachers as Standard Greek or Cypriot Greek speakers may consider correct or are even able to teach. Consideration of parents and children's reasons for learning Greek is necessary for determining the balance between Cypriot dialect and the introduction of Standard Greek. For example, whereas knowledge of Standard Greek may be most appropriate for jobs and visiting Greece, dialect would be more helpful for communication in the UK and visiting relatives in Cyprus (Sergides and Tansley, 1984; Constantinides, 1984).

There seems to be agreement amongst mother-tongue teachers that when literacy is introduced, the standard form of Greek is to be preferred. Tsatsaroni (1983), a teacher from Greece, averred that the Greek teachers' attempt to make pupils understand that even if they speak in Cypriot dialect they must learn to write in the Standard Greek. However, there appears to be a division of opinion amongst teachers as to the use of dialect during spoken discourse. Some teachers at the National Council for Mother Tongue Teaching Conference, 'Greek Outside Greece', considered it important to accept the dialect which the child brings to the classroom, starting from where the child is and using the child's own resources and life experience, to develop the motivation for personal and social learning. But others felt that Standard Greek should be taught, to be useful for jobs, and by allowing children to use English, dialect and Standard Greek, they were just being 'kept happy' (Sergides and Tansley, 1984; Constantinides, 1984). It was generally felt that a teacher who corrected all spontaneous expression to Standard Greek would be sapping motivation and creating conflict in the child who would be made to feel inferior. Some teachers thought that the standard words should be presented as alternatives, as in the case of one teacher who taught standard and dialect in parallel, saying to the children, for example, 'this is the word you will find in the literature, but your grandmother probably uses *this* word ...'. She found that by relating their learning to personal experience, children often actively enjoyed 'cracking the code'. Other teachers, however, thought that the standard form of the language should be presented as 'correct'. A related issue was whether to teach grammar formally or as the situation arose. Interestingly, Georgiou (1983) found that children attending Greek classes said they spoke a different language at home from the one they learnt at school, but most said the language they were being taught at school was a better, 'more proper' version.

These differences in approach to the language being taught are likely in practice to be reflected in the medium of instruction employed, although officially teachers teach in Standard Greek. Elliott (1981), observing a Greek mother-tongue school in Hackney, noted that although teachers spoke Greek for most of the time, pupils only sometimes answered in Greek and they spoke English amongst themselves. Special teaching skills may be required for the children of mixed parentage who do not have Greek as a mother tongue (Constantinides, 1984). Singleton (1979) reported that at one large church school there was a class for such children who were taught to speak Greek by a teacher using English and Greek before they moved on to other classes. However, several commentators have questioned the English fluency of some of the Greek teachers (e.g. Wright, 1983; Singleton, 1979).

Once again, there is generally little information on the teaching of Turkish, though the issue of dialect may not be quite so significant. However, Singleton (1979) reported that teachers in a community school claimed that children were better at listening and understanding than speaking Turkish, even though most spoke Turkish at home to their mothers. Pronunciation is one of the main differences between dialect and Standard Turkish. Children were said to have a good basis for learning to read. Again, there were particular difficulties for children of mixed marriages. In one class observed, the children spoke to each other in English but the teacher taught almost exclusively (and expected pupils to talk to him) in Turkish.

CURRICULUM CONTENT AND LEVEL   Although the mother-tongue classes are primarily for instruction in language, the content of the curriculum is wider and set in a cultural context of beliefs and traditions. The schools run by the Greek Orthodox Church and some of the Turkish schools also include some religious teaching although the emphasis is primarily on language acquisition (George, 1960; Tsatsaroni, 1983). The curriculum varies from school to school and may include literature, poetry, history and geography as well as music and traditional dancing. The annual report of the Cyprus High Commission for 1978–9 shows that Greek was taught for two-thirds of the time, and one-third of the time was spent on the teaching of culture, music and dance. In the church schools the curriculum is more likely to be limited to language, the history and geography of Greece and Cyprus and religion (Tsatsaroni, 1983). Although it is said that the religious teaching is more about religious festivals and traditions rather than religion as such (Tsatsaroni and Papassava, 1986), Wright (1983) has claimed that in the church schools emphasis may be given to religious activities at the expense of language work. Singleton (1979) has described an assembly and RE lesson at one church school. Some homework was given. The curriculum of Turkish schools has a similar focus (Memdouh, 1981). As one Turkish teacher of a community-run, embassy-aided school put it:

> Our main aim is to teach the mother tongue to the Turkish children. We also teach folk dances, music and religion once a month. We are trying to teach the Turkish culture and some general subjects such as history, maths, geography, etc. (LMP, 1985, p.259)

In one school run by the Cyprus Turkish Association, Singleton (1979) found that in addition to Turkish stories, legends, poetry, history, dancing and singing, some games and the general principles of Islam were taught. The school did not teach Arabic or the Koran, but Turkish national days were celebrated. There was no homework.

In the Greek schools the level of instruction was standardized in the mid-1970s (Constantinides, 1977). According to Aristodemou (1979), there are three main grades or stages, A–C, and the standard of each is fixed, so that the progress of the pupil may be ascertained. Some of the schools have a fourth stage, D, for more advanced students who may wish to take GCE O- or A-level in Modern Greek. In 1978–9 the Cyprus High Commission knew of 13 schools, all of them in London, which operated a course at this level for a total of 142 pupils. However, the position may now have changed. Miles (1983) reported that in Weston-super-Mare Cypriot pupils at the local community centre were studying to O- and A-level standard. About 20 church schools enable Modern Greek to be studied to O-level, though fewer run A-level courses. They do not set out to provide formal classes for A-level tuition, but if the demand is established and the pupils are sufficiently proficient, then two or three classes each year are organized in the larger schools. Evidence suggests that examination entries are often made through mainstream schools. The number of entrants (see pp.109–10) and linguistic proficiency data as a whole (see pp.58–9,65) suggest that some pupils attain a high degree of competence if not full bilingualism. Once again, there is less evidence of the level of instruction at Turkish schools or of examination entry (but see p.110). Singleton questioned whether the English of the Turkish teachers observed in one school would be adequate to teach exams involving translation work.

TEACHING MATERIALS It is clear that one of the main difficulties for the Greek and Turkish classes – common to many mother-tongue schools – is that of the suitability and availability of textbooks and teaching materials. From the inception of the earliest Greek classes materials have been provided free by the Greek Ministry of Education (George and Millerson, 1967; Tsatsaroni, 1983; Wright, 1983). The books were produced in Greece as the official set of reading texts used throughout Greece and Greek Cyprus. The books are sent from Greece to Cyprus and then to Britain at the expense of the Greek government. Singleton (1979), who described the 'Alphabetario', the first book in the series, claimed that the books had remained virtually unchanged since 1951. However, towards the end of the 1970s a new reading scheme – developed in 1977 – was imported from Greece and widely used in all community schools (Roussou, 1984a). Like the earlier materials, they suffered from two main disadvantages in the British context, namely, the difficult and archaic form of Greek used, and the illustrations which were set in rural Greece. Indeed one community teacher had imported textbooks from America written for Greek American children which were more appropriate (LMP, 1985). In 1978–9 a small working team of teachers attached to the Cyprus High Commission were involved in the preparation of teaching materials suitable for each of the different grades which were then sent back to the Ministry of Education in Cyprus for approval. However, Aristodemou (1979) also reported that it was necessary to establish a working group with appropriate qualifications to undertake the re-writing of textbooks. Indeed there was a movement by the Greek Teachers' Association to attempt to change the language and orientation of the textbooks to reflect life in contemporary Cyprus and London. Thus in 1981, as part of the Mother Tongue Project, a Greek Development Group of 12 teachers from mainstream and community sectors, and Greece and Cyprus, was formed to produce an alternative series of primary readers, workbooks and an alphabet frieze. The draft set of books had been produced and given to trial teachers in the autumn term of 1982, just as a new reading scheme in full colour arrived from Greece in January 1983. It was thus decided to link this with other MTP materials (see p.97) and produce a workbook addressing the special difficulties faced by children simultaneously learning Greek and Roman scripts (Roussou, 1984a; see p.50). Georgiou (1983) discovered that the independent schools were using books based on the Cypriot child in London and Greece and that two-thirds of 39 pupils who completed a questionnaire thought that it was more important for Greek Cypriots to learn about Cyprus than about Greece.

Similarly, materials for teaching Turkish have been imported from Turkey and the Turkish Federated State of Cyprus. Some are supplied free, others are purchased by the Cyprus Turkish Association or even by the ILEA direct from

Turkey (Memdouh, 1981; Singleton, 1979; Cronin, 1984). These books reflect life in Turkey, and although the teachers in a school visited by Singleton claimed that this was not a problem in view of the pupils' visits to Cyprus, she considered they would require explanation to a London child. Indeed the Cyprus Turkish Association in evidence to the Swann Committee claimed that 'we feel that the Turkish Cypriot children are not equipped for certain of these books and that special books must be prepared and printed for their specific needs' (Memdouh, 1981). Other Turkish teachers have wanted books relevant to UK-born students and to use mainstream teaching aids (LMP, 1985). Singleton (1979) found that in addition the Turkish teachers had written and duplicated stories set in London and also took along to the classes story-books set in Cyprus for children to borrow. This was the only school, out of a range of mother-tongue schools visited which represented seven languages in Haringey, where story-books as opposed to reading books were provided.

The availability and supply of textbooks and materials has been another problematic aspect of teaching in the mother-tongue schools. Aristodemou (1979) noted that the schools were lacking suitable textbooks to enable proper work to be undertaken and the inadequate supply of books, especially readers and background literature, was revealed in Leeuwenberg's (1979) survey in Haringey. There the Greek Parents' Association kept a collection of about 200 books suitable for children and adults but the demand was greater than could be met, especially as the Association was frequently approached by mainstream teachers for books in English about Cyprus. In a Greek school in Hackney, Elliott (1981) reported that teaching materials consisted of a booklet with stories about a page long for reading practice, duplicated sheets for younger pupils to colour and learn words, exercise books, grammar booklets and duplicated sheets for translation practice in preparation for Greek O-level. Yet teachers and pupils were said to lack materials appropriate in their language and orientation, despite the fact that this was one of the more prosperous schools visited. Indeed, in a survey of mother-tongue schools in London, Elliott found that only six out of 23 Greek schools and four out of 11 Turkish schools claimed to have book collections. Elliott recommended that better use should be made by mother-tongue schools of public library provision, and clearly some students do borrow books in Greek and Turkish where available (Clough and Quarmby, 1978; Elliott, 1981; see p.73).

On the subject of materials it is important to note the Schools Council/EC Mother Tongue Project (1981–5) which has developed materials in Greek (and Bengali), and a teacher's handbook for teaching Greek in part fulfilment of the aim of devising a framework for materials development which could be transferred to other minority languages in Britain. The project focussed on the primary age range. The project's evaluator and its Greek co-ordinator have both described the principles underlying the materials, their levels and content (Tansley, 1986; Roussou, 1984a, 1984b). The planning and production of the materials was based on several guiding principles: that the materials should be child-centred, recognizing the child's oral use of dialect without criticism and gradually introducing the standard language in its oral and written forms; reflect the child's experience of life in urban British multicultural cities and avoid racial, national or gender stereotypes; and be flexible, available for use by community and mainstream teachers with pupils of different ages and abilities, and transferable to other languages. Since the majority of children of Greek Cypriot origin involved with the project spoke Greek as their second language there was an especial need to stimulate oracy in Greek and for materials to extend literacy to be used with older children who had attended classes for some time and could already read Greek.

The materials were designed to cater for children at three stages of language development: pre-literacy, where learners have some knowledge of the oral language and in some cases are fluent in Cypriot dialect; beginning reading, where there is a need to extend the oral language especially in its standard form; and extending reading skills, where learners with a foundation of literacy skills in their mother tongue are ready to be introduced to more advanced aspects of reading.

The materials themselves may be divided into three broad categories: the Greek core materials devised by the project, selected Greek materials and selected, mainly text-free English materials with an emphasis on oral language. During 1982–3 the core materials were extensively trialled in mainstream and community schools (see pp.111–14). The resulting project core materials of especial relevance to teaching Greek were either text-free or literacy materials. The text-free materials comprise: *Picture Cards* – 15 text-free pictures of various topics of interest to children aged five to 11; *Our Neighbours* – figurines depicting Greek and Bengali families, a mixed marriage and an English one-parent family; and an *Outline Story Book* – a multicultural resource to stimulate oral and written language (all published by Philip and Tacey Ltd). The literacy materials comprise: a *Greek workbook* – phonic material designed for word recognition and to introduce writing practice; and two sets of *story readers* in Greek and English which have varied cultural and linguistic content, some based in Britain and others in Greece or Cyprus. There is also a teacher's handbook, *Teaching Greek as a Mother Tongue in Britain*, designed to give practical help to Greek teachers in mainstream and community schools (all available from SCDC Publications). In addition, each project class had access to £10 worth of selected Greek materials such as the Greek Ministry of Education's reading scheme, maths and environmental studies books, anthologies published by the Cypriot Ministry of Education, project books produced by a group of Cypriot teachers in London in the 1970s (see p.95), stories by Greek children's writers (see e.g. *Mother Tongue News*, **6**, page. 16) and some bilingual books in Greek and English. The trial classes also had examples of books and kits produced to develop language in English classes, some of which were specially adapted for project use. These included the Schools Council's *Break Through to Literacy* sentence maker and readers with Greek words, and the ILEA Learning Materials Service's *Language for Learning* materials.

Tansley (1986) has reviewed the varied response of community and mainstream teachers to the materials and reported that initial take-up of the Greek literacy materials has been almost equally divided between the two sectors. These materials are likely to be a useful resource to mainstream and community teachers concerned to promote children's mother-tongue development. Manley (1986, pp. 49–51) provides a case-study illustration of a Greek community class for five to nine year-olds where some Mother Tongue Project and other materials were used. For other bilingual materials (Greek/English and Turkish/English), particularly from the Learning Materials for Ethnic Minority Groups Project, see p. 123.

EXTRA-CURRICULAR ACTIVITIES   The Greek mother-tongue schools also engage in a number of extra-curricular activities such as open days, clubs, dancing, summer holiday camps, exchange visits and sporting activities. In an early account of an open day at one Greek school George and Millerson (1967) observed that the songs, poems and plays commemorated with nationalistic fervour the work of underground schools during the Turkish occupation of Cyprus and Greece, the lives of heroes from the Greek War of Independence and the most recent civil strife in Cyprus. The researchers doubted whether the children understood the real significance of these shows, though their parents clearly enjoyed them. Both the church and Greek Parents' Association schools place great emphasis on cultural activities involving both pupils and parents. According to the annual report for 1978–9 of the Cyprus High Commission, some 153 school and community functions were organized by the 42 community schools (Aristodemou, 1979). Each school gathered pupils and parents together at least three times during the year and provided opportunities not only for recreation and education, but also to reflect about the nature of the mother-tongue schools (see below).

In addition to the community schools four children's clubs were set up in 1978–9 with the same purpose of fostering the cultural identity of the Cypriot children, but through a more activity-based curriculum (ibid.). A total of 196 Cypriot children were involved in two clubs in Enfield, one in Islington and one in Barnet. Although the opportunity to attend was limited compared with access to mother-tongue classes, it is interesting to note that the children who attended the clubs claimed to prefer them to the mother-tongue schools. Some larger church schools also arrange dancing classes (Tsatsaroni and Papassava, 1986; Singleton, 1979).

Both the Greek Embassy and the Cyprus High Commission have since the 1970s organized a number of summer holiday camps which have enabled children to visit Greece or Cyprus (Constantinides, 1977; Singleton, 1979; Alkan and Constantinides, 1981; Tsatsaroni, 1983). In 1978 some 80 students visited Cyprus for a month (Aristodemou, 1979). However, applications are now in decline (Tsatsaroni and Papassava, 1986). Alkan and Constantinides (1981) recommended that these summer holiday excursions should become study trips in which British youngsters could also participate. Aristodemou (1979) also reported that, in 1977, 150 children from a choir in Cyprus participated in an exchange visit, staying with Cypriot families in London, and he recommended that further exchange visits should be arranged, perhaps during each of the three vacation periods each year. The Cyprus High Commission's annual report for 1978–9 also revealed that there was an attempt to link activities in the UK Cypriot community with those in the wider community, for example, through the organization of football teams associated with each community school.

PARENTS' ATTITUDES Clearly not only have many Greek Cypriot parents shown considerable enthusiasm in their desire for their children to attend mother-tongue schools, but these have also been well supported by an institutional framework through the church and 'home' governments. Indeed in many cases the mother-tongue schools have become a focal point of Cypriot community activities, as is shown in a case study of the Greek Cypriot community school and centre in Weston-super-Mare (Miles, 1983). The 1978–9 annual report of the Education Department of the Cyprus High Commission indicates the extent to which the Greek mother-tongue schools, supervised by the High Commission, had contact with the parents of the children attending. The schools were divided into six districts within London and one outside, each of which had a teacher who undertook the role of liaison officer to establish co-ordinating committees with parents in order to facilitate communication between teachers, parents and LEAs. The parents' associations held 227 meetings in London during 1978–9, in addition to parents' involvement with various school activities (see above), and liaison officers participated with OESEKA in 1979 in discussing the problems of community schools. Indeed it is clear from Aristodemou's (1979) report that the Cypriot parents are seen as having considerable power to influence the mother-tongue schools through their representatives on the school, district or community committees and, in contrast to their relative lack of contact with mainstream schools (see pp. 146–50), it would appear that the Cypriot parents whose children attend mother-tongue schools often have a high degree of contact with these establishments. In one Hackney community association school, Elliott (1981) discovered that the Greek Parent–Teacher Association met monthly and gave some support to the school. However, Tsatsaroni and Papassava (1986) have reported that Greek teachers in the church schools generally have less contact with parents than Cypriot teachers who teach in the parents' association schools. Even so, in some church schools teachers see parents termly. Greek teachers in the church schools are keen to consult with parents about the real needs of children attending mother-tongue schools, and there is some interest in assisting parents to organize various social activities not just in connection with the church, but to encompass a wide range of lectures and meetings. Singleton (1979) reported that although the Turkish community at large ran the Turkish schools through such organizations as the Cyprus Turkish Association, there appeared to be very little local community involvement through parents' support groups.

Although there is evidence that there has been a high degree of support by some Greek-speaking parents for mother-tongue classes, it appears that some Greek parents may have been ambivalent about the additional demands made on their children by attendance (Constantinides, 1977). Moreover, in some cases, as Elliott (1981) discovered, even when parents do send their children to classes, they may not necessarily be supportive of mother-tongue learning at home, partly because of a lack of time and partly because they may themselves speak to their children in a mixture of English and Greek. The ALUS of the LMP (1983a) provides information on Greek and Turkish parents' awareness of, and their child's attendance at, mother-tongue classes in London. Some 87 per cent of 126 Greek-speaking respondents and 80 per cent of 158 Turkish-speaking respondents with children or young people under 21 in the household knew of mother-tongue classes. However, of the 102 Greek-speaking households with children in the five to 18 age range, only 41 per cent had at least one child attending mother-tongue classes in the previous four weeks, and this compared with only 11 per cent of the 133 Turkish-speaking households. These attendance figures were above average for Greek speakers and below average amongst the Turkish-speaking households (see pp. 87–8). Reasons given by both Greek and Turkish speakers for non-attendance were that children were too young, or occasionally too old, or too proficient, to make it worth while, or that parents or children were too busy or thought that the classes were not very valuable given their other priorities. However, both linguistic communities expressed a high degree of support for mother-tongue maintenance, suggesting that there may be a considerable unmet demand for support in this connection. Indeed, in Haringey, Beetlestone (1982) found that both Greek and Turkish parents were concerned about the lack of money available for such classes and teachers, the need for coach transport to the classes, the timing of the classes and the cost of hiring premises. Parents are also often concerned about sending young children out in the evenings at the risk of attack, and violent racial attacks in one area led to the discontinuation of one Turkish class (Memdouh, 1981).

PUPILS' ATTITUDES   Just as with parents, there is likely to be wide range of attitudes amongst pupils to attending mother-tongue classes. As Roussou has observed:

Pupils in mother tongue classes may be either first, second or third generation immigrants with some fluency in spoken and written Greek or with very little grasp of the language or even none at all. Depending on either parents' attitudes towards mother tongue maintenance, the geographical location of their home and mainstream school and also the attitudes of their mainstream teachers, pupils may be involved in learning their mother tongue and participating in cultural activities or may be completely against or indifferent to any such opportunities. (Roussou, 1984a, p.11)

When starting mother-tongue classes, children may notice the contrasts with their mainstream schools. However, Aristodemou (quoted by Beetlestone, 1982, and Georgiou, 1983) has claimed that 'after an initial period of adjustment, children come to appreciate the schools because they feel they are accepted as individuals and because they achieve success in their work'. Cronin (1984) found that a small sample of eight to 11-year-old Turkish-speaking children from mainland Turkey had positive attitudes to attending Turkish classes, were motivated to improve their knowledge and skills in language, history, dance, music and traditions and felt that learning Turkish was important to affirm their Turkish identity, in case they should wish to return to Turkey and obtain employment there. Elliott (1981) observed that although children in a Greek community school appeared well-motivated, they were often tired, particularly if classes were held in the evening, and conversely were also often tired in their mainstream classes. Indeed Triseliotis (1976) has claimed that attendance at mother-tongue classes in evenings and at weekends adds considerably to children's physical if not emotional stress.

Indeed as pupils grow older, and as peer group influence increases, they may become more reluctant to attend classes, and it has been claimed numbers may fall off quite dramatically (Archimandritou-Xefteris, 1977; Aristodemou, 1979; Martianou, 1981). On the other hand the LMP Mother-Tongue Teaching Directory (MTTD) data (LMP, 1983b; Table 16) suggest that the numbers of pupils of secondary age enrolled in classes may hold up quite well. Alkan and Constantinides (1981) have reported that whilst some Cypriot pupils can cope with learning two languages and attending mother-tongue classes, others become unwilling to study Greek or Turkish at about the age of 12 or 13 and display embarrassment in using their mother tongue. One of the difficulties is that the mother-tongue classes are extra-curricular, which means extra time spent attending school when peers are at play, doing homework or socializing (Constantinides, 1977), and they 'reject the separateness implied in supplementary classes' (Krokou, 1985). Some pupils also experience stress in the latter years of secondary schooling from the competing claims of their mainstream and community language studies. Martianou (1981) found that amongst a small sample of Greek-speaking 14–19-year-olds the majority of those who attended mother-tongue schools for, on average, three to five years liked learning there and aspired to taking O-level, but some found that the demands of their mainstream schooling were too great in the fourth year. Constantinides (1977) claimed that children often develop a 'fierce resistance' to attending classes, and that if parents insist, they may attend but be unruly and disruptive. Others may attend for a short period and then drop out, particularly if they experience difficulties in reconciling their parents' lifestyle with the one to which they aspire, as this may lead to a general resentment about being seen as Cypriot or 'foreign'. However, Constantinides also observed that many young Cypriots who resist mother-tongue classes in their adolescence later regain an interest in culture and language.

TEACHERS' ATTITUDES   Unfortunately, there is little first-hand research evidence of Greek, Turkish or mainstream teachers' attitudes to Greek or Turkish classes in out-of-school hours. The attitudes of Greek and Cypriot teachers to the language taught and methods of language teaching have already been indicated (see pp. 92–3), as have views on textbooks and teaching aids (see pp. 95–6). Available evidence on mainstream teachers' attitudes to Greek and Turkish teaching in community schools, as for mother-tongue teaching in general, appears to be negative, with complaints lodged about the tiredness of pupils, the rearrangements of classrooms where community classes are held and concern about linguistic interference (see p. 198).

Some Cypriot bilingual Greek/English, Turkish/English teachers teach in mainstream schools either occasionally as teachers of Greek or Turkish (Singleton, 1979) or of other subjects (see p. 205). Some of these teachers undertake a liaison role between the mainstream school and the Cypriot community. However, it should not be assumed that all such teachers wish to adopt this difficult role. In general commentators such as Georgiou (1983), who studied the social and cultural effects of attendance at mother-tongue classes on Greek Cypriot pupils in a comprehensive school, have advocated that there should be more exchanges between teachers in mainstream and mother-tongue schools through visits and discussions. These might facilitate greater awareness and understanding of the position of a Cypriot child learning two languages and experiencing two forms of schooling and help to dispel some of the negative perceptions which teachers in each sector of education may hold about the other.

Clearly there is a need for a long-term, in-built, in-service education framework for exchanges between mainstream and community teachers, especially perhaps in relation to the less numerous and less extensive network of Turkish teachers. Certain initiatives such as that of the Mother Tongue Project (see pp. 111–14) and the first national language conference for Greek, organized jointly by the National Council for Mother Tongue Teaching and the Schools Council/EC Mother Tongue Project (Roussou, 1984b), in which both community and mainstream teachers participated, have made a valuable beginning in this direction. Another teacher training initiative, the RSA Certificate in the Teaching of Community Languages, is an important development in the training of teachers of minority languages who may be either part-time tutors in the community sector or qualified teachers of other subjects in the mainstream, and this provides an opportunity for both groups to work together and share experience (Smith, 1984; see also p. 116). Given the likelihood of a continuing need for teachers from Greece and Cyprus in the community schools and the desire of those teachers to be involved in further exchanges of ideas with mainstream teachers and in in-service courses (Roussou, 1984b), strategies for extending formal liaison need to be developed by the community organizations concerned in co-operation with LEAs and schools.

In conclusion, this review of publicly available research and reports on community provision for the teaching of Greek and Turkish has shown that despite a substantial organizational network, especially for teaching Greek, the mother-tongue schools, teachers and pupils often suffer considerable difficulties and disadvantages. The main problem for the teaching of Turkish is the apparent shortage of qualified teachers, and the lack of financial stability to cope with the employment of more teachers, the payment of rent for accommodation and the provision of transport for pupils to and from classes. To a lesser extent some of the Greek schools suffer similar difficulties, though the support of the church and governments, especially in supplying teachers, is much more significant. The very involvement of several agencies and interest groups in Greek and Turkish mother-tongue teaching nevertheless serves to diversify rather than unify approaches to provision and highlights differences in teachers' views about the relative value to be accorded to, for example, Cypriot dialects of Greek and standard Greek in the teaching–learning process. Indeed community teachers appear to hold significantly divergent views about teaching methods. Difficulties with textbooks in terms of level of language development and their cultural orientation towards the mainland, Cyprus or the position of pupils in multiethnic Britain are common to both Greek and Turkish schools. Recent joint initiatives between mainstream and community schools may have indicated ways forward on materials development. Yet there is much more which could be done by the mainstream education system to support community provision. For example, more LEAs could offer free use of school premises; schools could make available various teaching aids and foster links with community teachers; and INSET providers could facilitate joint courses involving mainstream and community teachers. However, the situation is rendered more complex by the involvement of both respective mainland and Cypriot governments in the financial provision for, if not the administrative organization of, teaching Greek and Turkish. Indeed the very presence in some community schools of pupils with backgrounds in mainland Greece or Turkey alongside those with a Cypriot background may not only complicate actual practice in terms of the language taught, the medium of instruction and the cultural orientation of the curriculum, but may also suggest different legal rights to mainstream provision for the children of migrant workers according to the terms of the EC Directive on Mother-Tongue Teaching accepted by the British government.

But to what extent have the original aims of Cypriot parents in sending their children to mother-tongue classes, namely, to raise their consciousness of belonging to a Greek- or Turkish-speaking ethnic group and to offset the Anglicization of mainstream schooling and cultural influences, been achieved? Even in the late 1960s George and Millerson (1967) doubted whether the mother-tongue schools had achieved their aims as they saw children's lack of proficiency in Greek as an outward sign of more fundamental differences between the two generations. Oakley (1970) also considered that attendance at mother–tongue schools only had a superficial effect in countering Anglicization and in instilling a positive appreciation of Greek or Turkish language and culture. It is possible that with the passage of time some parents' objectives and the aims of some community schools have been modified, perhaps to give greater emphasis to the linguistic development rather than the cultural and ethnic identity of the pupils. On the other hand, mother–tongue schools may have become more effective in achieving their aims or young Greek and Turkish Cypriot pupils may have become more interested in exploring the language and culture of their backgrounds, particularly if they receive encouragement from their mainstream schools. But without adequate research evidence on the attitudes of parents, pupils and teachers, it is only possible to gain a few insights into the extent to which the present albeit extensive community mother-tongue provision (for Greek speakers at least) is both satisfactory for, and satisfying to, those involved. The following sub-section considers to what extent mainstream education has been aware of and has explicitly recognized the interests of Greek- and Turkish-speaking parents and pupils in learning these languages, by making provision for the teaching of Greek and Turkish during normal school hours.

Modern Greek and Turkish in the mainstream
The teaching of Greek and Turkish in community schools has a long history. But to what extent is this reflected in provision in mainstream schools for pupils whose first language is Greek or Turkish and their peers? Does the concentration of Cypriot pupils in Greater London and especially north London, for example, affect attitudes towards provision and the opportunities for such pupils to learn their mother tongue in their ordinary school? Here we examine the extent of provision

by considering requests which LEAs and schools have received over the years for Greek and Turkish to be taught, attitudes towards mainstream provision, actual teaching arrangements which have been made and examination entry for Greek and Turkish at O- and A-level whether directly by mainstream schools or on behalf of mother-tongue schools. Research into teaching Greek in the mainstream will also be outlined and consideration given to further issues and resource constraints in extending provision. Once again, the evidence focusses on the teaching of Greek, rather than Turkish.

REQUESTS FOR AND ATTITUDES TOWARDS PROVISION There is very little recorded evidence of specific requests by Greek- or Turkish-speaking parents or community mother-tongue teaching organizations directly to LEAs or schools for mainstream provision for Greek or Turkish. However, Constantinides (1977) claimed that all the organizations involved in operating Greek community schools – the Greek Orthodox Church and the Embassy, the Cyprus High Commission, independent parents and left-wing voluntary associations – have put pressure on secondary schools in areas heavily populated by Greek Cypriots to include the teaching of Modern Greek in their curricula. But in 1979, in a national survey, Little and Willey (1983) found that only 12 LEAs with more than ten per cent ethnic minority pupils reported receiving requests from parents for the teaching of their mother tongue in schools; and of these, some were requests for the teaching of Greek from Greek Cypriot communities.

Fortunately, however, there are more reports of claims and evidence of the attitudes of parents, pupils and teachers towards mainstream Greek and Turkish provision. These suggest that there may be some division within the Cypriot community as to the desirability of provision for mother-tongue teaching in the mainstream. In addition to the claims made by Constantinides (1977), a number of others closely involved with the Cypriot community, for example, Alkan and Constantinides (1981), Cypriot liaison officers in the social services department in Haringey, Beetlestone (1982), a mainstream infant teacher in schools with Cypriot pupils and Tsatsaroni (1983), a Greek teacher in church mother-tongue schools, have argued that Greek-speaking Cypriot parents, the Cypriot communities and mother-tongue teachers themselves want provision to be made for the teaching of Greek in the mainstream school. In this way, the status of Greek can be raised, so that it can be seen as a valuable modern language in which to claim proficiency and which, in turn, may enhance the self-confidence of Greek-speaking pupils. In the ALUS in Haringey, in 1980–1, 94 per cent of 197 adult Turkish speakers and 88 per cent of 193 adult Greek speakers agreed with the assertion that 'the government should provide the teaching of our language as a right for all our children in state schools' (Reid *et al*, 1985). Martianou (1981) found that all of a small sample of predominantly Greek Cypriot parents, who either sent their children to mother-tongue schools or taught them themselves, wanted their language to be taught in the mainstream instead of other modern languages if a sufficient number of students were interested. They cited as their reasons: to improve communication between parent and child and also with relatives in Cyprus; to give the child a positive self-concept and hence, they argued, to improve academic performance; and to gain an additional O-level. The Cyprus Turkish Association argued in its evidence to the Swann Committee that mainstream provision should be made in order to give true equality of opportunity to linguistic minority pupils on a par with their majority peers and that immigrant children needed a sound knowledge of the mother tongue in order to study their own culture. It was not just conservative minority parents who wanted minority languages in the school curriculum, but 'even young parents are very conscious of the need of acquiring a working knowledge of their mother tongue to be learned by their children so that they may grow up in a multi–racial society without losing touch with his own identity and his national background' (Memdouh, 1981, pp. xiii–xiv). The Swann Committee stated in its Report (GB.P. H of C, 1985) that Cypriot community representatives were strongly in favour of mother–tongue teaching in mainstream schools and that, in general, parents would prefer some provision to be made during school hours. Those in favour argued for mother-tongue maintenance and mother-tongue teaching, rather than structured programmes of bilingual education, although it was felt that there was a clear need for some bilingual support in the early years for those with little or no English.

On the other hand, there is evidence of a certain ambivalence and lack of whole-hearted support for mainstream provision amongst Cypriot parents. In 1975 a Community Relations Commission (CRC) investigation in eight multiracial areas, which included Haringey and Hackney, found that a mere two per cent of the 48 Greek-speaking Cypriot parents interviewed wanted their own language to be taught to their children in their mainstream schools. This contrasted greatly with the responses of speakers of various South Asian languages, some 27–47 per cent of whom desired their language to be taught to their children in schools (CRC, 1977). Following a study of some Greek-speaking pupils in mother-tongue and main-stream schools, Georgiou (1983) whilst suggesting that the provision of Greek in the school curriculum might assist the integration of Greek Cypriot pupils, nevertheless was of the opinion that children attending such classes might feel singled out and might miss some other curricular subject. She suggested that Greek Cypriot parents might still prefer to send their children to an extra-curricular Greek school in order that they should receive tuition not only in language, but also have the opportunity to learn to appreciate Greek and Cypriot culture. Moreover, Miles (1983) claimed that Cypriot parents in Weston-super-Mare did not wish Greek lessons to interfere with children's normal education, preferring to make their own arrangements for extra-curricular tuition. Beetlestone (1982) suggested that Cypriot parents have seen community provision as additional to that of the educational system – partly because of the concern with a different set of values in the Greek and Turkish classes – and have not until recently considered the possibility of such teaching being a part of mainstream education. Indeed two prominent contributors of Greek Cypriot origin to the National Council for Mother-Tongue Teaching/Schools Council Mother-Tongue Project Conference on 'Greek Outside Greece' – Constantinides and Anthias – argued that community provision should not be reduced or weakened by the introduction of Greek in mainstream schools because it broadened the cultural context of the child's learning; as Anthias expressed it:

> These mother-tongue classes are very important because they do not only teach the children to read and write their own language but they play a role in maintaining the ethnic identity of the children. In these classes the children will learn about the history and culture of Cyprus (and Greece). They will come together with other Greek-speaking pupils and explore their shared experience as Cypriots. (Anthias, 1984, p.7)

Given the stress by Cypriot communities on the cultural and ethnic aspects of learning Greek and Turkish, perhaps it is not a question of either community or mainstream provision, but provision which can be complementary in respect of linguistic and cultural objectives.

What, then, is known of the views of pupils of Greek and Turkish Cypriot origin about mainstream provision for teaching Greek and Turkish? The Swann Committee reported that, in contrast with the attitudes expressed by community representatives and parents, Cypriot youngsters (mainly Greek and Turkish sixth-formers) in discussion were very much against mainstream provision. They preferred to study other subjects in school and to study Greek or Turkish in their own home and thus possibly gain an additional qualification. Community representatives suggested this reluctance might be a reflection of the low status accorded to Greek and Turkish by schools. Indeed Cronin (1984) reported that a small sample of primary-age Turkish pupils attending community schools were generally not keen to have Turkish in their state schools as they feared being ridiculed by their peers. It has also been suggested that Greek-speaking pupils tend to see community-run schools as places where they socialize as much as places for learning Greek (Couillaud, 1984). On the other hand, Martianou (1981) found that almost all of a small sample of Greek Cypriot pupils of secondary age thought that there should be mainstream provision for learning Greek as a modern language and for an extra qualification where sufficient numbers allowed. However, an HMI survey of mother-tongue teaching found that the take-up of Greek (and Turkish taught outside the timetable) in a few mainstream schools was not substantial relative to the number of pupils speaking these languages as mother tongues on roll (GB. DES, 1984). The LMP Secondary Pupils Survey in Peterborough and Bradford revealed relatively little preference by either the monolingual or bilingual secondary-age pupils surveyed for learning Greek – indeed it is not possible to tell if Classical Greek may have been intended (LMP, 1983a). Although some English pupils were reported to have taken an interest in learning Greek, in one school where it was timetabled and available after school few were said to persist because of difficulties they experienced in learning from the beginning (GB. P. H of C, 1985).

Unfortunately, there appears to be little evidence of the views of mainstream teachers about provision for teaching Greek and Turkish in the curriculum (but see the views of those involved in research, pp. 111–13). However, Prager (1977), head of a modern languages department in a boys' high school in Waltham Forest, argued that to teach Greek or Turkish to Cypriot pupils would be far more relevant than other European languages in the school curriculum, and that by not teaching pupils' first languages schools are ignoring the wishes of minority populations. Indeed contributors to the NCMTT/SCMTP Conference reported that even when Greek was 'officially' taught in the timetable it had, *de facto*, a low status compared with English and other modern languages and the teachers of Greek were 'marginalized', which was seen to be in line with most mainstream teachers' negative views of bilingualism (Couillaud, 1984). Even so, Krokou (1985) has argued that 'long-term language maintenance requires the legitimacy confirmed by the formal school curriculum'. We now consider to what extent schools have met this challenge.

MAINSTREAM PROVISION   Reports of teaching Greek or Turkish in mainstream curricula are both limited and, not surprisingly, more likely to occur in secondary rather than primary education. This provision may be compared with that in institutions of further and higher education. As might be expected, evidence of provision is largely related to those localities of greatest Cypriot concentration. Interestingly, Singleton (1979) reported that one of Haringey's then 52 primary schools had been teaching Greek and Turkish, mostly within the ordinary school timetable, for two years. This had come about largely because the head was convinced that increased competence in the mother tongue would lead to improved performance in English. In 1978 two teachers of Greek, financed by the Cyprus High Commission, taught a class of 20 Greek-speaking children and two teachers of Turkish, financed by the Turkish Federated State of Cyprus, taught a class of 27 Turkish-speaking pupils. No English mother-tongue speakers participated. Children were grouped according to their mother-tongue ability across ages, which was not usual within the school. Another problem arose because there was no spare timetable slot, and the Greek- and Turkish-speaking children were withdrawn from other lessons and were sometimes disappointed to miss swimming. A few children who originally started classes had opted out; it was not known how much parental pressure to continue was put on a child. Hunter-Grundin (1982) reported that in a junior school in the South Harringay district of Haringey, with a high proportion of pupils whose first language was Greek or Turkish, arrangements were made for Greek and Turkish parents to hold classes for pupils one afternoon each week. The classes included the teaching of the spoken language and also general cultural topics. In practice, only pupils of Greek or Turkish Cypriot origin attended, although the classes were open to all pupils. The headmistress of this school was herself taking lessons in Greek and Turkish in order to facilitate communication with parents. According to Beetlestone, who considered that experiments in teaching Greek and Turkish in infant and junior schools might be beneficial in extending a possibly superficial command of the mother tongue, one school in Haringey in 1983 experimented with a withdrawal group for Greek lessons as part of the timetable and another provided lessons in after-school hours, but there had been some opposition from the LEA to this practice. Evidence generally indicates that there is little direct provision for Greek or Turkish in the primary curriculum, especially in comparison with community classes. In a Schools Council Survey, in 1983, although 252 primary schools in 23 LEAs were providing mother-tongue teaching as part of the primary curriculum, Greek was only supported in two schools and Turkish in seven, despite the fact that seven LEAs had named Greek and three Turkish as being amongst the most frequently occurring languages (Tansley and Craft, 1984). In recent years, there has been a movement to encourage teachers in multilingual classrooms to recognize and support the mother tongue of all bilingual pupils as part of the everyday curriculum, as in a Hackney primary school with ten per cent Greek-speaking children. Several primary schools involve bilingual parents as aides in the classroom, especially in story telling sessions (Houlton, 1984).

In secondary schools Greek and Turkish classes may be offered as options in the modern languages curriculum or during lunchtimes or immediately after school hours. Research evidence indicates a pattern of *ad hoc* and localized provision. At secondary level, in a national survey in 1971, Townsend and Brittan (1972) found that only four out of 98 secondary schools provided any tuition in the languages of immigrants' countries of origin, which included tuition in Greek. Although the researchers suggested that the lack of mother-tongue teaching might have been due to the fact that headteachers did not see this as one of the school's functions, one headteacher mentioned that O-level Greek had been introduced into the school timetable mainly to prevent out-of-school tuition which was being used largely for political teaching. Apparently in north London Modern Greek classes were instituted at Stationers' School in the 1960s, as was a Turkish class at Archway (Martin-Jones, 1984). Originally the Greek classes were taught outside normal school hours, but by the late 1970s were mostly timetabled (Singleton, 1979). In 1975 Saifullah Khan (1976) found that about 110 boys were taking Modern Greek, the majority of them Greek Cypriots. In that year, ten students had taken O-level and it was planned to introduce A-level Modern Greek into the curriculum. The head was reported to be willing to teach another community language at the school but was waiting for pressure to come from the community (Singleton, 1979). In 1975 Greek classes up to O-level were available for members of the Greek Cypriot community in Liverpool at the Language Centre. Generally schools were more likely to facilitate examination entry by pupils attending community classes and there were only isolated examples of schools with curriculum provision (Clough and Quarmby, 1978). In another case, in a national survey in 1979, Little and Willey (1983) found that in only two out of eight LEAs in areas of high ethnic minority concentration which reported the teaching of minority languages Greek was said to be taught at two secondary schools and 'elsewhere where necessary'. This corresponded with a low response in another part of the survey from heads of modern language departments claiming that Greek was taught to O- and A-level standard. However, it appeared that Greek-speaking pupils and their parents had reacted favourably to the introduction of opportunities for studying their language in the mainstream curriculum. Another national survey in 1980 (Tsow, 1983) revealed a similarly parlous state in terms of LEA provision; only two LEAs claimed that Greek was taught to O-level and only one to A-level; and there was no mention of Turkish.

However, given the residential concentration of Cypriots, national surveys may not always provide the best evidence of curricular provision for Greek and Turkish, and it may be more illuminating to consider studies in north London and particularly the London Borough of Haringey. Martianou (1981) found that three out of five schools with Cypriot pupils studied in north London had mainstream provision. Two schools had timetabled Greek since 1975, about half the fourth years opted for it, and about 50 per cent were entered for examinations each year, although the results were said not to be very good unless pupils had previously attended community schools. One school operated classes for years 1–3 at lunchtime, but there was insufficient interest for a language option. Four schools entered pupils for O- and A-level examinations, sometimes in conjunction with community schools.

In Haringey in 1967 an Educational Consultant for Immigrant Children, after visiting and commenting on classes run by Greek Cypriot organizations, strongly recommended that the newly established comprehensive schools should carefully consider the possibility of introducing O-level Greek courses (Milstead, 1981). Although Haringey has officially had a positive approach to bilingualism, Milstead considered many schools had yet to advance to such a position. In 1979 Singleton found that in addition to Stationers', 'the pioneering School for Modern Greek', at two other secondary schools, Drayton and Alexandra Park, Greek was taught after school hours. She considered that the fact that Greek and Turkish (see pp. 44–5) were the only two languages taught within the state system in Haringey was due to the large number of speakers of these languages in the borough and the good organization of these two communities which, with the backing of their governments, had put pressure on the system. According to Christodoulides (1984), since 1980 the long-term liaison between the Greek Parents' Association and the LEAs has resulted in the integration of Greek teaching into mainstream curricula where possible or the creation of classes from 3.30–6.00 pm under the responsibility of the head. Classes are open to all pupils. Apparently the classes have served to strengthen relationships between the Greek parents and school staff and the exchange of information.

Others have commented on the extension of mainstream and LEA support (Alkan and Constantinides, 1981; Martin-Jones, 1984) and Houlton (1984) also mentions that some ILEA schools are offering Greek within the options system. The LMP Mother-Tongue Teaching Directory (MTTD) survey in Haringey, in 1982, found that the LEA financed the salaries of teachers and the accommodation of 12 out of 90 Greek classes and usually the accommodation of a further four Greek classes and one Turkish class. Three of the Greek classes took place entirely during school hours and a further six, partly in school hours and partly after school and at weekends. Two Turkish classes were taught during school hours, one once and the other twice weekly. A further 27 Greek classes and one Turkish class met entirely after school or on a weekday evening, though it is not clear if some of these were supported by mainstream schools (LMP, 1983b; see p. 84). However, the researchers observed that the extent of mainstream provision and support was noticeably small for an area with many quite old-established linguistic minorities and a sizeable Cypriot population. It appears that provision for Turkish at secondary level is more likely in the neighbouring Borough of Hackney (ibid.) either in the timetable or as an extended day. However, the Cypriot Turkish Association reported that sometimes pupils studying Turkish had to miss other lessons such as RE or PE. Indeed, examples of mainstream curricular provision for both Greek and Turkish, apparently remain somewhat exceptional, especially given the extent of community provision and the evidence of demand, and may depend greatly on the initiative, liaison and continuing input of Cypriot teachers themselves (see e.g. LMP, 1985).

By contrast, it is interesting to note that in a CILT report (1975) of a conference which considered less-commonly taught languages in further and higher education, it was said that a lively, if not widespread, demand existed, often based on commercial and cultural interest, for the teaching of Greek at this level. In fact the report revealed that in 1973 some 81 students were enrolled on courses in Modern Greek at polytechnics and colleges, second only to Italian in the number of students of Western European languages (other than French, German, Russian and Spanish). Two CILT guides which focus on opportunities for learning Greek (CILT, 1982) and Turkish (CILT, 1983) show that it was possible to study Greek at five universities and many other polytechnics and colleges, and although opportunities for studying Turkish in these latter institutions were more limited, first-degree courses were offered at six universities. However, by 1986 the number of universities offering first-degree courses in Greek or Turkish had declined to four and five respectively.

EXAMINATION ENTRIES AND PERFORMANCE   What kind of examinations are available in Modern Greek and Turkish? To what extent have mainstream schools been involved in making arrangements for Greek- and Turkish-speaking pupils to sit for examinations in these languages? To what extent can this be a guide to the level of achievement of such pupils?

Modern Greek is offered at O- and A-level for students studying as a foreign language by the University of London GCE Board. The Oxford Delegacy of Local Examinations offers O-level for students studying as a foreign language or mother tongue (Reid, 1984; CILT, 1982). Other GCE boards may offer O-level Modern Greek, but they borrow the papers from either London or Oxford (Wright, 1983). Other examining bodies which also offer Modern Greek are: the Institute of Linguists, for foreign language learners and rarely used by schools; the International Baccalaureate Office and the Greek Institute, both for foreign language or mother-tongue learners (CILT, 1982; Wright, 1983). There was no CSE provision in Modern Greek up to 1983 (Wright, 1983). Turkish is offered to foreign language learners at O- and A-level by the University of London Board. Until 1982 it was also offered at O-level by Oxford (Reid, 1984). The Institute of Linguists and the International Bacculaureate Office also offer examinations to students studying Turkish as a foreign language (CILT, 1983).

According to Wright (1983), potential examination candidates include: second- and third-generation children born in Britain of Greek and Greek Cypriot origin who have Greek as a first language; an increasing number of children of Greek or Greek Cypriot origin whose first language is English, and who learn Modern Greek as a second language; children without a Greek or Greek Cypriot background who wish to learn Modern Greek as a foreign language; and some overseas candidates from Cyprus and Greece. Currently the majority of candidates for Greek examinations are mother-tongue learners. The University of London GCE O-level examination in Modern Greek has since its inception in 1938 been used to test proficiency in English of intending settlers. Yet the examination, for which there is no published syllabus, is the same for overseas and home candidates, though the latter are seeking a certificate of proficiency in Greek. The three-hour examination paper consists of translation from Modern Greek (two passages, 40 marks), translation from English into Modern Greek (one passage, 20 marks) and an essay of 200 words in Modern Greek chosen from four topics (40 marks). The Oxford Delegacy GCE O-level, has a specially approved syllabus, and examinations have been set regularly since 1957. The paper consists of two passages for translation from Greek to English, one narrative or descriptive, the other dialogue, taken from books or magazines (45 per cent of marks); translations from English to Greek to test a particular range of vocabulary and construction (40 per cent of marks); and a passage of writing in Modern Greek of around 130 words on one of three topics. Neither the London nor the Oxford examinations have an oral component and since mainstream schools may enter small numbers of candidates, who may have studied at a community school, and may not have mainstream teachers competent to administer an oral test, the practical difficulties in arranging this are considered severe (ibid.).

Indeed given the widespread lack of mainstream teaching of Modern Greek and Turkish in the modern languages curriculum, it would appear that the majority of examination entries in these subjects may be on behalf of pupils who have actually studied in community schools. Usually parents pay the examination fee (ibid.). Singleton (1979) who reported that examination candidates must be entered for mother-tongue examinations through the state school which they normally attend, found that the three Haringey schools with double-figure O-level entries in Modern Greek in summer 1978 were curiously not those which actually taught the language. In a national survey, in 1979, Little and Willey (1983) found that more modern language departments claimed to make arrangements for pupils to sit Greek than actually taught the language, though in any case the number was very small. Both Martianou (1981), who noted examination entry for Modern Greek and Turkish from four mainstream schools in north London, and Elliott (1981), who investigated examination entry in the community schools, found that the numbers involved even for Modern Greek at O-level were small, rarely entering double figures, and those for Turkish were not above two or three, like the A-level entries for Modern Greek. The LMP MTTD survey in Haringey (LMP, 1983b) showed that in 1981 there were 82 entries for O-level in Modern Greek and 12 at A-level out of a total number of 2,073 pupils on roll in all the Greek mother-tongue classes. Although the LEA paid the examination fees in some cases, it was more likely to be the parents who paid. Some candidates were entered for Turkish but the number of entrants was not known.

Table 17 gives an indication from a variety of sources, of the number of UK entrants for O- and A-level examinations in Modern Greek and Turkish through several examining boards over the last 15 years. It is interesting to note from the tables cited by Reid (1984) that from 1978–80 the number of UK entrants through the London Board for O-level Modern Greek was the third highest (after entrants for Chinese and Persian) and the highest for A-level out of all 'specially approved languages'. According to Wright (1983), the University of London estimated that most of the home entries for Modern Greek were from candidates who have Greek as their first language. For example, of the approximately 400 London O-level candidates for Modern Greek in 1981, 300 were entered through mainstream schools, although the vast majority had been taught in community classes and the remaining 100 were from FE colleges, other institutions or private entries. Most of the 163 home candidates for the Oxford Board O-level in Modern Greek in the summer of 1982 were candidates of Greek Cypriot parentage who sat their examinations at centres in the London area, though a few were English speakers learning Modern Greek as a foreign language.

Table 17:   UK examination entrants for O- and A-level Modern Greek and Turkish, 1973, 1978–81 and 1983

		1973	1978*	1979	1980	1981†	1983‡
Greek	O-level	623	372	303	350	595	418
	A-level	134	267	231	233	225	224
Turkish	O-level	82	125	141	136	174	
	A-level	45	57	57	62	47	

* Figures for 1978–1980 O- and A-level are for University of London entries, summer only.
† O-level figures for 1981 are combined summer entries for Oxford Delagacy of Local Examinations and University of London: Modern Greek 184 + 392 + 19 other examining boards, and Turkish 10 + 155 + 9; in addition, London entrants for Modern Greek in January were 41; A-level figures are for London only.
‡ Figures for 1983 known to Greek Embassy; figures for Turkish entrants not known.
Sources: CILT, 1975, Table 1; Reid, 1984, Table 1 and 2, University of London, 'specially approved languages' – candidate numbers; Tsatsaroni, 1983.

Given the extent of examination entry, it would appear that despite the claimed lack of emphasis at community schools on teaching to examination level, a fair proportion of Greek- and Turkish-speaking pupils are in fact reaching the standard at which they can be entered for public examinations. Unfortunately, little information is available about their level of success. Singleton (1979) reported that in the summer of 1978, in Haringey, 81 students achieved O-level Modern Greek and 12 Turkish, and there were 14 A-level passes in Modern Greek and one in Turkish. The greatest number of A-level results were at schools where the languages were not actually taught within the timetable. Tsatsaroni (1983) stated that, at one of the largest Greek mother-tongue schools run by the church, in 1982 some ten pupils obtained A-level in Modern Greek and 28 O-level, mainly at the middle range of grades.

In the early 1980s, the Schools Council undertook a project on 'Assessment in a Multicultural Society', which considered to what extent available examinations were appropriate for the needs of a multicultural society. In her review of provision for Modern Greek (see p. 108) Wright (1983) argued that radical changes were required to bring the examinations up to date, by widening the reading and writing exercises and including tests of listening and speaking, more like the Institute of Linguists' examinations. Wright emphasized that although the examinations should be conducted through Standard Greek, the Cypriot dialect should not be heavily penalized especially during orals. However, the difficulties of setting up oral examinations and the need for collaboration between the examining boards,

OESEKA and the church were recognized, as was the necessity for practising teachers and the boards to devise a suitable syllabus starting from the experiences of young people in the UK, using as a base the syllabus and assessment guidelines proposed by the Schools Council Modern Languages 16+ Committee. It was recommended that a single examination in Modern Greek at 16 plus should be developed, which would be sufficiently flexible to meet the needs of mother-tongue and foreign language learners and would have parity with other established modern languages. It is not known to what extent proposals for GCSE may have affected developments. Moreover, there is no indication of the appropriateness of the examinations available to UK Turkish entrants, but given that the exams are offered to foreign language learners, it may be supposed that they require similar revisions to meet the needs of Turkish mother-tongue candidates. Moreover, research by Reid (1984) showed that the status of minority community languages such as Modern Greek and Turkish is not uniform with respect to university and polytechnic entrance. On behalf of a working party of the National Congress on Languages in Education, Reid argued that examination passes in minority community languages should have parity with examination passes in more common (European) foreign languages. In addition, a consistent and explicit admissions policy should be operated with respect to the distinction made between candidates offering such examination passes as a mother tongue or as a foreign language. It was recommended that the distinction employed should be that used by the University of London, whereby if a candidate had been educated in the medium of English, one of the languages could be counted as a foreign language; but if not educated in English, then English could be counted as a foreign language.

RESEARCH INTO TEACHING MODERN GREEK A focus of part of the Schools Council/ EC Mother Tongue Project (MTP) from 1981 to 1985 was on developing materials for the teaching of Greek at primary age. The project aimed to assist teachers of primary-age children both in mainstream and community schools by developing a variety of resources for teaching, learning and supporting minority languages (see pp. 96–7). Greek and Bengali were focus languages for the project, although the wider aim was to devise a framework for materials development, as well as a core of materials, which could be transferred to other languages. Tansley (1986), the project's evaluator and later director, has described the evolution of the project, and it is worth considering here that aspect which involved mainstream and community teachers in developing Greek materials and teaching Greek on account of the issues raised in relation to teaching and learning objectives, teacher liaison, outcomes and attitudes.

The project team initially worked with a group of 12 teachers from mainstream and community sectors on the development of draft materials in Greek. The mainstream and community teachers often had different perspectives in relation to the objectives of the project on account of differing needs and expectations which made the development of a single pack of materials very difficult. For example, one objective 'to enable children to achieve literacy and further extend their competence in their mother tongue' through 'direct mother tongue teaching' was controversial in the normal curriculum of mainstream schools, though an ongoing process in community mother-tongue schools. Moreover, the community schools were concerned to teach literacy in the mother tongue and an understanding of culture. On the other hand, mainstream teachers had to fit in with the aims and approaches of primary school pedagogy with an emphasis on the acquisition of language across the curriculum as part of the overall development of the child. It was decided to develop pupil materials and teachers' guides to meet specific needs or fill gaps in existing materials identified by the teachers rather than exemplars of pupil materials. The principles behind the materials, their levels and the composition and content of the final published materials are outlined elsewhere (see pp. 96–7; see also Roussou, 1984a).

During 1982–3 draft materials were trialled in five mainstream schools in Haringey, both infant and junior schools with different social class intakes and percentages of ethnic minority pupils, and seven community schools representing church schools and those run by the Greek Parents' Association, with differing social class intakes and children of both mainland Greek and Cypriot background. In the community schools the project was included in ongoing teaching programmes, although some groups of children were selected to work specifically with the project's materials. But in mainstream schools classes were specially set up for the work to take place, so that not only were the materials on trial but the concept of mother-tongue teaching itself. Many of the mainstream classes used the withdrawal model whereby the mother-tongue teacher withdrew children from the classroom on a regular basis; others followed the integrated model with the mother-tongue teacher working within the same teaching area as the class teacher and attempting to develop collaborative links; and in some classes there was a combination of these approaches. A minimum of four hours' mother-tongue teaching per week and one hour's liaison time between the mother-tongue teacher and class teacher were recommended. The mother-tongue teachers had wide-ranging backgrounds: one was a Greek-speaking, British-trained mainstream teacher; the majority were teachers from the Cyprus High Commission, two of whom including the Greek project co-ordinator trialled the materials in mainstream schools, the others in community schools; one teacher in two mainstream schools was provided by the Greek Embassy; of other teachers who worked for the Greek Parents' Association schools, one was a graduate but without teacher training qualifications and one voluntary mainstream helper was an unqualified but enthusiastic parent. Over 150 Greek-speaking children were involved in the five mainstream schools. They were mainly second- and third-generation speakers of Greek whose understanding of Greek outran their spoken fluency.

Most of the evaluation of the response to, and outcomes of, the project relates to the mainstream schools. In general, virtually all the schools reported increased confidence amongst the children which had beneficial effects on their work as a whole, enabling them to participate more fully in education. The project helped children mix more easily with other children and many project children experienced increased self-esteem and pride in home language and culture as the status of their home language was elevated by use of the project's materials. Although some of the children learning Greek actually spoke English as a first language and found learning Greek hard, after initial difficulties most seemed pleased enough to be learning Greek. Some older children were concerned about missing other lessons, though this did not generally happen. None of the schools suggested that the time spent on mother-tongue teaching had adversely affected the children's overall progress, or that in learning English, and some felt there had been an improvement in both English and Greek. Teachers were sometimes compelled to reappraise their perceptions of children: one said 'I thought Michael was very poor at language but now I find he is fluent in Greek' (Tansley, 1986, p.120).

On oracy tests in Greek and English two-thirds of the 20–30 Greek-speaking children tested made an overall improvement during the trial year and one-third stayed the same or did less well, though in English the results were affected by the ceiling effect of the test. Data on reading assessments in Greek for a small number of children showed that those able to complete a reading test made very good progress, and children tested in English also made good progress. The writing skills of almost all of the children tested in Greek improved, so that whereas at the beginning of the year over half the children could not write a simple sentence alone, at post-test all the children could, and some could write short stories in Greek. Most of the children tested also improved their writing skills in English. A case study of one Greek-speaking girl reveals some effects of the project (ibid., p.125)

Some other outcomes and effects of the project may be summarized in terms of the responses and attitudes of the schools, teachers, parents, communities and LEAs. Initially the project experienced indifferent or actively negative reactions by some mainstream schools which had been approached to participate. Even in the five schools which eventually agreed to participate, only five per cent of teachers responding to a questionnaire reported that ethnic minority children were encouraged to use their languages in the school, although by the end of the trial year teachers responding to a questionnaire had markedly increased their support for this behaviour. On the other hand, by the end of the trial year the percentage of teachers expecting pupils to speak English in the classroom had actually increased and there was no improvement in provision for all children to learn about each other's languages.

A particularly important issue in the mainstream schools where Greek was being trialled related to the use of teachers funded by the Greek Embassy and Cyprus High Commission. Mainstream teachers were apprehensive about the content of the classes, concerned that the children might be receiving religious or political instruction, and heads were unhappy about the presence of teachers in their schools who were not responsible to them and over whom they had no official control. There were also criticisms of the teachers' more formal teaching styles and sometimes lack of discipline in the classes. There were some changes in Greek and Cypriot teaching personnel due to the ending of their UK secondments. Moreover, some of the community teachers who faced English language problems of their own, for various reasons related to other commitments, age and personal beliefs, did not perceive favourably the project's philosophy of transferability, multiculturalism or methodology of language teaching based on a communicative dialect to standard approach rather than one focussing on literacy. This highlighted the importance of in-service training preceding any trials of new methodology and materials. In fact the most significant variables to emerge concerned teachers' attitudes. The mother-tongue teachers' qualifications, teaching experience, English language competence, familiarity with British primary school practice, personality and attitudes were important factors, but mainstream teachers' enthusiasm and willingness to understand and accommodate sometimes conflicting approaches were equally vital. These also had to be set in the context of the attitudes, expectations and support of the head and the rest of the staff.

As to the attitudes of parents the relative status of a language was an important consideration. Greek was perceived by many parents as having a higher status than Bengali and in one of the schools trialling Greek some middle-class parents were eager for their children to join the Greek classes. On the other hand, many of the Greek parents from established families considered achievement in English to be important and were a little concerned about time spent learning another language which might interfere with their child's progress in English. On the whole, however, they were reassured by events and most Greek-speaking parents who commented were pleased about the opportunity for their children to learn their mother tongue at school. But the political dimension of working with community groups was an undercurrent throughout the project. The Greek community was initially cautious and the choice of teachers proved difficult because of internal politics amongst the various Greek-speaking community groups. At the end of the day the four official bodies concerned with community mother-tongue teaching in Greek felt that the project's materials would have a limited impact and tend to be used to supplement the language programme materials already supplied free by their governments.

However, many individual teachers, especially those working with mainstream schools, have shown interest in the project's materials and the thinking behind the work. Indeed Tansley considered that, ironically, in view of the greater need for materials and support in the community sector, the project was likely to have a greater long-term impact in mainstream schools. In fact, in Haringey, the project was a contributory factor leading to pressure to formulate a policy on bilingualism and the realization by the LEA that a mainstream commitment to the development of mother-tongue teaching was required. Such a project represents an initiative towards greater collaboration between mainstream and community language teachers and provided an opportunity for increased awareness of the teachers' respective situations as well as the impetus to produce materials which can be used as a basis for further exchanges and co-operative developments. The experience of the Mother Tongue Project in attempting to form links between the community and mainstream sectors with respect to mother-tongue teaching should indicate to intending LEAs and schools some of the specific problems, of philosophy, practice and resources, as well as the benefits involved.

FURTHER ISSUES AND RESOURCE CONSTRAINTS   Throughout this consideration of mainstream provision for teaching Modern Greek and Turkish several issues and resource constraints serving to restrict developments have been encountered. In conclusion some of these will be reviewed briefly in respect of obligations, interests and feasibility in relation to mainstream provision.

One of the criteria for implementation of mother-tongue teaching in the mainstream is often the number of pupils speaking a minority language in a particular school or locality. As Derrick (1977) has argued, the presence of relatively large numbers of Greek-speaking pupils in a school should make it easier for the school to make decisions about the provision of mother-tongue instruction, especially if the community to which such pupils belong is fairly large and stable, considers the maintenance of its language and culture important, and is able to articulate its needs. There is abundant evidence to indicate that in certain areas of Greater London, and particularly in north London, these conditions apply, though, as yet, with the exception of a few long-running language option courses, provision is not widespread. But whilst it may be possible to introduce teaching in schools with a substantial number of pupils who share a mother tongue, demand may also exist from smaller numbers of other language speakers either in the same schools or others within the same LEA. In this case, teaching may be introduced in just one or two schools which may act as consortia within an LEA, and if this is made known, then parents may be able to choose to send their children to such a school (CRE, 1982). Thus it would, for example, be possible to avoid a situation where there was provision for the teaching of Greek to pupils of Greek Cypriot origin but none for the teaching of Turkish to pupils of Turkish Cypriot origin due to their generally smaller numbers in schools. Moreover, even though the research evidence suggests that mainstream provision for Modern Greek or Turkish in the areas of greatest Cypriot concentration is *ad hoc* or on an experimental basis, there is virtually no information on the availability of teaching of Modern Greek and Turkish to less numerous groups of mother-tongue speakers in towns and cities elsewhere in Britain.

Another factor of particular relevance with respect to Greek-speaking pupils is the implication of the EC's Directive in 1977 concerning the provision of mother-tongue teaching and culture in mainstream schooling for the children of migrant workers (GB. DES, 1982). Whilst this Directive – the catalyst for the current mother-tongue teaching debate – focusses on provision for the children of migrants, and in this sense would not apply to pupils of Cypriot origin whose parents are settled in the UK, it does nevertheless relate to Greek-speaking children of Greek parents of mainland origin. Greek nationals have been eligible to come to the UK more freely since Greece joined the EC in 1981, and there is evidence that they are particularly keen for their children to maintain their mother tongue, not least in the likelihood of a return to Greece (Archimandritou-Xefteris, 1977; Tsatsaroni and Papassava, 1986). The EC Directive will also apply to the children of Turkish migrant workers if Turkey becomes a full member of the EC. Indeed the Cyprus Turkish Association's evidence to the Swann Committee stated that 'a reasonably high percentage of our supporters and members are from mainland Turkey. Furthermore, Turkish children from mainland Turkey also attend our mother-tongue teaching classes' (Memdouh, 1981, p. xiv). The wider application of the EC Directive may have an impact on the extent of demand by Greek- and Turkish-speaking Cypriots (CRE, 1980).

Although some teaching of Modern Greek and Turkish already takes place in response to demand in a few schools the more widespread implementation of such teaching clearly involves considerable philosophical, logistical and methodological issues. A key factor is whether mainstream provision for Greek and Turkish is genuinely desired by Cypriot parents and by their children (see pp. 103–5). Since the inclusion of Modern Greek or Turkish in the mainstream curriculum would be most likely as a modern language (although at primary level it may be used as a basis from which to develop English), would this meet parents' interests in wanting their children to attend mother-tongue schools? Or could those only be satisfied by means of the cultural, ethnic and even religious orientation of community provision? Indeed might this not be complementary? Mainstream provision might not be seen as necessarily competitive in view of the avowed orientation of mother-tongue schools towards language development in a Cypriot, Greek or Turkish context rather than an emphasis on examination performance. Moreover, as the number of pupils from Cypriot backgrounds who have English as their first language grows, the argument for mainstream provision of Greek and Turkish as modern foreign languages, in which many pupils by virtue of their origins will have some interest, will gain ground. Clearly any intending mainstream providers have to be aware of such issues as the framework for consultation with the appropriate local Cypriot community, the role of the church and the place of religion in language teaching, the purpose and motivation for mother-tongue teaching and even the form of the language taught. The MTP project demonstrates that close knowledge of, and liaison with, the Cypriot community is vital even to initial exchanges between mainstream and community teachers. More research within the whole community is required to clarify perspectives.

Apart from other issues such as appropriate teaching materials (see pp.95–7), and examinations (see pp.108–9) the major constraint on the feasibility of more extensive provision for Greek and Turkish in the modern languages curriculum is the lack of suitably qualified and trained teachers. In 1982 a survey of 106 initial (ITT) and in-service (INSET) teacher training institutions in England and Wales (Craft and Atkins, 1983) revealed that nowhere could a graduate in Turkish or Greek obtain an appropriate training for teaching these languages. Moreover, there was apparently no specific interest in developing courses relating especially to those languages. A working party of the National Congress on Languages in Education in 1982 (Reid, 1984) recommended that both ITT and INSET courses should be systematically developed for 12 of the most widely used languages of minority communities, including Greek and Turkish, and welcomed the initiative of the Royal Society of Arts in setting up a one-year course leading to a certificate in the teaching of community languages. As a preparatory course leading to the RSA certificate, in 1983 Haringey College initiated a one-year evening course designed for those either already engaged in or intending to teach community languages but without formal teaching qualifications. The course also ran in 1985–6 (see *Mother Tongue News*, **4**, May 1984, p. 6, or **7**, August 1985, p. 14, for outline of course aims, and **6**, March 1985, p. 11, for some student responses). In 1984 Middlesex Polytechnic was a pilot centre for the RSA course in the teaching of community languages recruiting, for that year only, teachers of Greek. This ongoing course provides an important opportunity for community teachers and qualified teachers of other subjects in the mainstream sector to learn from one another and share expertise (Smith, 1984). However, given the apparent absence of widespread initiatives of this kind, and the lack of mention of Turkish, there is clearly considerable scope for further developments.

Since the availability of teachers qualified to teach Greek or Turkish in the modern languages curriculum of secondary schools is likely to remain limited for the foreseeable future (unless, perhaps, more Greek and Turkish Cypriots can be recruited into teaching and wish to teach Greek or Turkish), it is even more important for all teachers to be conscious of ways in which they can encourage, support and develop Greek, Turkish and other minority languages spoken by the pupils in their classrooms. However, in order to do this the class teacher, in turn, needs considerable support and information about language development and the languages most commonly encountered in schools. Taking the example of Greek, Rosen and Burgess illustrate the complexities involved and the extent to which teachers need to be informed:

> What differences are there between Cypriot Greek and mainland Greek? What are the differences between 'Dhimotiki' and 'Katharevousa'? What is known about the literate culture of Greek people in England (newspapers, books, religious works, etc.)? What works in English translation would be most useful to read? What are the special difficulties encountered by the Greek learners of English? (Rosen and Burgess, 1980, p. 170).

Clearly specific INSET courses are required to answer such questions in fine-tuned detail. However, there is a growing literature on ways in which teachers can support the mother-tongue skills of their pupils in ordinary classroom activities. One important booklet, *All Our Languages* (Houlton, 1985), developed as part of the MTP, offers guidelines to non-bilingual teachers who wish to develop strategies to recognize their pupils' home language in their day-to-day classroom practice (see also pp. 122–3).

This review, however, demonstrates that in recent years despite the relative groundswell of interest on the question of mother-tongue teaching and even support for mother-tongue speakers in the mainstream, and the evidence of substantial provision for Greek, and to a lesser extent Turkish, in community mother-tongue schools to meet the demands and interests of parents and children, it would appear that – except for a number of comparatively isolated cases – there has been little serious attempt to make provision for teaching Greek and Turkish in the mainstream. Thus although there may be an increased consciousness on the part of some teachers of the linguistic abilities of pupils whose first language is not English, this may have issued in controversy and debate about the philosophy and practice of language development and resource constraints, rather than examples of mainstream provision. Hence a statement made in the CILT report on *Less Commonly Taught Languages: Resources and Problems* over a decade ago in relation to all pupils with a mother tongue other than English would seem to apply with scarcely diminished force to pupils of Greek and Turkish Cypriot origin within the current educational context:

> No reliable statistics are available of the numbers of ... those .... who have Greek, Turkish ... as their mother tongues. We know however that they form part of the permanent population, and provide not only largely untapped resources for learning, but a virtually unexplored and undefined demand for teaching these languages, often in schools but also in further education. A lively demand for language maintenance certainly exists, if not yet for the use of such languages as media in education. The imperial responsibilities which remained in 1947 may well have been replaced by the domestic needs of 1975. But as yet there is little indication that these are being seriously studied in spite of much ostensible recognition given to the notions of multicultural and multiracial education. 'Immigrant' languages are still virtually ignored in schools except in so far as they get in the way of better English learning. Language maintenance is usually left to the immigrant communities to organize for themselves outside the public educational system. (CILT, 1975, p. 11)

TEACHING ENGLISH AS A SECOND LANGUAGE

The home background of pupils of Cypriot origin is usually predominantly Greek- or Turkish-speaking. Since the 1960s Cypriot children have tended to start school with little, if any, knowledge of English (Oakley, 1968). Despite the gradual acquisition of English by many Cypriot adults in succeeding years, this still appears to be largely true, even if parents may have been resident in the UK for 30 years or more (Clough and Quarmby, 1978). The oldest child in the family is particularly likely to start school with no English (Alkan and Constantinides, 1981). Beetlestone (1982), an infant teacher, has suggested, however, that whereas Greek Cypriot children tend to enter school knowing some English, Turkish Cypriot children tend to be exclusively Turkish-speaking. Sources have generally agreed that amongst the reasons why children of Cypriot origin tend to enter school with little or no English is the fact that they have often been exclusively looked after by family or Cypriot friends and have not had access to scarce pre-school facilities to stimulate play activity, general aptitude and language development, though such provision is widely recommended (GB. P. H of C, 1985; Anthias, 1983; Beetlestone, 1982; Alkan and Constantinides, 1981).

Since the first language of the overwhelming majority of second-generation Cypriot pupils, as well as those who arrived direct from Cyprus, is either Greek or Turkish, schools receiving such pupils have needed to give considerable attention to teaching them English in order that they might participate in mainstream English-medium schooling. Indeed Greek- and Turkish-speaking pupils, often in considerable numbers in certain schools, may have been amongst the first non-English-speaking pupils in some classes and with whom teachers had to devise strategies for teaching English as a second language (E2L). Over the 25 years or so during which Greek- and Turkish-speaking pupils have been present in British schools their E2L needs will have varied widely and will continue to do so with the arrival of the third generation in schools, according to family language background, with increasing knowledge of English and possibly a differential language shift between the Greek and Turkish speakers in the Cypriot population. It is, therefore, important to consider what is known of teachers' views of the English of pupils of Cypriot origin and the number thought to be in need of E2L teaching, the organizational arrangements for teaching E2L, any particular difficulties which might be experienced due to a difference in structure of the Greek, Turkish and English languages and recent approaches which may draw upon the pupil's mother tongue as a basis for E2L learning. However, since the following account is derived from research sources, it may not fully reflect the changes in thinking in this field and arrangements which have been made for teaching pupils E2L over the last 15 years or so because there appears to be far less documentation with respect to teaching E2L to Cypriot pupils compared with some other linguistic minority pupils. Nevertheless, this may not necessarily imply any less a degree of need.

Class teachers have usually been responsible for assessing the need of pupils from linguistic minority backgrounds for E2L teaching. In an ILEA survey, in 1965, Cypriot pupils formed the largest group out of 5,134 children who spoke 'little or no English'; some 2,000, one-fifth of the total number of Cypriot pupils in ILEA schools at that time, were said by their teachers to be 'those pupils who by reason of language difficulties were unable to follow a normal school curriculum with profit to themselves'. In a Schools Council survey in 65 LEAs across the country, in the same year, a further 2,000 Cypriot pupils were considered by their teachers to have 'inadequate English', 1,500 of these pupils being in the Haringey area (Schools Council, 1967). In 1975 a CRC investigation (1977) in eight urban education authorities (including Haringey and Hackney) found that the 46 teachers in 20 primary, middle and secondary schools considered that pupils of Cypriot origin, as well as some other ethnic minority pupils, had particular educational difficulties due to language. Teachers recognized that these difficulties were not necessarily confined to children born in Cyprus but that pupils of Cypriot origin born in the UK to a non-English-speaking mother might still enter primary school knowing no English. In schools in Brent, Camden, Haringey and Islington, in 1975, Clough and Quarmby (1978) found that infant teachers were concerned about Greek-speaking children who were said to learn English slowly in comparison with their Asian peers. However the ILEA Language Centre which they visited contained fewer Cypriot pupils of secondary school age than those from other linguistic minority groups, some 15 out of 110 11–15-year-olds. Moreover, Rosen and Burgess's (1980) survey in 28 secondary schools in 11 London boroughs revealed that only 12 per cent of both the 165 Greek-speaking and 97 Turkish-speaking pupils were considered by their teachers to be less than fluent speakers of English by the age of 11–22, thus suggesting that by this age most pupils of Cypriot origin may acquire a certain degree of competence in English.

Four ILEA language censuses provide evidence of the continuing need of some Greek-speaking and especially Turkish-speaking pupils for E2L teaching or support (see pp. 66–7). In the first census, in 1978, some 31.6 per cent of 3,802 pupils who had Greek as their first language and 44.5 per cent of 3,587 pupils who had Turkish as their first language were said by their teachers to be in need of additional English teaching (ILEA, 1979). In the subsequent censuses, in 1981, 1983 and 1985, around two-fifths to less than a half of pupils who used Greek other than or in addition to English at home, compared with just less than three-fifths to two-thirds of pupils who used Turkish other than or in addition to English at home, were said by their teachers to lack complete fluency in English. At every census just more than half the Greek speakers compared with considerably less than half the Turkish speakers who lacked complete competence in English were at the third stage of learning English (see Table 13, ILEA, 1982, 1983, 1986). Whilst it is possible that the relative fluency of these two groups of pupils may have been affected by differences in their age distribution (see pp. 56–7), the consistency of the difference in the proportion of Greek- and Turkish-speaking pupils rated as less than fully competent suggests that there is a real difference in the fluency of these two language groups as perceived by their teachers. Indeed the 1985 census suggests that as many as half of Greek-speaking pupils and two-thirds of Turkish-speaking pupils are in need of language support.

In another study in which 40 heads and teachers in a range of schools in Haringey were interviewed (Beetlestone, 1982) Turkish Cypriot children were seen as needing more E2L help than Greek Cypriot children. In explanation heads advanced a number of reasons, usually based on social or ethnic criteria, such as 'impoverished backgrounds' or 'less educated' parents; that the Turkish-Cypriot pupils were 'slower starters', some leaving the infants as non-readers; that they did not integrate as well socially, which was related to cultural differences, with Turkish Cypriot parents seen as 'not so forthcoming' or 'shyer' and that fewer Turkish than Greek Cypriot mothers had a good command of English, all suggesting that Turkish Cypriots were perceived as having a lower status than Greek Cypriots. Only two heads thought special linguistic differences or improved language teaching might make a difference. However, Beetlestone suggested that the language needs of Turkish Cypriot children were sometimes overlooked in schools, where they were either outnumbered by Greek Cypriot children or pupils from other ethnic minority backgrounds, and because they were British-born and teachers associated E2L needs with immigrant pupils. It was sometimes assumed that with the assistance of specialist teachers and in-service courses teachers were qualified to cope in the classroom or that nursery education was geared to meet E2L needs, but few Cypriot children were eligible for nursery places and many nursery assistants were not trained in E2L. Moreover, few heads were aware that problems with language structure might cause difficulties in secondary education for pupils of Cypriot origin. However, in another study involving secondary schools with numbers of pupils of Cypriot origin teachers suggested that their performance was hampered by difficulties with English and it was recognized that schools needed to make additional provision for E2L teaching (Martianou, 1981).

What evidence exists from research of the arrangements which LEAs and schools make for E2L teaching in relation to pupils of Cypriot origin? According to Bhatnagar (1970), in the early 1960s when many Cypriot pupils were arriving in schools in London, the Borough of Haringey operated a *laissez-faire* policy with respect to English language teaching, so that each headteacher made his own arrangements, which usually meant E2L teaching for Cypriot pupils on a withdrawal basis. Thereafter there has been a progressive phasing out of this arrangement and greater use of E2L specialist help in the classroom (see p. 43–4). An early study by Kawwa (1963) in one large secondary school in Islington showed that a wide range of immigrant children were receiving special English tuition in the remedial department including 79 Greek-speaking and 28 Turkish-speaking Cypriots, who constituted the largest proportion of non-English-speaking pupils. In 1971 Townsend reported that across the country 71 LEAs at secondary level and most at junior and infant level had created a range of E2L teaching arrangements which varied from additional tuition in the pupil's own class to peripatetic teaching, attendance at language centres on a full- or part-time basis, and full-time classes on a withdrawal basis in school, or part-time teaching at home. Although no specific information was available from this survey about the particular arrangements made for E2L teaching to pupils of Cypriot origin, Townsend noted that LEAs with such pupils were tackling E2L teaching with some urgency. In a follow-up survey of language teaching in 132 primary schools and 98 secondary schools Townsend and Brittan (1972) found that many of the headteachers in the 34 infant schools where there were greater concentrations of non-English-speaking infant pupils, such as pupils of Cypriot origin, tended to make special arrangements for language teaching. Indeed some saw the fact that Cypriot pupils came from non-English-speaking homes as in itself necessitating special treatment, and some schools reported receiving requests from Greek- and Turkish-speaking parents themselves for English language tuition (see p. 78). In the mid-1970s certain London boroughs such as Haringey, Camden and Islington recognized the need to organize crash-courses for the Cypriot refugee children arriving in schools and instituted a system whereby children attended language centres for half a day and then returned to their own schools, with the aim that they might be able to integrate with other children as soon as possible. It was said that girls had made more progress than boys, but that all had mastered English in three years and had started to make progress in other subject-areas (McCarty and Christoudoulou, 1977) In a Community Relations Commission (CRC) survey in 1975, involving interviews with 700 parents in eight urban areas, including Haringey and Hackney, only 16 per cent of 51 Cypriot parents said that their child had attended special schools or classes to help with learning English. Yet this proportion – the same as that for children of Pakistani parents – was the highest for any of the five ethnic minority groups. Cypriot parents whose children had not attended special schools or classes were less likely than Asian parents to think that it would have been helpful if the children had done so, as many thought that their children already spoke English. Indeed the Swann Report (GB. P. H of C, 1985) deprecated the practice of withdrawing pupils for language help, whether within schools or to separate language centres, partly because it is seen as potentially hindering socialization and promoting negative images of withdrawn pupils. Concern was also expressed about the 'lack of structured and ongoing language support beyond the straightforward "survival" stage'; the risk of second language learners being classified as slow learners or remedial when they needed further language help; and the inappropriateness of teaching materials for second-stage learners.

In view of the assessment of teachers that many Greek-speaking pupils, especially those in the younger age ranges, are in need of E2L teaching or additional English tuition (see pp. 118–19), are there particular difficulties for pupils of Cypriot origin in learning English? To what extent are the structures of the Greek, Turkish and English languages different, and how may this influence the learning of English for pupils whose first language is Greek or Turkish? The extent to which pupils of Cypriot origin have a knowledge of their mother tongue is germane to any consideration of their educational achievement in English-medium schooling both in the way in which it may affect their acquisition of or proficiency in English, and in the way in which it may be seen as enriching their own personal linguistic repertoire and the linguistic vitality of their school environment. However, until relatively recently reference to the mother tongues of linguistic minority pupils has usually been to the way in which these have been seen to interfere with the learning of English in mainstream schooling. For example, teachers in the infant and junior schools visited by Clough and Quarmby (1978) in Brent, Camden, Haringey and Islington in 1975 expressed concern about Greek Cypriot pupils learning English as their only opportunity to do so was in school and their parents emphasized their attendance at Greek classes on week-day evenings. Similarly, Derrick (1977) reported some teachers' concern that attendance at mother-tongue schools slowed down a child's development in English, and noted an agreement with one Greek community that children would not attend Greek classes until the age of seven, so that learning to read and write in Greek would not interfere in the development of literacy in English. Furthermore, the Swann Report recorded that several heads and teachers with Cypriot pupils had reported 'the noticeable effects which extended visits to Cyprus, which often required pupils leaving before the end of the school term, had on the level of English of especially the youngest children' (GB. P. H of C, 1985).

According to Derrick (1977), in the mid-1970s teachers were recommended to familiarize themselves with a descriptive knowledge of their pupils' first languages, so that they might understand mother-tongue interference in mastering English grammar or pronunciation. Yet it may be doubted to what extent hard-pressed teachers who are not E2L specialists have had occasion to acquire an understanding of these particular difficulties from the point of view of the Greek or Turkish speaker, even if materials were available to enable them to do so. Two guides compiled by CILT (1982, 1983) indicate some similarities and differences between Greek, Turkish and English (see p. 50). For example, both Greek and Turkish are phonetic languages, but English is not. Modern Greek is written in its original script and often with tones and breathing marks. It lacks an infinitive, but has much flexibility in word order. Although spelling may cause confusion, even to native language users, pronunciation follows a number of relatively simple rules. There are not many different sounds in Greek since it has only five vowels and 18 consonants compared with 12 and 22 respectively in English. Many Greek Cypriot children apparently have difficulty in recognizing Greek words in the English language (although 12 per cent are derived from Greek), for whilst Greek is phonetic, these words are not always translated phonetically into English and may be pronounced differently (Alkan and Constantinides, 1981). Georgiou (1983) has claimed that the main problem for Greek Cypriot children is spelling as Greek is spelt phonetically, so a child may try to spell English in the same way which does not always apply, and other teachers have noted 'poor vocabulary' (GB. P. H of C, 1985). Western Turkish – the form of Turkish spoken by pupils of Cypriot origin – is easier to write than Greek as it shares the Latin alphabet with English. There are, however, two major differences between Turkish and English. Although Turkish has a regular structure, the syntax is very different from English and hence the construction of sentences might cause considerable difficulty for the Turkish-speaking Cypriot pupil learning English. Secondly, the word structure is different with a sequence of suffixes added to an unchanging root, and the sequence of vowels occurring within the word are subject to laws of vowel harmony. Moreover, unlike Greek, there are few words which Turkish has in common with other Indo-European languages.

To date, it would appear that relatively little attention has been paid in detail to the differences between Greek, Turkish and English and teachers' understanding of the implications for pupils whose mother tongue is Greek or Turkish and who are learning English. However, a handbook from the Schools Council Project in English for Immigrant Children considered the particular pronunciation problems of pupils of Cypriot origin (Rudd, 1971). Moreover, although LEAs still focus on E2L as such, there is some limited but growing evidence of schools and LEAs beginning to recognize the mother tongues of pupils learning English as a second language either by directly developing skills in the pupil's first language as a basis for learning E2L or supporting a pupil's first language in the ordinary classroom. A national CRC survey in 1980–2 (Tsow, 1983) found that only very few LEAs responding had made arrangements to develop the mother tongue as a medium for teaching English as a second language. Turkish was amongst the languages mentioned. A Schools Council survey (Tansley and Craft, 1984) discovered that although Greek was named by seven LEAs and Turkish by three LEAs as languages occurring most frequently in primary schools with at least ten per cent bilingual pupils, Turkish was more likely than Greek to receive support – but only as part of the curriculum of seven primary schools. There are other reports of some teachers favouring a bilingual approach to E2L in Haringey (Beetlestone, 1982) and recognition being given to the mother tongue of bilingual pupils, including Greek-speaking children, as part of the day-to-day work of the classroom in Hackney (Houlton, 1984). In this, bilingual parents may be employed as aides in the classroom, especially in story-telling sessions, for as yet there appear from a survey in 1980–4 to be relatively few bilingual nursery assistants in training, though many more speakers of Greek than Turkish (Rathbone and Graham, 1983). However, as teachers contributing to the Schools Council/National Council for Mother Tongue Teaching Conference, 'Greek Outside Greece', recognized, there are a number of constraints facing monolingual teachers who wish to give more recognition to their pupils' home languages such as the claimed ambivalence of some bilingual parents towards the mother tongue; shortage of suitable classroom resources; teachers having insufficient information about the languages of their pupils; and resistance from other colleagues who are unconvinced of the importance of the mother tongue or uncertain about support in the normal classroom (Houlton, 1984). Indeed few teachers interviewed by Beetlestone (1982) recognized that the way in which the child's language is valued in the school might affect the way in which the child might learn.

Over the past ten years several reports, for example, the Bullock Report (GB. DES, 1975) and the Swann Report (GB. P. H of C, 1985), have recommended that schools should operate a language across the curriculum policy, in which all teachers should be involved, and that structured language support should be provided for E2L learners within the normal class. However, institutions engaged in initial and in-service teacher training are more likely to offer E2L courses as such, rather than preparing teachers to offer language support across the curriculum or to develop strategies for working in multilingual classrooms (Craft and Atkins, 1983). However, during the past decade several curriculum development projects have focussed on supporting children's bilingualism in relation to E2L learning. Some projects and materials which specifically relate to Greek- and/or Turkish-speaking pupils are briefly outlined here (see also pp. 202–4).

The Schools Council Language in the Multicultural Primary Classroom Project (1981–3), which involved teachers in Haringey and three other LEAs, was an action research project whereby class teachers explored the linguistic resources and cultural experiences of E2L learners, devised strategies to meet their language development needs and acknowledged the enriching contributions which their different experiences could bring to the curriculum for all children. Several broadsheets, tape–slide sequences and films are available from SCDC publications and Drake Educational (see also Mottram *et al.*, 1983). Part of another Schools Council/EC project, The Mother Tongue Project (1981–5) (see pp. 96–7, 111–14), also focussed on developing a handbook for monolingual teachers which outlines strategies for supporting classroom language diversity across the curriculum. The handbook *All Our Languages* (Houlton, 1985) was used in trials by 22 LEAs and over 150 teachers. Other project publications (Houlton and Willey, 1983; Tansley, 1986) examine issues of implementation and list a wide range of teaching materials which can be adapted for use in the teaching of any language (Manley, 1986). The EC-funded Children's Language Project (1983–4) has produced a teacher's book and activity packs of cards which focus on a theme based on particular aspects of children's language experience, with suggested follow-up activities for class and group work, as a starting-point from which teachers and pupils can explore the many forms of language which exist around them at home, at school and the neighbourhood.

A few materials have specifically set out to enable pupils to build on their knowledge of Greek or Turkish whilst learning E2L. Most publications relate to the primary age range, but unusually the Centre For Urban Educational Studies' Bilingual Education Project, set up in 1977, devised bilingual Greek–English and Turkish–English materials for recently arrived pupils of secondary age (1982; see also Wright, 1980). The *World in a City* materials, which provide survival information in a range of areas, are suitable for use in various learning situations and offer opportunities to practise developing particular skills. The Learning Materials for Ethnic Minority Groups Project which began in 1982 has been collecting oral material in several community languages, including Greek and Turkish, to use in the production of teaching materials in mother tongues and English; it has been involved with 16 schools from pre-school to secondary level in Haringey, Enfield and Barnet. The resulting series – Luzac story-tellers (several stories, fables and fairy-tales) – are available in a range of bilingual versions including Greek–English and Turkish–English. Other books and materials include: Ezra Jack Keats's books with Greek/Turkish–English texts; Terraced House books (in English) with stick-on words, and available in Turkish; and Co-print cut-and-paste lettering available in Greek with ideas for making materials (see Manley, 1986 pp. 36, 35, 39). In 1984–5 the BBC Radio 4 *Mother Tongue Song and Story* programme for four to seven year-olds included two stories, one using Greek and the other Turkish as spoken in Cyprus together with English, in its broadcasts, and produced an accompanying booklet. Islington Libraries and the Turkish Education Group have produced a bilingual video for Turkish-speaking children aged five to seven years, which offers children an opportunity to use their language skills (see the Mother Tongue Project newsletter, *Mother Tongue News,* **6**, March 1985 and **7**, August 1985). Other materials developed specifically to teach Greek and Turkish in mainstream and community classes are reviewed elsewhere (see pp. 95–7).

Overall the evidence indicates that many pupils of Cypriot origin, especially from Turkish-speaking backgrounds, still enter school with relatively little knowledge of English. Schools still focus on E2L teaching as such, though there is a gradual move towards supporting children's language development, sometimes using the home language as a basis for developing E2L, in the normal classroom situation, especially in those LEAs where pupils from Greek- and Turkish-speaking backgrounds are most numerous. Nevertheless, class teachers often need more information about these languages and the way in which they may influence their speakers' acquisition of English. Indeed teachers' assessments suggest that many Turkish- and Greek-speaking pupils may continue to need English-language support throughout their experience of schooling.

ENGLISH PROFICIENCY

In view of teachers' assessments of the language knowledge of pupils of Cypriot origin, and their perceived need on entering school to learn English as a second language, an examination of the performance of pupils of Cypriot origin on tests of English, and especially reading, is important complementary evidence when evaluating their attainment in English and their general educational achievement. Most of the evidence for the performance of Cypriot pupils in English and reading is derived from large-scale surveys undertaken by the ILEA on certain cohorts of pupils, either at transfer to secondary school or, in the case of reading, longitudinally over a period of seven years. Some other data from small-scale studies also exist. Thus the English-language development of pupils of Cypriot origin during their schooling can be checked over time, in relation to that of other pupils for whom English is not a first language, and distinctions can be drawn between the performance of Greek- and Turkish-speaking pupils.

Assessment of performance in tests of English proficiency, is available mainly from the two ILEA transfer surveys undertaken in 1966 and 1968 (Little *et al.*, 1968; Little, 1975a). In the first survey information was collected on the performance of 237 Cypriot pupils who represented 23 per cent of 1,051 immigrant pupils in the sample of 52 schools with more than a third immigrant pupils. The total number of immigrant pupils in these schools formed a quarter of the immigrant pupils aged 10–11 transferring to secondary education in 1966. Pupils were assigned on the basis of their teachers' assessments of attainment in English and scores on specific tests to one of seven profile groups. A mere six per cent of Cypriot pupils were placed in the top groups, one and two, compared with 57 per cent in the bottom groups, six and seven. Interestingly, the same percentages of Cypriot pupils were placed in the two top and bottom profile groups for verbal reasoning, though the distribution between the groups was different. The performance of Cypriot pupils was between the performance of Indian and Pakistani pupils and that of West Indian pupils. However, each of the groups of immigrant pupils had a distribution of performance which was significantly different from that of ILEA pupils as a whole (at the 0.01 level). When a further analysis was undertaken of the performance of pupils who were judged by their teachers to speak at least some English, almost twice as many Cypriot pupils (11 per cent of 124 pupils) were placed in groups one and two for English, although 35 per cent were still placed in groups six and seven. Indeed, in this analysis, the profile distribution of the Cypriot pupils was seen to be considerably superior to that of West Indian pupils. Unfortunately, no information was provided on the influence of length of schooling on these findings.

In the second ILEA transfer survey, undertaken in 1968, an analysis was made of the distribution of performance of 4,269 immigrant and 22,023 non-immigrant pupils according to their placement in seven profile groups for English. Teachers in primary schools ranked pupils in order of merit and provisionally assigned each to a group. Each child was then tested in English, the tests were marked in the school and the results were collated centrally. Schools then made a decision on which pupil was to be assigned to which group in the light of information as to the number of pupils who would be expected to fall in each of the seven groups compared with all pupils in the authority. This survey again involved a considerable amount of assessment by teachers in the pupils' own schools. To some extent, therefore, the findings may be compared with teachers' assessments of pupils' competence in English in subsequent ILEA language censuses (see pp. 66–7). Although in reporting the findings of the 1968 transfer survey Little (1975a) does not state the number of Greek and Turkish Cypriot pupils who were involved, it is clear that, as with other immigrant pupils, their distribution in the profile groups for English was inferior to that of non-immigrant pupils. Indeed only 8.1 per cent of Greek Cypriots and a mere 2.2 per cent of Turkish Cypriots were placed in groups one and two, compared with 50.3 per cent and 65.2 per cent respectively in groups six and seven for English. The performance of the Greek Cypriot pupils was very similar to that of the performance of immigrant pupils on average as a whole. It was inferior to the performance of Indian and Pakistani pupils in English but better than that of West Indian pupils, whereas the performance of Turkish Cypriot pupils, which was clearly inferior to that of their Greek counterparts, was in addition the lowest of all the immigrant pupils. Once again, there was no analysis according to length of stay or schooling of the Cypriot pupils. The distribution of performance of the 1968 cohort of Cypriot pupils as a whole was very similar to that for the 1966 cohort on transfer to secondary education. Thus early, the performance of pupils of Cypriot origin, particularly that of pupils of Turkish Cypriot origin, must have been a matter for some concern.

Research undertaken by Bhatnagar (1970) involving all the pupils of Cypriot and West Indian origin and a control group of British pupils in one secondary school in Haringey provides further complementary and comparative evidence. Proficiency in English was assessed on a five-point scale by teachers for written English, by the researcher for fluency of spoken English, and using the 68-item Mill Hill Vocabulary Scale Form 1 Senior for vocabulary. As might be expected, in all three areas of English the control group of 100 English pupils had superior levels of performance over those of the 76 Cypriot and 174 West Indian pupils (significant at the one per cent level). In all three areas, although the West Indian pupils' mean score was higher than that of the Cypriot pupils, the difference did not reach significance. There were inconsistent sex differences with, for example, the West Indian girls having a higher mean score for written English than Cypriot girls who had a significantly higher score (at the five per cent level) for spoken English, whereas West Indian boys had a significantly higher score (0.01 per cent) than Cypriot boys for spoken English. Although these findings are limited to one school and across the whole age range, they nevertheless confirm the inferior performance in English of pupils of Cypriot origin compared with that of their English peers and point tentatively to some possible differences between the performance in English of Cypriot pupils and West Indian pupils.

The Mill Hill Vocabulary Scale was also administered, in conjunction with Raven's Progressive Matrices (see pp. 48–9), by MacDonald (1975) as part of a battery of tests of English given to a sample of 114 Jamaican, 65 Greek and Turkish, and 55 British students in a further education college in Stoke Newington. There was no significant difference in the performance of the Greek and Turkish students compared with the Jamaican students, but there was a significant difference (at the 0.05 level) between that of the Greek and Turkish students and the British students. Moreover, there was a significant difference in performance (at the 0.05 level) in favour of the Greek students over the Turkish students on the Mill Hill Vocabulary Scale, though this finding must be interpreted with caution due to the small numbers involved.

Proficiency in English was also assessed by a range of tests including some which were specially constructed. All the students in the study were aiming to pass English at O-level or CSE grades. Performance on the 100-item multiple-choice tests showed that the Greek and Turkish, as well as the Jamaican students, found it easier to recognize 'Standard English' than to produce it. Greek and Turkish speakers had significantly higher mean scores (at the 0.05 level) than Jamaican students though their scores were, in turn, significantly lower, at the same level, than those of their British peers. Again, the Greek speakers, in both year groups (1972–3 and 1973–4) performed significantly better on the first test (at the 0.05 level) compared with their Turkish peers and in the first year (at the 0.01 level) on the second test. A repeat of the second test produced the same performance differentials between the three main groups of students. On the first of the two essay tests on 'Myself' the Greek and Turkish speakers had significantly fewer structural errors than Jamaican students (0.05 level), but again significantly more errors than their British peers (0.05 level). On the second essay test on 'The college' the Jamaican students had significantly more lexical errors (0.05 level) than the Greek and Turkish students. There was little difference in the performance of the Jamaican and Greek and Turkish students on either the written or the oral version of the picture test; both groups made more errors on the written form. Overall the differences between the Greek and Turkish speakers were less than those between them as a group and the Jamaican students, although MacDonald argued that these speakers generally had equal difficulty in producing Standard English. Interestingly, MacDonald found that although there was no significant relationship between the performance of the Greek and Turkish speakers on the English test battery, whether they had been born in the UK or not, there was a significant relationship (at the 0.01 level) between their years of education in the UK and also intention to settle in the UK and their examination performance in English at GCE O-level and CSE. These detailed findings are of interest in an analysis of the English-language difficulties experienced by pupils of Cypriot and West Indian origin, especially in coping with written English, as Bhatnagar's teachers' assessments also revealed. It appears that this difficulty may persist throughout the years of education.

Reading performance
The reading performance of pupils of Cypriot origin has been documented in the longitudinal ILEA literacy survey which commenced in 1968. The reading attainment of some 32,000 pupils aged eight was assesssed by means of the group-administered NFER SRA Sentence Completion Test involving silent reading and comprehension. Early findings (ILEA, 1969) revealed that the reading standards of immigrant pupils (mean 87.4) were markedly lower than those of non-immigrants, although even the mean score for the children of UK origin (at 96.9) was below the standard mean. On average the proportion of immigrants who were classified as poor readers with scores of less than 80 was almost double the proportion of non-immigrants who were poor readers: 28.5 per cent compared with 14.8 per cent. There was no difference in the proportion of West Indian and Greek Cypriot pupils aged eight who were poor readers (about 30 per cent), although these groups had slightly higher proportions classified as poor readers compared with the proportion of immigrants on average. But the proportion of poor readers amongst the Turkish Cypriot pupils (45.5 per cent) was more than three times the proportion of poor readers of UK origin. Clearly, once again (see also pp. 65-7) the reading performance of the Turkish Cypriot pupils, with a much higher proportion of poor readers, was inferior to that of the Greek Cypriot pupils. In a subsequent further analysis of this age group (Little, 1975a) the attainment of 381 Greek Cypriot pupils was very similar (ranging from 85.6 to 88.7), regardless of the degree of concentration of immigrant pupils in schools, whereas amongst the 264 Turkish Cypriot pupils there was no clear pattern in the relationship between reading attainment (ranging from 79.2 to 87.1) and immigrant concentration in schools, although the differences between the sub-groups were much larger. These mean scores show that the Turkish Cypriot pupils' performance in reading was below that of Greek Cypriot pupils; the mean reading score of the group of Cypriot pupils was below the mean reading score of immigrant pupils as a whole, and also of pupils in London as a whole; and they were themselves below the national standard mean. Thus at age eight Turkish and Greek Cypriot pupils had a reading age from just over a year to two years behind their chronological age.

It is interesting at this point to compare the reading performance of pupils aged ten plus in one London borough – as measured by the same reading test administered as part of a larger investigation in 1970 by Yule *et al.*, (1975). The mean reading scores of the 34 Greek Cypriot (84.2), 42 Turkish Cypriot (86.5) and 335 West Indian pupils (85.3) were significantly lower (at the 0.001 level) than that of the 1,660 indigenous pupils (94.8). Contrary to other findings, the Greek Cypriot pupils in this study actually had a slightly lower mean reading score than Turkish Cypriot pupils.

Interestingly, there was a significant difference (at the 0.01 level) in the reading performance of Turkish Cypriot pupils in favour of those born in the UK (UK-born 93.8, immigrant 79.3), whereas this did not obtain for Greek Cypriot pupils. Yule *et al.* claimed that their finding of particularly poor reading attainment amongst children of Cypriot parents replicated that of the ILEA Survey in 1968 (ILEA, 1969) and was 'both striking and worthy of further detailed investigation' (p. 12). However, subsequently – probably due to their larger numbers – the achievement of West Indian pupils has been the focus of attention. Overall findings indicate that though the mean reading scores of UK-born Cypriot pupils were closer to those of indigenous pupils, they were still inferior and indeed further below the national norm. However, it can be seen how such data may have given rise to the view prevalent in the 1970s that the reading attainment of such pupils would improve with length of stay or schooling in the UK.

But was this borne out? Such an hypothesis may be examined by returning to a consideration of the longitudinal ILEA literacy survey data. In 1971 the same cohort of pupils who were tested at age eight in 1968 were tested again at the ages of ten to 11 using the parallel SRB version of the NFER sentence completion reading test (ILEA, 1972). Once again, the attainment of immigrant pupils was markedly lower – on average a ten-point mean difference – than that of non-immigrants (96.2). The proportion of poor immigrant readers and the pattern of differences observed between the immigrant groups in 1968 were largely the same in 1971. Whereas Greek Cypriot pupils (86.1) occupied a mid-position after a mixed group of immigrant pupils and Indian pupils, as before the Turkish Cypriot pupils had the lowest mean reading score (82.3).

The final testing of pupils, in 1976, took place when they were aged 15. Mabey (1981) presented data for those children with complete test scores at eight, ten and 15 plus, so that a longitudinal assessment of progress might be made for the same group of children. Hence the number of pupils involved was much smaller than those in the original cohort. According to an ILEA report (1977), 21,122 pupils or 71 per cent of the original cohort were still attending ILEA schools at 15 plus and completed the NFER EH1 Reading Test, again a sentence-completion-type measure. However, of the original cohort, only some 62 per cent of Greek-speaking and 64 per cent of Turkish-speaking Cypriots remained, over a third of both groups having moved out of inner London during their schooling (see also p. 10). It was suggested that the mobility rate reflected differences between the groups in the occupational level and social class of parents, as in 1968 and 1971 it had been found that apart from West Indians and to a lesser extent Turkish Cypriots, the immigrants tended to be much more middle class than the indigenous population in inner London.

According to figures presented by Mabey (1981), which tended to be higher for those pupils tested on all three occasions, no group at any stage was reading at a level expected for its age on the basis of a national sample (see Table 18). Over the three occasions of testing only the mean for the Greek-speaking Cypriots remained constant, though at some 10–11 points below that of the UK group. In fact only the scores of the West Indian and Turkish Cypriot pupils declined during the period of their schooling on each of the three occasions when they were tested at eight, ten and 15 plus. Although the actual mean score of the Turkish Cypriots was the lowest for any of the groups at age 15, the West Indian pupils seemed to have deteriorated more markedly in their performance over their years of schooling – by more than 2 points. The ranking of the different ethnic groups was virtually identical on all three occasions, so that the Turkish Cypriot pupils were always ranked the lowest, whereas the Greek-speaking Cypriots improved slightly from seventh to sixth position between age eight and ten. When a further analysis was undertaken according to length of education, all the groups which had partial primary education made considerable improvement in their reading attainment between age eight and 15, with the exception of Greek Cypriots and West Indians who improved less than one point. Only the Turkish Cypriots and the West Indians fully educated in the UK had a lower reading attainment at 15 (by almost three points for the Turkish Cypriots) and hence their reading level had actually deteriorated during their years of schooling.

Table 18:   Mean reading scores at eight, ten and 15 years, by ethnic group, ILEA Literacy Survey, 1968, 1971 and 1976

Age in years	UK	WI	IND	PAK	GC	TC
8	98.1	88.1	89.6	91.1	87.3	85.4
10	98.3	87.4	89.6	93.1	87.8	85.0
15	97.8	85.9	91.4	94.9	87.6	84.9
N	12,530	1,465	137	74	194	139

Note: UK = United Kingdom; WI = West Indies; IND = India; PAK = Pakistan; GC = Cyprus, Greek-speaking; TC = Cyprus, Turkish speaking; pupils from these groups according to DES definition and teachers' assessments.
Source: Adapted from Mabey, 1981, Table 1.

This limited analysis indicated important differences in the effect of schooling on the reading attainment of the two groups of Cypriot pupils (see Table 19). The findings appeared to indicate that whilst UK schooling of any length was important for Greek Cypriot pupils to maintain or improve their reading performance, that of Turkish Cypriot pupils actually deteriorated with length of UK schooling. As Mabey commented, the performance of the Turkish Cypriots at roughly the same level as the West Indian pupils is interesting, but unfortunately the small numbers of Turkish Cypriot pupils in the study did not permit a more detailed analysis of various socioeconomic and school-based factors as was possible for West Indian pupils. Indeed it would seem that the absence of concentrations of pupils of Turkish Cypriot origin – their very encapsulation as a minority within a minority – has contributed to the complete lack of attention given to their consistently low performance on reading tests (and also on measures of IQ). Hardly a note of concern has been expressed. In the absence of social class and school background data from the ILEA literacy survey on this group of pupils, it is only possible to speculate about the extent to which their position as a minority within the Cypriot community *vis-à-vis* other immigrant communities – particularly other Muslim communities – specific school factors and matters of cultural orientation as well as particular difficulties for this group in learning English may account for the real deterioration in reading performance during their years of schooling. From an educational viewpoint it would, therefore, have seemed a matter of expediency for specific research to have been conducted into the performance of pupils of Turkish Cypriot origin during the last decade since the Literacy Survey was undertaken.

At about that time, MacDonald (1975; see pp. 125–6), also examined reading performance on the 60-item Manchester Reading Test of Greek, Turkish and Jamaican students in comparison with that of their British peers in a further education college in Stoke Newington. Although the Greek- and Turkish-speaking students performed at a significantly lower level than British students, their performance was significantly higher than that of their Jamaican peers (at the 0.05

Table 19: Mean reading scores at eight, ten and 15 years of Greek and Turkish Cypriot pupils in ILEA Literacy Survey, by amount of education in the UK

	Age	Fully educated	Full junior education	Partial primary education
Greek Cypriots	8	88.8	87.7	81.6
	10	89.4	88.1	82.5
	15	88.7	90.7	82.4
	N	136	15	30
Turkish Cypriots	8	87.5	79.2	78.3
	10	85.6	80.4	82.0
	15	84.8	79.0	85.0
	N	95	11	23

Source: Adapted from Mabey, 1981, Table 4.

level). Moreover, for all three sub-samples there was a significant positive correlation (at the 0.01 level) between results on the Manchester Reading Test and two multiple-choice tests, which suggested a common test element of reading comprehension or proficiency in Standard English. For the Greek and Turkish Cypriots, the number of years of UK education and intention to settle were again both significantly related (at the 0.01 level) to their performance on the Manchester Reading Test. The Greek Cypriots in the first-year group performed at a significantly higher level (0.05) than their Turkish peers on this test. Similar significantly different performance levels between the Jamaican, Greek and Turkish, and British students were found on a test of listening discrimination.

Overall findings on the performance of pupils of Cypriot origin on tests of English proficiency and on reading are clear, in accordance with teachers' assessments (see pp. 65–7), and show a remarkable degree of consistency. Evidence from the 1960s and 1970s showed that the performance of the Cypriot group as a whole on measures of English was poor, both in relation to other ethnic minority groups and to white British peers in neighbourhood schools, whose performance in English and on reading tests may in itself be lower than that nationally. Moreover, a distinction must be made between Greek- and Turkish-speaking Cypriots in this area of performance, as also in that of intelligence testing. For not only has the attainment in English of Turkish Cypriot pupils been lower than that of their Greek Cypriot peers, but it has in most cases been at a similarly low, if not lower, level than that of pupils of West Indian origin, about whom generally so much concern has been expressed. Hence it remains an interesting question as to why Turkish Cypriot parents themselves do not appear to have voiced greater concern about their children's performance, and also why their performance does not appear from publicly available evidence to have received detailed investigation within the ILEA since its Literacy Survey or by other outer London boroughs known to have relatively large numbers of Turkish Cypriot pupils in their schools. Apparently the London Borough of Haringey undertook a monitoring and screening programme in 1977 and analysis revealed clear differences between the performance of Greek- and Turkish-speaking pupils on Schonell, Spooncer and Carver reading tests with Turkish Cypriot pupils having the lowest level of reading attainment (Sharma, 1979, quoted by Beetlestone, 1982). More recently, a longitudinal study of 2,000 pupils in 50 randomly selected primary schools in the ILEA from age seven to secondary transfer discovered that Greek- and Turkish-speaking pupils continued to have significantly lower reading scores on entry to the junior school (Mortimore *et al.*, 1986).

With these exceptions, it would appear that pupils of Turkish Cypriot or even Greek Cypriot origin have generally not been the special focus of concern despite their low performance levels as indicated by research. Indeed in schools they may be perceived as a composite Cypriot group and their particular difficulties and needs in learning English, especially in the early years of schooling, may have been overlooked. Yet, given the research findings of lower literacy skills in English for Turkish-speaking adults, greater use of Turkish in the home and less access to Turkish mother-tongue schools compared with Greek-speaking adults, homes and communities, the language development needs of Turkish-speaking pupils in particular might have been considered to warrant greater attention. However, even relatively small-scale practical innovations, such as that described by Tizard *et al.* (1982), which involved collaboration between teachers and parents in assisting children's reading, may have a distinctive and lasting effect. This experimental study was carried out in six multiracial infant and six junior schools in Haringey in 1976–9 and included Greek and Turkish Cypriot pupils amongst the total of 1869 pupils. The one-year intervention project, compared the reading performance of three groups of pupils: one group which had practised reading at home to their parents from books selected by their class teachers; a control group with an ordinary teaching programme; and another group which had extra reading tuition at school. The pupils who were involved in the collaborative reading programme had higher mean scores on a battery of reading tests (Southgate Group Reading Test, NFER Test A and BD, Carver Word Recognition Test and Spooncer Group Reading Assessment). There was an improvement right across the ability range, and particularly amongst poor readers, which was maintained at the end of the second year of the project and one year after the project had ended when these children's reading performance was still superior to that of the other groups. Moreover, some parents with little formal education became excellent home reading supervisors, and parents who could not speak English adequately in the school environment were often found to do so in their own domestic situations. Many of the non-literate parents who spoke languages other than English placed a particularly high value on literacy in English and supported the programme and the closer contact which it meant with their children's school. The children clearly had great satisfaction in reading aloud in English to their parents, and this was in itself beneficial despite the limited correction of errors which their parents were able to make. Moreover, the children gradually came to take greater responsibility for their own learning, supervised their book exchange scheme and were reported by their teachers to be better behaved, motivated and more satisfying to teach. The project also led to greater parental support in other school activities. Although teachers' professional skills and responsibilities to encourage the language development of pupils whose first language is not English should not be underestimated, it is clear that collaborative innovations combining the resources of teachers, parents and pupils can positively affect pupils' reading performance and their adjustment and social and linguistic development as well as fostering home–school involvement and, in particular, promoting better understanding of and involvement with their children's schooling by their parents.

Mathematics and Other Curricular Areas
As in other curricular areas, with the exception of English, there is relatively little research evidence on the attainment of pupils of Cypriot origin in mathematics. Of four studies which include information on achievement in mathematics, two are large-scale, involving cohorts of pupils on transfer to secondary education in the ILEA in 1966 and 1968, and two are of relatively small-scale, one of which focusses on pupils of mainland Greek origin in relation to whom some illuminating comparisons with pupils of Cypriot origin may be made.

The 1966 ILEA transfer survey of pupils from primary to secondary education included some 237 Cypriot pupils, 23 per cent of 1051 immigrant pupils in 52 schools with more than a third immigrant pupils. Pupils were placed in one of seven profile groups according to teachers' assessments of mathematics attainment in school work and test scores. Like the other immigrant pupils, Cypriot pupils had a distribution of performance which was significantly lower (0.01 level) than that of pupils in the ILEA as a whole (Little *et al.*, 1968). A mere seven per cent of Cypriot pupils were placed in the top quartile, groups 1 and 2, whereas some 48 per cent were placed in groups 6 and 7. Nevertheless, their profile distribution in mathematics was slightly better than that for verbal reasoning or English (see pp. 47, 124). The performance of the Cypriot pupils in mathematics was inferior to that of Indian and Pakistani and 'other' immigrant pupils, though it was better than that of pupils of West Indian origin. When a further analysis was undertaken of the performance of pupils judged by their teachers to speak at least some English, although proficiency in English is generally reckoned to be a lesser handicap in assessing performance in mathematics than in other subjects, the percentage of 124 Cypriot pupils placed in the upper quartile again doubled, though their profile distribution remained inferior, but no longer significantly inferior, to that of ILEA pupils as a whole. Again, the profile distribution of the Cypriot pupils was considerably superior to that of the West Indian pupils and resembled that of 'other' immigrant pupils. Unfortunately, no information was provided on the influence of length of schooling on these findings.

In 1968, the ILEA transfer survey to secondary education which involved some 22,023 non-immigrant and 4,269 immigrant pupils again included an assessment of pupils' performance in mathematics. Each primary school ranked its pupils in order of merit and provisionally assigned each to a group. Each child was then tested in mathematics anonymously in the school where the tests were marked and the results centrally collated. Headteachers made a final decision on the pupils to be assigned to each of seven profile groups in the light of information from the ILEA as to the number of pupils who, compared with all pupils in the authority, would be expected to fall into each of the groups. According to Little (1975a), none of the immigrant pupils had profile distributions similar to the theoretical or actual ILEA non-immigrant distributions, each having smaller proportions in groups 1 and 2 and higher proportions in groups 6 and 7. Although the number of pupils involved was not cited, comparisons can be made between the mathematics performance of Greek and Turkish Cypriot pupils. Some 10.1 per cent of Greek Cypriot pupils and a mere 4.7 per cent of Turkish Cypriot pupils were ranked in groups 1 and 2, compared with 46.1 per cent and 64.8 per cent respectively in groups 6 and 7. This reveals a clear difference in performance between the two groups of Cypriot pupils. The ranking of the Greek Cypriot pupils in groups 1 and 2, and 6 and 7, was above average for all immigrant pupils, but even so their ranking did not match that of Indian and Pakistani or 'other' pupils. By comparison with Turkish Cypriot pupils, there was only a smaller percentage of West Indian pupils in the top two groups for mathematics, but there was still a higher percentage of Turkish Cypriot pupils in groups 6 and 7. The distribution of performance in mathematics of Cypriot pupils as a whole in the 1968 study was very similar to that of Cypriot pupils as a whole in the 1966 transfer study in groups 1 and 2, but actually inferior for groups 6 and 7. Thus the performance of Cypriot pupils in mathematics, in the late 1960s, must have given rise to some concern in ILEA.

A small-scale study, in 1966, in one secondary school in Haringey (Bhatnagar, 1970) enables further comparisons to be made between the performance of pupils of Cypriot origin and their West Indian and English peers on measures of academic and non-academic performance. Some 76 Cypriot pupils and 174 West Indian pupils of all ages throughout the school and a control group of 100 pupils were rated by their teachers on a five-point scale according to their relative position in their age-group for their performance in mathematics, science, geography, history and religious education – their academic achievement (for English see p. 125). Many of the ratings were based on written examination results. Although there was no significant difference between the academic achievement of the Cypriot and West Indian pupils, both these groups of pupils had significantly inferior ratings to those of their English peers (at the one per cent level). For Cypriot boys, academic achievement correlated at the one per cent level of significance with personal satisfaction, freedom from anxiety and a composite adjustment score, and at the five per cent level for social acceptability. But these measures only correlated at the five per cent level with academic achievement for Cypriot girls. The non-academic achievement of pupils was also assessed by summing the number of prizes won by an individual in sports, swimming or boxing at school, membership of any team counting as a prize. The performance of the Cypriot and also of the English pupils on this measure was significantly inferior to that of the West Indian pupils (at the one per cent level). Non-academic achievement did not correlate significantly with any of the measures of adjustment for any of the groups. Thus in this study the Cypriot pupils did not perform favourably compared with their peers either on measures of academic or non-academic achievement.

Another study investigated the performance of pupils with mainland Greek backgrounds as part of a comparative study of scholastic achievement and family background of pupils in Athens and London (Archimandritou-Xefteris, 1977). At the London end of this study, in 1974, 24 teachers, four in each of six Greek high schools, equally divided between south and north London, estimated pupils' motivation and knowledge of parents' methods of upbringing based on their contact with the pupils' families as private tutors, and comparisons were made with objective data on pupils' performance at school in the Greek language, maths and science. On the basis of these school grades pupils were assigned to one of three achievements bands – high, average or low. The 120 pupils whose achievement level was matched by their motivation level (out of 130 who formed 25 per cent of all Greek adolescents aged 13–18 attending part-time Greek schools in London) were considered further in terms of teachers' perceptions of characteristics of two groups – high-achievers (38 boys and 34 girls) and average and low-achievers combined (27 boys and 21 girls). Interestingly, teachers claimed that the attainment and adjustment of the Greek pupils was significantly greater in their English schools than in the Greek schools, which they attended from 5 to 7 pm each evening and on Saturday mornings. They suggested this was because of the extra fatigue and burden of homework which attendance at the Greek school entailed, and also because these immigrant adolescents were more attracted to English culture as it was transmitted in their ordinary schools and obtained more satisfaction from their achievement in British schools. By comparison, their parents were said to value their attainment in Greek rather than British schools. There were no sex differences in the assignment of pupils to the three achievement bands. The researcher attributed this to the influence of Greek mothers in the home who were significant role models for girls, who were better adjusted and less pressurized than boys. There was a tendency for first born and only children to be higher-achievers. According to teachers, average or high achievers were twice as likely to be assisted by their mothers, and teachers were three times as likely to identify the mothers of pupils in the lower-achieving group as interfering or neglectful. By comparison, there was no significant association between achievement and the proportion of available time which the father spent with the child. There was a highly significant correlation (at the 0.001 level) for both boys and girls between IQ as measured by the Georgas Test including two sub-tests of vocabulary, the 'Draw a man/woman test', the Beeny Visual Motor Integration Test and RPM and the level of achievement. But the researcher suggested that girls needed to have a greater intelligence than boys in order to succeed because males were expected to do well whatever their level of intelligence. Some 25 per cent more high-achievers than those in other groups were rated as having relaxed and cheerful dispositions, and high-achievers were twice as likely to come from families rated as rather, or very, happy and having a tolerant, warm and constructive attitude to problems. More than half the high-achievers were rated as having creative abilities, and there was a particular high association (0.01 level) for girls, especially for painting. Achievement levels were also closely associated with involvement in certain extra-curricular activities for both boys and girls, although there were almost twice as many high-achieving males in this category as females, which the author suggested was because of the expectation that Greek adolescent girls would spend time helping with housework and the family business. Moreover, there was a very strong association (at the 0.001 level) between concentration and achievement, girls especially showing higher concentration, which reinforced the impression that the pattern of achievement was different between the boys and the girls.

Though it would be imprudent to extrapolate these correlations and perceptions to pupils of Cypriot origin, they may nevertheless suggest some cultural insights which might be considered further in relation to pupils of Greek Cypriot origin. Such data provide, moreover, important information on the relatively small but increasing number of pupils with backgrounds in mainland Greece in British schools who may otherwise be generally subsumed in the category of Greek-speaking pupils together with their Cypriot peers. Taking the data on Cypriot pupils as a whole, their performance in mathematics, as assessed in the ILEA transfer surveys, though slightly superior to their performance in English and verbal reasoning, was nevertheless significantly inferior to that of indigenous pupils and to a lesser extent that of their Indian and Pakistani peers. In mathematics the profile distribution of the Cypriot pupils as a whole was slightly better than that of West Indian pupils, but only because of the superior performance of the Greek Cypriot pupils. However, the transfer survey evidence also demonstrated that proficiency in English had an effect on competence in mathematics. Unfortunately, there do not seem to be any small-scale, in-depth studies which indicate the kinds of difficulties which pupils whose first language is not English may experience when engaged in learning in other areas of the curriculum.

School Placement
Owing to the fact that Cypriots migrating to Britain in the 1960s tended to be in their twenties and thirties, their children, in comparison with other ethnic minority pupils such as those of Asian or West Indian origin, were more likely to enter British schools at primary rather than secondary age (Oakley, 1968). Although some pupils rejoined their families at a later date, in their adolescence, the majority of pupils of Cypriot origin both during the 1960s and since, as they have become a UK-born group, have tended to start school at the usual age and, in comparison with other ethnic minority pupils have often benefited from a more lengthy period of junior education. Unfortunately, little information exists on this. This section focusses on the placement of pupils of Cypriot origin in different types of school and in streams within secondary schools. However, the research evidence on school placement suffers from two major deficiencies. First, it is mostly very dated, thus failing to reflect the reorganization of secondary education during the past 15 years and the considerable differences which exist between and within LEAs and schools

in their organization and teaching arrangements. Secondly, much of the information about school placement has failed to distinguish either a group of pupils of
Cypriot origin or Greek or Turkish Cypriot pupils, who are frequently merged in an
amorphous group labelled 'other', or another broad category, 'Mediterranean',
including pupils of Gibraltarian and Maltese origin.

It appears that even before the reorganization of secondary education along
comprehensive lines there were relatively few pupils of Cypriot origin to be found
in grammar schools. Figueroa (1974, 1984), who conducted research in Haringey in
1966, reported that Cypriot pupils formed only 0.9 per cent of all pupils in grammar
schools in 1967, of which 0.7 per cent were Greek Cypriots and 0.2 per cent Turkish
Cypriots. Only 5.6 per cent of all Cypriot pupils totalling 815 were in grammar
schools. By comparison, there was a higher proportion of Indian and Pakistani
pupils (16.8 per cent, 173 pupils) and more Caribbean pupils (941), though a
smaller proportion (2.9 per cent). However, the ethnic minority pupils in grammar
schools were disproportionately fewer than the white British pupils (41.1 per cent).
In Townsend and Brittan's (1972) national survey, in 1970, seven per cent of 'other
immigrants' (a group including pupils from Australia and other European and
African countries as well as a high proportion of Kenyan Asians, Italians and
Cypriots) compared with 25 per cent of non-immigrant pupils transferred to
selective schools from the two-thirds of 132 primary schools sampled which
operated a selection procedure. Clearly the number of pupils of Cypriot origin was
very small, and most, like those involved in a subsequent NFER survey in 1972
(Jelinek and Brittan, 1975), are likely to have received their secondary education in
co-educational secondary modern schools. In recent years, despite widespread
provision of comprehensive schooling at the secondary level, especially in areas of
greatest Cypriot population, Beetlestone (1982) has interestingly observed that
Cypriot parents, particularly the middle class, are careful to select primary schools
which are associated with what they regard as the more desirable secondary schools
or even to move into their catchment areas at the time of their children's transfer to
secondary education.

Within secondary education, although there have been moves towards mixed-
ability teaching, banding, setting and, especially in earlier years, streaming, have
been a widely used means of organizing pupils for teaching. For example, reference
has already been made to the kinds of organizational arrangement involved in
teaching E2L to pupils of Cypriot origin which sometimes involved their placement
in remedial streams (see p. 119). Kawwa (1963) found that Cypriot boys and girls in
a large secondary school in Islington were concentrated in the lower streams,
usually, it appears, because they did not have an adequate command of English,
and many were receiving special English tuition in the remedial department. In a
mixed secondary modern school in Haringey, in 1966, Bhatnagar (1970) found that
Cypriot boys and girls tended to be placed in lower streams but where they were in
greater numbers in the lower forms, they were more evenly spread between
streams and some were placed in the top streams. Figueroa's (1974) research, also
in 1966–7 in Haringey, showed that the 48 Cypriot pupils in his sample, who had
mostly been born in Cyprus and lived in the UK for less than four years, tended to
be clustered in the lower streams of forms, together with a high percentage of West
Indian pupils. Indeed over two-thirds of the Cypriot pupils, and proportionally
more boys (over four-fifths) than girls, were placed in the lower streams of the
fourth and fifth forms. This proportion was greater than that for West Indian or
white British pupils. Yet data collected from a national sample of schools in 1971 by
Townsend and Brittan (1972) tended to confirm the pattern indicated in Bhatnagar's school. It was reported that although immigrant pupils generally tended to

be concentrated in the lower streams, in both two-thirds of the few primary schools providing information about the streaming of 'other' immigrant pupils and in the two-thirds of 98 secondary schools which streamed pupils 'other immigrants', including Greek- and Turkish-speaking pupils, were more evenly distributed across streams. Hence in the researchers' view linguistic difficulties were not the sole cause of any differences between the distribution of immigrant and non-immigrant pupils in streams. Many headteachers reported a more even distribution of immigrant pupils as they progressed through the secondary school, so that some pupils of Cypriot origin were clearly overcoming earlier educational difficulties. However, this has to be set alongside the fact that since fewer immigrant pupils tended to be selected for grammar schools, immigrant pupils in non-selective secondary schools represented a wider range of educational potential than non-immigrants.

However, at the other extreme it seems that it may nevertheless be the case, as Alkan and Constantinides (1981) have suggested, that since Cypriot children have tended to start school at the age of five speaking Greek or Turkish, inadequate testing methods have sometimes in the past led to some Cypriot children being classed as educationally sub-normal (ESN), when teachers have been unable to ascertain the child's educational potential. DES figures for 1972 (GB. DES, 1973), the last year in which data on immigrant pupils were collected, show that 242 pupils of Mediterranean origin (from Cyprus, Gibraltar and Malta), 142 boys and 100 girls, were classified as ESN. It seems unlikely that this would be an overrepresent-ation of pupils of Cypriot origin in this classification. Triseliotis (1976) has claimed that the percentage of Cypriot children deemed educationally sub-normal has been well below that of West Indian pupils. However, it is reported that in Haringey, in the 1970s, there was an overrepresentation of Turkish Cypriot boys classified as ESN and attending the local school for maladjusted children along with pupils of West Indian origin and parents were concerned about their placement (Milstead, 1981). Yet, according to the 1981 ILEA Ethnic Census of School Support Centres and Educational Guidance Centres, only eight Greek pupils, including Greek Cypriots and six Turkish pupils, including Turkish Cypriots, were found to be represented in 53 centres comprising some 640 secondary pupils. Hence it would not seem that pupils of Cypriot origin were considered by their teachers to be particularly in need of additional psychological assessment or educational guidance.

Considering other special school placement, Figueroa (1974) claimed that in 1967–8 Cypriot pupils were under-represented in Haringey in special schools for the blind, deaf and physically handicapped. Indeed DES figures for 1972 indicated that only 12 pupils of Mediterranean origin were classified as blind or partially sighted, 22 deaf or partially hearing and 36 physically handicapped. A total of 375 pupils of Mediterranean origin, 206 boys and 169 girls, were found to be in a range of special schools in 1972 (GB. DES, 1973). They comprised 5.6 per cent of immigrant pupils in special schools.

Generally, therefore, allowing for the age of some of this research evidence, it would appear that pupils of Cypriot origin, apart from their need of additional English teaching, have not been seen as particularly in need of special attention of any kind by their teachers and schools. Rather it would appear that, especially for those who have had the opportunity to progress through full junior and secondary schooling, pupils of Cypriot origin may often have been able to better their position within the type of teaching organization operated by their schools as they have become more proficient in English and more accustomed to the culture and environment of the school.

Examination Performance, Further and Higher Education
There appears to be an almost complete absence of publicly available information
about the entry of pupils of Cypriot origin for CSE or GCE O- or A-level
examinations and also about their performance in such examinations. Some figures
on the number of Cypriot pupils entering for examinations in Greek and Turkish
have already been cited (see pp. 109–10). However, the absence of information on
examination entry and performance from the DES School-Leavers Survey (quoted
in the Swann Report) is a serious gap in the data since it is impossible to test out at
school leaving earlier indications in the research literature on the performance of
pupils of Cypriot origin, usually but not exclusively at primary school level, on
measures of IQ, aspects of English and mathematics. One very small-scale study
and two reports of teachers' perceptions of performance provide the limited and
inadequate 'soft' evidence on examination performance.

From a questionnaire to five secondary schools with Cypriot pupils, and visits to
three, Martianou (1981) discovered that pupils of Cypriot origin were well
represented in GCE O- and A-level entries. However, schools generally suggested
that their performance in various subjects and at both levels was often hampered by
difficulties with English. There was a tendency to take CSE English, then O-level,
and often only low-grade passes were achieved or pupils had to retake English even
if they were doing A-levels in other subjects. Three out of five schools reported that
boys had a bias towards sciences and that few pupils of Cypriot origin took A-level
English – if so, they were more likely to be girls. According to these schools, the
academic performance of pupils of Cypriot origin was related to social class: in
three schools in 'middle-class' areas pupils of Cypriot origin were said to cover the
full range of ability and to perform as well as indigenous pupils; in two schools in
'working-class' areas they were said to perform slightly better than indigenous
whites. Cypriot parents and children were said to have high academic expectations
which were sometimes seen as unrealistic by schools. Parents wanted GCE entry.
Examination entry and performance data quoted by Martianou for one school for
1977, 1978 and 1980 show that, compared with the rest of the school, a slightly
higher percentage of pupils of Cypriot origin than those in the 'rest of the school'
were entered for GCE O-level, for a slightly greater number of subjects on
average, and that their pass rate per candidate was slightly greater – though hardly
high. Over the three years a greater percentage of pupils of Cypriot origin than
other examinees in school obtained O-level grades A–C. Moreover, in the two
years for which comparative data are cited for the ILEA as a whole, the Cypriot
pupils in the one school performed as well as or better than ILEA examinees as a
whole. Similar findings obtained for A-level grades A–C. However, these data
should be treated with great caution and due acknowledgement made to their
limitations.

Other evidence of performance is restricted to reports of perceptions. As a result
of 40 interviews with headteachers in schools, mostly at the primary level, in
Haringey, Beetlestone (1982) reported that pupils of Cypriot origin were not seen
as performing less well than other pupils. Some heads claimed that the performance
of Greek Cypriot pupils was higher. But Beetlestone in fact questioned the general
level of performance. The Swann Committee observed in its Report that in the
majority of schools with Cypriot pupils which it visited

> there was a strong feeling that those pupils as a group were underachieving and
> the Turkish Cypriots were often singled out as giving particular cause for
> concern ... even where Greek Cypriot pupils were apparently 'doing well', ie
> achieving on a par with their peers from other groups – they were still sometimes

regarded as failing to fulfil their true potential since in many of the schools which they attended achievement levels were below the national average. (GB. P. H of C, 1985, p. 687)

The Report goes on to put forward a number of wide-ranging institutional and interactive factors which teachers and community members suggested could affect the achievement of pupils of Cypriot origin and other supposed group differences and perceptions which might 'explain' the 'apparent differences in the achievement of Greek Cypriot and Turkish Cypriot pupils'. These, however, remain at the level of hypotheses to be assessed and refined in further studies. As a step in this direction, there must surely be more information, such as data on examination performance, available within LEAs with large numbers of pupils of Cypriot origin. As it stands, however, publicly available evidence does not permit any conclusions to be drawn about the examination performance of pupils of Cypriot origin or their achievement levels in comparison with those of their peers.

Another indicator of performance of pupils of Cypriot origin at the end of compulsory schooling is the extent to which they stay on at school or engage in further education. But the research data here are also slight and inadequate with respect to reasons for continuing in education. As part of a thorough but small-scale investigation in three London comprehensive schools, in 1972, Dove (1975) investigated the intentions of 545 pupils aged 15–16 to stay on at or leave school. The sample comprised some 78 Cypriot pupils, mainly Greek Cypriot, more than half of whom had been born in the UK, together with 298 white British, 109 West Indian and 60 Asian pupils. Some 53 per cent of the Cypriot pupils intended to leave school after taking CSE or O-level and a further 37 per cent after taking A-level. Very few wanted to leave school as soon as possible. This may, therefore, also be seen as an indication of the extent to which pupils of Cypriot origin were oriented towards entering for examinations. A greater percentage of each of the groups of immigrant pupils than of the white British pupils intended to stay on at school, and for longer. This tended to apply for girls as well as boys, except in the case of Cypriot girls who, according to Dove, appeared to expect less than the Cypriot boys, and rarely had the confidence to aspire to A-levels. This sex difference was perpetuated in the pupils' declared intentions after leaving school. The Cypriot pupils as a group were very ambitious for further full-time education – 42 per cent overall aspiring to this – a higher percentage than for any other group of pupils. But whereas half of the boys intended to enter further education, only one-third of the Cypriot girls had such an intention. Only 17 per cent of the Cypriot pupils envisaged not continuing in any form of education after leaving school. (For their vocational aspirations and transition from school to work see pp. 189–90.)

To what extent are aspirations for further education translated into actuality? In an early study in 1966–7 which included 48 Cypriot pupils, 261 British, 88 West Indian and 27 other white pupils, Figueroa (1974) found that a relatively large proportion of immigrant pupils, except Cypriot girls, expected to stay on at school and in fact did so. Four-fifths of the Cypriot girls said that they would prefer to leave school, but all in fact did so, compared with three-fifths of the Cypriot boys who preferred to leave school and three-quarters who did so. At a follow-up interview one year after school-leaving Figueroa found that one-tenth of Cypriot boys and a very slightly higher proportion of Cypriot girls were engaged in further education. More recently, Martianou (1981) discovered that almost all of a few Cypriot pupils interviewed wanted to stay on at school after school-leaving age. In the five schools investigated many were reported to stay on into the sixth form, often to retake O-levels, but some took A-levels. It was reported that fewer Cypriot girls stayed on at school, but this was more likely if the girls did well academically, or if the school had a commercial department. Otherwise, they often pursued secretarial courses at the FE college, where some boys took A-level courses. MacDonald's (1975) study in an FE college indicated that the majority of Greek- and Turkish-speaking students were pursuing O-level courses, some were in business studies or art and design courses, and a few were taking A-level courses.

Interestingly, data collected in the ILEA language censuses (ILEA, 1982, 1983, 1986) reveal differential rates of staying on at school after statutory school-leaving age for Greek- and Turkish-speaking pupils (Table 20). Whereas in each year the staying-on rate for Greek-speaking pupils exceeded that of the ILEA average, that for Turkish-speaking pupils was the lowest of all the main groups of minority language speakers and lower than that of the average for the ILEA as a whole. Unfortunately, there are no indications of reasons for this differential rate of staying on at school between the Greek and Turkish speakers. Moreover, there is no evidence of the types of course pursued nor of the length of time spent in school after statutory school-leaving age. Such information would be valuable. It may be noted, moreover, that in Leeuwenberg's (1979) sample 41.7 per cent of the Greek speakers compared with 17.9 per cent of the Turkish speakers had remained at school or college after the age of 19.

Table 20:   **Staying on rates of Greek- and Turkish-speaking pupils in ILEA, 1981, 1982 and 1984**

		1981		1982		1984	
		Greek speakers	Turkish speakers	Greek speakers	Turkish speakers	Greek speakers	Turkish speakers
1	Number aged 16–19 (1981) or 17 (1982 and 1984)	229	162	82	48	60	42
2	(1) as a % of pupils aged 15 in 1981, and in 1983 for 1984	66.8	46.3	23.9	13.7	19.4	13.2
3	(1) as a % of (2) for all ILEA pupils	52.2		19.9		17.9	
4	Staying on rates in relation to other language speakers, (1) as a % of (2)	8 language group speakers, higher rates than Greek speakers; Bengali 57.7%, Portuguese 55.1% lower; Turkish speakers lowest		9 language group speakers, higher rates than Greek speakers; French 21.3% lower; Turkish speakers lowest		10 language group speakers, higher rates than Greek speakers; Bengali 13.6% lower; Turkish speakers lowest	

Source: ILEA, 1982, 1983, 1986.

Turning to consider aspirations for, and participation in, higher education, the available evidence is again slight. In Figueroa's (1974) sample few of the Cypriot pupils aspired to a university or higher education, which he considered was because of their social class position and placement in secondary modern schools, which meant that higher education did not enter into their frame of reference. However, more recently Martianou (1981) discovered that four out of five schools with pupils of Cypriot origin reported that many entered a range of higher education institutions, most often colleges or polytechnics. Indeed in two schools there was evidence of over a third of pupils of Cypriot origin entering universities, with a few scholarships. Clearly some young people of Cypriot origin have also embarked upon teacher training courses, though there is no evidence of numbers. Indeed, as part of their studies, some of these students have shown a particular interest in undertaking small-scale research projects into aspects of the educational and cultural experiences of their communities. Reference has been made throughout this review to these researches (ibid; Ulug, 1981; Stamataris, 1983; Georgiou, 1983). Such research and the engagement of teachers of Cypriot origin in mainstream schooling can only serve to promote greater awareness and understanding of the interaction and effect of home, community and school experiences on the education of pupils of Cypriot origin. However, the identified gap in research data on the examination performance and participation in further and higher education of pupils of Cypriot origin needs to be rectified in order to evaluate the extent to which the educational aspirations of Cypriot parents and their children are satisfied.

Cypriot Parents

The attitudes of Cypriot parents to the education of their children may be assumed to have an influence on their children's attitudes to education and on their educational performance. Hence it is important to consider the education of Cypriot parents themselves, their knowledge of and attitudes to British education in general, the extent to which they have contact with their children's schools, their attitudes towards various aspects of school organization, the curriculum and extra-curricular activities and – on a more domestic note – the kinds of interaction and relationship which Cypriot parents and their children enjoy, plus parents' aspirations for their children's employment.

PARENTS' EDUCATION

Although there is very little direct information available on the educational level or experiences of Cypriot parents in the UK, it is important to gain a general impression of the educational provision which they will probably have encountered as this, in turn, is likely to influence their attitudes to and expectations for their children's education in the UK. An outline of developments of the educational systems in Cyprus during this century is sketched as a background to consideration of the educational characteristics of Cypriot adults in Britain.

According to Oakley (1968), Cypriots have generally enjoyed relatively good provision for educational opportunities compared with people in other developing countries. However, the educational experience of Cypriots has varied greatly both according to the time of their education – for it is only since the Second World War that at least some education has been universal – and gender – for the education of girls has generally been considered less important. Yet traditionally, education has been valued very highly both for intrinsic and instrumental reasons. The school has often formed the focal point in many Cypriot villages and the teacher has commanded respect.

The bipartite system of education on Cyprus whereby the Greek and Turkish communities manage separate schooling for the children of each community has developed from, and been perpetuated by, historical events and political conditions (LCSS, 1967; Oakley, 1968). Prior to British domination of Cyprus, under Ottoman Turkish rule organized education was only provided for Muslims, and most Greeks and Turks received only very elementary instruction from the village priest. Under British administration schools continued to be financed by villagers, appointing teachers who taught a curriculum modelled on that of Greece or Turkey and which emphasized national and religious loyalties. Schools came under the increasing supervision of central boards and district committees. Centralization of control over elementary education occurred by 1933 due to fears of the power of an increasingly secular Greek teaching force to promote revolutionary nationalist sentiment. Linked with this was the founding of a teacher training college in Cyprus in 1936. This operated a two-year course, directly influenced by British educational methods, which focussed on individual approaches to basic subjects and groupwork in the arts and social studies. The college became the main centre for teacher training for the majority of teachers, although teachers were also recruited from the UK and Cypriot students were enabled to study in Britain. However, despite British legal restrictions in 1952 on the provision of financial aid to secondary schools in Cyprus where teachers were the employees of the Department of Education, secondary schooling largely escaped British influence as many teachers, especially those educated in Greece, resisted the attempt to change the Hellenic bias of the secondary curriculum. Nevertheless, more scientific and technological subjects were introduced. According to Oakley, the British administration's attempts to modernize the curriculum and give it a 'Cypriot' orientation served only to modify, not transform, the national character of the Greek and Turkish education systems. Indeed after the independence of Cyprus in 1960, completely separate authorities were set up for teaching the children from the two communities, which in the opinion of the LCSS report (1967) 'has caused great financial difficulties and has had a disunifying effect on education generally' (p.52), with uncertainty about teaching methods and curricula in the respective mainlands.

In the post Second World War period considerable expansion of educational provision took place, and there was a gradual rise in the percentage of children receiving at least elementary education. This was accompanied by increases in literacy (see pp. 52–3) and expansion of library facilities (Leeuwenberg, 1979). Free primary education from the age of six to 12 was available before the Second World War but did not become compulsory until after 1960. Secondary education was fee-paying until the early 1970s and there was a high drop-out rate in the first two years (Triseliotis, 1976). Thus, whereas only ten per cent of those of secondary school age attended secondary school in 1939, this figure rose to 17 per cent in 1946 and 25 per cent in 1953. By 1960 some 40 per cent of 12–18-year-olds were considered to have received some secondary education, even though it was fee-paying (George, 1960; Oakley, 1968). By the late 1960s secondary education had been extended to the majority, but as the secondary and technical schools tended to be sited in urban areas or larger villages children from smaller or more isolated villages had less chance of secondary education. For example, in 1967–8, according to information supplied by Greek sources, there were 542 elementary schools in Cyprus, with 70,690 pupils and 2,110 teachers and 67 secondary schools, nine technical-vocational schools (set up to meet the perceived needs of industry) and one agricultural school having a combined total of 33,434 pupils and 1,500 teachers. Some 73 per cent of pupils transferred from primary to secondary schooling, a quarter on scholarships. By 1972, 81 per cent of pupils transferred and secondary education became free for the first three years (Steinberg and Paxton, 1969, 1973).

Oakley (1968) has described educational provision for Greek Cypriots in the mid-1960s when the village schools were beginning to take on a different, more outward-looking character. In the local community the teacher was a person of importance with power to influence the future of children – whether or not they would proceed to secondary education – and also the future of the village, and from this derived much respect and prestige. Despite the teacher's authority on educational matters, parents monitored activities and would make any serious grievances known. At that time, the teacher–pupil ratio was 34:1. For each ethnic community, the curriculum focussed on its own language, religion, classical literature and national history, using textbooks from the respective mainlands. Teaching methods were predominantly authoritarian with firm discipline and emphasis was placed on rote learning and homework from an early age. Children possessed their own school books (Butterworth and Kinnibrugh, 1970). Both primary and secondary schools were generally mixed, especially in rural areas, but boys and girls were usually segregated in the classroom. Work was regularly assessed and examined, each group proceeding on the basis of a minimum achieved standard. English and French were taught after the age of 12.

Only since the mid-1970s has secondary education become compulsory to the age of 15 in Greek Cypriot schools (Martianou, 1981). In Turkish Cypriot schools, although the majority of pupils proceed to middle school and continue until the end of the year in which the pupil reaches his fourteenth birthday, some ten per cent, mostly girls, leave at 12 as the school-leaving age is not enforced (Crellin, 1981). Crellin (1979, 1981) has described Turkish education in Cyprus since 1975 with particular reference to primary schools. The schooling pattern is now $6 + 3 + 3$ years from the age of six and there has been a move to larger teaching units in the bigger communities. The curriculum, which is centrally prescribed, overtly recognizes Turkish nationalism, but there are attempts, especially in the methods and planning of the school system and revisions to social studies texts, to pursue a Turkish Cypriot line. The emphasis in the curriculum is on Turkish, environmental studies and mathematics, and English is taught from the fourth year. Formal sex education is forbidden. Materials, especially set textbooks which come from Turkey, are scarce but some local texts are produced. There have been improvements in literacy, attendance, even in rural areas, and nursery education. Although there is apparently little scope for individual learning or initiative, and work is often repetitive children do not display signs of disaffection or behaviour difficulties. There are 170 elementary schools, some with up to 400 children in urban areas, others with one teacher catering for six age ranges in village schools. Class size is limited by law to a maximum of 35. There appears to be strong parental influence against the closure of village elementary schools and also co-operative parent–teacher associations in providing equipment and materials, yet there is no scope for participation in curricular decisions. Ulug (1981) has also briefly described upper secondary provision for three years from 15. There is a stress on science and mathematics in preparation for higher education, but there are also schools with commercial or technical orientations. There is also apparently a selective English college for 12–18-year-olds, where, after spending a third of the first two years learning English, students then learn some subjects through the medium of English in preparation for GCE O- or even A-levels.

The only full-time further education on Cyprus has been a three-year course for prospective elementary school teachers in the two teacher training colleges, which from 1936 to 1960 were sexually segregated and since independence ethnically segregated (Oakley, 1968). According to Crellin (1979, 1981), the Turkish college has been one of the least adequate areas of the education service, with unsuitable accommodation, poor library resources and fluctuating student numbers. Teachers in secondary education must be graduates, and since there are no institutions of higher education in Cyprus, this means they have either been educated or recruited from abroad. Young Cypriots pursue further and higher education in Greece,

Turkey or the UK. Thus there were, for example, many Cypriot students –
estimates varied from 670 made by an overseeing committee to 3,300 by the
Cyprus High Commission – studying in FE and HE institutions in the UK when
civil war broke out in Cyprus in 1974 (World University Service, 1977). Many of
these students, mostly Greek Cypriots, became destitute or lost their sources of
income and some were assisted to continue in full-time education in this country,
113 on development-related OND studies funded by the Overseas Development
Ministry and others on first degree courses financed by the DHSS. Although the
status of these students, as refugees, may have been unclear, it is likely that many
will have stayed on in the UK and possibly influenced the educational aspirations
of young Cypriots in this country.

However, it is important to distinguish such an urban educated élite as a
minority within the adult Cypriot population in the UK who have formed the
parents of children in schools. Indeed, according to Constantinides (1977),
education is one factor, together with status and reason for being in the UK,
employed by Greek Cypriots to distinguish amongst themselves. More specifically, the officials of the Cyprus High Commission, employees in banking,
trade and tourist offices, and Cypriot academics and students are clearly dist-
inguishable from the majority of Greek Cypriots of rural origin in the UK by
their high level of formal education. Similar distinctions can be drawn within the
Turkish Cypriot community and to an extent within the mainland Turkish
community, though this has been, like the mainland Greek community, a highly
educated group of students, officials and business people (see p. 5).

Sources are generally agreed that first-generation Cypriot parents generally had
low educational qualifications (Oakley, 1968; Constantinides, 1977; Anthias,
1983). The majority of young adult Cypriots who emigrated to the UK in the
1950s and early 1960s would have had some – if not a complete – primary
education. Moreover, since by the mid- to late 1960s the majority of school-
leavers in Cyprus had some secondary schooling, many of the young male
emigrants to the UK, particularly those who came in the 1960s, may well have
had some secondary educational experience and possibly some elementary knowledge of English. However, as George (1960) has observed, since it was traditionally considered less important for girls to attend school, there may well be
differences in the educational level of Cypriot men and women in this country.
The tendency for females to have received less education than males has
influenced the differential literacy rate amongst Cypriot men and women, though
George has suggested that the literacy of emigrants may have been higher (see
p. 52).

Studies in the UK which incidentally considered Cypriot parents' education have
shown that Greek Cypriot women have generally had six years' primary education
(Clough and Quarmby, 1978), as had half the parents of Greek- and Turkish-
speaking students in FE, very few of whom were able to receive help with their
studies from their parents (MacDonald, 1975). Archimandritou-Xefteris (1977)
observed that although lower-middle-class Greek parents working in shipping
companies or running their own small-scale food businesses had a limited
education, they were nevertheless educationally ambitious for their children,
sending them to Greek mother-tongue classes in the evenings and sometimes
employing private tutors, with mothers in particular monitoring their child's school
achievement. Moreover, Beetlestone (1982) found that although Cypriot parents in
Haringey who had left Cyprus around 1960 usually only had elementary school
experience, and generally the Turkish Cypriot parents had less educational
experience than Greek Cypriots, they remained in touch with educational

developments in Cyprus through news from relatives, students, newspapers and visits back. They were thus aware of the significance of education in Cyprus in contributing to its growing economy, industrial advancement, political stability and international status. These perceptions were contrasted with their knowledge of the educational experiences of their children in a large urban area: 'Thus the Cypriots have now come to see their system as very much superior, linked as it is to a notion of cultural superiority ... and their clinging on to a cultural heritage in the face of insecurities of life in a strange environment' (ibid., p.18). Parents' own relative lack of formal education may in fact serve to make them more conscious of its importance, increase their regard for it and intensify their educational aspirations for their children.

KNOWLEDGE OF AND ATTITUDES TO BRITISH EDUCATION
At this point, it is important to assess the attitudes of Cypriot parents towards education in general, and their understanding of the British education system and their children's schooling in particular, and the extent to which they feel that the British system of schooling takes account of their wishes for the education of their children. Available research evidence indicates changes in perceptions over a 20-year period.

Most sources are agreed that Cypriot parents value education highly. Like most parents, many Cypriot parents hold both intrinsic and instrumental views of education, valuing learning for its own sake and as a passport to better employment (Krokou, 1985). Early research evidence also indicated that Cypriot parents had a considerable regard for the British educational system (George, 1960; LCSS, 1967; Oakley, 1968). However, such generalizations may conceal a certain ambivalence about particular schools or aspects of schooling which may emerge as concerns over time or remain unexpressed as criticisms. For example, in the Community Relations Commission (CRC) survey conducted in 1975 (CRC, 1977), 80 per cent of parents from seven or more ethnic groups, including Cypriots, who were interviewed expressed satisfaction with the schools in their eight multiracial localities with few between-group differences. However, fewer parents were satisfied with the schools which their own children attended, and Cypriot parents, together with West Indian parents, were the least likely to like their children's schools. Unfortunately, no reasons were given for Cypriot parents' dislike. Indeed, in another national survey, teachers were marginally more likely to claim that European parents, including Cypriot parents, rather than English or West Indian parents usually showed considerable interest in the education of their children (Brittan, 1976a; see p.196).

Despite the generally positive attitudes which Cypriot parents hold towards education, many sources agree that they often have little understanding of the educational system as such, either in terms of its general aims or the particular objectives and practices in their child's school. For instance, the LCSS report (1967) claimed that many Cypriot parents did not understand what was expected of them by the education system; they had, for example, to learn that punctuality, which had not been very important in Cyprus, was vital once their children attended school in Britain. The report recommended that an independent agency should undertake to explain to Cypriot families the demands that would be made on their children at school, and claimed that, if this were done, because of the high value they placed upon education, Cypriot parents would then accept more readily the school's role in the lives of their children. As Oakley put it:

Cypriot parents have in general a great admiration and respect for the British education system, but in practice they have little understanding of its detailed workings. They see it not as a set of coherent principles or as a complex organisation of related activities, but simply in terms of what it does to their own children. Success or failure is judged largely in relation to the aims and assumptions of the educational system in Cyprus, and it is against this background that the worries and criticisms of Cypriot parents need to be understood. (Oakley, 1968, p.45)

Indeed evidence almost 20 years later suggests that although Cypriot parents may have a better general understanding of the organization of the education system, they may still remain mystified about some significant aspects of their children's schooling. There continues to be a great need for schools to educate parents about the purposes and methods of schooling (GB.P. H of C, 1985). As Alkan and Constantinides (1981) have pointed out, all parents are confused by a changing education system and varying teaching techniques, but Cypriot and other ethnic minority parents are even more bewildered. For example, they have not understood the true meaning of CSE performance, and especially the grading system, so that as a result parents may have had higher vocational expectations for their children than their educational ability or performance would warrant. In interview with a small sample of Cypriot parents Martianou (1981) found that they seemed to have little idea about how the education system functioned, especially in respect of examinations, discipline and homework. Although some knew about the age of transfer, relying on the recommendation of other Cypriots for choice of secondary school, they generally knew little about actual practice in schools. Many did not understand or approve of child-centred methods in the primary school.

Similarly, in a study of the perceptions of Cypriot parents in Haringey, Beetlestone (1982) discovered that they disliked the primary schools' emphasis on play, oral work and visual presentation; they found it difficult to understand the concept of 'the integrated day' or topic/project-based learning and would have liked more straightforward information on their children's progress, their stage of learning and how they were assessed. Yet parents were generally unlikely to complain. Beetlestone drew class and ethnic distinctions in her interpretations of the perceptions of Greek and Turkish Cypriot parents and communities. For the middle class, who were most likely to be Greek Cypriots, education was a means of increasing personal status and a contributory factor in the decision to emigrate: 'They had high expectations of a better life centred round the education of their children' (p.18). These parents were usually careful in their selection of primary and secondary schools. Any criticisms voiced by Greek Cypriots tended to be concerned with minor elements of the system which could be improved without fundamental change. By contrast, the working class were less mobile and often had to accept educational situations with which they were unhappy, fearing that their child's education would reinforce their class position, though they, too, wanted it as a means of acquiring skills and increasing social status and often had higher expectations than white working-class parents of their children gaining academic qualifications. Yet because of their employment position and language difficulties, they were often unable to take part in school activities. Beetlestone found that 'A difference in the attitude of the working-class parents towards the school is seen by some teachers as a reason for educational underachievement and this was particularly directed towards Turkish parents' (p.19). Indeed Turkish Cypriot community leaders were concerned with educational failure as part of a pattern of working-class failure. In particular, Cypriot parents found the idea that education was concerned with the whole person as very confusing:

Criticisms which they do advance centre round concern for academic learning.

They see lack of this as a real area of discrimination. Many are unimpressed by the social concern shown by schools in trying to create a multicultural atmosphere – one of social tolerance – such factors are seen as a bonus – but they mask the real job of the school which is to teach. They see these other factors as outside the province of the school. (Beetlestone, 1982, p.21)

Memdouh (1981) reported that Turkish Cypriot parents were concerned that academic students were not encouraged to study the sciences and that some were in favour of extending vocational preparation in schools such as design, cutting, mechanical studies, metalwork and woodwork and pottery.

Cypriot parents' desire for conventional educational success is powerful, but so also is the wish to maintain cultural identity. However much Cypriot parents want their children to do well in their mainstream schooling (Oakley, 1968; Alkan and Constantinides, 1981), it is clear that Cypriots make sterling efforts to maintain and transmit their linguistic and cultural heritage to their children. But despite their success in re-creating many of their customs, institutions and the spirit of community life in their UK settlements, Cypriot parents encounter difficulty in handing on their cultural traditions to their UK-born children, partly because of their exposure to a variety of new influences in the school environment. In 1968 Oakley suggested that the majority of Greek Cypriot parents did not take any particular measures to counteract what they perceived as the Anglicizing influence of their children's schooling, though he noted that a small minority were tending to discourage effort in British education and instead focussed the child's interest on Greek. But it would appear that over the years the number of parents who wish their children to have a greater appreciation of Greek or Turkish culture and language (though perhaps as well as rather than detracting from British education) has grown considerably to judge from the number of children who attend mother-tongue classes (see pp. 86–8). Indeed the very fact that Greek parents have banded together to form an association – now of over 35 years' standing – which actively promotes Greek culture and language amongst the young is a measure of their strength of feeling in this regard. As Constantinides has remarked:

> Prolonged participation in the British education system is thought by parents to cause a loss of 'Greek identity' as individual children conform to the values and behaviour of their school peers. Participation in the Greek-language schools is quite specifically designed to counteract some of the effects of State schooling. (Constantinides, 1977, p.284)

Moreover, Greek teachers interviewed in mother-tongue schools claimed that although many of the Greek-speaking pupils believed that their acculturation would make life easier, this belief was actively discouraged by their parents who sometimes even employed Greek tutors to supplement their learning of Greek at home and to further their immersion in Greek culture (Archimandritou-Xefteris, 1977). These parents apparently valued attainment in Greek rather than in British education. They viewed the serious competition as between Greek and Greek and family and family, and attainment in English schooling was seen rather as a necessary tool within an adopted culture.

Though it would appear that Turkish-speaking Cypriot parents may be less organized in their response to the Anglicizing influences of British schooling on their children, and there is certainly less available information about their attitudes towards and knowledge of British schooling, a small-scale study undertaken by a Turkish Cypriot student (Ulug, 1981) sheds some light on their views. Ulug reported that Turkish Cypriot parents feared the loss of their culture and considered it important to maintain a social distance from mainstream culture, whilst nevertheless retaining high educational aspirations for their children. They were horrified by what they perceived as the permissiveness of English schools. There appeared to Ulug to be both a lack of understanding and general mistrust by Turkish Cypriot parents of their children's schools. They felt that their own culture was considered inferior by educationists and that this might bring about the same sentiment in their children. Yet, at the same time, they wanted to retain their own culture and encourage an appreciation and adoption of it by their children and also greater recognition of it in the curriculum in their children's schools.

These various strands of evidence and comment suggest a considerable ambivalence on the part of Cypriot parents towards the British education system. On the one hand, they want their children to succeed and to do well, for they recognize that educational qualifications are important, but on the other, it would appear that they do not wish these to be acquired at the expense of their children losing their consciousness of their Greek/Turkish and/or Cypriot identities and culture. Though parents' understanding of the philosophy of British schooling and the particular teaching methodology and practices of their child's school may be imperfect, their perceptions of the influence of schooling lead them to wish to counteract its Anglicizing tendency, by encouraging in their children greater appreciation of and identification with their traditional cultures and outlook, not only through upbringing in the home, but by means of attendance at mother-tongue schools where a Greek or Turkish ethos and orientation prevails. Moreover, some parents feel that their cultural traditions are not merely ignored, but rejected as inferior by mainstream education. Hence it is important to examine the extent to which research evidence indicates that schools have attempted to appreciate parents' views in terms of differences in emphasis on particular matters of cultural and social practice, more fundamentally in terms of the orientation of the curriculum and whether they have established effective channels of communication with parents through home–school contact.

HOME–SCHOOL CONTACT

How do schools with pupils of Cypriot origin establish contact with parents, and to what extent have Cypriot parents sought to communicate with their children's teachers and schools? One important factor in assessing home–school contact must be the attitude of Cypriot parents to approaching teachers in their children's schools. In an early study Oakley (1968) reported that some teachers found it puzzling that Cypriot parents did not seem to display more interest in their children's schools, especially as an aim of some Cypriot families in coming to Britain was apparently to obtain a better education for their children. Oakley suggested that Cypriot parents' lack of involvement, at that time, needed to be understood in terms of the traditional attitude of respect for teachers and their professionalism, and the need to allow them to pursue their profession unhindered. However, according to Oakley, Cypriot parents soon began to understand that their relationship with the school in Britain was very different from that in the small village communities in Cyprus. Some realized that, in comparison with Cyprus, they had little power to affect the administration of the school. On the one hand, their reaction was to trust, albeit somewhat uneasily, in the authority of the teacher and the school system, and on the other hand to attempt to make their contact with the school more personal and direct by keeping in touch with the child's class teacher, as well as meeting the headteacher from time to time. For Greek Cypriot parents, these contacts serve to assess what kind of person the child's teacher is and whether according to their own perceptions he or she is suitable to stand *in loco parentis*. If parents are satisfied, then they will trust the teacher's opinion, take advice on the child's problems or decisions for his future schooling and be happy to meet the teacher from time to time to hear about the child's progress. According to Oakley, parent–teacher contact is both meaningful and important to Cypriot parents, whereas written reports and circulars are not: 'Greek parents are therefore in favour of closer parent–teacher relations, not out of interest in the school or in education in general, but because they provide a framework of opportunity for personal contact, opportunity they would be uncertain and reluctant about creating on their own initiative' (pp. 48–9).

To what extent have schools appreciated such attitudes and the uncertainty and timorousness of Cypriot parents in getting in touch with teachers? The attitudes of Cypriot parents tend to derive from their own educational experiences in Cyprus; the feeling that education is the responsibility of the teacher whose position is greatly respected, and that parents should not interfere. Lack of fluency in English and inadequate understanding of the curriculum may also make approaches to schools daunting for some parents (GB.P. H of C, 1985; Ulug, 1981). Even a decade ago, Triseliotis (1976) claimed that schools have an obligation to communicate to parents their expectations about parental involvement in schooling. Yet there has been a lack of clear communication by teachers as to the roles they see parents playing and a lack of sustained attempts to cultivate contacts with parents. In short home–school contact could be improved to increase an understanding of the different ways of life and expectations of school and home but, 'Over the years there has been a dismal failure to use the school, a familiar institution to all ethnic groups, to make easier the transition of both immigrant families and children from one culture to another' (ibid., p.373). Indeed only recently schools have again been criticized for failing to communicate effectively with parents especially over events in which they might participate (Anthias, 1984), and it has been recommended that schools need to 'reach out' and involve parents more in the education process.

Clearly practice varies enormously and there are individual schools to which such charges do not apply, especially perhaps as over the years some teachers have become more aware of the distinctive needs of Cypriot pupils and the interests of their parents and have been able to build up channels of communication. One significant factor in improving communication between parents and schools has probably been the establishment of parents' associations by Cypriot parents. The level of activity of such parents' associations may be related to the more established settlement of Cypriot communities in the UK and also to a growing awareness of increased parent–teacher interaction, particularly on such matters as school placement, closure, provision of materials and equipment and administration of the school buildings in Cyprus (Crellin, 1979, 1981; Beetlestone, 1982). One of the aims of the Greek Parents' Association in the UK is to facilitate liaison with schools on educational, cultural and social matters concerning Cypriot children (Alkan and Constantinides, 1981). The parents' association performs a significant role as it both organizes mother-tongue classes in conjunction with the Cyprus High Commission and aims to represent the interests of members in relation to their children's mainstream schooling. But the position of the association *vis-à-vis* each schooling system is clearly different. On the one hand, an aim of the Cyprus High Commission in supporting mother-tongue schools is to encourage the wide involvement of parents in a democratic governing structure where the power rests with the representatives of the parents on school, district or communal committees (Aristodemou, 1979). But the role of the parents' association *vis-à-vis* mainstream schools must be by invitation. Alkan and Constantinides (1981), for example, recommended that contact be established between schools with large numbers of Cypriot pupils and Cypriot parents by inviting parents' associations to organize social events in school which could be followed by relevant school business in Greek and Turkish, as in the case of the Stationers' Company School, where the Cypriot Parents' Association works closely with the school to promote matters of social, cultural and educational interest to the large number of Cypriot boys in the school. Conversely, some teachers attend functions organized by the Greek Parents' Association (see e.g. Hunter-Grundin, 1982).

How, then, has home–school contact between Cypriot parents and their children's schools seemed from the perspective of teachers? What attempts have schools made to facilitate interaction with Cypriot parents? Has the communication been as 'personal' as it would seem, from the accounts of Oakley and Triseliotis, that Cypriot parents would wish? Although research evidence is sparse, it does nevertheless indicate increasing awareness of the need to establish home–school contact, that some genuine attempts have been made to establish communication, and with some success. In an early survey Townsend and Brittan (1972) found that although 119 out of 230 schools in a national sample cited difficulties in establishing personal contact with immigrant parents, in over 100 cases this was with Asian parents as only six schools mentioned difficulty in contacting Greek and Turkish Cypriot parents. However, a smaller number of schools with pupils of Cypriot origin may have been involved in this investigation, and unfortunately no information is provided about the extent of involvement by Cypriot parents in different kinds of school functions or visits, as it is for other ethnic minority parents. Seven schools in the sample sent information home to parents in Greek and four in Turkish. But as the report by Alkan and Constantinides (1981) demonstrated, in some cases, such as school journeys, it may be necessary to organize meetings with Cypriot parents at school or home, rather than communicate by letter, if sufficient trust is to be established for Cypriot girls to participate. Over the years research surveys have shown that LEAs, especially those with a larger proportion and/or number of linguistic minority pupils, have provided information to parents in their own language and sometimes, where appropriate, in Greek or Turkish (Townsend, 1971; Little and Willey 1983). Haringey is one such LEA where a translation service is available for newsletters, invitations and letters to parents (Hunter-Grundin 1982). However, Beetlestone (1982) found that only eight out of 40 schools used the borough's translation service and few attempted to explain their teaching approaches, for example, to reading. In interviews heads generally saw Cypriot parents in positive terms as generous, friendly, supportive, enthusiastic, willing to help, interested, energetic and lively. Although some parents were involved in parent–teacher associations (PTAs) and various home–school activities, some parents, particularly Turkish Cypriot mothers, were seen as shyer and less forthcoming, and some Cypriot fathers were seen as hostile to female teachers in authority. Heads also sometimes saw parents as too busy to attend school and unwilling to give up time to see teachers. However, Beetlestone suggested that the expectation of parental participation might be seen as an unwarranted imposition on the lives of working-class parents.

Yet some schools have been successful in establishing direct personal contact and relationships with Cypriot parents through a variety of means, either in school or in the parent's home. Some LEAs, for example, Haringey, offer an interpreting service in Greek and Turkish. In some schools Cypriot teachers and adults other than teachers perform this function, interpreting for Cypriot parents and children and staff regarding a range of matters such as health examinations and school outings. Derrick (1968) noted that 'many schools have found that the services of an adult member of the immigrant community are the greatest help in making the life of the school run smoothly' (p.130). English-speaking Cypriot pupils may also act as interpreters. Markopoulou (1974) described a project in Camden whereby some Cypriot girls of secondary age who had been referred by teachers, social workers or parents after reaching the point of nervous breakdown or delinquency as a reaction to the conflicts between their lifestyles at school and the social restrictions placed on them by their parents, gradually engaged in various developmental groupwork activities and eventually realized that they could offer a 'service to the community' by acting as interpreters between the Cypriot and English communities. Whenever possible, the girls acted as messengers for social workers, keeping illiterate clients informed of the progress of their case, or interpreting for teachers to Cypriot parents about the development of their children's learning. This resulted in very practical benefits to both communities. In this case, through patient counselling and the continuous involvement of teachers, parents and social workers the disaffection of these girls was eventually transformed and turned into a beneficial arrangement for all parties.

Some LEAs have special schemes for liaison with the Cypriot community. For example, in Haringey there are special liaison officers who help school social workers in relation to the Cypriot community (Alkan and Constantinides, 1981; Little and Willey, 1983). Another scheme is that of educational home visiting as described by Hunter-Grundin (1982). The objectives of the South Harringay home-visiting scheme were to help parents to realize their own educational role in assisting the pre-school child's learning through play and toys, encourage pleasurable anticipation of school, establish strong home–school links and, in particular, to foster language development. In evaluating the project, Hunter-Grundin saw this as a key area for future development and one likely to be cost-effective, despite the investment of time and patience. Other schemes have involved working with whole families and bringing together groups of parents in order to discuss common problems and reduce social isolation (Martianou, 1981). Evidently this is a sensitive field and schools need to have reflected upon and developed consistent policies and practices with respect to home–school liaison. Ulug (1981) showed that schools were sometimes involved in mediating between Turkish Cypriot adolescent girls and their parents with respect to intergenerational and cultural difficulties, but needed in-depth awareness to perform this role adequately. However, evidence from case studies of a small sample of Turkish Cypriot girls indicated that home–school liaison might be considered by a Turkish Cypriot girl as an intrusion on her separate life at school, become an additional pressure and reinforce the culture conflict.

Clearly it is of the utmost importance to establish good home–school links in the early days of the child's education in order to build a firm foundation for later parent–teacher involvement. Any pre-school home–school visitor links should persist at the transition from home to school and, at this time, particularly Cypriot mothers should be encouraged to visit schools in order to give confidence to their children until they are settled (Alkan and Constantinides, 1981; Beetlestone, 1982). An example of good practice involving Greek and Turkish Cypriot parents who were shown by infant teachers how they might help their children at home in reading and mathematics is quoted in the Swann Report (GB.P. H of C, 1985, pp. 677–8). Another example, described by Hunter-Grundin (1982), is that where parents in the South Harringay area of Haringey were closely involved with the pre-school centre, infant and junior schools whose rolls included 37 per cent Greek Cypriot and 30 per cent Turkish Cypriot children. The pre-school centre, set up in

1978, served a culturally and socially diverse area, and was staffed by a co-ordinator, two part-time educational home visitors and two nursery nurses. Its work covered three main fields: child development, adult education and community support. In one week, in June 1981, it was visited by 90 adults, either parents or minders, with one or more children usually under three years old. The centre promoted small group discussion amongst the parents and encouraged inter-parental support. In addition to providing information and advice, it aimed to foster understanding between parents from different social and cultural backgrounds, especially in the discussion of child-rearing practices. Hunter-Grundin saw the adult education provision at the centre as a supremely significant feature and considered that the centre's success in giving local community support was dependent on the caring, friendliness and commitment of the staff, the absence of formality, sensitive approaches to both child-rearing and adult recreation and the proximity of the centre to local schools with which there was close collaboration. Indeed infant and junior schools in this area were also characterized by an unusually high degree of parent involvement. At the time of her report, the infant school had 170 children, aged four to seven, of 21 nationalities, speaking 17 different mother tongues, and many had no English at all on arrival. Parents were encouraged to visit the classroom and four para-professional teachers were employed to supervise classroom play if a parent wished to speak to a teacher. Parents were invited to stay for school assembly, to enrol in a choir with a multiethnic repertoire, to demonstrate aspects of their cultures to the pupils, for example, through cookery and dance, and were invited to tea once a month by the child's teacher.

Parental involvement was similarly encouraged in the junior school attended in 1981 by 200 children aged seven to 12, most UK-born, but mainly speaking English as a second language as only 17 belonged to the indigenous British population. Parents were invited to discuss any aspects of the child's performance, to attend open days and social evenings, sometimes arranged by the Greek Parents' Association, and discussions about books in the children's mother tongue and between the headmistress (who was herself learning Greek and Turkish) and parents concerning ways in which the school and home could work more closely together to enhance pupil progress. Although parents' fluency in English was an important factor in whether they felt able to accept invitations to school, there appeared to be evidence of a steady growth in the number of parents who were actively involved. Moreover, some pupils from local secondary schools also assisted younger children in the infant and junior schools with language development. The strength of the South Harringay project appeared to be that it recognized both the prior and simultaneous influence of the home on the child's learning and worked to improve the communication and connection between the home and the school to the benefit of individual pupils and the community as a whole. But it is worth echoing Hunter-Grundin's conclusion that in order for successful home–school contact to be achieved on a more extensive scale, teachers will need to adopt different roles and have more flexible working hours which can be spent partly in classrooms, partly in curriculum development with parents, and partly in home visiting. Though Cypriot parents are clearly interested in, and highly concerned about, the education of their children, it seems unlikely from research evidence that they will all enjoy such a degree of personal contact with their children's schools, even if this might be what they desire.

ATTITUDES TO ASPECTS OF THE SCHOOL AND CURRICULUM ORGANIZATION

One way in which to consider the attitudes of Cypriot parents to their children's schooling is to examine their views on aspects of school curriculum and organization. Parents' attitudes to British education are likely to be considerably influenced by their cultural orientation, the extent to which the social norms of their rural backgrounds and lifestyles are re-created in their communities in the UK, the conditioning influence of their experiences of education in Cyprus, the response of individual families to Anglicization and the degree of their understanding of British education in theory and practice. Since the religious background of Greek Cypriots is in the Greek Orthodox Church, their religious beliefs and practices are not at variance with the Christian basis of British schooling, yet significantly, this is not the case for Turkish Cypriots whose religious background is in Islam. Some slight evidence permits a limited insight into the extent to which the views of Turkish Cypriot parents differ from Greek Cypriot parents about aspects of their children's education, such as religious education and single-sex schooling, for religious and cultural reasons. However, such differences have generally – and certainly not until recent years – been unacknowledged, which perhaps also reflects the lack of assertion by Turkish Cypriots of their own interests and/or the lack of documentary evidence. Throughout the literature the following aspects of the curriculum and school organization are reported to have received comment from parents: discipline, teaching methods and curriculum approaches, homework, school meals, religious education, single-sex schooling and ethnic schooling.

One of the most significant and enduring criticisms made by Cypriot parents has concerned what they have perceived as a lack of discipline in schools. As Oakley (1970) explained, the difference in perspective is not merely about the morality of punishment or the role of formal teaching methods in the learning process. It springs from the manner of upbringing in which the child is very dependent on external pressures, such as those of family and local community, for enforcing good conduct, so that the notions of public honour and shame are much more pertinent than the internalized controls of conscience, guilt and pride more familiar to the English pattern of child-rearing. Though Greek Cypriot children, for example, may avoid misconduct for fear of being found out, the comparative relaxation of community ties in settlements in London means there may be less pressure for children to conform to traditional ways, and when at school they are further away from adult Greek supervision so increasingly loosening the system of control. There is thus a contrast between the relative absence of discipline in school and the external control over a child's behaviour exercised within the Greek Cypriot family. Oakley suggested that teachers would find that Greek Cypriot children required more guidance than the average child, and for this both children and parents would rely on the teacher. Furthermore, he opined that whilst girls would be more likely to seek guidance of their own accord, because of the emphasis upon dependence on others in their upbringing, they might need it less, since industriousness and application are instilled in them from an early age and they are more subject than boys to family supervision. On the other hand, Oakley considered that boys, controlled to a lesser extent by their families, aspire to be more independent and are less likely to solicit advice – but because they may be exposed to more influences, they might often have greater need of it.

Butterworth and Kinnibrugh (1970) also noted that the contrast between the upbringing of a Cypriot child in Cyprus and the more liberal atmosphere of the British school was a source of initial difficulty to some Cypriot children who arrived in the UK during the course of their schooling. Some were bewildered by the need to develop control over their own behaviour without the permanent threat of punishment. Butterworth and Kinnibrugh found this was also sometimes a cause of dismay to Cypriot parents (especially fathers) who might even perceive it as a threat to their authority over the child. Some older adolescents arriving in Britain after they had left school in Cyprus who found that they were legally obliged to return to school were unable to make the adjustment to their new environment and developed behaviour difficulties and occasionally truanted. Having undertaken clinical and social work with Cypriot families, Triseliotis (1968, 1976) claimed that many Cypriot parents were highly critical of schools for being too permissive and expected teachers to discipline the children on their own behalf even to the extent of using physical punishment. If teachers do not wish to operate a more authoritarian and directive learning environment, perhaps contrary to their personality or beliefs, this may be perceived by Cypriot parents as a failure to impose firm control, weakness or indifference. Thus the teacher's teaching style is called into question, the authoritarian role of the Cypriot father comes under strain and the Cypriot child may feel confused by the double standards of relative internal control at school and external control at home. Triseliotis argued that such children should not be encouraged to flout parental demands, rather more positive direction should be given and more clearly defined limits set in order to provide a framework in which Cypriot children might begin to develop the internalized control presupposed by the British system of schooling. Some behaviour problems do, however, result amongst Cypriot children on account of the conflicting expectations between the school and the home with respect to standards of behaviour and discipline.

Evidence from some educational research investigations supports these socio-anthropological descriptions of differences in disciplinary approaches between Cypriot parents and teachers. In Townsend and Brittan's national survey (1972), although primary teachers very rarely mentioned disciplinary problems with Cypriot pupils, a few secondary teachers noted that Cypriot parents and also Cypriot girls were sometimes distressed by the contrast between the restrictions placed upon them by their parents and the greater freedom experienced by many of their English peers. In a follow-up study, Brittan (1973, 1976a) reported that a few teachers from 25 schools in different parts of the country mentioned some behavioural difficulties with Cypriot boys, which were attributed to gender-based differences in parental discipline, but teachers have not generally perceived Cypriot pupils to display unacceptable behavioural traits. Again, a CRC survey (1977) in 1975 recorded that the majority of 46 teachers in 20 multiethnic schools in eight multiracial areas claimed that ethnic minority parents expected more or stricter discipline to be exerted at school than teachers believed appropriate, and Cypriot parents were particularly said to desire stronger discipline, especially for their daughters. This was borne out in another part of the survey. Although 51 per cent of 61 Cypriot parents did not perceive discipline to be a problem in their child's school – a higher percentage than other ethnic minority or white British parents – only nine per cent thought it was 'OK/all right/good' – a much lower percentage than other parents – and 31 per cent claimed that discipline was not strict enough or that lack of discipline was a problem – a slightly higher percentage than other parents. This suggests that the views of Cypriot parents were likely to differ from those of other parents on the question of discipline, especially since between 14 and 28 per cent fewer Cypriot parents than those in other groups – in fact a very small percentage – were positively satisfied with the discipline in their child's school. Although these investigations took place over a decade ago, the concerns of Cypriot parents about the standards of discipline and behaviour in schools and their perception of the lack of supervision of girls' conduct have continued to be acknowledged (Alkan and Constantinides, 1981; GB.P. H of C, 1985). Interestingly, Martianou's (1981) interviews with a small sample of Cypriot parents suggested that they might hold a broader concept of discipline as they criticized schools for failure to instil moral codes and some wanted schools to bring children up to be good citizens and to respect their elders as well as to offer a good academic education.

Just as the attitudes of Cypriot parents to discipline in the school environment are influenced by the social and cultural norms of their communities, so their own experience of schooling in Cyprus may lead them to have different expectations of schooling and teaching methods employed in the British educational system. Oakley (1968) reported that Cypriot parents were critical of the school curriculum and of the methods of teaching languages and mathematics and, in particular, they disapproved of play activities. This may be interpreted as an aspect of the question of discipline since traditionally young children were more likely to take part in the daily activities of the family, girls helping mothers in the home and boys working with fathers, than they were to play, and also because of the formal teaching methods in schools in Cyprus and the expectation of Cypriot parents that these will also obtain in schools in the UK (Butterworth and Kinnibrugh, 1970). Triseliotis (1976) also claimed that creative and self-directed learning was viewed by Cypriot parents as less 'efficient' compared with formal teaching. More recently, Martianou (1981) reported that Cypriot parents did not understand the primary or secondary school curriculum, disapproved of child-centred methods of learning and criticized the third-year secondary option specialism. The Swann Report (GB.P. H of C, 1985) noted that a difference of viewpoint was expressed by community representatives, for whilst some Turkish Cypriots claimed that many parents disliked the informality and flexibility of primary education, 'all play and no work', others stressed that such views were based on a lack of knowledge and understanding of the rationale behind such provision. Clearly there is a responsibility on schools to inform parents of the nature and reasons for their teaching approaches and curricular provision, especially perhaps in terms of the educational purpose of play, as in the South Harringay project described by Hunter-Grundin (1982; pp. 149–50).

Another source of parental complaint reported by several observers (Oakley; Triseliotis; Butterworth and Kinnibrugh; Martianou) is the lack of homework. Cypriot parents expect homework to be given from a relatively young age as in Cyprus children possess their own school books and customarily take home exercises, usually involving memorization, to do in the evening. This may be a case where cultural expectation can be put to good use, especially in language development, through, for example, collaborative learning exercises in which parents may hear children read (Tizard *et al.*, 1982). On the other hand, Archimandritou-Xefteris (1977) observed that in some Greek families children had difficulties in completing their homework assignments, especially when they were involved in mother-tongue classes in the evenings and in assisting in family businesses both before and after school. Martianou (1981), however, reported that Cypriot parents checked their children's homework at the primary level and supervised the homework of secondary pupils as best they could, and some paid for extra private tuition.

Another area of concern may be school meals. A Community Relations Commission (CRC) survey (1977) revealed that although half of the Cypriot parents claimed that there were no problems with the school meals available to their children, some 30 per cent – a higher percentage than any other group of parents – complained about the poor quality of school dinners. Like West Indian parents, they were twice as likely to make this complaint, though they were less concerned with the expense than West Indian parents. As Alkan and Constantinides (1981) have pointed out, whereas young Cypriots in the late 1940s and 1950s often had to adopt British food habits because of the lack of availability of traditional Cypriot food, since 1960 available fresh produce direct from Cyprus has meant that Cypriot pupils have not necessarily had to accommodate to a change in diet, though they may have become just as familiar and content with a British diet. Whilst it is possible that some of the parents in the CRC survey could have objected to school meals on religious grounds, in view of the Islamic prohibition on pork, relatively few of this sample of Cypriot parents were apparently Turkish Cypriots. Turkish Cypriot pupils are discouraged by their parents from eating pork at school (Memdouh, 1981). However, the extent to which their dietary preferences have been taken into account by the school meal service in the areas in which numbers of Turkish Cypriots are settled, in boroughs north and south of London, may be questioned.

Religious education may be a matter of concern, especially to some Turkish Cypriot parents. In the CRC survey (1977) 74 per cent of 61 Cypriot parents claimed that they were satisfied with the religious instruction which their children received in school, although a small minority were concerned that no religious instruction was given, that it was insufficient, or, there was inadequate instruction in their own religion. Though there was a clear contrast between the views of Cypriot and Asian parents, there was no explicit indication of the views of Turkish Cypriot parents. However, Turkish Cypriot representatives emphasized to the Swann Committee that they were concerned that greater attention should be given to Islam within the RE curriculum (GB.P. H of C, 1985). They considered that Cypriot parents were generally not formally informed by schools of their right to withdraw their children from religious education, although they preferred their children not to attend RE lessons (Memdouh, 1981). However, Ulug (1981) noted that some Turkish Cypriot girls did not attend school assemblies.

In the CRC survey parents also expressed their views about multicultural education. Only 25 per cent of Cypriot parents – the same percentage as West Indian parents but smaller than that of Asian parents – claimed that their children were taught nothing of their country's origin; however, a further 49 per cent, a higher percentage than any other group of parents, thought that they were not taught enough. This may serve to indicate the strength of Cypriot parents' orientation to their cultural background and their desire for it to be recognized and transmitted to the second generation. Moreover, Cypriot parents clearly thought that teachers from their own country would be helpful either in imparting their culture or in leading to a better understanding of their children's educational needs. Some 45 per cent of Cypriot parents claimed that their children had Cypriot teachers, and three-quarters of those who did not would have liked Cypriot teachers in their children's schools. Interestingly, only a minority of the 600 ethnic minority parents in the sample claimed that their child had problems because of being a member of an ethnic minority group, and of these a mere four per cent of Cypriot parents, a smaller percentage than any other group of parents, claimed that their child had experienced racial problems in school. Evidence to the Swann Committee also indicated that Cypriot parents were in favour of a multicultural curriculum which reflected 'a more balanced and less Anglo-centric view of the world', particularly in relation to history and geography and the use of Cypriot literature and folk tales (GB.P. H of C, 1985, p.685).

Many Cypriot parents apparently have a preference for single-sex schooling at secondary age in view of traditional cultural attitudes *vis-à-vis* the position of girls and boys (Townsend and Brittan, 1972; Milstead, 1981; Memdouh, 1981; GB.P. H of C, 1985). Yet Triseliotis (1976) suggested that Cypriot parents accepted the idea of co-educational schools, whilst restricting adolescent mixing between the sexes in out-of-school hours, and a majority of parents in Martianou's (1981) sample preferred mixed schooling. On the other hand, Little and Willey (1983) reported that of five LEAs in 1979 which claimed that they had representations from ethnic minority groups concerning the provision of single-sex schools, one of these was from Turkish Cypriot organizations. Moreover, the Swann Report recorded the strong preference of both Greek and Turkish Cypriot parents to have the option of single-sex provision for girls, that in one case strength of protest had led to the retention of this option in one area, and that some Turkish Cypriot parents had sent their daughters to a single-sex school rather than to a neighbouring co-educational school which they believed to have higher educational standards because of their preference for single-sex provision. According to Beetlestone (1982), for Turkish Cypriots 'this is seen as an important means of preserving the position of women in a way which is seen as desirable against adverse cultural influences' (p.20).

However, the Swann Report noted that, unlike some Asian Muslims, Turkish Cypriot Muslim representatives were unanimous in opposing in principle the concept of a Muslim voluntary-aided school as they were not in favour of the existing dual system and did not wish to see it extended. They objected to 'the use of the educational system to promote religious ends' and their suspicion 'was deepened by the association of religion with right-wing political views' (GB.P. H of C, 1985, p.678). Their apparent concern to divorce themselves from Islamic fundamentalism may also have been linked to the desire not to be associated in the minds of the British public with Pakistani Muslims, a 'coloured' ethnic minority group (Ladbury, 1977).

On the other hand, parental concern for the transmission of culture and language has led not only to community provision for part-time mother-tongue schools, but also to the establishment of some limited full-time provision for Greek and Greek Cypriot children. Oakley noted that in 1970 there were plans for a Greek secondary school in London, and Markopoulou (1974) recorded that there was a Greek school in Camden at that time. The Hellenic College was first established in the Greek Orthodox Church in Kentish Town and by 1980 occupied the premises of the former American School at Knightsbridge (Izbicki, 1983). This was a private fee-paying school for some 175 pupils, mainly the children of wealthy Greek shipowners and businessmen and some children from wealthy Cypriot families (Tsatsaroni, 1983). The school operated on a bilingual Greek–English basis and in respect of examinations and university entrance. Until February 1983 teachers were supplied by the Ministry of Education in Athens, when it became apparent that the more socialist values of the teachers and the ideology of the Greek government were somewhat at variance with the practices of the school. Moreover, as the parents' committee of the school were concerned that children were working too hard since the lessons were in both Greek and English, the school re-opened after a temporary closure with a new emphasis on lessons in English, Greek teaching being confined to language, literature, history and religion. Furthermore, since 1983 there has been a full-time, non-fee-paying school for approximately 90 pupils of Greek and Greek Cypriot origin, financed by and in premises adjacent to the Greek Embassy in Holland Park (Tsatsaroni and Papassava, 1986). Teaching is in Greek. Parents contribute to transport costs. There is apparently considerable interest on the part of some Greek Cypriot parents and a waiting-list for enrolment.

In conclusion, though research about Cypriot parents' views on aspects of the curriculum and school organization is largely limited to hearsay evidence and lacks quantitative rigour and in-depth analysis, it appears that Cypriot parents have some considerable concerns about aspects of the school curriculum and organization such as homework, religious education and single-sex schooling. In particular, complaints have focussed on questions of discipline, serving to illustrate not only differences in cultural attitudes and expectations, based on experience of schooling in Cyprus, but also lack of knowledge about and understanding of the philosophy and methods of British education. Oakley (1968) considered that parents ascribed any failure on the part of their children to perceived differences between their own experience of schooling and teaching methods in Cyprus and those experienced by their children. However, he suggested difficulties with language, motivation and self-discipline were more likely to be significant factors affecting the school performance of Cypriot pupils. Yet, interestingly, he noted that 'in one way or another ... almost every difference between the two systems [of education] is connected with this question of discipline, since the philosophies of learning which underlie them are almost totally opposed in character' (p.47).

Over the past 20 years the relative lack of documented evidence of Cypriot parents' voiced criticisms of their children's schools suggests that on balance they have preferred to leave curricular and organizational matters to LEAs and schools in line with traditional non-interference and respect for teachers' professionalism. However, whilst Cypriot parents may now have a greater awareness of the educational system, there is clearly much scope for schools both to recognize their responsibilities to enhance parents' understanding of the curriculum and teaching approaches and to appreciate the expectations of parents for the education of their children.

EXTRA-CURRICULAR ACTIVITIES

The attitudes of Cypriot parents, who attempt to maintain in the UK the traditional values of their rural origins to a greater extent than now obtains in Cyprus, are highlighted with regard to the participation of their children, especially adolescents, in school- or community-based extra-curricular activities. Though children are allowed considerable freedom and leniency in their behaviour, at adolescence social interaction between the sexes is actively discouraged. Great significance is attached to chastity before marriage and hence Cypriot parents, anxious lest their children become influenced by their adolescent peers, impose restrictions on what their children, especially girls, can do after and sometimes during school hours (Triseliotis, 1976). Such close supervision of their daughters by Cypriot parents may sometimes prevent them from taking a full part in school life. For example, Greek and Turkish Cypriot parents are often reluctant to allow their daughters to take part in school journeys or visits to theatres (Townsend and Brittan, 1972) and Turkish Cypriot parents may discourage their daughters from participating in school sports or plays because training or rehearsals require remaining in school at the end of the day (Ulug, 1981). School outings are sometimes sanctioned by parents if they have a clear educational purpose and are supervised by known staff, but geography may be avoided because of the fieldwork implications. The importance of greater home–school contact and building relationships of trust between teachers and parents is emphasized in an example cited by Alkan and Constantinides (1981), where parental uncertainty about a school trip and concern that girls should not be tempted into trouble led to last-minute organizational complications when one parent withdrew her daughter and other parents swiftly conformed in case the community accused them of irresponsibility. However, in the following year when parents received a full explanation of the school journey, the Cypriot girls were allowed to participate. With the move towards more practical and out-of-school learning experiences, greater attention will need to be given to the views of ethnic minority parents and the cultural and educational implications. Alkan and Constantinides recommended that lunchtime clubs be organized for Cypriot girls on school premises where they may have discussions and set up self-help groups. There may be a case for developing after-school clubs on school premises, possibly with joint teacher–parent supervision, just as there are also clubs attached to mother-tongue schools (Aristodemou, 1979).

There is, however, contrasting evidence of involvement in community-based youth clubs, whether these are run by mainstream or Cypriot organizations, though Cypriot boys may be the main participants in such associations. Indeed a Cypriot youth club was established by the Cyprus Community Party on the premises of a London school as early as 1952 (George and Millerson, 1967). Hylson-Smith (1968), the warden of an international residential club in Stoke Newington, observed that in that locality, in contrast to their parents, second-generation Cypriots often had more contact with mainstream institutions. Greek Cypriots joined freely with white British adolescents in the local youth club and in fact tended to have more English than Greek Cypriot friends. On the other hand, their Turkish Cypriot peers were less likely to belong to local youth clubs. By 1970, however, the Cypriot community had begun to extend facilities for its youth and there was some competition between the Greek Orthodox Church and the Communists for the allegiance of youth both through Greek mother-tongue schools and youth clubs (Oakley, 1970).

Despite this evidence of some early Cypriot youth club provision and attendance subsequent evidence in the mid-1970s is more conflicting. Triseliotis (1976) claimed that Cypriot adolescents usually had limited points of contact with other adolescents outside school hours as they generally made little use of local youth clubs and youth services and had not developed separate facilities. Indeed Triseliotis argued that if cultural and religious differences made it difficult for Cypriot adolescents to use local facilities, then it was necessary to enable separate clubs to be developed in order that young Cypriots could begin to interact with other young people from a position of strength and security when they felt more certain of their own position. Cross (1977), quoting from a CRC survey of new Commonwealth adolescents aged 16–20 in eight areas throughout England, claimed that Cypriots appeared much less likely ever to have been associated with a youth club (33 per cent) or to be attending one (11 per cent) than other young people (68 per cent and 26 per cent respectively). Yet young Cypriots, together with West Indians, were more likely to have been involved in a youth club than young Asians. Of those attending, almost two-thirds liked sporting activities best and Cypriots were even more likely than West Indians to want a club providing sporting activities.

It was probably during the mid- to late 1970s that the greatest expansion of Cypriot youth club facilities took place since Constantinides (1977) reported that a wide variety of youth and other clubs existed for Greek Cypriots. Although some aimed to be free of overt political affiliation, most were in fact associated with left- or right-wing politics, as in Cypriot villages. In Haringey in 1978, Leeuwenberg discovered two youth groups amongst nine Greek Cypriot voluntary organizations, though there did not seem to be similar facilities for Turkish Cypriot youth. Amongst a sample of 84 Greek and 84 Turkish Cypriots with a bias towards 15–24-year-olds, 11.9 per cent of Greek Cypriots and 7.1 per cent of Turkish Cypriots attended youth clubs and a further 8.3 per cent of both groups used sporting facilities. LEA provision was sometimes related to Cypriot provision. In a national survey, in 1979, 16 LEAs with more than ten per cent ethnic minority pupils and 14 LEAs with 2.5–10 per cent ethnic minority pupils had special youth and community provision. In some LEAs youth clubs catered exclusively or largely for specific ethnic minority groups, as in the case of the Greek Cypriot youth club affiliated to Enfield Youth Service (Little and Willey, 1983).

By the early 1980s there were at least ten youth clubs run by the Greek Parents' Association in London and held in school buildings and halls (Martianou, 1981). Singleton (1979) described one such mixed club for 11–20-year-olds with games, music and dancing activities. At that time, at least eight Cypriot associations in Haringey were involved in some kind of youth work, together with one association in Barnet, Enfield and Camden (Alkan and Constantinides, 1981). The activities provided ranged from dancing through drama, choirs, an orchestra, badminton, snooker and table tennis to football. The mixed youth clubs provide the main opportunity for social mixing amongst adolescents. Girls' involvement in these activities seems to be largely restricted to dancing, or perhaps some drama, and parents often inspect the clubs and collect their daughters at the end of sessions. The boys have a wider social outlet in various sporting activities including London-wide Cypriot football leagues which are separate for Greek and Turkish Cypriots. Within the Cypriot community there are a number of preventative and remedial social work therapy groups in which a range of games and drama activities and discussions about home–school problems take place. Alkan and Constantinides recommended the expansion of such groups on a gender or mixed basis and also that more community youth clubs should take account of the social needs of adolescent Cypriot girls. There may also be a particular need for facilities for the single 18-plus age-group, since, apart from large social gatherings, they often have nowhere where they can meet with parental agreement. Greater co-operation between teachers and parents would enable better use of school facilities and the development of school-based activities and clubs enjoying the same confidence which Cypriot parents have in their own community facilities.

PARENTS AND CHILDREN

In some Cypriot families, as in some other ethnic minority groups with strong cultural traditions, inter-generational differences and difficulties in the home may be confused with culturally differentiated perceptions and orientations, compounded by the loss of the mother tongue and the contrasting values transmitted in education and exhibited in the school environment. Such generational and cultural mismatch tends to be highlighted in the relationships between parents and children especially (but not only) at adolescence and also with respect to the behaviour of girls. Clearly relationships between parents and children, in so far as they are affected by two cultures, will not only vary from family to family, or even within families, but may also change over time, depending on a range of factors not the least of which is the strength of the surrounding ethnic community norms and sanctions. Relationships between Cypriot parents and their children, as documented in the research literature, will be examined through a consideration of traditional values; parents' perceptions of British culture and their reactions in terms of control over the behaviour of their children; differential cultural responses between the first and second generations, especially with respect to values and upbringing, language and communication; some cases where there are not just tensions between parents and children, but a breakdown in relationships; and the role of the school in promoting better inter-generational and inter-cultural understanding.

As already noted (pp. 151–2), a strong cultural influence is the extent to which Cypriot parents use externalized forms of behavioural control, which may conflict with the reliance teachers place on more internalized methods and which may lead to differing views of discipline on the part of Cypriot parents and children. Another traditional cultural value relates to a set of gender-differentiated attitudes and expectations about socially acceptable behaviour which are often the cause of inter-generational tension and dispute because of their perceived contrast with the observed social practices of British adolescents and their families. One matter in particular may often become the focus for inter-generational and inter-cultural conflicts where Cypriot girls are concerned, namely, the great significance attached to chastity before marriage and a good reputation. In this regard, Cypriot parents are much more concerned with the behaviour of girls than boys since Cypriot society tends to identify moral behaviour mainly with female sexuality, the sexual behaviour of the male being much less scrutinized (Triseliotis, 1968, 1976). Hence traditional attitudes tend to support double standards regarding male and female behaviour, prescribing a secluded and rigidly supervised life for Cypriot girls, whereas boys have traditionally been permitted more freedom (Oakley, 1968, 1970). The extent to which Cypriot parents attempt to uphold these traditional attitudes and behavioural norms in the light of their perceptions of contrasting and antipathetic British values and practices in school and neighbourhood may lead to particular inter-generational difficulties. Many Cypriot parents consider that what they perceive as the permissive attitude of British society towards relations between the sexes is a threat to their own values (Butterworth and Kinnibrugh 1970; Oakley, 1970; Triseliotis, 1968). Such perceptions on the part of both Cypriot parents and their children may be informed to a large extent by exposure to a range of conflicting values through the media, especially television, as well as parents' general observations of social behaviour in the locality and children's knowledge of the kind of freedom which many British adolescents enjoy in their relationships out of school (Derrick, 1968).

Cypriot parents' fears of 'immoral' influences on their children may lead them to attempt to keep adolescents closely supervised. Due to the high value placed on virginity and a good reputation, Cypriot girls in particular are very restricted in their activities outside the home since to be allowed out too freely may be considered 'loose' by the community, and Cypriot parents have an intense desire that the standing of their daughters should not be so diminished (Butterworth and Kinnibrugh, 1970; Constantinides, 1977; Alkan and Constantinides, 1981). Hence suspicion of the British way of life and social mores may lead Cypriot parents to deprive their adolescent children of the chance to mix with British teenagers, especially of the opposite sex, and girls' opportunities for socialization may be extremely limited (Markopoulou, 1974). For example, George (1960) recorded that Cypriot girls were not allowed to go out freely because this was regarded as morally wrong, and there were even restrictions on their dress, whereas boys were permitted to socialize widely, even with other communities. Girls are expected to spend more time at home helping with housework, the rearing of younger siblings or working in the family business (Archimandritou-Xefteris, 1977; Markopoulou, 1974). Martianou (1981) found that many 14-year-olds declined to accompany their parents on outings, but whereas boys were allowed to go out with friends, girls stayed at home. Protection is clearly much more extensive for girls than for boys (Khan, 1976; Alkan and Constantinides, 1981). Girls often resent the individual pressures upon them to conform to accepted codes of behaviour – to behave with decorum and propriety and to go out chaperoned – and the tremendous community pressure to keep up appearances; whilst some appreciate the support of the community, however, others feel stifled by the surveillance of their behaviour (GB. P. H of C, 1985). Any kind of relationship between the sexes is actively discouraged, but serious relationships either between Greek or Turkish Cypriots or with the wider community are particularly frowned upon. According to Triseliotis (1976), on occasion Cypriot girls have been sent to Cyprus to stop them seeing a particular boyfriend. Some adolescent girls see an early engagement arranged by their parents as the only prospect of leading a free life like that of their British contemporaries (Triseliotis, 1976; Constantinides, 1977; Ladbury, 1977; Alkan and Constantinides, 1981).

Gender-differentiated attitudes and practices appear to apply in both Greek and Turkish Cypriot families. A study by Ulug (1981) revealed beliefs and behaviour supporting the superiority of men, the protection of young girls and the importance of honour for the family within Turkish Cypriot households which were reinforced by the views and perceptions of Turkish Cypriot boys. As Ulug observes, however, some British families also impose restrictions upon their daughters, so it is perhaps the strength of feeling which Turkish and Greek Cypriot parents have about retaining cultural beliefs and practices which are socially sanctioned by the re-created community in the UK, and the determination and deliberate methods which they adopt to uphold them, which are the real points of conflict between parents and children in this respect. Anthias (1983, 1984) has argued that amongst Greek Cypriots there has been some easing of the expression of the ideology of sexual purity and young women have more freedom, for example, with respect to taking a job in non-Cypriot establishments, but girls have been brought up to submit to parental will and continue to do so as an obligation even when they have more opportunities to exercise independent judgement. Moreover, the geographical, social, economic and political links of the Cypriot communities act as 'policing' mechanisms preserving traditional roles and sexual relations. The strict upbringing during school days continues after school leaving with restrictions on freedom imposed by male authority, girls being discouraged from associating with English girlfriends and reverting to a more Greek Cypriot environment. Uneasy compromises are often made, but as though to compensate for loss of freedom, parents offer every financial support they can (Anthias suggests out of guilt and self-interest), often providing cars, clothes and food as well as allowing girls to keep their wages (see also Georgiou, 1983).

It is important, however, to look behind the issue of gender-differentiated attitudes and behaviour – and upon which the research literature tends to focus – to consider the extent to which this is symptomatic of other inter-generational differences relating to the retention of specifically Cypriot cultural values and traditions. Much has been written about the experience of ethnic minority children between two cultures. As early as 1967 the London Council of Social Service (LCSS) report warned that Cypriot children might develop divided loyalties, to their families and Cypriot background on the one hand, and to the school on the other, and that in some cases failure to reconcile the expectations of both might lead to rebellion or behavioural difficulties at school or home. Such observations continue to be made some 20 years later (GB. P. H of C, 1985). But it is important to attempt to get beyond these kinds of generalizations – a matter of extreme difficulty where both inter-cultural and inter-generational perceptions are concerned – in order to examine more closely those aspects of traditional Cypriot culture and values which are hotly disputed by the second generation, and those which generate less concern and are given a different emphasis. Although the literature tends to give more weight to matters of inter-generational disharmony, it is nevertheless possible to discern a certain value congruence.

Even in the 1960s, Hylson-Smith (1968) noted that whereas first-generation Cypriots had relatively little contact with the wider society and were orientated largely towards their own cultural norms, adolescents of the second generation often established friendships and had far more contact with the host society. Hylson-Smith considered that, at that time, because of their less developed community life and the greater affinity of the religious and moral basis of their cultural norms to those of the host society, Greek Cypriots appeared to be more assimilated than Turkish Cypriots. Second-generation Cypriots were aware that the main hindrances to assimilation were cultural differences, but they either thought these would be resolved in time or did not perceive it as a problem. However, Oakley (1970) suggested that Cypriot children's experience of the process of growing up within two cultural traditions was rather more painful, especially for those lacking a commitment to traditional Cypriot culture and the comforting institutional background from which their parents could derive support. In particular, the greater perceived autonomy and independence of their school peers and the development of critical thinking encouraged in the British system of schooling led some Cypriot children to question and challenge their parents to a greater extent than if they had been in the village communities in Cyprus. Some parents find this difficult to accept and may need help in recognizing the strangeness of their children's experience and attempts to reconcile two cultures. Importantly, in this context, as Triseliotis (1976) also points out, Cypriot parents may lack awareness of how much they mean to their children, for as they perceive most things as happening from forces outside themselves feelings from within may be somewhat underplayed. Just as the Cypriot parent may have difficulty in understanding the adjustment of the older immigrant child, so the child of Cypriot origin born in the UK may fail to appreciate parents' values and their continued orientation towards and identification with Cyprus. Hence a perceptual gap may often develop between these children and their parents as neither has experienced the world of the other. Some Cypriot parents' attitudes may have remained more traditional than current attitudes in Cyprus which have changed over time and with political circumstances. Where parents' sense of emotional and spiritual loss in their removal from their homeland is great, this may make them feel more misunderstood and more determined to ensure that their children conform to traditional cultural norms. In such cases, parents may also expect their children to fulfil what they themselves failed to achieve or to give them back what they have lost – 'the dream of a "good" life' (see Anthias, 1984).

Three specific educational research studies provide some insight into the ways in which the values held by Cypriot parents and the methods which they employ in the upbringing of their children influence the response of the latter to certain moral values, their home environment and their school achievement. In an interesting small-scale study Marvell (1974) investigated the formation of moral values of a multiracial group of 120 pupils in two mixed comprehensives in a large town in southern England. The adolescents comprised 20 Greek Cypriot, 20 Turkish Cypriot, 40 English, 20 West Indian and 20 Indian pupils, an equal number of boys and girls from each year in the schools. Following participant observation in the schools and interviews with staff, parents were visited and interviewed at home. The young people were interviewed at school and completed written tests and questionnaires including a sentence completion measure. Community leaders were also interviewed and visits made to clubs. Parents unanimously accepted both their responsibility for the moral character of their children and the value of the traditional mores of their particular cultural background. Though they had difficulty in verbalizing their conceptions of their moral values, which they tended to see concretely, many of the immigrant parents expressed distress at what they perceived to be the permissiveness of English society in general, and young people in particular. They differed from English parents not in the moral rules which they saw as necessary for society to function, but over whether control should be external or internal. In addition, whereas all groups of parents excepting Turkish Cypriots gave overall priority to honesty, in word or deed, the Turkish Cypriot parents considered obedience to be more important. This ranked as second priority for Greek Cypriot parents. Turkish Cypriot parents also thought hard work was an important part of moral training. Curiously, although only a few did so, the English parents were more likely than either Greek or Turkish Cypriot parents to mention chastity.

On the sentence completion test the overwhelming majority of the adolescents agreed with their parents on the importance of honesty. Yet although the majority named their parents as the people with whom they would talk if they had a problem, only 60 per cent of Turkish and 58 per cent of Greek adolescents, fewer than other group members, did so. The Greek and Turkish Cypriot pupils were less likely to give positive responses concerning their feelings when at home (half or less than half of these groups compared with three-quarters of the English adolescents) and a high percentage of the Greek and Turkish pupils (70 and 75 per cent respectively) made critical comments about their parents' lack of understanding and the lack of status accorded to them by their parents. Overall the responses of the Cypriot pupils indicated the greatest degree of parent–child tension. On the other hand, they were less likely than English or West Indian pupils, though slightly more so than Indian pupils, to say that the school had influenced the development of their character (Greek Cypriots 35 per cent, Turkish Cypriots 40 per cent). Some 42 per cent of Greek Cypriot and 30 per cent of Turkish Cypriot pupils, fewer than the English pupils, claimed that the school had influenced their judgement on moral matters. The Turkish Cypriot pupils were least likely to want to turn to somebody in the school for advice if they had a problem. Although the school did have a positive effect in the area of moral values, this was less marked than that of the home, particularly for Greek and Turkish Cypriot pupils, who experienced the greater tension at home. Moreover, it appeared that the Cypriot pupils were unlikely to be influenced in their moral values by those in the wider community (see p. 173), and although over half of the Greek Cypriot and four-fifths of the Turkish Cypriot pupils claimed to discuss moral questions with their friends, they were less likely to claim to have been influenced by them on moral matters.

Marvell's study serves as a reminder that though there may be parent–child tensions in the home, this may not necessarily be a negative state, but one which can be used for personal growth. Indeed parents and the home context apparently still had particular salience for these pupils in influencing their moral values and judgements. In a study in a London FE College MacDonald (1975) found, in interviews, that Greek and Turkish students were slightly more likely than British or Jamaican students to express contentment with their home situation. Another study which involved some 130 Greek-speaking adolescents aged 13–18 (Archimandritou-Xefteris, 1977) examined the relation between various aspects of upbringing and achievement (see pp.132–3). In these children's patriarchal families, where the mothers were responsible for child-rearing and supervising schooling, there was no significant association between children's achievement and the proportion of available time spent by the father with the child, and the researcher suggested that the physical presence of the father was less important than the way in which the father was represented to the child by the mother, as power and pressure could be exerted even in his absence. According to Greek teachers' estimates of the kind of upbringing experienced by these Greek adolescents, whereas those in the high-achievement group were more likely to have fathers who were inclined to be neither strict nor liberal, and those in the average or low-achievement group were likely to have very strict or erratic fathers, overall some 38–50 per cent in both groups had fathers who were said to have little or no direct influence on their upbringing. The high-achievers were more likely to have mothers who were firm but not strict or liberal in their upbringing, whereas the low-achievers tended to have mothers who were more likely to be erratic or very strict. Interestingly, for 60 per cent of the average or low-achieving group, teachers reported that maternal style of upbringing was in direct contrast to that of the father, i.e. authoritarian compared with erratic or uninfluential. Archimandritou-Xefteris pointed to a tendency to over-protection in Greek culture with high-achievers being only marginally less protected by their mothers. Despite a social veneer of democratic liberality amongst these Greek families, they still relied on traditional approaches to upbringing, stressed the importance of succeeding for the family's sake, strongly countered any tendency towards Anglicization (see p. 178) and invoked traditional values to encourage children to succeed educationally and occupationally (see p. 166).

According to Oakley (1970), few Cypriot parents have really attempted to confront the difficulties presented by bringing up their children according to their own traditional cultural values in a society and in a school context in which some specific values and practices are very different. Rather, as a number of commentators appear to indicate, parents may avoid the decisions which might enable them to resolve the tensions and conflicts with their children in a constructive way and changes often come about by default. On the other hand, relationships between parents and children may become bitter and hostile to the extent that in some cases communication may cease altogether. Conflict between two or sometimes three generations in a Cypriot household due to value differences and rural vs urban upbringing might well result in poor communication, compounded by lack of facility in the mother tongue which literally reduces the possibilities of communication at a meaningful level (Markopoulou, 1974). A communication barrier between Turkish Cypriot parents and daughters due to differential perceptions about cultural practices and lack of intimacy may give rise to a constant temptation to be deceitful at home (Ulug, 1981). As several sources indicate (see pp. 76–7), the very choice of language used may itself symbolize deeper problems of communication. A significant increase in communication difficulties is reported at adolescence, especially with mothers, partly because of superficial knowledge of the mother tongue, so that although children may be able to use everyday words, they may be unable to hold a more abstract conversation in that language. Some Cypriot children may refuse to speak their mother tongue except when essential, demonstrating not only the dominance of their fluency in English, but also the value which they accord to English and by implication the values inherent in the language itself (Saifullah Khan, 1980b). In order to counter the Anglicization of their children, many Cypriot parents choose to send their offspring to mother-tongue classes. But if they are already having difficulties reconciling their parents' point of view to the lifestyle to which they aspire, then such attendance may further increase their resentment (Constantinides, 1977). However, in some children an interest in their parents' culture and language may be rekindled in later years.

Where tensions in relationships between Cypriot parents and their children actually result in serious breakdowns in communication, the stress may lead to rejection or rebellion at home and behavioural difficulties at school. From his wide clinical and social experience, Triseliotis (1963) reported that the mental health of Cypriot children suffered as a result of inter-generational conflict. Frustrated ambitions frequently led to parental overambition with regard to their children. In other cases, parents' ambivalence towards their adopted country hindered their children's attempt to become part of it, or they might have found meeting the basic needs of their families so difficult that children's other needs were temporarily disregarded. All these situations existed amongst immigrant families, including a few Cypriot families, in the Sparkbrook district of Birmingham in the mid-1960s (Williams, in Rex and Moore, 1967). Triseliotis (1968) described a number of detailed case studies which illustrated these situations and showed in the child's emotionally disturbed behaviour in school in terms of aggression, anxiety or passivity, learning difficulties and truancy. Littlewood and Lipsedge (1982) describe the case of a Turkish family where the father's reassertion of traditional values after the simultaneous failure of various financial enterprises, in what had become a prosperous and Anglicized middle-class family, resulted in a serious physical effect on the younger daughter who experienced most of the unanticipated restriction on their lifestyle and was prevented from attending secretarial college. Lack of freedom to socialize with adolescent peers may lead to nervous breakdown or delinquency for Cypriot girls unless social workers and schools can join together to counsel such girls and their parents as Markopoulou (1974) has described. On the other hand, some older immigrant children, especially those who were refugees in the mid-1970s, sometimes found the greater freedom of the British school and social environment in general extremely frightening, and it served to compound their sense of loss of their previous lives (McCarty and Christoudoulou, 1977; Triseliotis, 1976).

Clearly many Cypriot and other ethnic minority children find themselves in conflicting situations with their parents and teachers as they attempt to make sense of their experiences at home and school and the often divergent values, on the one hand, those upheld by their parents and their cultural traditions, and on the other, those transmitted by education, the media and their peers. Cypriot children may be able to accommodate the contradictions between these two sets of values and expectations if they receive the support of their home and the understanding of the school. But 'it carries risk in the case of parents who may feel threatened or are so insecure as not to realise that their children, by accommodating some of the values of the host culture, do not necessarily reject them or their heritage' (Triseliotis, 1976, p. 375). Often the discussion of these matters revolves around gender-differentiated behaviour. Stamataris (1983) observed that although many Greek Cypriot parents seemed unable to accept the fact that their daughters were having to adapt their lives to suit two cultures, and this promoted conflict both within and without the family, the Greek Cypriot adolescent girls whom she studied continued to maintain a strong ethnic identity. However, the exertion of too rigid control and lack of trust by Cypriot parents has on occasion led to their daughters running away from home for brief periods, merely to establish a sense of freedom (Alkan and Constantinides, 1981). Ulug (1981), who studied a small group of Turkish Cypriot adolescent girls, concluded that many of the difficulties of living between two cultures not only continued to develop and remain unresolved but also sometimes went unrecognized. School might be considered as a place of freedom, as a place for deviancy, divorced from the restrictions of home. Anthias (1983) remarked on the degree to which Greek Cypriot girls 'manage' the dissonance they encounter. Most do not openly flout parents' expectations, but many develop situationally appropriate behaviour and are privately more likely to entertain different attitudes and behaviour. Whilst some researchers consider Cypriot pupils, especially girls, 'need to lead two separate lives in order to survive' (Georgiou, 1983), others suggest that Cypriot youth are learning 'to integrate both worlds' (Martianou, 1981). Commentators are generally uncertain as to whether parent–child tensions are primarily inter-generational or cultural.

What role should the school adopt in this process, and how much should it attempt to be involved in what may be seen primarily as a domestic matter, though one which has considerable implications for learning and hence achievement in the school environment? Whilst some teachers have long been aware of some of the culturally differentiated values held by some Cypriot parents, they may have lacked the more precise knowledge about Cypriot parents' thinking and feeling on controversial issues which would, in turn, enable them to be more sensitive in their approach and response to pupils. Schools are often caught in the complex position of trying to satisfy the demands of both parents and pupils and may have to arbitrate or engage in crisis management between both parties, sometimes as in a case reported by Ulug (1981), being asked by parents to operate surveillance procedures which may overlook the perspective of the pupil and collude with the home in punishing the pupil for what may only be a suspected misdeed. Clearly schools have to work towards consistent policies and practices on such sensitive matters. There are also significant and considerable tasks for the school both in terms of developing meaningful programmes of personal and social education and the proper function of the pastoral care system in relation to multicultural education. Alkan and Constantinides (1981) have argued that it is essential for young Cypriots to come to appreciate both the differences between their lives at school and home and those of their British peers and also to understand the similarities, perhaps by comparing Cypriot and British cultural practices and traditions. There is a need, too, for more counselling facilities, both for children individually and for children and parents. A study by Olowu (1983) of counselling with ethnic minority children in Manchester, including some Cypriot pupils, showed that ethnic minority pupils appeared to have more problems than their peers and that girls needed more counselling than boys, especially in schools with few ethnic minority pupils. Parent–child relationships are obviously a delicate matter as far as the school is concerned. On the one hand, parents need to establish a balance between control and trust, and on the other, children need to develop a greater appreciation of their parents' values and behavioural expectations, especially as these are upheld by community sanctions. But the school is in a unique position *vis-à-vis* both parents and children since it provides a continuing focus for the interaction of Cypriot parents and children with the wider British society. Moreover, as far as tensions and serious difficulties in parent–child relationships may affect the ability of children to benefit from their schooling and to realize both their educational and social potential, then this must surely be a matter of considerable concern to the school and one in which its mediation may be justified.

PARENTS' ASPIRATIONS FOR THEIR CHILDREN'S EDUCATION AND EMPLOYMENT

Most parents have high aspirations for their children to succeed in education and employment, and Cypriot parents are no exception. Though little research evidence is available on the precise educational and vocational aspirations of Cypriot parents for their children, various reports indicate general attitudes, possible differences in expectations for boys and girls and some ambiguities due to the desire to retain a strong ethnic and cultural identity.

In an early study in ten secondary schools in Haringey, in 1966, Cypriot pupils (31 boys, 32 girls) reported their mothers were slightly more likely to take an interest in their school work than their fathers (Figueroa, 1974). Although a minority of girls reported no interest on the part of their mothers, over half of the boys and girls reported that their mothers had great interest in their school work. In terms of parents' aspirations for their children's future employment, almost three-quarters of the Cypriot boys (18) and two-thirds of the girls (35) said that their fathers took an interest, and four-fifths of the boys and two-thirds of the girls said that their mothers took an interest. There was a higher reported rate of maternal interest for Cypriot than for West Indian or British boys. Moreover, whereas almost two-thirds of Cypriot boys (23) said that their father had named a suitable job for them, and over half claimed that their mothers had done so, a considerably higher proportion of Cypriot girls (22) – almost nine out of ten – claimed that their fathers and/or their mothers had named a suitable job for them. Cypriot parents thus appeared more concerned to exercise control over the future employment of their daughters than over that of their sons. Hairdressing, office work and sewing were occupations typically suggested by Cypriot parents for their daughters – being types of employment which may be compared with those of their parents (see pp. 16–17) and with the pupils' own vocational aspirations (see pp. 188–9).

In another study in London which attempted to relate scholastic achievement to various family background variables as assessed by Greek teachers Archimandritou-Xefteris (1977) found that high achievers (see pp. 132–3) were likely to have experienced very different child-rearing practices from those of low or average achievement. Parents of high achievers tended to reinforce successful performance by reference to similar achievement when they were at school, whereas parents of low achievers tended to see success as an aberration. The parents of high-achieving adolescents helped them with hobbies and to use their time creatively, and seemed to have a greater knowledge of the kind of pressure which could be applied to their children without demotivating them. They were also more aware of the children's limitations and, in co-operation with their children, worked out goals designed to match their capacities and inclinations. Moreover, whereas parents' occupational choice for high achievers was generally not connected with the father's own occupation, parents of low achievers assumed that the children would follow their fathers into the family business. Parents of high achievers tended to emphasise deferred gratification and encouraged their children to start again if there were failures. Parents of the average, low- and high achievers alike tended to stress the child's duty to succeed and, in addition, the parents of high achievers invoked the concept of 'philotimo' (literally love of honour in relation to self esteem (Oakley, 1968)) as a positive inducement to enable the family to feel pride in the child as one of its members. By contrast, the parents of low achievers tended to convey duty as an injunction upon the individual and pressurized the child to succeed. Generally the parents of high achievers tended to establish the limits of behaviour for their children, but left them free to make decisions within this framework, and were aware of the kind of stimulation children should receive, tending to have values which were consistent with their children's efforts.

A CRC (1977) survey in 1975 investigated the kind of education parents wanted for their children. Some 51 per cent of Cypriot parents compared with 63 per cent of East African Asian, 45 per cent of Indian parents and only 16 per cent of white parents wanted their children to gain academic qualifications at school. Only two of the 51 Cypriot parents wanted their children to have a practical training at school in order to acquire a skill or trade. Cypriot parents often expect considerable application and success. McCarty and Christodoulou (1977) found that relatives caring for children who had arrived as refugees from Cyprus in the mid-1970s were often inclined to put even more pressure on these children to succeed academically, without realizing their traumatic experiences in Cyprus, and sometimes became impatient if the children failed to achieve the sort of results they felt their parents would want. Triseliotis (1976) claimed over-aspiration on the part of some Cypriot parents due to lack of knowledge about the educational system (see pp. 143–6) but also a certain ambiguity in their attitudes. The educational ambitions of both Cypriot parents and their children are often much higher than those of the local population (see CRC, 1977), possibly, Triseliotis suggested, because they have not been exposed over many decades to an image of themselves as a class with limited abilities who must keep their aspirations low. Yet parents' lack of knowledge about the education system, for example, that only a small percentage of pupils proceed to university, may make it more difficult for teachers to explain a child's limitations in some cases where parents' aspirations are seen as unrealistic. Moreover, as Triseliotis has also argued, although Cypriot parents generally have high aspirations for their children's educational performance, they may also have contradictory attitudes related to a different cultural standpoint. Hence whilst most Cypriot parents consciously want their children to succeed, and encourage them to take advantage of opportunities, they may at the same time give them verbal or non-verbal messages which serve to hold them back by creating some confusion for the child.

More recent studies and comment suggest further interpretations and possible changes in Cypriot parents' educational and vocational aspirations for their children. For example, the Swann Report, confirming that in general Cypriot parents are ambitious for their children, suggested this was particularly true of parents who may themselves not have had the opportunity to progress beyond primary education in Cyprus. There was also a suggestion that as families had gained some social and financial security in the UK, they might 'push' their children less hard. This may be linked to other observations that Cypriot parents want their children to be professionals, and yet are not concerned about unemployment, since with the help of relations they are able to provide employment in businesses within the community if ambitions are unrealized (Alkan and Constantinides, 1981; Beetlestone, 1982). Hence, at least until recently, the transition from school to work may have been fairly smooth in view of the employment safety-net. However, there are difficulties here. To what extent do the existence of potential opportunities for employment within the Cypriot community lead to a certain ambivalence in pupils' occupational aspirations, as well as those of their parents? Moreover, might not some parents exercise covert pressure on a child to join the family business, as in a case described by Archimandritou-Xefteris (1977), where a high-achieving child wished to become an engineer whereas the father would have preferred him to continue with the restaurant business? Thirdly, if Cypriot pupils have vocational aspirations outside the ethnic community which are matched by their qualifications and yet poor general employment prospects push them towards opportunities within the Cypriot community, might this not increase the frustration felt by such young people and the tensions between them and their parents? Unfortunately, there are no research data to examine these issues. Indeed there is an assumption that the very high rate of self-employment amongst Cypriots and the strength of links between their ethnic businesses continues to permit the easy absorption of second- and third-generation Cypriots into employment. In fact such businesses may be severely hit by economic recession. Cypriot school-leavers and home-workers were the first to suffer when the recession affected the clothing industry in 1980 (Alkan and Constantinides, 1981).

The Swann Report (GB.P. H of C, 1985) noted that much evidence had been received which referred to gender-differentiated parental expectations and aspirations, suggesting that, whereas parents might be concerned for sons to perform well in public examinations and perhaps go on to higher education, they were less interested in their daughters' education and might prefer them to leave at the statutory age and prepare for marriage. Alkan and Constantinides (1981) pointed to such a differential amongst Cypriot parents in Haringey, suggesting that many girls are still encouraged to look upon employment as a temporary phase between school and marriage and that the preference of many Cypriot girls for a career is not widely understood by the Cypriot community. However, others reported to the Swann Committee that there was a 'growing acceptance of the need for girls to be accorded full equality of opportunity in educational terms' (p. 680), and that reflecting changing practice in Cyprus, even Turkish Cypriot parents would be prepared for a daughter to enter higher education whilst preferably living at or near home. Indeed higher education might be seen as enhancing marriageability and as a potential economic contribution to the family.

These claims tend to be supported by other evidence. Ulug (1981) reported that Turkish Cypriot parents wanted their daughters to do well at school and did not wish them to engage in machining at home as an occupation. Martianou (1981) found that a small sample of Cypriot parents were unanimous in wanting both their sons and daughters to go to higher education, preferably a university. All wanted their children to have a better job, and two were concerned that education should also help them to become better citizens. Parents offered moral and material rather than academic support, though some expected help with housework and cooking or in the family business. All expected their children to stay on at school or go to college if they did not do well at 16. Similarly, Georgiou (1983) noted that although these expectations also applied to Greek Cypriot girls, they still experienced more social restrictions than their male peers when at school or college. And Krokou (1985) observed that educational success may have contradictory implications for girls and their parents, for whilst it may enable a 'good marriage' to be made it carries with it the possibility of rejection of traditional mores.

Whilst Cypriot parents are generally considered to have high educational aspirations for their children, some may feel more ambivalent about the outcome of educational success in terms of the possible implications for the continuation of their own businesses and the social and cultural challenges which may result from the possible distancing of their sons and particularly daughters by taking up higher education or employment outside the community. As Alkan and Constantinides (1981) have observed, though parents may genuinely desire their children to do well academically, they may also expect and need help in their businesses, which they see themselves passing on to their children for their own benefit. On the other hand, the fact that parents often have a limited understanding of the grading and examination system may lead them to entertain unrealistic aspirations for their children and to expect them to obtain training for occupations for which they may not have the required ability or qualifications. Ambivalent attitudes and lack of understanding may lead to considerable frustration and friction between Cypriot parents and children. Clearly, especially in view of current examination changes and increased emphasis on vocational preparation schemes, there is an urgent need for schools to give parents more accurate, up-to-date information about the school's assessment system and curricular innovations relating to the transition from school to work as well as discussing an individual child's educational performance and ability. Regrettably, in the absence of research data on the educational achievement of pupils of Cypriot origin at school-leaving age, the nature of careers advice which they receive and the expectations of their teachers for their school performance, it is impossible to judge whether the aspirations of Cypriot parents and those of their children (see pp. 187–91) are realistic or not.

Cypriot pupils
In any attempt to assess the education performance of pupils of Cypriot origin, account must be taken of the views of those pupils themselves. Hence this section considers research evidence on Cypriot pupils' attitudes to race and their peers; to themselves, in terms of their identity and self-esteem; to their schools; and their

aspirations and expectations for their future careers. In comparison with some other less numerous ethnic minority pupils, there has been much more educational research on the attitudes of pupils of Cypriot origin, especially on their attitudes to their peers and their self-perceptions. This is largely because Cypriots have sometimes formed the third group of ethnic minority pupils in studies which have included pupils of West Indian and Asian origin. In approaching these research data, it is important to bear in mind that many of the attitude scales and measurements employed in these studies may be subject to bias like intelligence tests, largely having been constructed for use with the white majority population. Attitude testing may also, moreover, be particularly influenced by the colour of the tester, the testing context and what is perceived as the tester's expectation. Furthermore, since attempts to evaluate attitudes to race are likely to be influenced by both the racial composition of the school and neighbourhood and also the racial climate obtaining at the time of the research, the fact that the research studies reviewed in this context span a 20-year period makes for difficulties of comparison. Nevertheless certain trends are indicated.

ATTITUDES TO PEERS

The social adjustment of pupils in school may not only influence their attitudes to school, but also seriously affect their educational performance. What attitudes do pupils of Cypriot origin have towards their peers from other ethnic groups in neighbourhood schools? How do Cypriot pupils feel about other members of their own ethnic group? Do Greek and Turkish Cypriots interact? How do the ethnic attitudes of pupils of Cypriot origin affect their actual or desired friendship choices? Are there ethnic differences between the pupils whom Cypriot pupils choose as friends or best friends? Since only two studies, one very small-scale (Kawwa, 1968a) and one on a national scale (Jelinek and Brittan, 1975), have included Cypriot pupils of junior school age, the review considers sociometric investigations according to the date of the research. Moreover, as only two small-scale research projects have examined the attitudes of pupils of Cypriot origin to race as such (Dove, 1974; Young and Bagley, 1979, 1982a) and at opposite ends of the age range, these will be considered prior to the friendship studies, for which they may be seen as setting the tone.

In the first of two studies, involving pupils of Cypriot origin, to consider interethnic attitudes, Dove (1974), investigated the racial awareness of 15- and 16-year-old boys and girls in the fourth and fifth years of three London comprehensive schools in 1972. At the time of the research, there was 'a lull in racial "news"', but despite the multiracial and working-class composition of the schools and neighbourhood, there was little social mixing outside the school. Of the 545 pupils involved in the research, 78 (15 per cent) were of Cypriot (mainly Greek Cypriot) origin, more than half UK-born. Some 298 white British (55 per cent), 109 West Indian (20 per cent) and 60 Asian (11 per cent) pupils also took part. As part of the research a sub-group (N = 98) spent five minutes writing down anything they found of interest in a photograph showing a commonplace scene in schools or streets in England in which children or adults of various races and ethnic groups were inconspicuously depicted. The test was designed to assess spontaneous mention of race, ethnicity or nationality (REN). Dove considered that the school's emphasis upon tolerance and community appeared to affect the responses since over one-third of 'coloured' teenagers did not mention REN, though West Indian and Asian pupils were far more likely to mention these features than Cypriots or Britons. Only a third of Cypriots mentioned REN, compared with less than half the white Britons and half the West Indians and

Asians. Dove suggested that race might have seemed less important to the Cypriots because they 'are less obviously "different"', and they may also have preferred to ignore this dimension because they were sensitive and embarrassed. 'Immigrant problems' in the area tended to be seen as 'colour problems' and the Cypriots did not wish in any way to be perceived as belonging to, or identifiable with, such a group. This was reflected in a comment by a Cypriot boy: 'The photo shows children of various races playing happily together ... The children do not think themselves different from one another ... and this is the way things ought to be' (p.257).

The second research study, including an assessment of ethnicity and colour by Cypriot pupils, involved 400 four- to seven-year-old children of English, West Indian, African, Cypriot and Asian origin, 351 in north London schools and 117 West Indian pupils in Jamaica (Young and Bagley, 1979, 1982a). The sample included 30 Cypriot children. All the children were tested by a black Jamaican on two tests: the Colour Meaning Test (CMT), in which they were required to evaluate black and white animals; and the Pre-School Racial Attitudes Measure (PRAM), which required an evaluation of 24 pairs of pictures of black and white males and females of various ages. On both the tests over four-fifths of the Cypriot children displayed pro-white bias, indeed to a higher degree than their white British peers. The Cypriot pupils displayed almost no black bias at all, and the Cypriot boys were particularly likely to have high scores on the PRAM test indicating much white bias. In the Cypriot group as a whole there was also a significant tendency for pro-white bias to increase with age. Young and Bagley suggested that this trend could be related to increased exposure to, and internalization of, white-biased cultural norms in the curriculum with age.

Interestingly, these educational research findings tend to fit with socio-anthropological observations. Ladbury (1977) perceived that, despite uncertainty about the English, Turkish Cypriots have adopted many English racist attitudes towards members of other groups (especially West Indians and Africans) not because they are perceived as an economic or moral threat, but because, in working with or getting to know the English, Turks have found it expedient to identify with the English majority, and this can be most obviously effected by creating a common outgroup based on colour difference. Similarly, Constantinides (1977) claimed that Greek Cypriots were preoccupied with their relationship to the white British and were anxious that they should not in any way be identified with West Indians and Asians in order to avoid being perceived as members of an immigrant group. Such concerns may easily be transmitted to children within the family group and may be reflected in their responses in interethnic and sociometric studies. Georgiou (1983), for example, found that Greek Cypriot children 'expressed some apprehension' about the proportion of West Indians in their school, though this may have been 'a dislike for their behaviour which to them appeared "loud" and "rough" rather than a prejudice for their community' (p. 38). Many voiced their parents' concern that they would be negatively influenced by associating with West Indians. Earlier Townsend and Brittan (1972) noted some headteachers' reports of friction between Greek Cypriot and West Indian pupils as well as, for Cypriots, some dislike of mainland Greeks and Turkish pupils.

As part of a series of investigations on interethnic attitudes and friendship choices, in 1962 Kawwa (1963, 1968a) administered a sociometric test to children in one mixed London comprehensive school in an industrial lower-working-class area of Islington with a high proportion of Cypriot and coloured people. Some 41 Cypriot boys and 46 Cypriot girls, 340 British boys and 316 British girls and 16 'coloured' boys and girls were asked to list in order of preference their five best friends of the same sex in the school. The Cypriot pupils, like other groups, had a significant preference for their own group (at the 0.01 level). But although the Cypriots, who were not born in the UK, were concentrated in the lower streams of various forms and did not know English well, exchanged hardly any friendship choices with coloured children, about one-quarter of the Cypriot girls and boys cited British pupils as their best friends. Kawwa suggested that more research should be undertaken to discover the effect of linguistic barriers on friendship choice. In this connection Triseliotis (1976) suggested that the tendency of Cypriot children to mix and play with other Cypriots might reduce their opportunities for learning English and familiarizing themselves with British culture. But he considered this preferable to the isolation and withdrawal of some children in localities where the opportunities for play with other Cypriot children did not exist.

Kawwa (1968a) carried out a second study in 1964 in a boys' secondary modern school in north London, which involved some 385 British, 50 Cypriot, 43 black, 34 Indian and 16 other pupils. Two sociometric tests were administered. In the first each boy was asked to choose his two best friends, one from his own class (restricted choice), the other from the whole school (unrestricted choice), and also to name one boy in his class whom he disliked or liked least of all. In the second test each boy was asked to indicate one or more of 27 schoolboys' activities he enjoyed most and to name the boys with whom he shared or enjoyed sharing these activities. The results on the restricted choice test, which were not significantly different from those on the unrestricted choice test, showed that Greek Cypriot boys had an own-group preference, though overall they actually gave more choices to non-Cypriot, mostly British boys, as did the very small number of Turkish Cypriot boys. However, on the rejection test the British boys were rejected by the Greek Cypriots (41) and the Turkish Cypriots (7). Greek Cypriot boys tended to reject black boys more than other groups and showed similar anti-black feelings to those of British children, with more emphasis on what they perceived as the aesthetic unacceptability of negroid features and colour. Turkish Cypriots were inclined to reject Greek Cypriots, apparently for ethnic reasons.

A third study was also carried out in a primary school in north London, in 1964, involving 7–11-year-old pupils: 29 Cypriot boys and 24 girls, 55 British boys and 61 girls, 13 black boys and 12 girls, and two Indian boys and four girls. Each child was asked to name his/her two best friends without restriction as to class or sex. Greek Cypriot children gave more choices than they received (see p. 194). The choices were not significantly in-group: over half the Greek and Turkish Cypriot girls, half of the Greek Cypriot boys and just under half of the Turkish Cypriot boys gave their choices to British pupils of their own sex.

Two early studies (Bhatnagar, 1970; Figueroa, 1974), both undertaken in Haringey in 1966, permit a distinction to be drawn in terms of ethnic group membership of 'friends' and 'best friends'. In Bhatnagar's study, in the course of interviews with the Asian researcher, children in one secondary school were asked to list their friends and from this to nominate their 'best friends'. Although the school was generally regarded by teachers and others as having good race relations, few interethnic friendship choices were made. Yet even though only 14 per cent of Cypriot pupils chose an English child as 'best friend', this far exceeded the proportion of the more numerous West Indian children (3 per cent) who made such a choice. Furthermore, a much greater proportion of the Cypriot pupils (76 per cent, and again more girls than boys) than that of the West Indian pupils (22 per cent) claimed friendship with at least one English child. This may have influenced the differential 'social acceptability' of the two groups (see p. 193). Moreover, the mean adjustment scores and the mean scores on the four adjustment sub-scales of social acceptability, personal satisfaction, freedom from anxiety and objectivity of self-concept were found to be significantly higher for those Cypriot pupils, both boys and girls, who claimed an English friend as opposed to those who did not (at the 0.01 level). Bhatnagar concluded that the adjustment of an immigrant child may be helped by his friendship with English children (see also Hylson-Smith, 1968).

In Figueroa's study (1974), which involved 46 Cypriot school-leavers, 248 white British, 82 West Indian and 24 other white adolescents in ten secondary schools, some contrasting data on friendship emerged. Overall some 76 per cent of the Cypriot pupils, a higher percentage of boys than girls, claimed some Cypriot friends. This was a lower proportion than that of West Indian or British pupils claiming friends from their own ethnic group. Some 30 per cent of Cypriot pupils claimed to have some British friends – less than half the percentage in Bhatnagar's study (1970). Some 58 per cent of the (37) Cypriots claimed to have Cypriot best friends, there being a slight tendency for Cypriot girls to have best friends from their own ethnic group. Yet 30 per cent claimed to have British best friends – twice the percentage of Cypriot pupils in Bhatnagar's study who claimed an English child as their best friend – and the same percentage as those who claimed any British friends at all. Whilst this may indicate that a British friend is especially prized, it may not necessarily mean that the friendship is reciprocated (see p. 194). Some 94 per cent of the Cypriot school-leavers in Figueroa's investigation said that their best friend lived nearby, although the remaining six per cent stated that their best friend did not even live in Britain, which is perhaps not surprising given that most of the Cypriots were born in Cyprus and one-fifth had only been in the UK for less than two years. Indeed McCarty and Christoudoulou (1977) reported that some Cypriot refugee children who entered British schools in the mid-1970s claimed that their peers were more friendly in Cyprus, suggesting that they found it difficult to adjust and make friends.

The largest number of Cypriot pupils to be involved in a sociometric investigation, both at primary and secondary age levels, were those in the third NFER national survey in 1972 (Jelinek and Brittan, 1975). The actual and desired friendship choices of 1,288 pupils in the second and fourth years of 13 primary schools and 3,012 pupils in the second and fourth years of 12 secondary schools were investigated. There was a range of 18–84 per cent ethnic minority pupils in these schools who included Indian, Pakistani, West Indian, Kenyan Asian, Italian and 'other' pupils, as well as Cypriot pupils, hence the findings must be seen as illustrative rather than representative. A total of 221 Cypriot pupils were involved in the investigation, 28 (nine boys and 19 girls) at 8 plus, 23 (12 boys and 11 girls) at 10 plus, 92 (42 boys and 50 girls) at 12 plus and 78 (44 boys and 34 girls) at 14 plus. Pupils were asked to name up to three friends they played with at school and up to three children they would like to have as friends. Almost all of the Cypriot pupils were in co-educational schools, together with 70 per cent of the indigenous and 80 per cent of the West Indian pupils. About five per cent of each of these groups made inter-sex choices, although 25 per cent of Cypriot, 27 per cent of West Indian and 18 per cent of the indigenous pupils desired inter-sex friendships. The actual inter-sex choices were usually made to a pupil's own ethnic group, but at 14 plus the proportion of actual inter-sex choices approximately reflected the proportional distributions of Cypriot pupils in the mixed schools. Unfortunately, because of the smaller number of indices calculated for Cypriot pupils on the Criswell Index of Self-Preference, it was not possible to make formal comparisons with the actual and desired friendship choices of other ethnic groups. Though there were no marked differences in the primary schools – all groups having a preference for their own ethnic group – at the secondary ages there was a tendency for the Cypriots to show greater own-group preference in actual and desired friendships than indigenous pupils in the same schools. Thus ethnicity was shown to be a strong factor in both the actual and desired friendship choices of Cypriot pupils, and there was an indication that this intensified with age. Similarly, when Thomas (1975) asked 244 British, 172 West Indian and 48 Turkish Cypriot boys in the first, second and fourth years of a comprehensive school in London to write down up to three best friends from within their class, there was a strong in-group choice pattern (<0.001) which increased with age.

The preference of pupils for friendships within their own ethnic groups, though considerable, does not necessarily exclude friendships with pupils from other groups. In a study in two mixed comprehensive schools Marvell (1974) found that, unlike the English and West Indian pupils, who tended to belong to either exclusive or mixed friendship groups, the Turkish and Greek Cypriot adolescents divided three ways: into a nationalistic cluster (Greek ten per cent, Turkish 20 per cent); a multiracial cluster (Greek 26 per cent, Turkish 55 per cent); and a 'whites only' group (Greek 63 per cent, Turkish 25 per cent). There was, therefore, a considerable degree of interracial friendship. Over half the pupils in each ethnic group said that they discussed moral questions with their friends, the proportion rising to four-fifths for the Turkish pupils. However, fewer than half in each group claimed to be influenced by their friends on moral matters. A study at an FE college in Stoke Newington suggested a greater degree of interethnic mixing by Greek- and Turkish-speaking students than Jamaican or British students (Mac-Donald, 1975).

In a study which involved 120 pupils, categorized according to achievement ratings on Greek language, mathematics and science into three groups of 72 high achievers and 48 average and low achievers, Archimandritou-Xefteris (1977) discovered some interesting correlations with friendship patterns. Whereas a quarter of average and low achievers were said by their Greek teachers to have no friends, high achievers were said to be significantly more sociable (at the 0.01 level). Greek girls, in particular, had a different pattern of friendship according to their level of achievement: high achievers were much more likely than their average- and low-achieving girl peers to select both English and Greek friends, possibly because their parents had encouraged such friendships. However, half to a third of both groups had only Greek friends. High-achieving boys and girls tended to display leadership qualities; this was the case for nearly half of the high-achieving females compared with just over a quarter in the lower achievement group. By contrast, a study by Georgiou (1983) of the social and cultural effects of attendance at Greek mother-tongue teaching schools suggested that Greek Cypriots, especially girls, encountered difficulties with social integration. Martianou (1981) found that whereas within school Cypriot pupils had a range of friends, out of school they were mostly Cypriots. In detailed case studies Ulug (1981) illustrates the difficulties for Turkish Cypriot girls of having English friends, with the risk of jeopardizing their reputation amongst their community and of being misunderstood or ridiculed by English girls. Whilst some compromised with their friendships, others set a social distance between either Turkish or English peers.

In conclusion, though the findings of studies of interethnic attitudes and friendship patterns involving pupils of Cypriot origin have tended to be somewhat conflicting, certain trends do emerge. In particular, in their interethnic attitudes, Cypriot pupils are clearly very much pre-disposed towards white British rather than black pupils. This is reflected in their friendship preferences from which pupils of

West Indian origin, with whom they are most commonly to be found in schools in London, are almost totally excluded. Moreover, all the studies indicate a considerable in-group friendship preference. But it must not be assumed that reciprocal friendships occur between Greek and Turkish Cypriots, for there is indeed some evidence of hostility between the two groups. Though out-group friendship choice is clearly oriented towards white British pupils, there are conflicting indications as to the extent to which British friends are claimed as best friends. Whether the degree of ethnocentricity in the actual and desired friendships of Cypriot pupils is greater than the own-group preference of British children is also somewhat unclear. Other insights can be obtained by considering issues relating to the self-identity and self-esteem of pupils of Cypriot origin (see pp. 175–85) and the attitudes of white British and West Indian pupils to their Cypriot peers (see pp. 191–5). But generally it would appear that although Cypriot pupils may both desire to, and actually do have friends amongst their white British peers, they may nevertheless prefer to have friends from amongst their own ethnic group. This, however, they have in common with pupils from all other ethnic groups.

ATTITUDES TO SELF
Research on the friendship choice of pupils of Cypriot origin suggests that this is influenced not only by the attitudes which they may hold towards other ethnic and racial groups and their perceptions of them, but also the attitudes which Cypriot pupils have to themselves and their own ethnic group which, in turn, are affected by how they are seen by others. The attitudes of pupils of Cypriot origin to themselves are considered by means of research evidence on identity, self-concept, personality and self-esteem. It is important that findings should be set in the wider context of the lifestyles of pupils of Cypriot origin in Britain, the status of Cypriots as an ethnic community, the different position of Greek and Turkish Cypriots within that community, the ability of Cypriots to be independent in housing and employment and the strength of the influence of Cypriot family life. In addition, allowance should be made for the specific influence and interactive effect of the immediate school neighbourhood, the social and educational ethos of the school and especially the personal relationships within it between teachers, pupils and peers on educational research data.

There is a certain confusion when considering attitudes to self, partly because of the plethora of terms to describe such attitudes, namely, identity, self-concept, self-esteem, etc., which are often used interchangeably or to refer to aspects of the personality and functioning of the person in various social situations. Self-concept, for example, can be used to mean knowledge of characteristics of the self or an appraisal of those characteristics. Identity, which also has cognitive and affective aspects, is thereby respectively related to self-concept and self-esteem. Useful discussions of the theoretical bases of these concepts and their relation to multicultural and interethnic research may be found in two collections edited by Verma and Bagley – *Race, Education and Identity* (1979) and *Self-Concept, Achievement and Multicultural Education* (1982a) – and, in particular, in a paper by Young and Bagley (1982b) in the latter collection. Proper evaluation of the way in which concepts have been employed in educational research involving pupils of Cypriot origin would be extremely difficult – both because the terms are generally loosely used and, with the exception of research by Bhatnagar (1970) and Young and Bagley (1979, 1982a), the measures selected to assess these concepts have generally not been located by researchers in a theoretical context. Interestingly, most of the literature on Cypriot pupils focusses on identity which may be seen as including both self-concept and self-esteem. For example, Bhatnagar was especially interested in the way in which these aspects of the self could be said to be integrated and how these related to the personal and social adjustment of the individual. For ethnic minority groups, in particular, cultural factors are extremely significant in the formation of identity and it is important to be aware that the focus for assessment of identity, including self-concept and self-esteem, may change over time as various reference groups and factors become of greater or lesser salience. But the research tends to gloss over differences between individuals in terms of the cognitive and affective aspects of their self-identification and esteem and of necessity crystallizes these self-perceptions at a moment in time and is unable to monitor the ongoing process.

How do pupils of Cypriot origin perceive themselves? How do they choose to identify themselves? What concept do Cypriot pupils have of themselves? Do they have distinctive personality traits? And how do they evaluate themselves? Almost all the research has been undertaken with Cypriot pupils of secondary school age, reflecting the fact that this is a time when individuals become more self-conscious. Moreover, it is clear that several complex interrelated factors affect the self-identification of pupils of Cypriot origin: in particular, cultural differences especially in the UK context; the degree of orientation towards Cyprus and emotional ties with the country and people; the extent to which aspects of cultural and social life are maintained in the ethnic community in the UK; and the significance of the individual's relationship to the group, especially at adolescence.

By the end of the 1960s after the arrival of most Cypriot immigrants in the UK, Oakley (1968) observed that the Greek and Turkish Cypriots formed distinct ethnic communities and emphasized the 'Greek-ness' or 'Turkish-ness' in their identity. Many adults, and especially their children, referred to themselves as simply 'Greek' or 'Turkish'. Focussing on the Greek Cypriots, he claimed that the distinctive 'Greek-ness' in their lives consisted essentially in continuing to think about family matters in terms of the traditional cultural framework within which they evaluated their own and other people's behaviour. But other options began to be available to the second generation of Cypriot pupils as they came under other influences, particularly the values mediated through school. Oakley postulated that one choice was for the second generation to remain Greek (or Turkish); another was to become English and cause a division within the family; and a third was for the second generation to straddle both worlds. Though the personal cost in terms of divided loyalties might be very considerable, Oakley thought the third course would bring the English and Greek Cypriots closer.

At that time, Hylson-Smith (1968) also reported that although Cypriots in Stoke Newington tended to identify with either the Greek or Turkish Cypriot communities, reflecting social distinctions in their country of origin, this was less marked for the second generation who, unlike their parents, had begun to participate in wider social institutions and were acquiring the language and norms of society at large, though they remained aware of considerable cultural differences. Research in Haringey, in 1966, amongst school-leavers tended to bear this out. Figueroa (1974) found that young Cypriots were less likely than their West Indian peers to say that there was some considerable difference between them and their English schoolmates, but three-quarters of the Cypriots explained the differences in cultural terms, whereas the West Indian school-leavers focussed on colour prejudice or snobbery. In fact only just over half the Cypriots saw their future in Britain, expecting to live in the UK at the age of 25, whereas one-third expected to be living in Cyprus, Greece or Turkey and the remainder in another country. Moreover, Kawwa (1968a) found in schools in London, in the early 1960s (see pp. 170–1), that Cypriot pupils not only did not expect to be ignored by their British peers, as West Indian pupils did, but no matter how Anglicized Cypriot pupils might be, and some were almost fully so, very few expressed a wish to give up their group membership.

That cultural roots in Cyprus and an orientation towards or contact with the country can continue to influence the identity of pupils of Cypriot origin is shown in a study by Dove (1974). As part of research project in three comprehensive schools in London, in 1972, Dove asked 78 Cypriot pupils, mainly Greek, out of a sample of 545 pupils, including West Indian, Asian and white British pupils, to describe themselves in order to assist the researcher to identify the pupil on next meeting. These written responses were analysed according to the extent to which pupils mentioned racial, ethnic or national characteristics (REN) in self-identification. Almost one-third of the Cypriot pupils identified themselves by all three of these characteristics, a similar proportion mentioned ethnic group or nationality and, interestingly, one in ten specifically referred to themselves as white. Only half as many Cypriot pupils as West Indian pupils, and fewer Cypriot than Asian pupils, identified themselves according to racial, ethnic and national characteristics, though they were more than four times as likely to do so than white British pupils. Dove suggested that because of the rich communal life enjoyed by the Cypriot pupils and their consciousness of intercommunal strife in their country of origin, it was understandable that they should identify themselves primarily in ethnic or national terms and only secondarily according to race. On the other hand, the fact that a large proportion of Cypriot pupils did not mention race as a distinguishing feature of their identity might have been because their attitudes towards their own group and their evaluation of its status made them unwilling to identify publicly. Although they may have been proud of their group, they may have been aware of the social disadvantage to themselves of drawing attention to their race. Hence the very omission of self-identification by REN might have been an indication that it was very important to Cypriot pupils. Unlike their West Indian and Asian peers, however, Dove found that the Cypriot pupils who had been in the UK longer were more likely to identify themselves by REN. One-third of Cypriots born in Britain mentioned these characteristics compared with just less than a quarter of those born in Cyprus. Moreover, over a third of those who had been in the UK for more than ten years mentioned REN, compared with one in ten who had lived in Britain for less than ten years. Interview data suggested that Cypriot pupils born or living in the UK from early childhood, who felt secure culturally and linguistically in England, tended to romanticize the Cyprus which they had heard about from their parents' stories or knew of from holiday visits. Dove also noted that mention of REN might have represented aggressive self-assertion for those Cypriot pupils sensitive to British xenophobia and resentful of their low status as immigrants. Of all the groups, the Cypriots showed most confusion or hesitation about identifying themselves. Half were uncertain whether they were Greek because of their parents' origin or because they spoke Greek at home. Others wondered if they were English because they were born in the UK or had a British passport. They found it troubling to be asked to choose their identity and, according to Dove, it was clear that many retained close ethnic ties which sometimes conflicted with the claims made on them by the community in which they were growing up.

From her socioanthropological observations, Constantinides (1977) noted that during 1974, when civil war erupted in Cyprus, second-generation Cypriots in London became acutely conscious of their origins and of the emotional and kinship ties which bound them to Cyprus. Ironically, at the same time as this culmination of Greek Cypriot consciousness, there was also an awareness that their future lay in the UK and a change of orientation occurred which led them into greater social and political participation within the framework of UK politics. Constantinides considered that most second-generation Cypriots, whilst preoccupied with the question of Cypriot vs British identity, on the whole retained their sense of ethnic identity as Greek Cypriot, though this did not, as with their parents, necessarily extend to maintaining ties with a particular village in Cyprus. Attitudes to Cyprus developed on account of their parents' stories of village life as well as the cultural atmosphere of the home may be dramatically affected by a holiday visit back to the village of origin. According to Constantinides, the effect on British-born Cypriots may be profoundly positive or negative: many feel moved to identify with the island and their relatives and are inspired to achieve greater fluency in Greek; others become alienated by communication difficulties and restrictions placed on their freedom according to the relatively strict moral codes of village life (see also Krokou, 1985). A small survey carried out by the mother-tongue schools run by community organizations in Haringey found that children of Cypriot origin who had more recently visited Cyprus tended to claim that they were 'Greek' or 'Turkish', but that children who had not often or who had never been to Cyprus firmly identified themselves as English (Alkan and Constantinides, 1981). Ulug (1981) indicated that many pupils of Turkish Cypriot origin consider Cyprus merely as a foreign land, a holiday island and a place where relatives reside. They have great difficulty in sharing parents' emotions about their homeland and roots. Visits back often have little impact and may soon be forgotten. Ulug suggested that on visits the Turkish Cypriot child observes life in Cyprus as 'a "London Turk" of Cypriot parents' with feelings of mismatch with the home society. For some Turkish Cypriot girls, visits to Cyprus, where a greater degree of freedom may be permitted, may reinforce confusion when a stricter way of life has to be resumed on return to the UK.

Thus, although the Cypriot community may see its future in Britain, this may not mean a loss or lack of emphasis upon the cultural traditions and social values of the Cypriot village as they left it. Indeed in many ways Cypriot communities have attempted to re-create much of their previous social world through the establishment of various community groups and organizations in their settlements in the UK (pp. 28–32) not only for dance, theatre and music (Khan, 1976), but also for the second generation mother-tongue classes, sometimes associated with the church (pp. 80–1). All these institutions serve to enhance a Cypriot identity. Since the emphasis on linguistic and cultural maintenance in the UK may be considerable in view of the concentrated settlement patterns of Cypriots, and hence the relative ease of enforcing social sanctions, the Cypriot child will be exposed to the family's cultural orientation and the values of the wider society as transmitted by the school. How can the child build an identity on two value systems and cultures which are sometimes in conflict? Some cross-cultural differences relating to control and attitudes towards relationships between the sexes have already been discussed (see pp. 151–2, 158–60). Triseliotis (1976) observed that an identity can significantly be built on more than one set of values and that Cypriot children can accommodate the contradictions if these are understood. This is an additional task, but one which is part of daily life for the Cypriot child. In fact, by becoming familiar with differing values and expectations, the child may well respond by finding situationally appropriate responses. But what, it may be wondered, is the effect on the self-esteem or self-concept of such a Cypriot child?

It seems important, therefore, to explore this emphasis given by pupils of Cypriot origin to factors which need to be integrated into an identity, and the extent to which they draw upon aspects of Greek, Turkish, Cypriot or British culture and values according to the evidence from research studies. Language is one such factor. As Rosen and Burgess have argued, language is a highly salient dimension of ethnic identity. It is a highly explicit carrier of cultural meaning. Put very simply, a Greek child may feel Greek when speaking English but much more Greek when speaking Greek. (Rosen and Burgess, 1980, p. 52)

Yet in a study of Greek-speaking pupils attending mother-tongue classes in London, in 1974, Archimandritou-Xefteris (1977) found that in the opinions of their Greek teachers these adolescents were more attracted to British culture as transmitted in their mainstream school, and derived more satisfaction from their achievement in those schools than that in the mother-tongue classes which their parents insisted they should attend in order to retain their cultural identity. The Greek teachers said that their pupils believed that acculturation would make their lives easier, but this was discouraged in many ways by their parents. Greek adolescent boys and girls differed in their degree of identification with British culture. On the whole, the boys felt Greek and were treated as foreign, although they were attracted by succeeding in the British educational system. A British orientation was precluded by various family influences, religious observance, family loyalty and the family's commitment to transmitting Greek culture. Archimandritou-Xefteris concluded that these Greek boys were not fully either Greek or English and that they would only adjust by identifying with one or the other culture. By contrast, for Greek adolescent girls the family placed less emphasis on academic achievement than on social and moral codes of conduct which stressed the girls' future role as mothers and the importance of pre-marital chastity. There was a considerable drop-out rate from the mother-tongue classes in order to cope with the dissonance which these adolescents felt between their two school lives. But sometimes their parents countered with private tuition and family declarations of intention to return; indeed sometimes the adolescents were sent back to study in a Greek university. Similarly, Georgiou (1983) found that although Greek Cypriot boys liked both Greek and British cultures, whether or not they attended mother-tongue classes, they expressed more pride in the Greek culture than the girls, who played down their Greek nationality and tended towards British culture in spite of attending Greek classes.

The pressure to identify with one or other culture may develop greater and increasing poignancy in adolescence, and it is clear that Greek and Turkish Cypriot parents may go to considerable lengths, especially in regard to their daughters, to ensure that cultural values are maintained and a certain degree of identification obtains. Though many adolescents rebel against their Greek or Turkish affiliation, it is interesting to note that several commentators (e.g. Constantinides, 1977; Ulug, 1981) have claimed that once Cypriot pupils have left school the ties of ethnicity may be stronger and reasserted. Constantinides reported that for many Greek Cypriot adolescents, a type of identity crisis occurred after they had left school and sought employment as many found themselves poorly qualified for the jobs they aspired to, and additionally parental concern for the moral welfare of girls might restrict the distance from home they were allowed to work. Moreover, since the ethnic economy during the 1970s was able and willing to absorb school-leavers, particularly when family businesses were to be maintained, the period of attempting to find employment often marked the 're-entry' of Cypriot adolescents into their ethnic group.

But though the existence of a widespread and strong community network which provides opportunities for linguistic and cultural maintenance, employment and social and moral sanctioning may exert a considerable pull on Cypriot youngsters, the very fact of their growing up in a wider social and educational environment means that in different places or phases in their lives individuals may choose to adopt values more attuned to their Greek, Turkish or Cypriot backgrounds at one time and those of British society at another. The monograph by Alkan and Constantinides (1981) illustrates this point. They state that a Cypriot child in the UK, asked for an identity, will claim Greek or Turkish, but that his/her parents come from Cyprus. By the age of 12 or 13 Cypriot children begin to be particularly conscious about their identity and until about the age of 17 they apparently 'feel awkward and do not want to be distinguished as non-British'. After this age, many apparently take an interest and pride in their identity as British-born Cypriots, but may, nevertheless, continue to be confused about their background and situation. Alkan and Constantinides argue that it is extremely important for Cypriot young people to know in depth about their own and their parents' backgrounds in order to feel happy and secure and to avoid a sense of not belonging to or fitting comfortably in either country, and that it should be a specific function of education to develop an awareness of origin and of roots in the UK (see pp.199–206). However, evidence to the Swann Committee suggested that Cypriot pupils may feel that a part of their identity is being ignored in school and 'they learn to cope with the ethnocentrism of the school, but only at the expense of merging their own identity with that of the school culture' (GB.P. H of C, 1985, p. 682).

Other evidence suggests that Alkan and Constantinides may have overestimated the extent of identification as British-born Cypriots and oversimplified the range of factors which bear upon affirmation of identity. In a survey in Haringey, in 1978, Leeuwenberg (1979) found a considerable range in the self-identification of some 84 Greek and Turkish Cypriots, predominantly aged 15–24; four-fifths had been born in Cyprus and three-fifths had lived there until age 15. Perhaps not surprisingly, very few saw themselves as British, although more – especially the Greek Cypriots (almost one-fifth), a higher proportion of whom were UK-born – identified themselves as London Cypriots. Rather, the emphasis tended to be on their Greek or Turkish connections based on divisions in Cyprus – the majority, over two-fifths of each group, claimed to be either Greek or Turkish Cypriots. Yet there was an interesting difference, in that whereas almost one-third of the Greek Cypriots identified themselves as Cypriots, almost the same proportion of Turkish Cypriots ascribed to themselves full Turkish identity, even though only one in ten had roots there. Leeuwenberg suggested this was both a reaction to the political state of Cyprus and to living in the UK. He indicated three main factors in identity formation: the political situation in Cyprus, the nature of the London Cypriot community and the attitudes of the British host community, which both groups agreed was not sympathetic to outsiders and was largely hostile to language and culture main-tenance. Cypriot children were reported to identify quickly with their classmates and to move away from a Cypriot identity, although a core spoke Greek and looked to their Cypriot identity at work and home. The Turkish Cypriots had more problems with their identity because they were a smaller group and had a less widespread support structure. They tended to polarize – either shrugging off their Cypriot identity or holding on to it in as pure a form as possible. Leeuwenberg felt that it was easier for Greek Cypriots to envisage the alternative of identifying themselves as London Cypriots and they felt less pressurized to make a decision. Thus while birthplace is clearly a significant factor in identity, other factors, including orientation towards Cyprus, the Greek or Turkish mainland or their culture and place of residence may also come into play when Greek and Turkish Cypriots ascribe their identity, so that ascriptions may fail to have a clear or shared meaning.

It may, therefore, be more helpful and educationally significant to focus upon individuals rather than upon supposed or self-ascribed group membership. For although Alkan and Constantinides (1981) correctly pointed to the importance of promoting an awareness of Greek and Turkish Cypriot culture in schools to enhance a sense of origins, care needs to be taken to guard against the perception of individuals as primarily members of a certain group in such a way that the classification may ignore or weaken a need for individual identity. Indeed Ulug (1981) has claimed that the individuality of pupils may sometimes be overlooked when they are all considered to be of a certain 'type'. In her case study of a small group of Turkish Cypriot girls of secondary age she found that individuality was very dominant, so that although girls were suffering on account of their divided roles and loyalties as a result of living between two cultures, each girl was coming to terms with this dilemma according to her own level of maturity. Some of the pupils had decided to embrace a Turkish identity and cultural values and a few compromised between a British and Turkish cultural identification, but none of the girls had opted for a totally British identity. Yet, according to Ulug, this did not mean that the girls were free from culture conflict, or indeed that they were academically more successful. Those girls who had made a compromise between the two cultures, or adopted a 'bi-self-concept', saw themselves as living under false pretences or acting as if they were required to be two different people. Yet even those who had claimed to reject British culture expressed similar schizophrenic feelings which implied that neither rejection nor compromise permitted escape from the dual-role dilemma. Some of the girls found the matter of dual standards of expected behaviour for boys and girls particularly difficult to accept, resenting the freedom outside the home allowed to their brothers and sometimes responding by becoming mute, deceptive or alienated from the family. But some fascinating quotes from interviews with Turkish Cypriot boys, together with written material, demonstrated that, although they appreciated the confusion of living between two cultures, they upheld the importance of maintaining the traditional values and especially the code of behaviour and role of women, justified on account of their gender, and which the boys saw as their responsibility to protect. Detailed case studies of five girls demonstrated their awareness of and attempts to resolve differences in the values and practices of the two cultural worlds in which they were growing up, especially in connection with relationships with parents, attitudes to arranged marriages, role at home and relationships outside the home. One intelligent 17-year-old stated: 'I have sorted out two roles ... I live in two worlds ... it gets confusing because I'm pretending in school and at home ... so who am I? ... which is me? ... someone in between ... I'm proud of what I am and yet being what I am brings me so many problems.' Ulug claims that both English and Turkish societies presuppose a certain kind of person and that survival requires modification and adaptation of personal characteristics accordingly.

A few educational research studies have attempted to assess the self-concept, personality traits and self-esteem of pupils of Cypriot origin. Bhatnagar (1970) conducted research in one secondary modern school in Haringey in 1966 which attempted to measure the adjustment of 76 Cypriot, 174 West Indian and 100 English adolescents. A well-adjusted person was defined as socially acceptable, personally satisfied, having an objective self-concept and being free from anxiety. Four sub-scales of a test designed to assess adjustment were constructed to measure each of the variables (see p. 193 for social acceptability). Objectivity of self-concept which was defined as the degree of overlap between perceived self or the 'self as we see it' and the objective self or the 'self as others see it' was measured on a 25-item scale. The subject was asked to assess himself, and the five randomly selected peers were also asked to assess the subject on the same items, the difference between the two sets of assessments being computed. The 25-item scale covered various aspects of the self-concept, physical appearance, performance, relationship with teachers, relationship with others, abilities and overall success, each item being rated on a three-point scale. There was found to be a significant difference (0.01 level) between the mean score of the English pupils and the Cypriot pupils and, at a lower level of significance for the mean score of the Cypriots and West Indian pupils as a whole, but not for girls. Of all the scales of the composite adjustment scale, the objectivity of the self-concept sub-scale revealed the greatest difference. Bhatnagar suggested that the discrepancy between the 'self as I see it' and 'self as others see it' was much greater amongst Cypriot and West Indian pupils because the cues employed in the process of person perception in different cultures are likely to be different, and by moving between two cultures these children were handicapped when gauging the reactions of children from other cultures towards themselves. Thus they could not predict with any accuracy how they were perceived by other children.

A second sub-scale – freedom from anxiety – revealed an aspect of the pupils' personalities. Anxiety was defined as 'the fusion of low fear with the anticipation of possible failure and punishment'. Subjects were asked to indicate whether or not 20 items on a scale (which proved difficult to construct) applied to them. There was a significant difference (at the 0.01 level) between the mean score of the English and the Cypriots as a whole and the Cypriots and the West Indians on this scale, though the Cypriot girls did not differ significantly from the West Indian girls in terms of freedom from anxiety. These findings suggested that Cypriot girls were prone to greater anxiety and had a less accurate self-concept in the school context. Bhatnagar also used two other tests to assess pupils' character traits. On the 22-item extraversion scale of the New Junior Maudsley Personality Inventory the Cypriot pupils again obtained a mean score between that of the West Indian and the English pupils, but there was no significant difference between the mean score of the Cypriot and the West Indian pupils who were more extraverted than the English pupils. (For a comparison with teachers' views, see p.197.) Extraversion was related to all aspects of the adjustment measure, with the exception of the objectivity of the self-concept scale, so that an extraverted Cypriot child was more likely to be socially acceptable, personally satisfied and free from anxiety than an introverted child. Other aspects of personality were measured by three sub-scales of the 66-item Cotswold Personality Inventory. Of the three groups, the Cypriot pupils had the highest mean score on interest in things; the lowest mean score on interest in people, with significantly greater interest shown by Cypriot boys than girls, perhaps because of cultural restrictions; and the lowest mean score on the interest in ideas sub-scale.

The third sub-scale of the adjustment scale in Bhatnagar's study – the personal satisfaction sub-scale – may be considered to indicate self-esteem. Personal satisfaction was defined as the degree of satisfaction an individual derived from his perception of the self, his social environment and his personal relationships. This was measured by a 28-item scale, concerning the school, family relationships, the self, peer-group relations, teacher–pupil relationships and the neighbourhood according to ratings on a three-point scale. On this measure the Cypriot pupils were found to be the least satisfied with their personal lives. Their mean score and that of the West Indian pupils were significantly lower (at the 0.01 level) than that of their English peers. The Cypriots, though more socially acceptable than the West Indians (see p. 193), were nevertheless less personally satisfied with their lives than their West Indian peers. Finally, on the adjustment scale overall the Cypriots were between the West Indians (the least well adjusted) and English pupils (the most adjusted). There was a significant difference (at the 0.01 level) between the mean adjustment scores of the English and the Cypriot pupils for the group as a whole and boys and girls separately, and a significant difference (at the 0.05 level) between mean scores of the Cypriot and the West Indian pupils as a whole. Thus the adjustment level of the Cypriot pupils was much more like that of their West Indian than their English peers. Bhatnagar considered this difference in the pattern of adjustment 'alarming', and suggested that it might be a consequence of living in a culture with a norm of mild xenophobia and where the educational system aimed to inculcate English middle-class values and did little to enhance the pride of the Cypriot or West Indian pupil in his own historical and cultural inheritance.

In considering the self-esteem of pupils of Cypriot origin, a few other studies may also be mentioned. Marvell (1974) asked Greek and Turkish Cypriot, English, West Indian and Indian children in two mixed comprehensive schools to write an essay about their ideal person. Over 70 per cent of each of the ethnic groups chose 'myself' as the person they would like to be, although some chose glamorous models and a few family members or close acquaintances. The occupations of the persons selected demonstrated ambition rather than a desire for an idyllic existence. When the essays were analysed into those which expressed altruistic or egocentric viewpoints, over two-thirds of both Greek and Turkish Cypriot pupils, like the majority of other ethnic groups, expressed only egocentric views, although one in ten Greek and one in 20 Turkish Cypriots expressed altruistic views only. An essay test with the subject 'myself' which was given to Greek- and Turkish-speaking students in a further education college as part of a battery of tests administered by MacDonald (1975) was also revealing in terms of students' identifications and self-concepts and for demonstrating the cultural ambiguities in their social worlds.

At the other end of the age range, in the only study to have considered young children, Young and Bagley (1979, 1982a) measured the self-esteem of 30 pupils of Cypriot origin aged four to seven as part of an investigation of colour and ethnicity involving a multiracial group of children in London and West Indian pupils in Jamaica. On an adapted version of the Ziller self-esteem measure, an individually administered spatially oriented test, the Cypriot children had the lowest level of self-esteem of all the groups in the UK, lower than their West Indian, Asian, African and English peers. However, this finding, which is underplayed by Young and Bagley because of their primary interest in this context in West Indian pupils, was significantly correlated with the sociometric isolation of pupils ($r=0.413$, $p<0.05$) on several sociometric measures (see p. 170). Hence in this case lack of popularity in the classroom was related to poor self-esteem. Unfortunately, no information is provided about the number of schools involved in the study, or their ethnic composition, so it is not possible to ascertain whether pupils of Cypriot origin may have been isolated in small numbers. However, the finding is of interest since it tends to confirm the low level of Cypriot pupils' self-esteem found by Bhatnagar (1970) on the personal satisfaction measure. Yet the Cypriot adolescents who comprised approximately 10 per cent of the school roll in Bhatnagar's study had low personal satisfaction, despite their comparative social acceptability, whereas in Young and Bagley's study young Cypriot children's self-esteem was low, apparently because of their social isolation. Again, Young and Bagley argued that the school should transmit to all ethnic groups in the school an intimate knowledge of and pride in the language and culture of their traditional society, suggesting that thereby pupils would come to have a more positive self-assessment.

Verma and Bagley (1982b) have claimed that research has failed to show any differences in levels of self-esteem between white, West Indian, Asian and Cypriot children according to a study reported by Bagley, Verma and Mallick (1982) which was partly concerned with validating a number of measures of self-esteem for use with British children. A short version of the Cooper Smith Self-Esteem Inventory, a short version of the Piers-Harris Self-Concept Scale and an adjective rating list of self-characteristics checked on a five-point scale were administered in West Yorkshire and Outer London to 159 English, 68 West Indian, 47 Cypriot and 36 Asian pupils aged 11–14 in multiracial middle schools. The scores correlated equally well for these subjects and did not differentiate between these groups at a significant level, suggesting that in the late 1970s ethnic differences in self-esteem in older children in British schools were exceptional. There was again, however, a tendency for girls, except West Indian girls, to have poorer self-esteem than boys, and for Cypriot pupils to have poorer self-esteem than their peers. However, Bagley *et al.* argued that, although there are cross-cultural and cross-ethnic similarities in the structure and meaning of self-esteem as measured by these tests, it would be unwise to conclude that one ethnic group has 'poorer' self-esteem than another, for as part of a more complex identity structure self-esteem has a different grounding and meaning in different ethnic groups. Moreover, they suggested that it is necessary to investigate the relationship of self-esteem responses in girls to their lower status and lack of social power before this difference is interpreted in pluralistic terms.

Finally, Stamataris (1983) administered the Cooper Smith Self-Esteem Inventory and the Mooney Problem checklist, which enables the subject to review any problems in relationships at home, at school and career aspirations, to a small sample of Greek Cypriot adolescent girls, attending a London Greek School, who were also interviewed. The researcher claimed that the higher the degree of cultural pressure the girl received at home, the lower was her self-esteem. The parents of these Greek Cypriot girls seemed unable to accept that their daughters were having to adapt their lives to two cultural contexts and this promoted conflict within and outside the family. Interestingly, the girls, though resenting the restrictions placed upon them, nevertheless maintained a strong ethnic identity. Stamataris, a Greek Cypriot herself, considered that it was vital for Greek Cypriot girls to maintain a cultural identity 'especially when living in a society in which the culture is not one's own'.

What conclusions can be drawn from the research on Cypriot pupils' attitudes to themselves, their identity, self-concept, personality and self-esteem? Clearly the studies reviewed only represent individuals' choices at a particular moment in time and hence it is necessary to extrapolate considerably from the data when comparing different populations or considering changes over a 20-year period. Moreover, many of the studies are small scale, involving Cypriot pupils as the third or residual group, rarely the prime focus of study, and whilst in some investigations they have been spread over several schools, in others they are studied in depth in only one or two schools. Nevertheless, there appears to be a consistent cultural focus when Cypriot pupils' attitudes to themselves are examined. The context for consideration of identity, self-concept or self-esteem is not racial, nor one which focusses primarily on colour, although Cypriot pupils display some anxiety that they should be distinguished from their black West Indian and Asian peers. The identity of Cypriot pupils may well be influenced by a change in emphasis in the orientation towards Cyprus or the UK, which may vary from family to family and certainly over the period under study. Yet the fact that pupils of Cypriot origin may have been born or lived most of their lives in the UK may not prevent them from identifying with their parents' country of origin. Regardless of their length of time in the UK, emotional ties persist and a romanticized image derived from family stories, together with an increased consciousness of cultural and ethnic roots at times of war or from visits back, may serve to revive identity. In the UK there is, moreover, both strong family and community pressure to maintain the ethnic language, and traditional cultural values. Even in the early 1960s, Cypriot adolescents who became Anglicized did not necessarily lose their identity as Greek or Turkish Cypriots. In recent years, as a greater sense of community has developed through ethnic associations and organizations and, in particular, mother-tongue schools, considerable community pressure has been placed upon families to ensure the maintenance of the mother tongue and traditional cultural values amongst the second and third generations. These value systems assume gender-differentiated behavioural expectations and the restrictions placed on adolescent girls mean that cultural conflicts become the focus for the questioning of identity at adolescence. Though this may result in some rebellion and defiance, there are indications that after leaving school a further crisis of identity may occur if ambitions fail to be realized and there may be a reabsorption of Cypriot adolescents into the community through work and a reassertion of ethnic identity. Nevertheless, it is difficult to know whether self-identifications as Greek, Turkish, Cypriot, Greek Cypriot, Turkish Cypriot or British Cypriot have shared and commonly understood meanings, and what significance such labels have within or outside the community. Being born in the UK may influence affirmation of identity, but this is by no means the only significant factor. The ascription of identity by pupils of Cypriot origin in educational research studies may only be one aspect of a complex ongoing process of identity resolution in the Cypriot community as such, which may be heightened for the second and third generation by the degree of and, perhaps, their exclusive contact with the UK.

Hence, rather than considering the group, it may be more appropriate to focus upon the individual's attempt to make a proper self-assessment, of abilities, personal characteristics and social position. This is generally a matter of particular concern to adolescents as a feature of growth towards adulthood, but it may be especially troubling for those who live in two cultures and who may have need of sensitive guidance and counselling which the school might offer. It need not necessarily be a matter of concern that identity or self-concept should be stable, but rather that it should be secure. What should give pause for reflection is the degree of dissonance which pupils of Cypriot origin, and some other ethnic minority pupils, experience between their lives at home and school and the extent to which the inconsistency of value systems results in practical difficulties in daily life which affect self-concept, personality and self-esteem which, in turn, relate to self-ascribed identity. It would thus seem more illuminating to focus on the similarities and differences of living within two cultures and to explore the phenomenological meaning of Cypriot, Greek, Turkish or British identities for such pupils.

These cultural influences make it difficult for pupils of Cypriot origin to assess their self-concepts objectively and the need to negotiate between at least two value-systems complicates their perception of how they are regarded. Research tentatively suggests that they may be both anxious and extravert compared with their English peers. Indeed in tripartite investigations they appear more like their West Indian peers on measures of such traits. However, it must be a matter of some concern that, despite their greater social acceptability compared with West Indian pupils, their personal satisfaction levels remain low. The complex interrelationship of self-concept and personality may, in turn, influence pupils' self-esteem. Research again suggests that the self-esteem of pupils of Cypriot origin has been low, indeed lower than that of their West Indian peers. Though it is possible that such findings may be a feature of the particular samples under investigation, such as low proportion of Cypriots on school roll, or social isolation, nevertheless evidence of low self-esteem of pupils of Cypriot origin has been camouflaged by the general educational research focus on pupils of West Indian origin. Unfortunately, there are little or no data on differences in self-perceptions of Greek and Turkish Cypriot pupils. However, it may not be inappropriate to speculate to what extent the apparently low self-esteem of pupils of Cypriot origin may influence their school performance since measures of IQ, reading and other curriculum subjects suggest low levels of attainment similar to that of their West Indian peers. Although there are no simple explanations, community pressures for linguistic and cultural maintenance, and cultural contrasts which are not adequately taken into account in the school, may, together with other less readily identifiable factors, have a cumulative effect.

ATTITUDES TO SCHOOL

Although the attitudes which pupils of Cypriot origin hold towards their schools and teachers may be assumed to have considerable influence upon their school performance, relatively little research has been conducted in this area. Available information is generally derived from the same investigations of the attitudes of pupils of Cypriot origin to themselves and others and tends to focus on pupils of secondary age. Moreover, since the studies were largely undertaken in the mid-1960s and early 1970s they usually apply to Cyprus-born pupils, and also to secondary schools prior to the reorganization of secondary education in most LEAs.

George (1960; see also Triseliotis, 1968, 1976) reported that Cypriot pupils who arrived in the UK at the age of 14 plus often experienced particular difficulties since they had left school in Cyprus at the age of 12 and, being legally obliged to attend school in the UK, found it necessary not only to get used to being at school again, but also to learn English. Indeed some were inclined to play truant. Bhatnagar (1970) examined the attitudes of 76 mostly Greek Cypriot pupils to one secondary school. In Haringey, in 1966, nine out of ten of the Cypriot pupils had been born abroad, although nearly three-quarters arrived in the UK before secondary school age and their mean length of residence was 4.6 years. As assessed on a 20-item sub-scale of the Cotswold Personality Inventory, according to ratings on a five-point scale, the mean attitude to school scores of the Cypriot pupils were found to be midway between those of their English and West Indian peers who had the most favourable attitudes towards the school. Cypriot girls had a slightly higher mean attitude score towards school than Cypriot boys. There was a positive correlation (at the 0.01 level) between Cypriot pupils' attitudes towards school and their composite score adjustment. Thus Cypriot pupils who had a more favourable attitude to school were also likely to be well-adjusted. Another study in Haringey secondary schools, in 1966, by Figueroa (1974) involved Cypriot pupils, almost all of whom had been born in Cyprus and almost half of whom had been in Britain for four or more years by the time they came to leave school. Overall three-fifths of the Cypriot pupils, very slightly more girls than boys, claimed that they liked school very much and a third claimed neither to like nor dislike school.

A contrasting result was obtained by Dove (1975), who, in 1972, investigated the attitudes to school of some 78, mainly Greek, Cypriots, over half of whom were UK-born, and 298 white British, 109 West Indian, and 60 Asian pupils in three London comprehensive schools. Over half of the Cypriots claimed to like school, two-fifths to feel neutrally about it and less than one-tenth actively disliked it. They were less likely to like school than their Asian peers, but more likely to like it than their West Indian or white British peers. The converse applied in the case of those with neutral feelings to the school. There was a considerable sex difference in the attitudes to school of school-leavers, for whereas three-fifths of the boys claimed to like school, only just over two-fifths of the girls claimed to do so, with over half claiming to feel neutrally.

The largest investigation of pupils' attitudes to school was undertaken as part of the third phase of the NFER multiracial education project in 1972 (Jelinek, 1977). A total of 3,551 pupils in 13 primary and secondary schools were involved, 604 at 10 plus, 1,488 at 12 plus and 1,459 at 14 plus. British, West Indian, Indian, Kenyan Asian, Pakistani and 'other' pupils were included, together with relatively small numbers of Cypriot and Italian pupils – 42 at 10 plus (24 boys and 18 girls), 113 at 12 plus (55 boys and 58 girls) and 100 pupils at 14 plus (54 boys and 46 girls). Since their attitudes are reported in a composite form, it is not possible to be certain that they are necessarily those of Cypriot (or Italian) pupils alone. An attitude test of 33 items was constructed from a pilot survey of pupils' attitudes, sentence completion tests, picture presentation tests and essays, and subjects rated items on a five-point scale, ranging from 'strongly agree' to 'strongly disagree'. Generally the Cypriot/Italian pupils had fairly favourable attitudes towards the multiracial atmosphere of the school, midway between the attitudes of their Asian, West Indian and British peers. However, they were less favourably disposed towards the multiracial school than any of the other ethnic minority groups at 14 plus. Overall there were no sex differences in attitudes to the multiracial school, but the Cypriot/Italian boys had more favourable attitudes than the European girls at 10 plus and 14 plus. Overall indigenous pupils were less concerned about schoolwork and least anxious, though Cypriot pupils, like 'others', were also relatively little concerned in comparison with their Asian and West Indian peers. As for girls in general, Cypriot/Italian girls tended to be more concerned about schoolwork than the Cypriot/Italian boys at all age levels. Cypriot/Italian pupils, like 'other' pupils, generally held favourable attitudes to the school at 12 plus and 14 plus. Like their other ethnic minority peers, but in contrast to their indigenous peers, there was a marked improvement in their attitudes between the age of 10 plus and 12 plus, particularly for the Cypriot/Italian boys, as European girls generally had more favourable attitudes to school. Though these findings are of interest, especially as they tend to fit with other evidence, they should not be accorded too much weight in view of the aggregated data presentation and the fact that Cypriot pupils were only drawn from four schools. Indeed school-specific factors associated with school atmosphere, teacher–pupil relationships and teaching–learning methods are likely to affect the differential responses of individuals and groups of pupils to these kinds of attitude scales and make it difficult to accord meaning to generalizations across schools and ethnic groups.

The general attitude to school scale of this study, which included items on teacher–pupil relationships, suggests that the attitudes of pupils of Cypriot origin to their teachers may be of particular significance. Indeed in the second phase of the NFER project (Townsend and Brittan, 1972) some teachers reported difficulties in some relationships between Cypriot boys and women teachers as some boys took a time to accept women teachers, even Cypriot teachers. Cypriot pupils have, however, perceived British teachers to be less strict and to give less work than their teachers in Cyprus (McCarty and Christoudoulou, 1977). Yet in Dove's study (1975) three-quarters of Cypriot pupils claimed that they had favourable relationships with their teachers, although the remainder said they were favourable or did not reply. They resembled their white rather than Asian or West Indian peers in their perceived relationships with their teachers. However, in another relatively small-scale study in two mixed comprehensive schools Marvell (1974) found that although between two-fifths and a half of the sample, including Greek and Turkish Cypriot pupils, claimed that they would turn to someone in the school for advice if they had a problem, the Turkish Cypriots were least likely to do so. Cypriot pupils, like other pupils, found the headteacher a distant figure. Although the Cypriot pupils had positive attitudes towards their relationships at school, it seemed that they were less likely to be influenced by the school than the home in relation to moral values, the Greek Cypriots being less influenced in matters of character and the Turkish Cypriots less influenced in their judgement on moral matters. Indeed Ulug (1981) suggested that Turkish Cypriot girls often feel a lack of understanding by and mistrust of their teachers. By comparison, in another small sample of Greek Cypriot pupils in the fourth to sixth years of secondary schooling Martianou (1981) found that all except one girl were happy at school, three-quarters were happy with all of their teachers and the remainder with most of them, and none were afraid of their teachers. A quarter had difficulty in following some teachers, but if they did not understand in class only half would ask, the others claiming to be too shy or not liking to ask for an explanation. If they had problems, these pupils were almost equally divided as to whether they would turn to their form teacher, year head, parents or friends for help.

From the available anecdotal evidence (see e.g. GB.P. H of C, 1985) it is impossible to tell to what extent pupils of Cypriot origin may experience racism and hostility in school either overtly or unintentionally in terms of attitudes and expectations. Although studies reviewed have shown that between half and three-quarters of Cypriot pupils generally have favourable attitudes towards the school, clearly a significant minority either have neutral or unfavourable attitudes which may well, in turn, influence their school performance. Findings generally suggest that more attention should be paid to developing positive attitudes to school amongst pupils, for example, by allowing them more genuine curricular choice, and by promoting more sensitive teacher–pupil relationships in the classroom and in counselling situations. It may, moreover, be helpful for pupils of Cypriot origin to have a structured opportunity to discuss problems with school and with schoolwork amongst their peer group on neutral territory, in out-of-school hours, possibly under the auspices of community social workers, as in the case of some groups described by Alkan and Constantinides (1981).

VOCATIONAL ASPIRATIONS AND EXPECTATIONS

Research studies on the vocational aspirations and expectations of pupils of Cypriot origin are few, of small scale and considerable age: two of the three main studies in which such data were collected in Haringey are now 20 years old. Thus there is no research, as distinct from general comment, which takes account of changes in the employment situation of the Cypriot community and in the economic climate in recent years. However, the studies provide some insights into gender-differentiated vocational aspirations and expectations, and ideal and actual occupations through an exploration of the transition from school to work. Comparisons are, however, complicated by the variable use of social class and occupational categorization in different studies in relation to aspirations, expectations and actual jobs.

Bhatnagar (1970) pointed to the importance of distinguishing vocational aspirations and expectations suggesting that these might be different, especially perhaps for immigrant pupils who might feel that they might not be offered jobs which they might otherwise have expected to obtain. In one school in Haringey in 1966, Bhatnagar inquired of 65 Cypriot, 153 West Indian and 170 English pupils what job they thought they deserved to get when they left school. Some 85 per cent of the Cypriot pupils, virtually the same percentage as that of English and West Indian pupils, aspired to skilled, clerical or professional jobs. However, almost all of the Cypriot boys, compared with three-quarters of Cypriot girls (the least likely of all the groups to have such aspirations), thought that they deserved these kinds of work. Moreover, only just over a quarter of Cypriot and West Indian pupils, compared with just over half the English pupils, thought that they would actually obtain a skilled, clerical or professional job. On this the expectations of Cypriot boys and girls were alike. Indeed just less than three-fifths of Cypriot and West Indian pupils, compared with a third of English pupils, thought that they deserved a skilled, clerical or professional position, but did not expect to get such a job. Almost two-thirds of Cypriot boys, compared with half Cypriot girls, had different vocational aspirations and expectations. Correlations with tests of adjustment indicated that Cypriot pupils whose vocational aspirations and expectations were similar were better adjusted, though interestingly these were at a lower level of significance for the Cypriot pupils than both the English and West Indian pupils.

By far the most detailed study of Cypriot pupils' aspirations, expectations and actual jobs was undertaken in 1966–7 by Figueroa (1974). In fact the study focussed on all the West Indian fourth- and fifth-formers in ten schools in Haringey and included all the British, Cypriot and 'other white' pupils in the same forms. The sample of school-leavers comprised: 48 Cypriots (24 boys and 24 girls), though numbers responding to different aspects of the questionnaire fluctuated; 131 British boys and 130 British girls; 29 West Indian boys and 59 West Indian girls; and 16 'other white' boys and 11 'other white' girls. Most of the data derived from a questionnaire in 1966, but 43 West Indians in work and an equal number of British respondents, matched by sex and school class were followed up in interview one year later. Unfortunately, little follow-up information is available for Cypriot pupils; this concentrates on girls.

Just over half the Cypriot boys ideally aspired to engineering jobs – almost equally divided between mechanical and electrical engineering – compared with over three-quarters of West Indians and less than a third of their British peers. Almost a quarter of Cypriot boys ideally chose what Figueroa termed 'fantasy' occupations, and a similar proportion either miscellaneous occupations, woodwork or building. Over two-fifths of the Cypriot girls, unlike either their West Indian or British peers, ideally chose hairdressing as their future occupation. Almost a third of Cypriot girls ideally aspired to office work, whilst the remainder were divided between those who ideally chose professional, technical or artistic miscellaneous occupations.

By comparison, when asked what their job expectations were on leaving school, two-fifths of the Cypriot boys thought that they would become either electrical or mechanical engineers. However, the remaining majority had no clear idea of what job they expected to obtain on leaving school. Cypriot girls' expectations seemed, by contrast, to be more in line with their aspirations, as half expected to become hairdressers, almost a third to obtain office work and the remainder to work in factories or sewing. A higher proportion of both Cypriot boys and girls than their white British or West Indian peers expected to have skilled employment. Two-thirds of the Cypriot pupils expected to like their job very much on leaving school. The Cypriot girls' aspirations and expectations for their future occupation coincided considerably with those they said their parents held (see pp. 165–6). Two-thirds of Cypriot girls had long-term job expectations and very few, compared with over a fifth of their British peers, expected to be just a housewife. By the age of 25, over four-fifths expected to have a job only, and almost two-thirds expected this to be office or telephone work and a quarter expected to be hairdressers. Three-quarters, fewer than the British and West Indian girls, expected their long-term work to be non-manual and a further quarter specified skilled work.

In terms of general aspirations three-fifths of Cypriot pupils, more than either of the other two groups, thought that a good education was important. Cypriot pupils generally stressed hard work less and good luck more than their British peers, but also with their West Indian peers emphasized a good education and special training more. But all respondents placed much importance on obtaining jobs. Three-fifths of Cypriots felt it was important that they should have pride in their job and virtually all of the Cypriots thought that it was important to have interesting work. Over two-thirds of Cypriots thought it important that they should have a job where they themselves made decisions, and a similar proportion wanted to work with their hands or with other people.

One-third of the Cypriot pupils expected the transition from school to work to be positively easy, in contrast to one-third of West Indian pupils who expected it to be difficult. Interestingly, Figueroa found that Cypriot and 'other white' boys were more likely to be recommended to skilled employment than their British or West Indian peers who were more likely to be recommended to semi-skilled work. By comparison with their peers, Cypriot girls were less likely than British and West Indian girls to be recommended to clerical work but they, too, were often recommended to skilled occupations such as hairdressing. At the time when they completed the questionnaires, two-fifths of Cypriot and 'other white' pupils, like their British peers, did not have a job already fixed, compared with some three-fifths of West Indians.

At the follow-up one year later only two-thirds of the Cypriot boys, compared with over four-fifths of the Cypriot girls, were in work, and one in ten were in further education. Unfortunately, no indication is given as to why such a low proportion of the Cypriot boys were found to be in employment or how those who were working were occupied. Of the Cypriot girls in employment, two-fifths – a much greater proportion than their peers – were in skilled manual jobs and half in non-manual work, compared with well over four-fifths of white British and West Indian girls. In fact over a third of the Cypriot girls were in apprenticeships in hairdressing, another third were working in offices and a fair proportion of the remainder were doing sewing. For the Cypriot girls, then, there was considerable consistency between job aspirations, expectations, parental choice and actual job which suggests the absorption of Cypriot girls into the ethnic business community.

In a study by Dove (1975) in three London comprehensives, in 1972, which involved 78 15–16-year-old Cypriots, over half of whom were born in the UK, fewer than one in ten wanted to leave school as soon as possible. The Cypriots were more like their white British than Asian or West Indian peers, in that over half wanted to leave school after O-level and nearly two-fifths, more boys than girls, wanted to leave after A-level. Over two-fifths of the Cypriot pupils, one-third of the girls and half the boys, wanted full-time education. This was a higher proportion than for any of the other groups. Over a third of the Cypriots wanted an apprenticeship or day release and one in ten were prepared to study at evening classes. Dove attributed the attraction of apprenticeships to the opportunities for hairdressing and tailoring in the local Cypriot communities. The adolescents were asked to describe the jobs they would most like to do and those they expected to get. Over two-fifths of the Cypriot pupils opted for a job in social class 3, though almost as many aimed for class 1 and 2. In this, they were more like their white British than their West Indian or Asian peers. By comparison, however, fewer expected to achieve such employment status: a quarter expected jobs in social class 1 or 2; fewer than two-fifths in social class 3; and one in ten expected jobs in social class 4 or 5. Almost a third gave no answer. Their responses were most like those of white British pupils. Dove considered that the schools had failed to capitalize on the pupils' positive attitudes to their schools and teachers (see pp. 185–6) and that they did not prepare them for life beyond school, especially the transition from school to work. In Dove's view, ethnic minority pupils were as realistic in their job expectations as their white British contemporaries and took into account the economic situation and their qualifications. But Cypriots were less ostensibly conscious of the racial and cultural disadvantages which they might encounter once they left school and 'some thought of the "immigrant problem" as one for black people, not for themselves' (p.65).

In another study (Archimandritou-Xefteris, 1977), in which pupils were categorized according to their level of achievement in the Greek language, mathematics and science by their Greek teachers (see pp. 132–3), boys had a strong bias towards the physical sciences and girls had a strong bias towards languages and literature irrespective of achievement. Almost two-fifths of low achievers, compared with fewer than one in ten high achievers, had not decided on their future occupations. The high achievers were much more likely to be ambitious and to have conceptions of their desired occupation, even if these were unrealistic, whilst the low achievers tended to opt for occupations similar to those of their fathers or their teachers. The high achievers were generally seen by their Greek teachers as successful adolescents, well-adjusted and using their capabilities.

In the light of the reported vocational aspirations and expectations of pupils of Cypriot origin, what are the relative influences of teachers, parents and the employment situation on the likely realization of pupils' aims? Triseliotis (1976) argued that pupils of Cypriot origin may not have thought of themselves as a class with limited abilities who have to keep their aspirations low, yet teachers in working-class areas are sometimes astonished by the aspirations of such pupils which they may see as unrealistic. Triseliotis considered that realistic aspirations sometimes fail to be encouraged. On the other hand, how great is the influence of Cypriot parents in their aspirations for their children's future employment (see pp. 165–8)? Few studies have attempted to consider both these factors. For example, Martianou (1981) reported that schools saw Cypriot pupils as having as high educational (see pp. 196–7) and vocational aspirations as indigenous whites. Cypriot parents were also seen as having a high regard for education and ambitious for the vocational prospects of their children, sometimes unrealistically. But schools also saw parents as exerting pressure upon boys and not necessarily upon girls. None of the Cypriot pupils interviewed wanted to do the same jobs as their parents. Whilst parents have high aspirations for their children, they may be prepared to allow their sons more latitude in their choice of occupation than their daughters, upon whom they may also place certain restrictions such as the distance of the workplace from home (Constantinides, 1977). Indeed the research suggests a considerable congruence between the aspirations, expectations, parental choice and actual jobs of Cypriot girls who seem to be involved in three main occupations – hairdressing, office work and sewing. According to Anthias (1983, 1984), although young Cypriot men, and to a lesser extent women, still enter the catering and clothing industries, there is a general movement away from such employment and, in the case of Greek girls, towards clerical work and hairdressing, even in non-Cypriot establishments. Apparently some Turkish Cypriot girls are also working as secretaries and in banks (Memdouh, 1981). But to what extent are the vocational aspirations of Cypriot pupils constrained? To what extent has the reported expectation that they would not experience difficulties on account of race or ethnicity in the transfer from school to work been borne out in practice? How much is this in fact due to their absorption within the Cypriot community? And if this is so, to what extent is it a matter of choice or default? The Swann Report (GB.P.H of C, 1985) suggested that the tie with the 'internal economy' of their community seemed to have shielded Cypriot youth from rising unemployment, as well as limiting their experience of racial discrimination in employment, although in the current economic climate there was increasing pressure on some areas of Cypriot employment, especially the clothing trade. Young Cypriots were attempting to enter mainstream employment, but were finding that the current employment situation often led them to fall back on their community, with some reluctance. This suggests that there may be a considerable and possibly increasing discrepancy between the vocational aspirations and actual employment of Cypriot youth. However, in the absence of data on examination performance and up-to-date research on the transition from school to work involving Cypriot pupils, it can only be speculated to what extent this may be a result of unrealistic aspirations, inadequate qualifications, poor economic opportunities or actual discrimination in the job market. If young Cypriots do experience job discrimination, as is generally the case to a greater extent for ethnic minorities in times of recession, then this may become a major source of discontent for young Cypriots, which may affect not only their attitudes to school and educational achievement, but increase parent–child tensions. Clearly one of the functions of the school is to ensure that educational and vocational aspirations are realistic and match job prospects.

Teachers, Peers and Schools

How do the peers of pupils of Cypriot origin regard them? What opinions do teachers of pupils of Cypriot origin have of them, their behaviour, their language and their culture? What attempt has been made to take account of Greek, Turkish and Cypriot cultures in school curricula, especially in those schools where pupils of Cypriot origin are to be found? In particular, are there any teachers of Cypriot origin who may serve as role models for Cypriot pupils and negotiate between the Cypriot and British communities? Such matters will form the subject of the final section of this review of research into the education of pupils of Cypriot origin.

ATTITUDES OF PEERS

Although the few studies which have been undertaken investigating the attitudes of peers of pupils of Cypriot origin to Cypriot pupils are of some antiquity and of small scale, nevertheless it is important to consider to what extent they indicate that pupils of Cypriot origin have suffered from racial discrimination by their peers in the school context, the stereotypes held of them and the interethnic attitudes displayed by peers of white and West Indian origin, and whether such pupils claim friendship with Cypriot pupils.

'Bubble and squeak' – thus white pupils in a mixed comprehensive school in London in 1963 referred to Cypriot pupils. According to Kawwa (1963), they made no distinction between Greek and Turkish Cypriot pupils, all were considered Greek. In recent years, concern has been expressed that such name-calling demonstrates racist attitudes. But the literature of the 1960s on immigrant pupils did not portray Cypriot pupils as suffering particularly from prejudice or discrimination. Bowker (1968), for example, excluded consideration of Cypriot pupils because he claimed the evidence indicated that they were less likely to be the victims of prejudice and discrimination than other ethnic minority pupils. Yet he noted a general sociological ambivalence at the time, for whilst some writers referred to Cypriots as 'coloured' others did not. However, other researchers (for example, Figueroa, 1976; Bhatnagar, 1970) have stressed that although Cypriots may be considered phenotypically similar to white British pupils, there are great differences between Cypriot and British culture. Consideration of prejudice has, therefore, to extend to cultural as well as racial discrimination. The distinction between differences on racial, ethnic or cultural grounds is a continuous thread running through the research involving pupils of Cypriot origin. There is considerable concern amongst the Cypriot community and the second generation that they should not in any way be identified with other 'coloured' immigrants. Cypriots have, therefore, made consistent and concerted attempts to distance themselves socially from West Indians and Asians, aligning themselves in this respect at least with the majority white British population (Constantinides, 1977; Ladbury, 1977). Indeed, in a Community Relations Commission (CRC) survey (1977) out of five groups of ethnic minority parents, Cypriots were the least likely to claim that their children had experienced racial problems in school, and then only very few. But is this actually the case? What indications does research give as to whether pupils of Cypriot origin experience discrimination from their peers in school and, if so, is this on cultural or racial grounds?

In a follow-up study of young people in employment one year after leaving school, in 1966, Figueroa (1974, 1976) attempted to establish a racial frame of reference. Forty-three British youngsters were asked to say of 11 characteristics whether each fitted the English, West Indians or Cypriots best, and which of these three groups each item fitted least. Generally the Cypriots provoked the milder response from the British respondents; only on three or four of the items were the British more likely to rate the Cypriots rather than the West Indians negatively. About two-fifths of the British respondents said that Cypriots were dirty, slow workers or backward. On the other hand, over two-fifths to two-thirds of British respondents said that Cypriots were the least honest, bold or happy or strove least to improve themselves. Hence these respondents who had experienced their schooling with from 11 to 47 per cent of Cypriot pupils on the rolls of ten Haringey secondary schools held some distinctly negative views of them, though as in other areas of research, to a lesser extent than towards pupils of West Indian origin. More recently, Georgiou (1983) reported that Greek Cypriot children claimed little prejudice, though this might more accurately be described as resentment as their peers regarded them as being spoilt materialistically in terms of having more money or being bought more things by their parents. Georgiou suggested, however, that these children might have to pay dearly in emotional terms for such benefits.

Only a few studies have considered the interethnic attitudes of white and West Indian pupils towards pupils of Cypriot origin. Kawwa (1963, 1968b) conducted one of these studies in which 636 11–15-year-olds in a mixed comprehensive school in Islington, in 1962, where Cypriot and black pupils formed 15 per cent of the roll, were asked to state their attitudes to Cypriots and West Indians on a specially constructed eight-item questionnaire rated on a three-point scale. The open-ended questionnaire, which was designed to tap affective, cognitive and conative aspects of prejudice, was constructed from terms used by children in discussions, but was not piloted. The questionnaire inquired how white pupils felt towards Greek Cypriots and whether they liked them; what they would like to be done about them; how the individual pupils treated Greek Cypriots; how they would like other people to treat them; what they hated or liked about Cypriots; whether Cypriots were good for the country and in what ways; and whether Cypriots should be given council houses and why. Kawwa, a Lebanese, who was mistaken by many Greek Cypriots as Greek, administered the questionnaire, but claimed that this did not have a visible effect on the testing process as British children were explicitly told that he was not Greek. In fact Kawwa discovered that the 331 white British boys and 305 girls in the school displayed slightly, but not significantly more, prejudice towards Cypriots than blacks. Kawwa suggested that this was due to three main reasons. Cypriots were seen as more different culturally from British people than

West Indians, in that they had a completely different language which they used both in and out of school. Secondly, there had been a recent rapid influx of Cypriot pupils who, at 150, outnumbered black pupils in the school. Thirdly, there had been many complaints by the pupils that, from a British point of view, the Cypriots had not understood how they were expected to behave, i.e. what their place and status as a foreign group was, though there had not been any major open conflict in the school. The British pupils considered that as newcomers the Cypriot pupils were still learning to readjust, which was why they were less acceptable than black pupils, though in fact the British pupils displayed negative attitudes to both groups. Yet on the whole they did not believe in the innate inferiority of Cypriot or black pupils; they thought that if given the same chances, they would be the same culturally. On the other hand, some 438 British boys and girls in the school believed Cypriot and coloured children did not live in the way Britons do, especially in respect of food, lifestyle, dealings and attitude to life. They claimed that the Cypriots should not be allowed to have council houses, but were divided about whether they constituted an employment threat. Some of the pupils said that it was acceptable for them to have 'dirty' jobs, lacking in authority and responsibility.

As part of an attempt to measure the adjustment of pupils in one London secondary modern school in Haringey, in 1966, Bhatnagar (1970) administered a sub-scale to evaluate their social acceptability. This was defined as the degree of acceptance of the child by his peers in situations involving voluntary social interaction. Social situations were classified as those involving a considerable degree of interpersonal interaction, formal with minimal interaction, authority-based, those bringing recognition to the school and those showing extreme rejection. Every pupil rated and was rated by five randomly selected classmates on a three-point scale. Cypriot pupils were found to be less socially acceptable than English pupils, but more socially acceptable than their West Indian peers. There was a statistically significant difference (at the 0.01 level) between the mean social acceptability scores of the English and Cypriot pupils compared with those of the West Indian pupils, but no significant difference between the English and the Cypriot pupils. Bhatnagar concluded that the Cypriots were not seen as such a distant out-group as the West Indians, but that skin colour was an extremely important variable in social acceptance of a child at school since on all criteria except external appearance the West Indians were closer to the English than the Cypriots.

How likely is it, then, that pupils of Cypriot origin will be chosen as friends by white British and black pupils? Evidence from these small-scale, in-depth studies conducted by Kawwa (1963, 1965, 1968a, 1968b) provides some insight. In the first study in one mixed London comprehensive school, in 1962, 656 white British pupils (340 boys and 316 girls) and 32 black pupils (16 boys and girls) were asked to list in order of preference five best friends of the same sex in the school. Both the British and the black children (as well as the Cypriot pupils – see pp. 170–1) demonstrated significant in-group choice patterns (at the 0.01 level; Kawwa, 1963). Black pupils tended to choose British rather than Cypriot pupils as friends if they did not choose from amongst their own group. Of the few British pupils who made out-group choices, girls tended to give their choices to Cypriot girls rather than black girls, whereas boys tended to distribute their choices more equally though not proportionately. Interestingly, those British pupils who had chosen non-British friends were not necessarily found to be less negatively prejudiced than other children who had chosen friends from their own group (Kawwa, 1968b).

In the second study carried out in a boys' secondary modern school in north London, in 1964, some 385 British and 43 black 11–17-year-olds, as well as some

Indian and 'other' pupils, were asked to choose two best friends, one from their own class (restricted choice) and the other from the whole school including the class (unrestricted choice), and to name one boy in the class whom they disliked or liked least of all. Each boy was also asked to indicate which of 27 schoolboy activities he did or enjoyed doing most and to name the boys with whom he shared or enjoyed sharing these activities. Both the restricted and unrestricted choices of the British and the black boys showed an in-group friendship pattern. Few British boys chose Greek Cypriot or Turkish Cypriot friends and fewer black boys did so. But the British boys also rejected Greek and Turkish Cypriots more than they chose them, although they rejected their own group more. Interestingly, British boys who had chosen non-British friends were those who were most rejected by their British peers. Also Kawwa observed that a British boy might choose a Cypriot and reject a black boy as a friend or vice versa. Furthermore, the British boys demonstrated in-school and out-of-school in-group associations. Just as there were comparatively few friendship choices between black and Cypriot boys, so there were few rejections, although black boys were less likely to reject Greek Cypriots than vice versa. The black (and Cypriot see p. 171) boys who were more ethnocentric demonstrated a strong preference to socialize within their own group, which Kawwa attributed to their presence in significant minorities and also to cultural reasons.

In the third study carried out in a primary school in north London, in 1964, 116 British (55 boys and 61 girls) and 25 black (13 boys and 12 girls), as well as a very few Indian pupils, were asked to name their two best friends. The choices showed an in-group pattern, but the British (and Cypriot) girls did not make significantly in-group choices. The Greek Cypriots received fewer choices than they gave. The black children showed an in-group preference, choosing British rather than Greek or Turkish Cypriot peers for friends. In general Cypriots were far more accepted in the primary school than black children which, according to Kawwa, was because a number were Anglicized and because some British children reported parental objections to their association with non-British, especially black, children.

In a study of secondary school leavers, in 1966, Figueroa (1974, 1976) again found overwhelming in-group friendship choices. A mere five per cent of 248 British and six per cent of 80 West Indian fourth and fifth years claimed to have some Cypriot friends, although Cypriots comprised 12 per cent of these forms. Although fewer still of the British claimed West Indian friends, almost a third of the West Indians claimed British friends. Furthermore, a mere two per cent of 241 British, one per cent of 74 West Indian and one per cent of 21 other white pupils claimed Cypriot best friends. Hence, although almost a third of Cypriot pupils claimed British friends and best friends, this level of friendship choice does not appear to have been reciprocated. Indeed, several commentators (e.g. Constantinides, 1977; Leeuwenberg, 1979) have suggested that although Cypriot adolescents may quickly identify with their classmates and attempt to move away from their Cypriot identity, the supposed friendships on their part may not survive either in out-of-school contexts or on leaving school when in work and at home they look more towards their Cypriot origins.

Finally, in another small-scale study in an all-boys secondary school in London, in 1973, Thomas (1975) asked all first-, second- and fourth-year pupils (244 British, 172 West Indian, 48 Turkish Cypriots and 11 Asians) to write down in order of preference up to three best friends from within the class. Again, the distribution of friendship choices of all the group revealed a significant in-group choice pattern (at the 0.001 level) which was most marked by the fourth year. In addition, the cleavage was most marked between the British and West Indian groups with, by contrast, relatively little withdrawal from the Turkish Cypriots by either group.

Research evidence on the attitudes of school peers of pupils of Cypriot origin as manifested by their stereotypes, interethnic attitudes and friendship towards Cypriot pupils is somewhat parlous and dated, but certain common features can be identified. Although there is little overt research evidence of explicit racial prejudice on the part of their peers with respect to pupils of Cypriot origin, so that they do not appear to have been as exposed as some other ethnic minority pupils to name-calling, bullying or racial harassment, nevertheless it is clear from the data on stereotypes, interethnic attitudes and friendship patterns that they have been regarded somewhat negatively, if not with hostility, both by their white and West Indian peers in neighbourhood schools. On the other hand, neither white nor West Indian pupils had such negative stereotypes of Cypriot pupils as they did of each other. On interethnic attitudes there were conflicting findings: Bhatnagar found that the social acceptability of Cypriot pupils was nearly as great as that of white pupils, yet Kawwa discovered that British pupils displayed slightly more prejudice towards Cypriots than West Indian pupils, though it is possible that the recent arrival of Cypriot pupils in this school may have influenced this finding. Whilst, in general, friendship choice is ethnocentric, it appears that British pupils were slightly more likely to choose Cypriot than West Indian friends and West Indian pupils were more likely to choose British than Cypriot friends. Though more up-to-date investigations or more sensitive measures of interethnic attitudes and friendship patterns might indicate greater interethnic social interaction, the strong in-group preferences of British, West Indian and Cypriot pupils in these studies and the apparent lack of choice of friends from other ethnic groups should have been a matter of some concern. Indeed Beetlestone (1982) reported that teachers saw even Turkish Cypriot infants as less well integrated socially. Since objections to pupils of Cypriot origin seemed largely to be based on cultural differences, it is important to examine to what extent schools in which such pupils are found have made attempts to take account of the distinctive Greek, Turkish and Cypriot cultures, to which we now turn.

TEACHERS' ATTITUDES

In appraising the educational experience of pupils of Cypriot origin in multiracial schools, it is necessary not only to consider the attitudes of their peers, but also to take account of the attitudes of their teachers. However, once again there is a lack of research data on the attitudes of teachers to pupils of Cypriot origin, especially in comparison with those on teachers' views of pupils of Asian or West Indian origin. This suggests that Cypriot pupils may not have been the main focus of attention for teachers, and even where they may be found in schools in relatively large numbers, they have not been the prime subjects for research. Moreover, since teachers' opinions have been solicited on pupils of West Indian and Asian origin, the focus has tended to be on race, and explicitly colour, rather than on ethnicity or culture, although there is more available in terms of the cultural backgrounds of pupils of Asian origin. Does the fact that there is a dearth of research evidence on teachers' attitudes to pupils of Cypriot origin indicate that they have been overlooked or that the inherent difficulties in researching into attitudes, particularly in the sensitive context of teachers and race or ethnicity, have prohibited the conduct of such research? Perhaps further information is available in certain localities with greater Cypriot populations or in higher degree theses but none has come to light.

The main attempt to research the opinions of teachers about Cypriot pupils formed part of the series of NFER investigations undertaken in the early 1970s. But these researches were on a national scale and aimed to cover several groups of immigrant pupils. Also since a wide range of educational establishments and localities were involved, Cypriot pupils and their teachers were only found in a few schools, so data relating to them are fairly incidental. Moreover, a serious drawback in terms of unravelling information about pupils of Cypriot origin is that teachers' opinions from the first stage of the NFER study (Brittan, 1976a) are analysed in relation to the group of 'European' pupils as a whole including Cypriot, Italian and other European pupils. Yet there may well be important distinctions to be drawn between these groups of pupils – as the teachers responding were themselves aware. Some commented in general about the validity of comparing the behaviour of different ethnic groups, many others wished to qualify their answers to refer, for example, to Cypriots but not to other European groups, to boys rather than girls or to recently arrived pupils as opposed to those in the UK. However, in the absence of other large-scale quantitative data, general reference may be made to this investigation since it provides some information on teachers' attitudes to the academic standards, behaviour and language of 'European' pupils against which other small-scale qualitative data may be set.

In 1972, 510 teachers (171 primary and 339 secondary) in 25 schools with 18–84 per cent ethnic minority pupils generally had less marked opinions of European pupils in comparison with those which they expressed towards pupils of West Indian or Asian origin (Brittan, 1976a). However, their attitudes towards European pupils were not necessarily positive by any means; many teachers were unwilling to make the generalizations imposed by the questions and a sizeable number made use of the 'not applicable' or 'neutral' response categories. Whilst this may have been due to a lack of familiarity with European pupils or a recognition of diversity within the group, since the opinions actually expressed indicated a considerable consensus, at least within each age range, certain teachers apparently did have clear views about such pupils. For example, when asked to give their views on whether European immigrant pupils tended to raise the academic standard of the school, although 60 per cent of all teachers did not express a strong view (neutral or not applicable), 32 per cent of teachers – rather more primary than secondary – were of the opinion that European immigrant pupils did not tend to raise the academic standard of the school. Moreover, whilst a similar percentage of teachers (37 per cent) also held a negative view about the presence of Asian pupils raising the academic standard of the school, 15 per cent of teachers thought that they did raise academic standards, compared with only five per cent of teachers who claimed this of European pupils. On the other hand, teachers did not display such negative attitudes towards European pupils *vis-à-vis* the academic standard of the school compared with West Indian pupils since half the teachers disagreed with the statement that 'West Indian pupils tend to raise the academic standard of the school' and a further 27 per cent strongly disagreed.

Despite charges of low teacher expectations with regard to the academic performance of pupils of Cypriot origin (Memdouh, 1981; GB. P. H of C, 1985), there is very little direct research evidence to substantiate this. Martianou (1981) found that schools sometimes saw the high academic expectations of Cypriot parents as unrealistic. Anthias (1984), noting 'the enormous value given to educational achievement' by Greek Cypriot parents, which she suggested was not the case on the whole for the semi- and non-skilled working class, reported that teachers often misidentified Greek Cypriot children as sharing 'the working-class syndrome of low aspiration'. In 40 interviews with heads and teachers in a range of Haringey schools Beetlestone (1982) discovered that it was difficult for respondents to focus on the group of Cypriot pupils. Teachers were frequently unaware of how many there were in the school and did not see them as having special needs.

Individuals' problems were generally related to social or psychological factors, but teachers also appeared to invoke differential stereotypes of Greek and Turkish Cypriot pupils and parents with respect to fluency in English, reading performance, behaviour, general intelligence, social integration, the position of women and ethnic characteristics, which all tended to give lower status to Turkish Cypriots. Indeed the Swann Committee considered 'persuasive' the suggestion that 'the apparent differential in performance between Greek Cypriot and Turkish Cypriot children could, in part at least, be ascribed to the rather different stereotypes which existed of them in the minds of the majority community and particularly teachers' (GB.P. H of C, 1985, p. 692).

In the third phase of the NFER research teachers were asked to respond to the statements 'European immigrant pupils are usually better behaved than English pupils' and 'European immigrant pupils resent being reprimanded more than English pupils do' (Brittan, 1976a). Teachers appeared to display more divergent opinions on the first item. Whereas some 55 per cent of teachers did not express strong views (including some 39 per cent who checked the neutral category), 30 per cent in fact disagreed that European pupils were usually better behaved and only 11 per cent agreed. Interestingly, there was again a difference between primary and secondary teachers' opinions, more of the secondary teachers claiming better behaviour and fewer disagreeing with the statement. The responses overall indicated that whereas teachers were less favourably disposed towards the behaviour of European pupils than that of Asian pupils, they were more likely to consider European pupils as better behaved than West Indian pupils. But there were indications elsewhere, both in a more extensive description of the same data (Brittan, 1973) and in information from headteachers in an earlier investigation (Townsend and Brittan, 1972), that some teachers experienced difficulties with the behaviour of Greek Cypriots, especially boys, which was generally attributed to gender differentials in traditional Cypriot culture practised in the home, but not necessarily in the school, leading to difficulties of adaptation for certain pupils. On the other hand, whilst again some 37 per cent of teachers expressed a neutral view and 19 per cent claimed that it was not applicable or did not reply to the statement 'European immigrant pupils resent being reprimanded more than English pupils do', some 35 per cent of teachers disagreed – slightly more primary than secondary – suggesting that European pupils might be more prepared to accept correction. Again, the behaviour of European pupils was seen as more like that of Asian pupils in this respect than that of their West Indian peers. These findings must, however, be regarded with considerable caution since they are highly generalized and do not relate solely to pupils of Cypriot origin.

Two other studies provide some insights into or possible reasons for such responses. Martianou (1981) noted that teachers in a few secondary schools with Cypriot pupils reported that they were not more than usually indisciplined, and of those who were, it was said that they either experienced strict upbringing at home, were spoilt by their mothers or came from single-parent families. The participation of pupils of Cypriot origin in class was generally said to be good, although some pupils were said to be shy, which teachers put down to the fact that they were not encouraged to discuss things openly at home. Beetlestone (1982) also reported that heads did not generally see Cypriot pupils as presenting behaviour problems. However, some infant and primary heads reported that although the girls were quiet, hardworking, well-behaved and good at working on their own, some boys exhibited disruptive behaviour, had difficulty in settling into school, resented accepting discipline, especially from female teachers, were uncooperative and unwilling to do the kinds of task done by their mothers, or sought attention and were exhibitionistic.

Teachers interpreted these behaviour patterns in cultural terms; the importance and dominance of the male was seen as presenting problems for a profession whose workforce was predominantly female. This sometimes assumed larger proportions in secondary schools in the relationships between Cypriot boys and female teachers, since women teachers were sometimes said to be seen by Cypriot fathers as low in status and non-academic, and this perception was sometimes passed on to their sons.

Another context in which teachers' views have been expressed in relation to pupils of Cypriot origin is that of language and culture. Reference has already been made to teachers' opinions of the difficulties experienced by pupils of Cypriot origin in learning English (see pp. 120–1) and other aspects of their performance in English (see pp. 124–6) which demonstrate some concern. It appears that teachers have generally tended to be ambivalent over bilingualism and especially the development of language through the mother tongue as complementary to, rather than a limitation upon, developing fluency in English. According to Krokou (1985), prevailing attitudes have been assimilationist and 'the barely hidden message' was that continued use of Greek or Turkish at home or in school would militate against cognitive development. Evidence to the Swann Committee (GB. P. H of C, 1985) from the Cypriot communities indicated a clear perception that some teachers saw lack of fluency in English as a sign of lack of ability and adopted a negative view of second-language learners: 'Teachers tended to display a punitive attitude to the use of mother tongue in schools in a misconceived attempt to foster early learning of English. This gave children their first direct experience of racism' (p. 681). Cronin (1984) also reported that a small sample of Turkish-speaking children who were studied spoke little or no Turkish at their state school. Although half the sample's teachers knew their pupils attended Turkish classes in out-of-school time, they gave little encouragement. Pupils never spoke Turkish in front of their teachers and one had been severely reprimanded for doing so. Teachers have also been concerned about the strain on pupils of Cypriot origin attending mother tongue classes in the evenings or at weekends and the possible consequent tiredness, lack of concentration in schoolwork and homework and confusion in mastering English (Milstead, 1981; GB.P. H of C, 1985). These predominantly negative and ambivalent attitudes to bilingualism are illustrated by the following summary of the discussions of a group of teachers from mainstream and community schools:

> ... on the one hand teachers will tell their Greek-speaking pupils not to go to community-run schools because 'it impinges on their homework time and overall concentration on "what is important"; on the other hand, when Greek-speaking pupils choose Greek as an 'O' level subject and, therefore, to attend the mainstream Greek classes, teachers will discourage them from doing so, and encourage them to 'study Greek after school'. (Couillaud, 1984, p.22)

Teachers have also often regarded extended visits back to Cyprus with a degree of ambivalence. Whilst some have placed high educational value on the enriching experience of such trips, others have seen them as an impediment to continuity of learning and particularly as a setback in the development of proficiency in English. Visits in term time may, however, have been more common in the late 1960s or early 1970s. Owing to political upheavals, reorientation and the establishment of stronger community links in the UK, pupils of Cypriot origin may nowadays make less frequent holiday visits to relatives and friends in Cyprus and these are more likely in the summer vacations, even possibly in organized parties, such as those arranged by the Cyprus High Commission and Greek Embassy (Aristodemou,

1979; Constantinides, 1977). Attendance at school may also be affected by the need for children to act as interpreter if a parent, especially the mother, goes to the doctor or to hospital. Though this may increase the child's fluency and ability to switch between two languages, it may have the adverse affect that absences from school may mean lack of continuity in education and difficulties in making up work (Alkan and Constantinides, 1982).

Unfortunately, little specific information is available from research studies on teachers' attitudes towards aspects of the multicultural curriculum with specific reference to pupils of Cypriot origin. Any incidental data have been cited as appropriate, especially in comparison with the views of parents on aspects of school organization and the curriculum (see pp. 150–6). Although, for example, another part of the third phase of the NFER multiracial education project investigated teachers' opinions on aspects of school life (Brittan, 1976b), teachers' views clearly did not specifically focus in any way on pupils of Cypriot origin, but instead on the influence of Asian culture on the school curriculum and organization. Indeed it has been claimed that teachers generally lack knowledge and understanding of the languages and cultural background of pupils of Cypriot origin (GB.P. H of C, 1985), as illustrated, for example, by Ulug's (1981) brief case studies. Teachers had very limited knowledge of the patterns of behaviour and upbringing of Turkish Cypriot girls and lacked awareness of the degree of incongruence of Turkish and British cultures; lack of insight caused them to fail to observe the position of these girls with objectivity and often reinforced feelings of inferiority or of being misunderstood. Whilst the girls wanted more attention paid to aspects of their culture in school, they were reluctant to bring it into class discussions without the support of teachers for fear of ridicule but, at the same time, were dissatisfied with general lack of interest shown by their schools. It has been suggested that teachers need in-service training in order to examine their attitudes towards pupils of Cypriot origin and their culture (Beetlestone, 1982). The following sub-section considers research evidence on the extent to which teachers and schools have attempted to include Greek and Turkish cultures in curriculum innovation and the availability of resources to bring this about.

MULTICULTURAL EDUCATION: THE GREEK AND TURKISH CYPRIOT DIMENSION

To what extent have schools taken account of the specific educational needs of pupils of Cypriot origin by including their languages in the school curriculum and their cultures as perspectives permeating learning? Clearly there is an extensive demand and intense desire by many Cypriot parents for their children to have a greater appreciation not only of their Greek or Turkish mother tongue, but also of their cultural background. However, to date, with a few signal exceptions on the part of certain schools which have initiated opportunities for studying Greek or Turkish in the school curriculum (see pp. 105–8), the community organizations, embassies and the Greek Orthodox Church have largely had to attempt to satisfy these interests through the provision of mother-tongue schools and classes. But should it just be the responsibility of Cypriot parents to ensure that their children know something of their linguistic and cultural origins? The Cypriot parents interviewed in the CRC survey (1977) thought that schools should be doing more to teach the culture to their children, even if they were already doing something. Half the Cypriot parents, a much higher proportion than any other group of ethnic minority parents in the survey, claimed that their children were not taught enough about their culture in schools, and a further quarter said that they were taught nothing. This suggests that Cypriot parents were conscious of the curricular omission and that they were especially keen to see that their culture was maintained. Cronin (1984) reported that there was almost no opportunity for Turkish-speaking pupils in a small sample studied to celebrate Turkish holidays or festivals in their state schools, and like the girls in Ulug's (1981) study they did not generally welcome their friends asking questions about their country or language for fear of being ridiculed. Cronin suggested that since the Turkish pupils did not appear to have a preference for either their state or mother-tongue school, and that as these were 'simply not comparable', they may not have felt the inability to celebrate their 'Turkishness' at state school because attending Turkish classes helped to maintain the balance.

Cypriot professionals have in recent years become more vocal about what they perceive as the needs of children of Cypriot origin to have their cultural backgrounds recognized in the school environment, to have a more comprehensive and detailed explanation of these customs and traditions and for the similarities and differences between these present lifestyles in the UK and British culture to be explored. Alkan and Constantinides (1981) have suggested, for example, the introduction of Cypriot studies at secondary school level and the inclusion of Cyprus in European or Middle East studies, history, geography and religious education. In primary schools they consider that myths, tales and religious stories relating to Cyprus should be taught. Alkan and Constantinides, who have been active in promoting counselling and social therapy groups within the Cypriot community, argue that at secondary school level seminars should also be held about Cypriot culture and family life as well as greater provision being made within the school for counselling and guidance. However, although Ulug (1981) also recognized such a need, she found that Turkish Cypriot girls stressed the importance of trust between pupils and the teachers if they are to act as counsellers. The girls ideally preferred a female Turkish teacher who 'would understand'. Ulug pointed to the need, for example, for teachers to be aware that older Turkish Cypriot girls might be experiencing several offers of marriage – a process which might be affecting their academic achievement.

There is nothing particularly new or radical in such recommendations on the part of Cypriots *vis-à-vis* the school curriculum. But what research evidence is there of teachers' awareness of the cultural needs of pupils of Cypriot origin or of curricular initiatives? It is quite possible that research data may be unrepresentative in the context of curriculum development and give an unbalanced view. Initiatives may be better documented at local level, especially within those LEAs where Cypriot pupils are concentrated, but published reports are not widely in evidence. It appears more likely that once again the interests of pupils of Cypriot origin have not been foremost in the development of a multicultural curriculum. For example, a questionnaire sent to primary and secondary schools, multiracial and non-multiracial in immigrant and non-immigrant areas, to investigate teachers' views of the aims of school syllabuses with respect to multiracial education, to identify curricular innovations, the changes foreseen and the direction of development and the external help teachers would welcome, did not appear to unearth curricular innovations in relation to the cultural needs of pupils of Cypriot origin. Although Townsend and Brittan's report (1973) described a variety of new curricular approaches and identified a gap between training and resources, apart from mention of the probable future inclusion of Greek and Turkish music in the curriculum of a multiracial secondary school, Cypriot culture received no acknowledgement, and the focus was as usual on Asian and West Indian cultures. Similarly, in Townsend and Brittan's earlier survey (1972), although it was clear that some teachers were introducing a multicultural curriculum in multiracial schools, there were few references to Greek and Turkish cultures. One team teaching scheme for nine to 11 year-olds based on 'Our neighbourhood' involved a visit to a local Greek Orthodox Church, and in another school Greek dancing and choral singing from Cyprus had been included in the curriculum. Some teachers may have seen the variety of cultural backgrounds in the school as widening and enriching the experience of all pupils, but to all intents and purposes the mother tongues of Cypriot and other ethnic minority children were ignored by schools (Derrick, 1977).

It may have been the case that in the 1960s and 1970s teachers of pupils of Cypriot origin were preoccupied with practical matters such as teaching English and appreciating the traditional Cypriot naming system and method of determining age. Alkan and Constantinides (1981) have pointed out that the pre-war and immediately post-war Cypriots in London tended to Anglicize their names in order to be less conspicuously foreign, but they claim that Greek and Turkish names nowadays are used widely. Since it is a Cypriot custom for a wife and children to take the husband's first name as their surname, this might cause confusion in documentation, with the father bearing a different surname to that of his family. Interestingly, Alkan and Constantinides reported that the Cypriot community is realizing the need for obvious continuity in British society and they imply that this practice may be changing, though it seems likely that it will have given rise to some confusion for teachers over the years. Indeed evidence to the Swann Committee (GB.P. H of C, 1985) indicated that Cypriot names were frequently misspelt in records and mispronounced and that some pupils Anglicized their names. Moreover, the method of counting age in which the child is considered to be one year more than his chronological age – a practice common amongst several Mediterranean communities and other minority groups in the UK – may have had implications for school placement, assessments and certain administrative matters such as the ten-year rule, according to which headteachers recorded the number of immigrant pupils on Form 7 for collation in DES statistics up until 1972 (Butterworth and Kinnibrugh, 1970).

Yet even into the 1980s the lack of evidence of any structured curricular innovations primarily focussing on Cypriot, Greek or Turkish culture suggests that initiatives may still be tokenistic or incidental. This may be because of the need to accommodate several cultural backgrounds of different ethnic minority groups in one school. For example, Twitchin and Demuth (1981) in a book which accompanies the BBC series, *Case Studies in Multi-Cultural Education,* cite one school in which a sociology department had introduced a course unit on minority groups which reviewed the experience of Cypriots, Turks and other ethnic minority groups in Britain. But such specific courses are probably still the exception rather than the rule. Generally any curriculum development involving Cypriot pupils has failed to be documented. Nor did the 'Education for a Multi-Racial Society: Curriculum and Context 5–13' project redeem the omission of Cypriot culture from curriculum development which had been identified in earlier surveys. The project report noted:

> Although the presence of Irish or Cypriot children, say, in our schools may present similar issues, 'race' as it is defined by British society has been quite deliberately the focus. The team's overriding concern has been with the nexus of relationships binding white society (its teachers, its parents, its children) to the children of families it defines as racially different – that is, children of African, Asian and Caribbean descent. (Schools Council, 1981, p.5)

In this approach the project was perpetuating the societal definition which has come to be enshrined in education whereby the focus is on Britain's 'black' minority groups and largely ignores the cultural needs of other ethnic minority pupils.

But this may overlook significant initiatives in the localities in which pupils of Cypriot origin are represented in a substantial number of schools. Much of the research on pupils of Cypriot origin has taken place in the London Borough of Haringey. Haringey Council is committed to developing policies and practices to promote a just and harmonious multiracial community, and its Education Committee has paid attention to developing the curricula of schools to be multicultural in content and perspective (see pp. 43–5). In 1977–8 an Adviser for Multicultural Education was appointed and the Education Committee approved the establishment of a Multicultural Support Group to work towards the development of curricula which would meet the needs of pupils in a multiracial society (Milstead, 1981). The group has focussed on the development of resources on which schools can draw, such as historical materials linked with archive and museum resources and relevant audio-visual aids and library resources, as well as undertaking project work at primary school level and developing humanities materials at secondary school level. One of the group's functions is to support teachers who might be feeling uncertain and insecure in attempting to develop a multicultural curriculum. For example, the group meets with teachers to discuss concerns about bias in teaching materials, curriculum content or teaching methods, to enable teachers to examine their racial and cultural attitudes, and to advise on the development of appropriate materials. The aim of the Multicultural Support Group is to maximize the efficiency of the teacher as the greatest resource, and it would appear from some accounts (Alkan and Constantinides, 1981; Hunter-Grundin, 1982) that the Support Group has had a considerable influence on some local schools in making their curricula more appropriate to an ethnically plural community. An appropriate curriculum is likely to interest parents, as Hunter-Grundin observed in schools in the South Harringay district, where there was a high degree of parental involvement which, in itself, can further enrich the curriculum.

According to Krokou (1985), Haringey has also sponsored in-service courses specifically aimed at sensitizing teachers to the needs of children of Cypriot origin. As Rosen and Burgess (1980), for example, have argued, perhaps teachers' greatest need of support is for manuals, booklets, films and tapes related to language development which will enable them to respond positively to the linguistic diversity within schools, and, with respect to pupils of Cypriot origin, their Greek or Turkish mother tongue. But to date, linguists have shown a certain reticence in collaborating with educationists to undertake the popularization necessary for teachers to gain insights into the languages spoken by pupils in schools. In the case of Greek, teachers need to know the difference between Cypriot and mainland Greek, the attitudes of Greek speakers to such differences, the availability of Greek literature, newspapers, books, etc. in England and what special difficulties may be encountered by Greek-speaking learners of English. However, as Rosen and Burgess also point out, it may be very difficult for pupils who read and write in another language to make use of it in the learning context of mainstream schools, partly because of the difficulty of locating suitable materials, as in the case which they cite of trying to find a biology book for a Turkish-speaking pupil appropriate for his age and attainment. The availability at LEA level of carefully selected materials in the major languages of minorities in the area would facilitate teachers wishing to support the bilingualism of their pupils in the school environment. However, such innovations are comparatively recent and ongoing. For example, the BBC Schools TV series *You and Me* for four- and five-year-olds included stories in both Greek and Turkish which are available on tape for teachers who want to give some recognition to the significance of the mother tongues of their young pupils. At the primary level the Schools Council/EC Mother-Tongue Project has produced a handbook of procedures and strategies to guide monolingual teachers wishing to support pupils' mother tongues in learning across the curriculum (Houlton, 1985) (see p. 122). At secondary level the Bilingual Education Project has produced materials (CUES, 1982) to enable newly arrived secondary pupils to build on their mother-tongue knowledge and to develop English by using both languages in parallel through a series of learning activities with a social studies focus relating to life in contemporary Britain (see also p. 123).

But the human resources must not be overlooked. Older pupils from local secondary schools may be able to assist in language development with individual pupils at infant level who share a common mother tongue thereby engaging in a collaborative learning experience (Hunter-Grundin, 1982). Pupils may also act as interpreters and relay messages to homes where Greek and Turkish are spoken but not read, thus acting as significant links between home and school (Markopoulou, 1974). Pupils may themselves become a linguistic resource in the classroom by being called upon to explain the meaning and derivation of scientific terms with Greek roots (Twitchin and Demuth, 1981). Exchange visits between mainstream teachers of pupils of Cypriot origin and teachers in Greek and Turkish mother-tongue schools may not only serve to develop insights into aspects of the learning of pupils of Cypriot origin, especially when coping with two languages, but also promote interaction between two cultural life worlds. Indeed mainstream teachers may themselves be inspired to take up learning the Greek or Turkish languages of their pupils. The Centre for Information on Language Teaching (CILT) language and culture guides (1982, 1983) list many sources of information on courses at all levels in Modern Greek and Turkish. In addition, the Royal Society of Arts Examinations Board has instituted courses leading to a diploma in the teaching of community languages intended for teachers in mainstream or supplementary schools who wish to become language teachers (Orchard, 1983). Moreover, as Hunter-Grundin's (1982) case study amply demonstrated, the involvement of Cypriot parents in infant and junior schools can be a dynamic form of community participation and support, which as Alkan and Constantinides (1981) have suggested, often needs strengthening at secondary school level. Contacts may usefully be extended beyond the generation of parents to elderly people and professionals in the Cypriot community. Alkan and Constantinides, Cypriot liaison officers in the London Borough of Haringey, reported an increased interest in the early 1980s on the part of schools to which they regularly gave talks and by professionals in contact with the Cypriot community with whom they took part in seminars covering the history, cultural background, immigration and social and educational aspects of the Cypriot community.

Turning to a consideration of other resources for the development of a multicultural curriculum which takes account of Greek and Turkish cultures, the CILT guides (1982, 1983) on Modern Greek and Turkish also provide information for teachers on learning materials, resource organizations and centres, libraries, radio and TV broadcasts, booksellers, and film and video cassette distributors. Several public libraries, particularly in London boroughs, now have varying collections of Greek and Turkish books (see pp. 30–1). Some libraries offer reading and story-telling in Greek and Turkish for children in the library, liaison with schools on the provision of Greek and Turkish books, and materials in English on Cyprus for second-generation Cypriot and non-Cypriot pupils.

Community organizations may also be in a position to assist with materials. Leeuwenberg (1979) reported that the Greek Parents' Association in Haringey was frequently approached by teachers, especially for books in English about Cyprus, and regularly supplied books to schools, although the demand was often greater than its own supply, especially of readers and background literature. Moreover, the Cypriot High Commission, the Office of the London Representative of the Turkish Federated State of Cyprus, the Greek Embassy and the Turkish Embassy may also be able to supply useful materials on language teaching, aspects of cultural background or life in Cyprus. Indeed in 1978–9 Aristodemou (1979) recorded that the Cypriot High Commission dispensed over 5,000 leaflets or booklets on Cyprus and, according to Miles (1983), information is also available direct from the public information office in Nicosia.

Though such agencies may be an important supplementary source of teaching materials, there may be particular difficulties in obtaining well-produced materials in Greek and Turkish at levels appropriate for use in teaching. Moreover, up-to-date background information on Cyprus since the civil war may be less easy to come by than that relating to the 1960s and the situation at the peak of emigration. Miles cites a wide range of literature on history, poetry, painting, cookery, stories and festivals connected with Cyprus in English. But, as Ulug (1981) has pointed out, it is not only important to consider the traditional cultural background and contemporary life in Cyprus, but it is of perhaps greater significance that pupils of Cypriot origin should be aware of the development of their own communities in the UK. As for other ethnic minority groups, however, there is a relative dearth of information of this kind which can be easily utilized in school. An ILEA (1975) booklet is informative about the way of life of Cypriots in Cyprus and Britain, especially in relation to customs and foods. Alkan and Constantinides (1981) explain the differences between Greek and Turkish religious customs and give some account of modifications to traditional practices with respect to marriage, divorce and mourning amongst Cypriots in Haringey. Once again, however, there is a particular scarcity of books suitable for younger pupils. *Rebecca is a Cypriot* is a well-illustrated informative children's book about a Cypriot family living in London, and *A Turkish Afternoon* similarly describes the typical activities of a Turkish family (Bennett, 1983). There is an urgent need for books of such a kind. Some teachers of Cypriot pupils have developed their own materials and resources. Miles (1983) has produced a reference handbook entitled *Cyprus Studies*, containing useful contacts, book lists, films, etc. relevant to teaching about Cyprus and Cypriot culture. Information sheets on customs and the Cypriot community in the UK have also been compiled with the aim of informing the teacher about aspects of Cypriot culture relating to the school situation, for example, Cypriot parents' views about their daughters' social position and the reasons why some may not be allowed to attend extra-curricular activities. When multicultural education centres and support groups provide access to resource materials and offer support for curricular innovation, teachers are enabled to engage in school-based in-service training which may be directly related to their specific curriculum development needs. Whilst this may mean that there is more curriculum development taking place at the school level in localities where pupils of Cypriot origin are more numerous, this unfortunately does not facilitate dissemination of available expertise, experience and information which might be helpful to teachers with only a few Cypriot pupils scattered elsewhere in the country, particularly at various seaside resorts. Co-ordination of the dissemination of such resources would be of potential benefit to other teachers and stimulate greater awareness at a national level than otherwise appears to exist about the Greek and

Turkish Cypriot dimension to multicultural education which might take account of the interests of pupils of Cypriot origin and the needs of all pupils for a broad, balanced and relevant curriculum.

Teachers of Cypriot origin may, if they so wish, have a special part to play in effecting a multicultural curriculum, especially in schools with Cypriot pupils. At the start of the 25-year period covered by this review, a time when many recently arrived Cypriot pupils would have entered schools in Britain, attitudes towards the employment of ethnic minority teachers, including those of Cypriot origin, were often ambivalent, particularly with respect to their suitability to teach English as a second language. Over the years attitudes towards the employment of such teachers have generally changed, so that greater emphasis is placed on their special ability to liaise with pupils from similar ethnic, cultural and linguistic backgrounds, to serve as role models, to be a source of information to other teachers and to liaise between school and home. It is often assumed that ethnic minority teachers teach in schools with ethnic minority pupils, but there is little information on the likelihood that Cypriot pupils arriving in the early 1960s would have been taught by a Cypriot teacher, or on either the number or distribution of teachers of Cypriot origin at the present time. Hence it is difficult to assess the nature or extent of their influence within the Cypriot community and in the schools where they teach and in which pupils of Cypriot origin may also be present.

Townsend and Brittan (1972) found in a national survey that about one-third of 132 primary schools and just under half of 98 secondary schools employed immigrant teachers, fewer than one-sixth of whom mainly taught immigrant pupils. In the Community Relations Commission's survey (CRC, 1977)only 20 out of 468 full-time staff employed in 20 schools where research was undertaken in eight multiracial areas, in 1975, belonged to minority groups, and only one was of Cypriot origin. Yet in the same areas nearly half of the Cypriot parents claimed that there were Cypriot teachers in their children's schools, this being more likely for Cypriots than for any other ethnic minority group. Indeed Cypriot parents were particularly keen that their children should have teachers from their own group and three-quarters of those whose children did not have such teachers would have liked them to have done so. Martianou (1981) claimed that there were three Cypriot headteachers in London and a growing number of Cypriot lecturers and researchers in universities and colleges. In a sample of five secondary schools with 12–25 per cent pupils of Cypriot origin four schools had two part-time or peripatetic Cypriot teachers of Modern Greek and two schools had two Cypriot teachers of other subjects who also taught Modern Greek at lunchtime. All the Cypriot teachers acted as liaison teachers, translating documents and visiting Cypriot homes, but in only one case was this officially recognized by the school. But Hunter-Grundin's (1982) evaluation of the pre-school centre, infant and junior schools in the South Harringay district of Haringey revealed that even in an area with 30 per cent Greek-speaking Cypriots and 30 per cent Turkish-speaking Cypriots there was no Cypriot member of staff in the junior school. The Swann Report noted the concern of Cypriot community representatives about the very small number of teachers of Cypriot origin, since it was felt that they could be very supportive to Cypriot pupils and in home–school liaison. Some Cypriot teachers stressed the difficulties they felt they faced in gaining promotion and reaching positions of responsibility in the schools. Those who had undergone teacher training in the UK referred to the 'appalling' absence of realistic coverage of multicultural concerns in their courses and to what they felt was the hostile atmosphere they had encountered in staffrooms when on teaching practice.

In consideration of the special role of Cypriot teachers, however, it is necessary to be conscious of the considerable ethnic, cultural and religious differences between

Greek and Turkish Cypriots which may surface at times of tension in Cyprus, as Clough and Quarmby (1978) noted amongst the Greek and Turkish Cypriot staff of a secondary school in London during the civil war in 1975. On the other hand, McCarty and Christoudoulou (1977) opined that the presence of Cypriot teachers in Haringey had facilitated the provision made for, and integration of, Cypriot refugee children who arrived in the UK in 1975. Greek- or Turkish-speaking staff may be particularly helpful in the early years of schooling to facilitate language development with pupils with some degree of bilingualism in Greek or Turkish and English, and perhaps thereby also to establish confidence in the school environment. However, Couillaud (1984) reported that bilingual Greek-speaking teachers of other subjects who could be a resource for Greek-speaking and other pupils are often not taken full advantage of in mainstream schools. When convenient, they are used on a voluntary basis for home–school liaison and this may give a falsely coherent and consistently positive multicultural image of the school. It was recommended that the DES should fully recognize the expertise of bilingual teachers as part of an overall strategy to enhance the status of community languages in mainstream schools. Indeed some Cypriot teachers who teach in both mainstream and mother-tongue schools may be in a position to be particularly sensitive to the overall development and educational progress of pupils of Cypriot origin whom they see in both school contexts. Alkan and Constantinides (1981) list two teachers' organizations for Greek Cypriot and Turkish Cypriot teachers involved in both British mainstream and Greek and Turkish mother-tongue schools which include in their aims the improvement of relationships between these educational establishments and the Cypriot community. The experience and expertise of such teachers should be capitalized upon to enhance the awareness and understanding of other teachers in mainstream schools, to develop closer interaction between the two systems of schooling which many Greek and Turkish Cypriot pupils experience and to establish firmer relationships between Cypriot parents and their children's mainstream schools. Such teachers' organizations might be particularly helpful in establishing links between smaller Cypriot communities and schools outside London where there may be less awareness of Cypriot culture and community mother-tongue teaching arrangements. But it is with the second generation of Cypriot origin that the greatest hope must lie in terms of facilitating greater mutual appreciation and understanding between parents in the Cypriot communities and teachers in their neighbourhood schools and in order to promote educational provision which is more appropriate to meet the needs and interests of pupils of Cypriot origin. For it is the second generation, who were born in the UK after their parents settled as young adults in the 1960s, who have experienced their education in the British system and who now, as adults themselves, with first-hand experience of both British and Cypriot cultures, are training for and embarking on a career in teaching. Their particular sensitivity to both cultures, should enable them to assist other children with experiences of living in two cultural worlds to realize their full educational potential.

Part Two
Pupils of Italian Origin

Introduction and Background

HISTORY AND EMIGRATION   That there has been a sizeable number of pupils of Italian origin in British schools in the last 35 years might appear surprising to judge from the lack of attention they have received in educational literature. In fact Italians have been resident in Britain for many centuries as traders, bankers, musicians, craftsmen, artists and scholars. In 1861 there were about 2,000 Italians living in London. When Italy became a country of mass emigration, Italians arrived in increasing numbers, so that at the turn of the 20th century their numbers, mostly from northern Italy, tripled in 20 years to 20,000, many of whom were involved in the food trade. During the Second World War many Italians were interned as aliens or deported, and others returned to Italy. But in the late 1940s agreements between the British and Italian governments as part of the European Volunteer Workers Scheme, and the setting up of recruitment offices, opened up mass emigration from southern Italy, due to poverty and unemployment, to jobs in heavy industry in Britain which could not be filled by indigenous labour. Some 15,000 men came to work in the brick industry alone (King, 1979); in Bedford, its centre, Italians form one-tenth of the population. It has been estimated that 180,000 Italians have migrated to Britain since 1945. However, at the end of the 1960s repatriation exceeded emigration (MacDonald and MacDonald, 1972; Palmer, 1977). Statistics on the nationality of foreign workers employed in member states of the European Community (Commission of the European Communities, 1977, Table 3) show that in 1975 some 72,000 Italians were employed in the UK, but many more Italians were employed in Germany (292,435), France (230,000) and Belgium (90,000). Many Italians have settled in Britain, and, together with their descendents, according to an Italian Catholic Mission Census, about 200,000 in the 1970s (King, 1979).

DEMOGRAPHY   Census figures for people born in Italy and resident in the UK show that the greatest growth in Italian immigration was between 1951 and 1961, when women considerably outnumbered men (Table 21).

Table 21:   **Italian-born population resident in Britain, by sex, 1951, 1961, 1971 and 1981**

	1951	1961	1971	1981
Total	33,159	81,327	108,985	97,848
Males	12,661	36,017	52,045	47,920
Females	20,498	45,310	56,940	49,928

Sources: Census 1951, 1961, 1971, 1981; GRO, 1956, 1964; OPCS, 1974, 1983a.

An analysis of the 1981 Census figures, by age, shows that the Italian-born population in Britain is ageing (see Table 22).

Table 22:   Italian-born population resident in Britain, by age, 1981

Total:	0–19	20–4	25–9	30–4	35–9	40–4	45–60/65	60/65+
97,848	5,773	6,223	7,912	9,939	8,559	12,175	37,976	9,291

Source: Census 1981; OPCS, 1983a, Table 2.

However, these figures provide no information on the UK-born Italian population. A more realistic figure for the population of Italian origin which corresponds with the Italian census figure is provided by the Labour Force Survey in 1979. This involved half a per cent of the population, respondents being asked to name the ethnic group from which they considered they and other members of their household were descended (OPCS, 1982b). These figures indicate a greater age spread and suggest that 25,000 children of Italian origin may have been receiving education in Britain at any one time in the 1970s (Table 23).

Table 23:   Population of Italian origin in Britain, by age, 1979 (thousands)

<15	15–24	25–44	45–59/64	60/65+	Males/ females	All
37	35	63	54	14	99/100	201

Source: Labour Force Survey, 1979; OPCS, 1982b, Table 5.2.

RESEARCH STUDIES   As one of the groups of 'invisible immigrants' from southern Europe, Italians have largely been ignored both as a social group and as the focus for study (MacDonald and MacDonald, 1972; King, 1978). Although a few early studies were undertaken (Garigue and Firth, 1956; Sibley, 1962; Barr, 1964; Chadwick-Jones, 1965), only in the last decade have the Italians attracted the interest of social geographers, notably King (1977a, 1977b, 1978, 1979; King and King, 1977; King and Zolli, 1981) and socioanthropologists such as Palmer (1973, 1977, 1980), who have described the demographic patterns of Italian settlement and aspects of the socioeconomic circumstances and social interaction of the post-war Italian communities in Britain. Even less have pupils of Italian origin been the focus of educational research. But why should there have been a lack of educational interest in such pupils, at least as documented in research literature? The findings of social geographers and anthropologists suggest that the social and cultural background of pupils of Italian origin and the image of Italians as a group may indicate why, except in certain areas of more concentrated settlement, they have largely received little attention. King (1979) has suggested that the Italians' 'lack of conspicuousness' in their long period of immigration and their socioeconomic mobility as well as cultural, economic and political marginality – have all served to keep them out of the spotlight.

ITALIAN LINKS AND CHARACTERISTICS   Many of the Italians born in the UK have retained their Italian nationality, so that although they enjoy rights as EC nationals, they are also disenfranchized aliens. Italian identity has also been strongly maintained both culturally and economically. Kinship occupied an especially important place in social life in the poor villages of the south from which more than two-thirds of the ill-educated, post-war Italian immigrants have come (Levi, 1947; MacDonald and MacDonald, 1972). This implied certain rights and obligations and the need to uphold social standing by demonstrating ability to maintain and improve the family's economic position. Kinship was a strong feature of chain migration to Britain offering social assistance and cultural protection to other village members. Loyalty has, therefore, been first and foremost to kin, to the village and the region. Strong links continue to be maintained by visits 'home', but the 'myth of return' is now generally not considered a viable option either economically or socially (Palmer, 1980), although attitudes may remain ambivalent (King and Zolli, 1981; Weston, 1979; Bottignolo, 1983).

Indeed, as with some other expatriate communities, it has been suggested (see e.g. Tosi, 1979a) that Italians in Britain have failed to keep pace with linguistic, social and cultural changes in their regions of origin and have maintained their traditional attitudes and expectations which often show up most strongly in relation to the behaviour of the younger generation. Italians in the UK have received support in maintaining their cultural background through two official institutions: the Church and the Italian vice-consulates. The majority of Italians are Roman Catholic and, in addition to its spiritual role, the church has certain social, welfare and language teaching functions. Many children of Italian origin attend Roman Catholic schools, nurseries and youth clubs (see e.g. Farrell, 1983). The church is said to preserve Italian ethnicity through its various organizations (King, 1979). The Italian government, through its three local offices, offers administrative support, especially in settlement of families, organizes the teaching of Italian and, as Tosi (1984) has argued with respect to Bedford, often adjudicates between conflicting interest groups or associations, or in disputes and tensions between different kinship and family groups. In an analysis of the objectives, nature and meaning of communal activities of Italians in Bristol and Swindon, in 1975–80, Bottignolo (1983) identified the preoccupation with attempts to organize community and political affairs, but absence of collective responsibility led to failure. This also impeded full participation in the local British community, the Italians preferring the 'official' Italian organizations as a pivot for communal initiatives and to mediate relations external to their community.

FAMILY LIFE   There are strong ties of loyalty to the Italian community with the majority of young people of Italian background marrying within the group. At the same time, there are indications of social integration amongst the British-born as, for example, between 1977 and 1980 nearly one-third of the marriages at Bedford's Italian church were to non-Italian partners, with almost as many women as men marrying 'out' (Jeffcoate, 1984; see also Di Blasio, 1979, and King and Zolli, 1981). Various studies (e.g. Brown, 1970) have indicated the importance of family life to Italians. This is usually close and disciplined, with the identity of the individual subordinated to that of the family group (see e.g. Open University, 1982). Italians resemble the British in their health standards, despite their long exposure to hard physical labour (Brown, 1970), and have a lower than average rate of mental illness (Littlewood and Lipsedge, 1982; Cochrane, 1977). Although Italian homes may be male-dominated, men may undertake some domestic activities to enable their wives to work out of the home (Lobo, 1978). The family is very child-centred and demonstratively affectionate towards children. Mothers have close relationships with their children and may even be 'overprotective'. Grandmothers may also be involved in child care (Triseliotis, 1976; Simons, 1980). The extended family is highly significant in social life and close bonds are often formed between cousins.

EMPLOYMENT   Although the Italians are socioeconomically upwardly mobile, they are still predominantly working class. The Italian immigrants of the early 20th century from the north of Italy tended to be involved in catering – restaurants and cafés, hotel work and ice-cream manufacture – and a whole range of businesses associated with re-creating an Italian way of life amongst their communities in Britain (Palmer, 1977). Some became very successful entrepreneurs. During the war many Italians were interned and engaged in farming and other agricultural activities. After the war, 10,000 immigrants from the south of Italy found employment in horticulture to the north of London, but most arrived to do jobs in heavy industry such as in brickmaking or metal-working. They often became highly valued workers (Skellington, 1978), though there was some trade union opposition to coalminers (Crisp, 1980). Although correspondence testing in 1973–4 revealed that Italians seeking white-collar work were discriminated against in about ten per cent of cases, this was only a third of that experienced by black applicants (McIntosh and Smith, 1974). In Bedford, for example, some of the Italians in the brickworks have moved on to lighter 'managerial' jobs and there has been a general change in the employment pattern towards light industry, mainly food, drink, tobacco, textiles and clothing and service work such as hairdressing (MacDonald and MacDonald, 1972; King, 1977a). At least eight per cent of the Italian population in Britain are self-employed (King, 1977a), and as many as 85 per cent in the established Glasgow settlement (Colpi, 1979). In the case of northern Italians associations with food trades may have fitted with a desire for economic independence (King, 1978). Some of the earliest recruitment schemes involved Italian women who came to work in textiles, rubber, ceramics, food, clothing and light engineering industries, and as domestic workers in hospitals and hotels and in retailing (Brown, 1970; MacDonald and MacDonald, 1972; King and Zolli, 1981). Indeed King (1977a) and Di Blasio (1979) have shown that Italian women preceded men in the post-war immigration and played an important role in kin sponsorship. But the female dimension has been largely ignored in consideration of the Italian labourforce (see Table 6). Some Italian women arrived as war brides. More recently, there is some evidence of increasing movement into professional occupations, especially amongst longer-established communities (e.g. in Glasgow, see Colpi, 1979).

SETTLEMENT   Social geographers have been able to demonstrate direct links between areas, even villages, of emigration from Italy to employment in the UK and hence patterns of settlement. For example, Wilkin (1979) showed that the earliest Italian immigrants to Scotland were from two rural areas, Barga in Tuscany and Picinisco in Frosinone (see also Colpi, 1979). Most Italian immigrants to Bedford came from four remote villages – Busso in Molise, Montefalcione in Campania, Buonvicino in Calabria and S. Angelo Muxaro in Sicily (King, 1977b), thus they were speaking mainly Neapolitan or Sicilian dialects of Italian (Tosi, 1984). In Leicester, King and Zolli (1981) found that over a third of respondents came from Avellino and Benevento and one-fifth from Picinisco. Crisp (1980) studied the effects of migration on the immigrants and their village of origin.

Direct recruitment to various industries followed up by chain migration has naturally led to certain concentrations of Italian settlement, for example, to coalmining and steelworks in South Wales, Yorkshire and Lancashire; brickworks in Bedford; and agriculture and light industry in Peterborough. Thus the Italian population of certain towns (e.g. in Bedford at around 10,000) is greater than in larger cities or those with older-established Italian communities such as Glasgow, Edinburgh, Cardiff, Manchester, Leeds, Nottingham, Birmingham and Bristol, with numbers in the thousands. Bedfordshire and Huntingdonshire have settlements of Italians at five times the national ratio of Italians to the British population (King, 1977a). The majority of Italians – about 55 per cent – reside in the south-east with some 30 per cent in Greater London itself. Within London, Italians are found in significant numbers in most boroughs – in 1971, Islington, Westminster, Camden, Enfield and Lambeth all had Italian populations at over

2,000 (Campbell-Platt, 1978), though Italians are in fact less spatially concentrated than many other minority groups (King, 1977a). As with other minority groups with increased prosperity, there has been a trend to move out of central London into Greater London, particularly to the north, where they may comprise a greater proportion of the population, for example, 29 per cent in Waltham Cross (3,000 Italians) (King, 1979). Moreover, due to the increasing involvement of Italians in catering and service industries and their occupational mobility, they are to be found, like the Chinese, in medium and small towns across England and Scotland (King, 1978). The 1981 Census figures for the Italian-born population indicate the range of settlement (Table 24), though the Italian census in the 1970s, including the UK-born, gave 85,300 in south-east England, 47,000 in the Midlands, 15,000 in Scotland and 23,000 in Wales. A further census was undertaken in late 1986 by the Italian Embassy.

Table 24: Regional settlement in the UK of the Italian-born population, 1981

Wales	3,974	Greater London	30,752	South-	
Scotland	4,789	Outer metropolitan	14,639	east,	
North	1,360	Outer south-east	10,016	55,407	
Yorkshire and Humberside	4,411	South-west	5,447		
East Midlands	6,127	West Midlands	6,307		
East Anglia	3,810	North-west	6,216		

Source: Adapted from Census 1981; OPCS, 1983a, Table 1.

Many of the sources quoted in this background outline deal with the history and spatial evolution of certain Italian communities in some detail: for example, in Bedford (Brown, 1970; King, 1977b; King and King, 1977; Skellington, 1978; Tosi, 1984), Leicester (King and Zolli, 1981), Scotland, especially Glasgow (Wilkin, 1979; Colpi, 1979) and Bristol and Swindon (Bottignolo, 1983).

HOUSING   As with employment, so in terms of housing the Italians have been upwardly mobile. Sources for Bedford have documented in detail the changes in Italian accommodation patterns, from hostels adjacent to the brickworks for the first male migrants to lodging-houses in town where men on different shifts shared rooms and even beds (Barr, 1964). The arrival of women and families created a large-scale demand for housing, but the Italians were ineligible for council accommodation. Large early Victorian properties were sub-divided by landlords for multi-occupancy and over a third of Italians in Bedford were in multi-occupied housing in 1970 (Brown, 1970). Gradually in the 1960s Italians became owner-occupiers of smaller terraced properties, and although there was some movement into Victorian property in the west of the town and inter- and post-war housing in the east, it was not until the mid-1970s with the second generation setting up homes that the Italian population dispersed more widely into different areas of the town (King and King, 1977). For the immigrants, cheapness and a sense of community were apparently more important than comfort and status (Skellington, 1978). There continues, however, to be a nucleus of the Italian community in the central area which has the greatest social and environmental stress, and is now occupied mainly by West Indians and Asians, some of the Italians having become landlords themselves. This has also occurred in Leicester and Peterborough (King, 1979; King and Zolli, 1981) and Coventry (Smith *et al.*, 1984). Over 90 per cent of Italians in Bedford and Coventry now live in owner-occupied housing (Jeffcoate, 1984; Smith *et al.*, 1984) but a significant number in London live in council housing (see Table 26, p.225).

COMMUNITY PERCEPTIONS   In many ways the Italians have been regarded as model immigrants, hard working, family-centred, law-abiding and interacting mainly with their own group (King, 1977). At the end of the 19th century in London there were a number of Italian businesses, clubs, schools, newspapers, an Italian church in Clerkenwell and even a hospital, all contributing to the feeling of community identity (King, 1979). Palmer (1977) has charted the changes in the Italian community from this time through its heyday in the 1930s to the trauma of internment during the war years and the confiscation of property even of Italians born in Britain and the early years of post-war immigration. Immigrants at this time were often subject to xenophobic abuse and although Italians were often perceived as noisy and extrovert because of a disposition to display their feelings (Brown, 1970; Triseliotis, 1976; King, 1979), there are few reports of overt hostility or discrimination (Rose *et al.*, 1969). For their part, Italians see the British as friendly, but cold and unsympathetic, and they resent being identified by surnames and classified as immigrants (Brown, 1970; King and King, 1977). Weston (1979) found that Italians in London had few criticisms of English society, but lived in a state of linguistic and social isolation. Researchers have differed on the extent of integration of Italians with the host community. Italians in Bedford have been portrayed as having few hobbies and little leisure, being predominantly work-oriented (Tosi, 1984). Socialization is largely within the kinship group and there are tensions within the community centring on leadership struggles linked with the need for indigenous authorities to identify one official community association and spokesman. On the other hand, there are Italian clubs for dancing, singing and music, cafés, language classes and a business infrastructure, making a self-sufficient community. Some have observed a reassertion of regional folklore (Brown, 1970; Lobo, 1978; Mengon, 1980). But in Glasgow, Colpi (1979) found that it was characteristic of the Italian population to integrate into mainstream social and political institutions being linked more by common factors than community. In Leicester, King and Zolli (1981) found that although Italians were friendly with the British, less than a third of the sample exchanging visits infrequently, visits among the Italian community were widespread and at least weekly. Despite greater socioeconomic integration the loyalty of even second- and third-generation Italians to regional links with Italy and the strength of cultural roots has often been noted (e.g. Steedman, 1979; Simons, 1980) and with the acceptance of settlement and a future in Britain there may be a feeling of consolidation rather than security.

The stereotype of the Italians in Britain tends to obscure the heterogeneity of the community as a whole. It is necessary to distinguish between varied geographical origins of the first generation in Italy with implications for cultural background, dialect (see p. 221), time of migration and settlement in the UK as well as socioeconomic status in Britain, residence, community orientation and generation. Taken together, these factors indicate the lack of homogeneity in the Italian community. This diversity in the social background of pupils of Italian origin should be borne in mind when evaluating their educational experience and achievement in Britain.

Education

Quality of Research Data

With the exception of a paper by Steedman (1979), there has apparently not been any previous review of the education of pupils of Italian origin in Britain. Nor have such pupils been a major focus for research on minority pupils. The research which exists is often piecemeal and characterized by discontinuity. This review is, therefore, largely concerned with drawing together various statements and appraisals, factual information and research data from the educational literature. In view of the strong links between region of origin in Italy and settlement and occupation in the UK, it is not surprising to find that educational data on pupils of Italian origin relate almost entirely to the south-east, in particular London, and East Midlands and Bedford, the town with the greatest post-war Italian population. However, since available information tends to exclude the education of pupils of Italian origin from settlements related to other migration patterns and sometimes to older settlements, dispersed throughout the country, it cannot be assumed that educational data appertaining to Bedford are necessarily representative for pupils of Italian origin in the UK as a whole. Moreover, even at the local level the absence of publicly available longitudinal data and information on achievement at subject and examination levels suggests that, even where most numerous, pupils of Italian origin have not been subjects for educational inquiry. The major exception is the EC/Bedfordshire Mother Tongue and Culture Project (MTCP) (see pp. 274–8). Indeed it is only in those LEAs which have been involved in language surveys, such as the Linguistic Minorities Project (LMP) (see pp. 228–9), or which keep ethnic records where data explicitly on pupils of Italian origin are available. Attention is drawn to location, where known, during the course of this review.

Membership of the group of European pupils has meant that in educational research analysis pupils of Italian origin have sometimes been included with other European pupils in a composite but disparate group (for example, the longitudinal National Child Development Study) or, more specifically, with pupils of Cypriot origin, as in the third phase of NFER researches in the early 1970s (see Jelinek and Brittan, 1975, on interethnic attitudes and friendship, and pp. 300–1; and Jelinek, 1977, on attitudes to school, and pp. 299–300) or even in a general group of 'others', for example, in the ILEA transfer studies (Little *et al.*, 1968; Little, 1975b) or generally in a mixed group of pupils. Such superficial categorizations are of little assistance when assessing the educational achievement and experience of pupils of Italian origin as such. Moreover, the general lack of specific attention to such pupils in research overlooks their distinctive educational needs both as a group and in comparison with other minority and majority peers. Extant research on pupils of Italian origin tends to focus on the affective and attitudinal aspects of their educational experience, leaving considerable gaps with regard to educational performance. More evidence has, however, recently become available on the language knowledge, use and attitudes of Italian pupils, as a result of growing interest in language learning in mainstream schools and in out-of-school hours. Indeed the language background of pupils of Italian origin predominates in this review. The collection of such data, inspired by the EC Directive on mother-tongue teaching, which aims to facilitate reintegration in the country of origin, is doubly ironical with respect to pupils of Italian origin. Without it the research evidence on pupils of Italian origin, relating largely to the late 1960s and early 1970s, would be dated. Yet although the EC Directive has served to raise consciousness, both at LEA and research levels, as to the linguistic and cultural needs of minority pupils, this has occurred at a time when by far the majority of pupils of Italian origin are UK-born. Though such attention has come too late for most of the first generation of Italian pupils to benefit directly in their educational experience, in terms of mother tongue and culture maintenance, this may not be the case for UK-born pupils of Italian origin, nor in the context of emigration is it necessarily misdirected (Palmer, 1977, 1980).

In the context of language the major contribution made by various institutions and individuals within the Italian community itself should be mentioned. For example, the regional consular offices of the Italian government have clearly had a strong role in the organization and administration of mother-tongue teaching schools and classes through the *Direzione Didattica*. They have also undertaken some research into the operation of the language classes as, for example, in the Rapporto di Lavoro, 1977 (quoted by Steedman, 1979). The educational influence of the Italian church has also been evident in the provision of certain nursery schools for children of Italian origin such as that in Bedford since 1961 for about 50 children, including some of West Indian origin (Brown, 1970; Jackson, 1979). The Italian Catholic Mission conducted its own census during the 1970s (quoted by King, 1979) and one of its priests in London compiled a much quoted social history of Italians in Britain (Marin, 1969, 1975). Apart from these sources, with one or two exceptions, the Italian community seems to have lacked professionals conducting research into the education of its children, at least research available in English. This may shortly be rectified with the growth to adulthood of UK-educated, second-generation Italians. As already noted, some source material is in Italian, limiting its accessibility. Further information in Italian is available on mother-tongue teaching as, for example, in the *Journal of the Association of Teachers of Italian*. Papers from volume 29 of this journal in 1979 and from a subsequent colloquium on the teaching of Italian in the UK (Baldwin *et al.*, 1980) under the auspices of the ATI, published in English, have been drawn upon as appropriate in this review. Such material has proved a particularly informative primary resource in considering the educational position of pupils of Italian origin.

Mainstream quantitative educational research is severely limited. Not only is there an almost total dearth of objective assessment of performance, for example, in reading, subject-areas or at examination level, but in descriptive evidence the criteria for evaluation are usually unstated, so that overall it is impossible, other than in the context of language, to make an assessment of the educational experience of pupils of Italian origin or to make comparisons with their white British or other minority peers. Yet whilst the quality of the research evidence may be impugned, the observations and data assembled are not without insight into pupils of Italian origin. Clearly the evidence refers almost exclusively to the children of post-war Italian immigrants, for the educational experience of some children of early Italian immigrant families, now into their fourth or fifth generation, seems to have passed without comment. Indeed even the limited evidence available spans at least two generations. Documentation of the 1960s and early 1970s relates primarily to the first generation of Italian-born pupils who arrived as small children either during or shortly after the immigration peaks of 1951, 1955–7 and 1960–1 (King, 1979). A second generation of children, born in the UK, were simultaneously receiving their schooling in Britain, for by 1973 many were in their middle teens to early twenties (Palmer, 1980). By far the majority of these children had both parents of Italian origin, though some may have come from mixed Italian and British, Polish, Ukrainian or Mediterranean backgrounds, predominantly Catholic. Increasingly over the last 15 years pupils of Italian origin have been UK-born, as few first-generation Italian children now arrive in this country despite the freer movement for work within the EC (see Table 22). Research dating from the 1970s, therefore, pertains to the second generation of UK-born pupils of Italian origin, with some first-generation and increasing numbers of third-generation pupils of Italian origin. Indeed in some schools located in some of the larger and longer-established areas of Italian settlement there could well be pupils of Italian origin of three generations receiving education concurrently.

Numbers and Distribution of Pupils of Italian Origin
What, then, is known of the numbers of pupils of Italian origin during the last 30 years? Though data are incomplete at national and local levels, it is possible to construct some indication of numbers of Italian pupils from several sources: Census figures, Italian government and church figures, DES records, local language surveys and figures from Bedford. However, the usefulness of these sources is limited for different reasons. Country of birth figures may be obtained each decade from the Census figures, though these are less helpful as the number of UK-born children of Italian origin increases (see Tables 21–23). The Italian government records the number of emigrant workers and their children leaving Italy for Britain, and the Catholic Mission has conducted a census in the UK, but these figures are at variance. The accuracy of DES figures collected on the number of 'immigrant' pupils for the period 1966–72 according to the 'ten-year rule' was disputed in educational circles. Although recent evidence from language surveys on the number of Italian-speaking pupils gives a more accurate reflection of current numbers of pupils of Italian origin, unfortunately publicly available data are as yet restricted to the ILEA and five other LEAs surveyed by the Linguistic Minorities Project. A more detailed local picture of the distribution of pupils of Italian origin in Bedford and the county may be compiled from various sources. But the lack of continuity in publicly available data means that at present it is only possible to indicate numerical trends for pupils of Italian origin locally and nationally (see pp. 227–9).

The 1961 Census shows that there were some 6,713 Italian-born children (3,422 males and 3,291 females) aged 0 to 14 who formed less than ten per cent of the Italian-born population in the UK (MacDonald and MacDonald, 1972). The DES figures are the main source for the 1960s. In his fascinating description of Bedford and its immigrants in the 1960s Brown (1970) noted that a number of headteachers considered that restricting the classification of 'immigrant' to pupils who had arrived in the UK in the previous ten years was artificial and would only falsify numbers and be misleading. According to Brown, the teachers claimed that:

> They find no essential difference between the children of Southern Italian immigrants who came here in the early 50s and the children of those who came a decade or more later. At whatever time Southern Italians came to Bedford, they brought and preserved their own language and their own ways of life, and they will preserve them, only partially modified by the experience of Britain, until they die. (ibid., 232–3)

As a result, Brown suggested that up to 1969 teachers tended to return the numbers of all immigrant pupils, irrespective of when their parents arrived in the UK but that in the latter years of data collection practices varied by year and school, so that the figures were less likely to be accurate. Such concerns led to pressure from teachers and eventually the abandoning of the collection of statistics on a national basis, although some LEAs continued to collect statistics locally.

From the figures in Table 25, it would appear that the number of pupils of Italian origin in schools during the period 1967–72 did not increase greatly and that a peak may have occurred around 1970. However, these figures will have increasingly failed to pick up the number of pupils of Italian origin born in the UK to parents who arrived before 1960. Since in the period 1951–61 the Italian population in the UK

Table 25:   Number of pupils of Italian origin in schools in England and Wales, by sex, 1967, 1970 and 1972

Year	Total	Boys	Girls
1967	10,685	5,422	5,263
1970	13,162	6,744	6,418
1972	12,009	6,147	5.862

Sources: GB. DES, 1968, 1971, 1973.

increased by 145 per cent, and by about 19 per cent between 1961 and 1966 (MacDonald and MacDonald, 1972), it seems highly likely that the number of pupils of Italian origin was considerably under-enumerated in the DES figures.

The figure of 12,000 pupils of Italian origin has generally been cited, for example, by Willke (1975), who compares the number of children of Italian migrants aged from six to 16 in Germany, in 1974 (68,200), and in Sweden (900); and Steedman (1979) also quotes 12,000 pupils of Italian origin in British schools in the 1970s, attributing the figure to Italian church sources (Marin, 1975). But with the increasing birth of children to Italian immigrants in the UK, King (1978) commented that the 1971 Census figure of 108,985 for the Italian-born population in the UK easily would have been matched by the number of second-generation children and that, if the descendants of 19th century and pre-Second World War Italian immigrants were included, the figure for the group as a whole would probably have exceeded a quarter of a million. Although a figure of 100,000 children of Italian origin outdistances any other, it may not be an unrealistic estimate of the number of second- and third-generation Italian children who have passed through the British education system in the 30-year period under review. Figures from the last Census (OPCS, 1983a) show that in 1981 there were some 510 Italian children aged 0 to four years (264 boys, 246 girls), 2,710 five to 15 year-olds (1,380 boys and 1,330 girls) and 2,553 aged 16 to 19 (1,325 boys and 1,228 girls). These Italian-born youngsters were dispersed in various regions of the country according to the patterns of Italian settlement outlined in Table 24. Thus, although a few children born in Italy are continuing to enter the UK as immigrants, they now form only a very small fraction of pupils of Italian origin currently undergoing schooling. Indeed the LFS figures for 1979 suggest that around 25,000 children of Italian origin are currently likely to be in education in Britain.

Recent language censuses provide location-specific numbers of Italian-speaking pupils. In the ILEA survey in 1978 (ILEA, 1979) teachers estimated that there were some 2,272 pupils who spoke Italian as their first language. The 1981 ILEA language census (ILEA, 1982) recorded a total of 2,808 pupils considered by their teachers to speak Italian other than or in addition to English at home; in 1983 the figure was 2,421 and in 1985 2,102 (ILEA, 1983, 1986). Evidence from the Schools Language Survey of the Linguistic Minorities Project undertaken in five LEAs in 1980–81 is also of interest, since Peterborough – one of the main areas of Italian settlement – was one of the survey areas. According to pupils' self-reports, some 572 aged from six years to 15 plus spoke Italian dialects at home in Peterborough, 451 in Haringey, 368 in Bradford, 145 in Coventry and 105 in Waltham Forest (Couillaud and Tasker, 1983). With the exception of Peterborough, where speakers of Italian dialects formed the second largest number of speakers of languages other than English in the home, there were fewer speakers of Italian dialects than speakers of the other main minority languages in these locations, Italian speakers ranking fifth in Haringey and Coventry, sixth in Bradford and tenth in Waltham Forest. This again indicates the dispersal of pupils of Italian origin across the country.

In view of the greatest concentration of the Italian-born population in the UK in Bedford, and the fact that much research evidence relates to this town, it may be of interest to chart the growing number of pupils of Italian origin and their distribution within the town's schools. In the early 1960s the Borough Education Officer (Walker, 1963a) recorded the arrival of many Italian children, the earliest being predominantly of infant age, older children arriving subsequently. Walker noted the tendency for such children to return to Italy for long holidays and that sometimes a cousin or a friend would return as a substitute. In March 1954, 33 Italian pupils were enrolled in infant schools in Bedford but by 1963 their number had risen to 900 (Walker 1963a, 1963b). They formed 11 per cent of the maintained school population in Bedford, clearly outnumbering the 500 other immigrant pupils from 22 nationalities. Brown (1970, Table 2) documented the number of Italian pupils in schools in Bedford from 1955 to 1969 and showed that during the 1960s their numbers continued to rise, reaching a peak of 1,548 in 1966, levelling off and remaining at over 1,000 towards the end of the decade. The arrival of Italian children (and the presence of children of Polish and of other East European origin) clearly preceded the arrival of Indian and West Indian children in schools in Bedford in 1964, as was also the case in the East Midlands (Feeley, 1965) and in Huddersfield (Burgin and Edson, 1967). In fact by 1969 immigrant pupils formed 23.4 per cent of school rolls in Bedford, of which Italian pupils made up ten per cent.

According to Walker (1963b), a number of schools in Bedford at that time had 30 per cent or more immigrant pupils and only three out of 26 schools had no Italian pupils. Brown's figures for 1969 (1970, Table 3) show that the distribution of immigrant children in Bedford schools was then remarkably uneven, so that whereas some schools had no immigrant children, others had up to 80 per cent. Only five schools had no Italian pupils, and in some primary and secondary schools they comprised up to a third of the roll. Clearly the concentration of Italian pupils in certain schools reflected the pattern of Italian settlement in 1969 in Bedford. As the proportion of pupils of Italian origin varied on the roll of different schools, so their proportion *vis-à-vis* other immigrant pupils was also variable. It is clear, however, from Figure 1 that the majority of pupils of Italian origin shared their schooling, especially at the primary level, with pupils from other ethnic minority groups and were sometimes the largest minority group. A survey of ethnic minority pupils in primary and secondary schools in Northamptonshire in 1977 (Northamptonshire LEA, 1980) showed that pupils of Italian origin, numbering 642, were the third largest group of ethnic minority pupils out of a total of 4,575 ethnic minority pupils from at least eight nationalities. Kerr (1978) also noted that in Nottingham, another area of sizeable Italian settlement, pupils of Italian origin were often concentrated in certain schools.

Unfortunately, there is a gap in the publicly available figures in the 1970s for pupils of Italian origin in schools in Bedford, although King and King (1977) have claimed that in the mid-1970s 30 per cent of the Italian population was under 14 years of age. Disputing that Italian settlements ever formed ghettos in Bedford, even though there were clearly marked concentrations in the 1960s, they demonstrate that by 1974 the Italian community in Bedford was widely dispersed, which suggests that pupils of Italian origin were less concentrated in the schools shown in Figure 1. However, some pupils of Italian origin may still be drawn from the Midland Road area served by these schools, which during the 1970s was shown to present the greatest accumulation of physical, social and environmental problems (Skellington, 1978). By 1971 the area had a greater proportion of European-born residents than all other primary minority group areas in Bedford. It subsequently attracted an increasing Asian, and particularly Pakistani, population. The Italian

Figure 1: Primary school rolls showing proportions of children born to minority group residents, selected areas of Bedford, 1969

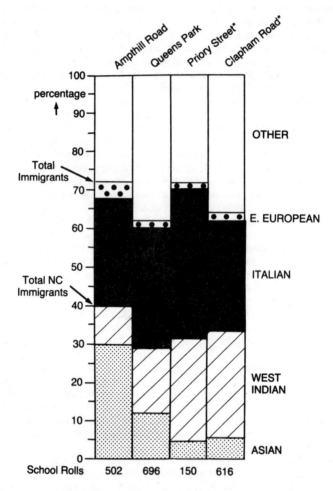

*Priory Street serves the Midland Road area, Clapham Road, Midland Road and Stanley Street areas.

Source: Skellington, 1980, p.41, on data from Brown, 1970, Table 3, p. 162.

Consulate offices, nursery school and club were located in this area. According to statistics from Bedford Social Services Department, in 1975 children in this area accounted for ten per cent of those in the town receiving educational welfare grants; in 1976 nearly half received free school meals and in 1974 the area had the highest concentration of children in the care of the local authority. Though it is by no means clear that such figures apply in particular to pupils of Italian origin, rather than of West Indian or Asian origin, the area may have acted as a residential 'trap' for minority families such as those Italians who settled early and bought properties. Such families would be sharing in the general socioeconomic and environmental deprivation of the area. On the whole, however, it is clear that Italians in Bedford have generally been upwardly mobile in socioeconomic terms.

Over the last decade there is a certain amount of research evidence on Bedfordshire LEAs' policies and practices specifically relating to pupils of Italian origin. For example, in the area of language development the LEA was involved in the Mother Tongue and Culture Project (MTCP) (see pp. 274–8) and there are indications of approaches used in the teaching of English as a second language (see pp. 284–6) and mainstream mother-tongue teaching arrangements. When the MTCP was set up in 1976–7, there appeared to be fewer primary-age, Italian-speaking pupils (Simons, 1979, 1980) which has subsequently been confirmed for other areas (Kerr, 1978; ILEA, 1982, 1983, 1986; Couillaud and Tasker, 1983), reflecting migration patterns and generations. Bedfordshire has a policy of collecting statistics on ethnic origin in order to identify special needs. In 1985–6, according to the Adviser for Multicultural Education, teachers' classifications using Form 7 returns showed there were 1,302 pupils of Italian origin in schools in Bedfordshire, 635 in Bedford itself, 250 in Luton and 417 in the rest of the county. Pupils of Italian origin thus now form a relatively small percentage of the county's ethnic minority pupils, numbering 13,672 (15.8 per cent of all school rolls), and of the school population of Bedford (10,987). However, it is likely that the method of classification under-enumerates pupils of Italian origin, the younger of whom will now be of the third generation. Since 1983 Bedfordshire has had a published paper on principles for multicultural education which are included, together with a policy statement on social services and ethnic matters, equal opportunities in employment and methods of monitoring the equal opportunities policy, in a brief document, *Policies for a Multi-Cultural Community* (BCC, 1983). The document's introduction notes that 'what is required is an acceptance of the pluralist society, recognizing and respecting differences and reflecting these differences in all aspects of the work of the Council, with the aim of creating and maintaining a total harmony' (p.1). The outlined principles of multicultural education aim to combat racism, to recognize and maintain pupils' mother tongue, recognize the needs of ethnic minority pupils in the organization of the school and the curriculum and note the importance of nursery education and equal opportunities in further education and other areas of the education service. However, although attention is drawn to pupils of Afro-Caribbean origin, there is no specific mention of pupils of Italian origin other than their involvement in educational visits and exchanges (see pp. 305–6). Currently this policy document is being redrafted.

Children of Italian origin now entering schools in Bedford and elsewhere will be of the third generation. Yet much available research evidence of pupils of Italian origin relates to UK-born, second-generation or first-generation pupils. As shown in Jackson's (1979) case study, the children in an Italian family may span a wide age range, for whereas the eldest son was setting up in the catering business in Huddersfield, the youngest was just starting school. Descriptions such as Jackson's provide insights into the varying educational experience of Italian children. Indeed, it is important to attempt to evaluate the extent to which pupils of Italian origin now starting school experience difficulties with language and differences in terms of cultural values and attitudes as did many first- and second-generation Italians.

It has been recognized that first-generation Italian pupils, who arrived in Britain during the course of their schooling, usually with their mothers, to rejoin their fathers some two years after beginning work here (King and King, 1977) experienced particular difficulties. Triseliotis (1976) noted, in general, the kinds of difficulty experienced by first-generation pupils of Mediterranean background adapting to British schools, such as behavioural difficulties, often symptomized by withdrawal, as a reaction to the change in school environment and teaching style (see also Brown, 1970) but made little mention of particular problems experienced by first-generation Italian pupils other than in connection with language. In Italy children would start to learn English in secondary schools. Perren (1979) has observed that, in Italy, English as a curriculum subject in schools is not of very long standing and has certainly not in the past been regarded as a better means for educational, social or cultural advancement than Italian. It has only recently acquired commercial, scientific and technical value and become the most widely learned foreign language with an internationalized cultural attraction, but one often unrelated to traditional literary or educational values, among the young. King and Zolli (1981) have claimed that first-generation Italian pupils may experience special linguistic difficulties when starting school in England, particularly if they have arrived in England just before going to school or, to an even greater extent, if they belong to the 'intermediate generation' who have already started schooling in Italy. 'Culture shock' made for additional difficulties in assessing the abilities of children, as in the example cited by Brown (1970) where the pupil's withdrawal was manifested by refusal to speak.

According to some sources (Triseliotis, 1976; King and Zolli, 1981), linguistic difficulties may be no less a problem for second-generation Italian children when starting school, as this may be their first meaningful contact with the English language unless the child has been lucky enough to have had nursery school experience. With the settlement of the Italian population, it is important to assess the degree of linguistic shift which has taken place between Italian dialects, Standard Italian and English as this is likely to have influenced the English facility of pupils of Italian origin commencing schooling in recent years. Part of the function of this review is to bring together the research evidence on the linguistic competence of pupils of Italian origin and their families (see pp. 222–36). Language is evidently one of the major factors in any consideration of the educational experience and achievement of pupils of Italian origin, as is clear from the weight of evidence marshalled in this review. It is also important to attempt to evaluate the extent to which the heterogeneity of the background of pupils of Italian origin relating to the diversity of their regional and cultural origins in Italy and their socioeconomic status and settlement patterns in the UK has been appreciated by schools, teachers and researchers, and whether the cultural orientation of pupils' home backgrounds and the significance of the Italian connection have been fully realized when consideration has been given to the distinctive educational needs of pupils with Italian origins.

Language
Since the weight of research concerning pupils of Italian origin bears on their linguistic position, this would suggest that from an educational perspective language has been regarded as of essential significance. Yet any attempt to assess the language knowledge, use and attitudes of Italian parents and their children at the present time is a rather fraught activity. This is due both to the evident complexity and subtlety involved in the evolution of language, particularly with respect to linguistic minority communities in a monolingual country such as Britain,

and also to the fact that research into the linguistic position of the Italian community has only recently begun. Hence there is both inadequate assessment of linguistic competence and also a lack of continuity in analysis of this long-standing minority linguistic community. It is necessary to rely upon researchers' subjective statements and anthropological description for the Italian adults who arrived in this country up to 30 years ago, whereas more recent research suggests that the generation of the speaker, the context of language use, the region of origin of the family and its location of settlement in the UK may have a distinct bearing on the linguistic evolution of this group. Hence consideration of the linguistic abilities of pupils of Italian origin has to be set in a wider sociolinguistic context.

The issue is further complicated by the fact that it is not merely a question of evaluating respective competence in, use of and attitudes towards Italian and English, but that on account of the regional heterogeneity of Italians and the Italian language it is also necessary to consider Italians' knowledge and use of various Italian dialects compared with Standard Italian. As Tosi (1980a) has pointed out, the languages spoken by the majority of Italian nationals living in the UK are substantially different from the Italian national language or Standard Italian. Reference is often made to these languages as dialects but, Tosi (1979a, 1980a) argues, that to consider these tongues as dialects may be misleading, especially if we think of dialects in terms of the English sociolinguistic context where they are regional or locally based variants of the national language. In both English and Italian, 'dialect' tends to be associated with a lower-class language and there may be a considerable variation in both the degree of structural similarity and mutual intelligibility between the dialects and the standard language. In fact the Italian dialects spoken by the families in this country are very dissimilar in grammar, lexis and phonetics from Standard Italian, which originated in the Florentine dialect. This has only become more widely accepted as the national language since the mid-19th century when other forms of Italian were demoted to the status of dialects. Italian families in Bedford, for example, speak dialects from the south of Italy – the area centro-meridional – which includes Neapolitan and Sicilian dialects, constituting one of the main sub-divisions of Italian dialects, the others being the northern Tuscan and central areas, whose dialects are spoken by Italians elsewhere in Britain. Awareness of these differences is necessary in attempting to identify whether the first language of the pupil of Italian origin is Standard Italian or a dialect form. It is important to be clear about the child's linguistic background in order to facilitate the development of potential in an educational context, especially in relation to second-language learning whether this be English or Standard Italian. Only fluency in Standard Italian can provide access to literacy as the dialects do not have a standardized spelling system. Tosi has argued that educationists need more information on the language backgrounds of pupils of Italian origin, especially with respect to instituting 'mother-tongue' teaching programmes, for an accurate assessment of pupils' linguistic competence is vital if misunderstanding in analysing language learning processes is to be avoided and objectives achieved.

In the absence of a linguistic map of Italian dialects spoken in Britain, this review draws chronologically upon various investigations involving several linguistic minority communities, predominantly in London, and smaller-scale sociolinguistic researches into Italian-speaking communities in areas of more concentrated settlement. Thus it is attempted to disentangle data on the linguistic knowledge, use and attitudes of Italian parents and their children with respect to dialect forms of Italian and Standard Italian and English in order to discern and evaluate the effect of the linguistic background of pupils of Italian origin on the ability of such pupils to profit from education in an English-medium school environment. A major factor here is the influence of Italian language classes, and a sub-section examines their organization and attitudes towards them (pp. 248–63). Mainstream provision for Italian is also considered (pp. 263–83), as is the teaching of English as a second language (pp. 283–87).

LANGUAGE KNOWLEDGE
This sub-section is concerned with Italian adults' and children's range of language knowledge in Italian, both standard and dialect forms, and English. Oral–aural competence and literacy as assessed by self-reports, interviewers' judgements and teachers' assessments are reviewed. Knowledge of Italian and English are considered separately and chronologically according to evidence from national and local surveys.

Knowledge of Italian
For several reasons there is no comprehensive national information about the extent to which Italian in standard and dialect forms is spoken, read or written, or by whom. Statistics on ethnic origin and country of birth (see pp. 207–8) can only give an increasingly imprecise and inaccurate guide to linguistic affiliation in the absence of a language question in the Census. According to Campbell-Platt (1978), who drew on data from the 1971 Census in an attempt to construct a linguistic map of minority groups in Britain in terms of their numerical size and the extent to which the mother tongue was widely spoken, Italians, numbering 108,980, formed the eighth largest linguistic group. But Campbell-Platt tended to ignore the differences between Standard Italian and dialects, claiming that the Italian language, unlike that of some other European minorities, is distinct and identifiable with relatively minor degrees of regional difference. This, however, is an oversimplification.

As Brown (1970) and Tosi (1979a) have pointed out, the first generation of Italian immigrants, recruited from secluded southern Italian villages in the 1950s and early 1960s to work in the brickworks in Bedford, invariably spoke almost exclusively their own village dialects. They were unaccustomed to Standard Italian, and had little competence in speaking the national language. According to Tosi (1984), their oral competence and literacy in Standard Italian depended on several factors: in particular, education, exposure to Standard Italian in Italy, gender, age and time of emigration. The overwhelming majority of Italians now living in the UK are of southern origin – Marin (1975, quoted by Steedman, 1979) suggested 172,000, compared with 43,000 from the centre and north. The majority of southerners are likely to have received their education during the period 1930–50. According to Steedman, in 1951 25 per cent of the population of southern Italy was officially classed as illiterate. A further 25 per cent had no primary school leaving certificate, i.e. they had experienced less than five years' elementary education. Steedman has suggested that at least 50 per cent of the immigrants to the UK from the south may have fallen into one of these two groups, although since the immigrants overwhelmingly came from the peasant classes, the proportion may well have been far higher. With respect to the first-generation adult immigrants to Bedford, all sources agree that the vast majority of men and women had little schooling (Brown, 1970; Simons, 1980; Tosi, 1979a, 1984). Most men left school before the end of primary school and even fewer women completed the course. The vast majority according to Tosi's research (1984) show only limited fluency in reading and poor writing skills since literacy was not required in everyday village life and work. Whilst some, usually men, could fully understand a speaker of Standard Italian in an informal mode and were able to express themselves without difficulty in near standard forms, they were unable to respond adequately to more formal registers. Others, mainly women, had great difficulty in understanding even colloquial and elementary forms of Standard Italian.

Tosi claims, however, that variation in the level of oral competence in the national language 'seems to be determined by the intensity of their exposure to that medium in Italy, rather than by the duration of their schooling' (p. 65). Maintenance of fluency was linked to personal events and closely related to the circumstances of their lives and their departure from the village. Prior to this time, only men were engaged in the few activities where the use of the national language was required such as in occupational functions, including military service and business contacts outside the village and with the provincial administration, and in traditional social roles, including contacts with the authorities, police and school. Women, living typically within the family circle, required only the local dialect for everyday life. At the time of emigration, older workers had experienced more opportunities to be exposed to the national language and to reinforce their competence and extend their language repertoire. Furthermore, recent immigrants had greater familiarity with the national language owing to the changing conditions of life in the south which occurred during the 1960s when greater social participation at national level, the extension of schooling, diffusion of the media and internal immigration, both urbanization and commuting, improved social and linguistic contacts between villages and towns. These more recent immigrants 'have maintained in their speech a repertoire of values, terms and structures in the national language' (p. 67), but the conditions of exposure were inaccessible to fellow villagers who left ten to 15 years earlier. For them, little schooling and hence low levels of literacy have been compounded by the fact that facilities for reading and writing in Italian have been 'drastically reduced' since moving to Bedford. The Italian government has, however, under the auspices of the Italian Consulate, gone some way towards recognizing this position by making provision for adult literacy classes in Standard Italian at the elementary and intermediate levels (see Northamptonshire LEA, 1980). However, the lack of oral and literacy skills in Standard Italian of many first-generation Italian parents restricts, in turn, their ability to pass these on to their children. Tosi (1984) claims that Standard Italian has only a small role to play in a first-generation Italian household in Bedford. The local dialect is the main medium of communication within the family and, where necessary, has incorporated English vocabulary. Apart from this, the three main dialects spoken in Bedford retain their local and conservative characteristics, especially as they are intelligible to the different speakers for the limited interaction which occurs between the different groups (see p. 237). Amongst the first-generation Italians linguistic differences still reflect the socioeconomic stratification of society in the country of origin.

Research evidence from a sociolinguistic study carried out in 1978–9 in two Italian communities in London (Weston, 1979) confirms these observations. The study, which aimed to investigate the language history, use, competence and attitudes and expectations of 47 Italian adults and 18 children, found that almost all of the parents, the majority of whom hailed from rural villages in central and southern Italy and had been in the UK on average for 20 years, had an Italian dialect rather than Standard Italian as their mother tongue, and it was their dialect with which they were most familiar. Weston discovered that a quarter of these adult Italians had difficulty understanding Standard Italian, and being understood in it. Interestingly, competence varied according to the area of London in which they lived. In one area the Italian community was highly organized and there were several community associations which provided opportunities for meeting. Since the community was composed of Italians from various regions, this was sufficient to ensure that it was necessary to use Standard Italian rather than dialects to converse with fellow Italians. By contrast, since the community in the other area was composed of people from the same region or even the same village, spoken communications were in dialect. Weston observed, moreover, that the Italian adults' knowledge of Standard Italian would be inadequate if they were to return to Italy to live (as over four-fifths wished to do), in view of the linguistic shift towards Standard Italian in Italy during the past 20 years, which has taken place alongside the development of the mass media, internal migration and the transformation from an agricultural to an industrial society. Hence figures such as in Tables 22 and 23 can only give a general guide to the number of Italian speakers.

Fortunately, some more detailed information is available on the extent of Italian language knowledge in two locations, Coventry and London, from the recent Linguistic Minorities Project (LMP) surveys. Two of these surveys, the Adult Language Use Survey (ALUS) and the Schools Language Survey (SLS), provide information on Italian language knowledge of adults and children. In the context of establishing adult language knowledge it is relevant here to describe the ALUS and findings in further detail; reference is made elsewhere in this and other sub-sections to other survey findings (LMP, 1985; Smith *et al.*, 1984; Reid *et al.*, 1985). In the ALUS, which involved several linguistic minorities, a random sample of 94 Italian speakers were interviewed in Islington and Barnet in 1981, and 108 Italian speakers were interviewed in Coventry in 1980. Amongst the respondents a sex balance was largely achieved, but there was a slight bias towards the older age-group as many younger people in both locations said they did not know the language at all well and there was some difficulty in securing interviews with them, and refusals in London. Although the data give a fair overall picture of Italian speakers in these two locations, the findings should not be interpreted as necessarily representative of Italian speakers in these cities or in England as a whole. Indeed there are some interesting contrasts.

Respondents' household members were concentrated in two age bands: in Coventry the first generation, who arrived in the 1950s, were aged 46–60, and in London the corresponding group were some five years younger. Their children were 16–25 in Coventry and 11–20 in London. Table 26 shows the main demographic features of the Italian respondents in Coventry and London. Very high proportions of the respondents in both locations were economically active, including seven out of ten women. In Coventry Italian women had been recruited to work at the Courtaulds textile factory and others had arrived as war brides, married to English, Irish, Polish or Ukrainian men. Italian women probably outnumbered Italian men in the first-generation migrants. There were contrasting patterns of employment between the two locations: in Coventry over half the respondents in work were employed in manufacturing, although nearly one in six were in the business and commercial sector; by comparison, in London nearly half worked in catering or retailing and another quarter were in service industries. In London nearly a quarter were self-employed or in family businesses, compared with one in ten in Coventry. Three-quarters in London and four-fifths in Coventry had manual jobs; one in three in London, almost twice as many in Coventry, had supervisory responsibilities; but almost a third in Coventry compared with a quarter in London had had professional or apprenticeship training. There were also contrasts in housing. A third of the Italians in London were in council housing, whereas almost all in Coventry were in owner-occupied housing. Although some families there had remained in the redbrick inner city housing, as their economic position improved many had moved into the northern and north-east suburbs of the city around the Italian Catholic church.

Table 26: **Demographic features of the Italian respondents in the Adult Language Use Survey, Coventry and London**

	Coventry	*London*
Estimate of total populations	600–800	31,000
Numbers of households with member interviewed	108	94
Numbers of people in the respondents' households	394	367
% of people in respondents' household aged below 17	22	30
% of people in respondents' household aged over 50	24	16
% of households in owner occupation	96	62
% of households in council housing	2	32
% of males aged 17–65 at work outside home or in family business	82	87
% of females aged 17–60 at work outside home or in family business	67	75
% of people in respondents' household brought up overseas	49	42

Source: Adapted from LMP, 1983a, Tables 5.1 and 5.3, ALUS, and LMP, 1985.

In the ALUS interviews took place in Italian. English was only used when the respondent asked to do so, or initiated a language switch. A section of the questionnaire investigated respondents' self-assessed language skills, including literacy in Standard Italian and English. Almost all of the respondents had at least a little Italian and English.

Table 27: **Extent of multilingualism amongst Italian speakers**

Italian speakers	N	Additional languages known, % of Italian speakers		
		French	Spanish	Italian dialects
Coventry	108	18	33	81
London	94	16	12	80

Source: Adapted from LMP, 1983a, Table 5.4.

In both Coventry and London very high proportions (over 80 per cent) of Italian speakers reported knowledge of three or more languages. This was largely owing to knowledge of dialects alongside Standard Italian but also knowing other European languages. Table 27 shows the extent of multilingualism amongst Italian speakers in the two locations. In addition, respondents reported on the oral skills of household members, including children and non-family members, said to know Italian (dialect or Standard) very or fairly well:

Coventry	N = 387	58 per cent
London	N = 339	76 per cent

Table 28: **Adults' competence in Italian**

Italian speakers	N	% respondents answering fairly or very well	
		Understand and speak	Read and write
Coventry	108	73	63
London	94	81	69

Source: Adapted from LMP, 1983a, Table 5.5.

The ALUS also supplies information on respondents' skills in Italian. Table 28 shows the percentage of respondents who reported that they understood and spoke and read and wrote Italian very or fairly well. As for their household members, the relatively low percentage of respondents claiming at least minimal aural–oral skills especially in Coventry – the lowest percentage of all minority language speakers – may be due to the fact that respondents may have interpreted questions about skills to relate to Standard Italian rather than to the dialects which many used more commonly, as Tosi also found in Bedford (see pp. 222–3). Further analysis showed that whereas in Coventry the main dialects spoken were Neapolitan and Sicilian (Smith *et al.*, 1984), in London they were Northern and Friulian and Neapolitan (Reid *et al.*, 1985). However, the younger respondents, especially in Coventry, may have felt that their Italian was weak in comparison with their English (see p. 233) and their productive skills (speaking and writing) were less well developed than their receptive skills (understanding and reading). Their order of skills was in fact understanding, reading, speaking and writing (LMP, 1985).

About two-thirds of respondents in both locations reported reading and writing Italian fairly or very well. Spoken and literacy skills in Italian varied mainly according to place of upbringing, with those brought up in the UK reporting lower skills. Length of schooling also had an influence on literacy skills. Further information on literacy is given in Table 30 (see p. 233).

Given this picture of Italian adults' knowledge of and competence in dialect and Standard Italian, how is this likely to influence the Italian language knowledge of children of Italian origin, particularly in their pre-school years and in out-of-school hours? Various factors such as generation, cultural orientation of the home, the language (dialect or Standard Italian) in question and the extent to which there is family and community support for mother-tongue maintenance – factors which may not have been adequately taken into account in research – are likely to have a bearing on any evaluation of available evidence. For example, Palmer (1980), writing of the second-generation, UK-born immigrants from the central Italian area of Emilia, who were largely engaged in catering in London, noted that by their late adolescence in 1973 they could hardly speak either Standard Italian or dialect. From research in Bedford, Tosi (1979a) has also claimed that although the second generation may speak their parents' dialect, they do not have competence in Standard Italian. The intermediate generation who arrived in the UK as small children might, however, have some competence in Standard Italian, depending on the time which they spent in school in Italy. Moreover, Simons (1980), evaluating the Mother Tongue and Culture Project (MTCP) in Bedford, reported the views of some teachers that although dialect might be predominant when second-generation children had only oral skills, since they also listened to other people besides their parents they could in fact understand some Standard Italian. Simple instructions, for example, would be understood partly through context, tone of voice and gesture. Hence children were able to understand more varied forms of Italian and Standard Italian than they were able to reproduce. Weston (1979) echoes this point. She noted that although the dialects spoken by some of the 18 children in her sample were very remote from Standard Italian, the majority of children had great competence in aural skills, so that they understood most of what was being said in Standard Italian. She further maintained that, when persuaded to speak, they showed a good mastery of the sound system, so that by building on this in time they could achieve all-round competence in Italian since their emotional link with Italy, and continued contact with it, provided the necessary motivation (see also p. 245–6). At pre-school age the language exposure of children of Italian origin depends largely on the home language background which varies from family to family. The majority learn their parents' dialect as their mother-tongue, whereas others learn a mixture of dialect and English, or even a mixture of dialect, Standard Italian and English.

Further research evidence permits consideration of the extent to which Italian is claimed as a spoken language for pupils of Italian origin. Four language censuses covering the whole of the ILEA in 1978, 1981, 1983 and 1985 (ILEA, 1979, 1982, 1983, 1986) provide evidence of considerable and increasing linguistic diversity amongst London schoolchildren and of the numbers of Italian speakers analysed according to their distribution within the ILEA and by age. Unfortunately, however, no distinction is drawn between different Italian dialects or between dialects and Standard Italian, nor is any assessment available of their competence in these languages as it is for English (pp. 235–6). In 1978 teachers in all primary and secondary schools collected information on a class basis for every pupil for whom English was not a first language. Italian speakers, numbering 2,272, formed the sixth largest group of speakers of the 128 languages recorded. With the exception of the City (24) and Greenwich (26), Italian-speaking pupils were fairly well spread across the ten divisions of the ILEA, most being found in Islington (514), Camden (456) and Wandsworth (304). An analysis of Italian-speaking pupils, by age, showed a greater percentage at the age of 12/13 and fewer children at the lower end of the primary range (ILEA, 1979). However, it was unclear whether this was because there had been fewer births to the Italian-speaking communities in inner London in the mid-1970s or because a higher proportion of young children from them had acquired English as a first language.

In the second ILEA survey, in 1981, teachers in all primary and secondary schools recorded the number of pupils who used a language other than or in addition to English at home. Although the number of pupils who spoke Italian had increased to 2,808, they then ranked as the seventh largest group of speakers of 131 overseas languages, forming some 6.3 per cent of the total of 44,925 foreign language speakers (ILEA, 1982). Moreover, by this time the distribution of Italian-speaking pupils, again with the exception of Greenwich (46) and the City (64), appears to have become more even. However, the ranking of distribution had changed with an increase in the number of Italian-speaking pupils in Camden to 521, compared with a decrease in Islington to 477, and other notable increases in Wandsworth to 412 and in Lewisham to 215, in the latter case doubling the 1979 figure. According to an analysis by age, in line with the general age distribution for the ILEA as a whole, there was found to be a decreasing number of Italian-speaking pupils in the younger age groups, so that pupils aged five constituted only about 75 per cent of the number aged 15. Interestingly, there were almost as many 16–19-year-old Italian-speaking pupils in secondary schools in the ILEA as those aged 15 (see pp. 290–1). Overall Italian-speaking pupils in 1981 had increased by 23.6 per cent over their 1978 number. However, of all the main language groups (apart from Greek speakers in the primary age range who actually declined), the number of Italian-speaking pupils of primary school age demonstrated the smallest increase, a mere 7.5 per cent. Whilst this may have been the result of the change in definition employed in the 1981 Census, it appeared to be more likely to reflect either a declining birth rate (between the second and third generations) at this particular time or some moving out of the ILEA area.

Further evidence of the changing age pattern of Italian-speaking pupils in the ILEA is apparent from the 1983 survey. This employed the same definition but extended its scope to include pupils in nursery and special schools. A total of 147 languages was recorded and Italian speakers, numbering 2,421, again fell, to ninth position (4.8 per cent) in the groups of overseas language speakers. As in 1981, the greatest number of Italian-speaking pupils lived in Camden (476) and numbers in

Wandsworth increased further to 347, overtaking declining numbers in Islington (331). In fact of all the groups of overseas language speakers, the overall number of Italian speakers showed the greatest decline, of 15.6 per cent, since 1981. This was almost double the overall fall in ILEA rolls of eight per cent between 1981 and 1983. Older Italian-speaking pupils outnumbered younger pupils, although they decreased too by 8.4 per cent compared with 23.5 per cent of primary-age pupils.

The ILEA census in 1985 revealed a further decline in the number of Italian-speaking pupils to 2102, now the tenth largest group (3.7 per cent) of speakers of overseas languages (161) (ILEA, 1986). Again, in 1985 the greatest number of Italian-speaking pupils lived in Camden (369) with almost as many (344) in Islington, an increase since 1983. As in 1983, of all the groups of overseas language speakers the overall number of Italian speakers showed the greatest decline, of 13.2 per cent in two years. Except at the beginning of primary school, where differences were quite small, speakers of Italian were more numerous in older age groups. A further decline in Italian speakers, particularly in secondary schools, is predicted. This distribution of Italian speakers suggests that the majority of second-generation Italian speakers have almost completed their schooling and the third generation are only just commencing school. It will be of interest to monitor to what extent Italian continues to be represented as a language spoken at home by ILEA pupils.

The Schools Language Survey (SLS) of the LMP, undertaken in 1980–1 in five LEAs, records the number of pupils speaking Italian at home and confirms the ILEA trend to declining numbers of Italian speakers in the lower age ranges. The SLS, developed to assist LEAs to document linguistic diversity, was administered by teachers in Bradford, Coventry, Haringey, Peterborough and Waltham Forest and records pupils' self-reports of the language(s) they spoke at home and their literacy in Italian. Table 29 provides information on the number of pupils speaking dialects and Standard Italian and, as a percentage of all minority language, speakers in the five LEAs, their age, sex and literacy (see p. 229). With the exception of Peterborough, where Italian-speaking pupils form the second largest group – almost a quarter – of pupils speaking a language other than English at home, Italian-speaking pupils were found to form only a small percentage of the total number of speakers of languages other than English at home in the four other LEAs. Most interesting is the predominance of unspecified or standard forms of spoken Italian, with relatively few pupils specifying regional dialects. However, it is not clear whether this is the result of lack of inadequate classification in data collection, or the reflection of a desire to claim knowledge of and spoken competence in Standard Italian, in view of its greater perceived status and the fact that this will be learnt by a high proportion of Italian-speaking pupils attending Italian language classes. However, as can be seen, a range of dialects is represented in each LEA, up to seven in the case of Haringey. In addition, in comparison with, for example, Greek-speaking pupils, Italian-speaking pupils are shown to be well distributed throughout the country, as represented by these five LEAs. Indeed a nation-wide survey in 1983 revealed that 12 out of 56 LEAs with primary schools with at least ten per cent bilingual pupils named Italian as one of the most frequently spoken languages (Tansley and Craft, 1984). There appears to be no evidence, however, in comparison with some other speakers of overseas languages, of pupils of Italian origin being multilingual, in addition to knowledge of their own dialect, Standard Italian and English.

These surveys demonstrate the dispersal of Italian-speaking pupils and also indicate the range of their Italian language background in terms of spoken dialects and Standard Italian. It is unfortunate that no study has been able to assess the

Table 29 Pupils' knowledge of Italian in five LEAs, 1981

		Bradford	Coventry	Haringey	Peterborough	Waltham Forest
Italian speakers:						
1	Numbers	368	145	451	572	105
2	% of all language groups in school	2.6	2.0	6.1	23.7	1.9
3	Literacy* % of total Italian speakers	72	63	59	63	68
4	Sex ratio: boy/girl	52/48	46/54	48/52	50/50	51/49
5	Age groups					
	6–8	42	19	83	107	29
	9–11	78	36	150	108	24
	12–14	111	47	131	140	41
	15+	114	41	–	108	–
6	Language groups					
	Standard or unspecified	339	134	410	466	96
	Unspecified dialect	3	3	3	38	–
	Central	1	–	2	–	–
	Neapolitan	21	1	15	29	4
	Sicilian	4	7	18	38	4
	Gallo	–	–	1	–	–
	Tuscan	–	–	2	1	–
	Venetian	–	–	–	–	1

* 'Literacy' here means reading or writing in one of the spoken languages given.
Sources: Adapted from Couillaud and Tasker, 1983; LMP, 1983a, Table 2.5.

relative oral competence of Italian-speaking pupils in dialect or Standard Italian, although as part of the MTCP Tosi (1979b, 1980a, 1984) attempted to devise tests of oral proficiency and investigated dialect and English interference and transfer in the learning of Standard Italian (see pp. 275–7). However, a few studies have considered the relative dominance of Italian and English for Italian-speaking pupils (see p. 235). The few children of Italian background amongst the 397 ethnic minority children of average age 11, interviewed by Clough and Quarmby (1978) in a large-scale investigation into library use by ethnic minority groups in six London boroughs, in 1975, claimed to speak Italian as well as English. A much higher proportion claimed bilingualism to some degree than most other linguistic groups. In another study in a school in Waltham Forest Prager (1977) found that Italian-speaking pupils were divided as to whether they spoke Italian better or as well as English or less well than English. The most informative data come from an investigation in 1977–8 of the linguistic competence of some 4,600 11–12-year-olds in 28 secondary schools in 11 London boroughs (Rosen and Burgess, 1980). Of this sample, they discovered that 46 pupils, some six per cent of the 749 bilingual pupils, spoke Italian. According to their teachers, 39 per cent of these Italian-speaking pupils were bilingual and regularly spoke their language, a similar proportion to French speakers, rather than Greek or Turkish speakers. Of the remainder, only two per cent had Italian as their dominant language and, at the other extreme, the majority, some 59 per cent, were considered to speak only some phrases of Italian. Italian thus seemed to be both less dominant for this group, compared with the mother tongues of some other overseas language speakers and to be less well known. This was reflected in the degree to which pupils were considered to be fluent and unambiguous speakers of English (see p 235).

Given these data about children's oral–aural competence, to what extent are Italian-speaking pupils literate in Italian, bearing in mind also the relatively low literacy skills of Italian adults (see pp. 225–6) and the dominance of dialect rather than Standard Italian in domestic use? Italian observers are divided about the influence of dialect. Tosi (1979a) claimed that second-generation Italians do not read or write Standard Italian and that biliteracy cannot easily be achieved by such children who hear their parents' Italian dialect in the home (Tosi, 1980a). Yet other teachers of Italian involved on the MTCP project (reported by Simons, 1980) thought dialect need not be regarded as an interference to learning to read and write in Standard Italian. On the other hand, dialect speakers might not develop literacy skills in Standard Italian in a predominantly English-speaking environment as quickly as if there was a supporting environment, as in Italy, through the media, the school itself and other aspects of the social environment and where being literate in Standard Italian would be seen as facilitating communication with other Italian dialect speakers, as well as being the language of schooling and commerce. In fact the EC/Bedfordshire Project demonstrated that children from Italian dialect-speaking backgrounds could be taught to read and write in Standard Italian relatively quickly (Tansley, 1981), for as Steedman (1979) reported after a visit to the project during its second year, children were observed to read Italian fluently and correctly, with evident enthusiasm and enjoyment. Tosi (1980b), however, suggested that these primary school age children of Italian origin were more likely to achieve higher levels in comprehension skills than in production skills of reading and writing.

Evidence of pupils' literacy in Standard Italian, and compared with English, is available from the same few studies but is somewhat conflicting. In Clough and Quarmby's (1978) study of ethnic minority groups' use of public libraries none of the Italian-speaking children claimed to read Italian. On the other hand, in a school in Waltham Forest two-thirds of the few Italian-speaking pupils claimed to read Italian better than or as well as English (Prager, 1977). Rosen and Burgess's (1980) study is again the most helpful in this context, providing assessments of reading and writing skills and enabling comparisons to be drawn with oral competence and with other language speakers. Yet only 21 per cent of the 46 Italian speakers in 28 secondary schools in 11 London boroughs were said by their teachers both to read and write in Standard Italian. In addition, a mere four per cent were said to read but not write in Standard Italian. Since 39 per cent were said to be bilingual, it is clear that this group of Italian speakers at least were more likely to have greater oral than literacy skills in Italian. Moreover, Italian-speaking pupils were considerably less likely to be able to read and write in their own language than Greek speakers (37 per cent), Turkish speakers (42 per cent), Portuguese speakers (43 per cent), French speakers (53 per cent) and Spanish speakers (66 per cent). However, these figures give no impression of the degree of literacy for Italian-speaking pupils.

Importantly, teachers' estimates of pupils' literacy are supplemented by further pupils' self-reports in both Italian-language schools and mainstream schools. As part of an investigation into the library needs of mother-tongue schools in London, Elliott (1981) interviewed some ten Italian-speaking pupils in one mother-tongue school in Hackney. All but one of the pupils were second generation, four being of primary school age and six of secondary age. Five of the Italian-speaking pupils claimed to be able to read in Standard Italian, and the other five said that they could do so a little (see p. 242). By far the most significant data are reported from the Schools Language Survey (Couillaud and Tasker, 1983). In all of the five LEAs surveyed – Bradford, Coventry, Haringey, Peterborough and Waltham

Forest – for the pupils aged six to 15 plus who claimed to be speakers of Italian in addition to English at home, there was a reported increase in literacy with age. Some 59–72 per cent of Italian speakers in these LEAs claimed literacy (see Table 29, p. 229). It is interesting that only in Peterborough, where Italian-language speakers were most numerous, comprising almost a quarter of minority language speakers and having an equal sex ratio, was there a statistically significant higher reported literacy for girls than for boys. This corresponds to widespread evidence of such differences in the educational literature on language achievement in general, and literacy in particular. Furthermore, over the five LEAs, average reported literacy of 65 per cent for Italian-speaking pupils was second only to that for Polish speakers (LMP, 1983a, Table 2.5).

Overall findings concerning the literacy of Italian-speaking pupils are ambivalent and the evidence does not lend itself to superficial generalization, especially since competence in reading and writing is unclear. Neither is it clear whether the extent or degree of their literacy in Standard Italian is greater than that of their parents (see pp. 222–3, 225–6). Though it seems probable that pupils from Italian backgrounds are less likely to be literate in Standard Italian than to speak a form of Italian, at the same time there is good evidence that literacy does increase with age. This suggests that literacy in Standard Italian must depend to a great extent on persistence with learning, and hence the likely influence of Italian language classes in schools, community and mainstream schools, their accessibility and attitudes towards language maintenance and development (see pp. 243–83).

In conclusion, the situation with respect to Italian adults' and children's Italian language knowledge is complex and as yet inadequately researched. Italian adults appear more likely to have greater oral skills in the dialects of their village or region of origin than in Standard Italian. A number of Italian dialects are spoken by Italian adults in the UK. Competence in Standard Italian is likely to depend on several factors such as exposure to it in Italy, education, gender, age, time of emigration and attitudes towards it and the need to use it in the UK. These factors apply to a greater extent for literacy than oral skills. This being the case, and given their additional exposure to English through schooling, the relative knowledge of dialect(s) and Standard Italian of pupils of Italian origin and their aural–oral and literacy skills are difficult to evaluate, especially since they have not been assessed with any degree of objectivity by research. However, available evidence suggests their aural skills may well be greater than oral skills, especially for Standard Italian, and that although literacy skills may increase with age, these are less likely to be developed and may depend on a whole range of factors such as attitudes to Italian (see pp. 244–6), use within the family and community (see pp. 237–41) and opportunities for developing Italian skills through language classes. Moreover, evidence suggests that it is also especially important to consider pupils' Italian language skills in relation to their knowledge of and competence in English.

Knowledge of English
The remainder of this sub-section focusses on Italian adults' and children's knowledge of English and considers to what extent Italian language skills interact with oracy and literacy in English. Bilingualism is likely to be a matter of the degree to which languages are spoken, ranging from minimum competence to complete mastery. Most bilinguals are likely to have a dominant language and those who speak English as a second language are likely to have degrees of mastery. Fluency is sometimes deceptive and literacy more difficult to assess. Again, Italian adults' and children's knowledge of English is reviewed through local studies and surveys.

Consideration of Italian adults' knowledge of and competence in English indicates that this is likely to vary at least according to the time when research is conducted, the generation of the subject, length of residence, areas of settlement and degree of interaction with the wider community. In particular, it would seem improbable that, due to lack of schooling and the lack of prestige of English in the Italian school curriculum until recently, Italian adults, other than a professional élite, will have had any English on arrival in this country.

Brown (1970) recorded that virtually none of the early Italian immigrants in Bedford had much command of English, and that the Italian Catholic Mission, run by the Scalabrini missionaries since 1954, performed a vital practical function, acting as interpreters in every sphere of life and in particular negotiating for the Italian immigrants in their relationships with authority, with respect to housing, the law, job applications and other bureaucratic matters. By 1970, however, Brown claimed that most Italian families had acquired enough English to cope with everyday needs, so that they could dispense with the help of the missionaries, rely more upon their English-speaking children when necessary, and turn to the Italian Vice-Consul and his staff for assistance with special problems. Even so, Brown also noted that lack of English in particular, as well as little education and few technical skills, restricted the advancement of Italians in employment; even though lack of competence in English made it difficult to adapt to mechanized processes, they enjoyed a high work reputation. Generally in this respect the relatively few Italians of northern origin were considered superior to southern Italians. By the mid-1970s Simons (1980) found that the English skills of parents of children involved in the MTCP in Bedford varied considerably and were often inadequate if their working and social environment was predominantly Italian in its cultural orientation. More recently, Tosi (1984) has noted that the English competence of women who work outside the home does not seem significantly below that of men. Yet employers often need the help of younger Italians to interpret organizational regulations, union activities and also in court, to the first generation, usually in dialect. Tosi studied the language patterns of Bedford Italians and analysed the interaction of Standard English, Transfer English, Standard Italian and dialects in some detail. He notes the immigrants' gradual acquisition of English vocabulary alongside their urbanization. First, the vocabulary of employment occupations, type of work, products and equipment, then relating to survival needs such as shopping, food, animals, landscape and city scenes and, finally, the vocabulary of houses, legal terminology and architecture. Children imported vocabulary related to ideas, concepts and objects associated with education. Finally, when the second generation left school to find employment and married, they introduced the vocabulary of the concepts and ideas related to their lives, work and aspirations.

Evidence from a sociolinguistic study by Weston (1979) amongst 24 Italian families in two London areas largely confirms the Bedford reports. Although hardly any of the adults had any English on arrival, all had learnt some during their residence. However, according to their self-assessments, which Weston felt might be overestimates, their range of English aural and oral skills was varied. For example, whereas one person seemed to understand and speak no English at all even after having lived and worked with English people in the UK for 18 years, a restaurant manager appeared to have native-like fluency. The majority, Weston observed, obviously only had 'linguistic survival kits', sufficient for simple day-to-day situations and elementary exchanges. Moreover, only just over half the respondents claimed to read English and only a quarter to write it. It is salutary to note the warning issued by King (1979, quoting Palmer, 1973) that it would be misleading to base any index of Italian assimilation solely on linguistic acculturation

– one of the common measures – as restaurateurs, waiters, hairdressers, etc., clearly have to learn English in order to function and communicate effectively, yet economically the Italian position is maintained by emphasizing and trading on their ethnicity. Ethnicity is encouraged at the same time as linguistic acculturation.

The ALUS of the LMP (1983a) provides up-to-date information on the oracy and literacy of Italian adults in English (see pp. 225–6 for survey and sample details). All of the Italian adults in the sample in Coventry and London claimed some knowledge of English. But self-rated ability to understand and speak and read and write English fairly or very well was considerably lower (Table 30). However, it is interesting to note the contrasts between the language repertoires of the Italian speakers in Coventry and London. A much greater proportion (over four-fifths) of the Coventry Italians claimed to understand and speak English fairly or very well than did the London Italians (only two-thirds). Indeed in Coventry more Italians – probably predominantly dialect speakers or younger respondents – claimed to understand and speak English fairly or very well than they did Standard Italian (see also pp. 225–6). This was apparently not the case for Italians in the London sample (see Table 28).

Table 30:   Italian adults' competence in English

Italian speakers	N	*Respondents answering fairly or very well*	
		Understand and speak English %	Read and write English %
Coventry	108	83	39
London	94	65	34

Source: Adapted from LMP, 1983a, Table 5.5.

In both locations claimed literacy skills in English were around half those of oral–aural competence in English and literacy in Italian (see Table 28), and were amongst the lowest for minority language speakers. However, almost none of the Italian adults was illiterate (only one per cent of the Italian speakers in Coventry). Indeed 55 per cent of Italian speakers in Coventry and 52 per cent in London claimed to be able to read and write at least minimally in two languages. Literacy skills in English related closely to country of upbringing and length of formal schooling. On balance, therefore, in these samples adults were more likely to have some literacy in Italian than English, although it is likely that at least a third have minimal literacy skills in Italian and at least half only minimal literacy in English.

Finally, the spoken language skills of respondents' household members, including children and non-family members, who were said to know English or English and Italian very or fairly well, are shown in Table 31. Almost nine out of every ten household members were said to know English at least fairly well. English skills depended on whether upbringing was totally or partly in the UK, and in Coventry Italian men had higher levels of English skills than women, probably due to a combination of shorter formal schooling for women and fewer opportunities to learn English at work outside the home (LMP, 1985). Half to two-thirds of household members were said to be bilingual in the sense of knowing both languages at least fairly well and had in principle the possibility of speaking in either English or Italian to the respondents. Indeed the particularly high percentage (exceeded only by Polish speakers in Coventry) of household members claiming a certain fluency in English suggests that children of Italian origin, in these locations at least, are likely to have access to other household members speaking some English. This is likely to have implications for their opportunities to learn and use English (see pp. 240–1, 283–4). Whilst for many people of Italian origin in these two locations English had become a major element in their linguistic repertoire, they had generally (see pp. 225–6) retained at least a strong base in Italian which could be developed with support.

Table 31: **Italian household members' English and bilingual skills**

Italian speakers	N	English %	Bilingual %
Coventry	387	89	50
London	339	86	65

Source: Adapted from LMP, 1983a, Table 5.7.

It appears that the spoken English proficiency of pupils of Italian origin, at least in the early years, will depend on a number of factors, especially whether they were born and received some education in Italy, the extent to which Italian (dialect or Standard) is spoken in the home, the generation of the parents and the position of the child in the family. Tosi (1979a) suggested that the English competence of the 'intermediate generation', who arrived in Britain as young children, might be proportional to the time spent in British schools and Italian schools. More recently (1984), he has claimed that since dialects are predominant in the language of the home amongst Italian first-generation families in Bedford, pre-school children rarely hear English spoken by adults, except when visiting relatives bring grown-up chilren who often respond in English, and when other second-generation members speak English amongst themselves. Contacts with older children inside or immediately outside the home and often long exposure to TV are other sources of English. However, whilst dialect is used to refer to home life, parents' speech also includes English words and expressions to describe the life and environment outside the home. Thus 'until they reach school age, children speak dialects with confidence and ease, switching occasionally and unconsciously to English' (p.107). Moreover, some teachers engaged on the Mother Tongue and Culture Project (MTCP) claimed that the generation of the parents of the children involved greatly influenced the extent to which children from Italian-speaking backgrounds went to school with some knowledge of English (Simons, 1980). First-generation parents who had arrived in Bedford in the 1950s tended to speak dialect to their children and this was the dominant language on entry to school. Even so, if the child was the youngest of three or four children in a family, then he was also likely to have acquired some knowledge of English, usually vocabulary rather than syntax, from his brothers and sisters already undergoing schooling. Hence the first child of primary school age in the family tended to have less English than the second or third child because he had not had the opportunity to speak English with siblings; Jackson's (1979) case study illustrates this. On the other hand, second-generation parents who had experienced their education in Britain and who had material, occupational and educational advantages over their parents, whilst retaining strong Italian cultural links, tended to speak English with their children, so that they would enter school having some knowledge of English. Moreover, in some homes the language background was clearly mixed, so one or other parent might tend to speak more in English or dialect or Standard Italian. The English competence of Italian children starting school may thus be very different according to their particular home language backgrounds; whereas some may arrive in school with little or no knowledge of English, others can already demonstrate certain aural–oral skills. Hence their needs with respect to language development may be diverse (see pp. 283–6).

Two research studies and the language censuses in London provide information according to teachers' assessments of the English language knowledge of pupils of Italian origin which may be compared with their knowledge of Italian (see p. 229). In 1978, Rosen and Burgess (1980) found that teachers considered 82 per cent of 46 Italian-speaking 11-year-old pupils were unambiguous speakers of English. The fact that only 18 per cent were considered to incorporate some features of Italian in their spoken English at this age might be taken to support the suggestion (see p. 227) that Italian-speaking pupils found it more difficult to encode rather than decode Italian and hence that there might be less interference from Italian in English. A similar percentage of Italian and French-speaking pupils were considered to be unambiguous speakers of English. Moreover, 91 per cent of these Italian-speaking pupils were considered by their teachers to be fluent in English and only nine per cent to have intermediate levels of English, none being in the initial stages of learning English. Taken together with their estimated relatively low skills in Italian (see p.229), these data overall suggest a considerable language shift towards knowledge of and competence in English for pupils from an Italian-speaking background by the early secondary school years. Moreover, this shift has apparently been greater than for pupils speaking other European languages coming from communities which have also become established in this country in the last 20–30 years. It is also of interest to note that when Weston (1979) contacted the schools of 18 children (of average age 14) of Italian families whom she studied, she found that some 51 per cent of these students were considered by their teachers to be above average and 42 per cent below average in English. Even though some were also said to perform below average in other subject-areas, Italian pupils were reported to be above average in the learning of foreign languages, excluding Standard Italian.

English competence has also been assessed by teachers in four ILEA language censuses in 1978, 1981, 1983 and 1985 (ILEA, 1979, 1982, 1983, 1986). In the 1978 census teachers rated the need of pupils for whom English was not a first language for additional English-language teaching. Although Italian-speaking pupils formed the sixth largest group of foreign language speakers, they fell to eleventh position numerically in terms of need of additional English teaching. Some 28.4 per cent (645) of Italian speakers were said to be in need of additional English teaching. The proportion in need was again similar to that of French speakers. They occupied a position midway between speakers from established East European communities and Greek speakers. Generally Italian-speaking pupils considered to be in need of additional English teaching were found in proportion to their distribution throughout the ILEA divisions.

In the subsequent surveys the fluency in English of pupils who used a language other than, or in addition to, English at home was assessed by teachers according to four categories: beginners, second- and third-stage learners and those with full competence (see p. 66). Thus findings in 1981, 1983, 1985 may be directly compared (Table 32). In 1981, 68.4 per cent of the 2,808 Italian-speaking pupils were considered to be fluent in English, a higher percentage than the average for the group of European language speakers as a whole (60.8 per cent). In this, their fluency was more like that of French, Maltese and Polish speakers rather than Greek, Spanish or Portuguese speakers. Indeed over two-thirds of Italian-speaking pupils were considered to be fluent in English, compared with less than half (46.7 per cent) of all foreign language speakers. Although 31.6 per cent of Italian speakers – a slight increase on the 1978 figure – were considered to be less than fully competent in English, over half of this group were placed at the third stage of learning English, again very similar to French speakers. In 1983, although fewer foreign language speakers overall were rated fluent in English (43.4 per cent), the number of Italian speakers rated as fully competent in English rose to 70.5 per cent, exceeding the average for all European language speakers (61.3 per cent) and again being most like Polish and French speakers in their levels of performance rather than other southern European language speakers. Similarly, in 1985, although only 36.7 per cent of foreign language speakers were rated fluent, 68.6 per cent of Italian speakers were considered fully competent in English, again exceeding the average for all European language speakers (57.5 per cent).

Table 32:   **Stages of competence in English of Italian-speaking pupils in ILEA, 1981, 1983 and 1985**

Year	Beginners %	Second stage %	Third stage %	Fluent %	Total N
1981	4.6	9.8	17.3	68.4	2808
1983	3.4	9.5	16.2	70.5	2421
1985	4.7	8.7	17.7	68.6	2102

Sources: ILEA language census, 1981, 1983 and 1985, adapted from ILEA, 1982, 1983, Appendix 4; 1986, Appendix 5.

These data are further indications (see pp. 226–31) of linguistic shift towards English on the part of pupils of Italian origin. Moreover, this appears to be greater and at a higher level of competence than for other pupils from other southern European backgrounds and communities with similar migration histories and cultural orientations. Unfortunately, however, research evidence does not make it possible to judge whether fluency in English is at the expense of fluency in the Italian dialect which is the mother tongue, or what part attitudes towards English, Italian dialects and Standard Italian may play in affecting the range of linguistic competence. Moreover, in the complete absence of explicit research data on performance on standardized reading and writing tests in English, it is not possible to assess the relative oral–aural and literacy skills of pupils of Italian origin. Undoubtedly, however, the English competence of pupils of Italian origin is likely to be influenced by that of their parents. Research indicates that although this will naturally vary from individual to individual, according to opportunity, need, interest and attitudes, for some Italian adults oral skills in English may be considerable. As more of the second generation of Italians wholly educated in the UK, become parents the language shift towards English seems likely to intensify, with implications for increased competence amongst the third generation.

LANGUAGE USE

It is important to attempt to assess claims made by researchers, teachers, Italian adults and pupils of Italian origin about language knowledge and proficiency. One way in which this may be done is to examine reported uses of languages and dialects in different social contexts. Several researches – usually the same studies and surveys from which information has been drawn regarding language knowledge and competence – have attempted some kind of sociolinguistic assessment of patterns of language use amongst different Italian communities and households, either by observational study, with varying degrees of involvement over time, or by questionnaire. Research evidence on language use by Italian adults and children focusses on language use in the community, in the home, between parents and children, siblings, friends and other household members. Information available for the Italian community in Bedford reveals changing patterns of language usage over 20 years, and this may be compared with evidence from other Italian communities in London, Coventry and Scotland. The studies indicate the diversity of factors involved in attempting to assess the rationale for language use. Interestingly, in view of findings on literacy, most available evidence concerns uses of oracy as, for example, the reading habits of Italians have not been studied as have those of some other linguistic minorities. Data are not divided here according to use of English, dialect or Standard Italian because the studies, largely reflecting practice, make no clear division. However, certain trends emerge. In particular, the language of communication between parents and children and between siblings is of especial interest in relation to its influence on a child's education. Obviously language use is affected by proficiency in a language and also attitudes to language (pp. 222–36).

The predominance of dialect in the oral skills of first-generation Italian adults and the reasons for competence in dialect rather than Standard Italian have been demonstrated (see pp. 243–7). Brown (1970) records that the Italian men who arrived in Bedford in the early 1950s to work in the brickworks wanted above all to live in their own way amongst their own people. By this, they did not just intend Italians as such, but those from their own district or village in order that they could speak in a local dialect. Even in the lodging-houses, they contrived to live with others from their own district to facilitate communication and accustomed lifestyles. Studies of the Italian community in Bedford indicate that for the first generation community contiguity continued to be of prime importance even when housing mobility became possible (see p. 211). Tosi's research (1984) describes in detail how Italians have continued to use the village dialect as the medium of communication at home, outside with kin members and with all Italians within the community. But it is mixed and alternated with elements of Standard Italian and English (see p. 223) according to the topic involved and the language of which the speaker feels the interlocutor has a better command. Amongst the first generation communication between children, close relatives and members of the extended family group is in dialect since the circle includes people from the same village and topics of conversation concern everyday life – the household, relations in Italy, family events, children and celebrations. Limited use of words in Standard Italian or English covering official business or administration not encountered in village life sometimes occurs, but may need to be paraphrased in dialect to ensure the interlocutor's comprehension. Standard Italian is more frequently used in conversation between a member of the community and a new arrival, to a northern visitor, in consulate offices or in the church confessional, though it includes continuous interference from dialect. When first-generation Italians come into contact with English people in shops, hospitals, schools and local authority offices, they use English. Old people, however, have not learnt English, but their interactions have been confined within their community.

The survival knowledge of English developed by most working people enables them to hold basic conversations, especially with a specific practical purpose, but interpretation is often still necessary at work (p. 232) between English and dialect. Two dialects rather than Standard Italian are used independently in informal interactions between members of different villages. Such conversations may also include English when the topics concern experiences and practical matters relating to life outside the community such as shopping, work, unions, transport, health and social security. This occurs in Italian shops, clubs and the consular offices as well as in the streets outside work, school and offices. English is usually incorporated into a sentence as a quotation or expression of, for example, approval or advice (see also p. 232). Tosi (1984) cites numerous examples of English transfers in the speech of Italians in Bedford which are necessary for basic communication as either the dialects lack equivalents or the interlocutors lack the vocabulary in Standard Italian. Tosi concludes that:

> In Bedford it appears that the significance of most cases of linguistic interferences among immigrants is to be found specifically in the conflict between their rural experiences and their new needs in an urban environment, rather than in phenomena of language contact typical of an 'incipient bilingualism'. (ibid., p. 101)

However, whereas the positions of English, Standard Italian and dialect appeared to be homogeneous for first-generation Italians in Bedford on account of their common social background, uniform level of education and similar life experiences in the new urban environment, for the second-generation in Bedford different patterns of language use, functions, competence and confidence apply in relation to dialect and English. These affect attitudes to learning Italian at school and interest in maintaining bilingualism and biliteracy. Until school age the second generation have an intensive exposure to hearing dialect relating to the essentials of home life spoken by their parents, with some English words, relating to experiences and concepts outside the home, interspersed. Many pre-school, second-generation Italian children in Bedford who are looked after by their grandmothers, often with other Italian children, because both parents are usually working, speak Italian dialect with their grand-parents (Tosi, reported by Simons, 1980). Second-generation children also tend to speak in dialect with their parents, copying them in the use of English loan words. Tosi (1984) has claimed that pre-school age children rarely hear English spoken by native-speaking adults unless they have been fortunate enough to enjoy the scarce nursery facilities in Bedford. However, they are likely to have increasing contacts with older English-speaking children, second-generation relatives, and to be exposed to English through TV (see also Jackson, 1979; Simons, 1980). When there are several children in the household, they often speak English amongst themselves. Thus, although second-generation children, according to Tosi, are predominantly dialect-speaking on entry to school many, especially younger siblings, have already become used to hearing English albeit mainly from non-native speakers and more often in a fragmentary form, and in terms of vocabulary rather than syntax. At the early stages of schooling English is used at school and with friends, and dialect is used with parents at home. By their early teens the responses of children in English even in the home and to parents have substantially increased.

It is not, therefore, surprising to find that as the second-generation Italians in Bedford have become adults – and, in turn, parents – they should increasingly use English in communications. Simons (1980) reported that teachers in the MTCP in Bedford in the late 1970s observed that second-generation Italian parents who had experienced their education in the UK tended to speak English to their children. In a few cases where the father, for example, had more education than usual and may have undertaken further education and training, Standard Italian was likely to be spoken to a greater extent. In some families there was a mixed use of language with, for example, the father speaking in Standard Italian and the mother in English. Third-generation children whose parents used English at home started school speaking English. Thus in Bedford a complex language pattern exists amongst the large Italian population. Amongst the first generation there has been a gradual evolution of dialect to incorporate some English and some Standard Italian features. Hence there is a considerable mixed use of language within families with an increasing emphasis on English amongst the second generation which is passed on to the third. This was demonstrated in Jackson's (1979) case study observation, even in the mid-1970s. The first-generation parents spoke in the dialect of the villages near Campobassa or Agrigento, and the mother had great difficulty in understanding Italians from other provinces. The language of the adult elder brother, one of the intermediate generation who experienced most of his schooling in the UK, was broken English. The mother spoke both dialect and English to the two younger second-generation children, who used dialect reluctantly with their parents and increasingly spoke English.

Similar patterns of language development have been described for Italians in Scotland (Farrell, 1983), London (Weston, 1979) and Leicester (King and Zolli, 1981), although the rate of change towards use of English and Standard Italian has depended on the distinctive characteristics and needs of the different communities. As in London, Italian immigration to Scotland is of long standing. By 1975 the Italian Consulate in Edinburgh estimated that there were 30,000 Italians in Scotland, but the Italian community there is widely dispersed and does not have a centre comparable to Bedford, with its post-war immigrants, partly due to their independence and self-employment. These factors militated against social interaction to facilitate linguistic and cultural maintenance. Farrell claims that the language of the second generation born in Scotland was English, and although some spoke Italian at home, few became fully bilingual. Parents conversed in dialect but would speak to their children in English. Even when children used Italian when small, its use at home diminished as they grew older to vanish at secondary school age, so that if they were able to study Italian at their Catholic schools, they learnt the language as foreigners. Farrell suggests several reasons for the widespread failure to develop bilingualism: the intention that immigration was permanent; the easy and quick integration of the Italian families; and the deeply rooted bewilderment and uncertainty over the validity of their dialects, felt especially by the southern immigrants in relation to those from Barga in Tuscany, though they also shared such doubts despite access to the Tuscan language which became Standard Italian. Yet Italian persisted in Christian names, the vocabulary of cuisine and family relationships. Like Tosi, Farrell gives examples of English words transferred into the dialect spoken. However, even in Italian clubs, banks and in various associational activities, the language most frequently used is English. Some claims, nevertheless, have been made of a revival of interest in Italian amongst the third and fourth generations.

A study of 24 Italian families from central and southern Italy in two areas of London suggests that the composition of the community may still have a considerable influence on first-generation Italian adults' language use. Weston (1979) found that in one highly organized community which drew Italians with varied regional origins together it was necessary for them to communicate in Standard Italian, whereas in the other area because their place of origin was similar they tended to use dialect. At home parents used dialect or a mixture of dialect and English, or dialect, Standard Italian and English, but by the age of 14 the children studied spoke only English even in response to their parents, and apparently with the same London accents as their friends.

In another study amongst the Italian community in Leicester, in 1978, King and Zolli (1981) also found mixed language use within the home. They interviewed 72 Italian adults – 18 per cent of the Italian families in Leicester. Sixty-four adults were married, nine Italian men married to English women and eight Italian women married to English, Polish or Ukrainian men. The majority of Italians were of rural origin from the central and southern provinces. Fifty-six had arrived in Leicester between 1956 and 1969, attracted by industrial employment in manufacturing and services, some migrating from other areas of Britain where they had been employed in agriculture. The researchers observed many varied patterns of language use in the families. Usually parents spoke to each other in Italian dialect, and to their children in Italian. However, sometimes parents addressed children in English, or addressed children in Italian, who replied in English. All younger children used English with their playmates.

Findings from these local observational studies are usefully complemented by more precisely categorized quantitative data reported from the LMP questionnaire survey. This tends to confirm differences according to location. Table 33 shows the patterns of language use between adult respondents in the ALUS (see pp. 224–5 for sample and survey details) and other household members, irrespective of language skills. All of these interactions involve at least one adult.

Table 33: Languages used between Italian adults and all other household members

N = household members excluding respondents		% of interlocutors using only or mostly minority language* reciprocally with respondents	% of interlocutors using only or mostly English reciprocally with respondents	% of interlocutors using both English and minority language reciprocally with respondents
Coventry	284	21	37	19
London	269	34	16	20

* 'Minority language' here includes Italian dialects.
Source: Adapted from LMP, 1983a, Table 5.8.

These figures exemplify a pattern of mixed language use both across households and locations. In fact in half the cases in London and over two-fifths in Coventry there was a mixed pattern of language use in which one person spoke in English, the other Italian, or both Italian or English were spoken by both parties (Smith *et al.*, 1984; Reid *et al.*, 1985). It is interesting to note that, whereas about a fifth of interlocutors and respondents in both locations used both English and Italian reciprocally, the percentages using only or mostly English or Italian are reversed for the two locations. Indeed the percentage of Italian households in Coventry where the members use only or mostly English was greater than for any other linguistic minority and over the three locations surveyed in the LMP as a whole, suggesting that the language shift to English has advanced further with them than with other linguistic minorities. This may have been related to the level of language skills available to speakers (see Table 31).

Further analysis of unconstrained choice of language use between respondents and family members with a fair knowledge of English and Italian revealed that under a third of Italian-speaking bilinguals in Coventry and only about a third in London claimed to use Italian all or most of the time (Table 34).

Table 34: Languages used between bilingual Italians and other bilingual family members

No. of persons in households including respondents		A No. of pairs of interlocutors both knowing English and minority language fairly or very well	B % of A where minority language used reciprocally all or most of the time	C % of A where English used reciprocally all or most of the time
Coventry	394	80	31	16
London	367	95	17 (+20)*	2

* Number in brackets is for Italian dialects used reciprocally.
Source: Adapted from LMP, 1983a, Table 5.9.

This was the lowest proportion across all locations of any minority language group claiming to use the minority language. Only persons brought up overseas were more likely to use the minority language reciprocally, even when bilingual. Although, as with other language speakers, only a small proportion of bilingual Italians in London claimed to use English reciprocally with other bilingual family members all or most of the time, some 16 per cent, a much higher proportion than for any other language group, claimed to do so in Coventry. In fact almost 16 per cent of the Italian-speaking adult respondents in Coventry claimed that their parents had used English in speaking to them when they were children (LMP, 1985). Overall the figures suggest predominant mixed use of Italian (Standard and dialect) and English amongst bilingual household members.

Further analysis of language use in the workplace, community and in free-time activities indicates that for the Italians in Coventry lifestyles and living conditions were less conducive to and supportive of use of Italian than for Italians in London. This may have been compounded by the low socioeconomic status and levels of formal education of the original migrants for many of whom Standard Italian was a second language (Smith *et al.*, 1984; Reid *et al.*, 1985). For example, two-thirds of the Italian-speaking respondents in work in London compared with two-fifths in Coventry had at least one fellow Italian-speaking worker in the same establishment, and over a quarter and nearly a third worked in establishments where all the staff could speak Italian or had a boss who spoke Italian compared with very few of the Italians in Coventry. This reflects the employment structure in these two locations and the occupations (see p. 224) of these workers, with almost two-thirds in Coventry speaking or reading only or mostly English in their work. Moreover, although nearly two-thirds of the respondents in both Coventry and London participated in at least one ethnic organization, in London three-quarters mentioned clubs or associations where all the members were Italian speakers compared with half in Coventry. Indeed a third of London Italians, compared with only a quarter of Coventry Italians, spoke Italian with the person with whom they spent most free time. Coventry Italians were far less likely than London Italians to have Italian-speaking neighbours or an Italian doctor, and three-quarters compared with almost all of the London Italians went sometimes to a shop where Italian was spoken.

The ALUS also reveals some interesting supplementary data on the language use of children in the household when speaking to each other. Some 86 per cent of the 57 children in Italian-speaking households in Coventry and 83 per cent of 59 in London were reported to use only or mostly English when speaking to one another. These were amongst the highest rates for any minority language group, exceeded only by children from Polish-speaking households in Coventry (91 per cent) and similar to those for children from Greek-speaking households in London (82 per cent).

Another part of the LMP, the Secondary Pupils Survey (SPS), which involved around 150 bilingual 11-year-olds in Peterborough in 1980 (the majority Italian, Punjabi and Urdu speakers, in almost equal numbers) and 230 bilingual 14-year-olds (mostly Punjabi or Urdu speakers) in Bradford in 1981, provides an analysis of language use with family members which confirms the general pattern indicated by ALUS and other studies reviewed here. In Peterborough 22 Italian-speaking pupils claimed to use Italian with their families and 16 both English and Italian, as did most of the few Italian-speaking children in Bradford. In Peterborough only seven out of 32 Italian-speaking children used only Italian when speaking to their fathers and 17 out of 23 reported using only English to their brothers, a single speaker using only Italian. The Italian-speaking children were much more likely to report a greater use of English with their families than South Asian language speakers. The SPS has also apparently been used in Bedford in 1981 and used as learning material within the ILEA, but unfortunately data do not appear to be available.

Finally, turning to consider the uses of literacy amongst Italian adults and their children, the research evidence is extremely sparse. Indeed research evidence on the literacy of Italian speakers is itself scant (see p.223,226). Available data from the

LMP indicate relatively low literacy skills amongst the working-class adult Italian population compared with other minority language speakers both for Italian and English. This is likely to influence considerably Italian adults' reading and writing habits, together with other factors such as access to books and leisure-time. Nevertheless, it appears that with the exception of the LMP data there is a genuine gap in research here, especially since the Italian population has not formed an object for study by research librarians as other linguistic minority groups in the London area have done. It is not known whether this is related to the spread of Italians throughout London and elsewhere, or whether assumptions have been made about the literacy of this group. But the lack of research on Italians' use of literacy is in line with the generally low level of mainstream research interest in Italians as a sociolinguistic group.

Although sources generally suggest that, for example, the majority of Italian immigrants to Bedford had low literacy skills (see p.222), the existence of *La Voce degli Italiani,* the fortnightly newspaper for Italians in Britain, produced according to Brown (1970) by the Scalabrini missionaries in Bedford, suggested that there was some proficiency in, and use of, literacy at this level. Indeed the ALUS of the LMP discovered that over two-thirds of the Italian respondents in Coventry and over four-fifths in London sometimes read newspapers in Italian, and four-fifths in each location read newspapers in English. Not surprisingly, this was much greater than their reading of textbooks or novels. Whereas somewhat fewer than half the respondents in both locations read textbooks in English, two-fifths of Italian speakers in London, twice as many as those in Coventry, read textbooks in Italian. Whereas half the Italian speakers in London read novels in Italian compared with less than a third in Coventry, the latter were more likely to read novels in English (two-fifths) compared with less than a third in London. Location did not, however, affect knowledge and use of the library service. Although about three-fifths of Italian-speaking respondents in both locations knew that local libraries stocked books in Italian, fewer than a third sometimes used the libraries at all, and of these only about a quarter sometimes borrowed books in Italian. Moreover, only one in five of the Italian speakers in Coventry and one in six in London sometimes used an interpreter, such as a family member or friend, to complete official forms. On the other hand, low-level literacy skills may result in some mixed language expedients. For example, it is interesting that Weston observed that since three-quarters of the parents in a sample of 24 families in London could not write in English, written communication, for example, with the milkman, was generally in two languages, Italian and English.

Similarly, there is little information about the uses of literacy of children of Italian origin. In Elliott's (1981) survey, involving ten Italian-speaking pupils in one Italian language school in Hackney, all except one of whom were second generation, and all of whom claimed to read Italian at least a little, it was found that only six books were claimed to have been read in Italian in the months prior to the interview, whereas ten books were said to have been read in English. Moreover, in all cases the book titles were mentioned in English, which as Elliott pointed out might indicate the pupils' preference for reading in English or that they wanted to show that they were more fluent in English or that there were insufficient books to read in Standard Italian. Furthermore, whereas the Italian children liked reading magazines, comics, stories, and factual books in English, they liked reading comics, stories and books about their parents' country of origin in Italian (see also Jackson, 1979). There may be a lack of suitable reading materials for children of Italian origin in this country (see Baldwin *et al.*, 1980). Certainly no mention has been found of books featuring pupils of Italian origin in a British context. Due to the lack of library research on the Italian communities in Britain, little is known of the current extent of library provision in Italian, though Cooke (1979) recorded that in the 1970s five local authorities outside London made provision for children's books in Italian. The evidence, such as it is, does not indicate extensive reading in Italian, apart from newspapers, either on the part of Italian immigrant parents or their children, who are likely to find it considerably easier to read in English than Standard Italian. The extent of their reading in Italian is likely to depend very much on whether their literacy has been encouraged by their parents and developed through their attendance at Italian language classes.

Overall research evidence of various kinds demonstrates the increasing use of English in everyday life by the Italian population in the UK, especially for the second, third and fourth generations. That several generations co-exist in certain locations makes for a varied and mixed pattern of language use. The language of communication between Italian adults in their communities, outside the home and kinship group, will depend on several factors such as generation, interaction with other dialect speakers and relative competence of the interlocutors in Standard Italian and English. The evident language shift towards English in the Italian-speaking communities is mirrored in the home. Although first-generation parents may still communicate in dialect, possibly interspersed with English, there appears to be a considerable use of both English and Italian at home, and increasingly and especially with second-generation parents use of English all or most of the time. As is to be expected, school is an important influence on the shift towards greater use of English amongst the second generation, as is the presence of older siblings and the TV, so that by adolescence children are likely to respond in English to parents who speak to them in dialect, and prefer to use English, tending to use Italian forms only when necessary. Evidence suggests that second-generation parents bring up their children as English speakers. All studies concur that children from the intermediate, second and third generations speak to one another in English. Although lack of evidence does not permit conclusions to be drawn about Italian adults' and children's use of literacy, indications of many adults' relatively low literacy skills, mainly due to lack of educational opportunities and need to acquire literacy skills in Italian or English, suggests that reading habits may not be a particularly significant aspect of first-generation lifestyles. Even if they have learnt Italian at language classes, the second and subsequent generations are likely to have greater literacy in English and hence their reading habits will tend to utilize these skills.

LANGUAGE ATTITUDES
Attitudes to a language are generally considered to be significant in affecting the acquisition of a proficiency in that language. It is, therefore, important to examine available research evidence on Italian parents' and children's attitudes to dialect, Standard Italian and English and the significance of these languages for their sense of identity. Unfortunately, although there is considerable evidence both from large-scale language censuses and surveys and closer observational studies of the knowledge of, and to a lesser extent, the use of dialect, Standard Italian and English by Italian adults and children, there is in contrast very little direct evidence on their attitudes to these different languages. Nevertheless, a picture can be built up from the observations and comments made by researchers who have been involved directly with Italian-speaking parents and children. Attitudes to languages will thus be considered more indirectly here through evidence on Italian parents' orientation towards Italy and towards their children learning Italian; children's attitudes to dialect and learning Standard Italian, and observations about the

interrelation of their language attitudes and developing identities. Comparatively
little information is available on adults' or children's attitudes to English.

In the research literature on first-generation Italians in the UK there is above all
a sense of ambivalence in their orientation towards Italy and the UK. Hence their
status as immigrants or migrants and their commitment to settle and a future in the
UK has, at least for the first generation, been a matter of serious debate. Clearly
such ambivalence affects attitudes to language, especially but not only amongst
Italian adults. The first generation have deep cultural roots in the Italian
countryside and their villages of origin, and their emotional attachment is renewed
by frequent return visits. During these visits the second generation also come to
have direct appreciation in their background of their Italian heritage. All the
evidence suggests that the majority of first-generation Italian adults have a strong
desire to return to their region of origin. This may also be strongly felt by the
intermediate generation, born in Italy but who have grown up in the UK, and even
some of the UK-born second-generation, though the evidence on this is less clear.
Indeed research and statistics (e.g. MacDonald and MacDonald, 1972; King,
1977a) demonstrate that the desire to return is not just a dream, but in the early
1970s at least return became an actuality for many when migration exceeded
immigration. This process appears to be unique to Italians amongst immigrant
groups. However, one of the major and increasing constraints on the return of
first-generation Italians to Italy (apart from social and economic processes of
'estrangement' and 'disengagement' described and analysed by Palmer, 1977, 1980)
is the very existence of the second and third generation in the UK. In view of close
family ties amongst the Italians, this provokes somewhat divided loyalties between
family and homeland.

Moreover, it is clear that both church and state, in the form of the Italian
Catholic Mission and the Italian Consulate, have taken significant positive action
towards maintaining the Italian connection for the Italian population in the UK.
Through religious, social and educational organizations, they have enhanced the
the Italian orientation of Italian adults and their children not just in a narrow local
or regional sense, but by introducing a wider national perspective. Probably the
most far-reaching way in which this has occurred is through the widespread
provision of language classes in Standard Italian both for Italian adults and
children. The classes financed by the Italian government, with help from the social
fund of the EC, are sometimes organized in conjunction with mainstream
schools. The very existence of such classes with the backing of government and
church support appear to have reinforced through community pressure any
personal inclination Italian adults may have had to ensure that their children
developed skills in Standard Italian in addition to oral skills in the parents' dialect.
Since the language classes are not engaged in mother tongue (dialect) maintenance
as such, their aim is not strictly to enhance communication between parents and
children or between children and their relatives in Italy. Parents' motivation for
sending their children to classes (see also pp.258–9) seems to be not only to
facilitate communication amongst different dialect speakers in the UK, but also to
ensure greater likelihood of adaptation to life in Italy in case of return, given the
increasing use of Standard Italian throughout the country in the last 20 years. But
the very fact that Italian parents are keen for their children to attend such classes is
in itself indicative not only of their attitude to the Italian language, but to their
Italian connection as such.

The strength of the attachment felt by Italians to their homeland and languages
may be illustrated by a few examples mentioned in the research literature. Simons
(1980) recorded that the cultural links of the intermediate generation of Bedford

Italians were still very strong, and their expressed desires to return to Italy had an important effect on the motivation and interest of their own children who were involved in learning Standard Italian as part of the Mother Tongue and Culture Project (MTCP). In his in-depth study of the linguistic repertoire of Italians in Bedford, Tosi (1984) observed that kinship and dialect loyalties were responsible for the maintenance of village vernaculars in their homes. The first generation were conscious of their mixed linguistic habits (see pp. 237–9) and keen to discuss their experiences, use of and access to English, Standard Italian and dialect but thought of their dialects as a corruption of proper Italian. Parents of children involved in the MTCP saw the programme as assisting their reintegration in the Italian school in case of return. Their unanimous support for the teaching of Standard Italian rather than their dialect was sustained by their eagerness to help their children overcome dialectism which they saw as an obstacle in the achievement of national identity and social emancipation. However, Tosi claimed that they underestimated their children's difficulties in learning Standard Italian as speakers of dialect.

Although lack of education and relatively low literacy of many first-generation Italian parents may have caused them difficulty in actively developing their children's skills in Standard Italian (see p. 226), they may not have prevented them encouraging their children's literacy in Italian in the home, as Jackson (1979) observed. Moreover, half the Italian pupils in an Italian class studied by Elliott (1981) reported that their parents read to them and told them stories in Italian, whereas only two parents were said to do so in English. The encouragement given by these Italian parents was, however, considerably less than that of other minority language speakers, for example, Polish, Greek, or Spanish parents, and more like that of Chinese and Gujerati parents. Italian parents may perforce be more inclined to rely upon language classes to instil in their children both positive attitudes towards Standard Italian and proficiency in it.

What attitudes are displayed by children of Italian origin towards dialect and Standard Italian? In the context of language learning Weston's (1979) observations on the attitudes displayed by pupils of Italian origin to Standard Italian are of great interest (see pp. 259–60). When teaching Italian, she experienced great difficulty in persuading the 14-year-old pupils to express themselves in Italian since they naturally spoke to her in English. They showed great reluctance to speak in Italian, reverting to English as soon as possible. However, she did not necessarily interpret this pattern in their language behaviour as a sign of resistance to learning Italian since all the pupils stated that they wished to learn Italian at their mainstream school rather than in out-of-school courses. The Swann Report (GB.P. H of C, 1985) also records that, according to Tosi, children studying Italian outside school hours 'sensed the negative connotations and wondered why it was not thought "good enough" for schools to teach, quite apart from the additional burden of having to attend classes in the evenings and at weekends' (p. 706). Weston (1979) felt that pupils' reluctance to speak Italian was because they felt shame when they realized the gap between their parents' dialects as spoken at home and the teacher's Standard Italian. The importance of community support for Italian language learning was also highlighted. In this area of London, which lacked a structured Italian community, adolescent pupils often displayed their resentment towards things Italian by rejecting the Italian language classes. In this, they attempted to identify with the majority group rather than what they perceived as a low-prestige minority group, using their rejection of the language class in an attempt to resolve their life between two cultures. On the other hand, Weston reported that such a regressive phase might be checked by encouraging suitable pupils to join an examination class. Although two-thirds said that if their parents emigrated to Italy they would do so too, and four-fifths claimed that they wanted to marry an Italian born and brought up in England, Weston thought these responses might have resulted from parental pressure. Many pupils seemed to have both an integrative and instrumental type of motivation towards learning Italian and intended to teach it to their children. But Weston argued that pressure exercised by British society, which assumes that a bilingual or bicultural individual may be at a disadvantage, acted upon these Italian adolescents whose desire to conform was greater than their natural enthusiasm for the language and culture of their parents' country of origin.

In common with many other second-generation children from minority language backgrounds, adolescent Italians have frequently been reported to be reluctant to address or respond to their parents in dialect, preferring to speak in English, even if this might invoke the ire of their fathers (Simons, 1980; Jackson, 1979; Tosi, 1984). In Bedford, Tosi (1984) has observed that speaking English is important to children of Italian origin in conferring membership of the peer group and that the local accent communicates cohesion across the diversity of surnames and skin colours. English is also associated with certain values absorbed through education and the TV. However, young Italians soon come to realize through personal and emotional conflicts that 'the two languages, their speakers and the different values that they independently communicate, were not naturally created to co-exist in the same environment' (p. 112). Tosi categorizes the second-generation's response in terms of the 'apathetic', 'in-group' or 'rebel reaction' (see also p. 303). Linguistically the 'apathetic reaction', which he considers to be that of the majority of adolescents and young second-generation Italians in Bedford, involves becoming as English as possible, thus 'a sharp tendency to monolingualism in English after a transitional state of bilingualism with the Italian dialect' (p. 116). Tosi considers this response is assisted by the lack of facilities in Bedford, both within the community and mainstream schools at primary and middle levels, to extend their bilingualism. By contrast, the 'in-group' reaction is to identify with Italian family life, community and the perpetuation of transitional bilingualism of English and Italian dialect. The two linguistic repertoires relate to separate roles, but since social roles requiring English are restricted to work and occasional contacts outside the community, opportunities for development of English are limited. Few members of the second generation are said to respond as 'rebels'. This reaction which involves an awareness of and an attempt to investigate the conflicting roles and values of both communities requires, according to Tosi, a deep familiarity with life and society in Italy, literacy in and a full command of Standard Italian. Linguistically the 'rebels' are bilingual individuals who can speak dialect and are able to function equally well in English and Standard Italian. In Tosi's opinion such a linguistic repertoire has not been observed amongst those merely exposed to community language classes as such provision 'seldom succeeds in helping the children overcome negative associations in their overall social and linguistic behaviour' (ibid., p. 118; Tosi, 1980a).

Such insights are helpful in indicating some of the factors involved in attempting to describe the attitudes of Italian parents and children towards dialect, Standard Italian and, by implication, English. But apart from the considerable evidence of language shift to English amongst the second generation (see pp. 234–6) there is little evidence of Italian adults' attitudes towards learning English or their children's acquisition of English. Here there is another gap in the research literature. The range of Italian adults' competence in English shown by research evidence (see pp. 232–4) – from the survival English of many first-generation Italians who rely on the help of their children in negotiations with the wider society to the considerable fluency, and possible literacy, of others, especially the second generation – suggests a range of attitudes to English. Even though the second generation educated in the UK – and increasingly the parents of the present and coming generation of pupils of Italian origin in schools – are apparently likely to speak English at home to their children (Simons, 1980), research has not directly assessed either their attitudes towards English or their use of it. Do Italian adults have an instrumental or integrative attitude towards English? Do they accept their children's acquisition of English as a practical necessity because of living in the UK in an English-medium environment with schooling in English, or resent and regret this? Do they see the use of Standard Italian, English and the continuation of dialect as compatible or mutually exclusive? Research can provide no direct answers to such questions. There is, moreover, a dearth of information on the attitudes of first-generation Italians towards learning English. Townsend and Brittan (1972) record that some mainstream schools had received requests from Italian adults to provide English-language tuition, but it is not clear whether provision was made in schools or through evening classes at further education colleges.

It seems possible that community pressure for Italian adults to attend classes in Standard Italian run by the Italian Consulate may have been greater, and that the orientation towards second-language learning amongst first-generation Italian adults may have been much more towards the acquisition of Standard Italian than English (Weston, 1979). The motivation was in order to facilitate communication between different dialect speakers amongst Italian communities in the UK and because of the continuing orientation towards the region of origin and the desire to return there. Ironically, however, first-generation Italians may consider themselves merely temporary residents in the UK, with a wish to return which may be partly linked to limited English skills and a consequent social isolation from the wider community. But also, conversely, their orientation towards the social and cultural values of their regions of origin at the time of emigration have considerably influenced their attitudes towards living in the UK (ibid.; Tosi, 1979a). These attitudes obviously vary from individual to individual and family to family, the area of origin and Italian community to which they belong in this country. But the irony goes further, as researchers have observed. Though the desire of first-generation Italians to return may be great, they would return to a country where industrialization and urbanization have displaced agricultural traditions and resulted in social and linguistic emancipation for many of their villages. Hence, as Palmer (1980) has described, returnees are increasingly estranged even on temporary visits. The retention of local dialects and traditions by the first-generation Italians in the UK may actually add to the difficulties of adaptation for those who return. Moreover, Weston (1979) has claimed that the Standard Italian of her subjects would prove inadequate, rendering them linguistically isolated in their home villages. Indeed Tosi has suggested that the first, intermediate and second generations have standards of linguistic competence which are below those required for re-integration into southern Italian rural communities and also for social emancipation in the UK. By contrast, Weston has claimed that the second generation have a basic competence in Standard Italian and the motivation to develop their knowledge, though they lack favourable learning conditions. In considering the education of pupils of Italian origin in the UK, it is therefore important to appraise research evidence on their learning of Standard Italian in classes both inside and outside mainstream schooling. For clearly the attitudes which pupils of Italian origin display towards the learning of Standard Italian, and their proficiency in it, may not be merely a matter of academic interest, but may vitally affect their future choices both as to lifestyle and actual residential location.

'MOTHER-TONGUE' TEACHING

Doposcuola
One way of assessing the strength of the Italian connection for Italian parents and their children in the UK is by examining the extent to which they participate in various organizations which reinforce their cultural and linguistic identity. The provision of Italian language classes for pupils of Italian origin in the UK may be seen as one of the most potent forces in encouraging and developing a link through language and culture with the parents' country of origin. Clearly the first generation of Italian adults have maintained a strong orientation towards their social and cultural origins in the villages of Italy. It is significant, therefore, to consider to what extent Italian parents desire that their children should develop a consciousness of their cultural roots and familiarity with traditions not only through everyday communication in the home, but by specifically encouraging their children to attend Italian language classes.

In considering the arrangements for Italian-language teaching for pupils of Italian origin, it is necessary to draw attention to two features which distinguish provision for Italian speakers compared with many other pupils who also speak a language other than English. As already described (see p.237), the home language of pupils of Italian origin is not usually Standard Italian, but an Italian dialect and often of southern origin. The precise way in which dialects differ from Standard Italian and the facility with which dialect speakers may learn Standard Italian seem to be matters for debate (see e.g. Tosi, 1984). But there is a real sense in which pupils of Italian origin attending Italian-language classes where Standard Italian is taught are not being encouraged to maintain their mother tongue as such, but are learning a new, though related, language. Thus it is misleading to refer to these classes as providing mother-tongue teaching in the same sense as mother-tongue classes for many other linguistic minority pupils.

Secondly, it is important to distinguish between Italian language classes which take place in out-of-school hours (*Doposcuola*) and those which take place within mainstream schooling, often as part of the timetabled curriculum. This is for two main reasons. First, Italian is sometimes taught as a second or third foreign language in secondary schools, often mainly to pupils of non-Italian origin. Secondly, the nature and organization of provision for the teaching of Italian to pupils of Italian origin has been greatly influenced by the direct support of the Italian government. The *extent* of involvement of the 'home government' in Italian teaching in the UK is a peculiar feature of language teaching arrangements for pupils from linguistic minority backgrounds, though other governments, such as the Spanish and Portuguese, also have mother-tongue teaching arrangements.

The *Corsi Integrativi*, under the auspices of the Italian government, take place in several contexts: after school or on Saturdays (*Doposcuola*) or in some cases as part of the normal school day, either in the timetable or on a withdrawal basis (*Corsi Inseriti*). Classes must have a minimum number of pupils and at least 50 per cent of pupils of Italian origin, although the remaining children can be of British or other ethnic backgrounds. Under this arrangement the Italian government supplies teachers and resources. A review of available information on provision for Italian language classes as part of the timetabled curriculum in mainstream schooling, which may be a joint enterprise by the Italian government and LEAs – or by LEAs and schools alone – and examination entries and performance in Italian is presented in the following sub-section (see pp.263–83). Clearly extra-mural classes and mainstream classes are complementary and may exist alongside each other in schools and towns. However, the *Doposcuola* system caters for greater numbers than mainstream provision. In 1980 there were about 12,000 pupils attending *Corsi Integrativi* distributed in about 800 classes, among which about 2,000 pupils were attending some 160 classes as part of the normal school curriculum (*Corsi Inseriti*) (Mengon, 1980). At the beginning of the academic year in 1985 there were 9,000 pupils enrolled in 770 classes, of which about a third were *Corsi Inseriti* (Brogi, 1986).

This sub-section examines the extent of provision for Italian teaching in out-of-school hours (*Doposcuola*), its organization and administration, the level of instruction and the attitudes of pupils, parents and teachers to the classes. It also highlights some significant issues relating to the teaching of Italian to pupils of Italian origin in the *Doposcuola* system and in comparison with mainstream provision.

HISTORY AND DEVELOPMENT   The existence of Italian language schools goes back to the mid-1800s when the growing Italian community in London established its own schools, a church and hospital (King, 1977a). The Republican intellectual Mazzini, exiled in London from 1837, promoted 'Italianita' amongst his compatriots in London and had a special influence in shaping the community (Palmer, 1977). Mazzini initially started classes in a room in Clerkenwell which was later to become the Mazzini–Garibaldi Club, still one of the most important Italian institutions in London (Walker, 1982). King (1979) has recorded that Mazzini established an Italian school in Hatton Garden in 1841. The fate of these schools is, however, somewhat unclear. Palmer (1977) claims that the school in Clerkenwell 'did not endure', but according to Walker the school founded by Mazzini did not close until 1981, though its existence in the intervening years has not been described. Prior to the Second World War, the education of the Italian community in London received another fillip when, as part of Mussolini's attempt to organize the Italian community along fascist lines, his government underwrote an Italian school at Hyde Park Gate. Mengon (1980) has also noted the development of *Doposcuola* in these years, mainly for reasons of nationalistic prestige. Not surprisingly, these schools were not to survive the end of the war.

With the growth of the Italian community once again in the early 1950s, any initiatives to organize Italian language classes were made by interested individuals or religious organizations (ibid.). It is likely that at this time the Italian church, which as Brown (1970) has recorded was very active in the settlement of Italians in Bedford, was particularly influential in protecting the linguistic heritage of Italians as part of its role in community life. Moreover, Italian parents have apparently always been keen for their children to learn Italian (Tosi, 1980a). In Bedford they made requests to mainstream schools when they realized that courses were not available (Walker, 1963a). During the 1950s and 1960s Italian children benefited from initiatives made by the efforts of the community itself to provide Italian language and culture classes. But the dispersal of Italians throughout the UK, many with little schooling and with low standards of literacy, together with wide variations in their socioeconomic status, were considerable obstacles to the establishment and large-scale development of provision by the Italian communities themselves (Steedman, 1979). Thus subsequent involvement of the Italian government in organizing the Italian language classes seems to have arisen from local demand and pressure on the part of Italian parents (Saifullah Khan, 1976).

In 1971 the Italian government became directly involved in the provision of classes in Italian in conformity with Law 153. This led to the establishment of an administrative organizational structure to promote the teaching of Italian language and culture to Italians of all ages throughout the UK. Within this framework the

UK is divided into three regions or *circoscrizioni consolari* based on London, Manchester and Edinburgh. Through the Italian consulates administering these areas a number of *Direttori* or *Coordinatori Didattici* and *Presidenze* set up and supervise classes to teach Italian wherever there is sufficient demand. According to Saifullah Khan, in 1976 the Italian Embassy had education advisers in ten centres throughout Britain. The *Ispettorato Scolastico*, the Italian Central Education Office, is responsible for co-ordinating the network of Italian classes throughout the country (Weston, 1979; Tosi, 1980a). In 1986 there were eight *Direttori Didattici* co-ordinating the teachers and inspecting the curriculum for primary Italian teaching (one in Birmingham, Bradford, Edinburgh, Leeds, Manchester and Nottingham and two in London), and two *Presidenze* with the same function in respect of secondary Italian teaching.

The Italian government appoints and pays the salaries of about 150 qualified teachers, supplies books and, where necessary, pays for accommodation for classes. Hence fees from parents are not required. In addition, a certain standard of teaching is assured (Saifullah Khan, 1976; Steedman, 1979). Approximately half of the cost is contributed from the EC Social Fund, the remainder funded by the Italian government. In 1975 the Italian Exchequer funded Italian classes in Britain to the tune of £456,494, a 30 per cent increase on expenditure in 1974 (Saifullah Khan, 1976). Such assistance serves to instigate and support schemes throughout the country since there is a powerful incentive to start schools when administrative and financial responsibilities are reduced. Indeed the well-developed organiz-ational structure for the provision of Italian language classes appears to have influenced the extent to which financial assistance for voluntary classes has been forthcoming from LEAs (Tsow, 1983; see p.253). Nevertheless, despite this organizational framework, Italian language schools and classes have had problems because of practical constraints, the characteristics of the Italian community itself, the position of the voluntary language classes *vis-à-vis* the British educational system and parents' perceptions of the aims and objectives of language classes (Steedman, 1979, drawing on insights from teachers who compiled the 1977 Rapporto di Lavoro).

AIMS The aim of the Italian government in supporting the language classes was initially to maintain the Italian language and culture amongst emigrant communi-ties in order to facilitate reintegration in the event of a return to Italy. Provision was extended to all age-groups, including adults, in an attempt to remedy the deficiencies in the education of many Italian migrants in the 1930s – 1950s in southern Italy. But their educational deprivation has had a number of fundamental implications for the work of the *Direttori Didattici* as recognized in the Rapporto di Lavoro (1977) (Steedman, 1979). In particular, the Rapporto calls into question the cultural aims of the classes, recommending an exploratory approach, so that instead of transmitting a standard cultural package, the role of the teacher should be to ensure that the adult Italian immigrant is enabled to integrate his own cultural roots within the wider history and development of Italy as a whole – perhaps, through a study of migratory movements and their historical, political and social origins. As the Northamptonshire LEA report (1980) noted, the adult classes at an elementary and intermediate stage are, in effect, adult literacy classes. According to Steedman (1979), the Rapporto (1977) recorded increasing demands by Italian adults to study at the Italian classes, some working towards the Lincenza della Scuola Media (School Certificate) which in Peterborough, for example, is used as a basis for obtaining technical qualifications leading to skilled worker status. Thus, for adults, the Italian classes not only aim to compensate for earlier lack of educational opportunity and extend knowledge of Standard Italian and Italian culture as a whole, but they may also serve to promote socioeconomic mobility in the UK.

However, the main educational objectives of the Italian language classes supported by the Italian government are directed towards the children of Italian immigrants. The aims of Italian language courses for such pupils are both instrumental and effective. Since, as Steedman points out, the major problems for children of Italian descent are often cultural identity and communication with parents with a different cultural frame of reference, the classes aim both to strengthen the links between the generations of Italian families and to develop the child's self-confidence and personal sense of identity. The declared aim of *Corsi Integrativi* is that pupils of Italian origin should retain a sense of their parents' cultural heritage, since it is considered that this will enable them to establish better communication with their parents, and also because the preservation of that heritage is considered to be an important factor in the construction of personal identity and thereby a prerequisite for participation in British social life. Another apparently somewhat contradictory aim is that children should be enabled to re-join an Italian school without serious educational disadvantage if the family should decide to re-emigrate (Mengon, 1980; Brown, 1970).

Like parents from other linguistic minority communities in the UK, Italian adults may have several reasons for wanting their children to attend Italian language classes. Unfortunately, there is relatively little direct evidence of this. Saifullah Khan (1976) suggested that Italian parents may wish their children to learn Italian in order to keep them within the community, and to assist with communication with relatives during visits. Indeed the idea of learning a second language may not be strange for Italian adults, for had they attended schools in Italy, their children would also have been taught in Standard Italian. In a study of 24 Italian families, in two London areas, Weston (1979) found that the most common reason given by Italian parents for their 14-year-old children attending voluntary language classes was that the children would need to know Italian if they were to return to Italy, as in fact 84 per cent wished to do. Another motivation was parents' painful awareness that they themselves were not able to teach their children Standard Italian. On the other hand, Steedman (1979) has claimed that some Italian parents may see Italian classes as providing an opportunity for both their own socioeconomic mobility and that of their children. Hence the Rapporto noted the interest of Italian parents in opportunities for children to be able to study to GCE O- or A-level standard, with a view to facilitating aspirations to a higher social level and financial security. Yet Mengon (1980) has stated that Italian parents regard the Italian classes as safeguarding at a personal and family and community level the social, cultural and emotional values which they see threatened by the immigration process. These claims about the Italian parents' reasons for encouraging the attendance of their children at Italian-language classes clearly may not be compatible. Moreover, it is most likely that they are given a varying emphasis by different individuals, families and communities. During the Swann Committee's consultations with the Italian community in Bedford 'mother-tongue' provision dominated the discussion, demonstrating the importance given by Italian parents to the 'mother tongue' as 'a key factor in preserving the community's "identity"' and as a means of strengthening family ties with relations still living in their country of origin and facilitating visits "home"' (GB. P.H of C, 1985).

NUMBER AND LOCATION OF SCHOOLS, CLASSES AND COURSES Using a variety of published sources some account of the development of provision for Italian teaching in the *Doposcuola* may be given, even though figures cited are often confused with regard to courses, classes and schools. Schools may have a number of classes or courses, and there are in addition the complications of mainstream school involvement and changes over time. Moreover, in view of the large number of *Doposcuola* classes and the absence of an available location list, it is only possible to give examples of class locations from research study references.

In 1974, three years after the Italian government legislation which led to the establishment of the organizational framework for teaching Italian language, 400 courses existed in the *Doposcuola* system (Tosi, 1980a) and a year later the number had risen to 583 (Saifullah Khan, 1976). Provision continued to increase such that by the end of the 1970s, in London alone, there were 400 courses operating at primary, secondary or GCE level (Weston, 1979), and in 1980 Mengon reported about 640 classes across the country. In 1985 there were approximately 520 *Doposcuola* classes (Brogi, 1986). However, Tosi has claimed this is still insufficient to meet demand.

One of the constraints is said to be the dispersal of the Italian community throughout the UK which causes organizational problems and a proliferation of small classes (Steedman, 1979, drawing on the Rapporto). It might be surmised that this may lead to a greater than usual fluctuation in the number of schools and classes. But, on the contrary, available evidence suggests the longevity and continuity of classes in certain locations. For example, there have been Italian classes in Coventry since 1956, the longest running with the exception of Polish and Ukrainian classes. By 1981 there were nine Italian classes offering a range of provision (LMP, 1982a; see also Table 35, p.255). Other researchers record classes enduring since 1968 in Slough and Maidenhead (Saifullah Khan, 1976) and Leicester (Wilding, 1981), and by 1970 in Bedford (Brown, 1970) and 1971 in Bradford (LMP, 1982b). As with many other linguistic minority communities, the greatest growth in provision for language teaching occurred in the 1970s, other Italian classes being recorded, for example, in Birmingham (Chapman, 1976), Northampton, Wellingborough, Rushden and Kettering (Northamptonshire LEA, 1980) and Hounslow (HCRC, 1982a). Thirty-three Italian schools were located across London, in 1980, in Elliott's survey (1981). Sometimes there was more than one class in an area: Lambeth (3 or 4); Barnet and Islington (3); Ealing, Enfield, Hammersmith, Lewisham and Wandsworth (2); and Brent, Camden, Croydon, Hackney, Haringey, Harrow, Hillingdon, Hounslow, Kingston, Merton, Newham, Redbridge, Sutton and Waltham Forest (1 each). In Scotland classes exist in the smaller towns as well as the big cities (Farrell, 1983). Clearly the locations indicated by these research sources are not exhaustive, but several of the documents cited include case-study data which have been drawn upon to compile this review of aspects of provision.

It appears that the organizational and financial assistance offered by the Italian consulates through the regional administration of language classes has influenced LEAs' awareness of their existence. Indeed in the light of the mother-tongue teaching debate and increased consciousness of the need to make greater provision for minority languages, LEAs appear to have increased their support for Italian language classes over the last decade (see pp.268–71). In the early 1970s a national survey of LEAs with immigrant pupils showed that it was beginning to be recognized that immigrant communities were encouraging the learning of their own languages, and amongst the more established immigrant communities Italians were reported to be particularly active in this respect (Townsend, 1971). In the second survey, in 1971 (Townsend and Brittan, 1972), 13 out of 230 primary and secondary schools across the country reported that Italian communities made arrangements to teach their language outside school hours. This was usually known because school premises were often used by Italian consulate classes. In another national survey, in 1979 (Little and Willey, 1983), only five out of 18 LEAs with ethnic minority concentrations of ten per cent or more reported that Italian was taught in out-of-school hours by the community, and in areas where there were between two-and-a-half and ten per cent ethnic minority pupils, only six out of 21 LEAs reported the teaching of Italian in community schools. However, another national survey for the Commission for Racial Equality (CRE) in 1980–2 (Tsow, 1983) revealed that the greatest support given by LEAs to voluntary language classes was given to Italian language classes. Some 47 per cent of LEAs responding (87) recorded the existence of some provision in the voluntary sector, in 90 per cent of cases in the form of accommodation. Some 52 per cent of LEAs responding (76 per cent) assisted voluntary Italian classes. In a further survey by the Schools Council, in 1983 (Tansley and Craft, 1984), 12 out of 63 LEAs responding mentioned Italian as a language occurring most frequently. Sixteen out of 49 LEAs able to give details about community schools knew of a total of 50 Italian schools in their areas. When figures collected by the Linguistic Minorities Project in Bradford and Coventry in 1981, and in Haringey in 1982, were added, some 90 'schools' could be listed for 19 LEAs (see Table 35, p.255). Even allowing for difficulties of classification and the apparently greater involvement of LEAs with Italian provision in out-of-school hours, these researches suggest that LEAs do not have a clear picture of local voluntary provision. However, in view of the involvement of the Italian Central Education Office with mainstream school provision and the teaching of Italian as a foreign language in some schools the account of LEAs' support needs to be supplemented further (see pp.268–71); it is also considered in more detail here under various aspects of provision. Indeed there is increasing collaboration on research between mainstream and community providers, as with the involvement of Italian teachers from community schools in the Mother Tongue Project (1981–5), developing primary teaching resources (see p.287) and under the auspices of the Ufficio Scolastico Italiano responsible for a team of *Corsi Inseriti* teachers working in mainstream schools in ILEA, where two secondary schools are involved in the Community Languages in the Secondary Curriculum Project (1984–7), developing strategies for teaching Italian and South Asian languages (see p.282).

PUPIL NUMBERS, AGES AND ATTENDANCE   Not surprisingly, as the number of Italian classes in out-of-school hours grew, so the number of pupils of Italian origin attending them increased, especially in the 1970s. A Council of Europe report for 1974 noted that Italian consulates made arrangements for 6,000 children of Italian origin to attend language classes in the UK (Willke, 1975), though Tosi (1980a) claimed that, in 1974, 9,000 pupils were enrolled. Indeed by 1975, 10,330 Italian children were said to be enrolled (Saifullah Khan, 1976), and by 1979 the figures had grown to 11,000 children attending courses in England, Scotland and Wales. Of these, 6,700 were in inner and greater London (Weston, 1979). Mengon (1980) indicated just less than 10,000 pupils of Italian origin attended *Doposcuola*. They represented more than a third of school-age children from Italian backgrounds at that time. Over the past five years there appears to have been a further decline in *Doposcuola* numbers, but an increasing number of pupils studying Italian in the *Inseriti* system.

It is difficult to be precise about the numbers and ages of pupils enrolled in schools since these fluctuate according to the fortunes of schools and classes, the age and establishment of different Italian communities and the date of research. Thus schools seem to vary from 100 to 300 pupils, but on average are likely to have between 100 and 150 pupils of Italian origin. Schools appear to cater for an age range on average of between six and 16. The Italian school in Slough, in 1975 (Saifullah Khan, 1976), seems to have been typical, although double the number (300) of pupils within primary age attended the Bradford school at the same time. In 1978 the Italian school in Leicester had 100 or more pupils aged seven to 15 (Wilding, 1981), and at that time King and Zolli (1981) reported that half the school-age children in 72 families whom they studied were following Italian language courses, mostly outside mainstream school hours.

It is perhaps more instructive to consider the extent to which provision in a certain locality is taken up according to the potential number of students. Fortunately, it is possible to make such an assessment in the case of Italian-speaking pupils in Bradford, Coventry and Haringey in the light of information collected in the Mother-Tongue Teaching Directory (MTTD) survey in 1981 and 1982 and the Schools Language Survey conducted by the Linguistic Minorities Project (LMP, 1983a, 1982a, 1982b, 1983b). The MTTD covered classes provided by community organizations as well as those initiated by the LEA or its schools, inside or outside LEA premises and during and after school hours. Table 35 gives details of the number of Italian classes, pupils and their ages in the three LEAs. The varying levels of attendance are of interest. Thus in Coventry 81 per cent of pupils who spoke Italian at home, amongst the highest percentage of any linguistic minority, were enrolled in Italian classes and 75 per cent were said to be regular attenders. On the other hand, whereas just less than two-fifths of such pupils were enrolled in Italian classes in Bradford and Haringey, nearly all were said to attend regularly. The data indicate that the proportion of Italian speakers and their attendance at language classes may vary considerably from locality to locality, suggesting varying degrees of commitment on the part of parents, pupils and communities, or that alternative opportunities exist (see also p.259). The majority of pupils in classes across the three locations were aged 11 or over. Indeed 33 pupils in Bradford and 15 in Coventry were aged over 16, amongst the highest numbers in this age-group. Whereas there might be a slight fall in numbers at early adolescence, as also indicated by data from the Secondary Pupils Survey (another part of the LMP) in Bradford and Peterborough, it seems that into the early 1980s there have been more Italian-speaking pupils at the higher age ranges. Taken in conjunction with ILEA Language Census data from this time (see pp.227–8), this again suggests the predominance of second-generation pupils of Italian origin in adolescence and the, by then, relatively small numbers of third-generation pupils being sufficiently old to commence language classes. However, in 1986 an Italian Embassy source indicated that provision was concentrated in the primary age range and that most pupils attended up to age 11. Attendance drops off during the year, possibly by as much as a third, especially amongst older pupils taking mainstream exams (Brogi, 1986).

ACCOMMODATION   In addition to any arrangements made by the Italian Central Educational Office for the teaching of Italian in the mainstream, it is likely that schools and LEAs will know of Italian language classes in out-of-school hours because of their use of local school accommodation. In particular, there is a considerable association with use of Roman Catholic schools, in line with the tendency for mainstream schooling in Roman Catholic schools and possibly indicating the further influence of the church (Saifullah Khan, 1976; Weston, 1979; Elliott, 1981; LMP, 1982a, 1982b). If LEAs permit free use of local school premises in out-of-school hours, this may represent a major source of provision to Italian language classes, but it seems LEA policy is variable and some LEAs may continue to demand rent (CRE, 1982; Tsow, 1983; Brogi, 1986). Thus, for example, in

Table 35: Number of Italian language classes, pupils and ages in three LEAs, 1981 – 2

		Bradford 1981	Coventry 1981	Haringey 1982
1	Year in which first surviving class began	1971	1956	1975
2	Number of classes in 1981 – 2	18	9	12
3	Number of pupils on roll	141	117	174
4	Percentage of pupils attending regularly	96	75	90
5	Pupils on roll as % of pupils in LEA using Italian at home (SLS)	38	81	39
6	Age-group of pupils			
	5–7	2	4	10
	8–10	12	29	47
	11–13	34	9	78
	13+	105	35	39

Sources: Adapted from LMP, 1983a, Tables 4.1, 4.2 and 4.3; 1982a, 1982b, 1983b, Table 6.

Coventry in 1981 the Italian government paid for accommodation for seven out of nine language classes, whereas the LEA only funded one source of accommodation; in Bradford the LEA supported at least four sources of accommodation, and the Italian government appeared to fund six classes; and in Haringey in 1982 the LEA did not appear to fund any accommodation for Italian classes. Premises in the ILEA are usually obtained free of charge, according to Italian consulate sources. High rents can be a considerable burden.

As the CRE survey (1982) showed, voluntary language classes experience a number of other common problems relating to accommodation in mainstream schools in out-of-school hours. Italian language classes may share accommodation with other language classes, as in the case of several Roman Catholic primary schools where groups of Spanish and Portuguese children were also learning their own languages at the same time (Weston, 1979). Sometimes Italian language classes are 'barely tolerated' and may indeed be 'openly antagonized' in the schools where they take place (ibid.; Jackson, 1979). Tosi (1980a) has observed that classrooms cannot normally be used for displaying or storing materials because they are used by other classes for other subjects, and this means that learning environments are often unsupportive or lacking in stimulation for the purpose of teaching Italian. Like other organizations engaged in voluntary language teaching, Italian consulate sources have also reported difficulties with caretakers and other aspects of accommodation provision (see also GB. P.H of C, 1985).

CLASS TIMING AND DURATION   There is a variable pattern in the timing and duration of Italian language teaching provision in research evidence from several locations and at different dates. Although classes may take place from one to three times per week, on average pupils appear to attend twice per week. Most Italian language classes seem to take place on weekdays, after school (4 – 7 pm) or in the evenings (5 – 8 pm) either once or twice per week, as in Wellingborough and Kettering (Northamptonshire LEA, 1980) and sometimes in London (Elliott, 1981) and Coventry (LMP, 1982a), or even three times per week in Scunthorpe (CRE, 1982); or on one or two weekdays plus Saturday, as for the most part in London (Weston, 1979), Bradford (LMP, 1982b), Haringey (LMP, 1983b), Slough (Saifullah Khan, 1976) and sometimes in Coventry (LMP, 1982a) and London (Elliott, 1981). Where classes are held on weekday evenings, there is little evidence of which days are preferred, though in Hounslow Tuesdays and Fridays are indicated (HCRC, 1982a). Classes may take place only on Saturday (Brogi, 1986), especially if accommodation is problematic, as in Northampton (Northamptonshire LEA, 1980). Classes on Sunday were only reported for A-level students in one location in a teachers' home (Saifullah Khan, 1976). In two cases classes are reported every evening and at weekends, but although it is unclear it is most likely that they are for different groups (ibid.; Elliott, 1981).

There is a similar variety in the duration of classes, although the average would appear to be two hours per session (Saifullah Khan, 1976; Jackson, 1979) and sometimes three hours (HCRC, 1982a). Since most pupils attend twice weekly, the average appears to be around four hours' teaching per week, as Brown (1970) found in Bedford. More recently, the LMP surveys found average weekly attendance in Bradford was three hours, in Haringey four hours and in Coventry it varied from an average of five-and-a-half hours for pupils less than 14 to two-and-a-half for those aged 14 and over (LMP, 1982b, 1983b, 1982a). Brogi (1986) has indicated that three hours' tuition is most common either at one time or in two one-and-a-half-hour sessions.

The variability in timing and duration of Italian classes is partly related to the variety of organizational arrangements which exist for Italian teaching as a whole as well as localized needs depending on numbers, residential spread of pupils and staffing availability. Some problems, also common to other minority language learning groups, have been noted. The Rapporto (1977) recognized that the motivation and attendance of pupils of Italian origin at the *Doposcuola* were seriously affected by the length of their mainstream schooling which may leave them with little time and energy for extra classes after school. It has also been claimed that the dispersal of the Italian population may also mean that some children of Italian origin have long journeys to language classes, though unfortunately there is no research evidence about the distance travelled, mode of transport or the length of time taken. On the other hand, attendance was rated very highly by the teachers in the Italian classes in the three locations covered by the LMP (1983a) survey. There is no research evidence on the length of attendance of pupils of Italian origin, though clearly many stay the eight-year course to O-level.

THE TEACHING FORCE   Teachers in the language classes are appointed by the Italian government and usually sent by the Ministry of Education on a minimum seven-year, full-time contract (Steedman, 1979; Elliott, 1981; Brogi, 1986). Only Italian nationals – though some may be UK residents – are accepted for employment by the Italian government within this programme. However, it has been claimed that there may sometimes be administrative difficulties in the renewal of contracts (GB. P. H of C, 1985) or an undesirably rapid turnover of staff (GB. DES, 1984). Teachers' salaries, which are said to be generous, are paid by the Italian government. The LMP data, for example, show that in both Coventry and Bradford the Italian government paid for the salaries and travelling expenses of five teachers and in Haringey for two teachers (LMP, 1982a, 1982b, 1983b; see also p.269 for LEA salary funding).

Somewhat strangely, despite the increasing number of classes during the 1970s, the teaching force appears to have remained constant, at around 150 (Saifullah Khan, 1976; Mengon, 1980; Brogi, 1986). This indicates one teacher's responsibility for several classes, probably amounting to 100 or more pupils as, for example, in Slough (Saifullah Khan, 1976) and in Leicester (Wilding, 1981). Teacher-pupil ratios are likely to vary from class to class. For example, in the six Italian language schools in London surveyed by Elliott (1981) teacher-pupil ratios varied from 1:15 to 1:40, with two schools having teacher-pupil ratios of 1:30. Teachers of primary-age pupils teach ten to 12 classes, whereas A-level teachers have fewer classes. The minimum teaching time is 24 hours per week in primary and 18 hours per week in secondary classes. Some teachers teach in both the *Doposcuola* and *Corsi Inseriti* (Brogi, 1986).

Teachers in Italian language classes are qualified, though Saifullah Khan (1976) questioned whether even well-trained Italian teachers are necessarily competent to teach children who are more proficient in English than Italian. An HMI report (GB. DES, 1984) observed that Italian teachers generally have no English teaching qualification or any teaching experience in mainstream schools so may be unfamiliar with aspects of the English educational system. Echoing these points, the Swann Report (GB. P. H of C, 1985) also noted the concern expressed by heads and community representatives about the different teaching styles adopted by some of the teachers sponsored by the Italian government. However, in the past two courses a year were organized for teacher training as part of an ongoing training scheme (Saifullah Khan, 1976; Tosi, 1980a). One LEA is also reported to have arranged in-service training for Italian teachers to exchange information about teaching skills (GB. P. H of C, 1985). In 1986 all Italian teachers had returned to Italy for INSET during the summer. There was to be some INSET in regard to GCSE arranged by one *Presidenze* in London. Every *Didattica* arranges some INSET, sometimes with mainstream teachers. The Italian authorities are keen to promote co-ordinated initiatives with the mainstream and to encourage the development of teaching of Italian as a modern language in the secondary curriculum (Brogi, 1986).

CURRICULUM CONTENT AND LEVEL What is known of the curriculum in Italian language schools? Does it consist entirely of language, or are other subjects included? To what extent is the Italian language pursued?

The Italian language classes usually seek to teach language in a wider cultural context in line with teaching objectives (see p.251) and syllabuses. Brown (1970) recorded that in Bedford, in the mid-1960s, Italian children were taught history, geography and culture in the Italian language classes, and in the late 1970s in the same town Jackson observed that mathematics was taught in Italian and some of the children also sang semi-religious Italian songs. Sometimes extra-curricular activities, such as trips to Italy, are arranged to enhance pupils' motivation (Brogi, 1986). The language taught in classes is Standard Italian. Steedman (1979) noted the exemplary sensitivity and awareness of the Italian teachers who produced the Rapporto di Lavoro (1977) about the problems of the dialect-speaking child learning Standard Italian, though a contemporary Ministry of Education document did not sanction any concessions to local dialect. Unfortunately, there are no reports of observations of the language of instruction used by teachers in the language classes or of their teaching methods.

It would appear that the level of instruction in Italian language classes ranges from the beginning stage to O- or A-level (Saifullah Khan, 1976; Weston, 1979). A full course is five years at primary level and three years at secondary level. It is interesting to note a certain change in emphasis on qualifications over the years. At the end of the 1960s, in Bedford, Brown (1970) noted that pupils could go on to take Italian secondary school certificates and GCE O-level examinations in Italian. A decade later, however, Steedman noted that although Italian adults were increasingly keen to obtain their intermediate school certificate for obtaining technical qualifications, they were more keen to support their children in taking GCE O- or A-level (Rapporto, 1977). Tosi (1980a) has claimed that only a few pupils attempt public examinations, the others having to settle for a certificate of attendance. He quoted a survey (without citing the source) which he claimed showed that pupils of Italian origin achieved lower examination results than those enrolled in courses of Italian as a foreign language, and attributed this to social background differences and difficulties of transferring from dialect to Standard Italian. Weston (1979) has also suggested that differences between Italian communities may affect GCE examination entries. One of the two communities in which she taught was highly organized, the courses were supported by a determined parents' association and were held in independent premises, attendance was good and most pupils were expected to study for O-level with a good number continuing to A-level. In the other area, which lacked a community framework, pupils often left the classes in their early adolescence, though they could sometimes be enticed back to join an O-level class, which increased motivation and was a spur to confidence and interest. Other teachers have also claimed that pupils are keen to take examinations (GB. P. H of C. 1985). Yet there appears to be relatively little evidence of the entry of pupils attending Italian classes in out-of-school hours for GCE O- or A-level in available case studies (Elliott, 1981). Although the Mother-Tongue Teaching Directory (MTTD) survey in Haringey listed 20 O-level entries in 1981, in Coventry only two of the O-level entries in 1980 were from Italian language classes not supported by the LEA; although more, as was also the case in Bradford, appeared to be entered from mainstream language classes (LMP, 1982a, 1982b, 1983b; see p.273). Brogi (1986) has claimed that hundreds of pupils enter for O-level each year and some for A-level. Entries are made through the *Doposcuola*, especially for pupils who are taking a full complement of O-levels in the mainstream.

TEACHING MATERIALS　Textbooks and teaching materials for the Italian classes in the *Doposcuola* system are supplied by the Italian Central Education Office and paid for by the Italian government. The textbooks feature life in Italy. In 1981 embassy sources were recorded as supplying textbooks and teaching aids to five of the nine Italian classes in Coventry and four of the 18 classes in Bradford and, in 1982, two of the 12 classes in Haringey (LMP, 1983a, 1983b). Moreover, in the case of two of the classes in Bradford and Haringey, the embassy also contributed towards exercise books and paper. However, Tosi (1980a) claimed that materials and equipment are limited both in quality and quantity. Elliott (1981) found that four out of six voluntary language classes surveyed in London had book collections. In 1975, as part of a study on the public library service for ethnic minorities in six London boroughs (Brent, Camden, Haringey, Islington, Wandsworth and Westminster), Clough and Quarmby (1978) found that in two it was reported that books in Italian were required by pupils from voluntary language classes. They were especially popular with 8–10-year-old girls 'who were now literate and still interested in their background, although, as they grew older, they were found to identify more with their immediate environment' (p.214). But Jackson's description of the reading primer in the Italian language class in Bedford in the late 1970s demonstrates the irrelevance of such texts to the present-day multiracial urban environment in which many pupils of Italian origin live, for they would fail to recognize themselves depicted in the illustrations in the text. As for some other voluntary language classes, appropriate teaching materials relevant to life in contemporary Britain remain wanting (see pp.281–2).

PARENTS' ATTITUDES TO ITALIAN CLASSES　Weston (1979) has claimed that different Italian communities may have varying attitudes towards, and an effect on, the attendance and success of their children at Italian classes. The 47 Italian parents involved in her survey in two London areas expressed some criticism of the Italian courses attended by their children, relating to the organization of the courses, the fact that children were tired after a day at their main school and that the lessons were not long enough. Weston suggested that a supportive parents' association may be of considerable assistance, but unfortunately there is little information on the extent of interaction between Italian parents and voluntary language classes. The Swann Report (GB.P. H of C, 1985) notes that Italian teachers working in mainstream curriculum time and in classes in out-of-school hours claimed to have some feedback from Italian parents, though they were said not to have much contact with schools. The Adult Language Use Study (ALUS) of the Linguistic Minorities Project (LMP) (1983a) provides information on Italian parents' awareness of and their child's attendance at Italian language classes in two LEAs. Whereas a relatively low 67 per cent of 78 respondents in Coventry with children or young people under 21 in the household knew of 'mother-tongue' classes, 97 per cent of 77 Italian householders in London were aware of classes. The high figure for the London Italians in fact reflected the ALUS sampling strategy for this local linguistic minority which included the use of lists from 'mother-tongue' classes. This also correlated with an extremely high attendance rate, as in 70 per cent of Italian households in London with children aged five to 18 at least one child has attended a class in the previous four weeks. By comparison, the attendance rate of 14 per cent for the children of Italian families in Coventry was below average. Italian respondents in Coventry were most likely to claim as reasons for non-attendance that they or their children were too busy or thought that the classes were not very valuable given their other priorities, whereas in London respondents were more likely to claim their children were too young, too old or already proficient in Italian. However, both communities expressed a high degree of support for mother-tongue maintenance, suggesting that there may be a considerable unmet demand for support in this connection.

PUPILS' ATTITUDES Various sources have claimed that Italian children, whether they were born in the UK or arrived as young children, feel considerable stress as a result of the strong pressure from their families and the church to improve their knowledge of Italian and to retain their Italian identity (e.g. Triseliotis, 1976). It has also been suggested that attendance at weekend or evening classes must contribute significantly to children's physical, if not emotional, exhaustion. Tosi (1980a) has claimed that pupils of Italian origin do not like attending Italian classes in out-of-school hours as they feel they cannot do their best when they are overworked. Italian teachers have also come to recognize that other school commitments and the necessity for some children to travel long distances to attend classes affects motivation and attendance (Steedman, 1979).

Other evidence appears to bear out these claims. In a pilot study involving 18 14-year-olds in Italian language schools, Weston (1979) found that most of the children seemed to resent attending classes and hinted that they would gladly have left if it had not been for their parents' insistence. However, this attitude did not relate to lack of motivation which was both integrative and instrumental since they considered that they needed to know Italian in case they went to live in Italy and it enabled them to remain in touch with their relatives and friends, especially on visits. They also thought if they remained in England their knowledge of Italian could help them to achieve more examination qualifications and possibly obtain a better job. Their objection to the language classes was to the condition and the times of the courses and to the fact that they took place out of the mainstream school environment. Weston considered that pupils' 'emotional' link and frequent contacts with Italians and Italy provided the necessary motivation to keeping up their attendance at language classes, and that some could be encouraged to join an examination class. As with other groups of young people learning their 'mother tongue', the period of early adolescence seems to mark a particularly testing time for their allegiance to attendance at such classes as these may often form the symbolic arena for their assessment of their personal, social and cultural identities (see also p.302–5). By contrast, Jackson (1979) noted that the primary-age pupils in a Bedford language class sat formally and were quiet, obedient and attentive.

Similar observations were made in the Swann Report. Pupils expressed less enthusiasm for classes in out-of-school hours, disliked attending and only did so because of parental pressure. Italian teachers noted a different motivation on the part of those whom they taught after school, who saw it as an 'imposition' on their time, whereas in the timetabled curriculum they were 'mentally prepared to work'. Its inclusion in the mainstream curriculum and the involvement of non-Italians enhanced its status in the eyes of Italian pupils (see pp.267,277). However, it must not be assumed that all pupils of Italian origin will necessarily wish to study in the mainstream. Some 'rebelled, seeing Italian as identified with the 'authority' of the family with which they might be in conflict, or resented missing other subjects against which Italian was timetabled and in which they were more interested (GB. P. H of C, 1985).

TEACHERS' ATTITUDES   Regrettably there is relatively little direct evidence either of Italian teachers' or mainstream teachers' attitudes to Italian classes in out-of-school hours. Weston, herself an Italian teacher, forcefully expressed her feelings of frustration regarding the position of these classes as

> often barely tolerated and sometimes openly antagonized by the schools where they take place (even if there are praiseworthy exceptions), mostly ignored by the English schools attended by the Italian children during the day, [and] are forced into a semi-clandestine, marginal sort of existence which is obviously detrimental to the balanced development of the children attending them. (Weston, 1979, pp. 46–7)

However, Tosi (1980a) has indicated that a constraint on developing a closer relationship between voluntary language classes and mainstream provision has been the fact that Italian teachers are in most cases peripatetic. Italian teachers in consultations with the Swann Committee (GB. P. H of C, 1985) confirmed that they were often unable to build up links with other teachers, pupils or parents if they taught in the mainstream, and if they taught after school, they might never meet the rest of the staff. They would welcome opportunities of exchange with other staff, especially to discuss a child's work in relation to progress in other subjects. They also saw it as part of their role to improve home–school links with Italian families. Italian families considered their success depended chiefly on the attitudes of the head and staff in a school. However, their perceptions of mainstream teachers' attitudes towards the teaching of Italian were that it was seen as of 'low status', that many regarded 'mother-tongue' provision as 'back-pedalling' in educational terms and that the teaching of English was of paramount importance.

Although research evidence of the attitudes of mainstream teachers towards Italian 'mother-tongue' teaching is similarly limited, it does on the whole appear to be negative. When Jackson (1979) questioned a few primary teachers in Bedford, he found that they were all very critical, arguing that the Italian children were too tired as a result of attending Italian classes and that, in addition, the time that they spent learning Italian made it harder for the primary teacher to teach them English. However, evaluation of Italian mainstream provision in the MTCP did not indicate any deleterious effects on the parallel development of competence in English (see p.285). Unfortunately, no research has been undertaken to evaluate the effects of attending voluntary Italian classes on mainstream educational achievement.

The Swann Report (GB. P. H of C, 1985) notes that mainstream teachers sometimes knew little about after-school Italian classes, although they complained about the untidiness of the classrooms after use. Often this sharing of the same premises seemed to be the only link between the Italian classes and the mainstream schools, so that 'separation' seemed 'particularly acute'. However, although several heads of schools where Italian government-sponsored teachers were working stressed their presence had improved the schools' links with Italian parents, concern was expressed that the peripatetic nature of the work did not allow for Italian teachers to build up relationships with other staff or to exchange views on pupils' needs, and there was some anxiety about different teaching methods employed by the Italian teachers (see p. 280).

SOME ISSUES RELATING TO TEACHING ITALIAN IN THE *DOPOSCUOLA* AND MAINSTREAM PROVISION   Clearly, despite the greater connection of the teaching of Italian with mainstream provision compared with the voluntary provision for language teaching for many other linguistic minority pupils, much remains to be done to improve and co-ordinate the relationship between mainstream provision and provision in out-of-school hours, particularly to the benefit of pupils and teachers. Some advances might be made by means of greater LEA support in terms of accommod-ation, teaching aids, fostering links between teachers and offering in-service courses for Italian teachers. However, the situation is complicated by a number of issues, concerning the financial and administrative involvement of the Italian government, the language and how it is taught, and the orientation of the current generation of pupils of Italian origin and the relationship between *Doposcuola* and mainstream provision.

Wilke (1975), who made a cross-cultural evaluation of the schooling of immigrant children in West Germany, Sweden and England, considered that in England the discussion of their bilingualism was reticent and in contradistinction to the approaches adopted in Germany and Sweden to provide instruction for migrants' children in their native language, history and culture and in that of the host country. Following the EC Directive in 1977, which has prompted much discussion of mother-tongue teaching arrangements in the UK, and doubtless without which much of the research referred to here would not exist, the charge of 'reticence', certainly with regard to discussion and to some extent to provision, may be less appropriate. Yet one of the key arguments, employed for example by the DES in reply to the EC Directive, and which displays reluctance to institute wider provision, revolves around the claim that ethnic minority children in the UK are not the children of migrants, but of immigrants. Though this may be asserted with some confidence with respect to children of some linguistic minority groups, with what degree of certitude can this be claimed in respect of children of Italian origin? Research in the 1970s revealed not only the expressed desire to return to Italy on the part of first-generation Italian parents, and in addition by some from the intermediate and second generations, but also the actual trend amongst the Italian population to re-emigrate to Italy (see p.304–6). It was the Italian government's original objective in its involvement in provision for Italian teaching in the UK to facilitate such a return. But such objectives are irrelevant for children of Italian origin who are British by birth, and are unlikely to go to the land of their ancestors other than on visits – a country from which even their parents may find themselves increasingly estranged. Indeed Saifullah Khan (1976) suggested that it has been difficult to assess whether the Italian government's investment reflected a genuine concern to make up the gap in provision in this country or whether it concealed other motives. Nevertheless, she conceded that the quality of teaching and facilities provided in schools supported by the Italian government was generally higher in the mid-1970s than that found in mother-tongue schools which were not centrally organized and lacked financial resources. Mengon (1980) endorsed the financial support of the Italian government but suggested that the measure of centralization and formalized uniformity which this seems to impose upon locally variable situations was less acceptable. Clearly the involvement of the Italian government in the organization of, and financial provision for, Italian language classes has considerable policy implications, not least perhaps concerning curriculum control and teaching methods, although unfortunately there appears to be little publicly available information on these. Indeed the Italian authorities are conscious of the anomalies of their position which they are currently reviewing with a view to legislative reform (Brogi, 1986).

Another major issue concerns the discordance between the Italian dialects spoken in the homes of pupils of Italian origin and the values implied, and the Standard Italian which they learn in schools and classes. Clearly Italian teachers in the UK have been aware of this (Steedman, 1979), though the Italian authorities may have shown less concern or interest. Indeed some time ago Brown (1970) pointed out that the very fact that Italian children attending voluntary language classes in Bedford in the 1960s were in effect learning a new language had the attendant danger that the children's sense of Italian achievements and traditions might remain academic and disconnected from their home environments, where even the language of that achievement was not in use. It is presumably such concerns which have influenced the statements expressed in the Rapporto (cited by Steedman, 1979) that pupils should be enabled to perceive the position of their own cultural experiences within the wider history and development of Italy, possibly through a study of migratory movements and their origins. Whether or not this covers the point for the UK-born children of Italian origin is, perhaps, open to doubt. Moreover, since pupils of Italian origin are almost in a position of learning a new language, the argument, for example, supporting voluntary language provision on account of enhanced conceptual development and literacy in the first language loses its strict force. Indeed the teaching of Standard Italian may cause the child to experience yet another discontinuity between his home life and that of the school, albeit the voluntary school. This may, in turn, have an effect contrary to that intended by one of the aims of such classes, by possibly complicating further the pupil's assessment of his personal identity. Steedman (ibid.) has argued that the grounds for encouraging the acquisition or maintenance of knowledge of the parents' mother tongue by children of immigrants must be on account of cognitive and personal development plus the practical considerations of the likelihood of a return to the country of origin or, on the other hand, the usefulness of fluency in a second or possibly third language. But in view of the increasing numbers of UK-born children of Italian descent, it becomes increasingly more appropriate to consider the role of Italian classes in promoting a reconciliation between the experiences of two (or three) linguistic, cultural and social-life worlds experienced by second- and third-generation Italian children, and to encourage them in appreciation of the mutual enrichment of the different facets of their own background and life experiences. This emphasis would differ from that in voluntary language classes, where the orientation is towards Italy, rather than the position of the Italian child in British society. Such a goal would be complementary and not necessarily contradictory to the objective of the development of oracy and literacy in Standard Italian which might lead to examination achievement. Whether these goals could be combined or whether they might be more appropriately pursued by two complementary systems of voluntary language classes and mainstream provision is a matter for further debate.

The very existence of a strong organizational framework for Italian language classes both in the *Doposcuola* and mainstream raises a different set of logistical and philosophical issues from those concerning most other minority language speakers for whom there is as yet generally little provision in the mainstream. Thus, for example, while the supply of teachers may not be such a significant matter (Baldwin *et al.*, 1980), other factors such as the role of a foreign government and issues relating to whether to teach dialect or Standard Italian may assume greater prominence. Above all, it would seem necessary to clarify aims and set out objectives for respective provision. Clearly, with regard to the Italian *Doposcuola*, the extent of provision indicates continuing and fairly stable and substantial demand and interest. But there appears not to have been an evaluation of this system (or at least not publicly available in English) outside the organizational structure itself. There are suggestions in Weston's work (1979), for example, that voluntary provision may not be satisfactory to pupils, teachers or parents. How much is this related to the internal arrangements of the *Doposcuola*, with respect to aims, objectives, teaching methodologies and materials, and how much is it related to the organizational position of the *Doposcuola vis-à-vis* mainstream provision? Apropos of the various arrangements for the teaching of Italian, the evidence of the Association of Teachers of Italian to the Swann Committee may again be cited:

> The provision of such classes would seem to help to counteract the problem of developing awareness of a personal cultural identity. Great benefit has been seen to be drawn from the integration of classes in schools, but the system generally is fraught with problems which affect all involved – the children, the Italian authorities and teachers, and the English authorities if they are involved or aware of this activity. The after-school classes have poor support and results as children often have difficulty in maintaining regular attendance, and often regard attendance at classes as an intrusion on their free time and a form of segregation from their contemporaries of other nationalities. The teachers frequently experience problems in finding suitable accommodation for the classes, and consequently their teaching style is severely limited. There is a general lack of continuity, and as the time available is very limited progress is slow. The regional organizers appointed from Italy often have little support from the British authorities, and frequently little knowledge of the British education system... *Corsi Inseriti* seem to be the best form of provision by the Italian authorities and function better when the classes are considered part of the language curriculum in the school and are open to all pupils – as well as children of Italian parentage. (GB. P. H of C, 1985, pp. 702–3).

Having considered the *Doposcuola* system, it remains therefore to attempt to assess through available research evidence the parallel state of Italian provision in mainstream schooling – both *Corsi Inseriti*, organized in conjunction with the Italian government channels, and that mounted by LEAs alone.

Italian 'mother-tongue' teaching in the mainstream
Given the extensive provision for teaching Italian in the *Doposcuola* system for pupils of Italian origin, it is important to examine whether this has influenced and has

been matched by arrangements in mainstream schooling. A feature differentiating mainstream provision for pupils of Italian origin is the extent to which the Italian government collaborates with some LEAs in establishing Italian teaching, either as part of the timetabled curriculum or in withdrawal groups, especially in schools with relatively high proportions of pupils of Italian origin. Such joint arrangements are made through schools' language departments to which a qualified Italian teacher is allocated with salary, textbooks and other equipment provided by the Italian authorities, so that the LEA effectively only provides accommodation. Since up to 50 per cent of non-Italian pupils can be enrolled in classes to make up a minimum number, this complicates any account of mainstream provision as it is not possible to ascertain to what extent pupils who hail from non-Italian backgrounds are included.

Further confusion arises because, after the predominance of French, Italian is one of the European languages most likely to be offered in the secondary modern languages curriculum. However, useful papers in the Centre for Information on Language Teaching (CILT) publication, *Italian in Schools* (Baldwin *et al.* 1980), the result of a colloquium held in 1979 by the Society for Italian Studies and the Association of Teachers of Italian, which includes consideration of present and future policies and practices with respect to Italian both as a mother tongue and as a foreign language, suggests that the prevalence of Italian in mainstream schooling should not be assumed. Carsaniga (1980), for example, cited HMI statistics claiming that only about 35 per cent of pupils aged 13 plus were learning a modern foreign language, and of these, a massive 97 per cent have French as their first foreign language. Only 0.8 per cent learn Italian. Even so, this percentage has to be recalled when considering examination figures and other data when there is no exclusive reference to pupils with Italian backgrounds.

The encouragement and resource support given by the Italian government to the teaching of Italian as a 'mother tongue' and a foreign language, and its inclusion in the modern language curriculum of some secondary schools, might suggest that compared with pupils from some other linguistic minority backgrounds, Italian-speaking pupils are in a privileged position with respect to potential access. But what is the situation of such pupils outside the main areas of settlement? Indeed, the Swann Report (GB. P. H of C, 1985) even suggested that Italian is less likely to be offered in schools with Italian pupils. This sub-section examines provision for Italian teaching in the mainstream by considering evidence of requests for Italian to be taught, attitudes and motivation towards provision and the actual teaching arrangements made in secondary and primary schools and in FE and HE, together with O- and A-level examination entrants and performance. Research into Italian teaching involving pupils of Italian origin will also be considered, and especially an attempt to teach Standard Italian at primary school in the EC/Bedfordshire Mother Tongue and Culture Project (MTCP). This raises many issues which should inform further general consideration of mainstream provision.

REQUESTS FOR PROVISION   Although there is relatively little evidence of requests made by Italian parents to schools or LEAs for provision for Italian language teaching in the mainstream curriculum, nevertheless an impression can be gained from a variety of sources. In the early 1960s, Walker (1963a) recorded that some 500 Italian parents in Bedford had signed a petition expressing concern that their children were forgetting their mother tongue. Although the Borough Education Officer was not unsympathetic and recognized that teaching in out-of-school hours was inadequate, he nevertheless claimed that there was no room in the curriculum for Italian teaching. Tosi (1980a) has suggested that Italian parents were prompted to start further classes when they realized that courses were not available in mainstream schools. Later the *Direttori Didattici*, backed by the Italian government, made considerable efforts to get Italian teaching integrated into schools' curricula (Steedman, 1979), especially where there were significant numbers of Italian children, and in some cases there was a co-operative response (see e.g. Northamptonshire LEA/NAME Working Party, 1980). However, parents may be ambivalent in their desires for Italian to be offered in the curriculum. Not only are there few records of Italian parents' requests, but Weston (1979) found that a mere 8.5 per cent of a small sample of 47 adults blamed the English schools which their children attended for failing either to provide Italian in the curriculum or at least to take an interest in the children's efforts to learn Italian in voluntary language classes. However, their adolescent children resented the conditions and times of the voluntary language classes and unanimously wanted to study Italian in the school curriculum. There may be scope for pupil initiatives in making requests (see pp.267–8).

In a national survey, in 1979, Little and Willey (1983) found that only one of 13 LEAs with between two-and-a-half and ten per cent ethnic minority pupils reported having received requests from Italian-speaking communities for language teaching, but that subsequently the group had opted to establish their own provision. Persistence is clearly required by parents and community groups pressing for language tuition or assistance with voluntary classes, for as the CRE survey of LEAs' responses to mother-tongue teaching in 1980–2 (Tsow, 1983) demonstrates, the primary responsibility for encouraging local authority interest has rested with the linguistic communities. On the other hand, the overwhelming support and interest shown by Italian parents, even of the second-generation, whose children were involved in the MTCP, shows that parents appreciate LEA initiatives (Steedman, 1979; Simons, 1980). But the whole process is in danger of becoming a vicious circle, for Carsaniga (1980) has observed that the fact that Italian is taught in only very few schools deters parents from requesting their children be taught even when it is available, in case they have to move to another school where it is not taught. Moreover, Tosi (1980b) has ironically claimed that although lack of demand seems to be the reason for the limited availability of Italian in the school curriculum, the extensive provision offered outside school seems inadequate to meet the demands of pupils of Italian origin.

ATTITUDES AND MOTIVATION TOWARDS PROVISION When considering the attitudes towards making provision for teaching Italian in mainstream schools containing pupils of Italian origin, it is curious to find the re-emergence, in a slightly altered form, of justifications advanced some 20 years ago and put in cold storage during the assimilationist phase of policy-making and curriculum development in the 1960s and early 1970s. Thus, Walker (1963a) asked why in principle Italian should not be taught as a foreign language for English children in some primary schools, particularly as they had Italian friends, even though there was no timetabled time. Moreover, the Schools Council Working Paper No.13 (1967) argued that although it was not suggested that both the English and non-English-speaking children should learn each other's language, even in schools where there was a large number of immigrant children, a case could be made for this where, as with Italian, the language was generally accepted as a foreign language for teaching purposes. It was implied that the social significance and status of Italian might have rendered it more acceptable for mainstream study. Perren (1979) , for example, has observed how in England attitudes towards minority languages are affected by social, historical and local prejudices and experiences and especially the socioeconomic status or colour of their speakers. Hence Perren suggested that Italian may have a relatively high status, together with German, Spanish and Polish, being accorded more prestige than Greek, Turkish and Chinese – and these, in turn, more than the languages of the Asian sub-continent. Following Walkers' earlier argument, it is interesting to see that Mengon (1980), who was a member of the Italian Embassy Education Inspectorate, also advocated that Italian taught in the mainstream education system should provide opportunities for study by pupils from both Italian and non-Italian backgrounds since positive recognition of the languages and cultures represented in the school can help to foster a school ethos contributing to the realization of a multicultural and multiracial society. Tosi (1980a) additionally suggests that Italian should be offered to all pupils as an option in order to derive best use of practical, economic and educative resources and to achieve the main intellectual and social goals of language teaching. The presence of near-native speakers in the classroom might be a stimulus to developing a new image for Italian not only as the language of a prestigious culture, but also as the popular language of peers, neighbourhood and community. This echoes Walker's argument 20 years previously. But as Steedman (1979) has argued, the assimilationist educational policies pursued in the interim appear to have ignored the potential need of children educated outside their parents' country of origin to acquire an awareness of their own personal cultural history through the maintenance of their parents' mother tongue. That British children might also benefit from opportunities to learn the language of their Italian peers – who were themselves a bilingual resource – or that Italian pupils should broaden their understanding of their social and cultural position by considering their lives in the UK compared with the lifestyles in their parents' villages of origin was hardly countenanced. Despite the relatively high prestige of Italian in the British education system, for historical reasons, the arrival of Italian migrant workers did little to encourage the expansion of mainstream Italian teaching.

Recognition of the importance of the mother tongue was given by the EC Directive (77/486 EC) on the 'Education of Children of Migrant Workers', issued in 1977, which ruled that Member States 'in accordance with their national circumstances and legal systems' should 'promote the teaching of the mother tongue and of the culture of the country of origin... with a view principally to facilitating their possible reintegration into the member state of origin' (GB. DES and WO, 1981, p. 53). This statement initiated a lively debate in the UK not merely with respect to the children of European migrant workers, but also by extension to the children of other nationals. Although many children with Italian backgrounds are UK-born, the ambivalence about returning to Italy displayed by many first-generation Italians and even their children makes the Directive particularly pertinent. Moreover, although the Directive does not cover children whose parents are UK nationals with family origins in other countries – the third generation of Italians now entering British schools – it should not be assumed that the significance of the Italian language, both for cultural reasons and in case of 'return' to Italy, has necessarily lost its force. Furthermore, it is not yet possible to discern the effect of Britain's membership of the Common Market, which makes it subject to laws governing the free movement of labour amongst EC Member States (see King, 1979), for although there are suggestions that a large number of migrants are young people who come as 'tourists' and take up temporary work (Palmer, 1973) and are unlikely to have children (similarly, domestic service workers are not allowed to bring over children – see MacDonald and MacDonald, 1972), nevertheless it is possible that there may be increasing numbers of Italian children arriving in British schools, even in a temporary capacity, hence justifying the language provision being made for them under the EC rules. The EC Directive required compliance by 1981. The DES Circular 5/81 (GB. DES and WO, 1981) advised that LEAs were not required to provide mother-tongue tuition as of right, but acknowledged the assistance of foreign embassies in some schemes and suggested that there was further scope for LEAs to encourage co-operation between teachers in community language and mainstream schools and to provide material help such as accommodation for classes. A further DES memorandum on compliance was issued in 1982 (GB. DES, 1982). As a result of the initial stimulus of the Directive followed by the Swann Report, many LEAs have been reconsidering their language teaching policies as a whole, re-examining the rationale for mother-tongue teaching and, in particular, secondary provision for minority language options. Apropos of the provision for Italian teaching, Tosi (1980a) noted that the funds available from the EC Social Fund for the education of the children of European migrants would cease with the implementation of the EC Directive in 1981 on the expectation that they would be replaced by national resources of the host country. Tosi claimed that as a result the 50 per cent grant towards costs was likely to be withdrawn from the *Doposcuola* system by the Italian authorities (and presumably this would also apply to contributions to mainstream schooling), so that unless mainstream schools began new courses in Italian, provision would be seriously undercut. This, Tosi suggested, was likely to increase the demand made by Italian parents and associations for Italian teaching in mainstream schools. However, in 1986 this position had not yet come about.

Another factor which should be taken into account in decisions regarding mainstream provision for Italian teaching are the attitudes of pupils of Italian origin and their peers. The Swann Report (GB. P. H of C, 1985) provided evidence that many pupils of Italian origin would have preferred to have studied Italian in school time, when teachers claimed their motivation was greater, and that timetabling considerations were vital in order to maximize opportunities for choosing Italian and meeting interests in other curriculum subjects. Indeed it should not be assumed that pupils of Italian origin naturally wish to study Italian in the mainstream. Sinclair (1980) and Devereux (1980) described the introduction of Italian into a secondary school in Reading in an area of small Italian population, but this failed to attract such pupils to the school. Indeed, as an HMI investigation into mother-tongue teaching found, take-up of Italian and other minority languages in the mainstream was not substantial in relation to the number of pupils speaking their mother tongues. However, Italian may be perceived as an attractive language to learn by non-Italian speakers (GB. DES, 1984). McGhee (1983) has argued that in Glasgow the introduction of Italian in three secondary schools at various times since the 1960s was enthusiastically received by pupils and not discontinued due to lack of pupil demand. In the Secondary Pupils Survey of the Linguistic Minorities Project many of the 1,600 monolingual 11-year-olds in Peterborough and 752 monolingual 14-year-olds in Bradford were aware that Italian was spoken by their classmates or in the locality, and many wanted to learn it. (Table 36).

Table 36: **Number of monolingual pupils aware of Italian spoken locally and wanting to learn it at school in two LEAs, Peterborough and Bradford**

	Awareness of Italian as:		*Wanting to learn Italian at school*
	classmates' language	local language	
Peterborough	572	275	250
Bradford	73	59	114

Source: LMP, 1983a, Tables 3.4 and 3.5.

In addition 27 bilingual pupils in Peterborough and 11 in Bradford (plus a few of those who had earlier used a language other than English) wanted to learn Italian. There is also evidence of interest in learning Italian amongst primary school pupils. Monolingual peers of Italian-speaking children involved in the MTCP in Bedford responded positively to the project and, as they became aware that the Italian-speaking pupils had some extra abilities, some also requested to be allowed to participate (GB. P. H of C, 1985). In another scheme for teaching Italian in five Edinburgh primary schools in 1981–4 (see p.278–9), where 300 Italian and non-Italian speakers learnt together, many of the non-Italian children considered it beneficial to know about a language other than English and a number specifically claimed that they felt the course would help them to learn languages generally. The involvement of native-speaking teachers was particularly appreciated (Hutchinson, 1984).

MAINSTREAM PROVISION   The following chronological account of provision for teaching Italian is derived from available research data on LEA- and school-based provision which attempts to distinguish the number of *Corsi Inseriti* jointly arranged with the Italian authorities. With the exception of such a scheme in operation since 1962 in five schools in Bedford (Open University, 1982), there is no record of any provision being made prior to the 1970s. Not surprisingly, when Italian is taught it is usually within the modern languages curriculum of secondary schools, though there is some evidence of limited primary school provision. It is also of interest to compare provision in Scotland and to consider the availability of Italian in institutions of further and higher education.

In a survey in England and Wales, in 1970 (Townsend, 1971) five LEAs claimed that languages of immigrants' countries of origin were taught in schools, and Italian was sometimes taught irrespective of the presence of pupils of Italian origin. In a follow-up survey a year later only four out of 98 multicultural secondary schools in the sample indicated that any tuition was provided in the languages of immigrant pupils' countries of origin, though Italian was numbered amongst them (Townsend and Brittan, 1972). Yet by 1974 some 250 courses under the auspices of the Italian Consulate were available in school curricula (Tosi, 1980a). Such courses were most likely in secondary schools with a relatively large number of pupils of Italian origin (see e.g. Kerr, 1978, regarding Nottingham), though pupils may not necessarily have been prepared for examination entry (Jackson, 1979).

The EC Directive in 1977 inspired considerable discussion and rhetoric, but to what extent in recent years has this led to activity in terms of provision of Italian language classes within mainstream schooling? In another national survey, in 1979 (Little and Willey, 1983), only five LEAs in areas with between two-and-a-half and ten per cent ethnic minority pupils reported that languages of minority groups were taught in schools, and in two LEAs this was the case for Italian. However, the response from such LEAs clearly failed to give a true reflection of provision, for although by 1980 the number of *Corsi Inseriti* had apparently declined, some 160 classes (2,000 pupils) nevertheless were being supported by the Italian authorities through the normal school curriculum (Mengon, 1980). Indeed in 1980 40 schools in the ILEA offered Italian at some level, twice the figure for the previous year (Sinclair, 1980). In view of the number of pupils of Italian origin in London schools (see p.227–8), it may perhaps be assumed that some of these classes would have included such pupils. Yet another national survey illustrated the difficulties of LEA response in this area, that many may not have a clear picture of provision and that a country-wide perspective may not properly indicate the level of provision in certain localities with relatively large numbers of pupils of Italian origin. In the CRE survey 1980–2 (Tsow, 1983) 26 per cent of the 60 LEAs responding (48 per cent) provided information on mother-tongue teaching in the maintained sector during and after school hours. Of these, five LEAs reported that Italian as a 'mother tongue' was taught in mainstream schools. In four of these LEAs the Italian government funded teachers' salaries. In three LEAs Italian was taught from a beginners' level up to A-level. Yet in 27 per cent of the 48 per cent of LEAs responding Italian was provided as a modern languages option. The BBC in-service training series, *Case Studies in Multicultural Education*, and the film *Languages for Life*, show how schools and LEAs can work together to provide classes in southern European and other languages on a consortium basis (Twitchin and Demuth, 1981). Indeed many have argued that Italian presents fewer difficulties than French to the adolescent learner and is more motivating for all ability levels. In 1987 the Association of Teachers of Italian was attempting to ascertain the number and location of schools in Britain where Italian is taught.

Survey data tend to suggest that although Italian may be more available as a modern language option than many of the other languages of minority communities in Britain, it is probably not more likely to be specifically provided for Italian language speakers as such, except where there is a sizeable number of Italian-speaking pupils and courses have been mounted in co-operation with the Italian authorities. For example, in Bradford the Mother Tongue Teaching Directory (MTTD) survey 1981 (LMP, 1982b) revealed that Italian was taught as a 'mother tongue' in three secondary schools. In these cases the Italian Embassy supplied the teacher(s), paid salaries and provided textbooks and teaching aids (in one case jointly with the LEA), and the LEA supplied exercise books and paper as well as accommodation. In fact in Bradford the Italian classes were the only classes other than those for South Asian languages to receive some LEA support. In Cambridgeshire, especially the Peterborough division, mainstream Italian is taught to pupils of Italian origin by teachers employed by the Italian government (Martin-Jones, 1984) and is taught in many schools as a second modern language by modern languages staff. According to the Adviser for Multicultural Education in Bedfordshire, in 1986, Italian was taught in the modern languages department of two 13–18 schools and in extra-curricular classes in one middle school by three full-time Italian teachers employed by the Italian Embassy. Apparently LEAs sometimes approach the Italian authorities for assistance; in other cases the embassy initiates arrangements to set up classes. Indeed by 1986 the number of *Corsi Inseriti* in the UK increased to around 250, with roughly as much as one third of the 770 classes administered by the Italian authorities. There are, for example, about 120 such classes in ILEA, 16 in Bedfordshire and 14 in Bristol (Brogi, 1986).

Evidence indicates, however, that there is little direct provision for Italian in the primary school curriculum, especially in comparison with community classes. In 1983, in a Schools Council survey, although 252 primary schools in 23 LEAs were providing mother-tongue teaching as part of the primary curriculum, Italian was only supported in two schools, despite its having been mentioned by 12 LEAs as one of the most frequently occurring languages (Tansley and Craft, 1984). However in 1986 Italian was taught in eight primary schools in Peterborough, Cambridgeshire in three schools by one teacher employed by the LEA and in five schools by Italian Embassy teachers. The Italian Embassy also supports other Italian classes for primary-age children and there are three classes for infants in Brixton run by the Scalabrini missionaries (Brogi, 1986).

Provision in England and Wales may be compared with provision in Scotland where Italian is the 'mother tongue' of the largest non-English-speaking immigrant community. Even so, Italian occupies fourth place in the modern languages curriculum after French, German and Spanish. According to McGhee (1983), the lack of status of Italian is due to its history as a school subject. In Glasgow, for example, Italian has been taught since the war, but always in Roman Catholic schools and, until 1960, the 'better' senior secondary schools, which tended to make it special. Until the late 1960s it was studied only as a second language and was available in only two comprehensive schools. Since then Italian has been introduced as a first foreign language in three Glasgow schools, with the result that more pupils continued the study of their first foreign language and opted for a second language. But apparently the textbooks, courses, methods and targets have not been adapted to teaching mixed-ability pupils in comprehensive schools. Yet McGhee claims there is evidence of pupil demand greater than that being satisfied. It is particularly interesting to note that Wilkin (1979) found a striking proportional relationship between the Scottish regions of settlement of early Italian immigrants (1877–1939) and the number of educational institutions in the various regions of Scotland where tuition in the Italian language was available in 1979. In view of immigration patterns, this would suggest that school provision is related to the third or, in some cases, the fourth generation in schools. In 1979, 110 secondary schools in Scotland offered Italian, some 66 in the Strathclyde region around Glasgow, and 15 in the Lothian region around Edinburgh (plus seven in Grampian, six in Tayside and Highlands, three in Central and Dumfries and Galloway, two in Fife, and one each in Borders and Orkney). The connection with Roman Catholic schools endures: all 19 in the Glasgow area teaching Italian (Farrell, 1983), and in Edinburgh in a small number of maintained Catholic secondary schools attended by most children of Italian origin (Hutchinson, 1984). At the primary level, again in contrast to the provision in England and Wales, a scheme in conjunction with the Italian Consulate has been operating in five primary schools in Edinburgh (Hutchinson, 1984; see pp.278–9). In 1986, 27 *Corsi Inseriti* classes were jointly organized by the Italian and local education authorities in Scotland, many at primary level (Brogi, 1986). Clearly, support from the Italian authorities has greatly influenced the extent of provision for the teaching of Italian to pupils of Italian origin, and others, in UK schools.

What, then, of provision for Italian teaching in further and higher education? In 1976 Saifullah Khan reported that an increasing number of technical colleges and FE colleges were introducing O- and A-level courses in minority languages, e.g. Italian. In Scotland, in 1979, a total of 48 colleges of technology, FE and commerce offered courses in Italian, 34 in the Strathclyde region (Wilkin, 1979). McGhee (1983) has acknowledged that in Glasgow Italian is more available and successful relative to other languages in FE than it is in secondary schools. The MTTD survey in Coventry, in 1981 (LMP, 1982a), discovered Italian classes in an FE college which included students from Italian language backgrounds and others wishing to learn the language. Where schools and FE colleges increasingly incorporate community languages into their mainstream provision, they are likely to have students for whom the language has family connections *and* those who have not, which illustrates why the term 'mother-tongue' teaching is becoming an unsatisfactory description of such provision.

In higher education the CILT report, *Less Commonly Taught Languages* (Perren, 1975), showed that 138 students in 1973 were enrolled on first-degree courses in Italian in England and Wales. Weston (1979) claimed that initial success in Italian by pupils of Italian origin has frequently led to continuing study and that many Italian departments at universities and polytechnics have a high quota of students of Italian origin, though no supporting figures are cited. She suggested that although the choice of Italian might be seen as a soft option, or might represent an attempt to handle feelings of alienation in respect of British society, it nevertheless shows an interest in their parents' country of origin and its language. From a questionnaire sent to universities Wilkin (1980) discovered that 35 universities in the UK offered courses at varying levels in Italian. However, although GCE A-level and SCE higher-grade examination pass rates in Italian indicated that around 800 school-leavers per annum would be nominally admissible for tertiary study during 1978-9, only 318 students were actually enrolled in first-year, post-school certificate classes in Italian available at 31 universities. These students represented a mere 12.7 per cent of all undergraduates reading Italian at university. Yet the *ab initio* courses in 34 universities and polytechnics for 1,119 students demonstrated that the demand for Italian was much higher than the 0.8 per cent of courses offered in schools. Almost three-and-a-half times as many students of Italian were generated from within the universities as were proceeding from secondary school for further studies in the subject. They accounted for 44.8 per cent of university enrolments for Italian and, according to Wilkin, were increasing annually, so that a disproportionate amount of university teaching time is increasingly employed at a level which should have been the province of secondary education. Hence Wilkin claimed that 'The educational authorities in the United Kingdom have, as yet, failed to activate the many recommendations that have been made with a view to honouring this nation's EEC commitment to make widespread provision of major community language teaching in our secondary schools' (1980, p.78). Unfortunately, there is no indication of how many students from Italian backgrounds are engaged on either the *ab initio* or higher-level Italian courses in universities. In a survey, in 1982, Craft and Atkins (1983) discovered that almost 30 universities offered first-degree courses in Italian but provision was limited to fewer than ten polytechnics (see Absalom, 1980), colleges and institutions of higher education. However, in 1986 six university departments of Italian were reported to have closed (Brogi, 1986). (For constraints on school-based developments and training opportunities in colleges of education see pp.279–83.)

EXAMINATION ENTRIES AND PERFORMANCE   Any consideration of examination entrants and performance for GCE O– and A–level and Scottish Certificate of Education, O and H grades, should take into account that figures will also include pupils from a non-Italian-speaking background. In summer 1980 GCE examinations in Italian were set by eight examination boards covering England, Wales and Northern Ireland, and for the Scottish Certificate of Education. After summer 1981, only six boards offered Italian. GCE O- and A-level Italian is offered annually by all these boards in the summer, and O-level is also examined in the autumn by three boards (Baldwin, 1980). Details about several schemes are given in the CILT book, *Italian in Schools* : on Lothian's approach to graded levels of achievement (Clark and Hutchinson, 1980); the Oxford Modern Language Achievement Certificate (Gordon, 1980); the West of England CSE Mode 3 scheme (Gupta, 1980); a review of GCE practices for Italian (Baldwin, 1980); and the International Baccalaureate (Lymbery-Carter, 1980).

Table 37 provides examination statistics for entries and passes for Italian at CSE and GCE O- and A-level for 1970-7. During this period there was a huge increase in CSE entries, though there was also a decrease of more than 20 per cent in the number of entries at GCE O- and A-level. Table 38 shows the entries and pass rates in the Scottish Certificate of Education O and H grades for 1970-8.

Some schools may make arrangements for pupils to sit examinations in languages not taught at school, as Little and Willey (1983) discovered was the practice of a third of 150 heads of modern language departments in 1979 in schools across the country. Of these, 12 per cent made arrangements for Italian to be taken at O-level,

Table 37:   Italian language and studies, CSE, GCE O- and A-level examination entries and passes, 1970–7

CSE all modes	Year	Entries	Grade 1	Grade 1 as % of entry	% change in entry over period 1970–77
Boys and girls	1970	153	35	22.9	
	1971	257	75	29.2	
	1972	243	90	37.0	
	1973	340	109	32.1	+ 247.7
	1974	393	105	26.7	
	1975	472	116	24.6	
	1976	385	124	31.4	
	1977	532	164	30.8	

GCE O-level: summer examinations	Year	Entries	Passes	% pass	% change in entry over period 1970–77
Boys and girls	1970	3,475	2,408	69.3	
	1971	3,456	2,291	66.3	
	1972	3,817	2,441	64.0	
	1973	3,943	2,319	58.8	− 22.3
	1974	3,576	2,216	62.0	
	1975	4,456	2,729	61.2	
	1976	3,615	2,319	64.2	
	1977	2,699	1,916	71.0	

From 1975 pass grades A–C are equivalent to previous grades A–E.

GCE O-level: winter examinations	Year	Entries	Passes	% pass	% change in entry over period 1970/71 – 1976/77
Boys and girls	1970–1	763	494	64.7	
	1971–2	776	495	63.8	
	1972–3	842	450	53.4	
	1973–4	836	460	49.1	− 54.7
	1974–5	858	368	43.0	
	1975–6	746	317	42.5	
	1976–7	346	280	80.9	

From 1975 pass grades A–C are equivalent to previous grades A–E

GCE A-level: summer examinations	Year	Entries	Passes	% pass	% change in entry over period 1970–77
Boys and girls	1970	934	720	77.1	
	1971	922	707	76.7	
	1972	943	712	75.5	
	1973	866	693	80.0	− 21.5
	1974	848	640	75.5	
	1975	833	619	74.3	
	1976	978	715	73.1	
	1977	733	568	77.5	

Source: CILT, 1980, pp.5–6.

Table 38: **Italian language and studies, Scottish Certificate of Education O- and H-level examination entries and passes, 1970–8**

Scottish Certificate of Education: O grade	Year	Entries	Passes	% pass	% change in entry over period 1970–78
Boys and girls	1970	339	239	70.5	
	1971	424	307	72.4	
	1972	481	340	70.7	
	1973	483	300	64.8	+ 19.5
	1974	424	304	71.7	
	1975	495	348	70.3	
	1976	535	376	70.3	
	1977	454	317	69.8	
	1978	405	307	75.8	

Before 1973, this was a pass/fail examination; from 1973 'passes' refer to awards in bands A–C.

Scottish Certificate of Education: H grade	Year	Entries	Passes	% pass	% change in entry over period 1970–78
Boys and girls	1970	233	174	74.7	
	1971	262	202	77.1	
	1972	311	238	76.5	
	1973	300	220	73.3	No change
	1974	282	208	73.8	
	1975	248	173	69.8	
	1976	272	181	66.5	
	1977	264	204	77.3	
	1978	233	176	75.5	

Source: CILT, 1980, pp. 7–8.

the second highest percentage after schools arranging for Polish; and three per cent made arrangements for Italian and Greek to be taken at A-level. (For examination entries from voluntary language schools see p.258.) The Mother-Tongue Teaching Directory (MTTD) surveys in Coventry and Bradford (LMP, 1982a, 1982b) showed that in 1980 five students, probably from an FE college, were entered for O-level with the examination fees being paid by the LEA. In Bradford there was a more widespread provision in three secondary schools: six pupils were entered for CSE, 30 for O-level and two for A-level Italian in 1980, the LEA paying the examination fees. Overall in the summer 1981 examinations in Italian held by the English and Welsh boards there were a total of 679 CSE, 2,962 O-level and 652 A-level entries in Italian (GB. DES and WO, 1983). Compared with the figures in Table 37, these show an increase for CSE and O-level and a decrease for A-level entries.

Unfortunately, there is no indication of the number of entrants from Italian-speaking backgrounds or of their examination performance. Tosi (1980a) claimed that relatively few pupils of Italian origin attempt public examinations and that an unspecified survey of examination results linked with candidates' nationality showed that candidates of Italian origin fared worse in O- and A-level examinations than those who had taken courses in Italian as a foreign language. Tosi argued that lower performance is due to difficulties associated with attendance at voluntary language classes, social background differences and the fact that the home language of pupils of Italian origin is dialect rather than Standard Italian. Tosi claimed that it is necessary to take into account the living language experience of pupils of Italian origin, and that there is a need for greater understanding of the structures of Italian dialect and their effect on learning Standard Italian in order that an assessment may be made of which structures are assimilated with native competence or as if they were a foreign language; whether lack of exposure to Standard Italian in the community affects natural transfer ability; to what extent this can be supplemented by the teacher in the classroom; which English loan words and interferences from English have displaced vocabulary and structure in the Italian dialect; and the optimum age for developing biliterate skills (see Tosi, 1984). The Swann Report (GB. P. H of C, 1985) also noted the concern of some Italian teachers about the appropriateness of O- and A-level examinations in Italian for pupils from Italian backgrounds as it was felt that they required an unnecessarily high level of English, rather than concentrating on a pupils' knowledge of Italian.

RESEARCH INTO TEACHING ITALIAN   It is curious that since any provision for teaching Italian is overwhelmingly at the secondary level of mainstream schooling (and F and HE) research into the teaching of Italian to pupils of Italian origin in mainstream schooling has, until recently (see p.282), only been undertaken at primary level. Two projects, the EC/Bedfordshire Mother Tongue and Culture Project and a scheme in five Catholic primary schools jointly organized by the Italian Consulate and the educational authorities in Edinburgh, for which evaluations have been published, are worth reviewing here for the insights which they afford into the teaching and learning of Italian and the issues which need to be considered in such language teaching projects. The EC/Bedfordshire Mother Tongue and Culture Project (1976–80) was sponsored by the EC in 1976 to study the organization, teaching and learning processes of mother-tongue teaching and to collect information on the logistics of implementing the scheme on a wider basis. The project involved the teaching of Italian to pupils of Italian origin and also the teaching of Punjabi to pupils of Punjabi origin. The project was clearly an innovation of major significance in the history of the education of pupils of Italian origin in the UK, serving to raise consciousness of their language learning situations. This has largely been achieved by extensive document-ation, in particular, the publications of the project's co-ordinator, Tosi (1979a, 1979b, 1980a, 1980b, 1982, 1984, esp. Chapter 4) and three evaluation reports which took an illuminative issue-centred approach. The three evaluation reports had a different focus. The first (Simons, 1979) evaluates the planning and operational structure of the project from January to September 1978 and the experience of those setting it up. The second evaluation report (Simons, 1980), covering September 1978 to September 1979, examined the issues concerning class and project teachers, and their perceptions of the pupils' learning experiences and their parents' cultural back-grounds. The third evaluation report (Tansley, 1981) related to the period September 1979 to July 1980, and concentrated on the espoused and actual aims of the project, liaison between class and project teachers and between home and school, the organizational and practical changes involved, difficulties of curriculum development, especially concerning teaching materials, and monitoring of pupils' progress in comparison with that of their peers in ordinary classes. These documents provide some fascinating insights into the mechanisms of research and development projects and the experiences of learning and schooling of pupils of Italian origin contrasted with those of their Punjabi peers. For further comments see also Wilson (1978) and project school headteachers' views in Hounslow Community Relations Council (1982b) and the Swann Report (GB. P. H of C, 1985).

The project included 34 pupils of Italian origin aged five to eight, who formed two groups, one of 15 children in one school and another of 19 children drawn from two schools. The majority of these children were second-generation Italians whose parents had come from an area approximately 100 miles south of Naples to work as unskilled labourers in Bedford up to 15 years previously. Most had been looked after by their grandmothers before starting school and had older siblings, through whom they were exposed to English, though the language of their homes was Italian dialect. Some had parents who, having arrived in the UK as small children, had experienced most of their own education here and tended to speak English to their children, though they encouraged them to learn Italian (Simons, 1980). Parents were asked to give their permission for their children to learn Italian at school and overwhelmingly indicated their support (Steedman, 1979; Simons, 1980). Although doubts have been expressed about the project teaching Standard Italian to pupils for whom it was not their mother tongue but, in effect, a third language after an Italian dialect and English, Tosi (1984, and in GB. P. H of C, 1985) has claimed that parents unanimously supported the teaching of the national language rather than the original dialect which they regarded as a corruption of proper Italian. They were keen to overcome dialectism and were aware that only fluency in the standard language could provide literacy. Moreover, they apparently saw the project not as a better opportunity for their children in the UK, but to help their reintegration in the Italian school in case of return. In fact a few did return during the course of the project. The children received tuition in Italian for one hour per day over a four-year period in classrooms specially reserved for the purpose. Initially two teachers of Italian, one an Italian national and one British, were engaged and, in 1979, another Italian teacher was appointed. At this time, 15 pupils of Italian origin at middle school and four (later 20) at upper school level were included in the project to test the conditions of continuity and timetabling. But although timetabling problems were explored to some extent, project arrangements did not provide for continuity, either organizationally for the schools or pedagogically for the children, as the groups were different in each school and the project ended by the time the five to eight year-olds reached middle and upper school (Simons, 1979).

The original aims of the project focused on enhancing the self- image of the pupils, facilitating their integration into the English education system and promoting esteem for immigrant pupils on the part of the indigenous children in the school, and an understanding of the host community's language, culture and education on the part of the immigrant group. However, it was soon recognized that these aims were too general, abstract and incapable of assessment. Curiously, it was not initially intended that the project should assess the pupils' linguistic progress. As the project developed, diverse aims existed and different institutions and individuals had varying priorities in their goals. These were reflected in the teaching approaches undertaken by individual project teachers, who generally followed established primary school practice, but did not adhere to a particular syllabus, which was only constructed later in the project. Teaching materials for primary-age pupils made available to the project by the Italian authorities were unsuitable in terms of content and language for their contemporaries in Bedford. One teacher developed a structured guided transfer method to facilitate the gradual change from dialect to Standard Italian which also attempted to take account of interference from English. As part of this process, a group of six to seven year-olds were recorded telling the story of Cinderella at three different times over intervals from three to six months. At the first recording, when the children had been learning for just over a year, a typical account was a mixture of Neapolitan dialect and English. It is interesting, for example, that the abstract and imaginative aspects of the story, such as 'pumpkin', 'fairy godmother', etc., were typically in English, whereas the practicalities, such as housework, were described in dialect (for details see Tosi, 1984). On the basis of this story a selection of interferences from sounds, morpho-semantic and lexical forms was made in an attempt to identify how the phenomenon of transfer from both English and dialect to Standard Italian was developing. Materials based on structures which would enable the children to find correspondences between dialect and Standard Italian were introduced into the classroom. After three months, when the children told the same story again interferences typically decreased by 56 per cent and three months later, in a further recording, had again decreased by 15 per cent (Simons, 1980). Another teacher of Italian, who did not regard dialect as an interference to learning Standard Italian, aimed to make pupils articulate bi-dialectally and literate in an undialectal way, and planned classroom activities to meet the specific needs of each individual child. By engaging in pre-reading approaches, children progressed towards early reading, and when they were fluent and able to read and write simple sentences story-books and topic-work were introduced. The third teacher who joined the project later, when the children were more fluent, concentrated on topic-work, with an emphasis on creative writing, such as children would experience in Italy, rather than on grammar.

As the project got under way, different emphases were placed upon various objectives and, partly in response to the ambivalent attitudes of some of the class teachers whose pupils were involved in the project, there was an increasing focus in the latter half of the project on the measurement of pupils' progress in Italian and English and the development of a resource bank for Italian language and culture – one of the original aims. Originally there were no plans for linguistic assessment, as no suitable tests were available, nor could pre- or post-experimental tests be organized and no control group had been set up. But the class teachers expressed some dissatisfaction about the lack of assessment, for although it was evident from talking to the project teachers that the Italian pupils were developing a fluency in Italian, there was no evidence that their experience in the project would facilitate their acquisition of English. This hope, together with support for the socio-psychological aims of the project, had led many class teachers initially to welcome it. On the whole they were inclined to think that the brighter children coped well with learning Italian and English, whereas the slower children experienced difficulty with both. Steedman (1979) reported that the 13 children of Italian origin whom she observed seemed to be learning enthusiastically and with enjoyment. They read Italian fluently and correctly and had a good grasp of the phonetic system of the standard language, although their speech still suffered from some interference from English. Simons (1980) observed that the majority of pupils involved in the programme had over the three years come to read, write and speak Standard Italian to a degree and that they had gained confidence and enjoyed the work, but she questioned whether any but the project teachers were in a position to establish what precisely the project meant to the particular children involved and their parents. Project teachers were asked to present descriptive profiles of three children of a different ability range – high, average and below average – which also corresponded with the judgement given of the child by class teachers. Case studies of two Italian pupils, quoted by Simons (ibid.), give some indication of the complex judgements which need to be made about pupils and their progress.

As part of the internal evaluation of the project (Tosi, 1984), some pupil profiles were drawn up in an attempt to systematize individual judgements. They consisted of the child's personal details and personality, linguistic background and assessment of competence in Italian, completed by the project teacher and the child's interaction with ethnic peers, other ethnic and indigenous peers together with assessment of competence in English completed by mainstream class teachers. An assessment of competence in both Standard Italian and English – in understanding spoken language, speaking the language, understanding the written language and the ability to write the language – was recorded on a four-point scale when the profiles were completed in October 1978, September 1979 and February 1980. Four variables were identified by Tosi as affecting progress in Standard Italian: the linguistic background of the family and degree of exposure to Italian and English; the degree of variation between language spoken at home and standard language taught; the consistency in the number of children and homogeneity in the age range and ability of the group; and the use of *ad hoc* teaching materials. According to Tansley (1981), most project and class teachers agreed that children had made considerable progress in learning Standard Italian. Summary tables of the successive administration of pupil profiles showed that teachers considered that 70–80 per cent of the Italian children had made 'exceptional progress' in understanding, speaking, reading and writing in Italian. Unfortunately, there is no indication of what factors distinguished those who did well compared with those who were less successful. Subsequently, Tosi (1980b) observed that Italian children seemed to have achieved a higher level of comprehension skills in oracy and literacy in Italian rather than in production skills of speaking and reading. He attributed this to the peculiarity of the dialect spoken at home by Italian children, competence in which led them to a degree of proficiency in decoding in Standard Italian forms which was higher than that achievable in encoding skills in the same language. Other assessments of the skills of pupils of Italian origin in Standard Italian were made in a survey of basic vocabulary, a test in Italian (the translation of the NFER English as a Foreign Language test) and in the recording of children's speech (see Tosi, 1984). The pupils also made progress in learning English, though not so dramatically (see p.285).

In addition to encouraging pupils' linguistic development, the project had other aims, one being to enhance the self-image of pupils. However, two of the Italian teachers and several class teachers did not consider this to be of great importance for the Italian children; they commented on the special position of the children in the Italian families and the natural confidence which they exhibited; some teachers even suggested that, as a result of the project, a few children had become too confident and had been set apart as an élite. It was also suggested that since many of the Italian children regarded themselves as English, the aim of building up their self-image through teaching them Italian was inappropriate. Pupils of Italian origin appeared to differ most from pupils of Punjabi origin in respect of self-image, thus indicating the need to tailor the aims of the project to a particular group of language speakers. Regarding another project aim, teachers suggested that the pupils of Italian origin had become more integrated though little evidence of this was cited. In view of the possible charge of 'élitism', it was more questionable whether another aim, that of increasing the esteem for immigrants on the part of the indigenous children, was achieved, although again this was not closely monitored. However, a headteacher of one of the project schools has reported that indigenous children became more aware of the Italian children's language skills and they, in turn, had 'an increased awareness of their own identity as people with "something of value"' (GB. P. H of C, 1985, p.706). The aim of increasing the understanding by pupils of Italian origin of British language, culture and education was again largely unmeasurable, and one teacher questioned its relevance to Italian children whose culture was seen as not being so very different. It would, however, have been interesting to monitor any longer-term affective consequences in reactions to conflicting cultural values and language attitudes.

In contrast to those less obviously achieved aims, one of the most successful aspects of the project was the establishment of closer home–school liaison. At the start of the project teachers visited parents of participating children, and during the life of the project parents visited the schools more often and became more involved in their children's learning. Good relationships were maintained by frequent visits to the children's families, and these continued on a weekly basis even at the end of the project. Tansley (1981) considered that this was an exemplary aspect of the project which should be observed by schools and teachers in general. However, relationships between mainstream and project teachers were more problematic, as was liaison between project teachers themselves. Even so, as the project developed there was a greater exchange of teaching methods and materials, which eventually resulted in the compilation of a valuable resources bank (see p.282).

An extended description of the MTCP project has been given because of the insights it offers into the learning of pupils of Italian origin and for the setting up and conduct of projects concerned with the development or maintenance of pupils' mother tongue and culture. As Tansley (ibid.) observed in the final evaluation report, there is a need to allocate sufficient time initially to determine the project's aims and procedures, especially with respect to aspects of liaison. The importance of formal assessment is also noted. There was, for example, no scope for long-term assessment of the effects of the project, which appears to have been a missed opportunity, particularly in view of the fact that according to a Commission for Racial Equality (CRE) survey in 1980–2 only six per cent of LEAs responding were conducting research into mother-tongue teaching or bilingualism (Tsow, 1983). Indeed apropos of the sociopolitical realities of such projects, several teachers have criticized the general lack of interest shown in the project by the DES (GB. P. H of C, 1985) and there appears not to have been any public discussion of the LEA's reasons for discontinuing the project after the cessation of funding, apparently this being predominantly on financial grounds (see Tosi, 1980a), although some Bedford schools continue to organize mainstream Italian teaching in conjunction with the Italian consulate.

Such a scheme which began in five Lothian primary schools in 1981 as a response to the EC Directive has been reported by Hutchinson (1984). Given that Italian is taught in some Catholic secondary schools attended by most children of families of Italian origin, it was thought appropriate to extend exposure to the language to some feeder Catholic primary schools, so that language contact could in theory continue on transfer. The absence of examinations and prescribed syllabus constraints were also intended to allow for the development of the study of Italian culture and geography. In 1981–2 mixed-ability P6 and P7 pupils in five primary schools, together with their class teacher who acted as a participant observer and fellow learner, experienced two periods of Italian per week taught by an Italian teacher. Language materials with an emphasis on games, songs and puzzles evolved as a series of visits covering a two-year course relevant to communicative needs in connection with visits to Italy, and family visits with Italian children. Class teachers were involved in the repetition and consolidation of materials and also introduced projects on aspects of Italian life which proved especially popular. Pupils enjoyed the shared experience with their teacher and many non-Italians liked learning another language. Although some of the more able found the repetition boring, a similar number of the less able expressed a sense of achievement. This was also noted by the teachers involved who commented favourably on the general educational benefits of the course, such as increased concentration and increased oral/aural skills rather than specific achievement in Italian, especially for those who were not otherwise high-fliers. This had a pay-off in other curriculum areas, as did the general interest in Italy, which stimulated a more global perspective. The primary teachers were generally enthusiastic and had many suggestions for improving and furthering the course.

Of the parents who commented, many echoed the teachers' perceptions in terms of enjoyment, increased awareness of language and culture and sense of achievement. Several parents were concerned about the lack of liaison with the secondary schools, as had been intended, and Italian parents felt that Italian should be available in the first form of the secondary school, whereas a few regarded the experiment as a waste of time unless it was directed towards examinations. On transfer, although some pupils would have liked to learn more language, none felt it had been a waste of time and most expressed confidence about learning other modern languages. Two-thirds of two classes asserted that they would prefer exposure to several languages than to learn one language well. Ironically the Italian teachers in two secondary schools were, not surprisingly, least satisfied as they found themselves teaching French to children who had done two years of Italian. Administratively, Hutchinson observes, it is too risky to offer Italian for five years with one teacher, and if offered to other year groups additional staff would be required but not permitted. The system does not allow for the degree of diversity in modern language teaching for which there is pupil interest. Hutchinson argues for increased flexibility given the project's success in developing pupils' language awareness and the new syllabuses and assessment being introduced in secondary education which emphasize communicative competence and language resource (see Clark and Hutchinson, 1980).

FURTHER ISSUES AND RESOURCE CONSTRAINTS Consideration of research and development projects brings into sharper focus a number of contentious issues in respect of the form of Italian taught, liaison between Italian teachers and mainstream teachers of Italian, their training and availability and the development of appropriate teaching materials. These will be examined briefly according to available research evidence.

The apparent discovery in the Mother Tongue and Culture Project (MTCP) that for many pupils of Italian origin in Bedford a decade ago their acquaintance with Italian was not with the national standard language, but the dialect of their family's village of origin raised a certain debate about which form of Italian should be taught – the dialect of the pupils' parents or Standard Italian. Tosi has argued that many pupils of Italian origin are in a situation of foreign language learning with respect to learning Standard Italian in school. Although their parents may have learnt some Standard Italian in school in Italy, the language of the home is a dialect and there is no surrounding environmental support for developing Standard Italian. This renders the concept of mother-tongue teaching *per se* problematic in connection with pupils of Italian origin, perhaps to a greater extent than for many other minority language speakers. Moreover, the language backgrounds of children of Italian origin are further complicated, and increasingly with each generation, by the development of English skills and in some homes the greater use of English than Italian dialect. This means that Standard Italian is becoming more of a third language for such children. Yet Mengon (1980) rejected the idea of following the EC Directive about mother-tongue teaching to the letter by teaching dialect not only because of the 'insurmountable' technical and practical problems, but also because of the evolving nature of language and various sociolinguistic shifts, not the least of which is the increasing encroachment of Standard Italian over the old dialects in Italy. He suggested that dialects should be used as a starting-point for further linguistic and cultural exploration and evolution rather than involution. Whilst acknowledging the importance of sociocultural origins, Mengon seemed on balance to favour an approach which recognizes that the future of pupils of Italian origin is probably in the UK. He suggested that Italian and British teachers should see their role as mediating between countries and cultures and aim to involve adults in the educational activities planned for children.

However, it would appear that to date a framework for liaison between Italian teachers in the *Doposcuola* system or even those teaching *Corsi Inseriti* in the mainstream and teachers of Italian in modern languages departments and others has not been established, despite recommendations such as those of Devereux (1980) for co-operation between both sets of teachers engaged in teaching Italian in the mainstream for the same examinations and more generally in DES Circular 5/81 (GB. DES & WO, 1981). Indeed the very position of Italian teachers working in the mainstream seems questionable. Tosi (1980a) has doubted whether if financial assistance to *Doposcuola* classes from the Italian government were to be withdrawn and *Corsi Inseriti* were extensively introduced into mainstream curricula, teachers trained and appointed by other bodies, with different teaching experiences, methods and practices, would be acceptable to LEAs and schools. He suggested that these teachers should be retrained, especially to acquire a knowledge of the education system and to design linguistically appropriate materials. This very objection was actually raised by headteachers in Bedfordshire, when it was suggested that the Italian government might provide Italian teachers for main-stream Italian classes to follow up the MTCP (Tansley, 1981). Headteachers were concerned about the control of, and responsibility for, Italian staff (see Mengon, 1980) and about teaching styles, and in order to exchange information about teaching skills one LEA organized in-service sessions for Italian teachers (GB. P. H of C, 1985). A UNESCO-funded project has investigated the co-ordination and development of INSET for Italian teachers and in relation to mainstream teachers in the UK. More structured opportunities for exchanges between Italian teachers in the *Doposcuola* system, those teaching on *Corsi Inseriti* and mainstream teachers of Italian and other subjects would seem beneficial in developing greater awareness of language learning and the educational needs of pupils of Italian origin.

On the other hand, Carsaniga (1980) has argued that the fact that Italian is relatively little taught in the mainstream is not because of the lack of qualified teachers, but because of failure to decide to make provision. The Swann Report provides evidence to indicate that financial considerations may be uppermost. Apparently headteachers in Bedford schools pointed out that they were unable to adopt Italian as the school's first modern language in case the Italian government were to withdraw support for its teachers. Only Italian-born teachers are accepted for employment in this programme by the Italian authorities. Moreover, as a British teacher of Italian observed, this tends to restrict the availability of teaching posts as the Italian teachers are available to LEAs at little or no extra cost.

An obvious requirement for extending provision for Italian teaching in the mainstream is the availability of trained teachers. However, there is evidence that, even though a relatively large number of universities offer courses in Italian (see p.271), there may be few teacher training opportunities, and that both may be declining. Clearly not all graduates in Italian intend to teach it, though some may teach other subjects. In 1979–80 Powell (1980) found that 15 university depart-ments or colleges offered part-courses to Italian graduates and 12 were prepared to offer varying amounts of specialist help. There were only about 64 Postgraduate Certificate of Education (PGCE) students in training offering Italian as a teaching subject. The lack of availability of convenient and adequate teaching practice places, the scarcity of suitably qualified teacher trainers and the relatively low-level Italian skills of some of the students for whom Italian may only have been a subsidiary undergraduate course (see p.271) were all serious problems. Powell recommended designated centres for minority languages, such as Italian, if possible in areas providing appropriate opportunities for teaching practice and close links between Italian and education departments in universities.

These points were examined further with respect to all community languages in another survey, in 1982, of 106 initial (ITT) and in-service (INSET) teacher training institutions in England and Wales (Craft and Atkins, 1983) and again revealed very limited opportunities. In terms of ITT only two institutions offered main and three subsidiary methods courses in Italian to very few students without previous knowledge, and although there were no B.Ed. courses with Italian some institutions did offer self-instructional facilities. In terms of INSET, only one institution offered a short methods course requiring previous knowledge (see also Bristow, 1980). There was slightly more potential in education department staff, five qualified to work on new courses for Italian and six to contribute to teaching method. However, only one institution was interested in developing a new Italian course in the PGCE and two in the B.Ed., all as a short or subsidiary language course or as a subsidiary or short teaching methods course. One institution was interested in developing new named award language and methods courses for Italian and two short courses for mainstream teachers. These institutions were situated in the north-west. There was apparently no interest in developing short courses for supplementary schoolteachers of Italian. By comparison, McGhee (1983) reported that in Scotland five colleges of education claimed to train teachers of Italian but that, in practice, this usually meant a few classes added on to the French course and that Italian 'has had less of the benefits of Colleges' expertise than other traditional second languages'. Specific Italian INSET and resource support was being developed, but tended only to have token education authority support.

A working party of the National Congress on Languages in Education in 1982 (Reid, 1984) recommended that both ITT and INSET courses should be systematically developed for 12 of the most widely used languages of minority communities, including Italian, and welcomed the initiative of the Royal Society of Arts in setting up a one-year course leading to a certificate in the teaching of community languages. Although there has been discussion of priorities for the development of training for minority language teaching in an attempt to break the vicious circle of recruitment and provision between schools, universities and training institutions (see e.g. Atkins, 1985), there is clearly scope for improvement in relation to Italian (see e.g. Andrews, 1980; Wilkin, 1980).

A further difficulty relating to provision for the teaching of Italian in the mainstream concerns the availability of appropriate teaching materials. It appears arguable (see Carsaniga, 1980; Sinclair, 1980) whether there is a suitable range of published teaching materials for teaching Italian in general. The joint 1980 ATTI/SIS/CILT report and the CRE Mother-Tongue Teaching Conference Report (1980) provide many examples of initiatives by enthusiastic teachers of Italian, conscious of curriculum development and INSET needs (see e.g. Devereux, 1980; Farrel, 1980; Clark *et al.*, 1980; Gordon, 1980; Gupta, 1980; see also McGhee, 1983). More specifically in relation to teaching Italian to pupils of Italian origin, Tosi (1980b) reported that in the MTCP it soon became apparent that existing materials and methodology to teach Standard Italian in Italy or as a second language abroad, were unsuitable for primary-age children of Italian origin developing their mother-tongue dialect to Standard Italian. There is generally little information about appropriate materials or stimuli to interest pupils in Italian as a mother tongue, although the BBC TV series for schools, *You and Me*, has produced stories in printed form and on cassette for four and five year-olds in Italian. The CRE survey in 1980–2 (Tsow, 1983) found that only one LEA was developing materials for 'mother-tongue' teaching in Italian. Materials were being developed on a consortium basis in Peterborough (Twitchin and Demuth, 1981). As a result of the MTCP, teachers produced a wealth of teaching materials in Italian (and Punjabi) (see Tansley, 1981; Tosi, 1964). The materials are divided into two sections at a pre-reading and a reading level. The pre-reading-level materials include picture and letter cards, phonic practice cards, alphabet and symbol cards, letter and word completion cards, sound blending exercises, etc. The reading level includes work in sentence building cards and sheets, workbooks and reading-books. There is an emphasis on topic-work in Italian materials. Following the completion of the project, materials were in circulation within Bedfordshire LEA, included in in-service training and were made available to Italian teachers through the resources bank in Bedfordshire. Part of the EC-funded Schools Council Mother Tongue Project (1981–5) which worked with teachers of primary-age pupils in community mother-tongue and mainstream schools to produce materials and resources for teachers to support their pupils' bilingualism was related to Italian (Tansley, 1986; Tansley *et al.*, 1985; Manley, 1986). Under the auspices of the Italian Consulate eight Italian teachers produced a range of materials for six to nine year-old pupils using a basic vocabulary of 953 words, including eight units of cards with exercises. A 'Breakthrough to Literacy Sentence Maker' in Italian, other cards, games, a cassette and picture-book are available from the Direzione Didattica Italiana. At the secondary level part of another EC-funded project, 'Community Languages in the Secondary Curriculum', based at the University of London Institute of Education (1984–7), is working with 12 Italian teachers employed by the Ufficio Scholastico Italiano, four of whom are working in two ILEA Roman Catholic schools to explore opportunities and constraints for the inclusion of community languages in normal curricular arrangements, the production of materials for diverse age and ability groups and exchanging ideas on teaching methodology and assessment.

The foregoing review might suggest that, compared with other minority language speakers, pupils of Italian origin might be in a relatively privileged position in terms of the opportunities open to them to learn Standard Italian in mainstream schooling, due to its inclusion in the modern languages curriculum of some secondary schools and the initiatives of some LEAs and schools in collaborating with the Italian authorities to introduce *Corsi Inseriti* where there are larger numbers of pupils of Italian origin. Yet it is clear that there are many problems associated with Italian teaching *per se* in the mainstream. Moreover, there are suggestions throughout the literature that the availability of such courses is by no means sufficient to meet the interest of pupils in general or the demand by pupils of Italian origin in particular. Pupils of Italian origin might prefer to learn Italian in the mainstream alongside their peers. Even if provision is made, the fact that the teaching is of Standard Italian and not of dialect makes it clear that it is not a question of mother-tongue maintenance or teaching which is at issue here. A number of significant questions need to be raised both with respect to the future teaching of Italian in schools as such and in relation to pupils of Italian origin. The experience of the MTCP (see pp.274–8) provided useful insights, and other recently completed (such as MTP, see above and pp.111–14) and ongoing projects (such as CLSE, see above) are gradually building up a more comprehensive evaluation of progress and problems in practice to inform policy. There is a continuing need for more research and curriculum development work. Meanwhile generations of minority language speakers are passing through schools, and communities such as the Italian are becoming increasingly English speaking. The existence of the EC Directive and the need for its implementation make consideration of the development of provision for Italian and other minority language teaching in mainstream curricula a matter of urgency.

TEACHING ENGLISH AS A SECOND LANGUAGE
In contrast to the relative profusion of information on other aspects of language knowledge, use and attitudes, and on provision for teaching Italian in community language classes and in the mainstream, there is little evidence on the teaching of English as a second language (E2L) to pupils of Italian origin. This, like other aspects of school-based provision for pupils of Italian origin, has not often formed a particular focus of research attention. Yet the first pupils of Italian origin to enter British schools – the intermediate generation, who would have been in the vanguard of immigrant pupils in many schools – are likely to have formed an experimental group for many teachers in their first encounters with non-English-speaking pupils. With such pupils, teachers may have developed language teaching strategies later to form the basis of more systematic and structured approaches as the number of pupils for whom English was a second language steadily grew. Lack of comment on the acquisition of English of pupils of Italian origin may also, perhaps, indicate that this may have occasioned less difficulty in view of the linguistic affinities of Italian and English, compared with the experience of other E2L learners whose language might bear little resemblance to English. Moreover, over the 30 years or so that pupils of Italian origin have been present in schools in Britain the needs of individual pupils and indeed generations of pupils in E2L teaching will have varied widely and will continue to do so, according to their family language background, as English may become a first rather than a second language. A limited account can be given from research evidence of teachers views' of the English of pupils of Italian origin and the number thought to be in need of E2L teaching, the organization and methods adopted for E2L teaching and current approaches, especially in relation to the relationship of E2L and mother-tongue teaching.

A study of race relations in Leamington Spa (Jenkins, 1971) suggested that in the 1950s the children of Italian immigrants spoke little or no English and in consequence were severely held back in local schools. By contrast, in the early 1960s in Bedford, Walker (1963a) suggested that with special English tuition pupils of Italian origin soon acquired competence in English. But as more pupils of Italian origin entered schools their need for E2L teaching became more apparent. In an ILEA survey, in 1965, 400 out of 2,500 or more Italian children were assessed by their teachers as speaking 'little or no English' and as 'pupils who by reason of language difficulties were unable to follow a normal school curriculum with profit to themselves' (Schools Council, 1967). Nationally, apart from the ILEA, a total of 7,200 European pupils were considered to have inadequate English, a number which in view of the settlement patterns of other European immigrant pupils is likely to have included a majority of pupils of Italian origin. Unfortunately, the NFER survey of pupils' need for E2L teaching in the early 1970s did not distinguish groups of pupils from European backgrounds. At the end of the 1970s a survey of linguistic diversity in 28 secondary schools in 11 London boroughs, in 1978, revealed that only nine per cent of the 46 pupils of Italian origin aged 11–12 involved were said by their teachers to speak English less than fluently at an intermediate level (Rosen and Burgess, 1980). Four ILEA language censuses provide evidence of the continuing need of some pupils of Italian origin for E2L teaching or support (see pp.235–6). In the first census, in 1978, some 28.4 per cent of the 2,272 pupils who had Italian as their first language were said by their teachers to be in need of additional English teaching (ILEA, 1979). In the subsequent census, in 1981, 31.6 per cent of 2,808 pupils, in 1983, 29.1 per cent of 2,421 and, in 1985, 31.1 per cent of 2,102 pupils who used Italian other than or in addition to English at home were said by their teachers to lack complete fluency. However, in each census more than half of these pupils were at the third stage of learning English (see also Table 32) (ILEA, 1982, 1983, 1986).

However, the Swann Committee received a considerable amount of evidence from teachers of the continuing need of pupils of Italian origin for help and support with mastering English. Some children were said to enter school with only a very limited knowledge of English, and apparent fluency might mask more complex second-stage E2L needs. It was suggested that teachers might fail to recognize the possible difficulties of pupils of Italian origin such as being able to apply knowledge of English to increasingly complex and abstract concepts (GB. P. H of C, 1985). Writing of pupils of Italian origin in Bedford, Tosi (1984) has claimed that fluency with the local pronunciation and accent is often interpreted by teachers as a sign of native command of English: 'Yet beyond the initial stages of the curriculum when more conceptual and less practical linguistic functions are demanded by the teacher, difficulty in elaborating abstractions and in using sophisticated vocabulary may arise' (p.111). Tosi suggests that these might be mistaken for cognitive rather than linguistic problems. Some teachers have been reported to claim that inadequate English and the complexity of examination language could militate against pupils of Italian origin demonstrating true ability in a subject (Open University, 1982; GB. P. H of C, 1985).

Although there is little specific information available on the organization of E2L provision for pupils of Italian origin, a chronological account, revealing the development of arrangements and approaches which can be pieced together largely from researches based in Bedford, is not without interest in view of the concentration of Italian pupils there. Brown (1970) recorded that initially in the late 1950s and early 1960s *ad hoc* strategies were devised, including separate 'English progress' classes which aimed to develop newly arrived children's competence in English to enable them to take a full part in school life and work. According to Brown, the absence of a common approach to E2L teaching at this time reflected a lack of clear direction in local policy-making. Teachers of immigrant pupils were not given official encouragement or special training, nor allocated special funds for their work. Some Bedford teachers formed the Association for the Teaching of English to Pupils from Overseas (ATEPO). However, as concern began to grow special English classes were instituted on a partial withdrawal basis for selected junior and senior pupils who spent their day mainly with specialist teachers rejoining their peers for assembly, meals and games (Walker, 1963a). By 1967 the Schools Council Project, 'English for Immigrant Children', was operating in Bedford schools. By then E2L teaching took place in both remedial streams and 'withdrawal' classes. Interestingly, Brown recorded that despite their greater number compared with other ethnic minority pupils, pupils of Italian origin did not form the major group in the separate language classes. More recently, Tosi (1984) has observed that on starting school in Bedford pupils from Italian backgrounds are taught in classes with pupils who are speakers of other languages including English. If they fail to make satisfactory progress, they are either taught in separate remedial classes or sent to a language centre. Just as organizational provision for E2L teaching has varied in Bedford over more than 25 years, so the form and quality of E2L provision has varied between LEAs. Indeed Triseliotis (1976) claimed that no special provision was made for the considerable number of Italian children outside London and other areas of large Italian settlement, so that their distinctive needs may not have been met. Restrictions on the use of money under Section 11 of the 1966 Local Government Act for Commonwealth immigrants may have affected E2L provision for pupils of Italian origin, though as Jeffcoate (1984) has argued, there was a good case for including Italian immigrants in view of their sociocultural backgrounds and lack of English.

There is little evidence of specific E2L techniques developed for pupils of Italian origin. In the early 1960s, as the Italian children were predominantly of infant age, it was relatively easy to introduce a vocabulary of nouns, adjectives and verbs to the children through the ordinary classroom environment by, for example, labelling items of furniture. But the arrival of older children required more specialized techniques and intensive courses in basic oral English, drawing heavily on repetition and ignoring the complexities of spelling and syntax. In the partial withdrawal groups teaching focused on conversational skills, based around real-life episodes, and tape recordings were used to develop good accents (Walker, 1963a). Tosi (1984) has briefly described how the principles espoused in Derrick's popular work, *Teaching English to Immigrants* (1966), have been implemented in infant classes of Italian and other non-English-speaking pupils. A handbook from the Schools Council Project in English for Immigrant Children deals with particular pronunciation problems of pupils of Italian origin (Rudd, 1971).

Similarly, there appears to be little documented evidence of any special difficulties which pupils of Italian origin experienced in the learning of English, or to what extent teachers have understood the relationship between the pupils' Italian dialects and their attempts to learn English. Bedford LEA has been involved in Italian teaching projects which, whilst not directly concerned with providing a language basis for the later development of English, contributed some subsidiary insights. In 1963 Bedford LEA and the Italian vice-consulate established a scheme of Italian teaching in 12 schools, and in five of these teaching occurred in the ordinary curriculum (Open University, 1982). However, Jackson (1979) found that primary school teachers were very critical of the attendance of pupils of Italian origin at Italian classes arguing that the time which they spent learning their 'mother tongue' made it more difficult for them to learn English. The teaching of English is seen by many teachers as of paramount importance (GB. P. H of C, 1985). Yet in the Mother Tongue and Culture Project (MTCP), in the late 1970s (see pp.274–8), although it was recognized that the language needs of pupils of Italian origin differed depending on their language backgrounds, and on generation, their position in the family and the degree to which the Italian dialect, Standard Italian and/or English were spoken in the home, it was generally agreed by most of the project and class teachers that the teaching of Standard Italian to these primary school pupils over a four-year period did not adversely affect their learning of English. Indeed the majority of pupils of Italian origin involved in the project were considered both by the project and class teachers to have made 'exceptional progress' in reading and writing and 'normal progress' in understanding and speaking English. Evaluations of the project (Simons, 1980; Tansley, 1981) imply that the majority of the Italian pupils were performing in English as expected for their age by the end of the four-year project. However, Tansley properly cautioned against generalizing from these findings with a small number of pupils and concluded that 'mother tongue teaching, whilst it does not actively hinder progress in English, does not necessarily help it' (p.23).

Attitudes to language learning may significantly affect progress. One of the most successful features of the MTCP project was the interest and support of Italian parents who were keen for their children to participate. Parents did not seem at all concerned that to learn Standard Italian their children might miss some lessons in English, and had no doubt that they would be able to pick it up subsequently. Indeed they may have welcomed this redressing of the balance, for as Mengon (1980) observed the insistence on the study of English may appear to Italian parents as evidence of the education authorities' intention of ignoring and neglecting their own culture and language. Even when parents do not have great competence in English, they can have a significant effect on the development of reading ability merely by hearing their child read regularly, as was demonstrated by a project which involved collaboration between teachers and parents in assisting with children's reading (Tizard *et al*, 1982).

It would seem that to date even though consideration of the relationship of mother-tongue teaching to the acquisition of English as a second language, and developing the language of the home as a basis for transfer later to learning English, are becoming rather more than merely of academic linguistic interest the subject of practical research (see pp.274–9), the policies and methods of schools and LEAs may be directed primarily towards E2L teaching as such. This is supported by the findings of the CRE survey in 1980–2 (Tsow, 1983) in which only a quarter of 83 LEAs responding recorded the existence of a policy on multicultural education. Only in 29 per cent of those LEAs with a policy did it specifically relate to mother-tongue teaching. Moreover, a quarter of the 57 per cent of LEAs with policies on multicultural education which responded made specific reference to the fact that provision of English classes for 'immigrant' children was the main priority of their policy. None of the LEAs was developing Italian as a 'mother-tongue' medium for teaching E2L. Indeed there is little evidence of other support for such an approach, either in terms of Italian-speaking bilingual nursery assistants (Rathbone and Graham, 1983) or teaching materials, and a Schools Council inquiry (Tansley and Craft, 1984) discovered that although Italian was named as the seventh most frequently occurring language by LEAs with multilingual primary schools, it had relatively little recognition in primary schools.

The Swann Report, claiming the support of the majority of teachers of pupils of Italian origin who were consulted, recommended that such pupils should not be withdrawn for E2L help, but that structured language support should be provided within the normal classroom situation. Language needs should not be seen as the concern solely of specialists, but all teachers should have an understanding of how linguistic difficulties might bear on a child's performance and be involved in a full language across the curriculum policy, as advocated by the Bullock Report (GB. DES, 1975). However, there is evidently a need to develop teachers' awareness of the language needs of pupils of Italian origin as such within linguistically diverse classrooms and in all subject-areas. A survey undertaken in 1982 for the Swann Committee (Craft and Atkins, 1983) revealed that institutions engaged in initial and in-service teacher education offered a range of E2L courses rather than courses for teaching minority languages, although E2L courses might be developing to include greater study of the minority community languages themselves. Student teachers were likely to emerge from initial teacher training with some awareness of linguistic diversity in schools, but they were much less likely to be trained to offer language support across the curriculum or strategies for working in multilingual classrooms. Only a little more than a quarter of institutions offered this in the core course and in nearly half the institutions instruction there was no opportunity to prepare for teaching in a multilingual classroom at all.

Although there is a dearth of evidence on strategies for E2L teaching where there are only a few pupils of Italian origin without specialized support and materials depicting pupils of Italian origin in Britain, over the last decade several curriculum development projects have considered E2L approaches for linguistic minority pupils as a whole and, more recently, support for children's bilingualism in the mainstream at primary level. The Second Language in the Primary School Project in the ILEA from 1975 developed materials to support learning English through collaborative learning in phased learning activities. The Bilingual Under Fives Project from 1978 developed materials which provide the bilingual child with opportunities to communicate in the mother tongue in school and to involve parents and siblings in a task- and activity-orientated programme. Materials from both projects are available from the Learning Materials Service of ILEA. The Schools Council's Primary Classroom Project (1981–3) devised strategies linking language growth with conceptual development across the curriculum, based on the enriching contribution of bilingual pupils to the education of the whole class. Some of the Schools Council/EC Mother Tongue Project's work (1981–5) has focussed on developing a handbook for monolingual teachers, *All Our Languages*, outlining strategies for supporting classroom language diversity across the curriculum by working with parents and local communities and developing resources, especially taped stories in pupils' mother tongues (see p.122–3). Other useful sources include *Supporting Children's Bilingualism* (Houlton and Willey, 1983) which cites recent projects; an annotated bibliography of materials supporting E2L learning (Hester *et al.*, 1977); Brown's book (1979) on the young bilingual child; Ch.12 on the mother tongue and Ch.13 on E2L in Twitchin and Demuth's book (1981); and publications from the National Council for Mother Tongue Teaching and Centre for Information on Language Teaching.

In conclusion, there is evidence that despite the longer residence in the UK of many Italian families compared with other ethnic minority groups, some pupils of Italian origin still enter school with relatively little knowledge of English, or a knowledge of vocabulary but not of syntax, and may need specific E2L support. However, even when specific arrangements exist to help with the initial stages of learning English, there may be a lack of suitable teaching materials or inadequate understanding of the particular difficulties experienced by pupils of Italian origin. There is little evidence of using the home language as a basis for learning English. Most importantly, attention needs to be given to providing continuing support in the development of full competence in English by pupils of Italian origin across the curriculum and throughout their experience of schooling.

School Placement, Examination Performance, FE, HE and School to Work
Consideration of the educational achievement of pupils of Italian origin should take into account pupils' language background and their personal linguistic range in English and Italian. In comparison with pupils from some other minority groups, there is little quantitative research evidence of a statistical nature relating to the achievement of pupils of Italian origin at school. Available evidence consists mostly of description and general statements based on knowledge and observation of Italian pupils, and has a largely subjective and qualitative basis. However, by drawing these insights together it is possible with a certain measure of consistency to sketch out a general framework for considering the school placement, qualifications, participation in further and higher education and transfer from school to work of pupils of Italian origin.

According to Steedman (1978), who reviewed the education of migrant workers' children including Italians in EEC member states, whilst Western European governments during the 1960s and early 1970s pursued policies of assimilation of migrants and their children with the host country's language and culture, resulting in very uneven levels of achievement of immigrant children within national systems, Italian children found themselves advantaged with respect to other immigrant groups and did not manifest the same dismal picture of educational underachievement as the children of Turkish, Greek or Portuguese migrant workers. Given that there are fewer children of Italian origin in the UK compared with other European countries (see Willke, 1975; Palmer, 1977; see p.216), and their somewhat ambivalent status as the children of Italian migrants or immigrants, to what extent have pupils of Italian origin succeeded in the British educational system? Steedman quoted two Italian sources (Marin, 1975, and the Rapporto, 1977) which emphasized that children of Italian origin do not experience 'major difficulties of discrimination or incomprehension of their cultural background within the English school system' (p.36). Moreover, Steedman (1979) claimed that pupils of Italian origin do not display the same degree of difficulty experienced by other ethnic minority pupils within the British educational system. On the other hand, other sources have suggested that the level of achievement of pupils of Italian origin may not be particularly high. For example, Tosi (1979a) claimed that on the whole second-generation Italian pupils in Bedford achieve poor standards at school. Researchers for the Open University Unit on Bedford (1982) encountered concern about underachievement amongst the Italian community and three Roman Catholic voluntary aided schools felt that Italian children were performing appreciably below their potential because of inadequate English. Even so, other schools and teachers argued that Italians did as well as other pupils. However, an LEA in Little and Willey's (1983) national survey warned against complacency about third- and fourth-generation European pupils whose home backgrounds were largely linguistically and culturally related to their origins in other European countries, and who might be underachieving in the British school system. The Swann Report noted that:

> whilst it appears to be generally felt that Italian pupils achieve 'reasonably well' in academic terms, there was a widespread belief amongst the teachers, parents and indeed pupils whom we met that the ability of some Italian children might be under-estimated by schools because of a lack of appreciation of their language needs. (GB. P. H of C, 1985, p. 699)

SCHOOL PLACEMENT   Evidence generally suggests that many pupils of Italian origin attend Roman Catholic schools (see e.g. OU, 1982; Farrell, 1983). This, according to Steedman (1979), ensures some cultural continuity between educational institutions in Italy and the UK, and especially for the intermediate generation may be a factor facilitating their integration. Italian parents' preference for their children to attend Roman Catholic schools may cover both primary and secondary education, as Brown (1970) showed in Bedford. When it may not be possible for pupils of Italian origin to attend Roman Catholic schools, special arrangements may be made for their religious education. For example, in a national survey, in 1971, Townsend and Brittan (1972) found that although only 13 out of a sample of 98 secondary schools reported making special arrangements for religious education for immigrant children, mostly for Muslim children, at one secondary modern school 60 Italian children were visited by a Roman Catholic priest who gave instruction in the faith and in Italian. In addition, the only primary school out of 132 in a national sample to mention that special arrangements were made for the religious education of immigrant children was one where Italian children who comprised 25 per cent of the school roll of 320 were withdrawn for 30 minutes per week for RE. Evidence also suggests that many voluntary Italian classes in out-of-school hours are held on the premises of Roman Catholic schools in areas of Italian settlement (see p.254).

Figures for Bedford schools in 1969 quoted by Brown (1970) (see p.217) also indicate that a fair proportion of pupils of Italian origin were to be found in single-sex secondary schools, thus suggesting some preference for such schooling on the part of Italian parents. Indeed, in the third phase of the NFER surveys of immigrant pupils which investigated interethnic friendship patterns and pupils' attitudes to the multiracial school, about 70 per cent of the 95 pupils of Italian origin were found in single-sex schools, mainly at secondary level, in an area of Italian settlement in the Home Counties (Jelinek and Brittan, 1975).

There is little evidence about the within-school placement of pupils of Italian origin. Early evidence suggested that they might be placed in remedial or lower streams whilst acquiring competence in English (Walker, 1963a; Brown, 1970; see p.284), and an early study of social integration (Feeley, 1965) found that Italian pupils tended to be placed in the lower streams of a boys' secondary modern school in the East Midlands. But Townsend and Brittan (1972) observed from their national survey that Italian pupils were more evenly distributed across streams, suggesting that initial linguistic difficulties might be overcome. However, the Swann Report noted that Italian pupils might be mistakenly placed in remedial streams due to difficulties with English. Although they made initial progress at infant school, they sometimes fell behind later in junior and secondary schools unless they received adequate support across the curriculum.

Early evidence suggests that there may have been some initial confusion between the linguistic functioning, social adaptation and cognitive abilities of Italian pupils, though there are few reports of their placement in schools for the educationally sub-normal (ESN). Walker (1983a) reported that a few of the Italian immigrant children in schools in Bedford at that time were suspected to be 'intellectually retarded', but this proved difficult to assess until teachers got to know them well. Some, it seemed, needed to be placed in residential schools which was often an acute social hardship for the close and loving Italian families. Triseliotis (1976), apparently drawing on information from Townsend and Brittan's national survey (1972), claimed that the percentage of children of Italian origin deemed as subnormal was well below that of pupils of West Indian origin and nearer that of the non-immigrant population. However, the data in Townsend and Brittan's report are not distinguished with respect to pupils of Italian origin.

If pupils of Italian origin were not generally to be found in ESN schools, nor were they particularly likely to be selected for grammar school education in the late 1960s and early 1970s. Triseliotis (1976) suggested that the proportion of Italian and Cypriot children who proceeded to grammar schools was only about two-fifths that of non-immigrant pupils, but this figure is derived from that cited by Townsend and Brittan relating to DES Form 7 statistics for 1970 in which Italian pupils are not distinguished from other immigrant pupils. Indeed Townsend and Brittan's figures for 1971 suggest that the percentage may have been lower for this group as a whole. Brown's data (1970) show that pupils of Italian origin, like other immigrant children, were very poorly represented in the selective schools of Bedford in 1969.

EXAMINATION PERFORMANCE There is a complete gap in research evidence concerning the performance of pupils of Italian origin in reading and in other subject-areas of the school curriculum throughout their school lives. Clearly pupils of Italian origin have not engaged the attention of educational researchers in this regard. Only one piece of research provides tentative indications of the examination performance of pupils of Italian origin on completion of their secondary school education (Driver, 1980). One of Driver's five case-study schools, situated in a regional centre in the

Home Counties, had a largely working-class multiracial catchment, equally divided between West Indian, Asian and English plus ten per cent of Italian pupils. In this school the teachers had made particular efforts to initiate a curriculum relevant and sympathetic to the special social and educational needs of their ethnic minority pupils. Driver provides data on 19 pupils of Italian origin: nine in 1976 and ten in 1977, 11 boys and eight girls. The performance of the pupils of Italian origin in CSE and GCE O-level examinations was generally as good as, if not better than, that of their peers. Overall Italian boys seemed to perform at a higher level than Italian girls, especially in mathematics and sciences. However, these figures should be regarded with extreme caution because of the small number of such pupils involved in only one school, variations between the year and gender groups in terms of course entrants and examinees and difficulties in the classification and interpretation of the performance data (see Taylor, 1981). The Swann Report suggests that pupils of Italian origin who have English as a second language might be penalized by the 'unnecessarily complex' language used in public examinations, so that they were unable to demonstrate their true ability in a subject.

FURTHER AND HIGHER EDUCATION   Some insights can be had into the involvement of pupils of Italian origin in further education in Bedford, Leicester and London. In 1970, Brown noted the importance of the local technical college in Bedford in the education of immigrant children, particularly those who had experienced little schooling in the UK, who had left school with little basic competence in English or low academic achievements. However, Brown suggested that this may have applied less to pupils of Italian origin than to those from Asian and West Indian backgrounds. In the Department of Production Engineering 24 out of 307 students at craftsman level were Italians, a greater proportion than for students from other minority groups, and there were 11 European students out of 215 studying for technician examinations, but no Asians or West Indians. It is interesting to note that in 1979 the Open University (1982) researchers found that Italian (and Asian) students were quite well represented on full-time courses for O- and A-level, business and secretarial studies, represented on various part-time engineering craft apprenticeships, but less so on technician-level courses and not at all on building trades, foundation arts ONC or HNC courses. Italian girls were well represented on hairdressing courses. The larger, more conservative and church-orientated workers' association in Bedford organized vocational training for second-generation Italians funded by the EC and Italian Ministry of Labour in conjunction with the college. A study of 72 Italian families in Leicester (King and Zolli, 1981) found that a small proportion of those over 15 were pursuing full-time further education, most often associated with employment-related training, although ten of the 84 children were working for A-levels.

Language census data (ILEA, 1982, 1983, 1986) show the high percentage of pupils of Italian origin staying on at school after the legal school-leaving age. Their staying on rate was (almost) twice that of the ILEA average and only (marginally) exceeded by three other groups of minority language speakers in each of the three surveys (Table 39). Unfortunately, no information is available on the types of course pupils of Italian origin are pursuing when staying on.

Information on the participation of pupils of Italian origin in higher education is less reliable. Weston (1979) claimed that pupils of Italian origin may continue their interest and success at O- and A-level in Italian by going on to universities and polytechnics to study it at degree level, and she suggests that many Italian departments have a high quota of such students. Very limited evidence from a survey of languages offered for entrance to higher education in 1981 tends to confirm this (see Reid, 1984). From their study in Leicester, King and Zolli (1981)

Table 39: Staying on rates of Italian-speaking pupils in ILEA, 1981, 1982 and 1984

Italian speakers	1981	1982	1984
1 Number aged 16–19 (1981) or 17 (1982 and 4)	237	92	89
2 (1) as % of pupils aged 15 in 1981, and in 1983 for 1984	91.9	35.7	38.4
3 (1) as % of (2) for all ILEA pupils	52.2	19.9	17.9
4 Other minority language speakers with higher staying on rates, (1) as % of (2)	Gujerati, 120% Urdu, 105% Chinese, 103%	Chinese, 55% Gujerati, 43% Urdu, 40%	Chinese, 45% Yoruba, 39% Urdu, 39%

Source: Adapted from ILEA 1982, Table 3; 1983, 1986, Table 6.

claimed that although Italian parents were ambitious for their children, this did not usually extend to encouraging them to continue to higher education. They noted that 'only' four out of 84 children receiving full-time education were at university, but this may not appear to be so low a number especially in relation to the whole school age range presumably covered by the figures.

SCHOOL TO WORK Studies in Bedford and Leicester offer evidence on the upward occupational mobility of second-generation Italians compared with their parents. In 1970, Brown predicted that most of the young Italians then undergoing schooling would have vastly different job expectations than those of their parents. He thought that they would be attracted by further education opportunities and apprentice training facilities and predicted that few second-generation Italians would join their fathers in the Bedfordshire brickyards or replace them when they retired. If they did so, it would be in apprenticeships for skilled machine work rather than for manual work. By 1979, Simons noted that the intermediate generation of Italians who had arrived in the UK as small children, had acquired qualifications during their progress through the British education system and usually had some kind of trade, as panel beaters, welders, technicians or mechanics. Though their educational and occupational level exceeded that of their parents, their cultural roots remained the same. Tosi (1984) reports that it is an obligation and matter of family honour for all members to contribute some income when they leave school. A small minority of the second generation have achieved white-collar, mainly clerical, occupations, whilst the majority who perform manual work prefer to be self-employed rather than have a routine job with long hours, like their parents. Some who have 'invested in the marketability of their ethnic orgin' have achieved moderate success with ice-cream vans, small restaurants and hairdressing (see Jackson, 1979).

In Leicester, King and Zolli (1984) found that the general trend amongst second-generation Italians was to leave school, get a job and then pursue further employment-related training. In nearly all cases the second generation had reached higher educational levels than those of their parents and there was an interesting contrast between the socioeconomic status of the two generations who comprised approximately 18 per cent of the Italian population in Leicester (see Table 40).

Whereas almost two-thirds of the first-generation Italians were semi-qualified manual workers, three-fifths of the second generation were qualified manual workers, and over a quarter of the second generation were no longer in manual occupations. The majority of these first- and second-generation Italians in Leicester, like Italians as a whole, were engaged in manufacturing industry and

Table 40: Socioeconomic status of first- and second-generation Italians in Leicester

	First generation (% out of 96)	Second generation (% out of 44)
Professionals, employers and managers	0.0	0.0
Other non-manual workers	3.1	27.2
Qualified manual workers	19.9	59.2
Semi-qualified manual workers	63.5	13.6
Unqualified manual workers	16.5	0.0

Source: King and Zolli, 1981, Table 2.

services. Men were employed in mechanical industries and also in largely self-employed service trades, such as shopkeeping, hairdressing and catering, whereas women worked in textile factories and hospitals. Unfortunately, no specific information is given on the occupations of the second generation who had experienced most, if not all, of their schooling in the UK.

The research data presented in this section are grossly deficient in terms of examining educational achievement during schooling, so that it is not possible to offer reliable conclusion about the relative strengths and weaknesses of pupils of Italian origin in the school system. However, in general trends suggest a range of performance as reflected in school placement. Suggestions re-occur that continuing attention to the language needs of pupils of Italian origin is necessary for them to achieve their full potential in secondary school examinations. Reliable evidence demonstrates that a high proportion of students of Italian origin pursue their education beyond school-leaving age in further education, often acquiring employment-related skills and training. It would appear that in occupational terms second-generation Italians have been upwardly mobile. There are indications that some young people from Italian backgrounds retain an especial interest in their cultural origins either through further study in their 'mother tongue' or by capitalizing on the food and trade skills associated with their Italian connection. However, further research is badly required to augment these tentative observations.

Italian Parents

ATTITUDES TO EDUCATION

It is likely that Italian parents' attitudes to the education of their children will, in turn, influence their children's attitudes and may even affect their educational performance. However, there has again been a lack of specific research interest in the attitudes of Italian parents to education in general, and aspects of school organization and the curriculum, or the degree of their contact with their children's schools. The evidence presented here is largely descriptive, derived from observation and knowledge of Italian communities, so that although an impression of Italian parents' attitudes may be gained, it is difficult to compare and contrast these directly with those of other ethnic minority parents.

In view of the strong cultural orientation to Italy which Italian parents (even those of the second generation) are widely said to maintain, their own educational background and experience is likely to have an important influence on their attitude towards the British education system and inform their perceptions of it *vis-à-vis* the schooling of their own children. However, many first-generation Italian parents have experienced little education in Italy. Few will have had more than primary school education and hence their degree of literacy may be limited (see p.222). The attitudes of Italian parents to the schooling of their children in Britain will also have been affected by their perceptions of British society and their position within it, with regard to other Italians, other immigrant groups and the white British majority. The combination of such factors distinguish the attitudes of Italian parents from those of parents from other groups. Additionally, attitudes vary from family to family, and individual to individual, just as they do for any other group of parents.

Researchers such as Brown (1970) have observed that Italian parents have much respect for education and for their children's teachers. Despite the linguistic and socioeconomic heterogeneity of the Italians in the UK, they are united by their strong interest in making their children benefit fully from local educational provision. Mengon (1980) has suggested that many Italian parents see education as having an instrumental value, serving to advance their children socially and economically, though they would generally also be prepared to recognize education as intrinsically valuable. This distinction is illustrated by King and Zolli's (1981) observation that Italian parents in Leicester, though ambitious for their children, did not usually encourage them to continue into higher education. Any apparent economic motivation may be explained culturally (see p.212) and is also realistic for first-generation immigrants anxious to secure socioeconomic stability and status in a new environment.

In a study of 24 Italian families, 47 adults with 18 teenage children in two London areas, Weston (1979) found that on the whole the Italian parents offered very little criticism of English schools or society at large. Though the Italian parents expressed favourable attitudes towards British society, in Weston's opinion they were not sufficiently articulate in their dialect, Standard Italian or English to explore the contradiction between their praises and discontent. Other researchers have noted a similar phenomenon. Steedman (1979) has argued that the sociocultural characteristics of the Italians, and other immigrant groups, constitutes an important factor in conditioning relations between parents and the British school system, quoting the Rapporto (1977) which observed that many Italian parents do not have the sociocultural framework to enable them to investigate and understand the ways in which the objectives and methods exemplified in the British school system differ from their own experiences of education in Italy. Hence they tend to interpret new cultural experiences in the form of the education experienced by their children in terms of a different educational model derived from their own limited educational experience in another country many years ago. Thus any criticisms which they may wish to make are likely to be related to knowledge of a more authoritarian, disciplined and formal system. Mengon (1980) also suggested that Italian parents may feel concern and unease because the educational experience which they see their children undergoing is new and they find it difficult to relate to the same sort of experience they had in school, yet

> Italian parents like the educational efficiency of British schools, their exact timetabling, their sense of tradition and continuity, all things which give an impression of order, and may induce their children to a desirable composure of behaviour. Some, though not all, like the British non-political approach to education. (ibid., p.25)

But at the same time, some Italian parents are distrustful of the apparently more liberal atmosphere of their children's schools and wonder whether their children can grow up to be serious, industrious and hard-working in such an environment. Some Italian parents would like schools and teachers to be more disciplined and authoritarian. Furthermore, Brown (1970) quoted a case where Italian parents objected to an Indian teacher and demanded that Italian children be placed with an English teacher and, in another incident, an Italian mother arrived in her child's classroom demanding that her offspring be moved from sitting next to an Indian child. Such instances – perhaps extreme and unrepresentative – may be seen as examples of Italians' responses to perceptions of their position as immigrants in the UK and a desire not to be identified with other coloured immigrant groups, feelings which may also have been transmitted to their children (see pp.212,300–1).

Triseliotis (1976) has suggested that there are many parallels between the attitudes of Italian and Cypriot parents with regard to the education of their children both in the school situation and in the wider sense of upbringing (see pp.139–68). Moreover, research has tended not to distinguish pupils of Italian and Cypriot origin from amongst pupils of European origin as a whole as, for example, in the third phase of the NFER survey in the early 1970s. In the second phase, which examined organizational aspects of multiracial schools, difficulties in establishing contact with Italian parents were reported by only two out of 119 schools, in contrast to their experience with parents of Asian, and to a much lesser extent, of West Indian origin. Lack of English was probably a reason for communication difficulties, though there may have been few schools with Italian pupils in the sample (Townsend and Brittan, 1972). In fact of the 66 (out of 230) schools in the survey which claimed to send information to parents in languages other than English, six communicated with parents in Italian. However, in view of doubts about the literacy of some Italian parents, this may not be the most effective means of communication.

Some indication of teachers' perceptions of Italian parents may be found from the third phase of the NFER survey in 1972 which involved 510 teachers, 171 primary and 339 secondary, in 25 multiracial schools with 18–84 per cent ethnic minority pupils. However, in the survey, reference was only made to parents of Italian origin, together with Cypriot and other parents under the umbrella term 'European'. Indeed many teachers clearly wanted to qualify their answers to distinguish different groups of European parents and pupils, and as a considerable proportion of teachers were obviously unwilling to generalize, there was a higher percentage use of the neutral or nil response categories than in connection with other minority groups. Nevertheless, some 37 per cent of primary and secondary teachers agreed or strongly agreed with the statement 'European parents usually show considerable interest in the education of their children', although 18 per cent would not comment and 36 per cent gave a neutral reply. Teachers were marginally more likely to affirm that European parents displayed considerable interest in their children's education than they were to say this of English or West Indian parents, and conversely were less likely to disagree that European parents showed considerable interest in their children's education than for any other group of parents. It should not be assumed, however, that these responses necessarily applied to Italian parents rather than to Cypriot or other European parents.

Some British headteachers have expressed regret at their lack of contact with parents of Italian children in schools, which is often attributed to the incomplete grasp which parents have of one or more languages (Steedman, 1979). One of the most successful outcomes of the EC/Bedfordshire Mother Tongue and Culture Project (MTCP) was an increase in home–school interaction (see p.278). The project teachers made a much greater than usual investment of time in getting to know the families of the children involved, undertaking an initial visit to explain the project and continuing regular home visits, on average once per week, up to the end of the project. As a result, not only did the Italian parents support their children's involvement in the project but they also increased the frequency of their visits to their children's schools. Another spin-off was an increased interest on the part of heads and other teachers in the home backgrounds of the Italian children (Simons, 1980; Tansley, 1981).

In this specific case Italian parents may have responded favourably to the visits which they received from their children's teachers not just because the project was demonstrating an interest in developing their children's knowledge of the Italian language, but also because it was an opportunity for teachers both to explain aspects of the educational system and to learn of parents' background and views on their children's schooling. The desire of many Italian parents for their children to maintain and develop an awareness and appreciation of their Italian cultural origins is clear from their support of voluntary language classes. But apart from increasing interest in such provision in recent years, how much attention has been paid specifically to inquiring into the views of Italian parents about aspects of the curriculum and organization of their children's schools? There is, for example, the question of Italian parents' attitudes towards school meals. Lobo (1978) reported that although Italian children in Bedfordshire eat school meals, their mothers take the view that this meal cannot be sufficient nourishment and often try to give children another, Italian, meal as a supplement. Clearly attitudes to food may symbolize a variety of cultural and sociopsychological attitudes on the part of mothers not only with respect to their particular child or children, but in regard to their attitude towards living in a society with different food habits. It would be of interest to know to what extent schools in areas of Italian settlement have taken account of the food preferences of pupils of Italian origin. Other data (see p.288) indicate that Italian parents may also have considerable preferences for sending their children to Roman Catholic and/or single-sex schools, especially at secondary level, when such a choice is available.

It is often generally assumed that the sociocultural backgrounds of the families of pupils of Italian origin and the values and attitudes which they hold and transmit to their children are sufficiently similar to those exemplified in British schooling for there to be no marked conflict for pupils of Italian origin in their experience of the culture of their schools and peers and that at home. However, evidence from the Association of Teachers of Italian to the Swann Committee explicitly calls this into question and reinforces the main points in their review, namely that

> Parents whilst being ambitious for their children, are often alienated from the school and its teachers through:
>
> 1 communication difficulties caused by their limited knowledge of English;
> 2 little understanding of the educational system and supporting systems from which advice may be sought;
> 3 the system's failure to conform to the school of their own experience;
> 4 their own limited education and background. (see GB. P. H of C, 1985, p. 699).

It was felt that schools could offer much more help to such parents, for example, in understanding the examination system, so that they, in turn, would be able to help and support their children. Indeed the literature generally suggests that the sociolinguistic background of first-generation Italian parents and their preoccupation with establishing themselves in work, and maintaining close family ties, may not have enabled them to express their views about their children's schooling, even if these had been solicited. Yet it would seem that the opportunity to ascertain the attitudes of first-generation Italian parents to education has largely been missed. Second-generation parents who have themselves experienced most if not all of their schooling in the UK may be more vocal! But parents' anxieties, not expressed to educational authorities or researchers, may have manifested themselves in their relationships with their children.

ATTITUDES TO THEIR CHILDREN

The relationship between Italian parents and their children has been described as both a 'key' and a 'major' problem area (Brown, 1970; Steedman, 1979). As early as 1970, Brown considered that there had been little or no public recognition of what he termed the 'crisis within the Italian family' since there had been few interpretations of the difficulties experienced by some immigrant families in cultural terms. According to Steedman, the extent to which Italian parents may have been able to adapt to the English way of life, or have retained a cultural frame of reference very different from that learnt by their children in school, may pose communication problems between the generations. As Mengon (1980) has also observed, for pupils of Italian origin the school's most important function is to introduce them to the English language and the British way of life. As a result, they are enabled to mediate between their parents' culture and that of society at large. This may give them a position of privilege in their own family, which in itself may sometimes be the cause of conflict as there is a tendency to see individuals as part of an overall family unit. Other agencies of socialization, such as siblings, peers, TV and the neighbourhood environment, may also have considerable and diverse influences on young Italians. These influences may be seen by Italian parents as threats to the social, cultural and emotional values which they wish to preserve within their close-knit families. Moreover, according to Mengon, Italian parents often feel forced into a defensive position because of what they perceive as not only the rejection or hostile attitudes of British society as a whole, but the fact that they are largely ignored. Such a response which may cope with rejection since it implies some form of communication but cannot support the kind of neglect which does not permit any emotional points of reference, may be distinctively Italian. Mengon suggests that this may also induce an isolationist position in which parents revive regional folklore to give themselves a social identity and refuse to admit even the most positive or least threatening influences of the society at large. In such a climate many Italian parents see voluntary language classes as safeguarding at an individual, family and community level the value which they hold most dear and which they feel to be most at risk.

These interpretations may be exemplified by reference to Brown's (1970) observations of Italian families, in the late 1960s, in Bedford. Interestingly, he drew comparisons between the Italians and Indians in the town at that time, noting their similar capacities for hard work, the self-regulation of their communities and the influence of religious faith on their lives, together with their close, disciplined patterns of family life. However, he pointed to a major difference, in that whilst the first-generation Italian adults attempted to preserve their social and cultural values, rooted in southern Italy, most of their children wished to break with these traditions and merge with the English. By the late 1960s the reaction of the intermediate and second generation against their parents was creating profound unhappiness, which Brown predicted could lead to further disharmony between the generations, and even to delinquency amongst the young. Italian parents kept to the ways they knew, and lacking education and opportunities to see and compare other people, places and standards, including the changes in their homelands, became more inflexible:

The world of the first generation is the static world of Southern Italy. Its intense feeling for the primacy of the family group, its religious respect for the authority of the father, its seclusion and control of unmarried women, its devotion to the Church: all have the force of permanent, unquestioned values. (ibid., p. 90)

According to Lobo (1978), a consultant paediatrician in Luton and Dunstable, Italian parents advocate strict standards of behaviour and discipline which their children increasingly reject as they grow to maturity. Consciousness of family honour and prestige is of less significance to the second and third generations. Italian parents seem to desire to attempt to control their children, even as young adults, and stress their responsibility to their parents. But as comments from second-generation Italians in the Open University Unit (1982) on Bedford show, although Italians are well known for their great sense of family unity, very often parental authority and a child's duty are masked as respect. Even in the 1960s, Brown noted that new ways of thinking and feeling learnt by the second generation through their education, interacting with their peers in and out of school, and living in a changing urban environment, divorced them from the values of southern Italy espoused by their parents and made them identify more with Bedford. The distance between parents and children especially by adolescence was evident in the languages spoken within the household, food preferences and disputes about parental authority, and sometimes became a conflict of values and attitudes with parents and children inhabiting the same house but living in two different worlds:

The two worlds implicitly deny each other, Inevitably, the young people who inhabit both worlds are divided in consciousness. As children they learnt to move between these worlds with relative ease. As they grew older, the divisions became to them increasingly explicit. As they developed as individuals, with new needs and aspirations, they came to feel the conflict almost as a conflict of physical forces. The tensions are explosive. (Brown, 1970, p.91)

Like some other ethnic minority parents in the UK (e.g. Cypriots and Asians), Italian parents tend to uphold traditional differential attitudes and expectations towards their sons and daughters based on the lifestyle of their village of origin. These attitudes usually result in their being accorded differential treatment and permitted different behaviour. Italian boys have greater independence with almost complete freedom, and as they experience more education, their parents are sometimes more willing to come to terms with their ideas. Yet even in the 1960s, Brown observed that rejection of their Italian origins was more overt on the part of young Italian males who, in their need to belong, often sought out their British contemporaries in proportion to the degree to which they rejected the traditional values of their parents' background and sometimes became vulnerable to the sociocommercial pressures of British culture. Moreover, by 1977 the kind of delinquency predicted by Brown and observed to a limited extent in the use of drugs was becoming a reality as Lobo (1978) cited figures showing that, although the number of Italian boys becoming involved with crime were still relatively few, it was nevertheless increasing. These Italian boys were apparently those most anxious to emulate their white peers and who found themselves in conflict with the standards of their families. In view of the very low crime rate of the adult Italian community in Bedfordshire and the country as a whole, the criminal involvement of these boys only served to set them more apart from their families.

Traditionally, Italian girls have been expected to conform to fairly strict controls on their behaviour and to be more closely confined within the family because of the need to preserve honour and reputation before marriage, in the belief that this would make them more respected, appreciated and sought after. Italian parents in this country have, above all, tended to uphold this practice and with a greater degree of control, often unaware that attitudes to relationships between the sexes and other values are gradually changing in their home areas. It has been suggested that Italian girls experience the tensions between the generations and within the family more deeply than boys and may be more keenly conscious of moral values and loyalties (Brown, 1970). Sometimes greater conflict is induced within Italian families because mothers may want more freedom for their daughters than fathers are prepared to allow (Lobo, 1978). Yet, at the same time, they also seem to deplore the extent of the freedom of English girls in their local neighbourhoods. Contrivance might be the only way in which many could escape parental control. However, according to Brown, some Italian girls were allowed to join a mixed youth club, established under the auspices of the Italian church in Bedford, which attempted to bridge understanding between the generations and also to create some measure of continuity in faith and values, and which offered for many a release from the tension, and sometimes anguish, of their home lives. By contrast, more recently, Palmer has claimed that the daughters of first-generation Italians from Emilia living in London have considerable freedom. This serves to highlight differences between Italian communities in their orientation and sociocultural adaptation. Whilst some parents have felt able to modify traditional views about acceptable behaviour and the freedom accorded to their daughters, and parents and children may have come to a better understanding of their different life worlds, some cases have been recorded of inflexible attitudes on both sides, leading to breakdown in communication and even the severing of family relationships with Italian girls leaving home (Brown, 1970). The attitudes of first- and second-generation Italians to such events tended to polarize, especially where Italian girls had left home to join West Indian boys.

Various sources have commented on the preference of Italian parents for their children, particularly their daughters, to marry within the Italian community in Britain or back in Italy (e.g. Saifullah Khan, 1976) as this is thought to increase the likelihood of preservation of traditional sociocultural values. But in the late 1960s Brown predicted that many of the young Italian men, as they developed their own lifestyles and felt their roots to be more in England, would marry English girls. However, the evidence seems to call this into question. For example, King (1977a) noted a strong preference amongst second-generation Italians, which may be partly dictated by their parents, for marriage to someone from the same Italian village of origin. Weston (1979) found that a large majority of a sample of second-generation Italian adolescents in London wished to marry an Italian, who had preferably been born and brought up in England. This suggests an increasing consciousness of being Italian in Britain. Social anthropologists are, moreover, agreed that many third-generation Italians in London socialize and marry within their ethnic group (Palmer, 1977; King, 1978). Palmer, who discusses this in some detail and cites interesting examples, indicates that the continuity of chain migration, the existence of community associations and institutions and their geographical separateness all favour the 'non-assimilation' of the third generation, in London at least. King has observed that what may be perceived as the comparative liberalism of British attitudes favours the integration of the immigrant at one level and, at the same time, permits difference and foreignness, so that there are few pressures to shed culture and even the British-born second- and third-generation Italians are able to feel, and sometimes stress, their Italian connection, or *Italianita* (Garigue and Firth, 1956). The extent to which marriage takes place within the community continues to be an important indicator of

Italianita, and the evidence suggests that the majority of marriages take place within the community (see Open University, 1982). So despite the stresses experienced between the generations, which tend to assume an intercultural focus, it seems that the Italian connection continues to be perceived as meaningful.

Italian Pupils' Attitudes to School, Peers and Identity
If the cognitive development of pupils of Italian origin has been largely ignored by educational research, and the views of Italian parents as to the schooling of their children given little attention, nor has the personal and social development of pupils of Italian origin, especially in a school context, become a matter of serious interest to educationists. Where data exist, pupils of Italian origin are sometimes included together with pupils of other European, mainly Cypriot origin. Nevertheless, by drawing on a range of observational and psychometric research it is possible to point to certain trends in the social and personal education and development of pupils of Italian origin in terms of their attitudes to school, their friendships and extra-curricular activities and, in a wider sense, their self-perceptions and identities.

There is a consensus in the literature that although pupils of Italian origin may find starting school a bewildering experience, especially if they arrived from Italy as small children or had no English, once they have settled, they have generally been favourably disposed towards their schools. The largest investigation of pupils', including Italian pupils', attitudes to school was undertaken in 1972 as part of the third phase of the NFER Multi-Racial Education project. Some 3,551 pupils in 13 primary and 12 secondary schools were involved, 604 at 10 plus, 1,488 at 12 plus and 1, 459 at 14 plus. The majority of pupils were of British, West Indian, Indian, Kenyan/Asian, Pakistani and 'other' origins. However, a relatively small number of Italian pupils were involved in the investigation, and unfortunately for this purpose their attitudes, together with those of a relatively small number of Cypriot pupils, are reported in a composite form. Nevertheless, the data on these pupils' attitudes to the school in general, the atmosphere of the multiracial school and to schoolwork are of some interest. A total of 255 Italian and Cypriot pupils rated 33 test items on a five-point scale, ranging from 'strongly agree' to 'strongly disagree' (Jelinek, 1977). Attitudes towards the atmosphere of the multiracial school reflected the extent of acceptance or willingness to mix with boys and girls from different ethnic backgrounds. Pupils of Italian origin generally had fairly favourable attitudes towards the multiracial atmosphere of the school, midway between the attitudes of their Asian, West Indian and British peers, although at 14 plus they held the least favourable attitudes of any of their ethnic minority peers. Boys and girls did not generally differ in their attitudes to the multiracial school, though at 10 plus and 14 plus the Italian/Cypriot boys held more favourable attitudes than their female compatriots. Attitudes towards schoolwork reflected the extent of feeling of being afraid or ashamed when the work was too difficult or incorrectly done. Italian/Cypriot pupils were relatively little concerned about their schoolwork, displaying less anxiety than their Asian and West Indian peers, though more concern than indigenous pupils. The Italian/Cypriot girls of all ages, like the girls as a whole, tended to be more concerned about schoolwork than the Italian/Cypriot boys. General attitudes to school related to pupil/teacher relationships, discipline and the help pupils obtained from their teachers. Italian/Cypriot pupils, like other pupils, generally held favourable attitudes to the school at 12 plus and 14 plus. In contrast to their indigenous peers, but like their other ethnic minority peers, their attitudes improved markedly between the ages of ten plus and 12 plus. This was particularly significant for the Italian/Cypriot boys as European girls generally had more favourable attitudes to school. It is unfortunate that the usefulness of this research, the only evidence on the attitudes of Italian and Cypriot pupils to school, is diminished because the data are combined for Italian and Cypriot pupils. Moreover, Italian pupils were only represented in three (and Cypriots in four) of the 25 schools. Since it is likely that the atmosphere, teacher–pupil relationships and the work environment of these particular schools affect pupils' responses to attitude scales, it may be more informative to use in-depth, case-study approaches to compare the attitudes of different groups of pupils within a few schools rather than attempt to compare and contrast the attitudes of different groups of pupils across a wide variety of school environments.

An influential factor in pupils' attitudes to school, which also affects their social and personal development, is attitude to their peers. In the case of pupils of Italian origin these may be assessed through researchers' observations, teachers' comments and sociometric investigations in school as well as some information on extra-curricular activities in youth clubs and the social relationships enjoyed by Italian families. In the early 1960s, in Bedford, Walker (1963a) reported that some white British children had Italian friends and that some contacts were retained, even if the Italian children returned to Italy. By the late 1960s Bedford had become much more multiracial, with the increasing immigration of West Indians, Indians and Pakistanis, but according to Brown (1970) the Italians, who had won respect and acceptance by hard work, self-discipline and obedience to the law, resented being classified with other immigrants. Italians had particular antipathies towards West Indians and Pakistanis, which they tended to pass on to their children and, as a result, there was antagonism in some school playgrounds. Brown also noted that even in informal gatherings in school pupils tended to form distinct national groups. Two headteachers in a national sample of schools surveyed by Townsend and Brittan (1972) also reported 'Italians don't like other immigrants, especially at first: they didn't want to dance with "black" children', and 'Friction, if any, is invariably between the Italians and Indians. Italians are less tolerant of the Indians than the English' (p.131). More recently, the Swann Report (GB. P. H of C, 1985) commented on the tendency of some of the Italian community to regard themselves very much as 'élite' immigrants and thus to disassociate themselves from more recent arrivals, especially Asians. On the other hand, it was a surprise to the Committee to learn from teachers, pupils and parents of the 'racial antagonism' between pupils of Italian origin and their 'English' peers, usually at the level of name-calling.

One way of checking these observations is to examine the interethnic friendships of pupils of Italian origin. Fortunately, a number of Italian pupils were included in a large-scale sociometric investigation undertaken nationally in 1972 as part of the third phase of the NFER Multi-Racial Education Project (Jelinek and Brittan, 1975). The actual and desired friendship choices of a total of 1,288 pupils in the second and fourth years of 13 primary schools and 3,012 pupils in the second and fourth years of 12 secondary schools were investigated. The schools contained 18–84 per cent ethnic minority pupils, and the research involved Indian, Pakistani, West Indian, Kenyan/Asian, Italian, Cypriot, 'other' and white British pupils. The 95 Italian pupils, however, were drawn from only three schools, one junior and two secondary, and comprised only 2.5 per cent of the total number of pupils involved in the research. Hence, with respect to them, the sociometric data must be seen as illustrative rather than representative. Pupils were asked to name up to three friends they played with at school and up to three children they would like to have as friends. As only about 30 per cent of the pupils of Italian origin were in mixed schools at the primary level, this reduced the opportunity for inter-sex friendships at school, but in fact they, like Asians pupils, reported no actual or desired choices from the opposite sex. At the primary level, like all other groups of pupils, Italian pupils preferred friends from their own ethnic group. At secondary level, by contrast, there was a tendency for Italian pupils to show greater own-group preference in terms of actual friendships than indigenous pupils, though not all other ethnic minority pupils, in the same schools. The pattern for desired friendships was less clear-cut, but only apparently at the age of 14 plus and in one school did Italian pupils indicate greater own-group preference than indigenous pupils. Compared with other ethnic minority pupils in the same school they were apparently more likely at the secondary level, especially at 12 plus, to desire friendships with pupils from other ethnic groups. However, these findings must be viewed with caution, given the sample limitations. Clearly ethnicity was a strong factor in the friendship choices of pupils of Italian origin, though there was a slight indication that, especially at secondary age, they would have liked more friends from the other groups than they actually had.

Given this position, what chance do pupils of Italian origin have for interacting with their peers in out-of-school contexts either at youth clubs or with their families? Clearly opportunities and attitudes will vary with individuals, over time and in different areas of Italian settlement. In Bedford, in the late 1960s, every major group of second-generation immigrants, including Italians, had its own youth club. The Italian youth club was established in 1966 on the premises of the Italian church and, in 1969, had some 120 members of both sexes aged 13–21, 60 per cent Italian and 40 per cent of other nationalities. As the most cosmopolitan youth club in Bedford, it offered an environment for music and games playing within an atmosphere of friendly interchange between Italian, English, Egyptian and Maltese young people, but apparently no Asian or West Indian youth participated. The club consciously aimed to help young Italians 'integrate' with the life of Bedford and, according to Brown (1970), was the one institution which bridged the world of the Italian parents and contemporary Bedford.

Some ten years later research undertaken by King and Zolli (1981) showed that second-generation Italians were even less involved than first-generation Italians in Leicester in clubs and associations. Fewer than a third of the 72 Italians interviewed attended these clubs (three recreational, one cultural and one political) even occasionally, apparently because of lack of time, their dispersal in Leicester and diverse regional origins. However, young Italians were not much more likely to meet young people from other ethnic groups through their families. Italian families tended to be most friendly with other Italians, and if they had friends other than Italians, they were more likely to be English. Italians were more likely to have links with Eastern European families through Catholicism and marriage than with Italian families in Leicester. Even though more than three-quarters of the respondents claimed some English friends, relationships may have been largely superficial in the workplace, as close social relationships did not develop for the first generation, at least, because of the language gap and the contrast between the individualistic British culture and the familistic Italian culture. Fewer than a third of the Italians exchanged regular visits with English people and then only about once a month. By contrast, Italian families were much more likely to visit one another, at least once a week. Another investigation in Clerkenwell, the 'little Italy' of London, also discovered a high degree of in-group activity amongst Italians in the Mazzini-Garibaldi Club and in the youth club attached to the church (Walker, 1982). Even for the second generation and students in higher education, social relationships were predominantly with other Italians. Cumulatively, therefore, the evidence suggests that, socially and culturally, the Italian connection continues to be of significance for second- and third-generation Italians and their close social relationships are more likely to be within the Italian community (see also p.212). Though interaction with other group members naturally varies according to individuals, time and place, the existing evidence appears to cast doubt upon the predictions of social anthropologists studying the Italian community in London 30 years ago, who suggested that, although the integration of Italians into English society was very slow, it would probably become effective with the third generation (Garigue and Firth, 1956).

But if second-generation Italians are not necessarily socially integrated, does this mean that they see themselves as Italian rather than as English, or as Italians in England? It has been said that one of the major problems for pupils of Italian origin is that of their personal and cultural identity (Steedman, 1979). Amongst ethnic minority families in the UK at adolescence – a time of increased interest in the self and identity – inter-generational relationships tend to become an arena for testing out the relative emphases to be given to the dual aspects of personal and cultural identities. Thus the attitudes which pupils of Italian origin display towards themselves and their identities, have to be seen in terms of the socioeconomic and political position of the Italian communities in the UK, and the loyalties and cultural orientations of their families towards Italy. Again, there will be tremendous variation between families and generations, and even within families, and the questioning of identity by pupils of Italian origin may assume various manifestations.

Even in the late 1960s, in Bedford, Brown (1970) observed that not only adolescents, but children by the age of ten, had been shaped to such an extent by their life experiences of schooling and an urban environment that both those who had arrived as small children and those born in Bedford had come to have the accents and attitudes of Bedfordians. Their interest in Italy was vicarious, rather than that of belonging. But with increasing exposure to life in the UK, as they grew older and developed as individuals, conflicts with the sociocultural origins and values of their parents became more explicit and intensive. Where these could not be resolved, a few Italian youth made dramatic breaks with their families. Rejection of their backgrounds was more overt on the part of Italian boys. In some cases, their need to belong made them vulnerable to the pressures of their British contemporaries – some being involved in drugs or crime – and the general sociocommercial exploitation for which their background made them unprepared; and some, by desiring individualism and rejecting traditional values and family bonds, acquired materialistic orthodoxies. Brown provided examples demonstrating that even those closely involved in Italian community organizations, such as the youth club, felt themselves to belong in the UK. They identified with Bedford both in terms of their future personal relationships and in their socioeconomic expectations. King (1977a), another observer of the Italian community, has also noted that the second generation has experienced, in addition to the usual generational problems, a cultural transformation from a familistic to a personalistic-societalistic culture, and that, although they will remain bilingual and bicultural in varying degrees, they will probably increasingly regard England as their home. And in another paper King and King (1977) have claimed that the young Italians in Bedford are far more English than Italian in culture and outlook. Lobo (1978) has also observed that the children of European immigrants, including those of Italian origin, are much more willing and able to develop a British identity, values and behaviour than children from other ethnic minority groups. But Weston (1979) has questioned whether the apparent integration of adolescents from Italian backgrounds into the British way of life, as in the case of those in two Italian communities in London, who looked and talked and behaved like their British contemporaries and had similar socioeconomic backgrounds, clothes, accents and tastes, means that they have really become whole-heartedly British. Weston found that in the less structured Italian community the questioning of identity amongst the Italian adolescents often took the form of rejection of things Italian, a regressive phase in their competence in Italian and a desire to drop out of language classes. Their way of coping with personal and cultural identity conflicts was to reject associations with the low status of their minority group and identify instead with the majority, but in so doing they neglected many vital aspects of their life experience.

From his observations and involvement with the Italian community in Bedford, Tosi (1984) has characterized the psychological reactions of the second generation in their search for identity as 'apathetic', 'in-group' or 'rebel' (see p.246 for linguistic implications). The 'apathetic' individual tends to submit to the stronger pressures of the wider social context and the values of the majority group which requires ridding himself of the habits, values and associations which mark him as Italian and becoming as English as possible. This reaction occurs when the individual feels unable to cope with the conflicting values of the two environments. But whilst declaring himself English and obsessively trying to conform with this environment, he may still retain a certain amount of Italian background and conditioning. Tosi claims that this is the response of the majority of the second generation in Bedford. The 'in-group' reaction is similar, but instead the goal is affiliation with the Italian community, with the individual striving to please fellow Italians. This is usually the response of individuals who feel particularly close to the family. It does not imply a lack of inter-generational conflict, but an attempt to find refuge in the family's values and habits. The 'rebel' reaction represents the position of only a few young people who have a strong interest in investigating the conflicting presentation of the values of the two communities for their personal and social implications. According to Tosi, these individuals have benefited from close personal guidance, stronger motivation in their studies, personal contacts with Italy and higher education. In particular, Tosi claims, access to new role and linguistic repertoires through Standard Italian and the cultural values expressed in Italy has added an awareness and understanding differing from that provided by the families and Bedford's Italian community. They are then seen in a wider social and linguistic context that accounts for migration and opposition to a new environment and 'clarifies the relationship between inadequate values and restricted linguistic repertoires'. However, Tosi claims such an awareness requires a deep familiarization with both British and Italian life and society, and bilingualism and biliteracy in English and Standard Italian.

The children of Italian immigrants have clearly experienced strong social and educational pressures which draw them away from their sociocultural roots in Italy and the conservatism of traditional attitudes and values practised in everyday life by their parents in the UK. But what links with Italy and the Italian village culture persist for second- and third-generation Italians? Brown (1970) thought a few young Italian men would return to live in Italy, being deterred by the prospects of military service. Apprentice training facilities and further education, as well as developing their own lifestyles, were more attractive prospects. In addition, King (1977a) has claimed that although Italy may be looked upon emotionally by the second generation as a cultural heritage and a place to go on holiday, few of the second generation have sufficient enthusiasm to return permanently. Though they may become more and more critical of aspects of Italian village life, few wish to deny their Italian ancestry, whilst feeling that they belong more in Britain. As for the third generation, they will be distinguished only by their surnames and perhaps by a slightly darker than average colouring (King and King, 1977). A lack of regard for their parents' unsophisticated cultural standards is also reported by Lobo (1978) of the second-generation Italians in Bedfordshire.

It is for just such a reason that the Italian church and government have been concerned to provide Italian language classes, in order to encourage an awareness and appreciation of the Italian language and culture as a means of sustaining a personal and cultural identity with Italy amongst the second generation. Other aims of the language classes (see pp.250–1) include strengthening the relationships between the generations and the development of the child's self-confidence. But there appear to be divided views on this. On the one hand, teachers involved in the Mother Tongue and Culture Project (MTCP) claimed that this was an unnecessary aim, for many of the Italian children exhibited natural confidence and had communicative personalities, and one teacher commented that since many of these children of primary school age regarded themselves as English the aim of building up their self-image by teaching them the Italian language was inappropriate. Moreover, Weston (1979) observed that one effect of the attendance of Italian children at voluntary language classes was to make them more aware of the gap between the dialect which they spoke at home with their parents and the Standard Italian of the language classes, evoking feelings of shame rather than enhancing self-confidence. On the other hand, Weston claimed that the apparent rejection of Italian together with the other aspects of an Italian identity, might be reversed if the adolescent pupil were encouraged to join an examination class which could boost a pupil's confidence and interest. However, Tosi (1984) argues that voluntary language provision outside mainstream schooling seldom succeeds in helping young people develop an awareness and understanding of the two sets of roles and values which they experience or to overcome negative associations in their overall social and linguistic behaviour.

Although some of the parents of the children of Italian origin involved in the MTCP in Bedfordshire, who had themselves arrived in the UK during their primary school years, were reported to have been socially upwardly mobile compared with their own 'first-generation' parents, they had nevertheless maintained their cultural roots, so that whilst they had their own home and car, they had Italian friends, ate Italian food and were closely involved with their families and caring for the older members. Their ways were traditional, cultural links were strong and some even expressed a desire to return to Italy. Palmer (1980) also discovered that the intermediate generation, perhaps on account of difficulties of adjustment in their early years, have retained an over-romanticized attitude towards the villages of their birth, more like that of their parents. Many first-generation Italian adults have actually fulfilled their desire to return to Italy. But it is also significant that many of the families who returned to Italy, for example, after the brickyard redundancies in Bedford in 1967, re-emigrated because of the unhappiness of their children in the rural environment in southern Italy to which they could not adapt (King and King, 1977). Palmer (1977, 1980) indicates the processes of estrangement and disengagement which make it difficult for first-generation adults to reintegrate in the life of a changed village community. However, it seems likely that were it not for the ties of the second and third generation born in the UK, more first-generation Italians might return to Italy in their retirement. For example, Weston (1979) discovered that over four-fifths of the 47 adults interviewed in two communities in London wished to return to Italy, even though they had been here on average 20 years. Indeed two-thirds admitted regretting coming to Britain, even though they had all found jobs and were often self-employed or managers. Although two-thirds of their children claimed that they would follow their parents if they went to Italy, their attitudes seemed more ambiguous, for this prospect produced great anxiety and it seemed that a decision to follow their parents would be as a result of parental pressure. They seemed to have an open mind about whether they would be likely to stay in Italy or return to England, and since they also expressed a preference to marry an Italian who was born and brought up in England, Weston suggested that the second-generation Italians seemed to feel that they belonged to a minority group formed by the Italians in England. Thus they were motivated to learn Italian because they perceived its utility either if they went to live in Italy or if they stayed in the UK.

One of the aims of the EC in setting up the MTCP was to assist children of Italian origin to learn Italian in the context of a possible return to Italy, and this was also an aim on the part of some of the children's parents, notably those of the intermediate generation. During the course of the project three children actually returned to settle. Indeed two of the teachers of Italian considered that Italians in Bedford should be considered not as immigrants, but as migrants (Simons, 1980). In support it was claimed that 70–80 per cent of the Italian children born in the UK who experienced their schooling in Bedford chose an Italian passport at 18. The loyalty to Italy which this indicates gains added force given that unless they revoke their nationality, Italians are denied political rights in the UK and are not entitled to vote, so that many first-generation Italians, and now apparently the second-generation also, despite having lived in this country for 25 years or so, have had no influence on local or national politics. The history of the experience of Italians in the UK, especially that of internment during the war and the abuse of the early post-war immigrants, which has been handed down in oral folklore to successive migrants and generations (Palmer, 1977; Bottignolo, 1983) is obviously relevant to a consideration of the extent to which Italians in the UK retain their identification as Italian, the close family links and associations with other Italians, especially those from the same regions and villages of origin, and the fact that some loyalty to their Italian connection is felt by even a second and third generation.

In addition to maintenance of various cultural traditions through the family, Italian language classes, Italian clubs and associations and choice of a passport, the most significant connection for children of Italian origin with the attitudes and values which inspire their parents is probably the return visits made to the villages of origin. These visits which occur on average every two years (Brown, 1970; Palmer, 1977; Weston, 1979) are important for the parents in reaffirming their loyalty, ties and identity and may serve to crystallize the attitudes and cultural orientation of their children. Another reason for the return visit is to show off the children to grandparents and family friends. In the 1970s, Palmer (1980) noted that an image of prosperity on the part of the migrants was essential, so that they usually travelled in a new car and ensured that the whole family, especially their daughters, were well dressed and behaved in a way which both they and the villagers perceived to be commensurate with their improved socioeconomic position. However, these attitudes and behaviour were often outmoded in terms of the changed conditions in the village communities themselves and served to heighten the distance between the villagers and the migrants. Children's reactions to the visit may be very mixed, even within one family: enjoyment might be limited to food (Jackson, 1979). Children are more likely to suffer from the heat, and Lobo (1978) has pointed out that children risk exposure to infectious diseases to which they may have no resistance through the more primitive sanitation of the village; some cases of tuberculosis have been reported amongst Italian children returning from abroad. But the major difficulty experienced by children of Italian origin visiting their relatives in Italy is that of language. For although the Italian language classes are intended to enable children to speak to their grandparents and relatives and to enjoy and learn from their visit to the full (Saifullah Khan, 1976), even those who have attended such classes may not be able to understand their relatives' spoken dialect and, in turn, the second- or third-generation form of the dialect which the children speak may be unacceptable in the village (Jackson, 1979; Rosen and Burgess, 1980, quoting Tosi). On the other hand, contact with the language community may act as a spur to further learning of Italian (Simons, 1980).

An investigation of various Italian associations in London (Walker, 1982) suggests that many young adult Italians born in Britain nurture their Italian identification, but through rather romanticized links – long summer holidays, Italian cars, films and cuisine – all of which, except the visit, can be enjoyed in London itself. In Britain it is clearly the family which maintains the main allegiance with the Italian connection and, specifically, the links to the village of origin. But in Italy place of birth is next in importance to the family in the formation of character and outlook. Palmer's (1977) anthropological investigations suggest that the orientation towards the village of origin may be strong not only amongst the first, but also the second (intermediate) and third generation, to the extent that some seriously debate the prospect of returning to these villages to develop the areas for tourism. Differences in perspective amongst the first-generation Italian migrants and the villagers have meant that, in the case of Emilians, repatriation has not resulted in resettlement in the natal village, but on the plains nearby, where some have invested in the growing urbanization in that area. But Palmer opines that should economic recession in Britain outlast that in Italy, another chain migration might ensue in which the pioneers would be British-born entrepreneurs emigrating to the homelands of their ancestors with the purpose of exploiting the growing developments in hotel and restaurant businesses to which many would be able to bring first-hand knowledge from their experience of the catering trade in London.

The significance of considering return visits and prospects for (re-)emigration to Italy in examining factors involved in the self-perceptions and identity formation of children of Italian origin is to demonstrate the strength and continuity of the Italian connection for their families, ties which they themselves may choose to accept or reject as they become more conscious of their own identities in adolescence. Not surprisingly, being born, educated and living in Britain increasingly influences the development of the personal and cultural identity of pupils from Italian backgrounds. Nevertheless, apart from those who actively and overtly reject the Italian connection, ties with Italy supported by the closeness of the family, the network of families with similar origins and community associations may continue to be strongly felt. Thus, though even the third generation may appear to adopt a British identity and lifestyle, it may by no means be assumed that they have necessarily lost their emotional ties to Italy.

Teachers' Attitudes and the School Context

The existence of little specific information on teachers' views of pupils of Italian origin is consistent with the lack of attention which they have generally received in educational research. How should this dearth of evidence be interpreted? Is it because pupils of Italian origin have not been a particular concern of their teachers, or compared with other ethnic minority pupils in the same schools, have they caused less concern? Is it that researchers have not sought the opinions of teachers who have taught Italian pupils over some years and know about their particular needs and interests? Or is it that inquiries into teachers' attitudes about ethnic minority pupils have become too sensitive, professionally and politically, in the racial climate of the 1970s and 1980s? Despite the lack of hard and precise data, this section attempts to give some indication of teachers' views, the academic standards and behaviour of pupils of Italian origin and the racial, social and cultural context of their schools. (For teachers' views on the English of pupils of Italian origin see pp.235–6.)

It is unfortunate that the major research evidence on teachers' attitudes to pupils of Italian origin from the third phase of the NFER investigations undertaken in the early 1970s (Brittan, 1976a) treats of Italians in a composite group of European pupils, including Cypriot and other European pupils. Clearly there may well be important distinctions to be drawn between these groups of pupils, as the responding teachers were themselves aware. Some commented in general about the validity of comparing the performance or behaviour of different ethnic groups, and many others wished to qualify their answers, so that their replies might refer, for example, to Italians but not to the other nationalities, to boys rather than girls or to recently arrived pupils as opposed to the UK-born. The earlier, second, phase of the NFER research (Townsend and Brittan, 1972) covered organizational arrangements for the teaching of all immigrant pupils, and Italian pupils and their teachers were present in few schools and localities, so teachers' comments relating to pupils of Italian origin are sparse and incidental. Having regard to these reservations, in the absence of other data, it is appropriate to draw on these researches in this context since they do provide some general information on teachers' attitudes to European pupils' academic standards and behaviour and in comparison with their attitudes to other ethnic minority pupils.

In the third phase of the project, in 1972, the opinions of 510 teachers (171 primary and 339 secondary) in 25 schools with 18–84 per cent ethnic minority pupils were generally far less marked with respect to European pupils, compared with the attitudes which they expressed towards pupils of West Indian or Asian origin. Many teachers were unwilling to make the generalizations imposed by the questions, and a sizeable number made use of the 'not applicable' or 'neutral' response categories. Although this may have been due to a lack of familiarity with such pupils, or a recognition of diversity within the group, the fact that when opinions were expressed there was a considerable consensus, at least within the two age ranges, suggests that teachers did have clear views about such pupils and that they were not necessarily favourable. For example, 19 per cent of all teachers did not express a view on the statement 'European immigrant pupils tend to raise the academic standards of this school', 41 per cent were neutral and 32 per cent disagreed. There was a contrast between primary and secondary teachers' views, 40 per cent of the former and 28 per cent of the latter disagreeing with the statement. Teachers were more likely to think that Asian pupils raised the academic standard of the school (15 per cent compared with five per cent for European pupils), though about a third held negative views of the academic achievement of both Asian and European pupils. Teachers did not, however, display as negative attitudes towards the position of European pupils *vis-à-vis* the academic standard of the school as they did towards West Indian pupils. Since it is evident that the English language competence of pupils of Italian has formed the main focus of teachers' assessments of the academic ability of pupils of Italian origin (see p.288), it is unfortunate that this research does not provide the specific insights teachers in schools in areas of Italian settlement have of the distinctive linguistic needs of pupils of Italian origin or appropriate teaching techniques or the expectations they have for the academic performance of pupils of Italian origin compared with their peers.

Teachers were also asked to give their opinions of the behaviour of European pupils and whether they resented being reprimanded more than English pupils. Teachers appeared to display more divergent opinions on the item 'European immigrant pupils are usually better behaved than English pupils'. Thirty per cent disgreed, 11 per cent agreed and 39 per cent checked the neutral category. More of the secondary teachers claimed better behaviour, and fewer disagreed with the statement compared with primary teachers. Interestingly, headteachers in an earlier part of the survey (ibid.) indicated that a few difficulties had been experienced with the behaviour of Italian children. These were generally attributed to differential standards of discipline between home and school, leading to difficulties of adaptation in the school context for certain pupils. By contrast, 35 per cent of teachers in Brittan's survey, slightly more primary than secondary teachers, disagreed with the statement 'European immigrant pupils resent being repri-manded more than English pupils do', although 37 per cent of teachers were neutral and 19 per cent claimed it was not applicable, or did not reply. This suggests that European pupils might be seen by their teachers as more prepared to accept correction. However, these generalized findings must be approached with caution, especially in this context, since they do not relate solely to pupils of Italian origin.

Another aspect of the education of pupils of Italian origin, upon which research might have been expected to offer some evidence, is teachers' views of their culture and its place in the school curriculum. According to Steedman (1979) two Italian sources (Marin, 1975; Rapporto di Lavoro, 1977) emphasized that Italian children did not experience major difficulties of discrimination or incomprehension of their cultural background within the English school system. This might be interpreted as indicating that pupils of Italian origin are socially well integrated and that their cultural backgrounds are recognized as an integral feature of their schools' curriculum. Italian pupils do not appear to have suffered particularly acutely from racial discrimination, although Palmer (1977, 1980) suggested that some of the intermediate generation may have experienced discrimination or abuse, and there continue to be reports of name-calling (see p.300). There is slight evidence of discrimination by Italian parents and their children against their black neighbours and school peers. But the relative absence of discrimination does not necessarily mean racial or social integration (see p.301). Moreover, it has perhaps been too readily assumed that the cultural background of pupils of Italian origin has been easily accomodated within the school curriculum because of its presumed simi-larities, especially the connection through Catholicism. For example, Tansley (1981), evaluating the MTCP, recorded that although, compared with Punjabi-speaking pupils, Italian pupils had to cope with greater linguistic interference problems – as they were learning Standard Italian and not their parents' dialect – since the Italian pupils' culture was more similar to that of the host country, they had fewer integration difficulties (p.26). But does presumed cultural similarity necessarily facilitate integration? Even if it is true that pupils of Italian origin have not suffered 'incomprehension' of their cultural background in the British school system, what evidence is there of aspects of their cultural background being positively incorporated in a multicultural curriculum? Research on teachers' attitudes towards aspects of the multicultural curriculum with specific reference to pupils of Italian origin is strangely silent. For example, another part of the third phase of the NFER multiracial education project investigated teachers' opinions on aspects of school life – race relations and the school curriculum, religious education and assemblies, dress and diet, culture and languages of countries of origin, English as a foreign language, the adaptation of the school, adjustment of newly arrived immigrant pupils, arrangements for English language teaching, non-English speaking infants, immigrant teachers and use of non-teaching staff (Brittan, 1976b). Views were expressed by these same teachers who gave opinions on the academic standards and behaviour of 'European' pupils, some of whom had Italian pupils in their schools, but their views were not specifically focused on pupils of Italian origin. The focus was primarily on Asian cultures, which have consistently gained the overwhelming attention of teachers considering the multicultural curriculum. Research or documentation may be lacking apropos of the Italian cultural background, but apart from the relatively few schools where pupils of Italian origin are enabled to study Standard Italian through the *Corsi Inseriti* jointly established by the Italian government, LEAs and schools, there is little evidence of any appreciation of the need to incorporate the cultural backgrounds of Italian pupils and their contemporary British lifestyles in the normal curriculum. Information may be lacking, either because it is erroneously assumed that in view of the Graeco-Roman influence on British culture, especially on etymology, the cultural background of Italian pupils is somehow taken into account as part of mainstream European culture, or because teachers just do not have the resources actively to include an awareness of the culture and lifestyles of pupils of Italian origin. In this respect, assistance may be gained from the Schools Council *Lifestyles* pack (Thomas *et al.*, 1984) which offers a means of opening up a more effective and sensitive appreciation of the cultural differences and similarities to be found in comparing family backgrounds and lifestyles through information on seven families, including one of Italian background.

Any opinions teachers may have expressed about pupils of Italian origin have concerned stress, tiredness, lack of concentration in their work or attention to homework which Italian pupils show on account of attending Italian language classes at evenings and weekends. Teachers have also been alarmed at long visits made by pupils to their parents' homeland during the summer holiday because of a concern for possible effects on progress in learning English. This was in fact the main concern of class teachers whose Italian pupils were withdrawn for daily tuition in Standard Italian for a four-year period in connection with the MTCP. The title of the project, 'Mother Tongue and Culture', itself indicates that one of the original project objectives was to include 'the teaching of the languages, history, geography, music, games and social studies of the country of origin' (Simons, 1979). The project teachers agreed, however, that at age five plus, and in view of the time constraint, the emphasis should be on language teaching, drawing upon cultural illustrations where appropriate, and these were actually as much from the cultural experience of the children in England as from Italy. Teachers generally considered that to ignore that the experience of such pupils is typically a mixture of parental culture and language, exposure to TV and the talk and behaviour of older siblings and to teach them only aspects of the culture of their parents' country of origin would have been artificial. But one Italian project teacher suggested that teaching about culture should be the responsibility of all class teachers. Interestingly, several of the class teachers, who were less committed to the language teaching than project teachers, suggested that adolescence was the most appropriate time to introduce teaching about the culture, and perhaps even the language, linking language study with O- and A-level examinations. Just as a question can be asked about which language to teach – dialect or Standard Italian – the question of which culture to teach also needs to be asked, and since the educational interests of a linguistic group might differ according to the cultural complexity and intercultural relationships within a local community, community needs and values should be ascertained. It was the view of one of the Italian teachers in the MTCP that in teaching the Italian pupils their culture,

We're not teaching them finance, institutions, banking, social politics or sociology. The culture they bring with them, the culture they have at home, the culture lies in the religion they have, in the baptism, the food they eat at home, the holidays they have, the letters they write... the emphasis they put on certain aspects of life, the emphasis they put on the family... this is their culture. Culture is not Dante, Petrarch... or the Roman Empire. This is their history if you want, this is their social and economic history, it's their political background, and so many things. It's not their culture as such. (Cited by Simons, 1980, p.25)

The teacher in the extract above believed it inappropriate to teach cultural norms directly and that the historical, literary and political heritage could be taught in curriculum subjects at a later stage of schooling. The emphasis was to be on teaching the children through the language, using it as a vehicle to give them access to other knowledge and experience. Thus mother-tongue teaching was using the language as a vehicle for developing the innate knowledge possessed by native speakers of the tongue. If this approach is accepted, then to include the cultural background of pupils of Italian origin in a multicultural curriculum is to teach the Italian language, drawing on aspects of their home culture in a family setting in the UK, involving their religious beliefs, food habits and their relationships with the extended family in Italy, and also by teaching about wider aspects of the historical, literary and political heritage in other aspects of the curriculum, which would be experienced by all other pupils. Indeed other aims of the MTCP were to promote general educational interest on the part of both indigenous and immigrant groups and to increase esteem for immigrants on the part of indigenous children in the school. The latter aim was somewhat contentious: ethnic minority pupils were in the majority in three out of the four schools; teachers' opinions varied according to whether the project pupils were seen as an élite or were ignored by the other children; and many teachers argued that it was not necessary to have the stimulus of the project in order to encourage indigenous children to find out more about other cultures as this already happened. There was some doubt, however, as to whether the indigenous children had actually become more aware of other cultures during the course of the project. On the other hand, the project had increased the interest shown by Italian parents, and teachers and headteachers in the schools from which the pupils were drawn, so that they became more appreciative and understanding in their dealings with ethnic minority pupils and parents. Furthermore, the class teachers thought the involvement of Italian teachers in the project had been particularly beneficial in establishing better home–school relationships with Italian parents as the teachers had devoted much more time than would normally be available to liaison and home visiting. Indeed Bedfordshire LEA has a specialist liaison teacher for the Italian community and also organizes visits and exchanges to Italy.

Unfortunately, just as there is a lack of information about mainstream teachers' attitudes towards pupils of Italian origin and provision for including their language and culture in the school curriculum, other than that in the MTCP evaluation, so there is also an absence of information on the number of teachers of Italian origin teaching in British schools. Clearly some Italian-born teachers, such as those employed on the MTCP, are involved in language-teaching arrangements in connection with pupils of Italian origin, for which purpose they are employed by the Italian government (see pp.256–7). The register of the Association of Teachers of Italian might include more information but this would still not indicate how many teachers of Italian origin might be teaching in other subject-areas. There are, moreover, no indications of how many second-generation Italians who have experienced all their schooling in the UK may have entered teaching. Such teachers may occupy a special position, enabling them to facilitate interaction between mainstream schools and the parents of pupils of Italian origin. The experience of the MTCP clearly demonstrated that Italian parents of the first, intermediate and second generation welcomed the special interest which mainstream schools displayed in their language and culture. But apart from the MTCP initiative, the absence of serious research effort and significant evidence on the personal, social, cognitive and linguistic development of pupils of Italian origin means that, although it is possible to infer broad trends in these pupils' experience of schooling, it is only possible to guess at the range of their abilities, skills and achievements. The participation of the third generation of pupils of Italian origin in education, therefore, presents new opportunities for teachers and researchers to make good this deficiency.

Part Three
Pupils of Ukrainian Origin

The Ukrainians, amongst Britain's invisible immigrants, are distinguished, like other East Europeans, by being political exiles. As far as can be ascertained, the Ukrainians and their children do not appear to have received the special or focussed attention of either social scientists or educationists. This may be due to several factors: the lack of research in the period immediately after the end of the Second World War when the Ukrainians settled in the UK; their relatively small numbers compared with other immigrant groups and their dispersal across the country; and, not least, the lack of awareness of their distinctive characteristics, historical and social background which distinguish them from other East European immigrants. A range of sociological and educational sources have thus been used to build up a description of the Ukrainian community in the UK and the education of their children over the last 40 years.

History and Social Background

HISTORY The Ukrainians, by all accounts, are deeply conscious of their distinct identity as a people and their long cultural history, even though the Ukraine has been almost continuously denied a separate political existence. The history of the Ukraine, famed as a plentiful agricultural area, is one of foreign domination and division. In the 17th century, under Peter the Great, a treaty aimed at defining the relations between the Ukraine and Russia, which in practice had preserved the independence of the Ukraine, was abolished. In the 18th century the Ukraine was divided: the eastern region of the Ukraine came under Russia and the western region of Galicia fell under Austrian rule. In this area, which was allowed greater freedom, Ukrainian national consciousness developed most strongly. East–West differences were further emphasized by religion: most of the Western Ukrainians belonged to the Greek Catholic Church, most of the easterners were members of the Russian Orthodox Church (Brown, 1970). During the 19th century national consciousness grew and intensified in an oral literary tradition. There is a distinct Ukrainian literature and language. At the end of the First World War the Eastern Ukraine was incorporated as a socialist republic into the Soviet Union, and in 1923 Western Ukraine was made part of a re-created Poland. During the 1930s there was deep resentment and strong opposition to Soviet policies of land collectivization because of the long traditions of peasant ownership and farming in the Ukraine. The Soviet-engineered famine of 1932–3 and the deportation of millions to labour camps also entered into the consciousness of the Ukrainians. With the advent of the Second World War, many Western Ukrainians at first welcomed the coming of the Germans in 1941 as an opportunity to proclaim their independence. But this was short-lived. Underground resistance increased, first against the Germans and later against the Russians. But in 1942 with the Russians advancing some Ukrainians joined the German army, some fighting the Poles, and millions were transported to Germany to serve as industrial and agricultural workers. At the end of the war they formed two-thirds of all 'Eastern workers' in Germany, and many found them-selves overtaken by the Allied forces.

EXILE IN BRITAIN An awareness of their historical and social background is essential to an understanding of the Ukrainians who arrived in Britain at the end of the Second World War. At that time, the Western Ukraine was absorbed into the USSR, where the Ukraine now forms the largest of the 15 republics occupying land three times the size of Britain, with a population of 50 million. Most of the Ukrainians had become refugees in the wake of the advancing Red Army and all rejected communism as a way of life (Haxell, 1979). Brown's (1970) account of Ukrainians in Bedford includes some first-hand accounts of their wartime hardships and indignities, tracing their varied routes as displaced persons and prisoners of war to the UK. At the end of the war many Ukrainians were recruited from amongst the million displaced persons in camps in Europe, in 1946, by the British Ministry of Labour under the European Voluntary Worker Scheme (EVWS) by which the British government aimed to recharge its labourforce in order to carry out the rebuilding of the country and the economy (Krausz, 1971). Most of the Ukrainians in Britain arrived here from Germany in 1947–8 (Khan, 1976). According to Zubrzycki (1956, quoting a statement made by the Home Secretary in the House of Commons, 31 March 1950), 8,238 Ukrainians were admitted under the EVWS during the period 1945–9. They were amongst some 80,000–90,000 other workers recruited under this scheme, mostly Poles, Latvians, Lithuanians, Yugoslavs and others from the Baltic and East European regions (Krausz, 1971), However, Smith *et al.* (1984) assert that over 20,000 Ukrainians, about a quarter women, from the displaced persons' camps were admitted between 1947–50 as EVWs, as were 8,400 Ukrainian prisoners of war brought to Britain from Italy in 1947. The younger, more active men and boys from amongst those in the displaced persons' camps opted to come to Britain, most of the older people, including the intellectuals, chose to go to the USA (Brown, 1970). There is now a sizeable Ukrainian community in the Canadian prairies and an estimated half a million Ukrainian speakers in North America (Smith *et al.*, 1984). Clearly unlike many other immigrant groups, and even other exiled East Europeans, such as the Poles, the Ukrainians have had little, if any, chance of returning to their homeland, even on temporary visits. Yet despite tenuous connections with their homeland and any remaining relatives, and a consciousness of their continued hardships, Brown (1970) reported that Ukrainians in Bedford in the late 1960s had not lost hope of returning. Indeed it appears that even though over the years the Ukrainians have developed commitments and roots in the UK, their resolve to keep alive their Ukrainian identity and cultural heritage has remained firm.

WORK For the most part, Ukrainians were recruited as single men and women, without dependents, to work in essential industries and services in Britain for which British workers were not available. Many Ukrainians spoke little or no English and did not possess relevant skills. As EVWs, their civil and social rights were severely restricted. They were compelled to accept employment selected by the Ministry of Labour and allowed to change only with the consent of that department for at least three years after arrival (Rose *et al.*, 1969; LMP, 1985). The Ukrainian men were usually directed to agriculture (45 per cent), coalmining, quarrying or brickmaking (17 per cent) or domestic service (eight per cent); the women were mostly placed in textile manufacturing (42 per cent) or domestic or hospital services (40 per cent) (LMP, 1985). Thus many Ukrainian men described by Brown (1970) in Bedford had begun working in the brickfields there, living initially in large hostel accommodation. Others had worked in agriculture, farming in Suffolk and Cambridgeshire, or temporarily in coalmining. Some Ukrainian women worked in the cottonmills in the North and in Scotland, others as nurses and hospital workers in Bedford. Rose *et al.* (1969) recorded some initial reluctance on the part of trade unions to accept EVWs and to accord them rights under the new welfare state, and there were also some reservations on the part of the majority of the society to accept Ukrainians and East European immigrants socially.

DISPERSAL AND SETTLEMENT   The numbers of Ukrainians in the UK have not been documented in succeeding years, as they are not separately enumerated in the Censuses. It is clear, however, that the initial dispersal of Ukrainians to employment has continued, so that although nuclei of communities remain in certain original locations of settlement, Ukrainians have become more widely scattered across the country with the years as restrictions on their employment were removed and their economic stability has increased. Brown (1970) has recorded how, as the young Ukrainians started to marry and attempted to move out of the hostels in Bedford in the early 1950s, they experienced extreme difficulty in finding accommodation. Data cited show that the number of Ukrainian families in multiple occupation of housing in Bedford was at a peak in 1956 and thereafter slowly declined, although it continued well into the 1960s. Smith *et al.* (1984) claim that in the mid-1950s half the Ukrainians in Britain were still living in hostels and that a high proportion were engaged in agricultural work. By 1970 most of the Ukrainians in Bedford were living in owner-occupied dwellings, and despite their origins in the land, were still working mainly in the brickyards in Bedford. Some pursued other trades or professions as shoemakers, electricians or teachers.

There are other indications that the settlement of the Ukrainians was increasingly widespread. According to Smith *et al.* (1984), in the mid-1950s nearly half the Ukrainians in Britain lived in the East Midlands and the North of England, the remainder in smaller numbers throughout the country. In the 1960s Brown noted that the Ukrainian priest in Bedford also served 550 parishioners in 15 places from Northampton to Peterborough. Other sources indicate that many Ukrainians settled in the textile towns of the North – Oldham, Rochdale and Bradford (Khan, 1976). Similarly, in Huddersfield, Burgin and Edson (1967) recorded that most of the European immigrants, including Ukrainians, who had arrived in the 1950s, were involved in the textile trade or chemical and other industries and had started to move away from the cheaper dwellings in the town centre to the suburbs in the 1960s as they became more economically established. Bradford became the centre for the Ukrainian population in the North. The 1971 Census listed some 2,205 inhabitants in Bradford from the USSR (presumably mostly from the Ukraine), and by 1979 it was estimated that the Ukrainian population had reached 2,500 (Haxell, 1979). There are also Ukrainian communities in Manchester and Leicester, and in the mid-1970s an estimated 300 Ukrainians in Derby (Khan, 1976).

Owing to a continuing process of dispersal, some of the Ukrainian communities, such as that in Grimsby, are very small and this may limit their ability to support their own community groups. The Association of Ukrainians in Great Britain (AUGB) has estimated the Ukrainian population including children born in the UK to be around 35,000. They are dispersed over 70 community centres, the larger in the industrial North, Midlands, London and Edinburgh, with smaller communities radiating from them (Maryniuk, 1985). The Swann Report which acknowledged estimates of 20,000–30,000 including the descendants of 'mixed' marriages, suggested that probably a third of the Ukrainian community is now UK-born (GB. P. H. of C, 1985).

SOCIAL STATUS Partly because of the predominance of single people in the Ukrainian immigration, but also because of their dispersal and their gradual acceptance socially, there has been considerable intermarriage with the British and with other Europeans. In Bedford, in the 1960s, by far the majority of Ukrainians had mixed marriages; only in a quarter were both partners Ukrainian. Amongst the 86 families there were a larger number of marriages between Ukrainian men and British women (34) or Italian women (19), the remainder being married to other southern, central or East European women. The community also comprised 47 men, some of whom had been forced to leave their wives in the Ukraine (Brown, 1970). According to Khan (1976), less intermarriage took place in the north, which may have been a factor influencing stronger community support. But for some Ukrainians, Brown (1970) reported that the strain and suffering of the war and post-war years left a lasting legacy. Some individuals, who were separated from their land and families, had endured intense physical and mental hardships, long periods of undernourishment and the degradation of jobs for which they were unfitted by nature and intelligence, combined with years of loneliness in lodging-houses. These experiences had sometimes led to alcoholism, breakdown and suicide, and as with other exiles, there was a high incidence of mental illness and coronary disease (ibid). On the other hand, over the years the public invisibility of the Ukrainians may have facilitated individual social mobility as by the early 1980s many were in higher-status housing and occupations than the average for linguistic minorities as a whole (LMP, 1985).

IDENTITY AND COMMUNITY ASSOCIATIONS If there is any consciousness of the Ukrainians in the UK, then they are likely to be known for their assiduous activity in preserving their cultural heritage, which is sustained by a passionate love for their motherland. According to Brown (1970), 'As a community, no other national group in Bedford is more single in purpose and being' (p.56). Their purpose was to keep the Ukraine alive within themselves. Despite the unrecognized political identity of the Ukraine, the Ukrainians in Bedford had a sense of their distinct identity as a people, which they had clung to throughout the war, defying attempts at classification as Polish or Russian, and preferring, despite the lead of their priest, to remain stateless rather than compromising their identity by taking British nationality. Therefore, it is particularly ironic that if Ukrainians in the UK have been the subject of research, they should generally appear in some generalized East European category. This not only denies their distinct characteristics and heritage, but fails to distinguish them from the Poles, the largest East European immigrant group, who have received the greater attention. The Ukrainians and Poles were, moreover, deeply divided on account of their experiences of war. Indeed, as Patterson (1977) has pointed out, although pre-1939 Poland was an ethnically plural society which included unassimilated Ukrainian communities as well as smaller numbers of assimilated Ukrainian Poles, after their arrival in Britain, a large number of Polish-born Ukrainians disassociated themselves from Polish state loyalties and joined local Ukrainian communities. The division between the Poles and Ukrainians in Bedford, in the 1960s, was apparent from Brown's (1970) descriptions, although there was no open hostility.

Experience of post-war Britain and the contrasting 1960s had served to strengthen the Ukrainians' resolve to preserve their identity. According to Brown (ibid.), the Ukrainians in Bedford lived abstemiously and were gradually accorded respect in the town. Though they retained links with their homelands, the arrival of the second generation strengthened their communities in England. Indeed Brown reported that despite reservations, there was a deep sense of obligation to and even some affection for Britain as the country which gave them asylum. However, their respect for the Britain of the 1960s was diminishing. Being a self-sufficient community, they favoured discipline, order and authority, and condemned apparent British laxity in morals and the weakness of the authority of parents and teachers. Yet they were content with a modest way of life, not having great expectations or ambitions. These attitudes were matters of both temperament and experience. They appeared to aim simply to live peaceably and to preserve their own cultural identity. In many ways, then, they felt self-consciously different from other immigrants in Bedford whom they perceived as coming to Britain to earn money for a better life. Hence their relationships with other immigrant groups, though fairly amiable, were not close. They felt little kinship with other Slavs, the Poles, Serbs or Slovenes, and Brown suggested that they were perhaps closest to the Latvians who were also descendants of smallholders and peasant farmers. The Ukrainians were particularly reserved about the later immigrants to Bedford – the Italians, West Indians, Pakistanis and Indians – suggesting that they, too, should follow the Ukrainian tradition of self-help. Brown considered that their pride, industry and devotion to upholding their Ukrainian identity and cultural traditions would be assured in the second generation.

Maryniuk (1985) claims that the Ukrainian community has not suffered from racism in the same way as the Asian, West Indian or some other ethnic minority communities, rather they have been positively received and have benefited from living in Britain. She asserts, moreover, that the Ukrainians have had a choice in matters of integration and assimilation and have chosen to sustain their cultural heritage through their language and religion, whilst also actively engaging in British society. As a Ukrainian community organization expressed it in evidence to the Swann Committee:

> The Ukrainian community seeks to preserve its identity by passing on to new generations the Ukrainian language, knowledge about the Ukraine and its history, and Ukrainian cultural and religious traditions. The objective is to minimize the extent to which people of Ukrainian origin lose their Ukrainian identity through assimilation with the society at large, at the same time encouraging them to be successful members of British society. Assimilation cannot be totally avoided, but it is likely that the community will exist in this country as a distinct entity for the forseeable future. (GB. P. H of C, 1985, p.712)

Since the early years of their arrival in Britain, the Ukrainians have maintained their identity through their determination to preserve their cultural heritage, so that some 40 years later the community has many 'vibrant and active' cultural, political, educational, youth and women's organizations which meet in large houses, churches and schools in the main centres of settlement and are centrally co-ordinated by national full-time organizations (Maryniuk, 1985). From the beginning the focus of community life was the church either the Ukrainian Catholic or Ukrainian Orthodox Church where Ukrainian is used in services. For the first-generation Ukrainians in Bedford, religion in the Ukrainian Catholic Church was a primary bond and a natural part of their consciousness as a people. As early as 1958 the Ukrainian community in Bedford purchased a hall which it converted for use as a church and, in 1962, a house was purchased to form a community centre. These two institutions gave the Ukrainian community in Bedford a focus and stimulus. In the 1960s there was a busy programme of meetings and community activities each week and celebrations of literary and political anniversaries of national importance.

In Bradford and Coventry the Ukrainian community established their own churches, or church services, clubs and mother-tongue schools (see p.321), in order to ensure the preservation of their traditions and their continuity amongst the second generation (Haxell, 1979; LMP, 1985). By 1970 there were several national Ukrainian organizations: the Association of Ukrainians in Great Britain (AUGB) (influential in mother-tongue teaching), the Association of Ukrainian Former Combatants, the Association of Ukrainian Women and the Ukrainian Youth Association. Musical activities were central to the Ukrainian community's activities in Bedford, in the form of an adult choir, a youth orchestra, dancing and folklore groups (Brown, 1970).

Indeed during the 1970s, whilst researching into ethnic minority arts, Khan (1976) noted that the Ukrainians had 46 community centres throughout the UK, and that their activities were largely music-orientated. There were some 20 Ukrainian dance groups and choirs in existence and, in addition, a youth centre for 800 in Derbyshire and a scout camp in Wales. Drama groups could, however, no longer be sustained because of the dispersal of communities. Khan showed that there was little local authority funding for Ukrainian choirs or dance groups. Despite this, and the increasing distances participants needed to travel, the choir and dance groups in Manchester in particular were thriving. The choir performed at least monthly throughout the UK and had had an international tour. Khan also singled out the intense cultural activity amongst the 300-strong community of Ukrainians in Derby who had formed two dance groups, two orchestras and a male voice choir. The performers were overwhelmingly young and the dance group met, together with Ukrainians from Leicester, in a large, commodious Victorian house which formed the Ukrainian Club. Members of the youth music group were particularly conscious of the erosion of Ukrainian folk traditions and wished to tape songs recalled by elderly Ukrainians, to develop materials to teach children to play Ukrainian instruments and to manufacture these instruments in the UK. The group was in great demand for performances, travelling throughout the country. Khan commended the self-sufficiency of the Ukrainian communities in their cultural activities, but suggested that they were beginning to feel the need for wider support and patronage and that their song and dance activities should have a much wider appeal.

Evidence from the AUGB to the Swann Committee reveals that many children and young people continue to be members of two Ukrainian youth organizations, participating in choirs, folk dancing groups and summer camps. There is even a Ukrainian university in the UK with strong links with Ukrainian universities in Rome and Munich and students are encouraged to attend courses in Ukrainian studies at various times. There is also a Ukrainian publishing company which produces books, magazines and a weekly paper (GB. P. H of C, 1985; Marynuik, 1985).

Language

Language is one of the primary means of preserving cultural traditions. Thus, in addition to the church, cultural and club activities in which the Ukrainian communities are actively engaged, it is necessary to consider the extent to which knowledge and use of the Ukrainian language has been maintained and transmitted to the second generation in the UK. For the Ukrainians, the oral tradition in poetry and literature gives an additional stimulus to the preservation of language. Ukrainian as a Slavic language is closely related to Russian and more distinctly to Polish, and is written in a partly Roman, partly Cyrillic alphabet. Across the world there are about 35 million speakers of Ukrainian. Many of the older Ukrainians in the UK who were born in the Western Ukraine which was then part of Poland also have some knowledge of Polish (Smith *et al.*, 1984).

Knowledge and Use of English and Ukrainian amongst Adults and Children
Sources are generally agreed that most Ukrainians, many of whom arrived in the UK in young adulthood, had little English and few had any education beyond the age of 14 (McCrea, 1964; Rose *et al.*, 1969; Brown, 1970). Moreover, Brown suggested that their knowledge of English continued to be limited even 15 years after their settlement in the UK, and in some cases this restricted employment opportunities. There is no information about the influence of marrying out of the Ukrainian community on the English knowledge of adult Ukrainians. A national survey conducted in the 1970s (Mobbs, 1977) reported that there were few East European women amongst participants in language tuition schemes.

Fortunately, however, the Linguistic Minorities Project (1979–83) included a survey of the Ukrainian community in Coventry as part of its Adult Language Use Survey and also provides information on maintenance of and attitudes to Ukrainian in its Mother-Tongue Teaching Directory Survey and, incidentally, through the Schools' Language Survey and Secondary Pupils Survey (see p.53). As well as supplying data on the linguistic repertoires, skills in Ukrainian and English and language use in the household, at work and in leisure-time of the Ukrainian respondents in Coventry, the ALUS also usefully provides up-to-date demographic information on this particular community in Coventry. However, in view of the small sample involved, which was drawn from a community association record and hence may be biased towards its more active members, the picture given may not be representative overall. On the other hand, the findings relate to at least half the families of Ukrainian origin in Coventry, in 1980–1, and may therefore be seen as indicative for that location (Smith *et al.*, 1984).

Some 48 respondents were interviewed, men outnumbering women and more in the older age-groups as many of the younger people were hesitant because they said that they did not know the language at all well (LMP, 1985). Altogether they had 144 family members in their households, of whom 60 per cent were brought up overseas. The population was predominantly middle-aged and elderly – 53 per cent over 50 – and men clearly outnumbered women. The second generation was concentrated in the 16 – 25 age-group, with only 11 per cent under 17. Most families lived in owner-occupied accommodation (88 per cent) and only 10 per cent in council housing. Some 78 per cent of males and 63 per cent of females aged 17 to 60–65 worked outside the home. Two-thirds of respondents in work (32) were in manufacturing industry. The remaining third were equally divided between working in the civil service or local authority, retailing or catering and other services. Most were in manual work, and very few had supervisory responsibilities, although nearly half had at least an apprenticeship qualification. None were in family businesses or self-employed.

About half of the respondents claimed to know three or more languages. Almost all respondents claimed knowledge of at least a little Ukrainian and English. Approximately a tenth claimed to know Italian and almost a third Polish, though this was rarely used. Over nine out of every ten respondents claimed to understand and speak Ukrainian either very or fairly well and over eight out of ten said they had the same level of skills in reading and writing Ukrainian. Those brought up in Britain reported lower literacy skills. Fewer respondents claimed skills in English at the same levels. Nearly one-half reported that they could understand and speak and nearly a third that they could read and write English very or fairly well. Again, these skills depended on length of formal schooling and country of upbringing. Nine out of ten respondents had at least minimal literacy in both languages and none were unable to write in either language. About four-fifths of respondents' household members were said to know Ukrainian and about the same proportion English fairly or very well, and six out of every ten were said to be fluently bilingual in both languages. English skills depended very much on whether the household member had been brought up totally or partly in the UK rather than overseas.

Ukrainian was the language most often spoken to and by the respondents' household members. Nearly two-thirds of respondents and their interlocutors (94) in the households used only or mostly Ukrainian. Only about one-sixth of pairs used only or mostly English. The remainder used both Ukrainian and English in some combination. Indeed in the 18 cases where there was a real language choice available to both speakers as many as 16 used only or mostly Ukrainian. At work nearly a third of the working respondents had at least one Ukrainian-speaking colleague, but over two-thirds spoke only English to their workmates and thought it essential to read English in their job. However, most of the respondents spent their leisure-time with other Ukrainian-speaking friends and two-thirds used Ukrainian with the person with whom they spent most of their free time. But only one in ten had Ukrainian-speaking neighbours and one in 20 a Ukrainian-speaking doctor. Although three-quarters sometimes went to a shop where Ukrainian was spoken, none had seen a Ukrainian film or video in the previous four weeks. Over half of the respondents were church members, over one-fifth belonged to a Ukrainian social club and almost as many to music and dance associations (ibid.).

Respondents reported a high level of reading and library use. Nearly nine out of every ten read newspapers in Ukrainian, just over half read textbooks and novels in Ukrainian and just under half read these in English. A third of respondents knew there were Ukrainian books in local libraries, but although nearly three-fifths had sometimes used the libraries, only one in five had sometimes borrowed books in Ukrainian. Only a fifth had ever needed to use a family member or friend as an interpreter, mostly in complicated official contacts or paperwork.

These data from the ALUS in Coventry indicate a fairly strong degree of bilingualism, indeed trilingualism, and strong language maintenance on the part of Ukrainian speakers in Coventry. In present-day Ukrainian-speaking households, especially where all the adults have knowledge of the language, it appears to be in regular everyday use. The language of the home is likely to have a considerable influence on the linguistic competence of pupils of Ukrainian origin, especially in their early years of schooling.

What, then, of children's knowledge of Ukrainian? Brown (1970) considered that the second generation might read or write Ukrainian, despite difficulties which might be encountered with the alphabet. Yet whilst visiting Ukrainian community centres and clubs, Khan (1976) noted that few adolescents of Ukrainian origin spoke really fluent Ukrainian and that dance classes, for example, were conducted in a mixture of English and Ukrainian, with English predominating. Unfortunately, the ILEA language censuses which have become an important source of data on minority language speakers are not helpful with respect to Ukrainian pupils, presumably because inner London has not been a principal area of Ukrainian settlement or because the second-generation had completed their education. Although in 1978 Ukrainian is listed amongst the languages spoken by ILEA pupils for whom English was not a first language, such speakers are not distinguished and are included amongst the category 'other European', and in the censuses in 1981, 1983 and 1985 only 15–12 pupils were recorded as speaking Ukrainian other than or in addition to English at home (ILEA, 1979, 1982, 1983, 1986). Furthermore, they were not distinguished according to division of the ILEA, age or stage of fluency in English, but were categorized with 'other European' pupils, of whom in these years around 60 per cent were said by their teachers to be fluent in English.

The Schools Language Survey of the LMP provides evidence of Ukrainian speakers in five LEAs (Couillaud and Tasker, 1983; LMP, 1983a). In Bradford, already noted as one of the principal areas of settlement for Ukrainians in the UK, 104 pupils aged six to 15 plus claimed to use Ukrainian other than English at home. They formed 0.7 per cent of the speakers of a language other than English at home, the eleventh largest minority group in Bradford. Of the Ukrainian speakers, 53 per cent were girls and 47 per cent were boys. There were declining numbers in the lower age ranges, for although there were 45 Ukrainian speakers aged 15 plus, their numbers dropped to 24 12–14 year-olds, 12 nine to 11 year-olds and nine six to eight year-olds. According to the pupils' self-reports, their literacy in Ukrainian increased with age, and there were no significant differences between girls and boys in this respect. In view of the estimated Ukrainian population of Bradford at 2,500 in 1979 (see p.314), it is perhaps surprising to find only 104 Ukrainian speakers amongst the school population. However, these declining numbers probably represent the last of the second-generation from Ukrainian backgrounds, with the arrival in schools of the third generation yet to come, or they may indicate declining knowledge of Ukrainian. In comparison with the numbers of Ukrainian speakers in Bradford, there were relatively few Ukrainian speakers in the other four LEAs surveyed: 40 in Coventry, 14 in Peterborough, two in Haringey and none in Waltham Forest, which incidentally confirms the settlement of Ukrainians outside London. Since two-thirds of the very few Ukrainian respondents in the ALUS survey in Coventry with children in their households (18) said that the children used only or mostly English when talking to each other, and as the second generation now becoming parents will have experienced their schooling in Britain, it is most likely that the third generation from Ukrainian backgrounds will enter school with some competence in English, and for many it is likely to be their first language.

'Mother-Tongue' Teaching

In addition to other religious, political and social activities, Ukrainian communities, in common with other minorities, have also attempted to preserve their identity and cultural traditions through mother-tongue classes for the second generation. Indeed it has been suggested that certain East European exile communities may feel a greater concern to maintain their traditions than those who can voluntarily return home and be assured of their cultural and linguistic heritage (Saifullah Khan, 1976). Ukrainians have clearly felt it to be a matter of paramount importance to pass on to their children an awareness and appreciation of their background, for many Ukrainian classes have been in existence since the 1950s and were well established in the 1960s (Khan, 1976; Saifullah Khan, 1980b). These were amongst the earliest mother-tongue classes to be set up, usually shortly after or about the same time as Polish classes. For example, the oldest mother-tongue class in Bradford was a Ukrainian class initiated in 1948, and this was still surviving in 1981 (LMP, 1982b). In Leicester the Ukrainian Saturday School has been in existence since 1954 (Houlton, 1980; Wilding, 1981). Furthermore, in 1981 one of the Ukrainian classes still held in Coventry was initiated in 1955, second only to the Polish classes in longevity (LMP, 1982a).

AIMS   The Ukrainian classes aim to keep alive a sense of cultural identity and knowledge of and appreciation of the Ukrainian language and traditions. In evidence to the Swann Committee Ukrainian representatives emphasized that the purpose of the Saturday schools is to reinforce home practices and not to supplement the teaching of mainstream schools. It was acknowledged that second-generation, British-born Ukrainians were having to make determined efforts to provide a consistent language environment at home in which they spoke to each other as well as to their children in Ukrainian. But it was recognized, and accepted, that apart from in the home and in social settings with other Ukrainians children would speak together mainly in English (GB. P. H of C, 1985).

ORGANIZATION AND FINANCE The Ukrainian mother-tongue schools and kindergartens have been developed as a result of voluntary community effort. In a national survey of mother-tongue teaching in Britain, in 1975, Saifullah Khan (1977) found that Ukrainian teachers, especially in the older-established schools which were running efficiently, considered mother-tongue provision the community's responsibility. Apparently some teachers implied that financial help for existing schemes was not necessary and that any control or interference with their provision would be resented. Evidence to the Swann Committee shows that the Educational Affairs Council of the AUGB reviews provision and with the increasing number of third-generation births is, for example, currently renewing efforts to plan and organize playgroups and kindergartens. At these, teachers and children speak in Ukrainian and, as well as the usual aspects of children's pre-school development, children are also introduced to Ukrainian culture. The kindergarten and Saturday school teachers usually receive a small remuneration, though the work of the Council and local organizers is voluntary. The school in Leicester, for example, was run on weekly subscriptions (Houlton, 1980; Wilding, 1981) and fees were also levied from parents in the Ukrainian classes in Bradford and Coventry (LMP, 1982a and b). Maryniuk (1985) confirms that the expense of running the Ukrainian school is borne by parents and communities – an increasingly onerous financial burden as the Ukrainians who founded the schools are now mainly old-age pensioners. She suggests that as only a minority of the community schools receive some form of grant from their LEA, some sort of financial assistance, especially for the acquisition of books, would be welcome.

NUMBER OF SCHOOLS, CLASSES AND PUPILS The existence of Ukrainian classes is clearly related to the largest areas of settlement which can support them and make them worthwhile. There are reports of Ukrainian classes in Bradford (Saifullah Khan, 1976; LMP, 1982b), Leicester (Saifullah Khan, 1976; Houlton, 1980; Wilding, 1981), Coventry (LMP, 1982a) and Bedford (Brown, 1970), and these case studies have been drawn upon to indicate the following organizational and curricular features. However, caution must be exercised in extrapolating from the limited and possibly unrepresentative data available, especially in view of the terminological confusion between schools, courses and classes. Most importantly, provision is variable over time and related to migration history and the birth of subsequent generations.

Maryniuk (1985) claims that in the 1960s there were about 42 Ukrainian schools with 2,000 pupils. Information from mainstream sources may, however, under-enumerate provision due to lack of awareness and information. In a national survey, in 1971, Townsend and Brittan (1972) found that only one out of 230 schools reported that arrangements were made by a local Ukrainian community to teach their language outside school hours. By 1979 when Little and Willey (1983) undertook a further national survey, two out of 18 LEAs with ten per cent or more ethnic minority population and three out of 21 LEAs with 2.5–10 per cent ethnic minority population reported that Ukrainian was taught out of school hours by community groups. One LEA claimed to support a Ukrainian supplementary school. In 1975, Saifullah Khan (1976) recorded eight classes in Leicester, two for older pupils and six for younger children. At that time, there were three Ukrainian schools in Bradford. But by the time of the Mother-Tongue Teaching Directory (MTTD) survey in 1981 there were 15 Ukrainian classes in Bradford, run by three different interest groups: ten by the Ukrainian Association; four by the Ukrainian Catholic Church and one by the Ukrainian Orthodox Church (LMP, 1982b). By contrast, Coventry, with a smaller Ukrainian population, supported two language classes in 1981 (LMP, 1982a). A Schools Council survey of mother-tongue teaching and support for primary-age pupils in 1983 (Tansley and Craft, 1984) showed that there was less awareness by LEAs of Ukrainian classes than those known to exist from the LMP survey, and there was no evidence of Ukrainian being taught in the mainstream curriculum, which is perhaps not surprising as it was not amongst the most frequently occurring languages named by LEAs.

Similarly, pupil numbers vary according to location and fluctuate over the years. In the late 1960s 25 Ukrainian children attended classes in Bedford (Brown, 1970); in the mid-1970s there was a fairly stable enrolment of over 100 students in the Ukrainian classes in Leicester (Saifullah Khan, 1976) and 150 students of Ukrainian amongst at least 1,000 children from East European backgrounds attending mother-tongue classes in Bradford (Beaumont 1976; Saifullah Khan, 1976). More recently, LMP data provide an interesting gloss: in 1981 the MTTD Survey revealed 87 pupils regularly attending Ukrainian language classes in Bradford (LMP, 1982b), representing 84 per cent of those who claimed in the SLS to speak Ukrainian at home (Couillaid and Tasker, 1983). Commitment to attendance at language classes may vary in different locations as further evidence from the LMP shows. By contrast, in Coventry there were only 19 pupils attending Ukrainian classes in 1981 (LMP, 1982a), representing 48 per cent of those who claimed to speak Ukrainian at home in the SLS. However, oversimplified interpretations of such findings may be misleading as evidence from the ALUS of the LMP reveals. Although 96 per cent of Ukrainian-speaking respondents (48) in Coventry were aware of a mother-tongue class, in only six of the 19 households with children aged five to 18 had at least one child attended the class in the previous four weeks, usually because children were too young or too old or too proficient in the language. Indeed respondents expressed a very high degree of support for mother-tongue maintenance with a strong feeling, especially amongst older respondents that mother-tongue teaching should be provided as a right (LMP, 1985). Generally the decline in the number of pupils and Saturday schools in recent years appears to be due primarily to a gap between the second and third generations. Evidence from the AUGB suggests currently a total of 20 schools (with a maximum of ten classes in each) with five to 70 pupils per school (GB. P. H of C, 1985) or 350 pupils in 14 schools (Maryniuk, 1985).

AGE RANGES   The Ukrainian language classes appear to cater for a wide age range of pupils, usually from six to 16 (GB. P. H of C, 1985; Wilding, 1981). In the mid-1970s schools in Bradford took pupils from the age of five, but in 1981 the age range varied from under five to 16. Interestingly, although there were equal numbers of pupils in the under-five, five to seven and eight to ten age ranges and only slightly more in the 11–13 age range, there were more than twice as many pupils in the 14–16 group (LMP, 1982b), thus tending to confirm the declining numbers of the second generation in the lower age range. However, by contrast, the age range of the pupils attending Ukrainian language classes in Coventry, in 1981, was limited to eight to 16 year-olds, with more than half the pupils aged between eight and ten (LMP, 1982a).

ACCOMMODATION   Ukrainian classes are accommodated either in the Ukrainian community's premises or in local schools, but accommodation used may vary from location to location, over time and according to the age-groups meeting. In Bedford, in the 1960s, Ukrainian classes were held in the community centre specially purchased by the Ukrainian community (Brown, 1970). In Leicester the older children attended classes in the Ukrainian Association's house, whereas younger children studied in a local school (Saifullah Khan, 1976; Wilding, 1981). In Coventry the Ukrainian classes are held in a local school rented by the organiz-ation, whereas in Bradford the Ukrainian schools provide their own accommod-ation (LMP, 1982a, 1982b). There is no information on the distance which pupils have to travel in order to attend Ukrainian classes, the length of travel time, or the mode of transport used.

CLASS TIMING, DURATION AND ATTENDANCE   Ukrainian classes are usually held on Saturday, either as in Bradford in the mid-1970s in the morning (Saifullah Khan, 1976) or in the afternoon as in Bedford in the 1960s (Brown, 1970), and class duration may vary. In Leicester the older children attended classes on Saturday morning for three-and-a-half hours and the younger children studied for three hours on Saturday afternoons (Saifullah Khan, 1976). The MTTD survey revealed that classes were held once a week at weekends for two hours in Coventry and, as in the 1970s, for two to four hours in Bradford (LMP, 1983a). Attendance at mother-tongue classes tends to fall off during early adolescence, and Saifullah Khan reported less enthusiasm amongst some adolescents attending Ukrainian language classes in Leicester in the mid-1970s, though they were not allowed to drop out. By contrast, in the MTTD, 84 per cent of the Ukrainian pupils in Coventry were said by their teachers to be regular attenders and a 100 per cent attendance rate was claimed in the classes in Bradford (LMP, 1982a, 1982b). However, data from another part of the LMP, the SPS, show a certain pre-adole-scent decline in attendance and understanding of the language (LMP, 1983a).

TEACHING CONDITIONS   The teacher-pupil ratio, teachers' qualifications and teachers' salaries and expenses seem to vary across schools, classes and time. In the mid-1970s, 12 teachers with varied qualifications taught 150 pupils at the three Ukrainian schools in Bradford (Saifullah Khan, 1976), and by 1981, although there were no funds to pay teachers' salaries, in two cases teachers' travelling expenses were funded from parents' fees (LMP, 1982b). In Leicester in the mid-1970s all the staff at the Ukrainian classes taught voluntarily, but received a small sum for travelling expenses (Saifullah Khan, 1976). But by 1979 Wilding reported that there were ten teachers for the 67 students, three of whom were qualified and who received travelling expenses plus £1.00 per day. Teachers in the Ukrainian classes in Coventry are also apparently paid from parents' fees (LMP, 1982a). Although many of the teachers are second-generation Ukrainians and some are also mainstream teachers by profession (Maryniuk, 1985; GB. P. H of C, 1985), the extent to which local communities are able to command well-qualified teachers and provide proper remuneration may be questioned.

THE CURRICULUM: MATERIALS, METHODS AND LEVEL OF INSTRUCTION   Pupils are divided into classes by age and ability as in Bradford and Leicester in the mid-1970s (Saifullah Khan, 1976). According to AUGB evidence, the medium of instruction is Ukrainian and most textbooks in use are published by the University of Toronto Press. However, it is unlikely that even if these books are Western in orientation, they will relate to the position of Ukrainian-speaking pupils in the UK. In Coventry and Bradford the community's organizations and parents' fees paid for textbooks, teaching aids and exercise books and paper in use in the Ukrainian language classes (LMP, 1982a, 1982b), but Maryniuk (1985) has indicated that financial assistance from LEAs would be welcome for book purchase. Clearly the main object of the classes is to teach Ukrainian language, but the curriculum may also be wider. Ukrainian classes in Bradford, for example, also teach history and geography (CRE, 1982) and classes in Leicester include in addition other cultural and religious studies (Saifullah Khan, 1976; Houlton, 1980). In some places the Ukrainian Orthodox Church combines religious and language teaching (Martin-Jones, 1984). Ukrainian literature and the history of Ukrainian culture are also taught and the practice of folk traditions is encouraged (GB. P. H of C, 1985).

In the larger Ukrainian schools, at least, instruction is pursued to examination level. In the mid-1970s in Bradford, many children were said to take O- and A-level Ukrainian, and in Leicester three or four students took O-level Ukrainian each year (Saifullah Khan, 1976), as also in Coventry (LMP, 1985). But by 1979, Wilding reported that in Leicester although Ukrainian was taught up to O-level, Russian was taught at A-level because of the unavailability of Ukrainian. A survey of the availability and currency of ethnic minority languages in public examinations for the National Congress on Languages in Education, in 1981 (Reid, 1984), confirmed that the Joint Matriculation Board offered O-level in Ukrainian and was considering provision for A-level in Ukrainian. Recent sources (Maryniuk, 1985; GB. P. H of C, 1985) indicate that the Ukrainian community is still keen for an A-level course to be established. Nationally there are about 40 entrants annually for O-level Ukrainian: 37 O-level entries through the JMB in 1978, 46 in 1979, 38 in 1980 and 41 in 1981 (Reid, 1984). Maryniuk (1985) reports that teachers in the community schools have devised curriculum guidelines which culminate, after ten years' study, in a matriculation certificate in Ukrainian studies, based on written and oral examinations administered by the Ukrainian Teachers' Association and Inspectorate. The examination covers Ukrainian language, literature, history, geography and culture and is said to be more demanding than the O-level course.

MAINSTREAM LINKS   Overall available information shows that an interest in maintaining the mother-tongue has been sustained in Ukrainian communities as demonstrated by the provision of community language classes. There is no indication, however, of any provision being made for the teaching of Ukrainian in mainstream curricula, even in localities where children from Ukrainian backgrounds are most numerous. Although the ALUS survey in Coventry (Smith *et al.*, 1984) discovered that the Ukrainian respondents were almost unanimous in their agreement with the statement that 'The government should provide the teaching of our language as a right for all our children in state schools' other Ukrainians have considered that because of their dispersal and the relatively small numbers of the community in education, mainstream provision for teaching Ukrainian is impractical (Maryniuk, 1985; GB. P. H of C, 1985). Maryniuk has questioned whether even peripatetic teaching would prove administratively or financially viable. But community representatives have generally indicated that LEA grants towards the forming of community classes, and co-ordination of these outside the main areas of settlement, would be welcome, as would the encouragement which might be given to pupils by mainstream teachers to develop their bilingualism. They have also suggested that voluntary teachers would be glad to participate in LEA INSET programmes to enhance their teaching skills.

Mainstream Education
It would appear that the presence of pupils from Ukrainian backgrounds in mainstream schools has scarcely had any impact and they have received little attention specifically. If any account has been taken, it has generally been in the context of consideration of pupils from a wide variety of East European backgrounds, as in the case of examination performance. Apart from this, specific mention has usually been confined to knowledge of English and the personal and cultural identities of pupils of Ukrainian backgrounds.

It seems likely that the problem of lack of familiarity with English or fluency which pupils of Ukrainian origin experienced 30 years or so ago will have diminished with the current arrival of the third generation in nursery and primary schools. In common with other industrial areas which received immigrant pupils, increasing, though relatively small, numbers of children from Ukrainian backgrounds were reported in the 1950s and 1960s in schools (especially Catholic and single-sex schools) in Bedford (Brown, 1970) and Huddersfield (Burgin and Edson, 1967). Such pupils sometimes came from mixed Ukrainian–British or Ukrainian–other European marriages, but when their parents were both of Ukrainian origin the children, who heard little or no English spoken at home, normally formed the nucleus of the special English class. Although evidence to the Swann Committee indicates that parents of Ukrainian origin may continue to make determined attempts to maintain Ukrainian as the language of the home, so that some children may enter school with limited English, it was also suggested that such children were able to gain a basic competence in English in three to four months and did not suffer any subsequent disadvantage *vis-à-vis* their peers. Indeed community representatives expressed concern that children might be withdrawn into special language classes, a practice which was seen as possibly labelling the child as 'remedial' and as hindering progress.

It appears that generally Ukrainian parents have had high expectations for their children and have been keen to motivate them to have a positive view of education and the opportunities which were previously unavailable. Community sources suggest that there is no evidence of general underachievement of pupils of Ukrainian origin and even indicate that a higher proportion than the national average are successful in public examinations and enter higher education. Many of the second generation are said to have found employment quite readily, often employed in professions such as teaching, journalism, law, medicine and finance (Maryniuk, 1985; GB. P. H of C, 1985). Early anecdotal evidence from Brown (1970) in Bedford tends to support their educational achievement, as does other generalized and highly circumspect evidence from studies of examination course entrants and examinees which included limited numbers of pupils from East European backgrounds in two schools in the north, showing that they were mostly found in the GCE and some CSE, GCE or CSE with GCE crafts streams or courses (Verma and Ashworth, 1981), and that although performance levels were individualized, there may have been some difficulty with English (Driver, 1980). In a study, in 1971–2, which investigated the differential experience of job search of ethnic minority and indigenous school-leavers in Bradford and Sheffield (Allen, 1971; Allen and Smith, 1975), a higher than average proportion of the achieved sample of East Europeans in Bradford, which included Ukrainians, had O-level and CSE qualifications, and in Sheffield their distribution of performance seemed to resemble that of their white indigenous peers, rather than those from other ethnic minorities. However, no weight can be placed on these studies as their findings are vitiated by the lack of analysis undertaken on the group of East European pupils as a whole and the failure to distinguish the achievements of the residual numbers of pupils of Ukrainian origin.

Indeed, the same lack of specific focus given to pupils of Ukrainian origin in educational research is evident in the absence of attention to their special needs and interests in terms of the multicultural curriculum in schools. In evidence to the Swann Committee community representatives were concerned that 'the educational environment is not conducive to the development of the children's Ukrainian identity' (GB. P. H of C, 1985, p.713) and described the 'appalling ignorance' of the majority of teachers about the cultural life of the Ukrainian community and children's home background. They cited several examples of the way in which teachers could be insensitive, both in informal contacts and in the formal curriculum, by confusing being Ukrainian with being Russian or Polish, which they considered both insulting and a denial of their particular ethnic identity (see also Maryniuk, 1985). This was highlighted in the mispronunciation or simplification of children's names – clearly an important and integral aspect of the child's identity. Community representatives argued that if teachers fail to show an interest in a child's country of origin a negative attitude and even inferiority complex could be developed, but asserted that 'the development of a national identity is an important element in the development of a child's personality' (p.714) and that teachers should inform themselves about immigrants' countries of origin and the reasons for migration, particularly through teacher training courses, so as to be able to bring these to bear in discussions with pupils.

Although the formal and hidden curricula of schools have largely ignored the cultural backgrounds of pupils of Ukrainian origin, home backgrounds will be of particular influence on a pupil's identity. Whether a pupil comes from a mixed European or solidly Ukrainian background is likely to determine the degree to which a Ukrainian orientation is upheld within the family and the extent of its participation in the cultural activities of the Ukrainian community. It is worthwhile to quote at length a 17-year-old Ukrainian boy, who was studying A-level mathematics, physics and chemistry in a Bedford school during the 1960s, which illustrates an ambivalence about his identity in early adolescence and how he came to embrace a Ukrainian identity with increasing age:

Years ago, I felt more English than Ukrainian. When I went to school, all my friends were English. Then, when I was about 12 or 13 I started to turn back towards my parents. I began to find, in many ways, that to be Ukrainian, there was much more interest, more meaning, like. Now I am proud to say I am Ukrainian. Anyway, if I said I am British, my name would give me away. It's more honest just to say 'I am Ukrainian.' And I found out over the years, that with the British, if you say, 'I am Jaroslav Madylus' straight out, then they accept you. But if you are, well, apologetic, or if you try to hide that you are Ukrainian, or if you cover it up, then they are not so keen on being friends. When I first went to grammar school, you know, they would laugh at me. Some used to call me 'wog'. I suppose they did not know a better word. Just joking it was with most of them. In the end, I told them: 'Look, my parents came here because they are political refugees. My mum and dad could not go back now, or if they did, maybe they would never come back. Perhaps it would be the same for me, unless I had a proper British passport.

Now I know what I am, that I am Ukrainian, I no longer have to worry. I feel at ease ... I think you gain so much from having, like, two ways of life. Here in this house, this room, it's all Ukraine – outside, it's all England. It gives you a chance to compare, choose what you think best. (Brown, 1970, pp.63–4)

Brown, however, reported that other young people from Ukrainian backgrounds were far less certain of their identity. In particular those from mixed Ukrainian and British or other European backgrounds felt that they could not be other than English, being born in the UK. Although they might like Ukrainian things and read or write Ukrainian, they were primarily English in instinct, values and tastes, as they lacked any real connection with the Ukraine. Khan (1976), who visited Ukrainian community centres in Derby and Manchester, found that second-generation Ukrainians, who claimed they were typical, resembled other adolescents in these localities and spoke with regional accents, though they claimed an unshakeable allegiance to their parents' culture and felt that the Ukrainian part of their lives was extremely important and wished to develop it further by participating in Ukrainian dance classes, clubs or choirs. Striking though their adherence to their parents' culture might be, it did not prevent them from otherwise identifying with the society at large. An apparently British persona may, therefore, mask a distinctive Ukrainian dimension to an individual's identity.

In 1970, Brown observed that the extent to which the mother's way of life prevailed within families with a Ukrainian connection determined the orientation of the children's lives and the extent to which they participated in Ukrainian community activities. In addition, the apparently larger number of mixed marriages in the south and marriages where both partners were Ukrainian in the north might indicate a greater degree of commitment to a Ukrainian orientation in the north, and this appears to correlate with linguistic survey data (see p.318–9). However, the Swann Report observed that 'this sense of being Ukrainian appears to have persisted even through mixed marriages, particularly where the mother is Ukrainian' (GB. P. H of C, 1985, p.712). The will to preserve Ukrainian cultural traditions and the Ukrainian language by the first generation has been very strong and the community's clear sense of its own ethnic identity has been transmitted to many of the second generation who have continued to participate in communal cultural activities. But the significance of the Ukrainian connection in the lives of second-generation Ukrainians in this country, especially in their attendance at mother-tongue classes, has failed to be appreciated by the British education system. It will be of interest to see to what extent the Ukrainian language and cultural traditions can be transmitted to the third generation, and whether the current interest shown in minority communities and their bilingualism and the potential support to community organizations from LEAs will be sufficient and in time to support and regenerate community resources and commitment.

Part Four
Pupils of Vietnamese Origin

Introduction and Background

Since 1975 more than one million people have left Indo-China for various destinations in other South-east Asian countries and around the world. Approximately half of these have been Vietnamese. Few came to Britain in the first instance, but the number increased after 1979 when the British government agreed to accept 10,000 Vietnamese from transit camps in Hong Kong. Other arrivals – from other camps, from sea rescues and from family reunions – boosted the total to over 16,000 by the end of 1982.

The Vietnamese experience of the UK is different from that of most ethnic minorities, in that they are refugees rather than migrants in the familiar sense. Several distinguishing features follow from this: the number of arrivals, though small in overall terms , has been concentrated into a short space of time; they have been highly visible both to officialdom and to the popular media; they did not in general have access to existing kinship networks or familiar cultural patterns; and there has been a relatively high level of formal provision for them.

The available literature can for present purposes be grouped into four areas:

> background material, covering life in Vietnam before the migration and the migration itself;
> UK reception, covering the establishment and functioning of reception centres, including language education;
> educational experiences;
> miscellaneous topics.

Background Material

Many of the reports covering the Vietnamese experience of Britain present some background information on Vietnamese people and life in Vietnam. The most detailed account is by Mares (1982). Pearson (1982a, 1982b, 1982c) summarizes a good deal of anthropological information. Briefer accounts are given by Fitchett (1981), including a historical overview from early times to the fall of Saigon in April 1975; Nuffield Foundation (1981), which outlines the interwoven history of Vietnamese and Chinese people along with a note on the languages; and Dalglish (1980).

The book by Mares is subtitled 'A Handbook for Health Workers' and is the outcome of a project (run by the Health Education Council and the National Extension College) set up to improve resources and information for health workers dealing with people from ethnic minorities. It has four sections covering background, health, diet and resources. The first section offers a short history of Vietnam, languages and the naming system, background to the migration, life in Vietnam and family life. The second and third sections are geared explicitly to health workers, but contain much well-presented information that would be useful to teachers as well. The final section is also of general use, including a sub-section on communication and language for health.

The account by Pearson is brief and accessible, also intended for health visitors but of general interest. It is based on first-hand experience both in UK reception centres and a study trip to Hong Kong, Macau and China. It covers numerous topics in the space of a dozen pages, broken down into background and family life; marriage, death and religion; and health beliefs, birth and child care. As well as outline information on ethnicity and language, the background refers to cultural patterns and to family life and structures. The latter detail is particularly useful.

Dalglish provides information on the occupational backgrounds of refugees from Vietnam. This is based on Hong Kong government figures relating to about 70,000 Vietnamese in transit camps in Hong Kong. Most of the refugees in the UK came from Hong Kong. The figures are exceedingly vague and scanty,but do provide some useable pointers. For example, only three per cent of the group described themselves as coming from a professional background and four per cent from a merchant background. A total of 21 per cent were semi-skilled or unskilled workers. The breakdown is incomplete, however.

An important fact to emerge from the background information is the ethnic diversity of the Vietnamese refugees. The great majority of people living in Vietnam are indigenous Vietnamese but there are significant minorities. In particular, some two per cent of the population has been estimated to be Chinese. This reflects the long ties between China and Vietnam. Many Chinese people have lived in Vietnam for several generations and still speak their own regional Chinese languages; they may not speak Vietnamese well. The particular significance of this is that some three-quarters of the Vietnamese in Britain are ethnic Chinese.

A further consideration is that the Vietnamese refugees who came to the UK were by and large greatly disadvantaged in comparison with those accepted by other resettlement countries. Whereas almost all those accepted by the USA were from South Vietnam and had contact with Western languages and ways of life, many from professional and managerial backgrounds, this was not so in the UK. Selection criteria for entry were widely drawn and very few people who wished to come were rejected. This generous approach and the fact that the UK programme began rather later than those of other countries have meant that of the Vietnamese accepted by Britain few had any knowledge of English or of Western culture. Many were in Western terms unskilled, and many had been previously rejected for settlement by other countries.

Education in Vietnam is described in Fitchett (1981), Evans (1980) and Mares (1982). In South Vietnam prior to 1975 there were effectively three education systems: a state system, and two forms of private education. Primary schooling covered ages six to 11 years and the state sought to provide education for all children, using large classes and split shifts in order to do so. Between ten and 20 per cent of children passed – by means of competitive examination – to secondary school, studying for four years for a qualification broadly equivalent to O-level in the UK and a further three years for an A-level equivalent. Private schools were available for those who failed to get into the state secondary schools. Fees in these were often high; facilities were generally poor and teachers unqualified. For the very wealthy, a small number of exclusive schools, modelled on French lines, were available in the cities.

After 1975, when schools were shut for five months to facilitate educational reforms and political re-education, all private education was abolished. Kindergartens were introduced for children aged three to six. Schools were divided into schools of the first degree (six to 11 years), schools of the second degree (11–16) and schools of the third degree (16–18). Schooling is free but parents are expected to contribute towards books. Details on the extent of access to education are not available, but it is clear that it is limited by British standards particularly in rural areas.

The curriculum in Vietnamese schools is heavily academic with lessons geared to rote learning and repetition. Teaching methods are formal and discipline strict (though corporal punishment has been abolished since 1975). Pupils have little responsibility for their own learning and creativity is not encouraged.

The background to the Vietnamese migration is described in various places, notably by Jones (1982a, 1982b) and Mares. The pattern of migration is not to be explained in simple terms. Initially, many people left South Vietnam after the American departure in 1975 because their known identification with the former regime did not auger well for their future. The political and economic uncertainty of the following years seems to have been a significant motivation for others. Finally, the war in Cambodia and the Chinese invasion of Vietnam's northern border added to the instability and led to numerous departures from North Vietnam.

Few people came to Britain in the early years of the mass migration. Most movement was from South Vietnam at this stage and the USA was the preferred destination. Numbers of people rescued at sea by British-registered ships did come to Britain. However, 1979 was the real beginning. The British government agreed first to receive 1,500 refugees from camps in Hong Kong, Malaysia and Thailand, and subsequently to a further 10,000 from Hong Kong. As noted earlier, this number was increased by family reunions and further sea rescues.

UK Reception
Overall responsibility for the refugee programmes lay with the Home Office. The broad aims of the programme were to bring the refugees to the UK and, after an initial stay in a reception centre, to resettle them throughout the country. This was handled by three agencies receiving financial support from the Home Office: British Refugee Council (initially, British Council for Aid to Refugees); Save the Children Fund; and the Ockenden Venture. The Joint Committee for Refugees from Vietnam, set up in 1979, was charged with co-ordinating the programme and acting as a forum for policy discussion.

The reception period was meant to be a short – three months – orientation along with English language tuition. In the event, only ten per cent were rehoused within three months and many stayed in the centres for upwards of a year. Provision of tuition in English varied a great deal in the reception centres; when combined with the dispersal policy, it is not surprising that the achieved competence in English was generally low.

Information on the reception and resettlement of Vietnamese refugees can be found in Jones (1983), GB. HO (1982), Edholm *et al.* (1983), Somerset (1983) and Fitchett (1981). The report from the Joint Committee (GB. HO, 1982) concentrates on the lessons to be learned from the programme for any future reception/ resettlement programmes and the problems affecting the long-term adjustment of refugees in the community. Particular issues emerging were language tuition, the dispersal policy, inter-agency co-ordination and the nature and level of funding for the programme. Edholm *et al.* present data on the resettlement programme from both client and provider perspectives, covering housing, benefits, (adult) education and the reception centres. They also look at three providing agencies. Somerset (1983) reports on the resettlement experiences of 22 families who had recently settled in Hereford, Worcestershire and Shropshire. Fitchett (1981) briefly describes the settlement of families in Derby.

The most detailed information on the resettlement programme is provided by Jones (1982a) (some of this appears in summary form in Jones, 1983). This is the report of a study carried out by the Home Office Research and Planning Unit. The aim of the study was to examine the nature of the refugee population, together with the functioning of the reception and resettlement programme. The study was carried out by gathering basic social and demographic information on a large sample of the refugee population and by surveying attitudes to the programme on the part of the staff involved.

In summary, the typical refugee was from North Vietnam (62 per cent), of ethnic Chinese origin (71 per cent), had little proficiency in English and came from an unskilled or semi-skilled background. Most (82 per cent) came in the years 1979–80. Assessments of the standard of English conducted by resettlement staff revealed very low levels of attainment in speaking, writing and comprehension, even after individuals had been in the country for some time and had received language tuition. Younger refugees (aged 12–19) scored considerably better than did older people; but even of the former only 40 per cent were deemed to have at least a minimum working proficiency.

The Joint Committee report (GB. HO, 1982) refers to the considerable variation in language education in the reception centres, from 'extremely high standards in certain centres' (para. 30) to uncoordinated and unsatisfactory provision in other centres. A critical factor was the working relationship between the language teachers and the administrative staff in the centres. On the whole there was good communication between the two groups, but when there was not, various negative consequences followed – such as friction between individuals, unnecessary anxiety for the refugees and general distraction from established objectives.

These findings were corroborated by Edholm *et al.* (1983). English-language tuition was patchy at the outset and progress slow – there was no common language scheme or a ready-to-use textbook for teachers setting up classes. The amount of time available meant the teachers could only aim at basic survival English. From the side of the Vietnamese, two factors militated against successful learning: many had received very little formal education and may have been illiterate, and they were in a state of stress arising out of the trauma of the migration and anxiety for the future.

Education

The Joint Committee Report (GB. HO, 1982) refers briefly to education. With regard to pupils of school age, it is believed that provided they come to school at an early age there is usually sufficient time for total integration into the educational stream towards O- and A-level examinations. The report cautions against complacency, however, and points to reports received of some able Vietnamese children being placed in ESN classes. The difficulties facing older pupils are inevitably greater and special measures – such as the 13+ Project and the Bingley School, described below – are urged.

For those beyond school age, educational opportunities – specifically in language – are limited. A government-funded project under the management of the Joint Committee gathered information on adult education. This covered the cultural needs of the Vietnamese, their dispersal around the country and the range of available funding schemes. It found that in areas where there was substantial provision in English language teaching, the arrival of the Vietnamese had placed a heavy burden on resources which were already stretched. When settlement was in areas where there was no provision, the problem was to establish new arrangements. A further difficulty facing older students and adults was that studies leading to professional re-qualification did not attract LEA mandatory awards and very few discretionary awards were made.

These findings were echoed by Edholm *et al.* (1983). When the refugees left the reception centres to be re-settled, their access to English depended very much on where they went. Big cities which had existing ethnic minority communities and experience of English as a second language tuition were generally making the most suitable provision. Small towns with no such experience made the least provision. The result was enormous variation in the number of hours of tuition a week available. Some received nothing at all within the first months of settlement, while others had 12 hours a week.

The Adult Language Use Survey (ALUS) of the Linguistic Minorities Project (LMP) (Morawska *et al.*, 1984) provides data on 50 Vietnamese families who had passed through the Save the Children Fund (SCF) resettlement programme in Bingley and, in 1981, were living in Bradford. Most respondents were aged between 25 and 40, almost all were unemployed and were still attending daily classes which aimed to prepare them for life in Britain and teach them English. The respondents came from a range of socioeconomic backgrounds: peasant farmers, factory workers and unskilled craftsmen. More than nine out of ten knew three or more languages: Vietnamese, Cantonese and English. However, only one in ten of the respondents reported that they could understand and speak English and fewer that they could read and write English very or fairly well. Fewer than one in five household members were reported to know English at all well. None reported their children using only or mostly English. Few families were involved in social activities beyond those of mutual support and entertainment with other refugees, when naturally they again used either Vietnamese or Cantonese. Although they had a moderately high level of interest in reading, their awareness and use of libraries was very limited. Respondents expressed support for mother-tongue maintenance, but there was no widespread recognition of the need for support beyond the family. The refugees were predominantly concerned with learning English.

The most detailed information on educational provision relates to two SCF projects: the 13+ Project in Hounslow (Murray *et al.*, 1981) and a residential school in Bingley (Save the Children Fund, 1982). The 13+ Project was set up by the Hounslow Schools' Language Unit in April 1980 to provide English language teaching to Vietnamese teenagers whose schooling had been interrupted. It ran for four terms, providing tuition in English language for Vietnamese teenagers whose schooling had been interrupted by their departure from Vietnam. There were 15 students, ranging in age from 13 to 18, divided into two groups, seven of whom knew some English and eight who were beginners.

An independent evaluation of students' progress over the first six months was carried out. The NFER tests of proficiency in English were used with the beginners' group. All showed a marked improvement in the skills of listening, reading and writing; their speaking skills were considered to be less well developed. The other group was tested on material designed to measure capacity to cope with O-level reading material. Most were found to be performing below the target level.

Performance in the long term was considerably more positive, however. All pupils went on to school or colleges where they took O- or A-level courses, or if they were too young joined a course that would lead to O-level work. Those who had taken examinations had all performed well. The contrast between test results after six months and subsequent school and examination performance tends to support the staff's view that a considerable period of time was required for effective language teaching.

The second SCF project was a residential school for 13–16 year-old Vietnamese students who would in the normal course of events have entered higher education. It was set up in Bingley, in West Yorkshire, in the wake of positive reports on the 13+ Project in Hounslow. It ran for two years from September 1980 and catered for some 40 students. A summary report has been prepared by Butcher (n.d.). Detailed termly reports are also available.

Most of the information provided is descriptive in nature. The setting up and funding of the school are documented in detail. Most of the students took public examinations before leaving, but results were not available at the time of publication. Staff did acknowledge that initial expectations had been pitched too high. The hope was that students would be ready in two years for O-levels in a range of science subjects and in Vietnamese or Chinese. In the event, it soon became clear that this aim would be realized by only a minority of students, and science teaching was restricted to two subjects.

Other accounts consist of notes of particular local situations or general comments on educational provision. Fitchett (1981) contains brief impressionistic accounts of the experience of Vietnamese pupils at both a primary and a secondary language centre in Derby and also at a summer school. Apart from providing basic data, the accounts concentrate on the pupils' social and emotional development and their interactions with peers. Mackillop (1981) refers briefly to educational arrangements in Sheffield. Morris (1980) describes educational provision for the group in a general way.

Ye-Chin (1980) offers a personal perspective on the educational aspect of resettlement. This emphasizes the acculturation aspect of education, draws attention to the linguistic adjustments required of Indo-Chinese refugees in England and describes relevant social and survival skills which may need to be taught. Where children of school age are concerned, he agrees with other commentators that the principal problem is with the older ones, particularly adolescents who have received the bulk of their formal schooling in their own country. Four main problems are noted: language; adjustment to the English school system; difficulties of isolation and response to authority arising out of being a single refugee; and the psychological stresses associated with adolescence. The importance of pre-school provision is emphasized, particularly for the sake of promoting language development.

Miscellaneous

Two further studies of the Vietnamese experience in Britain have educational implications. One, reported by Dalglish (1982), concerned a reorientation course for teachers from Vietnam. The other, reported by Simsova (1982), related to the library needs of Vietnamese in Britain.

Over 100 Vietnamese had identified themselves as teachers on arrival in Britain. Their professional qualifications were not recognized for teaching in the maintained sector and some retraining was clearly necessary. The British Council for Aid to Refugees decided to mount a pilot course in order to gather information on the feasibility of retraining.

The course was held over a three-week period in August 1981 at the West Sussex Institute of Higher Education. On the basis of responses to a questionnaire to all adults who had identified themselves as teachers and some additional coroborative information, 18 candidates were offered places on the course. The aims of the course were broadly to assess their teaching competence and suitability for retraining and to advise on career prospects. The general conclusion reached was that most of the group had potential for retraining in this country, but it was unlikely that any would gain places on higher education courses as their English and level of social and cultural awareness were not sufficient to convince institutions of their ability to complete a degree programme successfully. It was considered that a longer period – say six to 12 months – of preparation was necessary before they would be ready for higher education geared to a teaching career in Britain.

Simsova (ibid.) conducted a survey of Vietnamese readers and materials in public libraries. Questionnaires were sent to 168 library authorities, with an achieved response rate of 70 per cent. About half of the respondents were aware of the Vietnamese using their library, and one-fifth were providing material in Vietnamese, though the latter was in some cases limited to a Vietnamese dictionary. Most were in favour of a back-up service offering Vietnamese books on hire to public libraries.

Part Five
Liverpool Blacks

Liverpool, like the other old major sea-ports of Cardiff, the north-east and London's East End, has numbered amongst its population the representatives of many different ethnic groups since their arrival during the last century. Although their numbers were augmented with post-war immigration, Liverpool, unlike other cities which then became multiracial for the first time, already had some 50 years' experience as a multiracial city. During this time because many of the original immigrants of African, West Indian, Arab, Asian and Chinese origin were single men, there had been considerable intermarriage with the white population in Liverpool. Their descendants, now in the third or fourth generation, are generally known as 'Liverpool blacks'. By considering the literature on the educational, social, employment and housing experiences of these diverse ethnic groups, who form a significant proportion of the population of Liverpool, it is possible to examine the extent to which a long-standing multiracial community has offered equality of opportunity and social harmony.

Over the years a considerable quantity of sociological data has been amassed on the development of the black community in Liverpool, which has focussed primarily on race relations, employment and housing. These themes have been reflected in the post-war educational literature, which has been concerned mainly with the social integration of Liverpool-born black pupils and their transfer from school to the world of work. In comparison with the sociological accounts, however, educational research is rather limited since there have been, for example, no longitudinal studies of the black community in Liverpool 8 and the educational performance of their descendants. Furthermore, although during the 1960s there was increasing interest in the educational performance of immigrant children in other cities which were becoming multiracial, this seems to have been overlooked in Liverpool, possibly in part because the number of black pupils from established families did not show up in, for instance, the DES figures because of the 'ten-year rule'. Reference in the literature was only made to Liverpool in terms of trying to draw on its experience – which ironically is not particularly well documented, or exemplary. In preface to an analysis of the contemporary educational position of Liverpool blacks, it is thus important to describe the composition and size of the group and to chronicle the evolution of the black community in Liverpool and its experiences of urban deprivation.

Definition

What is meant by the term 'Liverpool blacks?' In the 17th and 18th centuries as a sea-port Liverpool, together with London and Bristol, played a prominent part in the slave trade, particularly the movement of slaves from Africa to the West Indies and mainland America. After the abolition of slavery, Liverpool continued to prosper by trading with the expanding colonial empire and importing raw materials such as sugar, tea, tobacco and cotton for Britain's growing industries. In the late

19th century many African and Asiatic seamen, such as Arabs from Aden, Somalis, Indians and Chinese, were recruited abroad to serve on British ships (Krausz, 1971). Many jumped ship or settled at the British port of call, such as Liverpool, in order to escape poor working conditions and pay on board (Humphreys, n.d.). Often these seamen married and set up home with local working-class women. There was also a small African Negro élite who came to be educated in England, the precursors of larger numbers of African students, but they have always formed a minority of the black population in Liverpool. However, the early Negro seamen were joined by some of their countrymen who were recruited to work in munitions factories and as general labourers during the First World War. These two main groups formed the black working class in Liverpool (Krausz, 1971). During the inter-war years the black community in Liverpool continued to grow, diversify and intermarry with the local white community.

In the Second World War there was some additional recruitment, particularly from the West Indies, to help with the war effort, and this continued after the war in order to fill a manpower vacuum in Liverpool (Humphreys, n.d.). Thus by the late 1940s the 'coloured population' of Liverpool came mainly from West Africa and the West Indies, but there were also small numbers of Somalis, Indians, Arabs, Burmese, Malays and Chinese (Silberman and Spice, 1950). As Jeffcoate (1984) has observed, Liverpool attracted little of the mass immigration of the 1950s and 1960s due to the state of its local economy. There are therefore relatively few West Indians dating from this time, or South Asians or European immigrants generally. The largest group, of Irish Catholic ancestry, represents between a third and a half of the city's total population. With the exception of the Jews, the minority communities are solidly working class.

It is thus important to distinguish between those long-established families with overseas origins, the Africans, Arabs and Chinese who intermarried with the local English or Liverpool Irish communities – the Liverpool blacks – and the post-war immigrants who augmented the ethnic minority communities in Liverpool. Many of the Liverpool blacks are:

> blood relations of Liverpool 'whites' and have 'black' grandparents and great-grandparents born in Liverpool; they speak 'scouse' with a vocabulary, grammar and intonation identical with those of 'white' Liverpudlians, and in short there is nothing but their colour and their hapless situation to distinguish them from other long-established residents. (GB. P. H of C, 1985, p.733)

However, there is a tendency on the part of the local white population to perceive both the longer-established Liverpool blacks and the newer immigrants from varied backgrounds as one group, differentiated only by colour. This confusion makes for difficulties in accurately estimating the size of the Liverpool black population.

Numbers

There appears to be no reliable information on the size of the black population before the 1950s due to lack of records (Silberman and Spice, 1950). Collins (1957) recorded, however, that since the Second World War the negro population in Liverpool had increased tenfold to about 6,000. Although subsequent figures for the black population of Liverpool lack precision, ignore important distinctions and require qualifications, they may be outlined here. The 1971 Census showed that 0.7 per cent of the population of the Merseyside conurbation comprised some 9,040 people born in the New Commonwealth (CRC, 1974, Table 2, p.6). A subsequent analysis (CRE, 1978) revealed the diverse origins of the New Commonwealth-born population of Liverpool, but like the figures for the Merseyside this also overlooked the second, third and fourth generation of UK-born Liverpool blacks (Table 41).

Table 41: **Population born in the New Commonwealth in Liverpool, 1971**

Total Population	Total born in NC	East* Africa	Rest of Africa	America†	Cyprus	India	Pakistan	Rest of Asia
610,115	5,435	235	990	1,115	345	1,145	330	1,095

*East Africa includes Kenya, Malaysia, Tanzania, Uganda and Zambia.
†America includes the West Indies and Guyana.
Source: Census 1971; CRE, 1978, Table 7.

In response to a request by the House of Commons Select Committee on Race Relations and Immigration (SCRRI), in 1973, Liverpool LEA provided information on the number of coloured/immigrant children in its area (Liverpool Education Committee, n.d.1). According to the DES Form 7 (i) definition, whereby the number of immigrant children in each school was recorded in terms of their country of origin, the total number of such children in Liverpool in 1973 was 801, representing 0.67 per cent of the school population of 18,905 (LEC, n.d.2). A breakdown of figures for 1970–3 gave an indication of the number of pupils from different countries included in the DES definition (Table 42).

Table 42: **Number of immigrant pupils in Liverpool schools, according to DES definition, 1970–3**

Country of origin	1970	1971	1972	1973
West Indies	176	159	137	138
Africa	84	94	109	121
Pakistan	67	85	84	82
Asia	189	215	242	267
India	71	80	94	66
Others	200	171	134	127
Total	787	804	800	801

Source: LEC, n.d. 2.

However, these figures were unrealistic in that they, too, failed to include the Liverpool-born second- and third-generation of Asian, African and Carribean immigrants. Hence a more accurate figure of 2,500 – two per cent of the school population – was suggested to the SCRRI (LEC, n.d.1). As a result of this and other evidence, the SCRRI (GB. P. H of C. SCRRI, 1973) recommended the abolition of the collection of national statistics in this manner, which was agreed by the DES. One of the tasks of a subsequent working party in Liverpool (see p.344) was to consider ways in which statistics might be collected. Liverpool teachers were strongly opposed to the collection of statistics and there were uncertainties amongst members of the working party itself, especially community relations workers and representatives of immigrant communities. There was, in addition, the need to gain the approval of the city council and, some argued, the agreement of parents in co- operating in any such exercise. However, although a face-count of 'coloured' pupils was rejected by teachers, other methods, including photography, were considered , as some members of the working party argued that Liverpool's low rating as an educational priority area and in terms of race relations was due to a serious underestimate of its black population. In any case, an application for assistance under Section 11 of the 1966 Local Government Act, or the 1969 Urban Aid Programme, required that statistics be presented. It thus seems to be argued in the early 1970s that it was necessary to attempt to assess the size of the Liverpool black population in order to determine the scale of necessary provision. But the problems of mounting a census are formidable and increasingly difficult, and it would appear that this has not been undertaken.

More recently, an investigation by the House of Commons home Affairs Committee (GB. P. H of C, 1981) reported that Liverpool's ethnic minority population was estimated by Merseyside CRC to be 40,000. This figure comprises (see Somerfield, 1983):

Liverpool-born blacks	20,000
Chinese	8,000
West Africans	3,000
West Indians	3,000
South Asians	4,000
Somalis and Arabs	2,000

Of these 40,000, approximately 80 per cent, reside within Liverpool, mainly in the southern parts of the city, and comprise some eight per cent of the city's population. Yet until relatively recently at least, the criteria for Section 11 funding have excluded Liverpool as having fewer than two per cent of Commonwealth immigrants. The Labour Force Survey of 1981 provides information on the ethnic origins of the Merseyside population, whose diversity is once again evident (Table 43).

Table 43:   **Merseyside population by ethnic origin, 1981 (thousands)**

White	West Indian/ Guyanese	Indian	Chinese	African	Mixed	Other	Not stated
1,465	2	6	4	1	10	2	7

Source: Labour Force Survey, 1981; OPCS, 1983b, Table 6.

Of particular interest is the large population of mixed ethnic origin – some 10,000 persons. The non-white population of mixed ethnic origin varies considerably across the country and reaches its highest proportion, 40 per cent, in Merseyside. In the UK as a whole some three-quarters of the population of mixed ethnic origin were born in the UK and 94 per cent of this group were under 16 (OPCS, 1983b). This implies that in Liverpool by far the majority of pupils of mixed ethnic origin, and probably those of other ethnic minority origin, are UK-born. Moreover, whereas across the country as a whole the population of New Commonwealth and Pakistani origin tend to live in households headed by a person born in the New Commonwealth or Pakistan, Merseyside is exceptional, in that a large part of its population belonging to specified ethnic groups live in households headed by a UK-born person (OPCS, 1983b, Table 18, p.9). In addition, many of the 10,000 persons of mixed ethnic origin may be assumed to live in households headed by a UK-born person. This confirms the long-standing settlement of the ethnic minority population of Merseyside.

Evolution of a Community
In order to provide a context for subsequent description of post-war educational provision and practice in the Liverpool area, it is important to consider the development of the ethnic minority communities over the last 60 years. An historical outline of the evolution of the minority communities in Liverpool focusses predominantly on race relations, employment, intermarriage, housing and com-

munity development and the effect of the arrival of post-war immigrants and especially on the social organization of the Liverpool blacks.

At least from the 1920s onwards, as in other sea-ports, race relations were exacerbated at times of unemployment. Competition for the few available jobs in the shipping industry was made more fierce by the presence of coloured workers, and in 1919 there were racial disturbances with attacks on African settlers and their families by unemployed ex-soldiers (Bowker, 1968; Humphreys, n.d.). Again, in the 1930s, with the depression, there was widespread prejudice against the employment of coloured people in Liverpool (Little, 1948). Two reports of social investigations undertaken in the 1930s contrasted the position of the West African Negro communities with those of the Chinese in Liverpool. Fletcher (1930) concluded that the West African community presented a serious social problem. In confirmation Jones (1934) also noted that, although the Chinese and the Negro communities had both intermarried with the local white population, the negro-white families were less stable, and when grown up their children were reported not to get work easily or to mix with the majority population. On the other hand, a researcher employed by a group of white professionals – the Liverpool Association for the Welfare of Coloured People – in 1937 discovered that many firms would not employ coloured people and it was recommended that further immigration should be prevented (quoted in GB. P. H of C, 1985). There were further racial disturbances in Liverpool, in 1948, due to lack of work (Humphreys, n.d.; Jeffcoate, 1984). Broady (1955) claimed that the Negroes in Liverpool experienced more discrimination from local residents than the Chinese, and that there were some clashes between Chinese and Negroes. In 1954 Richmond reported on research into the problems of race relations, particularly with regard to Negro and West Indian communities in Liverpool in the 1940s and early 1950s. Race relations were aggravated by the influx of immigrants as racial incidents in Liverpool in the 1950s and elsewhere demonstrated. Collins (1957) suggested that Asians and Negroes were resisted by the majority society because they were considered a threat to economic security, as competitors for jobs and economic status. Moreover, black men were resented for their liaisons and marriage with white women, for miscegenation is a challenge to notions of white superiority. These perceived threats in employment and intermarriage seem from the early years of the century to have been the main reasons for discrimination and poor race relations, which seem to have continued in Liverpool at some times more overtly than others, despite the view which has prevailed at least until recently, that Liverpool is a harmonious multiracial city.

In the late 1940s Silberman and Spice (1950) distinguished three main types of employment for the adult black population in Liverpool. The majority were seamen, though others were amongst the long-term unemployed, and a third group had found work in industry. Some of the latter were West Africans and West Indians recruited for war service in the forces in Britain or as skilled artisans in the factories, who had either remained in the UK or returned to Britain at a later date to seek employment because of the economic depression in their homelands. Silberman and Spice cited occupational data for the fathers of 106 coloured children attending two schools in two areas of Liverpool where most of the coloured population lived in the 1940s. Twenty-two out of 39 West African and West Indian fathers and 13 out of 19 Arab and Indian fathers were seamen. A further five of the Arabs and Indians were dockers, six were semi-skilled workers and one was unemployed. Fifteen of the West African and West Indian fathers were general labourers, six in semi-skilled work and seven unemployed. Other data also indicated that the coloured adults at that time were predominantly engaged in semi-skilled or unskilled work, if they were employed at all. Silberman and Spice opined that many highly skilled coloured men and women were unable to gain suitable employment and were forced into unskilled labouring in factories and public works.

As the pre-war immigrants had married into the native white population by the late 1940s there was a fairly large group of mixed ethnic origin (ibid.; Krausz, 1971), but it was not until the 1960s that a local black community relations officer (Kuya, 1967) began to consider the special problems which children of mixed marriages might face. In the 1940s the coloured population lived in two decaying neighbourhoods which had previously housed middle-class families who had moved out to new suburbs. Most of the large houses were shared by the working-class coloured families. In their neighbourhoods there were two community centres, one social and the other offering opportunities for educational and cultural development, and also many ethnic clubs and cafés. As well as many social welfare agencies, particularly related to seamen's missions, there were two black self-help groups, the Negro welfare centre and the African Churches Mission. But despite their intermarriage and their concentration as a minority in two areas in Liverpool, the coloured population did not constitute a community. Silberman and Spice (1950) suggested that it was more appropriate to see them as a localized group of urban poor, joined together by their common experience of discrimination but distinguished within the group by their backgrounds, colour, cultures and experience of life in Britain.

It has been suggested that a distinction should be made between the long-established ethnic minority families in Liverpool and the post-war immigrant families, especially as the latter have tended to marry within their own ethnic groups, to be better organized socially and to have more associations formed on a religious, cultural or national/regional basis (Humphreys, n.d.). Collins (1957) researched into the environmental, occupational, community and housing conditions in the early 1950s and the effect of the newly arrived immigrants on the already established black community. The predominantly seafaring black population was augmented by West Indian immigrants, including West Indian women, and sometimes complete families. Most were better educated and more likely to be skilled or semi-skilled. By working on shore, they tended to be better paid than the earlier migrants, and also increased their contacts with the majority population. There was also a small middle-class élite. An extremely unstable social situation was created in the early 1950s as the older immigrants had no social control over the new. Numerous associations emerged but changeable leadership and internal conflicts made them short-lived. Relationships *vis-à-vis* the white population were also sometimes disharmonious.

Collins (1957) contrasted the position of the three main occupational groups: the seamen; the war-time technicians who as skilled workers were more readily accepted; and the post-war skilled, semi-skilled and unskilled male and female workers. The latter group tended to be employed in factory work and their position varied from firm to firm depending on their personal qualities and the attitude and policy of the management. Skill and numbers were important factors affecting race relations in the factories. Coloured workers were employed as general labourers in the railways and docks, in foundries and other heavy engineering trades. Some were engaged in a variety of skilled work, also as semi-skilled machine operators, minders and in transport, and other unskilled workers assisted craftsmen and worked as railway porters, bus conductors and drivers. However, as Humphrey (n.d.) recorded, this was only after a ban by Liverpool transport on black employees was challenged by the Colonial People's Defence Association in the mid-1950s, prior to the Race Relations Act. Other, but varying, evidence of discrimination in employment was cited by Collins and other observers. Lack of prior experience and a tendency to move rapidly between jobs affected the attitude of employers to the efficiency and adjustment of black employees. The attitudes and perceptions of white workers and trade unions were also significant. The African workers sometimes had more difficulty in adaptation due to lack of familiarity with the language and cultural context of working relationships.

Although the black community in Liverpool was perceived solely in terms of colour by the wider society, within it members differentiated themselves nationally and regionally as West Indians, West Africans, Guyanans, Nigerians, and so on, and in the case of West Africans a further differentiation based on tribal groupings was also significant. Yet voluntary associations and clubs often cut across regional and tribal boundaries. The various social organizations of the 1950s, many aiming both to provide welfare aid and to promote relationships with the wider community in Liverpool are described in detail by Collins (1957). Social status was ranked primarily on an occupational basis within the black community, in a similar way to that of the white population. Although the main black population was concentrated in one area, it was also dispersed over the city and its outskirts. The main district of settlement, which was the least desirable housing area of the town, had predominantly overcrowded and expensive accommodation. Common law unions predominated within the West Indian population, although the skilled Negroes, especially West Indians, sometimes had British wives. The role of the British wife tended to be more dominant if the mixed marriage was of long standing, and especially if the man was a seaman. The prestige of recently arrived immigrants tended to be lower if they had British wives. Collins claimed that there were twice as many illegitimate coloured children in this neighbourhood as there were white. The Anglo-coloured child did not mix easily with the immigrant child and there was often some tension between them. However, he concluded that although the early social environment of many Anglo-coloured children might have had an adverse effect on their upbringing, some had nevertheless shown great strength and determination in achieving success.

Education and its Socioeconomic Context

There was an absence of research and comment on the education of the children of the black population in Liverpool until after the Second World War. This was probably related both to the increasing awareness of the need for research in education at that time and, specifically in the Liverpool context, to the fact that since many children would have been of mixed marriages with English-speaking mothers, they would not necessarily have been noticeably disadvantaged in the school context with respect to English. Hence the primary emphasis of the post-war research was not language – though this was to come later with consideration of the curriculum and the transition from school to work – but sociometric studies of social relationships.

The first such research (Silberman and Spice, 1950) was undertaken in Liverpool in 1946–7 in the social context described earlier (p.339) when there were already considerable numbers of second-generation, mixed-race children with white mothers and fathers of West African, West Indian, Asian or Chinese origin. The study was conducted in six schools with a combined population of 1,048 children. Three were local authority schools, three Church of England schools, an infant, junior and senior school of each type. Some 135 'other coloured' children with one or both parents of African, West Indian, Arab, Malay, Burmese or Indian origin,

861 white pupils and 52 Chinese were involved. An assessment was made of the standard of clothing of the pupils, the coloured pupils (excluding the Chinese children) being found to be the least well dressed: 68 per cent had clothing which was well kept or mended, compared with 75 per cent of the white pupils and 94 per cent of the Chinese pupils. Pupils were given a friendship test, in two parts. They were first asked to send a letter to their best friend in the classroom, and a week later to send a second letter to their second-best friend followed, in the third week, by another letter, once more directed to the claimed best friend. In practice the procedure varied, so that sometimes a Christmas card was sent to a friend and sometimes a vote was made for a friend. The second part of the test aimed to assess antipathies. Children were asked to imagine a trip in a charabanc to the sea, but the pupils were requested to nominate 'the three children you would leave behind; three spoilsports, the nastiest children in the class'.

Detailed statistical analysis revealed that, according to the first friendship test, white children did not discriminate against coloured children when choosing friends and neither did coloured children discriminate against white children. Generally, however, each group of children demonstrated preference for other members of the same group. Significant prejudice was revealed in the case of the white children in the A stream in the local authority junior school, white girls in the local authority senior school, the C stream of the local authority senior school and in all local authority schools taken together, but amongst coloured girls only in the church junior school. Indeed when discrimination was analysed according to type of clothing, it was found that children with superior clothing discriminated in their friendship choices against those with inferior clothing. Nevertheless, children with inferior clothing nominated their friends without regard for clothing standard. On the rejection test coloured children, those with inferior clothing and boys were more often rejected (p < 0.05). There was a significantly greater rejection of coloured children and those with inferior clothing in the local authority schools, and as the size of the coloured group increased, so the proportion of outcasts increased (p < 0.01). By contrast, in the church school whilst some coloured children were popular, others were very unpopular, especially in the junior school.

This study appeared to show that prejudice on the basis of colour did not occur between the white and the coloured pupils. However, the coloured group comprised over a quarter of Chinese pupils whose clothing standard was shown to be better than that of the other coloured children. Since discrimination on the basis of clothing standard was demonstrated, it is possible, as Silberman and Spice argued, that had it been possible to analyse the findings separately for the 'other coloured' and the Chinese groups, then prejudice might have been demonstrated against the 'other coloured' but not against the Chinese pupils. This early study is of interest not because the results are clear-cut, but because it capitalized on the opportunity to examine the social relationships between mixed-race and white pupils at that time.

Over the following 15 years several small-scale studies were undertaken in Liverpool for higher education diplomas. For example, Melsher (1958, according to Feeley, 1965) found that amongst older children of an all-age school the group self-preference of white children increased with age, but that of coloured children mainly from settled coloured families and 'mulattos' diminished. McCrea (1964) considered the effect of the arrival of immigrant children in schools in Liverpool on the effectiveness of educational provision compared with approaches in other LEAs broadly in agreement with the then current assimilationist perspective. Some 20 years after Silberman and Spice's research, Feeley (1965) investigated the social integration of coloured immigrant children in three selected secondary schools, one in the most socially deprived area of long immigrant settlement in Liverpool. Interestingly, the researcher experienced some difficulty in finding suitable schools as, in some cases, 'immigrant groups were not distinct, being merged with coloured native born children'. The Liverpool school included 48 coloured boys, distributed between six classes, amongst the school roll of 304. A sociometric test was given to every class with an immigrant group. Pupils were asked to choose who in their class they would like to sit next to, play with in the school yard or to help do a job for the teacher. There was found to be more segregation between the ethnic groups if the immigrant pupils were in larger numbers in classes and less if they were in higher streams, though these tended to include relatively small numbers of such pupils. Dress, ability and willingness to speak English, and willingness to mix socially, were all found to be relevant factors overcoming racial differences in choice of friends. It was presumably such findings which prompted Bowker (1968) to suggest that, in contrast to areas in which immigrant children were arriving in considerable numbers in the mid-1960s, in some schools in Liverpool with its history of coloured settlement a degree of tolerance and understanding of the kinds of educational and social problems involved might be expected, and that little stress would be experienced because of the accepted presence of coloured children. But was this in fact the case? And what attempts had been made to ensure that Liverpool-born black children were able to derive maximum benefit from their experience of education?

Although relatively little publicly available educational research seems to have been undertaken in Liverpool in the 1960s, the increasing interest in the provision being made for immigrant children then arriving in schools in other localities tended to renew concern about the position of Liverpool-born black children and the children of post-war immigrants, especially in the wider social context of race relations and employment. In 1968, the year of the Race Relations Act, concern within Liverpool focussed upon a report of a working party of the Liverpool Youth Organizations Committee (1968) which caused considerable controversy. The working party had found that second- and third-generation coloured youth in Liverpool suffered psychological handicaps, discrimination in employment and felt insecure outside their own neighbourhood. For example, their survey of 19 stores found that only 75 out of 10,000 employees were black, very few indeed served on counters and seven stores employed no black workers at all. The working party questioned 'the long-standing myth in Liverpool of non-discrimination between people of different racial characteristics', claiming that it was a cloak for indifference and lack of understanding. Evidence of hostility was found even in those inner urban areas which had had coloured populations since the 1920s. The report warned of a danger of conflict unless an active policy of integration was urgently adopted (see also Gardiner, 1972–3). In 1971 a survey by the Runnymede Trust Industrial Unit showed a clear disparity in the employment of school-leavers aged 15–19 in Liverpool 8: 32.5 per cent of the blacks compared with 19.5 per cent of whites were unemployed (Whitfield, 1971). In 1972 South Liverpool Personnel, an independent employment agency, was set up in Liverpool 8 to provide a free counselling service, help to find employment or training and advice against discrimination. Since 1974 it has been supported by Liverpool City Council, and since 1979 funded through the Inner City Partnership Scheme. The majority of its clients are Liverpool blacks. Increasingly the agency has been effective in promoting equal opportunities in employment and positive, affirmative action by some city stores (see Ben-Tovim, 1983, pp.124–6).

It was between 1968 and 1973 that the SCRRI visited Liverpool as part of its investigation into school-leavers and education. The Committee discovered that immigrants and their descendants were at a disadvantage in school and out and in its Report (GB. P. H of C. SCRRI, 1973) Liverpool was criticized for allowing the problems of its black population to go unrecognized. The Committee was also disappointed that it was unable to give a lead to other LEAs with immigrant pupils. Meanwhile, in preparation for the SCRRI, a working party had been set up by Liverpool Education Committee to examine the educational needs of, and provision for, the children and Liverpool-born descendants of immigrants. The working party which met over two years comprised a number of black members, including Liverpool-born blacks, representing the CRC, teachers, schools and various ethnic communities. The working party's deliberations are summarized in two documents, a report and recommendation (LEC, n.d.1) and working papers (LEC, n.d.2), which are of interest not only for their descriptions of the background to policy and provision in Liverpool, but also as examples of the thinking at that time about the education of ethnic minority pupils. The first report (LEC, n.d.1) describes the terms of reference of the working party, its background and origin and its response to the SCRRI report, and examines statistics on educational priority and disadvantage, religious education, school meals, language, books, multicultural education and research. These matters are considered in greater detail in specially prepared papers for discussion by the working party in the second report (LEC, n.d.2), which also includes a useful bibliography of research investigations in Liverpool and lists black associations, organizations and their representatives, demonstrating the variety of distinctive ethnic groups in the Liverpool black community. A specific association for British-born blacks is to be noted. There has also been considerable interaction between the different ethnic associations, notably in connection with community arts festivals in Liverpool in the 1970s (Khan, 1976). Ben-Tovim (1983) provides an updated list. In conclusion the LEC working party recommended the strengthening of home–school links, the desirability of more resources, especially at pre-school and nursery level, for more appropriate books and materials, extended language provision, and career and vocational guidance.

Language and the curriculum were central to the focus of the working party. The work of the Crown Street Language Centre, co-ordinating a number of developments across the whole age range was described (LEC, n.d.1, n.d.2). The Centre's primary concern was to teach English to junior and secondary children referred by their schools. In 1973, following the criticism of the SCRRI, the staffing of the centre was increased, allowing for a greater number of pupils to receive tuition both in the centre and in their own schools. Pupils from up to 23 different nationalities received tuition in English at any one time at the Centre: large numbers of pupils from Chinese backgrounds and pupils from African and Asian backgrounds, mainly Sudanese and Somali. These pupils may well have been children of relatively recent immigrants or immigrants themselves, rather than the children of Liverpool-born blacks of long standing. Since 1971 the Language Centre has also been involved in arranging summer holiday school activities and in co-ordinating the parent–school partnership. One of the Centre's functions was to establish a course for demoralized black students who were conscious of their poor employment prospects in an economically and socially deprived area and were rejecting education. The working party also examined other aspects of the curriculum. It considered that religious education teaching was sufficiently flexible and notes that the Agreed Syllabus in Liverpool accepted that for the more mature pupils an understanding of other faiths was essential. There was thought to be sufficient access to single-sex schooling in Liverpool to meet the choice of ethnic minority parents, and on school meals the working party claimed that although there was provision for the identifiable dietary needs of all children, selected international dishes were to be introduced.

It was perhaps in consideration of the multiracial permeation of the curriculum that the working party was most exercised. During its life a multiracial teacher adviser had been appointed whose aims were to increase the self-image of Liverpool-born blacks and other ethnic minority pupils by increasing their respect for themselves and for others, and that of others for them. The working party had also been involved with the Schools Council/NFER project, 'Education for Multiracial Society', and had examined the implications of a committed approach to multiracial education for further education in the context of the Community Relations Commission/ Association of Teachers in Technical Institutions conference (CRC, 1975) and for teacher training and in-service education in general. During the lifetime of the working party Merseyside CRC had introduced a multicultural element in an induction scheme for student teachers. Statistics, collected for the working party, had shown that 40 per cent of 200 probationer teachers in Liverpool had no previous training in multiracial education. Thirty-five per cent had only experienced a brief mention of multicultural education in their teacher training, and although 22 per cent had covered it in some lectures, only two per cent had attended courses where it had received full coverage and was an integral part of the other subjects. The induction courses were initiated as a result of the working party's recommendation that priority should be given to the need to change teachers' attitudes.

The induction course in 1975 focussed on a series of lectures about the historical and social background of Liverpool's ethnic minority groups and analyses of the disadvantages they suffered with respect to employment, housing and education. A synopsis of these lectures by Humphreys (n.d.) drew attention to the many myths, generated from what were claimed as a few instances, surrounding Liverpool blacks and their children: for example, that since many came from mixed marriages, this made for unsettled family backgrounds. Such perceptions were said to condition teachers' expectations of the children, leading to an underestimation of the child's abilities and a misinterpretation of behaviour, with the child in turn responding, possibly becoming uncooperative, discouraged and refusing school, thus confirming the myth. It was also suggested that the young Liverpool blacks' expectations after leaving school markedly influenced their attitudes towards learning, and that with a restricted choice of jobs in the inner city it often seemed pointless to them to attempt CSE, O-levels or to enrol for further education. The Charles Wootton Centre – named after a young black man who died by drowning in the Mersey in the 1919 race riots – was inaugurated in 1974 to investigate the reasons why black people were not attending colleges and universities and to offer advice. It subsequently initiated preparatory courses for college entrance, advice on job applications or examination qualifications, as well as a technology centre and a workshop for trainees on the Youth Opportunities Programme (YOP) (see Ben-Tovim, 1983, pp.127–9). By the mid-1970s inner Liverpool was already an area of high unemployment, especially for school-leavers, and black school-leavers often had to wait longer than their white peers for their first job, were the first to lose their jobs in any cut-backs and were underrepresented in white-collar employment (Humphreys, n.d.; Rogers, 1975). For example, in one study (Ben-Tovim, 1976) over 30 per cent of employers were found to discriminate against black applicants applying for jobs by post. A report for South Liverpool Personnel (Watts, 1978) also indicated that half the young blacks on their books complained of discrimination at interviews. Yet Liverpool-born blacks did not move out of Liverpool 8 because of the high friction experienced in other neighbourhoods which were not used to black populations. This had led to the investigation by Merseyside CRC of many acts of aggression against black people on housing estates outside Liverpool 8.

In the school context the induction course was concerned, as Humphreys (n.d.) summarized, to suggest ways in which the curriculum could be permeated by a multicultural element, though not the introduction of Black Studies as such. However, 77 per cent of probationer teachers believed that too little time had been spent upon multiracial education in the induction course and an overwhelming majority wanted further training (LEC, n.d.2). Yet some years later an HMI report (GB. DES. HMI, 1982) noted that Liverpool LEA had no clear policy for in-service training, nor an induction programme for newly qualified teachers. The HMI found this surprising, in view of Liverpool's involvement in the pilot induction programme funded by the DES from 1974, and a matter of some concern. Such courses serve an important function, as even during the initial induction course reported views of members of the working party and examples quoted by Hopkins (1977) showed that teachers' attitudes towards the multicultural permeation of the curriculum were clearly slow to change and many preferred to ignore questions of 'race' and diminish their significance. Moreover, it appears that Liverpool lacked black teachers who might act as role models in the improvement of the self-image of Liverpool-born black pupils.

Developments in the 1980s

Into the 1980s the city of Liverpool and its education service have continued to be the subject of investigation by local watchdog bodies, government committees and, in the specifically educational context, an HMI report. In its 1980–2 session the Home Affairs Committee of the House of Commons visited Liverpool and also received oral and written evidence as part of its consideration of racial disadvantage. The persistence of black inequality in all aspects of social, political and economic activity were documented by local researchers (Ben-Tovim *et al.*, 1981). The Home Affairs Committee's report was critical of the position of the ethnic minority population in Liverpool. Noting that Liverpool was not widely perceived as a city with race relations problems, the Committee's report stated:

> The situation of Liverpool's ethnic minority population is, however, of particular interest because of the way in which patterns of disadvantage in employment, education and housing so far from disappearing with the passage of time, have if anything been reinforced over the years, to the extent that Chinese or Asian 'newcomers' are in a better position than Liverpool's indigenous blacks. If we cannot combat racial disadvantage in our cities now, we will soon have a dozen Liverpools but on a far greater scale. (GB. P. H of C, 1981, p.xlvi)

The report noted that the most visible symptom of racial disadvantage was unemployment, not least amongst black Liverpudlians of three or four generations. The Afro-Asian-Caribbean Standing Committee in Liverpool estimated that 60 per cent of the Afro-Caribbean population were unemployed. Indeed the risk of being unemployed was four times as great for inner city dwellers, and given that over 60 per cent of Liverpool blacks lived in the inner city, they were at a further disadvantage (Ben Tovim *et al.*, 1981; Morris 1983). The Home Affairs Committee approved the decision of Liverpool Council to declare itself an equal opportunity employer. But it affirmed that black unemployment was exacerbated by a degree of racial concentration in housing, including council housing, in which the allocation system made it difficult for those in housing need to move away from areas such as Liverpool 8. A general sense of alienation and disaffection amongst Liverpool blacks was also reported. However, the appointment of black social workers since 1974 to liaise with ethnic minority communities was commended.

On the other hand, the Committee was severely critical of educational provision and practice. In particular, it deprecated the closure of many inner city schools due to falling rolls and a reorganization plan, suggesting that this might have destroyed the possibility of community-based schools and the participation and involvement of parents in their children's education, so that expertise might be built up in overcoming the effects of generations of discrimination and disadvantage: 'There is a particular responsibility on the local education authority to ensure that Liverpool's black children are properly catered for in any further reorganization plans, and that full weight is given to the views of ethnic minority parents' (p.xlvii). Although the Committee noted evidence from the CRC and others criticizing the education of Liverpool's blacks who, it was claimed, underachieved although they had no language difficulties, it found 'no firm evidence of underachievement by Liverpool's black children, and a 1980 careers service report suggests that blacks may gain equivalent educational qualifications' (p.xlvi). However, the Director of Education recognized the need for curriculum changes and an increase in in-service training. The section of the Committee's report dealing with Liverpool concluded:

> Racial disadvantage in Liverpool is in a sense the most disturbing case of racial disadvantage in the United Kingdom, because there can be no question of cultural problems of newness of language, and it offers the grim warning to all of Britain's cities that racial disadvantage cannot be expected to disappear by natural causes. The Liverpool Black Organization warned the Sub-Committee 'what you see in Liverpool is a sign of things to come'. We echo that warning. (GB. P. H of C, 1981, p.xlviii)

This presentiment was somewhat ironical since in the period intervening between the Committee's visit to Liverpool and the publication of its report civil disturbances had already occurred in Liverpool's Toxteth, as in several other multiracial areas across the country. In Liverpool this had already been presaged by Ridley (1981, quoted by Jeffcoate, 1984) and the publication of a pamphlet by the Race Relations Sub-committee of the Liverpool Teachers' Association (1981) which also drew attention to what it claimed was 'an undisputed fact that black children in the city are underachieving in education'. According to Jeffcoate the disturbances were neither anti-police, nor black, riots, but 'a spontaneous expression of bitterness and disaffection on the part of the city's undereducated and unemployed working-class youth' (p.169). After the civil unrest in Liverpool in July 1981, reviewed in Lord Scarman's report (GB. HO, 1981), and a further disturbance at a primary school in Toxteth, there followed the publication of an HMI report (GB. DES. HMI, 1982) based on an HMI investigation over the previous two years which particularly focussed on the Toxteth area. The HMI report noted that 1971 Census data classified Toxteth as the second most deprived area of urban deprivation in Liverpool, but evidence suggested that it had since suffered further decline. Although the Anglican and Roman Catholic cathedrals and the university are situated in Toxteth, Liverpool 8, it is an area of decaying property, 'glaringly impoverished' (Jeffcoate, 1984) and 'marked by poverty and lack of opportunity' (GB. P. H of C, 1985). As the HMI Report observed in 1981, long-term unemployment, job instability, delinquency, infant mortality, health and housing problems were more than twice the city average; the incidence of children in care was six times the city average; and 18.7 per cent of the children lived in single-parent households, illegitimacy being four times the city average. Toxteth contained about 25 per cent of Liverpool's New Commonwealth population and most of the long-established Liverpool blacks. However, the area was losing its population twice as fast as that of the city as a whole, as those who were able to do so moved out. A general atmosphere of distrust within the community was reported.

The HMI report (GB. DES. HMI, 1982) focussed on 25 primary schools (13 voluntary) and 16 maintained schools (11 voluntary) which took pupils from Toxteth. Only 12 of the primary schools and none of the secondary schools were located in Toxteth. During 1981 the HMI had visited 11 of the primary schools, ten of the maintained secondary schools, two further education colleges nearby and a third of the 32 youth centres. The report criticized the LEA for mismanagement, particularly its failure to come to terms with the problem of falling school rolls, wasting resources because of lack of clear guidelines for schools, a lack of in-service training, staffing instability and low teacher morale, and narrow curriculum policies with few initiatives. It acknowledged, however, that teachers, especially in primary schools, were endeavouring to establish caring and co-operative educational environments, even though the standards of their pupils' achievements were not very high. The report noted the emphasis accorded to numeracy and literacy within the Toxteth primary schools and that between 1969 and 1981 annual tests of reading attainments in 16 Toxteth junior schools showed steady improvement. Nevertheless, many children still experienced difficulties when transferring to secondary education and in one comprehensive school only 30 per cent of the intake had a reading age on entry of ten plus. On the other hand, the report praised the Parents' Support programme set up under the Inner City Partnership scheme, which involved two primary schools and one nursery school in Toxteth. In these schools parents had become more involved in the life of the school and also in English language classes, toddler's clubs and cultural outings. Since there were no secondary schools in Toxteth, pupils from this area went to a wide range of secondary and two comprehensive schools outside the area; one primary school sent 11-plus transfer pupils to seven secondary schools. In such circumstances there was little opportunity for curriculum liaison and social cohesion was fragmented. In terms of the teaching and learning experience in secondary schools:

> HMI have seen work that is soundly prepared and shows the dedication of the teachers, but it is often limited in range and its expectations of pupils. There is a great deal of passive learning and mechanical work and, frequently, a lack of match between the work and the ability of the pupils. (ibid., p.5)

In consequence, external examination results, especially in some small secondary schools, were noted to be poor. With regard to the 1980 results: 'The low attainments noted appear in some measure, to be the result of low expectations on the part of teachers, parents and pupils themselves' (loc. cit.). Elsewhere the HMI report again noted the low aspirations of parents and their indifference and, often, hostility to education.

Low expectations were reflected in the low numbers staying on into the sixth form in schools with Toxteth in their catchment, so that in one comprehensive school there was a sixth form of only 26 pupils, nine on an A-level course. On the other hand, another comprehensive school with an open sixth form with full-time, part-time and day release students was an evident success. However, the HMI report also noted considerable social aggression between pupils, discipline problems, truancy and cynicism among pupils about examination courses and MSC courses. The position with respect to employment was scarcely better. Toxteth was said to have the second highest number of unemployed 16–18 year-olds in the whole of Liverpool, estimated at 35 per cent by the careers service and MSC in 1981. However, it was thought another 30 per cent might be registered at job centres. Of the 532 registered unemployed known to the careers service and MSC, 179 had no formal qualifications on leaving school, and although 164 were described as having average CSEs, only 19 had GCE A- or O-level or CSE grade 1 qualifications. Moreover, although there were 774 YOP places in Liverpool 8, some 338 were unfilled. Some reports suggested that this reflected the disillusionment of young people about the quality and relevance of the opportunities. The HMI suggested that it might also reflect a mismatch of the types of places available and those who had not enrolled. Moreover, although initiatives by the Secretary of State for the Environment had established 1,100 traineeship places in co-operation with private employers, only 24 of the 500 places being filled had been taken by young Liverpool blacks.

Another report concerning the employment of young people, including blacks in Liverpool, also confirmed the general body of research evidence on the transition from school to work/unemployment for young blacks. In 1979–81 between 80 and 100 16–20-year-olds in six multiracial areas – Liverpool, Brixton, Harlesden, Shepherds Bush, Wolverhampton and Manchester – were asked about their experiences since leaving school and the strategies which they had devised in coping with unemployment (Roberts *et al*, 1982). Of all the areas Liverpool was found to have the highest rate of unemployment, at 45 per cent. There was evidence of considerable job switching and the prospect of unemployment was not sufficient to deter young people from leaving the jobs which they had eventually obtained. In Liverpool respondents held their jobs for eight or nine months on average. Hence there was a pattern of temporary and sub-employment in the early careers of these school-leavers. Young people of Afro-Caribbean backgrounds comprised the main ethnic minority group in all the multiracial areas studied. Levels of unemployment amongst the black respondents, even those born and educated in Britain, were approximately 40 per cent ahead of those of white school-leavers, although blacks had apparently left school with superior qualifications and higher aspirations (no data are cited). The researchers found that racial discrimination delayed entry into occupation at all levels. Although young blacks were just as likely to have obtained apprenticeships in non-manual jobs as equally qualified whites, the majority, and even those with modest qualifications, had been obliged to take unskilled posts. Indeed in all the areas the black school-leavers were more likely to have enrolled in part-time further education, often to add to CSE and O-level passes, in the expectation that these would enhance future employment prospects.

There continues to be depressing evidence from publications since 1983 of a cycle of urban deprivation and institutional discrimination in terms of employment, housing and health. Outlining this serves to reinforce an appreciation of the extent to which the interrelation of local social, political, economic and institutional factors cumulatively disadvantage the Liverpool black population and affect educational opportunities, aspirations and expectations.

Merseyside's economy has traditionally been based on its port and related trading and manufacturing activities. These have declined greatly and been eroded in recent years. For example, over 100,000 jobs in manufacturing industry have been lost since 1976 (Jeffcoate, 1984). In 1983 the overall unemployment rate in the area was estimated at 20 per cent, but was said to be twice as high in the inner city and on some council estates. The Swann Report (GB. P. H of C, 1985) recognized unemployment as 'the overriding problem' both for its long-term effect – some men never having had a job – and the 'grave difficulty' faced by school-leavers in obtaining any employment (p.734) (see also Ridley, 1981). According to Jeffcoate (1984), of the 8,000 school-leavers in Liverpool, in 1982, one-third remained in full-time education, one-third joined the YOP and only 6.5 per cent were in paid employment six months after leaving.

Early in 1982 a conference on 'Equal Opportunities and the Employment of Black People and Ethnic Minorities on Merseyside' was organized and sponsored by Merseyside County Council and others, and subsequently the conference papers by employers, trade unionists, local authority personnel, community relations officers and academics, together with useful resource materials, were drawn together by Ben-Tovim (1983). This informative collection not only documents the racial disadvantage and discrimination in employment in Merseyside, but also outlines local and national initiatives to promote equality of opportunity. However, their marginal impact on, and the overwhelming absence of black people from, most of the existing employment opportunities in Liverpool are clearly documented. According to Keidan (1983), ethnic minorities suffer three times the level of unemployment of the local white population. Research on Merseyside shows that one of the most significant reasons is because employers and trade unions practice unintentional discrimination in their employment policies. For example, less than a quarter of employers have adopted an equal opportunities policy. A report by the Liverpool Careers Service (1980) showed that the success rate of placements of a sample of school-leavers in inner Liverpool was markedly lower for blacks than whites (27.8 per cent compared with 45.5 per cent). Indeed in its 1982 Annual Report Merseyside Community Relations Council suggested that 'real black youth unemployment in the Liverpool 8 area [was] currently between 70 per cent and 80 per cent' (p.9).

As several contributors to the conference (e.g. Brown, 1983) observed, the problem in Liverpool is not to get black people into *better* jobs but to find *some* jobs for black people, especially those in Liverpool 8, 'a community that is trapped without any real choice' and where black people are said to be discouraged from applying for jobs because they will not be successful. Opportunities may be assessed by considering recruitment procedures, implementation of equal opportunities policies and positive action. In July 1982 the Commission for Racial Equality (1983) in a survey of major employers with jobs involving public contact discovered that less than half the total employees were black and less than half of them were in visible public contact jobs. Torkington (1983) also cited evidence of very few black nurses or student nurses. Employers reported a lack of black job seekers from their usual recruitment sources, but job centres, the careers service and community organizations claimed that the root cause was discrimination over several decades which resulted in mutual distrust, stereotyping and the creation of segregated social and economic areas. As the Swann Report (GB. P. H of C, 1985) observed, large firms tend to advertise within the firm, so 'where there are no "black" employees already racial inequality is thus perpetuated' (p.737).

Gradually, however, a number of employers have agreed to implement equal opportunities policies and to take more positive action with respect to the recruitment and employment of Liverpool blacks. Some examples may be cited (see also Brown, 1983). In 1980–1 Liverpool City Council adopted an equal opportunities policy and set up a structure to work towards the employment of more blacks on the city council: a survey in 1980 revealed that black employees represented only 0.8 per cent of the workforce and in 1982, only 0.9 per cent

(Ben-Tovim, 1983, pp.111, 158–66). South Liverpool Personnel (see p.343) is an agency which is actively attempting to persuade employers to consider employing blacks and trying to get blacks into vacancies. Since 1979 the Probation Service in Liverpool 8 has operated a MSC-funded Community Assistance Scheme which enables some long-term unemployed blacks to have work experience within the service prior to further training, study or employment (see ibid., pp.194–7). The Social Services Department has a scheme, funded by Urban Aid, whereby blacks can be brought into the social services (see ibid., pp.199–203). Littlewoods is one of the firms which have seriously examined recruitment policies in relation to blacks (Moores, 1983). These and other initiatives documented in the conference collection (Ben-Tovim, 1983) have certainly made a start in redressing the balance in the employment opportunities of Liverpool blacks in an area where employment opportunities as such are severely limited. However, the implementation of equal opportunities policies, recruitment procedures and positive action projects need close monitoring, especially since doubts have been expressed about employers' commitment (Torkington, 1983; Ben-Tovim, 1983).

The current employment position of Liverpool blacks is related to their situation with respect to housing and health, where there is also evidence of discrimination. Jeffcoate (1984) has observed that the economic decline of Liverpool has been mirrored in a physical decline. Between the mid-1960s and mid-1970s the inner city population was halved in a policy of slum clearance, but outer city council estates are now said to be as disadvantaged as the inner city dereliction (Ridley, 1981). Amongst those left behind in the inner city, the unemployed or poorly paid have little opportunity to raise the money to buy a house in another area. Torkington (1983) claims that the discriminatory practices of estate agencies, mortgage companies and residents' prejudices combine to ensure that even those blacks who have the means to buy property may be excluded from certain suburbs. There is also evidence that blacks have not achieved equal access to good-quality public sector housing (Ben-Tovim, *et al.*, 1980). If rehoused, blacks are frequently subject to racial harassment and violence which housing authorities, the police and media are often reluctant to acknowledge as racist in origin, and requests to rehouse such victims are frequently ignored (Merseyside Community Relations Council, 1981). Indeed, according to Torkington, some black people have chosen to return to Liverpool 8 for protection.

However certain initiatives in the field of race relations and housing have also been taken. Since 1979 specialist staff have been appointed to Merseyside Improved Houses (MIH), Liverpool Housing Trust (LHT) and Liverpool City Council to consider the housing situation of ethnic minorities; training courses have been arranged; advisory committees set up to advise on policy and oversee monitoring; equal opportunity statements produced and other publicity circulated (see Ben-Tovim, 1983, pp.187–93). In particular, MIH and LHT are monitoring the ethnic origins of housing applicants (ibid., pp.153–5) and, in 1981, LHT set up a project in Liverpool 8 aiming to provide housing and support for predominantly black and Chinese youth considered to be at risk and to help them develop their independence and a sense of responsibility. Torkington (1983) reports the findings of research in Liverpool in 1980–2 relating to the influence of social factors, such as housing and employment, on health; and also health provision in Liverpool, including the distribution of hospitals, working conditions and attitudes of general practitioners, institutionalized racism and diseases specific to black people, individual and cultural racism in general health provision and reports of moves towards positive action in health care for ethnic minorities in Liverpool. Torkington concludes that existing health provision is inadequate for black people in

Liverpool because of lack of consultation with them about their needs, and that they experience considerable individual, institutional and cultural racism in health care.

Finally, it is important to consider the effects which local, social, political and economic factors have recently had on educational institutions and experiences in Liverpool. The Swann Report (GB. P. H of C, 1985) bore out the findings of the HMI Report three years earlier (see p.347–9) and expressed greater pessimism and concern. It observed that:

> ... it was apparent from the written and oral evidence submitted to us that the Liverpool Black children were particularly low in attainment: partly because of the negative attitude towards them of some teachers, and, despite the dedication of other teachers, partly because of their own and their parents' sense of alienation, in a social structure that offers them no hope for the future. (ibid., p.736)

In visits to Liverpool 8 the Swann Committee discovered that, despite the individual commitment of some teachers, they generally lacked a clear sense of direction because of the absence of a clear LEA policy on educational reorganization. Difficulties observed earlier by the HMI had been heightened by rapidly falling school rolls. Jeffcoate (1984) has claimed that due to ten years of political stalemate, seven or eight secondary schools surplus to requirements were kept open: for example, Paddington, a multiethnic comprehensive school built for 1,700 had 320 pupils on the roll in 1983. Smaller schools often meant a narrower range of curricular options and lack of specialist teaching. However, the Swann Committee found that despite very low morale amongst teachers in both primary and secondary schools, some teachers were still 'resilient and resourceful'. Jeffcoate reported on the LEA's school reorganization plans in 1983, which included closure of the single-sex and selective schools and the establishment of coeducational 11–18 neighbourhood comprehensives. The Swann Report noted that secondary reorganization had brought about the redistribution of some Liverpool black children into mainly white schools. It was concerned about their lack of social integration and low educational and employment expectations – few ever reaching higher education. Access courses leading to higher education courses in humanities, social work and teacher training have, however, been instituted under Inner City Partnership Funding (see Ben-Tovim, 1983, pp.177–8).

The Swann Report recognized that the educational position of Liverpool blacks was greatly affected by the special character of Merseyside. Established social and political structures perpetuated old practices and attitudes – 'the "blacks" are simply left out of the pattern' (p.737). Liverpool blacks lack employment opportunities and in the city centre they risk abuse and insult, so that their absence from the city's social life and power structure has become institutionalized. In the education service black teachers are scarcely better represented: a survey by Liverpool City Council in 1982 (see Ben-Tovim, 1983, pp.160–6) revealed that there were only 69 black teachers in a teaching force in primary and secondary education of over 7,000. Moreover, criticisms have repeatedly been made over the years of the lack of multicultural, anti-racist permeation of the curriculum and in-service teacher training in Liverpool. There have been continuing claims of black under-achievement in Liverpool schools, but there is little quantitative or specific evidence on this point, either because data have not been collected or are not publicly available. Nevertheless, there are consistent reports of low expectations on the part of teachers, parents and pupils and it is commonly suggested that the educational attainment of Liverpool blacks at school-leaving age is low, though not necessarily lower than that of white peers.

Indeed, some would argue that in this area of economic collapse and environmental blight, although Liverpool blacks have consistently faced discrimination and interethnic hostility, there is a common sense of shared identity and deprivation which requires a *general* regenerative programme to alleviate Liverpool's severe economic, environmental and educational difficulties rather than positive action in favour of blacks or other minority groups (see e.g. Jeffcoate, 1984). In recent years, there have been a number of local initiatives both supporting the promotion of equal opportunities and positive action in employment (see pp.350–1), housing (see pp.351–2) and education, for example, in terms of the appointment of an adviser for multiracial education, statements and recommendations by Liverpool Teachers' Association, the National Association of Schoolmasters/Union of Women Teachers and the National Association of Teachers in Further and Higher Education in Liverpool, as well as the setting up of a Race Relations Liaison Committee (see Ben-Tovim, 1983). Such developments are important because there is much evidence, as outlined here, to demonstrate that the disadvantages experienced by Liverpool blacks long predate the current economic crisis and are now endemic in the fabric of Liverpool's social structure. Moreover, as the reports on Liverpool blacks during this century for several generations have testified, at times of economic recession this group is likely to suffer disproportionately. Their present position can, therefore, only add to the cumulative effect and continuing cycle of all aspects of urban deprivation on the socioeconomic lifestyles of this group with consequent implications for the education of its youth.

With the exception of travellers' children, the Swann Report considered that Liverpool blacks had fared worse educationally than any of the other groups considered and hence had a particularly strong claim 'to positive action'. Yet it also noted, with great concern, that despite numerous reports over many years expressing 'the extreme degree of the problems facing this community, little real progress has yet been made to bring about the necessary changes in education and beyond' (GB. P. H of C, 1985, p.738). The significance of transforming the rhetoric of policy statements and increased awareness into changed attitudes, behaviour and institutional practices which can affect the daily living conditions of Liverpool's black community should not be underestimated. Otherwise the short- and long-term implications are dire – for current generations of Liverpool blacks, their descendants and the communities and city within which they live.

Part Six
Gypsy Children

Introductory Note

The term 'gypsy' is used throughout this account in preference to 'traveller' or other terms that are used in the literature. While some object to the term, many of those to whom it applies use it themselves, and its use is well-established in the literature. The use of a single term of designation should not be taken to mean that gypsies are a homogeneous group; the opening section – on background – demonstrates that this is far from being the case. It should be noted that most of this account, reflecting the literature available, is concerned with mobile caravan-dwelling gypsies. Where particular studies refer in a significant way to settled gypsies, this is noted.

Background

Gypsies are a unique group in the present context to the extent that they are both indigenous and members of an ethnic minority. Defining gypsy status is difficult and much effort has been expended on it. Acton (1974a) argued that the myth of the 'true gypsy' is archaic and misleading. Cripps (1977) could find no improvement on the terms of the Caravan Sites Act 1968 and defined gypsies as 'persons of a nomadic way of life, whatever their race or origin, other than travelling showmen or persons engaged in travelling circuses' (p.2). Smith (1975) confined himself simply to 'those who travel' (p.3). These definitions are complicated, however, by the fact that some persons who are gypsies in terms of values, customs, language and self-ascription have opted for settled accommodation and no longer travel.

In 1984 the Gypsy Sites Branch of the Department of the Environment examined the definition of gypsies on the basis of a literature review and discussion with people knowledgeable about gypsies. It concluded that there seemed to be 'little point ... in changing the legislative definition for the purposes of excluding non-gypsies' (GB, DOE, 1984). The study found that there was a group of people known as gypsies who had a distinctive way of life easily identifiable by those who worked with gypsies, and they were not readily confused with others who superficially resembled them.

Historically, the gypsy population is an amalgam of people of Indian/Romani, Irish and indigenous origin. While there has been some intermarriage, the three groups can be distinguished from each other, at least as ideal types. Acton (1974b) refers to two waves of migration from the East to Western Europe, the first occurring between about 1420 and 1550, the second from the middle of the 19th century onward. As Reiss (1975) pointed out, these arrivals came into a society with a tradition of nomadic craftsmen and entertainers, whose number was swelled from time to time by people 'dropping out' from conventional society. In addition, there has been a long tradition of Irish travellers, often called tinkers. Reiss (ibid.) estimated that people of Romani extraction constituted at least 80 per cent of all travellers in England and Wales, whereas Irish and Scottish tinkers were well under 15 per cent.

It is clear that gypsies are an ethnically diverse group. Doubtless some could lay claim to being of pure Romani or Celtic stock, but since this neither defines gypsies in practical terms nor relates to their educational needs, it would seem to be of little relevance. (The fact that some trace their roots in this country to the 15th century highlights the difficulty of making an indigenous/ethnic minority distinction!) There is in fact some uncertainty as to their status in relation to race relations legislation. Initially, The Race Relations Act 1976 was not held to apply to gypsies in general, but a recent view of the Commission for Racial Equality was that they do 'constitute an ethnic minority group and as such are protected against discrimination under the Race Relations Act 1976' (CRE, 1981b). More to the point for presents purposes, the education of gypsy children raises quite specific issues and presents problems which are different from those arising with most other children.

The linguistic situation of gypsies remains a grey area. It is generally assumed that they are competent in English, though there appear to be no detailed studies of their use of English, as distinct from studies into the structure and use of gypsy languages. Reiss (1975) has suggested that gypsies' use of English is sufficiently different from mainstream English to 'create major educational difficulties' (p.83). Reiss gives some information on Romani and Shelta, the two main gypsy languages. Hancock (1984) provides a detailed linguistic account. There are an estimated 60 dialects of Romani world-wide. British Romani comprises two mutually unintelligible languages – Romanos and Angloromani. Shelta is associated with gypsies of Irish origin and its currency it relatively restricted.

As might be expected, precise information on the number of gypsies in Britain is not available. A 1965 Census (GB. MHLG & WO, 1967) came up with a figure of 1,500 for England and Wales but this was acknowledged to be an underestimate. Cripps (1977) estimated a population size of 40,000 in 1976. The best current estimate comes from the Department of the Environment caravan counts. Figures for 1982 (quoted in GB. DES, 1983) suggest that there were 7,000 – 8,000 gypsy families in England making up an overall population of 30,000 – 50,000. Reiss (1975) has pointed out that there are no data whatsoever on the size of the housed gypsy and traveller population (p.65).

Educational Background
The educational situation of gypsy children is extremely unsatisfactory. The Plowden Report regarded their educational needs as 'extreme and largely unmet' (GB. DES. CACE, 1967, Vol.2, p.595) and described gypsy children as 'probably the most severely deprived children in the country' (Vol. 1, p.59). Unlike with other minority groups, the problem is not just one of the adequacy of the education received but whether they received any education at all.

Given the imprecision in the figures on the total gypsy population, estimates of school attendance rates must be speculative. The 1965 Census would suggest that some 25 per cent of the gypsy population were aged between five and 15. In 1970, Reiss (1975) estimated the number at between 6,000 and 12,000. In the mid-1970s, Buckland (1977) suggested a figure of between 15,000 and 20,000. (Apart from the passage of time, the school-leaving age had been raised in the interim.) The Plowden Report claimed that less than ten per cent of children of school age were attending school (Vol.2, p.598). Reiss conducted a survey which found that 1,500 gypsy children attended school in the academic year 1969/70; this pointed to an attendance rate of between 12 and 25 per cent, though the pattern of attendance varied from full-time to very irregular. Buckland (1977) presented national estimates (Table 44). Broadly similar estimates are given in evidence gathered by HM Inspectors (GB. DES, 1983).

Table 44:   Estimated percentage of gypsy children receiving education nationally

	%
Pre-school	5–7
Primary	40
Secondary	10–12
Adult	1–2

Whatever the precise attendance figures at any given time, it is clear that large numbers of gypsy children do not receive education. Also, attendance rates are much lower for secondary schooling than for primary. Acton (1982) argues that the provision of education is closely connected with site provision. Most of the children not receiving education (estimated by him to number over 5,000) are those on illegal sites. According to Department of the Environment figures in 1981, quoted by Acton, at least half of gypsy caravans are on illegal encampments. For that reason, he puts forward the widely held view among activists in this area that 'the provision of legal stopping-places may yet prove to be the most important factor in educational progress' (ibid., p.3).

Types of Educational Provision
Numerous different arrangements have been made to provide education for gypsy children, and a good deal of the available literature consists of descriptions of one or other approach. General accounts include those by Wallbridge (1972), Plowden (1975), Reiss (1975), Worrall (1977), Steyne and Derrick (1979), Advisory Committee for the Education of Romany and other Travellers (ACERT) (1981) and Plowden (1982). Some local education authorities have also published descriptions of their own provision – see Hertfordshire LEA (1981) for a good example. By far the most detailed accounts come from Reiss and Worrall respectively. Reiss described arrangements made in primary and secondary schools, special measures in the maintained sector, innovations such as a separate school and an extension classroom on a gypsy site and the role of the independent schools. Worrall documents provision in four locations, subjecting each to detailed and at times highly critical analysis. Plowden outlines briefly the efforts being made by a small number of local authorities to bring education to gypsy families. The other three publications are general symposia on gypsy education and contain a number of short accounts of educational practice.

Three broad categories of provision for children may be identified: placement based on normal school arrangements; separate, school-based provision; and on-site provision. Normal school arrangements entail having gypsy children in classes on an individual basis just like other children, but they may also involve withdrawal, small-group work or any of the special measures that schools take for the benefit of pupils with special educational needs. Besides the examples given in Reiss (1975), other published documents include a report on a study conducted in a secondary school in the South of England (Ivatts, 1975), an account of the arrival of gypsy children in a small first school in Dorset (Bateman, 1977) and brief accounts of primary schools' experiences of gypsy children in Wandsworth (Bourton, 1979), Trafford (Hare, 1979) and Lincolnshire (Kent, 1981) Most of these accounts were written by headteachers of the schools concerned and concentrate on describing the arrival of the children, the links between parents and the school, the assimilation – or lack of it – of the children and the various practical difficulties encountered.

A second approach to educating gypsy children is to make separate provision in schools or close by them, possibly feeding children into normal classes as deemed appropriate. This may take the form either of mixed-age special classes or units or of a set of classes following the normal age grouping of the school. They may be relatively self-contained, providing a parallel system of education for gypsy children, or they may serve a reception/induction function seeking to incorporate them into mainstream classes wherever possible.

Again, Reiss (1975) provides several examples. At primary level he described three different models: infant induction classes followed by dispersal at junior level; a separate system of classes at infant and junior level, using caravan classrooms and unattached teachers; and schools undertaking teaching on caravan sites where there is a community building. At secondary level he reported on substantial periods of remedial class withdrawal, but also 'an ESN-traveller unit' with a specially trained teacher in a comprehensive school. A good deal of the much-described West Midlands Educational Service for Travelling Children would seem to fit this pattern (Grayson, 1975; West Midlands Education Authorities, 1976; Worrall, 1979). A significant feature of this regional provision is the use of mobile classrooms which can provide schools with additional accommodation at short notice so as to enable them to cope with a sudden and possibly temporary influx of pupils. The classrooms are not intended to be confined to gypsy children, but they would appear to be the basic users of them, in a relatively segregated way.

Educational provision outside schools on sites has taken a variety of forms – summer schools, playgroups, mobile classrooms, peripatetic teachers, and classrooms and even schools established on sites in a relatively permanent way. These cover different purposes: running conventional playgroup and pre-school activities; preparing children for going to school; providing specific remedial or follow-up work; and serving functions of conventional schools albeit on a restricted basis.

On-site educational provision has been described in numerous reports and papers. These include: a playgroup in Hemel Hempstead (Jessel, 1971); playgroups and induction arrangements generally (Bryers, 1972); a playgroup and some remedial teaching in Perth (Hurry, 1972); a summer school in Wisbech (Oakley Smith, 1972); a playgroup summer project (Vinson, 1973); pre-school activities and basic teaching in Harlow (McGrath, 1973); a mixed-age teaching group in Hertfordshire (Waterson, 1976); building up provision in West Glamorgan (Johns, 1977); mobile teaching unit in Hertfordshire (Males, 1977); adult literacy and child education in a mobile bus in the London area (Kiddle, 1978); and various initiatives in Somerset, Manchester and inner London described in the Centre for Information and Advice on Educational Disadvantage Report (Steyne and Derrick, 1979). These are generally sketchy and anecdotal with the most substantial accounts coming from Bryers, Vinson, Waterson, Johns and Males.

Reiss (1975) has described a site provision in East Yorkshire and outlines initiatives relating to on-site pre-schooling, summer school projects, mobile educational units and educational visitors. Worrall (1979) provided detailed description and analysis of the West Midlands Travellers' School, a voluntary provision which predated the local authority service; the East Yorkshire provision referred to by Reiss; a site school in Northamptonshire; and the effort to build up educational provision on sites in Swansea.

Despite the novelty and the variety of the educational arrangements made, there would appear to have been little formal monitoring of them and certainly very little that has been published. Most of the accounts of provision are essentially descriptive and do not seek to evaluate the provision or analyse it in a systematic way. The main exceptions are the two studies reported by Ivatts (1975) and Worrall (1979).

Ivatts studied a secondary school in the South of England which had 22 gypsy children (all living in houses) on roll. They were integrated into the school's educational provision, with most however finding themselves in remedial classes. Their presence was giving rise to educational and organizational problems in the school and the study took place in response to a request for advice in dealing with the problems. The main contribution of the study was to illuminate how the 'gypsy problem' was perceived differently by the school and by children and their parents. The school saw them as a troublesome group – regularly late or absent, frequently disruptive, generally uncooperative, quite lacking in motivation and grossly underachieving at all levels. For the children and their parents, this pattern of behaviour and lack of achievement was a simple consequence of their intense dislike of secondary schooling, bolstered by a conviction that it had little relevance for them. They had some regard for literacy and basic educational skills, but education beyond that was perceived to have little to offer in their way of life. This analysis led to various recommendations based in particular on taking account of the different cultural backgrounds and aspirations of gypsy children and on establishing stronger links with the homes.

Worrall was attached to the action research project known as the West Midlands Travellers' School as a full-time teacher/researcher from 1971 to 1976 with a brief to carry out an evaluation of the project. In the course of this time he also studied and evaluated educational provision for gypsy children in other parts of England and Wales. The resulting publication provided a detailed description of the development of the programmes, along with searching criticism of them. The author argues the necessity of taking a comprehensive view. The educational provision made for gypsies, and the deficiencies in it, cannot be understood outside the context of the pervasive discrimination experienced by gypsies. The frequent harassment and evictions, the meagre allocation of resources and the failure to consult or involve gypsies in educational decision-making were all factors that served to define what was possible in educational terms. Other writers have mentioned these factors in passing but none with the vigour and the analysed detail that Worrall has provided. His case studies offer a valuable account of the process of setting up and developing educational provision for gypsy children. While the educational considerations seem sometimes to be lost amidst the invective and the discussion of contextual factors, and while some accounts would probably be couched rather differently by other participants, the broad thrust of the report is focussed directly on setting up educational provision.

Finally, mention may be made of educational provision for adults. Very little has been written about this, and the few initiatives reported have been confined to adult literacy programmes. The one available research study (Taylor-Brown, 1977) identified a broader set of needs relating to information and advice on dealing with non-gypsy society. This theme has been taken up in an action research project based on a University of London consortium. An interim report (Taylor-Brown *et al.*, 1982) points to the importance of defining adult education for gypsies in terms of the perceptions and practical goals of gypsies themselves and declares an intention of focussing on 'the need for various types of educational action that might be particularly appropriate for gypsies and for those gorgios (non- gypsies) who have dealings with gypsies' (p.6). Gartland (1982) describes a literacy centre in Sheffield set up specifically for gypsies.

The Curriculum

There is an ambivalence within the gypsy community about the nature of an appropriate curriculum for their children. On the one hand, there are demands for an education that is similar to that offered to other children. Thus the statement issued after the CED conference read in part: 'Traveller representatives at the conference argued that the major educational objective was that children should attend ordinary schools' (Steyne and Derrick, 1979, p.52). The implication of this is that they should be exposed to the same curricular opportunities as other children and – assuming special provision is made for any initial difficulties they experience – have the same teaching needs as them.

On the other hand, there is considerable evidence that a much narrower view of education has prevailed within the gypsy community, even among those who are well disposed towards education. Adams *et al.* (1975) noted that while parents' attitudes had become more positive over the preceding ten years, some still did not view formal education with favour. Primary schooling was acceptable for the grounding it gave in basic skills, particularly reading and writing, but the broader curriculum of the secondary school was held in low regard. This has been advanced by Ivatts (1975) and others as a main reason for the poor attendance at secondary level. Reiss (1975) pointed to various parts of the curriculum which were problematic for other reasons: sex education because of taboos on discussing sexual matters; physical education because of reluctance to expose the body; and vocational training or careers guidance because of the direct threat they presented to gypsy society.

The central problem seems to be the twin effects of early socialization in gypsy communities and the gypsy way of life. Adams *et al.* (1975) report on one of the few studies of socialization in the gypsy family, writing that:

> Gypsies principally have relied on the family for all educative functions that would prepare the child for the travelling way of life. This has involved the teaching of vocational skills and the responsibility for the transmission of its own culture, including the languages Anglo-Romany or Shelta. As such the Traveller family has retained substantial responsibilities across a wide range of services... for which among contemporary house-dwelling families responsibility has been transferred to an institution. (ibid. pp.90–1)

Okley (1975) also observed the crucial rule of the nuclear gypsy family in the socialization process and pointed out that it had many functions fulfilled by schools and other institutions for non-gypsy families. Associated with this socialization process and the distinctive identity it generates are the early maturity and the acquisition of vocationally appropriate skills that many other writers have noted. To the extent that school curricula fail or are unable to take adequate account of these factors, their relevance to gypsy children is constrained. Childs (1976) provides further discussion of gypsy child-rearing patterns in relation to schooling, arguing that 'the poor verbal contact between gypsy parents and their children is not only dysfunctional for the adjustment of the children at school, but also for future adjustment to the majority society in general' (p.10).

Several writers have pointed to the lack of congruence between conventional schooling and the gypsy way of life, evident in terms both of skills and of value systems. Smith (1972) and others have argued that schools fail to provide the social and economic skills specific to gypsy children's well-being and future life and, at the same time, seek to transmit other skills that are irrelevant if not actually dysfunctional to the gypsy way of life. Ivatts (1975) reported that school attendance for teenagers interfered with family work patterns, and by depriving parents of the work traditionally done by older children could result in loss of income. On the broader front, Reiss (1975) drew attention to the widespread notion that education and nomadism were incompatible, for reasons which seem to be a mixture of the logistical and ideological. Though he takes issue with this notion, his study does in fact document the considerable mismatch between gypsy aspirations and what schools conventionally offer. Smith (1975) argued that enforced participation in education could 'entail the destruction of precisely those characteristics that helped to define the individuality of the culture in question'. In this, he concurs with an impassioned statement from a leading gypsy spokesman on education:

> My children never had education. I reckon education destroys a lot, I do... The young people today, the moment they sit down they got to have a book in their hands. It's all wrong. I don't reckon that a lot of education is any good. If you've always got a book in your hands you ain't got no time to do anything else. (Quoted in Wallbridge, 1972, p.8)

An education system and curricular provision that take little account of gypsy values and lifestyles are unlikely to win much support in the gypsy community and indeed, as Reiss (1975) has pointed out, are likely to fail. He argues that schools must be aware of the distinctive cultural heritage of gypsies and must capitalize on it. This is no easy task, however, not merely because schools exist primarily for non-gypsy children and teachers are orientated towards mainstream education, but also because of gypsy resistance to having their culture exposed. Gypsy children may shrink from the attention that even a sensitive handling of topics from gypsy culture in the classroom may entail, while undue interest in the gypsy languages – Angloromani and Shelta – may be taken amiss by members of the gypsy community who regard their language as 'one of their last refuges against the power of the social worker' (ibid., p.154). It is clear that much work has to be done in determining an appropriate curriculum for gypsy education so as to achieve an effective combination of mainstream schooling and gypsy culture and aspirations.

In addition to the nature of the curriculum on offer to gypsy children, thought must also be given as to how it is to be implemented. Apart from the brief account of teachers' practice cited earlier, the main study to look at classroom practice and teaching approaches was the Schools Council project directed by Reiss. Conducted in 1971–2, this study sought information on the backgrounds of travelling children, their educational difficulties and the educational approaches found most successful. Information was gathered by questionnaire (to LEAs and schools) and visits (to some 40 schools). Worrall (1979) also reported on classroom practice in some of the situations he studied, documenting in particular process variables and the difficulties staff encountered in establishing their practice.

Reiss (1975) pooled the information on teaching approaches and materials together into a single lengthy chapter, covering: objectives and principles; the bridge into school and socializing into the classroom; teaching the basic skills – an integrated programme in oracy, literacy and numeracy; the wider curriculum; utilizing cultural background; and vocational aspects. This offers a detailed review of the most successful teaching studied during the project, along with a compendium of materials and activities which teachers might find useful. Patterson (1984) also offers some practical guidelines for children.

Moran (1983) examined gypsy children's experience of education in a Cambridge primary school run exclusively for gypsy children. She spent five months working as a helper for one day a week. She found that parents had positive attitudes to education and concluded that separate schools did offer advantages, at least in the early years of schooling. Children received a positive socializing experience and did not encounter the discrimination or threat to cultural identity often alleged to turn gypsy children from schooling.

Experience of Schooling

Gypsy children's experience of schooling is clearly different as between attendance at ordinary schools and site provision. Adams *et al.* (1975) and Ivatts (1975) provide some information on the former. While experiences differed considerably, a number of common patterns emerged. At a practical level, their spasmodic attendance, whether caused by family mobility, eviction from unofficial sites or general unconcern for education, led to an uneven and unsatisfactory experience of schooling. When they did attend regularly, gypsy children brought a set of cultural norms, expectations and skills which were at variance with those of the school, often leading to mutual incomprehension and even hostility. At secondary level in particular, as documented by Ivatts, their conviction that continued education was irrelevant resulted in an absence of motivation and a rejection of the ideology of the school. In addition, gypsy children lacked the socialization experiences that would enable them to fit easily into the way of life of the school, and in consequence could be a source of disruption through their obvious lack of conformity.

In some cases this was associated with prejudice and hostility which they regularly encountered from both teachers and other pupils. Adams *et al.* observed that gypsies tended to dramatize their school experience for sake of effect, but maintained none the less that 'the most common characteristic of school experience related by Travellers concerns the animosity of the entire school community to their presence in the school' (p.101). Ivatts likewise found evidence of 'a social cleavage of significant proportions' (p.18). The gypsies regarded the other children as being prejudiced against them, and their social mixing in the school was limited (and mostly confined to other children at the bottom of the school's social hierarchy). This picture is corroborated by anecdotal evidence from several of the brief reports cited above.

The situation is not entirely negative, however. Bateman (1977) found that it was possible to establish a *modus vivendi* in his school, even when the two groups stayed quite separate from each other. Adams *et al.* (1975) found that hostility to gypsy children could decline substantially. Many gypsy children, moreover, were attending school enthusiastically and received considerable encouragement from their parents in their efforts to learn and in their display of new-found literacy skills.

Children's educational experience on sites was very different from this. Most detail is given by Worrall (1979) and Males (1977) but the other shorter accounts cited give some information as well. Clearly, the fact that the educational provision was contained within the site meant that there was no occasion for the hostility and discrimination that many gypsy children have experienced in schools. (Equally, however, there was no opportunity for mixing with the broader community that when well managed is of benefit to gypsy and non-gypsy alike.) Also because it was on site in their own territory as it were, it was perceived as less threatening, though it was sometimes taken less seriously for the same reason.

In terms of education, on-site schooling tended to be limited both in aims and possibilities. Some of the provision was for the express purpose of building a bridge to normal schooling: by breaking down barriers of anxiety and suspicion and equipping gypsy children with some of the requisite social skills, staff sought to prepare them for school and encourage them to attend willingly. Even when the aim was to educate them in the narrower sense of developing academic skills, staff had generally to set themselves modest goals. This was for various reasons: contact time was limited, particularly in the case of mobile classrooms; continuity of attendance was difficult to achieve; and resources and accommodation were often limited.

Teaching groups were usually small, composed of children of widely different ages and often based on family groupings. Discipline had to be informal since attendance was optional, though staff did not report problems in this regard. Teaching tended to be individualized and child-centred, often related to things in the environment of the site and to aspects of the gypsy experience. The major emphasis was on basic literacy, since that was what the children and their parents wanted and because there was so little time in any case for teaching to a broader curriculum.

Comparative Information

Very little data comparing gypsies along psychometric measures with the majority population are available. A few small-scale studies relating to children will be described. It may be noted that there is no real evidence to take seriously the claim that gypsies are of low intelligence. The point would hardly seem worth making indeed were it not for the fact that this claim does surface from time to time. The studies reported here do provide evidence of underachievement on the part of gypsy children and low scores on a range of cognitive tasks. These have to be interpreted in the light of environmental factors, especially socialization patterns, and while they may be of some relevance to planning educational provision, they imply little of any substance about the innate abilities of gypsy children.

MacCallum (1975) reported verbal reasoning test scores (administered at secondary transfer) for gypsy children in Caithness. These numbered 120 out of a total of some 5,000, over the years 1964–73. The mean score for the gypsy children was 78, as compared with 98 for all children. Moreover, their attainments in English and arithmetic at the time of secondary transfer were at a level of the average eight-year-old. Disproportionate numbers of them were referred to the Child Guidance Service because of backwardness and retardation (47 per cent compared with nine per cent of the total school population) and were placed in special classes. MacCallum noted the disadvantaged backgrounds of these children and its likely effect on test scores. He also pointed out the limited validity of group tests with children who had such poor reading skills.

Childs (1976) studied the linguistic and cognitive development of children in the West Midlands, comparing three groups: gypsy children; children from similarly disadvantaged backgrounds; and middle-class children. Each group comprised ten children aged four to five years, all attending nursery school or playgroup. The gypsy children lived in caravans on sites in one of two areas; they attended a playgroup near the site in one case and a playgroup attached to an on-site school in the other. The socially disadvantaged children all attended a family centre which served families experiencing some form of difficulty or deprivation: the group was characterized by poverty, ill-health and broken homes. The middle-class children all attended nursery school and came from well-off homes where there was a high regard for education.

All the children were tested individually at their playgroup, family centre or nursery school on four tests: the English Picture Vocabulary Test, Columbia Mental Maturity Scale, Boehm Test of Basic Concepts and a Sentence Comprehension Test. These measured respectively receptive vocabulary, general reasoning ability, mastery of basic concepts and understanding of sentences. As might be expected, the middle-class group obtained significantly higher scores on all measures than the other groups. The gypsy children, however, performed as well as and in some respects better than the disadvantaged group. Their scores on the vocabulary test were lower, but were higher on the reasoning and conceptual development tests. Both groups scored similarly on the sentence comprehension test.

While the scale of the study was modest and some of the claims of significant differences are exaggerated, some tentative pointers do emerge. Gypsy children's language scores were low, being comparable to or less than the scores obtained by the disadvantaged group. It is not clear whether this was due to generally retarded language development or to second-language factors. Scores on reasoning ability and conceptual development, by contrast, were not unduly low and Childs argues that 'the Traveller lifestyle, far from hindering conceptual development, may actually be preferable to that of many settled but similarly economically disadvantaged children' (p.23).

Davies (1976) carried out a study comparing the use of English by gypsy and non-gypsy children. The aim was to test the hypothesis that in their use of language gypsy children were 'egocentric' in the sense of being poor communicators: they tend to lack awareness of their hearer's perspective and do not orient verbal expressions towards it. This was tested by means of a card discrimination task where a child had to describe a picture so as to enable another child to identify it. The children were seated on opposite sides of a screen; each had three cards which were similar but not identical, and the speaker had to specify – by verbal description only – a particular card. Raven's Progressive Matrices were also administered to the children.

The comparison groups comprised 40 gypsy children, drawn from three different locations and experiencing different forms of schooling, and 16 non-gypsy children. The latter were matched roughly with the gypsy group in terms of socioeconomic status: they attended an educational priority area school and came from homes which were judged by the headteacher to be culturally impoverished and where there was evidence of family poverty. The children were aged seven to 12, with an average age of just over nine years. The mean age of the non-gypsy control group was, however, four months less than the mean age of the gypsy group.

The results showed that the gypsy children performed at a significantly lower level on both measures than the non-gypsy children. Moreover, analysis of the speech used in the card test showed a marked inferiority in communicative skills on the part of the gypsy children. These findings were held to support the initial hypothesis. Not only did they concur with the view that 'Traveller culture places little value on excessive verbalization' (p.40), but they also pointed to the fact that gypsy children failed 'in communicating the relationships between the elements [in the pictures] adequately for the listener to identify the target' (p.39). This supported the hypothesis on egocentricity, namely, that they did not consider the listener's need of precise definition of the relationships in order to identify the pictures.

This study was subsequently discussed by Acton and Davies (1979) in an attempt to set it in the broader context of culture-fair testing and of gypsy dialects. There is some mention of the literature on the possible cultural bias in the use of Raven's Progressive Matrices. It is pointed out that the card task was carried out in English by a non-gypsy experimenter, whereas English is not part of the habitual structure of communication in the gypsy children's families. These various considerations, along with the limited nature of the study itself, would certainly urge caution in interpreting its findings. On their own, however, they do not justify the total dismissal of the initial findings. In order to do that, further empirical evidence rather than just speculative argument is required.

Summary

Research literature on the education of gypsy children is sparse. A few substantial studies have been carried out, but most of the available literature consists of policy discussion and statements, accounts from practitioners and general comment and opinion. These non-research documents contain much useful information and have been drawn on accordingly, but they cannot be taken as a body of systematic knowledge.

It is clear that there has been a substantial failure to meet the educational needs of gypsy children. Some receive no formal education at all. Others attend school part-time or receive occasional lessons from peripatetic teachers. Many gypsy children attending school full-time derived little benefit from it, particularly at secondary level. From the perspective of schools and local authorities there seems to be great disparity in levels of provision and concern to meet the needs from one area to another. There have been claims, too, of mismatch at local level between education departments which seek to make educational provision and other local authority departments which effectively obstruct them in doing so.

It is clear that educational provision for gypsies is a political matter. Numerous writers have drawn attention to the educational difficulties consequent on the eviction of gypsy families from unauthorized sites. Some argue that little educational progress can be made until the shortage of site accomodation is resolved. There would appear to be considerable legislative difficulties both in regard to implementing existing legislation, especially the Caravan Sites Act 1968, and in framing new legislation. The Education Acts of 1980 and 1981 would appear to have considerable relevance but it remains to be seen how they will be interpreted in practice with regard to gypsies.

Underlining these practical and logistical difficulties, and fundamental to any consideration of the problem, are the specifically educational issues. There is a question over the function of schooling for the gypsy community. It should not be taken for granted that schools serve the same purpose for gypsy children as for non-gypsy children. This question must be resolved and then the associated curricular and pedagogical matters tackled. School curricula and teaching practices assume certain cultural values, expectations and lifestyles. It is only to be expected that gypsy children with a radically different culture and lifestyle will be distanced by some aspects of conventional schools (as is frequently argued indeed in respect of many non-gypsy children). There are also considerable attitudinal barriers – prejudice and hostility on the part of schools and the settled community, lack of interest in schooling on the part of gypsy children and parents.

The numerous difficulties and the uneven progress achieved to date should not obscure the fact that progress has been made. The latter has been too modest to give grounds for complacency, but it does demonstrate the possibilities. Gypsy children – and their parents – can respond positively to educational opportunities, and schools can cope effectively with their presence and benefit from it. To that extent, the essential problem perhaps is to identify good practice and study it with a view to establishing and disseminating its characteristic features. In that way, educational provision for gypsy children would be shaped not by the manifold constraints and difficulties, but by a knowledge of good practice and what can be achieved.

References

ABSALOM, R.N.L., (1980). 'Italian in degree courses. The polytechnic view.' In: BALDWIN, T.D. *et al.* (Eds) *Italian in Schools*. London: CILT.

ACTON, T.A. (1974a). 'True gypsies – myth and reality', *New Society*, **28**, 563–5, June 6.

ACTON, T.A. (1974b). *Gypsy Politics and Social Change*. London: Routledge and Kegan Paul.

ACTON, T.A. (1982). 'New weapons in the struggle for gypsy education', *Traveller Education*, **17**, June (London: Romanestan Publications).

ACTON, T.A. and DAVIES, G. (1979). 'Educational policy and language use among English Romanies and Irish travellers (tinkers) in England and Wales', *Int. J. Soc.Lang.*, **19**, 91–110.

ADAMS,B. OKELY, J., MORGAN, D. AND SMITH, D. (1975). *Gypsies and Government Policy in England: a study of the Travellers' Way of Life in Relation to the Policies and Practices of Central and Local Goverment*. London: Heinemann Educational Books.

ADVISORY COMMITTEE FOR THE EDUCATION OF ROMANY AND OTHER TRAVELLERS (1981). *Reports and Papers*. London: ACERT.

ALKAN, F. and CONSTANTINIDES, S. (1981). *Cypriots in Haringey*. London: London Borough of Haringey.

ALLEN, S. (1971). Youth and Work: A Study of Differential Ethnic Group Experience. Unpublished report, University of Bradford, School of Studies in Social Sciences.

ALLEN, S. and SMITH, C.R. (1975). 'Minority group experience of the transition from education to work.' In: BRANNEN, P. (Ed) *Entering the World of Work: Some Sociological Perspectives*. London: HMSO.

ANDREWS, R. (1980). 'Secondary and tertiary education: interdependent levels or watertight compartments?' In: BALDWIN, T.D. *et al.* (Eds) *Italian in Schools*. London: CILT.

ANTHIAS, F. (1982). Ethnicity and class among Greek Cypriot migrants – a study in the conceptualization of ethnicity. Unpublished PhD thesis, University of London.

ANTHIAS, F. (1983). 'Sexual divisions and ethnic adaptation: the case of Greek-Cypriot women.' In: PHIZACKLEA, A. (Ed) *One Way Ticket: Migration and Female Labour*. London: Routledge and Kegan Paul.

ANTHIAS, F. (1984). 'Some issues affecting Greek speaking migrants in Britain – an ethnic profile.' In: ROUSSOU, M. (Ed) *Greek Outside Greece*. London: National Council for Mother Tongue Teaching.

ARCHIMANDRITOU-XEFTERIS, I. (1977). Scholastic achievement and family background in Greek secondary school pupils: comparative studies in Athens and London. Unpublished M.Phil. thesis, University of London, Birkbeck College.

ARISTODEMOU, T. (1979). Annual Report of the Education Department of the Cyprus High Commission in London for the School Year 1978–1979.

ATKINS, M. (1985). 'Minority community languages: problems, strategies and issues for teacher educators', *Brit. J. Educ. Studs,* **XXXIII**, 1, 57–69.

BAGLEY, C. (1971). 'Mental illness in immigrant minorities in London', *J. Biosocial Science,* **3**, 449–59.

BAGLEY, C., VERMA, G.K. and MALLICK, K. (1982). 'The comparative structure of self-esteem in British and Indian adolescents.' In: VERMA, G.K. and BAGLEY, C. (Eds) *Self-Concept, Achievement and Multicultural Education.* London: Macmillan.

BALDWIN, T.D. (1980). 'The "state of the art": a review of current practice in GCE examinations in Italian.' In: BALDWIN, T.D. *et al.* (Eds) *Italian in Schools.* London: CILT.

BALDWIN, T.D., CARSANIGA, G., LYMBERY CARTER, S., LEPSCHY, A., MOYS, A. and POWELL, R.C. (Eds) (1980). *Italian in Schools.* Papers from the Colloquium on the Teaching of Italian in the United Kingdom 1979, Association of Teachers of Italian, Society for Italian Studies. London: CILT.

BARR, J. (1964). 'Napoli, Bedfordshire', *New Society,* **3**, 79, 7–10.

BATEMAN, J. (1977). 'Gypsy intake', *Trends in Education,* **1**, 9–15.

BEAUMONT, E.B. (1976). 'Bilingualism in Bradford.' In: CENTRE FOR INFORMATION ON LANGUAGE TEACHING *Bilingualism and British Education: The Dimensions of Diversity.* London: CILT.

BEDFORDSHIRE COUNTY COUNCIL (1983). Policies for a Multi-cultural Community.

BEETLESTONE, F.S. (1982). A study of the Cypriot community in Haringey with special reference to the early years of schooling. Unpublished MA dissertation, University of London Institute of Education, and personal communication, 1983.

BENNETT, O. (1983). *A Turkish Afternoon.* London: Hamish Hamilton.

BEN-TOVIM, G. (1976). *Discrimination by Post.* Liverpool: University of Liverpool/Commission for Racial Equality.

BEN-TOVIM, G. (Ed) (1983). *Equal Opportunities and the Employment of Black People and Ethnic Minorities on Merseyside.* A Report of a Conference (plus resource materials) organized by Merseyside County Council on 7 January 1982 at the University of Liverpool. Liverpool: Merseyside Association for Racial Equality in Employment/Merseyside Area Profile Group.

BEN-TOVIM, G., BROWN, V., CLAY, D., LAW, I., LOY, L. and TORKINGTON, P. (1981). *Racial Disadvantage in Liverpool – An Area Profile.* Liverpool: University of Liverpool Press/Merseyside Area Profile Group.

BERGER, J. (1975). *A Seventh Man. A Book of Images and Words about the Experience of Migrant Workers in Europe.* Harmondsworth: Penguin.

BHATNAGAR, J. (1970). *Immigrants at School.* London: Cornmarket Press.

BOTTIGNOLO, B. (1983). Italian immigration in the Bristol region. Unpublished PhD thesis, University of Oxford.

BOURTON, J. (1979). 'Travellers' children in a multi-cultural primary school.' In: STEYNE, H. and DERRICK, D. (Eds) *The Education of Travellers' Children.* Report of a Conference held by the Centre for Information and Advice on Educational Disadvantage, 8–9 November 1977, Manchester.

BOWKER, G. (1968). *The Education of Coloured Immigrants.* London: Longman.

BRISTOW, A. (1980). 'A retraining scheme for modern language teachers.' In: BALDWIN, T.D. *et al.* (Eds) *Italian in Schools.* London: CILT.

BRITTAN, E.M. (1973). The opinions of teachers in multiracial schools on aspects of multiracial education. Unpublished M.Sc. thesis, University of Surrey.

BRITTAN, E.M. (1976a). 'Multiracial education 2. Teacher opinion on aspects of school life. Part 2, Pupils and teachers', *Educ. Res.,* **18**, 3, 182–92.

BRITTAN, E.M. (1976b). 'Multiracial education 2. Teacher opinion on aspects of school life. Part 1: changes in curriculum and school organization', *Educ. Res.*, **18**, 2, 96–107.

BROADY, M. (1955). 'The social adjustment of Chinese immigrants in Liverpool', *Social Rev.*, **3**, 65–75.

BROGI, F.R. (1986). Personal communication for Italian Embassy, 25 September.

BROWN, D.M. (1979). *Mother Tongue to English. The Young Child in the Multi-cultural School*. Cambridge: Cambridge University Press.

BROWN, J. (1970). *The Un-melting Pot. An English Town and its Immigrants*. London: Macmillan.

BROWN, W. (1983). 'Unemployment and the black community on Merseyside.' In: BEN-TOVIM, G. (Ed) *Equal Opportunities and the Employment of Black People and Ethnic Minorities on Merseyside*. Liverpool: Merseyside Association for Racial Equality in Employment/Merseyside Area Profile Group.

BRYERS, P. (1972). 'The under 5s in Gypsy education and community projects on sites.' In: WALLBRIDGE, J. (Ed) *The Shadow on the Cheese*. London: National Gypsy Education Council.

BUCKLAND, D.G. (1977). 'The education of travelling children', *Trends in Education*, **1**, 3–8.

BURGIN, T. and EDSON, P. (1967). *Spring Grove: The Education of Immigrant Children*. London: Oxford University Press/Institute of Race Relations.

BUTCHER, A. (n.d.). A Report Focussing on the Implications for the Education of Ethnic Minorities. Bingley School Vietnamese School Project, Save The Children Fund.

BUTTERWORTH, E. and KINNIBRUGH, D. (1970). *The Social Background of Immigrant Children from India, Pakistan and Cyprus*. SCOPE Handbook 1. Harlow: Longman/Books for Schools Council, pp. 69–75.

CAMPBELL-PLATT, K. (1978). *Linguistic Minorities in Britain* (rev. NICHOLAS, S.). Runnymede Trust Briefing Paper. London: Runnymede Trust.

CARSANIGA, G. (1980). 'Foreword' and 'Introduction: the task before us.' In: BALDWIN, T.D. *et al.* (Eds) *Italian in Schools*. London CILT.

CENTRE FOR INFORMATION ON LANGUAGE TEACHING (CILT) (1975). *Less Commonly Taught Languages: Resources and Problems*. CILT Reports and Papers No.12. London: CILT.

CENTRE FOR INFORMATION ON LANGUAGE TEACHING (1980). *Italian Language and Studies – Some Basic Examination Statistics*. London: CILT.

CENTRE FOR INFORMATION ON LANGUAGE TEACHING (1982). *Modern Greek*. Language and Culture Guide 10. London CILT.

CENTRE FOR INFORMATION ON LANGUAGE TEACHING (1983). *Turkish*. Language and Culture Guide 26. London: CILT.

CENTRE FOR URBAN EDUCATIONAL STUDIES (CUES) (1982). *The World in a City*. Bilingual Education Project. London: ILEA Learning Resources Branch.

CHADWICK-JONES, J.K. (1965). 'Italian workers in a British factory: a study of informal selection and training', *Race*, **6**, 3, 191–8.

CHAPMAN, R.D. (1976). 'Bilingualism in Birmingham.' In: CENTRE FOR INFORMATION ON LANGUAGE TEACHING *Bilingualism and British Education*. London: CILT.

CHEETHAM, J. (1972). *Social Work with Immigrants*. London: Routledge and Kegan Paul.

CHILDS, J.A.(1976). The linguistic and cognitive development of young traveller children: a comparative study. Unpublished B. Phil. (Ed) thesis, University of Birmingham.

CHRISTODOULIDES, M.Z. (1984). 'Cooperation between LEAs and Parents' Associations – examples from the life/efforts of the Greek Parents' Association (GPA).' In: ROUSSOU, M. (Ed) *Greek Outside Greece*. London: NCMTT.

CLARK, J.P.A.A. and HUTCHINSON, C. (1980). 'Lothian region's graded levels of achievement in foreign language learning.' In: BALDWIN, T.D. *et al.* (Eds) *Italian in Schools*. London: CILT.

CLOUGH, H.E. and QUARMBY, J. (1978). *A Public Library Service for Ethnic Minorities in Great Britain*. London: The Library Association.

COCHRANE, R. (1977). 'Mental illness in immigrants to England and Wales. An analysis of mental hospital admissions', *Social Psychiatry*, **12**, 23–35.

COLLINS, S. (1957). *Coloured Minorities in Britain*. London: Lutterworth Press.

COLLISON, P. (1969). 'Immigrants' varieties of experience', *New Society*, 26 June, and in *Race and Immigration*, New Society Social Studies Reader, pp. 16–18.

COLPI, T. (1979). 'The Italian community in Glasgow with special reference to spatial development', *Association of Teachers of Italian Journal*, **29**, 62–75.

COMMISSION FOR RACIAL EQUALITY (CRE) (1978). *Ethnic Minorities in Britain. Statistical Background*. London: CRE.

COMMISSION FOR RACIAL EQUALITY (1980). *Mother Tongue Teaching Conference Report*. Bradford College, 9–11 September 1980. London: CRE.

COMMISSION FOR RACIAL EQUALITY (1981a). *Race Relations in 1981: An Attitude Survey*. London: CRE.

COMMISSION FOR RACIAL EQUALITY (1981b). *Report of Four Formal Investigations into Alleged Pressure to Discriminate by Brymbo Community Council*. London: CRE.

COMMISSION FOR RACIAL EQUALITY (1982). *Ethnic Minority Community Languages: A Statement*. London: CRE.

COMMISSION FOR RACIAL EQUALITY (1983). 'Regional initiatives in Liverpool', *Employment Report*, **V**, 2, 2.

COMMISSION OF THE EUROPEAN COMMUNITIES (CEC) (1977). *The Children of Migrant Workers*. Collection Studies, Education Series No.1. Brussels: ECSC, EEC, EAEC.

COMMUNITY RELATIONS COMMISSION (CRC) (1974). *Ethnic Minorities in Britain. Statistical Data*. London: CRC.

COMMUNITY RELATIONS COMMISSION (1975). *The Further Education Service in a Multiracial Community*. Report on a joint CRC/ATTI Conference, 7–10 July, Goldsmiths College. London: CRC.

COMMUNITY RELATIONS COMMISSION (1976). *Who Minds? A Study of Working Mothers and Childminding in Ethnic Minority Communities*. London: CRC.

COMMUNITY RELATIONS COMMISSION (1977). *The Education of Ethnic Minority Children. From the Perspectives of Parents, Teachers and Education Authorities*. London: CRC.

CONSTANTINIDES, P. (1977). 'The Greek Cypriots: factors in the maintenance of ethnic identity.' In: WATSON, J.L. (Ed) *Between Two Cultures: Migrants and minorities in Britain*. Oxford: Basil Blackwell.

CONSTANTINIDES, P. (1984). 'The children of mixed marriages: Greek as a second language.' In: ROUSSOU, M. (Ed) (1984) *Greeek Outside Greece*. London: NCMTT.

COOKE, M. (1979). *Public Library Provision for Ethnic Minorities in the UK*. Report of an investigation carried out on behalf of the British National Bibliography Research Fund. Leicester: Leicestershire Library and Information Service.

COUILLAUD, X. (1984). 'Links between mainstream and community teachers from the point of view of the child.' In: ROUSSOU, M. (Ed) *Greek Outside Greece*. London: NCMTT.

COUILLAUD, X. and TASKER, J. (1983). The Schools Language Survey, Summary of Findings from Five Local Education Authorities. LMP/LINC Working Paper No.3, May.

CRAFT, M. and ATKINS, M. (1983). Training Teachers of Ethnic Minority Community Languages. Nottingham University School of Education.

CRELLIN, C.T. (1979). Turkish Education in Cyprus. An Outline of Current Provision with Particular Reference to that in Elementary Schools. Unpublished report, Middlesex Polytechnic.

CRELLIN, C.T. (1981). 'Turkish education in Cyprus since 1974: an outline of some of the changes in curriculum organisation and the professional standing of teachers', *Internat. Rev. Educ.*, **27**, 3, 315–30.

CRIPPS, J. (1977). *Accommodation for Gypsies*. London: HMSO.

CRISP, S. (1980). A study of the effects of migration on a South Italian hill village and on the migrants themselves. Unpublished PhD thesis, University of Cambridge.

CRONIN, A. (1984). 'Supplementary schools: their role in culture maintenance, identity and underachievement', *New Community*, **XI**, 3, 256–67.

CROSS, C. (1977). 'Youth clubs and coloured youth', *New Community*, **V**, 4, 489–94.

DALGLISH, C. (1980). 'Occupational backgrounds of the refugees from Vietnam', *New Community*, **VIII**, 3, 344–6.

DALGLISH, C. (1982). 'Reorientation for teachers from Vietnam', *New Community*, **X**, 1, 127–31.

DANIEL, W.W. (1968). *Racial Discrimination in England*. Harmondsworth: Penguin.

DAVIES, G. (1976). Egocentric verbal behaviour in traveller children. Unpublished B.Phil. (Ed.) thesis, University of Birmingham.

DAVISON, R.B. (1966). *Black British*. London: Oxford University Press/Institute of Race Relations.

DENCH, G. (1975). *Maltese in London. A Case Study in the Erosion of Ethnic Consciousness*. Report of Institute of Community Studies. London: Routledge and Kegan Paul.

DERRICK, J. (1966). *Teaching English to Immigrants*. London: Longman.

DERRICK, J. (1968). 'School – the meeting point.' In: OAKLEY, R. (Ed) *New Backgrounds. The Immigrant Child at Home and at School*. London: Oxford University Press/Institute of Race Relations.

DERRICK, J. (1977). *Language Needs of Minority Group Children*. Slough: NFER.

DEVEREUX, D. (1980). 'Italian as first foreign language: two viewpoints from one school: 1.' In: BALDWIN T.D. *et al.* (Eds) *Italian in Schools*. London: CILT.

DI BLASIO, N. (1979). 'Italian immigration to Britain: an ignored dimension', *Association of Teachers of Italian Journal*, **29**, 17–30.

DOVE, L. (1974). 'Racial awareness among adolescents in London comprehensive schools', *New Community*, **III**, 255–61.

DOVE, L. (1975). 'The hopes of immigrant school-children', *New Society*, **32**, 653, 63–5, 10 April.

DRIVER, G. (1980). *Beyond Underachievement: Case Studies of English, West Indian and Asian School-leavers at Sixteen Plus.*. London: CRE.

EDHOLM, F., ROBERTS, H. and SAYER, J. (1983). *Vietnamese Refugees in Britain*. London: CRE.

ELLIOTT, P. (1981). *Library Needs of Mother-Tongue Schools in London*. Research Report No.6. London: Polytechnic of North London, School of Librarianship.

EVANS, I. (1981). *Vietnam – a Resource List*. Bransgore: Sopley Education Centre.

EVANS, J. (1980). 'Education in Vietnam', *New Approaches in Multiracial Education*, **8**, 3, 14–16.

FARREL, J. (1980). 'Italian at Catford County School.' In: BALDWIN, T.D. *et al.* (Eds) *Italian in Schools*. London: CILT.

FARRELL, J. (1983). 'Italian.' In: McCLURE, J.D. (Ed) *Minority Languages in Central Scotland*. Aberdeen: Aberdeen Association for Scottish Literary Studies.

FEELEY, M.R. (1965). An investigation of the social integration of coloured immigrant children in selected secondary schools. Diploma in Secondary Education thesis, University of Liverpool.

FIGUEROA, P.M.E. (1974). West Indian school-leavers in London: a sociological study in ten schools in a London borough, 1966–1967. Unpublished PhD thesis, London School of Economics and Political Science.

FIGUEROA, P.M.E. (1976). 'The employment prospects of West Indian school-leavers in London, England', *Social and Economic Studies*, **25**, 3, 216–33.

FIGUEROA, P.M.E. (1984). 'Minority pupil progress.' In: CRAFT, M. (Ed) *Education and Cultural Pluralism*. Lewes: Falmer Press.

FITCHETT, N. (1981). *Vietnamese Children in Derby*. Primary English Language Centre, Rutland Street, Derby.

FLETCHER, M.E. (1930). *Report on an Investigation into the Coloured Problem in Liverpool*. Liverpool Association for the Welfare of Half-Caste Children and Economic Status of Coloured Families in the Port of Liverpool. Liverpool: Liverpool University Press.

GARDINER, S. (1972–3). Liverpool – Racial Situation 1972 – Report for CRC. Unpublished report. Liverpool: CRC.

GARIGUE, P. and FIRTH, R.W. (1956). 'Kinship and organisation of Italianates in London.' In: FIRTH, R.W. (Ed) *Two Studies of Kinship in London*. LSE Monographs in Social Anthropology No.15. London: LSE, pp.65–97.

GARTLAND, A. (1982). 'Gypsies write here', *Voluntary Action*, **11**, 24–5.

GENERAL REGISTER OFFICE (GRO) (1956). *Census 1951. England and Wales. General Tables*. London: HMSO.

GENERAL REGISTER OFFICE (1964). *Census 1961. England and Wales. Birthplace and Nationality Tables*. London: HMSO.

GEORGE, V. (1960). The assimilation of the Cypriot community in London. Unpublished MA thesis, University of Nottingham.

GEORGE, V. and MILLERSON, G. (1967). 'The Cypriot community in London', *Race*, **VIII**, 3, 277–92.

GEORGIOU, M. (1983). Study of social and cultural effects of attendance at additional evening and weekend schooling in their culture and language by Greek Cypriots from a North London comprehensive school. Unpublished B.Ed. dissertation, Middlesex Polytechnic.

GORDON, K. (1980). 'The Oxford Modern Language Achievement Certificate.' In: BALDWIN, T.D. *et al.* (Eds) *Italian in Schools*. London: CILT.

GORDON, P. (1983). 'Back to Cyprus?', *New Society*, 4 August, 170–1.

GRAYSON, D. (1975). 'For gypsies – a card, a mobile and a specialist', *Education*, 2 May, 90–1.

GREAT BRITAIN. DEPARTMENT OF EDUCATION AND SCIENCE (1968). *Statistics of Education, 1967. Vol. 1, Schools.* London: HMSO.

GREAT BRITAIN. DEPARTMENT OF EDUCATION AND SCIENCE (1971). *Statistics of Education, 1970. Vol. 1, Schools.* London: HMSO.

GREAT BRITAIN. DEPARTMENT OF EDUCATION AND SCIENCE (1973). *Statistics of Education, 1972. Vol. 1, Schools.* London: HMSO.

GREAT BRITAIN. DEPARTMENT OF EDUCATION AND SCIENCE (1975). *A Language for Life.* Report of the Committee of Inquiry appointed by the Secretary of State for Education and Science under the Chairmanship of Sir Allan Bullock, FBA. London: HMSO.

GREAT BRITAIN. DEPARTMENT OF EDUCATION AND SCIENCE (1982). Memorandum on Compliance with Directive 77/486/EEC on the Education of the Children of Migrant Workers.

GREAT BRITAIN. DEPARTMENT OF EDUCATION AND SCIENCE (1983). *The Education of Travellers' Children: An HMI Discussion Paper.* London: DES.

GREAT BRITAIN. DEPARTMENT OF EDUCATION AND SCIENCE (1984). *Mother Tongue Teaching in School and Community.* An HMI Enquiry in Four LEAs. London: HMSO.

GREAT BRITAIN. DEPARTMENT OF EDUCATION AND SCIENCE. CENTRAL ADVISORY COUNCIL FOR EDUCATION (1967). *Children and their Primary Schools.* Vol. 1, Report and Vol.2, Appendix 12: Gypsies and Education (Plowden Report). London: HMSO.

GREAT BRITAIN. DEPARTMENT OF EDUCATION AND SCIENCE. HM INSPECTORATE (1982). *Educational Provision by Liverpool Education Authority in the Toxteth Area.* London: DES.

GREAT BRITAIN. DEPARTMENT OF EDUCATION AND SCIENCE AND WELSH OFFICE (1981). Joint Circular No.5/81 (DES), No. 36/81 (Welsh Office). Directive of the Council of the European Community on the Education of Children of Migrant Workers. London/Cardiff, July.

GREAT BRITAIN. DEPARTMENT OF EDUCATION AND SCIENCE AND WELSH OFFICE (1983). *Foreign Languages in the School Curriculum: A Consultative Paper.* London: HMSO.

GREAT BRITAIN. DEPARTMENT OF THE ENVIRONMENT (1984). *Defining a Gypsy.* London: DOE, Gypsy Sites Branch.

GREAT BRITAIN. HOME OFFICE (1981). *Police Act 1964. The Brixton Disorders, April 10–12, 1981. Report Of An Inquiry* (Scarman Report), Cmnd 8427. London: HMSO.

GREAT BRITAIN. HOME OFFICE (1982). *Report of the Joint Committee for Refugees from Vietnam.* London: HMSO.

GREAT BRITAIN. MINISTRY OF HOUSING AND LOCAL GOVERNMENT AND WELSH OFFICE (1967). *Gypsies and Other Travellers: A Report of a Study Carried Out in 1965, and 1966, by a Sociological Research Section of the Ministry of Housing and Local Government.* London: HMSO.

GREAT BRITAIN. PARLIAMENT. HOUSE OF COMMONS (1981). *Fifth Report from the Home Affairs Committee. Session 1980–81. Racial Disadvantage. Vol. 1, Report with Minutes of Proceedings.* London: HMSO.

GREAT BRITAIN. PARLIAMENT. HOUSE OF COMMONS (1985). *Education For All.* Report of the Committee of Inquiry into the Education of Children from Ethnic Minority Groups (Swann Report), Cmnd 9453. London: HMSO.

GREAT BRITAIN. PARLIAMENT. HOUSE OF COMMONS. SELECT COMMITTEE ON RACE RELATIONS AND IMMIGRATION (1973).

Session 1972–3. Vol. 1, Report and Recommendations and *Vol. 3, Evidence and Appendices.* London: HMSO.

GROOCOCK, V. (1983). 'Cutting the tongue ties', *Education Guardian*, 15 February, 1.

GUPTA, J. (1980). 'CSE Mode 3 Italian examination: West of England scheme.' In: BALDWIN, T.D. *et al.* (Eds) *Italian in Schools.* London: CILT.

HANCOCK, I. (1984). 'Romans and Angloromani' and 'Shelta and Polar'. In: TRUDGILL, P. (Ed) *Language in the British Isles.* Cambridge: Cambridge University Press, pp.367–83, 384–403.

HARE, G. (1979). 'Meeting the needs of Travellers' children.' In: STEYNE, H. and DERRICK, D. (Eds) *The Education of Travellers' Children.* Report of a Conference held by the Centre for Information and Advice on Educational Disadvantage, 8–9 November 1977. Manchester.

HAXELL, M.A. (1979). European immigration and Bradford. Unpublished paper. Bradford and Ilkley Community College, West Yorkshire.

HEGARTY, S. and LUCAS, D. (1978). *Able to Learn.* Windsor: NFER.

HERTFORDSHIRE LEA (1981). *Travellers in Hertfordshire.* Hertford: Hertfordshire LEA.

HESTER, H., WAINWRIGHT, C. and FRASER, M. (1977). *English as a Second Language in Multiracial Schools.* London: National Book League.

HEWITT, R. (1982). 'White adolescent Creole users and the politics of friendship', *J. Multiling. and Multicult. Develop.*, **3**, 3, 217–32.

HILL, C. (1970). *Immigration and Integration: A Study of the Settlement of Coloured Minorities in Britain..* Oxford: Pergamon.

HILL, D. (1976). *Teaching in Multiracial Schools.* London: Methuen, pp.76–81.

HOPKINS, A. (1977). 'If it doesn't happen in Liverpool...' *Times Educ. Suppl.*, **325**, 8–19, 3 June.

HOULTON, D. (1980). A study of bilingualism in education and the response of the Asian community. M.Ed. thesis, University of Leicester, School of Education.

HOULTON, D. (1984). 'The "role" of the monolingual teacher in supporting the mother tongue of Greek-speaking children.' In: ROUSSOU, M. (Ed) *Greek outside Greece.* London: NCMTT.

HOULTON, D. (1985) *All Our Languages.* London: Edward Arnold.

HOULTON, D. and WILLEY, R. (1983). *Supporting Children's Bilingualism.* London: Longman/Schools Council.

HOUNSLOW COMMUNITY RELATIONS COUNCIL (HCRC) (1982a). Mother Tongue Teaching in Hounslow by Voluntary Organisations.

HOUNSLOW COMMUNITY RELATIONS COUNCIL (1982b). Report of the Education Forum 'The Bilingual Child in Primary Schools' held at the Civic Centre, Hounslow on 13 November 1981.

HUMPHREYS, A. (n.d.). 'Liverpool – a multiracial city.' Paper based on lectures given in Liverpool's Probationer Teachers' Induction Course, 1975.

HUNTER-GRUNDIN, E. (1982). Case Study on Parent Involvement in Education: a Multi-ethnic Project in the London Borough of Haringey. Council for Cultural Co-operation of Council of Europe, School Education Division, Strasburg.

HURRY, D.M. (1972). 'Teaching the Travellers', *New Era*, **53**, 7, 189–93.

HUTCHINSON, C. (1984). 'Italian in five Lothian primary schools', *Modern Languages in Scotland*, **25**, 81–7.

HYLSON-SMITH, K. (1968). 'A study of immigrant group relations in North London', *Race*, **IX**, 4, 467–76.

INNER LONDON EDUCATION AUTHORITY (ILEA) (1969). Literacy Survey: Summary of Interim Results of the Study of Pupils' Reading Standards. Proposals for Further Action. Rs 382/69.
INNER LONDON EDUCATION AUTHORITY (1972). Literacy Survey: 1971 Follow-up. Preliminary Report. Rs 567A/72.
INNER LONDON EDUCATION AUTHORITY (1975). *Lifestyles of Cyprus*. London: ILEA, Learning Resources Branch.
INNER LONDON EDUCATION AUTHORITY (1977). Literacy Survey: 1976 Follow-up. Report of the Education Officer to the Schools Sub-Committee on 24 November 1977. Report 412.
INNER LONDON EDUCATION AUTHORITY (1979). Report on the 1978 Census of those ILEA Pupils for whom English Was Not a First Language. Report 9484.
INNER LONDON EDUCATION AUTHORITY (1981). Ethnic Census of School Support Centres and Educational Guidance Centres. Research and Statistics Report.
INNER LONDON EDUCATION AUTHORITY (1982). 1981 Language Census. Report Rs 811/82.
INNER LONDON EDUCATION AUTHORITY (1983). 1983 Language Census. Report Rs 916/83.
INNER LONDON EDUCATION AUTHORITY (1986). 1985 Language Census. Report Rs 1026/86.
INNER LONDON EDUCATION AUTHORITY ENGLISH CENTRE (1979). *Our Lives: Young People's Autobiographies*. London: ILEA English Centre.
IVATTS, A.R. (1975). *Catch 22 Gypsies. A Report on Secondary Education*. London: Advisory Committee for the Education of Romany and other Travellers.
IZBICKI, J. (1983). 'Titles row closes Greek School', *Daily Telegraph*, 12 February.
JACKSON, B. (1979). *Starting School*. London: Croom Helm.
JEFFCOATE, R. (1984). *Ethnic Minorities and Education*. London: Harper and Row.
JELINEK, M.M. (1977). 'Multiracial education 3. Pupils' attitudes to the multiracial school', *Educ. Res., 19*, 2, 129–41.
JELINEK, M.M. and BRITTAN, E.M. (1975). 'Multiracial education 1. Inter-ethnic friendship patterns', *Educ. Res., 18*, 1, 44–53.
JENKINS, S. (1971). *Here to Live. A Study of Race Relations in an English Town*. London: Runnymede Trust.
JESSEL, C. (1971). 'Gypsy children learn to fit in', *Times Educ. Suppl.*, **2939**, 6, 24–5, August.
JOHNS, A. (1977). 'Education provision for travelling children in the West Glamorgan area 1975–6', *Traveller Education*, **10**, 4–16.
JONES, C. (1934). *Social Survey of Merseyside. Vol. 1, Liverpool*. Liverpool: Liverpool University Press.
JONES, J. (1982). Ethnic minorities in education – a Turkish mother-tongue supplementary school. Unpublished Research Project for BA (Soc), Polytechnic of North London, Department of Sociology.
JONES, P.R. (1982a). *Vietnamese Refugees*. Home Office Research and Planning Unit Paper 13. London: HMSO.
JONES, P.R. (1982b). 'Indochinese refugees in the United Kingdom', *Home Office Research Bulletin*, **13**, 2, 10–11.
JONES, P.R. (1983). 'Vietnamese refugees in the UK: the reception programme', *New Community*, **X**, 3, 444–54.

JOWELL, R. and PRESCOTT-CLARKE, P. (1970). 'Racial discrimination and white-collar workers in Britain', *Race*, **11**, 398–417.

KAWWA, T. (1963). Ethnic prejudice and choice of friends among English and non–English adolescents. Unpublished MA dissertation, University of London Institute of Education.

KAWWA, T. (1965). A study of the interaction between native and immigrant children in English schools with special reference to ethnic prejudice. Unpublished PhD thesis, University of London Institute of Education.

KAWWA, T. (1968a). 'Three sociometric studies of ethnic relations in London schools', *Race*, **10**, 2, 173–80.

KAWWA, T. (1968b). 'A survey of ethnic attitudes of some British secondary school pupils', *Brit. J. Soc. Clin. Psychol.*, **7**, 161–8.

KEEN, L. (1985). 'Weaving in the strands', *Mother Tongue News*, **7**, 12–13, August.

KEIDAN, H. (1983). 'Introduction.' In: BEN-TOVIM, G. (Ed) *Equal Opportunities and the Employment of Black People and Ethnic Minorities on Merseyside*. Conference Report and Resources Pack. Liverpool: Merseyside Association for Racial Equality in Employment/Merseyside Area Profile Group.

KENT, G. (1981). 'Going on the knocker', *Times Educ. Suppl.*, **5381**, 10 April, 28.

KERR, A.N. (1978). Mother Tongue Teaching in Nottingham and Stockholm. University of Nottingham.

KHAN, N. (1976) *The Arts Britain Ignores: The Arts of Ethnic Minorities in Britain*. London: CRE.

KIDDLE, C. (1978). 'A school for Gypsies', *New Society*, **45**, 825, 189–90.

KING, R.L. (1977a). 'Italian migration to Great Britain', *Geography*, **62**, 3, 176–86.

KING, R.L. (1977b). 'Bedford, the Italian connection', *Geographical Magazine*, **49**, 7, 442–9, April.

KING, R.L. (1978). 'Work and residence patterns of Italian immigrants in Great Britain', *International Migration*, **16**, 2, 74–82.

KING, R.L. (1979). 'Italians in Britain: an idiosyncratic immigration', *Association of Teachers of Italian Journal*, **29**, 6–16.

KING, R.L. and KING, P.D. (1977). 'The spatial evolution of the Italian community in Bedford', *East Midland Geographer*, **6**, 7, 337–45.

KING, R.L. and ZOLLI, L. (1981). 'Italians in Leicester', *Association of Teachers of Italian Journal*, **33**, 3–13.

KRAUSZ, E. (1971). *Ethnic Minorities in Britain*. London: MacGibbon and Kee.

KROKOU, A. (1985). 'The educational needs of Cypriot children', *Multicultural Teaching*, **III**, 2, 40–2.

KUYA, D. (1967). Mixed Marriages and the Problems the Children face. Unpublished monograph, IRR Library.

LADBURY, S. (1977). 'The Turkish Cypriots: ethnic relations in London and Cyprus.' In: WATSON, J.L. (Ed) *Between Two Cultures: Migrants and Minorities in Britain*. Oxford: Basil Blackwell.

LEE, T.R. (1973). 'Immigrants in London: trends in distribution and concentration 1961–71', *New Community*, **II**, 2, 145–58.

LEEUWENBERG, J. (1979). *The Cypriots in Haringey: A Study of their Literacy and Reading Habits*. Research Report No.1. London: Polytechnic of North London, School of Librarianship.

LEVI, C. (1947). *Christ Stopped at Eboli: The Story of a Year*. London: Cassell.

LINGUISTIC MINORITIES PROJECT (LMP) (1982a). Coventry Mother-Tongue Teaching Directory Survey 1981. Findings, First Report. University of London Institute of Education.

LINGUISTIC MINORITIES PROJECT (1982b). Bradford Mother-Tongue Teaching Directory Survey 1981. Findings, First Report. University of London Institute of Education.

LINGUISTIC MINORITIES PROJECT (1983a). *Linguistic Minorities in England*. A report by the Linguistic Minorities Project for the Department of Education and Science. London: University of London Institute of Education/ Heinemann Educational Books, LMP and LINC.

LINGUISTIC MINORITIES PROJECT (1983b). Mother-Tongue Teaching in Haringey. A First Report on the Findings of the Mother-Tongue Teaching Directory Survey in 1982. University of London Institute of Education.

LINGUISTIC MINORITIES PROJECT (1985). *The Other Languages of England*. London: Routledge and Kegan Paul.

LITTLE, A. (1975a). 'Performance of children from ethnic minority backgrounds in primary schools', *Oxford Review of Education*, **1**, 2, 117–35.

LITTLE, A. (1975b). 'The educational achievement of ethnic minority children in London schools.' In: VERMA, G.K. and BAGLEY, C. (Eds) *Race and Education Across Cultures*. London: Heinemann Educational Books.

LITTLE, A., MABEY, C. and WHITAKER, G. (1968). 'The education of immigrant pupils in inner London primary schools', *Race*, **IX**, 4, 439–52.

LITTLE, A. and WILLEY, R. (1983). *Studies in the Multi-Ethnic Curriculum*. Full Report from the Schools Council Project on Studies in the Multi-Ethnic Curriculum based at Goldsmiths' College, University of London, 1978–80. London: Schools Council.

LITTLE, K.L. (1948). *Negroes in Britain*. London: Kegan Paul.

LITTLEWOOD, R. and LIPSEDGE, M. (1982). *Aliens and Alienists: Ethnic Minorities and Psychiatry*. Harmondsworth: Penguin.

LIVERPOOL CAREERS SERVICE (LCS) (1980). Outreach Workers Report. Unpublished internal report, Liverpool Careers Service.

LIVERPOOL EDUCATION COMMITTEE (n.d.1). Meeting their Needs. Working Party Examining the Educational Needs of and Provision for the Children and Liverpool-born Descendants of Immigrants 1. Report and Recommendations.

LIVERPOOL EDUCATION COMMITTEE (n.d.2). Meeting their Needs. Working Party Examining the Educational Needs of and Provision for the Children and Liverpool-born Descendants of Immigrants 2. Working Papers.

LIVERPOOL TEACHERS' ASSOCIATION (1981). Before the Fire. LTA Race Relations Sub-Committee.

LIVERPOOL YOUTH ORGANISATIONS COMMITTEE (1968). *Special but not Separate: A Report on the Situation of Young Coloured People in Liverpool*. Liverpool: Liverpool Youth Organizations Committee.

LOBO, E. de H. (1978). *Children of Immigrants to Britain: Their Health and Social Problems*. London: Hodder and Stoughton.

LONDON BOROUGH OF HARINGEY (1978). Racialist activities in schools. London Borough of Haringey Education Service.

LONDON BOROUGH OF HARINGEY (n.d.). Equal opportunities in Haringey: an Education Service policy statement. London Borough of Haringey Education Service.

LONDON COUNCIL OF SOCIAL SERVICE (LCSS) (1967). *Commonwealth Children in Britain*. London: National Council of Social Service.

LYMBERY-CARTER, S. (1980). 'The International Baccalaureate.' In: BALDWIN, T.D. *et al.* (Eds) *Italian in Schools*. London: CILT.

MABEY, C. (1981). 'Black British literacy: a study of reading attainment of London black children from 8 to 15 years', *Educ. Res.*, **23**, 2, 83–95.

MACCALLUM, R.E. (1975). 'The Caithness tinkers: a people out of line', *Education in the North*, **12**, 3–4.

McCARTY, N. and CHRISTOUDOULOU, P. (1977). 'Children without roots', *Times Educ. Suppl.*, 15 April, 26.

McCREA, W. (1964). A study of some problems presented by immigrant children in the schools of one authority with additional reference to the work being done by other authorities. Dip. Ed. Dissertation, University of Liverpool.

MACDONALD, J.S. and MACDONALD, C.D. (1972). *The Invisible Immigrants*. London: Runnymede Trust Industrial Unit.

MACDONALD, M.I. (1975). Language acquisition by a multicultural group – a comparative study of a sample of Jamaican, Greek, Turkish and British students attending a London college of further education in an attempt to assess their progress in achieving a command of Standard British English. Unpublished PhD thesis, University of London Institute of Education.

McGHEE, M. (1983). 'The Question of Italian', *Modern Languages in Scotland*, **23**, 107–10.

McGRATH, K. (1973). 'Gypsy or gorgio?', *New Society*, **23** 112–13, 18 January.

McINTOSH, N. and SMITH, D.J. (1974). *The Extent of Racial Discrimination*. Broadsheet 547. London: Political and Economic Planning.

MACKILLOP, J. (1981). Ethnic Minorities in Sheffield. Sheffield Metropolitan District Education Committee.

MALES, S.E. (1977). 'A mobile teaching unit for Gypsy children', *Trends in Education*, **1**, 16–20.

MANLEY, D. (1986). *Look, No Words!* London: SCDC.

MARES, P. (1982). *The Vietnamese in Britain: A Handbook for Health Workers*. Cambridge: Health Education Council/National Extension College.

MARIN, U. (1969). *Emigrazione Italiana in Gran Bretagna*. Pts 1 and 2. Rome: Centro Studi Emigrazione.

MARIN, U. (1975). *Italians in Gran Bretagna*. Rome: Centro Studi Emigrazione.

MARKOPOULOU, C. (1974). 'A project of social work with Cypriot immigrants in London', *Internat. Migration*, **XII**, 112, 3–13.

MARTIANOU, C. (1981). Expectations of Cypriot parents and aspirations of their children, in the age-group 14–19 years-old of the British educational system in north London. Dissertation for Dip. Ed. for a Multicultural Society. Roehampton Institute of Higher Education, Southlands College.

MARTIN-JONES, M. (1984). 'The newer minorities: literacy and educational issues.' In: TRUDGILL, P. (Ed) *Language in the British Isles*. Cambridge: Cambridge University Press.

MARVELL, J. (1974). 'Moral socialization in a multicultural community', *J. Moral Educ.*, **3**, 3, 249–57.

MARYNIUK, M. (1985). 'The educational needs of children of Ukrainian origin', *Multicultural Teaching*, **III**, 2, 42–3.

MELSHER, E. (1958). Social and emotional attitudes of a group of coloured children. Dip. Ed. dissertation, University of Liverpool.

MEMDOUH, F. (1981). The Report of the Cyprus Turkish Association on the Educational Needs of the Turkish Community in London and in England. London: Cyprus Turkish Association.

MENGON, G. (1980). 'Italian as a mother tongue: its place in British schools.' In: BALDWIN, T.D. *et al.* (Eds) *Italian in Schools*. London: CILT.

MERSEYSIDE COMMUNITY RELATIONS COUNCIL (1981). Reports on Racist Attack and Housing Response. June.

MERSEYSIDE COMMUNITY RELATIONS COUNCIL (1982). Annual Report.

MILES, P. (1983). The Greek Cypriot School and Community Centre. One of a number of information sheets on the Cypriot community in Avon. Multicultural Education Centre, Bristol.

MILSTEAD, A. (1981). Education in a multicultural society: some responses of the London Borough of Haringey, 1965–81. Unpublished dissertation.

MOBBS, M.C. (1977). *Meeting their Needs – an Account of Language Tuition Schemes for Ethnic Minority Women.* London: Commission for Racial Equality.

MOORES, J. (1983). 'The Littlewoods Equal Opportunity Programme.' In: BEN-TOVIM, G. (Ed) *Equal Opportunities and the Employment of Black People and Ethnic Minorities on Merseyside.* Conference Report and Resources Pack. Liverpool: Merseyside Association for Racial Equality in Employment/Merseyside Area Profile Group.

MORAN, S. (1983). The 'underachievement' of travelling children: a case study. Project and dissertation for CNAA degree in Sociology, Polytechnic of North London.

MORAWSKA, A., REID, E. and SMITH, G. (1984). *Languages in Bradford.* CLE/LMP Working Paper No.11 London: Community Languages and Education Project, University of London Institute of Education.

MORRIS, B. (1983). 'Why equal opportunities? A national trade union perspective.' In: BEN-TOVIM, G. (Ed) *Equal Opportunities and the Employment of Black People and Ethnic Minorities on Merseyside.* Conference Report and Resources Pack. Liverpool: Merseyside Association for Racial Equality in Employment/ Merseyside Area Profile Group.

MORRIS, L.A. (1980). 'The educational reception of the boat children in the United Kingdom', *Trends in Education*, 1, 10–14, Spring.

MORTIMORE, P., SAMMONS, P., STOLL, L., LEWIS, D. and ECOB, R. (1986). *The Junior School Project. A Summary of the Main Report.* London: ILEA Research and Statistics Branch.

MOTTRAM, J., WRIGHT, T.A. and PARR, N. (Eds) (1983). Role of the Primary ESL Specialist. English Language Resource Centre, Haringey.

MURRAY, S., WARMAN, F. and YU, V. (1981). The 13+ Project: May 1980–July 1981. A Report on the teaching of Vietnamese pupils at Schools' Language Unit. Schools' Language Unit, Hounslow.

NORTHAMPTONSHIRE LEA (1980). Report of LEA/NAME Working Party on Mother Tongue Teaching and Mother Culture Maintenance in Northamptonshire.

OAKLEY, R. (1968). 'The Cypriot background.' In: OAKLEY, R. (Ed) *New Backgrounds. The Immigrant Child at Home and at School.* London: Oxford University Press/Institute of Race Relations.

OAKLEY, R. (1970). 'The Cypriots in Britain', *Race Today*, 2, 99–102, April.

OAKLEY, R. (1971). Cypriot migration and settlement in Britain. Unpublished D. Phil. thesis, University of Oxford.

OAKLEY, R. (1979). 'Family, kinship and patronage: the Cypriot migration to Britain.' In: SAIFULLAH KHAN, V. (Ed) *Minority Families in Britain. Support and Stress.* London: Macmillan.

OAKLEY SMITH, B. (1972). 'The turnings in the road to gypsy education', *Education*, 139, 25, 603–5.

OERTAL, B.A. (1978). A study of the Punjabi component of an EEC mother tongue and culture project in Bedford. MA thesis. King's College, University of London.

OFFICE OF POPULATION CENSUSES AND SURVEYS (OPCS) (1974). *Census 1971. Great Britain. Country of Birth Tables.* London: HMSO.
OFFICE OF POPULATION CENSUSES AND SURVEYS (1982a). *Labour Force Survey 1981.* London: HMSO.
OFFICE OF POPULATION CENSUSES AND SURVEYS (1982b). *Labour Force Survey 1979.* London : HMSO.
OFFICE OF POPULATION CENSUSES AND SURVEYS (1983a). *Census 1981. Country of Birth.* London: HMSO.
OFFICE OF POPULATION CENSUSES AND SURVEYS (1983b). 'Labour Force Survey 1981: Country of birth and ethnic origin', *OPCS Monitor*, 22 February.
OFFICE OF POPULATION CENSUSES AND SURVEYS (1984). Labour Force Survey 1983: Country of birth, ethnic origin, nationality and year of entry', *OPCS Monitor*, 18 December.
OKLEY, J. (1975). 'Gypsies travelling in Southern England.' In: REHFISCH, F. (Ed) *Gypsies, Tinkers and Other Travellers.* London: Academic Press.
OLOWU, A.A. (1983). 'The counselling needs of immigrant children: a study in some North of England secondary schools', *New Community*, **X**, 3, 410–20.
OPEN UNIVERSITY (1982). *Bedford: Portrait of a Multi-ethnic Town.* Open University Coursebook E 354. Block 1, Unit 1. Milton Keynes: Open University Press.
ORCHARD, H.E. (1983). 'Training tip', *Times Educ. Suppl.*, 5 August, 12.
PAINE, S. (1974). *Exporting Workers, the Turkish Case.* Occasional Paper 41. Cambridge: Cambridge University Press.
PALMER, R. (1973). Immmigrants ignored: an appraisal of the Italians in Britain. Unpublished MA thesis, University of Sussex.
PALMER, R. (1977). 'The Italians: patterns of migration to London.' In: WATSON, J.L. (Ed) *Between Two Cultures: Migrants and Minorities in Britain.* Oxford: Basil Blackwell.
PALMER, R. (1980). 'Processes of estrangement and disengagement in an Italian emigrant community', *New Community*, **VIII**, 3, 277–87.
PATTERSON, J. (1984). 'Educating Travellers' children', *Junior Education*, **8**, 5, 11.
PATTERSON, S. (1977). 'The Poles: an exile community in Britain.' In: WATSON, J.L. (Ed) *Between Two Cultures: Migrants and Minorities in Britain.* Oxford: Basil Blackwell.
PEARSON, R. (1982a). 'Understanding the Vietnamese in Britain. Part I, Background and family life', *Health Visitor Journal*, **55**, 426–30, August.
PEARSON, R. (1982b). 'Understanding the Vietnamese in Britain. Part II, Marriage, death and religion', *Health Visitor Journal*, **55**, 477–82, September.
PEARSON, R. (1982c). 'Understanding the Vietnamese in Britain. Part III, Health, beliefs, birth and child care', *Health Visitor Journal*, **55**, 533–8, October.
PERREN, G.E. (1975). 'Introduction.' In: CENTRE FOR INFORMATION ON LANGUAGE TEACHING. *Less Commonly Taught Languages: Resources and Problems.* London: CILT.
PERREN, G.E. (1979). 'Languages and minority groups.' In: PERREN, G.E. (Ed) *The Mother Tongues and Other Languages in Education.* NCLE Reports and Papers 2. London: CILT.
PLOWDEN, B., Lady (1975). 'Bridging the gap between the Gypsy child and school life', *Education*, **146**, 11, 262–4.
PLOWDEN, B., Lady (1982). *Looking Back, Moving Forwards.* London: ACERT.
POWELL, R.C. (1980). 'Teacher training and Italian.' In: BALDWIN, T.D. *et al.* (Eds) *Italian in Schools.* London: CILT.

PRAGER, P. (1977). 'Minority languages, *Times Educ. Suppl.*, **3233** 27, 20 May.
RAPPORTO DI LAVORO (1977). Problematiche e Prospettive delle Iniziative Scholastiche Italiane in Gran Bretagna, Segreteria della Direzione Didattica di Manchester.
RATHBONE, M. and GRAHAM, N. (1983). *Bilingual Nursery Assistants: Their Use and Training.* London: SCDC.
REID, E. (1984). 'Public examinations in ethnic minority languages: availability and currency.' In: REID, E. (Ed) *Minority Community Languages in School.* National Congress on Languages in Education Papers and Reports 4. London: CILT.
REID, E., SMITH, G. and MORAWSKA, A. (1985). *Languages in London.* CLE/LMP Working Paper No.12. London: Community Languages and Education Project, University of London Institute of Education.
REISS, C. (1975). *The Education of Travelling Children.* Schools Council Research Studies. London: Macmillan.
REX, J. and MOORE, R. (1967). *Race, Community and Conflict. A Study of Sparkbrook.* London: Oxford University Press.
RICHMOND, A. (1954). *Colour Prejudice in Britain: A Study of West Indian Workers in Liverpool, 1942–51.* London: Routledge and Kegan Paul.
RIDLEY, F.F. (1981). 'View from a disaster area, unemployed youth in Merseyside', *Political Quarterly*, **52**, 1.
ROBERTS, K., DUGGAN, J. and NOBLE, M. (1982). 'Out-of-school youth in high-unemployment areas: an empirical investigation', *Brit. J. Guidance and Counselling*, **10**, 1, 1–11.
ROGERS, J.A. (1975). Young Black People in Liverpool 8. Merseyside Community Relations Council.
ROSE, E.J.B., DEAKIN, N., ABRAMS, M., JACKSON, V., PESTON, M., VANAGS, A.H., COHEN, B., GAITSKELL, D. and WARD, P. (1969). *Colour and Citizenship.* London: Oxford University Press.
ROSEN, H. and BURGESS, T. (1980). Linguistic Diversity in London Schools: an Investigation Carried Out in the English Department of the University of London Institute of Education (mimeographed); also *Languages and Dialects of London School Children: An Investigation.* London: Ward Lock Educational.
ROUSSOU, M. (1984a). 'Aspects of teaching Greek speaking pupils in Britain.' In: ROUSSOU, M. (Ed) *Greek Outside Greece.* London: NCMTT.
ROUSSOU, M. (1984b). *Greek Outside Greece.* A profile of a Greek speaking community in contemporary Britain. Proceedings from the First National Language Conference for Greek organized jointly by NCMTT and SCMTP. London: National Council for Mother Tongue Teaching.
ROUSSOU, M. (1984c). 'Reflections on the first three years', *Mother Tongue News*, **5**, 2–3, September.
RUDD, E. (1971). 'SCOPE Handbook 2. Pronunciation for Immigrant Children from India, Pakistan, Cyprus and Italy. Schools Council Project in English for Immigrant Children. Harlow: Longman.
SAIFULLAH KHAN, V. (1976). 'Provision by minorities for language maintenance.' In: CILT *Bilingualism and British Education: The Dimensions of Diversity.* CILT Reports and Papers 14. London: Centre for Information on Language Teaching and Research.
SAIFULLAH KHAN, V. (1977). Bilingualism and Linguistic Minorities in Britain, Developments, Perspectives. A Briefing Paper. Runnymede Trust, London.
SAIFULLAH KHAN, V. (1980a). 'Linguistic Minorities Project.' In: COMMISSION FOR RACIAL EQUALITY *Mother Tongue Teaching Conference Report.* Bradford College, 9–11 September. London: CRE.

SAIFULLAH KHAN, V. (1980b). 'The "mother-tongue" of linguistic minorities in multicultural England', *J. Multiling. Multicult. Devel.*, **1**, 1, 71–88.

SAVE THE CHILDREN FUND (1982). *Bingley School Vietnamese School Project Pack*. London: Save the Children Fund.

SCHOOLS COUNCIL (1967). *English for the Children of Immigrants*. Working Paper No.13. London: HMSO.

SCHOOLS COUNCIL (1981). *Education for a Multiracial Society, Curriculum and Context 5–13*. London: Schools Council.

SERGIDES, N. and TANSLEY, P. (1984). 'Recognizing the Cypriot dialect in the classroom: does it affect the selection of materials?' In: ROUSSOU, M. (Ed) *Greek Outside Greece*. London: NCMTT.

SHARMA, K. (1979). Parents' attitudes to literacy and attainments of indigenous and multiethnic groups. Unpublished dissertation.

SIBLEY, D.E. (1962). 'The Italian and Indian populations in Bedford – a contrast in assimilation', *N. Universities Geographical Journal*, **3**, 48–52.

SILBERMAN, L. and SPICE, B. (1950). *Colour and Class in Six Liverpool Schools*. Liverpool: Liverpool University Press.

SIMONS, H. (1979). EEC Pilot Project 'Mother Tongue and Culture' in Bedfordshire. Evaluation Report January 1978 – September 1978. Cambridge Institute of Education.

SIMONS, H. (1980). EEC Sponsored Pilot Project 'Mother Tongue and Culture' in Bedfordshire. Second External Evaluation Report, September 1978 – September 1979. Cambridge Institute of Education.

SIMSOVA, S. (1982). *Library Needs of the Vietnamese in Britain*. London: Polytechnic of North London, School of Librarianship and Information Studies.

SINCLAIR, A.J. (1980). 'Italian as first foreign language: two viewpoints from one school: 2.' In: BALDWIN, T.D. *et al.* (Eds) *Italian in Schools*. London: CILT.

SINGLETON, E. (1979). An investigation into the provision of mother-tongue teaching for the children of ethnic minorities in the London Borough of Haringey – some initial findings. Unpublished dissertation.

SKELLINGTON, R. (1978). *The Housing of Minority Groups in Bedford: A Descriptiive Account*. Occasional Paper No. 1. Faculty of Social Sciences, Open University. Milton Keynes.

SMITH, D.H. (1972). 'Problems, perspectives, prospects.' In: WALLBRIDGE, J. (Ed) *The Shadow on the Cheese: Some Light on Gypsy Education*. London: National Gypsy Education Council.

SMITH, G., MORAWSKA, A. and REID, E. (1984). Languages in Coventry. CLE/LMP Working Paper No.10. London: Community Languages and Education Project, University of London Institute of Education.

SMITH, H. (1984). 'Report on discussion group on teacher training.' In: ROUSSOU, M. (Ed) *Greek Outside Greece*. London: NCMTT.

SMITH, M. (1975). *Gypsies – Where Now?* London: Fabian Society.

SOMERFIELD, P. (1983). 'Implementing an equal opportunity policy on Merseyside.' In: BEN-TOVIM, G. (Ed) *Equal Opportunities and the Employment of Black People and Ethnic Minorities on Merseyside*. Liverpool: Merseyside Association for Racial Equality in Employment/Merseyside Area Profile Group.

SOMERSET, F. (1983). 'Vietnamese refugees in Britain: resettlement experiences', *New Community*, **X**, 3, 454–63.

STAMATARIS, A. (1983). An investigation into the effects of cultural pressure on the developing self-esteem of a sample of Greek Cypriot adolescent girls attending a London Greek school. Unpublished B.Ed. dissertation, Middlesex Polytechnic.

STEEDMAN, H. (1978). 'The education of migrant workers' children in EEC member states.' In: *Proceedings of Annual Conference*. Edinburgh: Comparative Education Society in Europe.

STEEDMAN, H. (1979). 'The education of Italian immigrants' children in Britain', *Association of Teachers of Italian Journal*, **29**, 31–40.

STEINBERG, S.H. and PAXTON, J. (Eds) (1969, 1973). *Stateman's Year Book*. 1969–70 and 1972–3. London: Macmillan/St Martin's Press.

STEYNE, H. and DERRICK, D. (Eds) (1979). *The Education of Travellers' Children*. Report of a Conference held by the Centre for Information and Advice on Educational Disadvantage, 8–9 November 1977. Manchester.

STOKER, D. (1969). The Education of Infant Immigrants. A Report Prepared for the Schools Council Project in English for Immigrant children. University of Leeds, Institute of Education.

TANSLEY, P. (1981). EC Sponsored Mother Tongue and Culture Pilot Project. Bedfordshire Education Service Final External Evaluation Report, September 1979 – July 1980.

TANSLEY, P. (1986). *Community Languages in Primary Education*. Report from the SCDC Mother Tongue Project. Windsor: NFER-NELSON.

TANSLEY, P. and CRAFT, A. (1984). 'Mother tongue teaching and support. A Schools Council inquiry', *J. Multiling. Multicult. Develop.*, **5**, 5, 367–84.

TANSLEY, P., NOWAZ, H. and ROUSSOU, M. (1985). *Working with Many Languages: A Handbook for Community Language Teachers*. London: SCDC.

TAYLOR, M.J. (1981). *Caught Between. A Review of Research into the Education of Pupils of West Indian Origin*. Windsor: NFER-NELSON.

TAYLOR, M.J. (1986). *Chinese Pupils in Britain. A Review of Research into the Education of Pupils of Chinese Origin*. Windsor: NFER-NELSON.

TAYLOR, M.J. and HEGARTY, S. (1985). *The Best of Both Worlds...? A Review of Research into the Education of Pupils of South Asian Origin*. Windsor: NFER-NELSON.

TAYLOR-BROWN, M. (1977). Problems in training outreach workers among minority groups with special reference to Gypsy education. Unpublished M.Ed. dissertation, University of Manchester.

TAYLOR-BROWN, M., MARTIN, P., ARMSTRONG, D. and PARROTT, S. (1982). Adult Education and Gypsies. Interim Report. University of London Department of Extra-Mural Studies.

THOMAS, K.C. (1975). 'Race in the curriculum', *New Era*, **56**, 7, 10–13.

THOMAS, K., GIBSON, T., ATKIN, J. and CRAFT, M. (1984). *Lifestyles Pack*. Nottingham: University of Nottingham, School of Education/Schools Council Development Unit in Multi-Ethnic Education.

THOMPSON, S. (1986). 'Pupils' ethnic origin to be put on file', *Daily Telegraph*, 26 July, 2.

TIZARD, J., HEWISON, J. and SCHOFIELD, W.N. (1982). 'Collaboration between teachers and parents in assisting children's reading', *Brit. J. Educ. Psy.*, **52**, 1, 1–15.

TORKINGTON, N.P.K. (1983). *The Racial Politics of Health – a Liverpool Profile*. Merseyside Area Profile Group. Department of Sociology, University of Liverpool.

TOSI, A. (1979a). 'Mother-tongue teaching for the children of migrants', *Language Teaching and Linguistics Abstracts*, **12**, 4, 213–31.

TOSI, A. (1979b). Test of Basic Competence in Standard Italian for Primary School Children Bilingual in English and Italian Dialect. Bedfordshire Education Service.

TOSI, A. (1980a). 'Mother tongue maintenance as an extra- curricular provision: the state of Italian.' In: BALDWIN, T.D. *et al.* (Eds) *Italian in Schools.* London: CILT.

TOSI, A. (1980b). 'The EEC/Bedfordshire Mother Tongue Pilot Project.' In: COMMISSION FOR RACIAL EQUALITY *Mother Tongue Teaching Conference Report.* Bradford College, 9–11 September, 1980. London: CRE.

TOSI, A. (1982). 'Between the mother's dialect and English.' In: DAVIES, A. (Ed) *Language Learning at School and Home.* London: Heinemann.

TOSI, A. (1984). *Immigration and Bilingual Education.* Oxford: Pergamon.

TOWNSEND, H.E.R. (1971). *Immigrant Pupils in England: The LEA Response.* Slough: NFER.

TOWNSEND, H.E.R. and BRITTAN, E.M. (1972). *Organization in Multiracial Schools.* Slough: NFER.

TOWNSEND, H.E.R. and BRITTAN, E.M. (1973). *Multiracial Education: Need and Innovation.* Schools Council Working Paper 50. London: Evans/Methuen Education.

TRISELIOTIS, J.P. (1963). 'Immigrant schoolchildren and their problem of adjustment', *Case Conference*, **9**, 7, January.

TRISELIOTIS, J.P. (1968). 'Psycho-social problems of immigrant families.' In: OAKLEY, R. (Ed) *New Backgrounds.* London: Oxford University Press, pp.93–116.

TRISELIOTIS, J.P. (1976). 'Immigrants of Mediterranean origin', *Child Care, Health and Dev.*, **2**, 365–78.

TRUMAN, A.R. (1965). 'School.' In: HOOPER, R. (Ed) *Colour in Britain.* London: BBC Publications, p.99.

TSATSARONI, A. (1983). Personal communication, on behalf of Greek Embassy.

TSATSARONI, A. and PAPASSAVA, J. (1986). Personal communication, on behalf of Greek Embassy.

TSOW, M. (1983). 'Analysis of responses to a national survey on mother tongue teaching in local education authorities, 1980–82', *Educ. Res.*, **25**, 3, 202–8.

TWITCHIN, J. and DEMUTH, C. (1981). *Multi-Cultural Education.* London: BBC.

ULUG, F. (1981). A study of conflicting cultural pressures with particular attention to the Turkish Cypriot community and a small group of secondary school Turkish girls now living in North London. Unpublished B.Ed. dissertation, Middlesex Polytechnic.

VERMA, G. and ASHWORTH, B. (1981). 'Education and occupational aspirations of young South Asians in Britain.' In: MEGARRY, J., NISBET, S. and HOYLE, E. (Eds) *World Yearbook of Education 1981. Education of Minorities.* London: Kogan Page.

VERMA G.K. and BAGLEY, C. (Eds) (1979). *Race, Education and Identity.* London: Macmillan.

VERMA G.K. and BAGLEY, C. (Eds) (1982a). *Self-Concept, Achievement and Multicultural Education.* London: Macmillan.

VERMA G.K. and BAGLEY, C. (1982b). 'Introduction: issues in multicultural education.' In: VERMA, G.K. and BAGLEY, C. *Self-Concept, Achievement and Multicultural Education.* London: Macmillan.

VINSON, P. (1973). Road-side Families: a Short Report on the Circumstances of Some Gypsy Families on the Road-side in Hertfordshire. London: Save the Children Fund, Playgroups Department.

WALKER, E.C. (1963a). 'Bilingualism in Bedford', *The Teacher*, 19 July.

WALKER, E.C. (1963b). 'Sinking roots in Britain', *The Teacher*, 12 July.

WALKER, I. (1982). 'Garibaldi was here', *Observer* [Suppl.], 4 April.

WALLBRIDGE, J. (Ed) (1972). *The Shadow on the Cheese: Some Light on Gypsy Education*. London: National Gypsy Education Council.

WARD, B. (1982). 'The use of the Haynes test of learning ability to assess children whose mother tongue is not English', *AEP Journal*, **5**, 10, 12–17.

WATERSON, M. (1976). 'The traveller's child', *Engl. in Educ.*, **10**, 2, 1–10.

WATTS, C. (1978). Black Prospects: A Report of the Job Prospects of Liverpool-born Blacks. Unpublished report, South Liverpool Personnel, Liverpool 8.

WEST MIDLANDS EDUCATION AUTHORITIES (1976). Gypsy Education in the West Midlands. Wolverhampton.

WESTON, M. (1979). 'A pilot study on twenty-four Italian families from two London areas', *Association of Teachers of Italian Journal*, **29**, 41–7.

Which Degree? (1986). London: New Opportunity Press.

WHITFIELD, S. (1971). Unemployment and Young People in Liverpool 8. Unpublished report, for Runnymede Trust Industrial Unit.

WILDING, J. (1981). Ethnic Minority Languages in the Classroom? A Survey of Asian Parents in Leicester. Leicester Council for Community Relations and Leicester City Council.

WILKIN, A. (1979). 'Origins and destinations of the early Italo-Scots', *Association of Teachers of Italian Journal*, **29**, 52–61.

WILKIN, A. (1980). 'A view from the universities.' In: BALDWIN, T.D. *et al.* (Eds) *Italian in Schools*. London: CILT.

WILLKE, I. (1975). 'Schooling of immigrant children in West Germany, Sweden, England – the educationally disadvantaged', *Int. Rev. Educ.*, **21**, 3, 357–82.

WILSON, A. (1978). 'Pilot in trouble', *Times Educ. Suppl.*, 19 May.

WORLD UNIVERSITY SERVICE (1977). *Education for Refugees*. London: WUS.

WORRALL, D. (1979). Gypsy Education: A Study of Provision in England and Wales. Walsall Council and CRC.

WORRALL, R.V. (1977). Gypsies, education and society: case studies in conflict. Unpublished M.Ed. thesis, University of Birmingham.

WRIGHT, J. (1980). 'The World in a City: ILEA Bilingual Education Project.' In: COMMISSION FOR RACIAL EQUALITY *Mother Tongue Teaching Conference Report*. Bradford College, 9–11 September. London: CRE.

WRIGHT, M. (1983). 'Modern Greek.' In: BROADBENT, J., HASHMI, M., SHARMA, B. and WRIGHT, M. (Eds) *Assessment in a Multicultural Society. Community Languages at 16+*. York: Longman/Schools Council.

YE-CHIN (1980). The Educational Aspect of Indo-Chinese Refugee Resettlement in South England – A Personal Perspective. Southeast Asian Outreach, Swindon.

YOUNG, L. and BAGLEY, C. (1979). 'Identity, self-esteem and evaluation of colour and ethnicity in young children in Jamaica and London', *New Community*, **VII**, 2, 154–69.

YOUNG, L. and BAGLEY, C. (1982a). 'Identity, self-esteem and evaluation of colour and ethnicity in young children in Jamaica and London.' In: VERMA, G.K. and BAGLEY, C. (Eds) *Self-Concept, Achievement and Multicultural Education*. London: Macmillan.

YOUNG, L. and BAGLEY, C. (1982b). 'Self-esteem, self-concept and the development of black identity: a theoretical overview.' In: VERMA, G.K. and BAGLEY, C. (Eds) *Self-Concept, Achievement and Multicultural Education*. London: Macmillan.

YULE, W., BERGER, M., RUTTER, M. and YULE, B. (1975). 'Children of West Indian immigrants. II, Intellectual performance and reading attainment', *J. Child Psychology and Psychiatry*, **16**, 1–17.
ZUBRZYCKI, J. (1956). *Polish Immigrants in Britain*. The Hague: Martinus Nijhoff.

Index

102–16, 253–5, 261–83, 321, 324, 327
parents' attitudes to
Cypriot 75, 98–9, 113–14
Italian 249, 251, 258–9
pupils' attitudes to
Cypriot 76–7, 99–100
Italian 245–6, 259–60
requests for 103–5, 249, 264–5
teachers 90–2, 256–7, 323
teachers' attitudes 100–2, 105, 113–14, 260–1, 280, 309-11
teaching materials 95-7, 115, 258, 281-2, 323-4
Turkish 82–9, 91–2, 94–6
Ukrainian 320–5
Mother-Tongue Teaching Directory Survey (MTTDS) *see* Linguistic Minorities Project
Mottram, J. 122
multicultural education
Cypriot 199–206
Italian 308-11
Liverpool Blacks 335–53
Ukrainian 326
Multicultural Support Group (Haringey) 202
multilingualism 53-5, 61, 76
Murray, S. 332
music and dance 30, 32, 92, 94, 98, 100, 200, 317, 327

National Child Development Study 213
National Congress on Languages in Education 111, 116, 281, 324
National Council of Mother-Tongue Teaching 45, 93, 101, 104, 105, 122, 287
National Extension College 328
National Foundation for Educational Research in England and Wales (NFER) 48, 126, 127, 130, 134, 186, 195, 196, 197, 199, 213, 277, 283, 289, 294, 299, 300, 307, 308, 332, 345
Newcastle upon Tyne 10, 84
Newham, London Borough of 252
North London Cypriot Association 83
Northampton 84, 252, 314
Northamptonshire LEA 217, 223, 250, 252, 255, 256, 265

Norwich 84
Nottingham 10, 84, 210, 217, 250, 268
Nuffield Foundation 328

O- and A-level examinations 94, 95, 96, 100, 102, 103, 104, 105, 106, 107, 108, 109, 111, 125, 126, 136, 137, 138, 141, 189, 251, 252, 256, 257, 258, 264, 269, 270, 271, 272, 273, 274, 290, 309, 324, 326, 329, 331, 332, 333, 345, 348, 349
Oakley, R. 1, 3, 4, 5, 7, 8, 10, 12, 13, 14, 16, 18, 19, 20, 21, 22, 23, 25, 27, 29, 33, 35, 37, 39, 47, 62, 65, 69, 71, 75, 77, 79, 102, 117, 133, 139, 140, 141, 142, 148, 151, 153, 155, 156, 157, 159, 161, 163, 166, 175
Oakley Smith, B. 357
OESEKA (Union of Greek Cypriot Educational Assocations in Britain) 80, 91, 98, 111
Office of Population Censuses and Surveys (OPCS) 3, 5, 6, 7, 8, 11, 12, 13, 14, 16, 40-3, 51, 56, 338, 355, 366
Labour Force Survey (LFS) 5, 6, 7, 42, 208, 216, 338
Okley, J. 359
Oldham 314
Olowu, A.A. 165
Open University 209, 268, 284, 285, 288, 290, 297, 299, 338
Orchard, H.E. 203
Organization of Greek Teachers 91
Orkney 270
Oxford 84

Paine, S. 5
Palmer, R. 208, 209, 212, 213, 214, 226, 232, 244, 247, 249, 266, 288, 298, 304, 305, 306, 303
Papassava, J. 80, 81, 88, 89, 90, 91, 92, 98, 155
parents
aspirations for children 165–8, 325
attitudes to children 158–65, 296–9
see also family life, family strife
attitudes to extracurricular activities 156–8